Advanced Praise for *Make the Wor*

The world is facing multiple crises. But what can we do? Make the World a Better Place *helps answer that question. Kozma's deep analyses, coupled with case studies of groups already at work, makes this an essential book for everyone: citizens, designers, and most importantly, decision-makers in business and government.*

Don Norman, Ph.D.
Distinguished Professor and founder of the Design Lab, Emeritus
University of California, San Diego
Author of *Design for a Better World*

Has design lost its moral compass? Kozma's Make the World a Better Place *comes at important time in human history as unintended consequences of design are causing harm and benefits at scale. This book is a must read for all with an interest in the future of design.*

Jim Spohrer, Ph.D.
Apple and IBM retired executive
Board of Directors, International Society of Service Innovation Professionals

Dr. Kozma shares decades of his experience designing and studying designs for the audacious goal of making our lives and world better. He offers concrete principles and processes to help us design better and to think critically about the designs in our lives. The book is fun to read with informative case studies that demonstrate the myriad ways design impacts us all. The world is in need of better design, and Kozma's book shows us how to get there.

Mark Guzdial, Ph.D.
Director, Program in Computing for the Arts and Sciences,
College of Literature, Science, and the Arts
Professor of Electrical Engineering and Computer Science,
College of Engineering
University of Michigan

I have come to see that, at one level, democracy is a design problem—from the writing of a constitution to the structure of a Town Hall meeting to the layout of a ballot. But today's crisis of democracy runs deep and turns on the function of society itself. To address this larger societal problem, Kozma expands the scope of Design in this comprehensive and compelling book. Here, broad theory and detailed application inform each other, pointing the way toward a society in which individuals and communities can flourish and the ideals of democratic governance may come to fruition.

Robert Cavalier, Ph.D.
Director, Program for Deliberative Democracy
Emeritus Teaching Professor of Philosophy
Carnegie Mellon University

Following on Don Norman's landmark books (Design of Everyday Things *and* Emotional Design), *Kozma's* Make the World a Better Place *crystallizes, in accessible prose, with plenty of detail, where the field of designing "everyday things" needs to be going. Kozma's book is a GPS for HCI.*

Elliot Soloway, Ph.D.
Arthur F. Thurnau Professor
Computer Science and Engineering, College of Engineering
University of Michigan

This book is true to its title in helping the reader understand at the deepest level how each of us can make the world a better place. It neither preaches nor simplifies the task, but rather presents through captivating real-world examples of design successes and failures across multiple fields the moral imperative of designing well. Reading the manuscript has taught me that we are all in some way designers, and it has enhanced my work as a law professor and foundation executive.

Jay Folberg, J.D.
Professor and Dean Emeritus
School of Law
University of San Francisco
Founding Executive Director, The JAMS Foundation

I highly recommend Bob Kozma's new book Make the World a Better Place: Design with Passion, Purpose, and Values. *This book is an important—and timely—addition to that of other pioneers in many fields who have been promoting the importance of students' learning design thinking/doing in K–16 (and graduate school) education. But more than this, it deals with issues that are often not emphasized—values, ethics, and connecting passion with purpose. This book will be invaluable to learners and designers of all ages and backgrounds in collaborating together to deal with solving complex, sometimes called "wicked," problems and issues requiring transdisciplinary, systems thinking, on a global scale—and critical to our survival and continued growth.*

Ted M. Kahn, Ph.D.
CEO and Chief Futurist and Learning Architect
DesignWorlds for Learning and
DesignWorlds for College and Careers

As a society, we have the means to design our way out of wicked problems. Good design can reduce harm, increase happiness, and improve equity and shared prosperity. This knowledge is powerful. It can fill us with optimism. Kozma gets to the very root of design's relationship to culture and the real human consequences that flow from the design process. The book is a must read for those interested in design for the greater good.

Robert Ferry
Registered Architect LEED AP
Co-founder, Land Art Generator Initiative

With his meticulous research, multifaceted thinking, and marvelous prose, Robert Kozma takes us on a quite memorable journey to make the world a better place.

Curtis J. Bonk, Ph.D.
Professor of Instructional Systems Technology
Indiana University

Make the World a Better Place

Make the World a Better Place

Design with Passion, Purpose, and Values

Robert B. Kozma, Ph.D.
Emeritus Principal Scientist
SRI International
Menlo Park, California
US

Published by John Wiley & Sons, Inc., Hoboken, New Jersey.
Published simultaneously in Canada.

For general information on our other products and services or for technical support, please contact our Customer Care Department within the United States at (800) 762-2974, outside the United States at (317) 572-3993 or fax (317) 572-4002.

Wiley also publishes its books in a variety of electronic formats. Some content that appears in print may not be available in electronic formats. For more information about Wiley products, visit our web site at www.wiley.com.

Library of Congress Cataloging-in-Publication Data applied for:

Paperback ISBN: 9781394173471

Cover Design: Wiley
Cover Image: © RapidEye/Getty Images

Set in 9.5/12.5pt STIXTwoText by Straive, Chennai, India

SKY10044724_032023

So, let us leave behind a country better than one we were left with.

Amanda Gorman
National Youth Poet Laureate
The Hill We Climb
2021 Presidential Inauguration

To Dad
We call them the Greatest Generation
not because they made the most money
but because they sacrificed the most
for the greatest good.

Table of Contents

Author Bio

Robert B. Kozma, Ph.D.
Emeritus Principal Scientist,
SRI International

Robert Kozma is a retired professor, research scientist, and international consultant living with his wife in San Francisco and Lake Tahoe. He was a professor at the School of Education and a research scientist at the Center for Research on Learning and Teaching at the University of Michigan as well as a center director and principal scientist at the Center for Technology and Learning at SRI International in Silicon Valley. During his research career, he wrote extensively on media theory, the design and evaluation of educational technology systems, technology in science education and technology policy in support of educational reform. He and his research teams also designed advanced multimedia systems, primarily in the area of science learning.

His work was funded by the National Science Foundation, the U.S. Department of Education, The World Bank, and UNESCO among other organizations. His academic research was published in *Review of Educational Research, Journal of the Learning Sciences, Cognition and Instruction, Learning and Instruction, Educational Technology Research and Development, Journal of Research on Computers in Education, Journal of Computer Assisted Learning, Journal of Research in Science Teaching, Chemistry Education, Journal of Computers in Mathematics and Science Teaching,* and *Computers and Composition* among other journals and chapters in numerous edited books.

He consulted internationally, having visited more than 80 countries. His consultation focused on technology policies in support of educational reform that fostered economic and social development, preparing students for the knowledge economy and information society. His clients included ministries of education and other government and nongovernment agencies in Singapore, Norway, Jordan, Egypt, Thailand, and Chile among other countries; multinational organizations, such as UNESCO, OECD, and the World Bank; and high-tech companies, including Intel, Microsoft, and Cisco.

Preface

Who Should Read This Book

Well, first of all, if in your design work, you are primarily focused on making tons of money and retiring to a beach villa, this book may not be for you. There are ways to make tons of money in design and there are books to help you do that. But that's not the point of this book. This book is for people who want to make the world a better place. Design can help you do that as well. Indeed, I contend, it is the best way to do it.

This book does not focus on a narrow audience. Whether you are an engineer or a teacher, a musician, hobbyist, or homemaker, you are capable of designing. We are all everyday designers and all of us can help design a better world. Here are some specific groups of people who might find this book interesting:

Professional designers and design students

There are, of course, professional books in specific areas of design, such as engineering, architecture, interior design, product design, user experience design, graphic design, and so on. They detail how design should be conducted in each field. This book does not intend to replace those books. Rather, it provides an insight into the more general issues, particularly social and moral issues that are often not addressed in those more technical, area-specific books. If you are a professional designer, this book will help you to think about your personal actions, as a designer, and those of your employer and clients in a larger context and how the contribution your work might make toward creating a better world. It may help you adjust your career path or select projects or an employer who can help you make the world a better place. If you are a professor in a design field, you may find this book an important supplement to your traditional textbooks.

Other professionals

Lawyers, doctors, teachers, legislators, and other professionals rarely think of themselves as designers. Yet the main focus of your work is to create artifacts—legal briefs, medical treatments, lesson plans, legislation—intended to make changes or improvements for your clients, patients, students, and so on. As with professional designers, the book will help you to think about your work in the larger context, and help you focus your professional goals and the outcome of your actions, particularly as they might make the world a better place.

Corporate, investment, and foundation officers

Perhaps you are an officer or director of a corporation that is engaged in developing products or services. If so, you probably have many designers on your staff or you hire design firms. This book may help you think about your products and services in a larger context and, perhaps, rethink your business model, not to only create profitable products and services, but to improve society and the health of the planet. If you are an investment officer, this may help you focus on the social responsibilities of companies in which you invest. You may also come to include in your portfolio social-innovation startups that may not have the potential for large return on investments but may make significant contributions to social well-being, if they only had access to needed capital. If you are a foundation officer, read this book with an eye for reviewing your funding portfolio so as to create resources for design projects, big and small, global and local, that address the crucial problems that we face today. Of course, you are probably already doing this, but consider including in your qualifications not only universities, R&D institutes, and large nonprofits, but also small community groups and individual designers with great design ideas to improve their communities and the world.

Consumers of designs

Daily, all of us purchase and use products, take advantage of services, and are impacted by policies that elected representatives enact. These products, services, and policies are designs. This book is meant to give you a very different perspective on these everyday things. It will help you understand the thinking that went into them—or should have gone into them. And it will help you be a more critical, demanding consumer. It will help you decide to buy or not to buy certain products or services. It will help you demand better designed products, with more positive social impact, less impact on our environment, or less use of limited resources. It encourages you to engage in the political process so that public policies benefit the greater good, rather than narrow special interests.

Everyone else who wants to make the world a better place

Hopefully, this is all of us. It could be you. We all face challenges that affect our world, from climate change, plastics filling our oceans, and homelessness to arranging our work environment and putting a healthy meal on the table. These are all designs. We can all benefit from thinking more deeply about design; we can all benefit from your involvement in the design process. You could be a student deciding on a career, or be mid-career looking to change focus, or at the end of your career searching for purpose in retirement. If your passion is directed toward creating a better world, this book is for you. It is designed to give you a different way of thinking about the world and your role in it. And when it comes down to it, YOU are the product of your own design; you set your purpose in life and act on it to achieve your goals. You can choose to make the world a better place.

How to Read This Book

I, like most authors, hope you find value in every chapter, section, and word of this book. On the other hand, I'm reasonable enough to know that within the diverse audience I'm addressing, there are likely to be some chapters you find compelling while others will be irrelevant. Here is a layout that might help you read this book more selectively.

I highly recommend that everyone read Part I, Chapters 1–5, on design and the moral urgency for designing a better world. Part II, Chapters 6–10, presents five design traditions: Scientific, Technical-Analytic, Human-Centered, Aesthetic, and Community Organizing and Social Movements. Each chapter presents the history of the tradition, describes its characteristics, gives a case study, and explores the sociocultural and moral implications of the tradition. You can read these chapters as a set, of course, or read them selectively, depending on your profession or interest, or skip them altogether.

I recommend that everyone read Chapter 11, "Design with Passion and Purpose," that leads off Part III, "Design with Passion, Purpose, and Values." The other chapters in Part III drill down into specific values: Chapter 12, "Reduce Harm and Increase Happiness"; Chapter 13,"Advance Knowledge, Reasoning, and Agency"; Chapter 14. "Promote Equality and Address Injustice"; and Chapter 15, "Build Positive, Supportive Relationships and Community."

With Part IV, "Redesigning the System," I turn to larger themes. You may want read Chapter 16, "The Economy, Government, and Design," to help you understand the larger context that both influences and is influenced by design. Finally, I highly recommend that you read the last chapter, "Where Do We Go from Here?" This chapter helps you think about how to structure you career and life to design a better world and help create a culture of design.

Why I Wrote It

I bring a certain personal background to this book that has influenced me and informed my writing task. I was born in 1946, post-WWII USA, coincidentally the same year that the ENIAC was born, the first general purpose computer. I was the oldest of five boys in a working-class family that, over a couple decades, entered the middle class. I was raised in the suburbs of boom-town Detroit, the engine of America's 20th-century manufacturing capacity. As a middle school student, I attended a predominantly Black school in our more-or-less integrated suburban town, and I attended a Catholic high school. I was in high school when Dr. Martin Luther King Jr. had a dream and when President John F. Kennedy, at his inauguration, said, "Ask not what your country can do for you. Ask what you can do for your country." During my senior year in high school, President Kennedy was assassinated.

In my late teens, I worked on the assembly line at Ford Motor Company in the summers to pay the rather reasonable tuition of the University of Michigan, a high-quality, public post-secondary institution. At Michigan, I started my studies in aeronautical engineering but as the U.S. space program wound down and the Vietnam War ramped up, I transferred to political science and got a B.A. in that field. When I was in college, there was much social turmoil related to the Vietnam War and the Civil Rights Movement. During my senior year, Dr. King ascended to the mountain top. The next day, he was assassinated. Two months later, Bobby Kennedy was assassinated. One of his quotes I found particularly inspirational is, "Some men see things as they are, and ask why. I dream of things that never were, and ask why not."

I got married at 21 as a college senior. Fresh out of the university with a degree in political science, I wondered what to do with my life. I applied to the Peace Corps, Vista (a domestic version of the Peace Corps), and the Teacher Corps. I was accepted into the Detroit Teacher Intern Program, a project between Detroit Public Schools and Oakland University to take B.A. generalists and turn them into teachers. I received my M.A. in Education while teaching at inner-city grade schools in Detroit for four years. During two of those years, I taught in an experimental program that emphasized mastery learning and gave teachers both accountability and professional autonomy in achieving it.

While I was teaching, and my wife and I were starting a family, I also got a Ph.D. in Educational Technology at Wayne State University, a public, urban institution in Detroit. Upon completion, I returned to Ann Arbor as a research associate for two years at a small, private social science R&D company. For 20 years subsequently, I was a research scientist and professor at the University of Michigan, where I conducted research on the impact of technology on education, and taught graduate courses in technology and design. This was at a time when the personal computer was sweeping the country's educational system and beginning to make its mark on other parts of society. In 1984, I started a small software company to design educational software for the new Macintosh computer. And during 1989–90, I took a sabbatical and was a Dana Fellow for Educational Computing in the Humanities at the Center for Design of Educational Computing at Carnegie Mellon University and took courses from Nobel Laurette Herbert Simon.

In 1994, as the World Wide Web was exploding and Detroit's auto industry was imploding, I moved to Silicon Valley to head up a research center at SRI International, one of the nation's most renowned high-tech R&D institutes. Shortly after, I met and married my current wife and soulmate, Shari Malone. My charge at SRI was to develop and evaluate applications of advanced technology to improve education. During my career, I had many research grants and wrote more than 90 academic journal articles and chapters in edited volumes. Topics were on how software designs can improve the understanding of complex concepts in chemistry and improve the process of written composition, on the evaluation online learning, and on technology policy and education reform.

In 2002, I left SRI to consult with multinational organizations, the high-tech industry, and ministries of education on technology-based educational reform policies and programs that support economic and social development. My international clients included the World Bank, the Organization for Economic Cooperation and Development (OECD), the United Nations Education, Scientific and Cultural Organization (UNESCO), Intel, Microsoft, and Cisco as well many ministries of education and governmental agencies in Singapore, Norway, Chile, Jordan, Egypt, India, Thailand, and other countries. In total, I visited more than 70 countries, in both the developed and developing world, to explore how technology could be used to advance educational reform and innovation. Shari and I also volunteered in rural African villages to help villagers explore how basic technologies might improve their access to education and markets for their farm produce.

In the course of my work, I have examined some of the best—and worst—uses of technological designs. I was *inspired* to write this book by the amazing designs that I've seen, as well as the awesome power of the technologies that have enabled them. I was *compelled* to speak by some of the terrible designs, both trivial and significant, that have been imposed on us—sometimes out of carelessness and sometimes out of malice—and the increasingly awesome implications that such designs have, not only on the quality of our lives but on the survival of our species.

Above all, I am motivated by my late father, who told me when I was a young man, "whatever you do, leave the world in a better place than you found it." My father was very much of the old school, where principles and values mattered. He was a card-carrying member of the Greatest Generation. It is to his memory that I dedicate this book as well as to my wife, Sharon Malone; my kids, Sean Kozma and Nicole Kozma Tieche; my son-in-law, David Tieche; and my grandkids, Justus and Jaelle Tieche, for they are the ones closest to me who will be affected most by the designs we create. I also dedicate it to my younger brother, Brian, whose premature passing caused me to reconsider priorities in my retirement and decide to write this book. And finally, as I sit here writing, at times sequestered in place by the coronavirus pandemic of 2020–2022, I dedicate this book to the world's medical researchers and healthcare workers. They are the ones who designed the cures and vaccines for this scourge and who are on the front line, putting their lives at risk to save others. They are, indeed, making the world a better place in the face of this catastrophe and sometimes, sadly, in the face of abuse and personal threats. I also dedicate it to our essential workers—farmers, truck drivers, store clerks, and others who we had to count on to get us through this pandemic and who, too often, we take for granted.

Who Helped Me Write It

I would like to acknowledge the help and support of my wife and soulmate, Shari, who encouraged me to follow my passion, who tolerated our regular separations while I was "in my bubble," who critiqued numerous early drafts, and who gave me valuable feedback. I am particularly indebted to Scott Paris for his thorough reading and invaluable comments on all the chapters and to my daughter, Nicole, who proofread and commented on each. I would like to express my deep gratitude to those who have read and commented on early drafts of various chapters: Alec Bash, Julius and Barbara Cassani, Robert Cavalier, Robert Cliff, Chris Dede, Ola Erstad, Paul Fagin, Robert Ferry, Jay Folberg, Mark Guzdial, Ted Kahn, Gary Kozma, Kurt Kozma, Nancy Law, Elizabeth Monoian, Tetyana Nanayeva, Freya Pruitt, Thomas Reeves, Larry Sutter, Tim Unwin, Don Weil, Jane Weil, Tracy Williams, and Andy Zucker. And I would like to thank my men's dinner group for 15 years of stimulating conversation and fellowship that lead up to this book.

I want to thank a number of people who helped me get photographic images for the book: Rex Cabaniss, Dominique Debucquoy-Dodley, Vanessa Franking, Sandra Garcia Giraldo, Madeleine Hebert, Ciaran O'Connor, Dan Perkins, Tricia Prewitt, Leslie Rose, and Brent Spirnak.

A special thanks goes to the editorial team at Wiley: Todd Green, Judy Howarth, and Kelly Gomez, and to copy editing, initially by Traci Tieche, and by Barbara Long.

Finally, I dedicate this book to you, dear reader. For this book is not just a series of personal reflections, observations, and recommendations on design, it is a challenge to you. Design is sometimes thought of as a rarified domain restricted to specialists, such as engineers, computer programmers, architects, industrial designers, graphic designers, and fashion designers. But because, as I contend, design is a fundamentally-human activity, I would like you to consider how we are all designers and capable of designing a better world.

The major challenge to the human race—and to you, personally—is to develop and harness this human capacity, and the tools, materials, and technologies at our disposal, to address the myriad problems facing us, individually and collectively, in the 21st century. These problems play out in small, local ways and in grand, global ways. And they will require the contributions of all of us to solve them. I am asking you to follow my father's advice and design a world that is better than that which you found.

Who Helped Me Write It

Part I

A World by Design

1

Moral Imperative

If you see something that is not right, not fair, not just, you have a moral obligation to do something about it.

Rep. John Lewis
U.S. Congressman

When I was a young man and my father told me to leave the world a better place than I found it, it appealed to me as a nice sentiment. Now, his advice strikes me as a moral imperative.

The world is screaming to be made better. We look around: tragedy and misery abound.

Foreign states hack the infrastructure of governments and their economies.[1] Deep fakes, bots, trolls, and fake news are capitalizing on our political and cultural divisions.[2,3,4] Malware monitors our computer activity and steals our passwords.[5] And ransomware captures our computers and holds our companies, records, projects, finances, and health hostage.[6] Our preferences are sold to advertisers, our privacy lost.[7]

Our excesses are overloading our trash dumps, fouling our oceans, and polluting our rivers and air.[8] Each year, U.S. municipalities dispose of approximately 250 million tons of solid waste left over from our consumption.[9] The "Great Pacific Garbage Patch" of plastic waste is estimated to be at least 79,000 tons of stuff that doesn't make it into the dumps, but instead floats inside an area of 617,000 square miles, an area more than twice the size of the state of Texas.[10]

In the U.S., more than 33 million people, including five million children, are going hungry, according to the US Department of Agriculture.[11] 12.8% of Americans live in poverty.[12] Throughout the world, 183 million people in 47 countries are on the edge of hunger, with 135 million more suffering from malnutrition.[13] The World Bank reports that in 2020, after nearly a quarter of a century of steady global declines in extreme poverty, poverty reduction had its worst setback in decades.[14] The report estimates that as many as 115 million more people have been pushed into extreme poverty during the COVID pandemic. This is a level of poverty that economist Jeffrey Sachs calls "poverty that kills."[15]

As I write this in January 2023, the world has experienced 6.7 million deaths due to COVID-19.[16] 1.1 million COVID deaths have occurred in the United States and over 100 million Americans have been infected. At it at its worst, 10 million jobs in the United States were lost due to the pandemic.[17] And each day, 800 small business were closing for good.[18] Globally, the equivalent of 255 million full-time jobs were lost with $3.7 trillion in lost income.[19]

In 2021, due to the pandemic, drug overdoses, and the rise in diseases, life expectancy in the United States dropped to 76.1 years from a peak of 78.8 years in 2019 and is the lowest life expectancy among countries with large economies. [20,21] Americans can now expect to live only as long as they could

Make the World a Better Place: Design with Passion, Purpose, and Values, First Edition. Robert B. Kozma.

back in 1996. This continues a trend since 2016 that represents the longest consecutive decline in lifespan since World War I.[22] Addictive drugs have taken hundreds of thousands of lives.[23] In 2017, the U.S. suicide rate was 33% higher than in 1999 and was the highest rate since World War II.[24] One in three Americans know someone who has committed suicide,[25] the same number who know someone who has died from drug addiction.[26] In 2020, aggravated assaults and gun assaults rose significantly in the United States, and homicide rates were 30% higher than in 2019, an historic increase.[27]

In 2021, 3,597 children in the U.S. died by gunfire and guns are now the leading cause of deaths for children ages 1–18 and more die from gunfire than from auto accidents, cancer, or drug overdoses.[28]

Human-generated greenhouse gasses have resulted in melting glaciers, rising ocean levels, extreme weather events, and lost species.[29] From 2010 to 2019, the world saw nearly twice as many days (14 days per year) above 122°F as in the previous three decades.[30] The United Nations' panel of climate scientists (IPCC) warned that based on the most recent action plans submitted by 191 countries to curb greenhouse gas emissions, the planet is on track to warm by more than 2.7°C by the end of the century, far above what scientist and world leaders have agreed is the acceptable upper limit of global warming.[31]

But climate change is not some far-off prediction; it is happening now and extreme weather is having devastating effects. In 2018, a raging forest fire in my home state of California destroyed the town of Paradise, killing 85 people and the population of the town fell by 92%.[32] Since 2000, the annual average of 7 million acres burned is more than double the annual acreage burned in the 1990s.[33] In February of 2021, Texas and other southern states experienced a severe cold snap that killed 58 people, knocked out power for millions, and froze pipes that burst and flooded homes.[34] In July 2021, a heat wave killed hundreds of people in western U.S. states as temperatures reached all-time highs.[35] And in September 2022, Hurricane Ian hit the coast of southwestern Florida, causing $60 billion in insured loses[36] and at least 114 deaths.[37] The latest IPCC report concluded that things will get much worse unless systemic transitions and transformational changes are made to safeguard human well-being.[38]

Much of the misery we see is human-made. Even the impact of natural disasters, such as extreme weather and COVID-19, are caused or worsened by human behavior and policies. The world we live in today—for good and bad, better and worse—is the result of our own doing, the consequence of our own personal, corporate, and governmental actions.

Is this the world we want?

In many ways we got ourselves into this mess. And in any case, we can get ourselves out of it—we must. There is hope. We can change things. It's in our nature. But Nelson Mandela reminds us, "As long as poverty, injustice, and gross inequality persist in our world, none of us can truly rest."[39] And as Dr. King would say, "We are confronted with the fierce urgency of now."[40].

To Design Is Human

I contend that the characteristic that makes our species distinctively human—that which defines us and leaves our mark on the world—is not our exceptional intelligence, our language, or our use of tools, but humankind's ability to use these powerful resources in combination to create objects, processes, policies, institutions, and environments that go beyond the current condition in which we find ourselves to fashion a world that does not yet exist. That is, what defines human beings is our ability to plan, to create, to solve problems, and in so doing, to aspire to a different world. What is distinctively human is our ability to *design*. If other species are evolutionarily tuned to blend in, run, or hunt, we are evolutionarily tuned to design. It is through our designs that we will have a better world, that we will survive. . .or if we fail at it, perhaps not.

Design is the organizing concept that we explore in this book. We will see how it is that we've designed the world we live in, for good and bad. And we will see that by thinking of design as the everyday way that we all cope with and change our world, we can design not just to make new things, new services, and new experiences but to make the world a better place.

The prospect that our world will get more unequal, more hot, more contentious, more complex, and more challenging, means that our response—our designs—will need to meet those challenges. More and more people will need to take on the role of designer, in one way or another. And this role need not only include professional designers and specialized design teams and companies, but encompass everyday people, neighborhoods, and communities, as these complex challenges playout differently in local situations. Do we need product designers, software developers, engineers, architects, and urban planners? Most certainly. But also, teachers, healthcare providers, social workers, lawyers, managers, legislators, social influencers, and retirees. Church congregations and social clubs, men's groups and women's groups, fraternities and sororities, block clubs, and book clubs. Working together in twos, tens, and hundreds, we can improve our neighborhood, our city, our country, our world.

By participating in designs, we all have a moral obligation. Each of us, in our own way, has an obligation to see that designs make the world a better place by funding, creating, supporting, implementing, purchasing and using designs that improve not only our own condition, but also the condition of our fellow humans, our community, our country, and the world.

In this book, you will see some appalling designs that create harm and destroy people's lives, sometimes inadvertently, sometimes through casual disregard, and too often, through greed and malice. You will also see designs that solve problems, save lives, and bring great joy. This book will lay a foundation for telling the differences between them. It will provide you with analyses, ideas, and moral principles that have practical implications for real design situations and for making the world better.

I hope this book convinces you of the urgency of our situation and inspires you to act. The designed world surrounds us, defines us, and challenges us. The future of the world and the human race may very well depend on our ability to develop the creative, innovative, and moral capacities of each of our citizens so that our future designs will meet the challenges of the increasingly complex and critical problems we face. It is your passion, purpose, and values, coupled with your creative ideas and efforts, and those of many others can help get us from where we are today to where we ought to be. We do now and will forevermore live in a designed world. And it is imperative that we—all of us—design it better.

Moral Responsibility of Designers

Designs can be good or bad. And I firmly believe that designers have a special moral role in making the world a better place. I'm convinced that, in light of the immense challenges we face, it is the passion, purpose, and moral values of designers that will make a difference in the world.

But, a voice from the sidelines says that it is none of your business. In his book *The Philosophy of Design*, professor Glenn Parsons claims:

> One might agree that Design has the potential to reshape society in profound ways, but still maintain that this is not really the Designer's concern. The Designer, it might be said, should not concern herself with these larger problems, or try to engage in "comprehensive designing." Rather, she should merely "stick to the brief." These larger issues are the proper concern, not of Designers, but of someone else—perhaps the companies who decide which sorts of designs to commission or put into production, or perhaps the politicians whose job it is to regulate the use of certain products.[41]

He goes on to say:

> It is true, of course, that Designers, like other professionals, are significantly constrained by the economic system in which they work—they are not free to reshape the world at their whim, but must satisfy their corporate masters.

By denying designers the right or obligation to participate in the moral aspects of their designs, Parsons assigns that right to those with the monetary resources needed to hire others—their "corporate masters." Corporations, politicians, and regulators have moral responsibilities, of course. However, one must ask, why would the possession of money give those that have it a special moral status that allows them to, in effect, set the moral agenda for society and shape it in the way they see fit? And why should designers assume that politicians and regulators have all the moral bases covered?

Unfortunately, the motives of business owners and investors—those with the resources to hire people—are too often driven by the bottom line rather than a desire to make the world a better place. Too often the bottom line favors design ideas that make money in the short term, but degrade the overall quality of our society and world. And too often, politicians are beholden to special interests and regulating agencies are headed by people from the industries they regulate. So, why should we put our well-being and our lives exclusively in the hands of corporations and regulators? We have moral rights, responsibilities, and obligations, too. All of us are moral agents.

Neither designers nor anyone else give up their moral agency merely because they are employees or subject to being fired. Professional designers do not give up their humanity along with giving their labor, when hired. We are responsible for our own behavior. And as professionals, we owe an employer or our client not just our labor, skill, and expertise but our professional advice, including advice on the ethics or morality of a design, if the project implies it.

However, I do agree with Parsons on at least one thing: designs have the potential to reshape society in profound ways. Designers are in a unique position—maybe even more so than pastors, rabbis, mullahs, and philosophers—to shape our moral behavior. In his book *What Things Do,* philosophy professor Peter-Paul Verbeek, contends that the way we perceive and act in the world is mediated by designs and interacting with designs shapes our behavior.[42] Designs are created with certain functions, or affordances, that enable users to act in the world in ways that are easier or more efficient, increasing or decreasing the likelihood of these actions. Or they make certain behaviors possible that users couldn't do otherwise. Hammers are designed to be pounded, cars to be driven, cigarettes to be smoked, guns to be shot; so, with these artifacts, we pound, drive, smoke, and shoot.

In these ways, Verbeek contends, designs "materialize morality"[43] With the creation of designs, designers are often building in features and capabilities that, with their use and impact, have moral implications. It is in this way that designers have a special moral responsibility. They must think not only about the features they invent and intensions of their designs—what they would like to happen—but think about the moral impact, the consequences of their use.

The Designed World

Humans have been designing since the beginning. But human invention has grown exponentially and it has only been in the last 200 years that humans have come to be enveloped in the designed world, with all its desired benefits . . . and unintended consequences.

The Industrial Revolution was a major turning point in human history. It started with refinements of steam-powered engines in Great Britain in the mid-18th century that made them useful initially in the production of textiles. By the late 18th and early 19th century, the revolution was fully developed in Great Britain and established in the United States. Steam engines were particularly important in the growth of the United States, where they powered locomotives and river boats, facilitating movement across the huge land mass and river networks as the new nation expanded.

In 1844, a new power source, electricity, proved its practical use with the invention of the telegraph, introducing what some call the Second Industrial Revolution.[44] By 1866, a telegraph line had been laid across the Atlantic between Europe and the United States.[45] Ten years later, Alexander Graham Bell was awarded the first U.S. patent for the telephone. Thomas Edison invented the first practical electric light bulb in 1878.[46] With the widespread generation and transmission of electricity, electric lightbulbs replaced the use of candles and gas lights. The potential of this Second Industrial Revolution was fully realized with the invention of the AC electric motor by Nikola Tesla in 1887.

In 1946, the year I was born, the first electronic general-purpose computer, ENIAC, was also born and it launched the Third Industrial Revolution. It filled a 50-foot room and weighed 30 tons.[47] At the time, Thomas Watson, the President of IBM, thought the worldwide market for computers was five, at the most.[48] The early internet was established in 1969 and the World Wide Web in 1989.

The Fourth Industrial Revolution, which builds on the computer revolution, consists of three technological megatrends—physical, digital, and biological—that are impacting our economy, businesses, governments, society, and individuals.[49] These trends are the result of an explosion of digital devices and their interconnectivity, including the internet of things (IoT), sensors, virtual and augmented reality (VR and AR), biotechnologies, neuro-technologies, artificial intelligence and robotics, and blockchains.

These revolutions have had a dramatic impact on our world and our everyday lives. Prior to the Industrial Revolution, most humans survived off the land. Objects were made by hand in cottages or small shops. Most people lived a relatively simple life, rarely traveling far from their home or place of birth. Since then, there has hardly been an aspect of daily life these revolutions have not touched, often in ways not anticipated.

While Watson believed that the world would only need five computers, 349 million personal computers were sold around the world in 2021 alone.[50] There are now 15 billion mobile devices in the world[51] and approximately 5 billion of the world's 7.7 billion people have accessed the internet.[52] The world's internet users make approximately 3.5 billion Google searches of the World Wide Web every day,[53] 2.45 billion users are active Facebook members,[54] \$4.2 trillion worth of online purchases were made in 2020,[55] and 293 billion emails were sent and received every day in 2019.[56]

To give you a sense of how fast things have changed, my grandparents were born in an era of horse and buggy; they raised my parents in the age of the automobile; and before they died, my grandparents saw Neil Armstrong take "one small step." In the span of a single lifetime, humankind moved from a form of transportation that they had used for 4,000 years to one that landed them on the moon.

The best of times

During the last 200 years, we came to live in a fully designed world, from the clothes we wear, the houses we live in, the food we eat, and the cars we drive to the "natural" world that surrounds us—the grass in our yard and 51% of U.S. land mass that are crops and pastures.[57] But has all this made the world better?

Despite my bleak assessment, so far, the answer is a qualified "yes."

The design of new machines, products, and processes have become a principle driver of our economy, and since the 19th century, have created a vast amount of economic wealth, as shown in a chart of gains in per capita gross domestic product (GDP) (see Figure 1.1).

These revolutions also unlocked a different way of thinking about the world. We've come to think that if there is a problem, if there is a need, a new invention or a new idea can take care of it. Prior to the Industrial Revolution and its intellectual cousins, the Scientific Revolution and the Enlightenment, the world was pretty much taken for granted as it was. Change was incremental and came slowly. Since the Industrial Revolution, change is the norm, and the faster, the better.

Take, for example, the biological and health sciences. Plagues have wreaked havoc on the world throughout history.[58] And as late as 1900, the three leading causes of death were pneumonia, tuberculosis, and diarrhea and enteritis, which caused one third of all deaths while 30% of all deaths occurred among children aged less than 5 years.[59] It was less than 100 years ago, in 1928, that the antibacterial properties of penicillin were discovered and the drug was applied to treat a range of illnesses, including diarrhea, pneumonia, urinary tract infections, meningitis, syphilis, and gonorrhea. A vaccine was discovered for tuberculosis in 1921, for polio in 1955, and for measles in 1968. Smallpox was declared eradicated in 1977. And, the cocktail of drugs to treat human immunodeficiency virus/acquired immunodeficiency syndrome (HIV/AIDS) was designed in 1997. In late 2019, the world was hit by COVID-19. In response, the pharmaceutical industry, with government encouragement and support, designed the first approved vaccine within 7 months. Within 9 months, 11 vaccines had been approved for use around the world.[60]

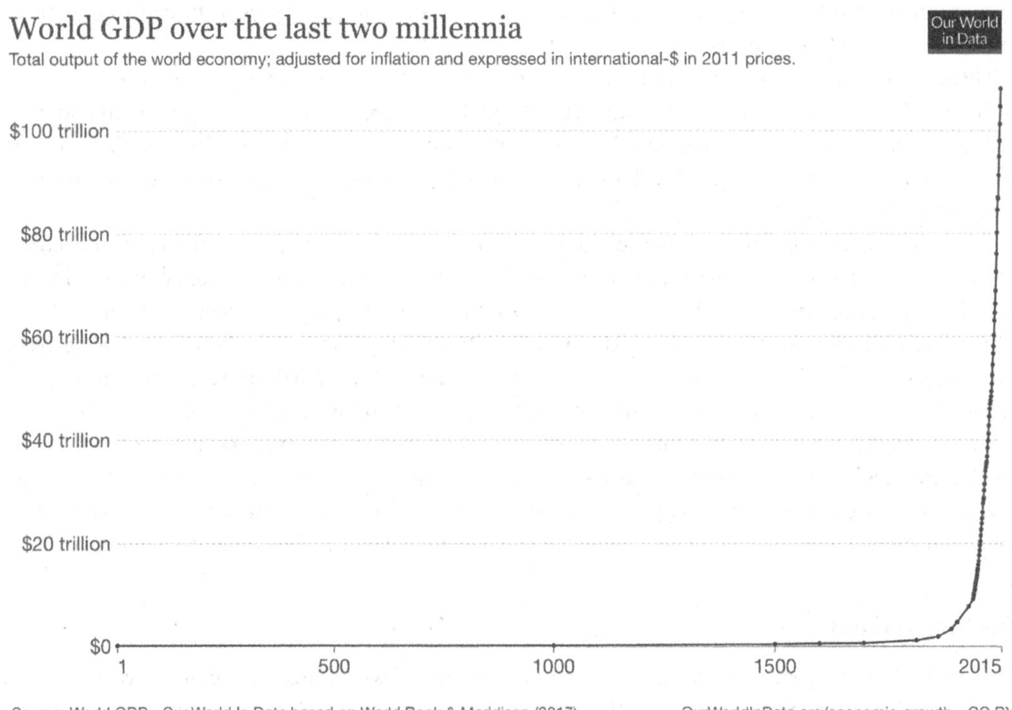

Figure 1.1 World GDP (*Source:* Our World in Data).

In his book *Enlightenment Now*, Harvard professor Steven Pinker documents a wide range of positive social impacts of these developments.[61] For instance, from 1990 to 2017, child mortality across the world dropped from 9.3% to 3.9%. During that same period, deaths around the world due to diarrhea dropped from 1.7 million to 580,000. The share of the earth's children under 5 years old who suffer from malnutrition dropped from 25% in 1990 to 13.5% in 2017.[62] The number of people in the world living in extreme poverty dropped from 1.9 billion in 1990 to 730 million in 2015.[63] Correspondingly, life expectancy around the world grew from 32 years in 1900 to an amazing 72 years in 2018.[64] The global literacy rate grew from 21% in 1900 to 86% in 2016.[65] The global rate of primary school completion rose from 74% in 1970 to nearly 90% in 2016.[66]

We have designed a truly amazing world.

The worst of times

However, our designs have not always made the world a better place, as noted in the opening of this book. There is a dark side to Pinker's rosy picture of progressive improvement. And then, of course, in 2020, there was a pandemic reset.

While, as Pinker claims, new designs and developments have driven dramatic economic growth, huge inequities remain in wealth between countries, most dramatically played out in GDP, the market value of all the goods and services produced by a country. In 2016, the per-person GDP for Singapore was about $65,000; it was $50,000 in the United States, $45,000 in Germany, and $37,000 in the United Kingdom, but it was only about $8,000 per person in Paraguay, $6,100 in India, and $3,500 in Zimbabwe.[67] While the child mortality rate was .7% in the United States and .3% in Norway in 2017, it was 7.5% in Pakistan and 12.7% in Somalia.[68] In education, the rate for completion of lower secondary school is universal in Sweden, France, and South Korea as well as many other rich countries.[69] But it's only 71% in Brazil, 48% in Iraq, and in Chad, it's only 15% overall, with only a 10% completion rate for girls.[70]

But even within rich countries there are huge disparities in the distribution of the benefits of our designed world. For example, in the United States, wealth distribution is highly unequal. The top 1% of the wealthiest people own 32% of the country's wealth and the top 10% own 69%.[71] The bottom 50% own only 2.8% of the wealth.

There are significant wealth and income differences among other groups. For example, there is a significant pay gap between men and women, particularly with a college degree, with women making only 74 cents for every dollar that college-educated men make.[72]

The income gap is even larger for some racial/ethnic groups. In 2019, the median annual family income for Black Americans was $58,500, and $61,000 for Hispanics, while it was $97,000 for Whites and $112,000 for Asians. As for accumulated wealth, the median for Black families was $17,000 and $21,000 for Hispanic families, while it was $171,000 for White families.[73] Even with a college degree, Blacks have a lower income and the difference between them and Whites with a degree has increased in recent years.[74]

Prior to the pandemic, there were 34 million Americans living in poverty, and the poverty rate was 10.5%.[75] Black Americans are more than twice as likely as Whites to be living in poverty; 26% of Blacks compared with 10% of Whites in 2014.[76] In 2016, 31% of Black children and 26% of Hispanic children under the age of 18 were in families living in poverty, while the poverty rate was only 10% for White and Asian children.[77]

Homelessness is a major problem in most U.S. cities. Among the country's richest cities, New York City has over 78,000 people living on the streets and there are 56,000 in Los Angeles, 11,000 in Seattle, and over 8,000 people sleeping on the streets in my home city of San Francisco.[78]

Across the United States, African Americans make up 40% of the homeless population, yet account for only 13% of the general population.[79] In 2015, while 72% of White household heads owned a home in the United States; only 43% of Black household heads owned one.[80] Evictions are far more likely in neighborhoods that are predominantly Black than in other neighborhoods.[81]

Prior to the Fair Housing Act of 1968, there was a widespread practice, called "redlining," that resulted in poor quality of life patterns that persist to this day.[82] The practice was used by the housing and mortgage industries to deny minority populations loans to buy homes in certain neighborhoods as well as to deny them improvement loans for their own homes. This practice not only reduced the value of homes, it created a cultural understanding that these areas were not only undesirable, they could also be used for other undesirable practices, such as the location of factories and toxic waste dumps.[83]

As for health, nearly 11% of the non-elderly population in the United States did not have health insurance as of 2019.[84] And with the increased health risk of the pandemic, it is estimated that roughly 2 to 3 million people may have lost employer-based coverage between March and September 2020.[85] Black Americans are more than twice as likely as Whites to be uninsured.[86] The fact that Blacks have less access to healthcare contributes to a 2.5 times higher prostate cancer mortality rate for Black men, for example, compared to non-Hispanic White men.[87]

Quality education is also unevenly distributed within the United States and it has an impact on employment, income, and other quality of life conditions. Studies show that schools with high concentrations of low-income and minority students receive fewer instructional resources than schools in wealthier neighborhoods.[88] Minority students have fewer and lower-quality books, curriculum materials, laboratories, and computers; significantly larger class sizes; less qualified and experienced teachers; and less access to high-quality curriculum. Many schools serving low-income and minority students do not even offer the math and science courses needed for college, and they provide lower-quality teaching in the classes they do offer.

All of these factors—income, wealth accumulation, poverty, homelessness, health, and education—interact with each other to systematically impact certain groups—race, gender, age—to the advantage of some relative to others. These systemic differences drive the products, services, and policies that are designed and for whom they are designed. This skews the distribution of benefits of our designed world.

If you are White, middle-age or older, and live in the United States, Western Europe, or certain parts of East Asia, you are able to take advantage of all the delightful discoveries, inventions, devices, and services our designed world has to offer. On the other hand, if you are someone of color or from much of the rest of the world, you are likely to be living a simple life and not able to take advantage of the much world's wondrous designs. You are more likely to be poor, sick, and to die young. If you are Black in the United States, you are particularly disadvantaged.

It doesn't have to be this way. We have the capability of creating new designs that allow us to respond to the impact of our previous ones. We are able to design new products, services, policies, and economic responses that address these problems and the ills of society. We can create designs that benefit more people and reduce harm.

The question that hangs in the air is: Why hasn't that happened?

How Has Design Failed Us?

To create better designs, those that make the world a better place, we must first understand why design has failed us so often and so spectacularly. The list of reasons is long and varied.

Designs and users fail

Sometimes it is designs themselves that fail: materials fatigue, parts corrode, structures collapse: the design was well conceived and executed but time and natural processes take their toll—over time, parts fail, bridges crumble, airplane wings crack. In the United States, over 46,000 bridges, or 7.5% of the nation's total, are aged and considered structurally deficient.[89]

In 1979, the failure of the Three Mile Island nuclear reactor in Dauphin County, Pennsylvania, started when a release valve in the primary system failed, sticking open to allow large amounts of nuclear reactor coolant to escape putting the lives and health of approximately 2 million people at risk.[90]

Often, failures are due to user error, where the design is fine but used in ways not intended by the designer, where users implement the design outside the designers' specifications or fail to follow procedures. The 1986 Chernobyl nuclear power plant disaster started with a planned safety test that was delayed, resulting in an unprepared crew to be on duty at the time, which then triggered a reactor shutdown that caused an uncontrolled nuclear chain reaction. The accident caused the deaths of 30 workers, radiation injuries to over 100 others, and years later, 6,000 cases of thyroid cancer reported in children and adolescents.[91]

The design process fails us

Sometimes design failures are due to errors during the design process. Failure is an inherent risk in the design process, according to Professor Henry Petroski. In his book *To Engineer Is Human: The Role of Failure in Successful Design*,[92] Petroski acknowledges that a designer's duty is to avert failure, but he admits that the demands of the design process require compromises. In their designs, engineers try to achieve more speed, lighter weight, more heat tolerance, more comfort, more safety, and to finish the product sooner and at lower cost. Often, all of these demands cannot be met at the same time. Compromises are made and compromise implies a risk of failure. And maximizing or minimizing any single variable—speed, weight, cost, profit—increases the likelihood that others will suffer.

As a result of risky compromises in the design process, the first commercial jet airliner, the Havilland Comet, suffered three crashes within a year of entering service due to catastrophic in-flight breakups. In 1940, the newly-opened Tacoma Narrows Bridge in the state of Washington collapsed as the deck oscillated in a heavy wind in a twisting motion that increased until the deck tore apart, while people watched in shock.

Sometimes the process fails because it doesn't include entire system thinking during the design process, focusing instead on only one kind of situation, one target population, or one kind of impact and ignoring others. Among the most egregious examples of this are what economists call "externalities," the imposition of costs on others who do not participate in a production or transaction. Think of the local factory that dumps its waste that pollutes your river or the exhaust from your car that contributes to global warming. These designs intentionally offload responsibility for their consequences onto someone else.

For example, in 1945 the DuPont de Nemours Company designed Teflon as a coating for cooking products that made them nonstick and easy to clean. The product worked as intended and was a great seller. But its manufacture involved the use of a toxic chemical, perfluorooctanoic acid (PFOA), which DuPont dumped onto property it owned. It ran into streams and leached into groundwater causing illness, including cancer, in thousands of people in the area of Ohio near the plant.[93]

Designers fail us

Sadly, designers fail us in many ways through commission and omission. The failure of the Teflon design was not only a failure to account for secondary consequences during the design process, it was also a moral failure of designers who ultimately knew the consequences of their designs and its externalities, and continued dumping anyway. It was a failure of commission. The negative impact of their design was no longer their problem; they made it someone else's.

Some designers are knowingly malicious, often masquerading the design as good; take John Kapoor, for example. Kapoor was CEO of Insys Therapeutics, a drug manufacturer. Insys designed a fentanyl-based synthetic opioid product, called Subsys, which was 100 times more powerful than morphine and was approved by the Food and Drug Administration (FDA) for cases of extreme pain, such as end-stage cancer. Kapoor and his executives designed a sales scheme to motivate doctors to prescribe Subsys for off-label conditions, such as back pain and migraine headaches, by paying them bribes as high as $140,000 a year, disguised as medical conferences, consultations, and speaking engagements.[94] And because Subsys is highly addictive, addicted patients created a constant stream of profit for Insys. But it also meant that far more patients suffered the devastating effects of addiction, from the pain of withdrawal, or loss of jobs and families, and even death. In May 2019, Kapoor and his top executives were found guilty of a range of crimes, including racketeering, illegal distribution of a controlled substance, and fraud.[95] In January 2020, Kapoor was sentenced to 5½ years in prison for his crimes.[96]

On the other hand, designers often fail us not by commission, but by omission. The designs they create are not immoral or harmful, but they don't solve an important need and they crowd out the possibility of more-important, more-helpful designs. Designers may only choose projects or only create designs that are likely to bring them fame or riches. They want their name to become a household word, to become an international brand. They want their designs to fill the racks of high-end stores on New York's Madison Avenue, LA's Rodeo Drive, Berlin's Kurfürstendamm, Paris' Rue du Faubourg Saint Honoré, and Dubai's Sheikh Zayed Strip. They want their designs to be seen on the streets of London, the beaches of Maldives, the night clubs of Ibiza, the casinos of Monte Carlo, the catwalks of Milan. They create designs for the 1%. These are "Veblen goods," designs for which demand increases as the price increases because of the item's exclusive nature and appeal as a status symbol and for which the profit margins are the highest.[97] There isn't room for designs that solve everyday problems for everyday people in a world of Veblen goods.

And some designers look only for easy problems where success is assured, those with short-term solutions—a quick fix and move on. It's easier to come up with the latest version of the iPhone or another installment of the *X-Men* than to come up with something truly novel that might contribute to solving hunger, poverty, inequality, and injustice. If something is too complex, they pass it by.

Systems fail us

Many of the world's biggest problems are not addressed because the economic or political systems are not structured to address them or cultures do not value their solutions. System structures and processes shape and constrain our activities, including our designs, as Parsons reminded us at the beginning of this chapter. Projects that get funded are the ones that support the system's function. Some designs are valued; other design ideas are ignored.

Typically, in our culture, the designs that are valued are the ones that make the most money. It isn't sufficient for designs to make people happy or to solve important problems unless they also generate significant profits. Designs that cannot be monetized, that don't bring a significant return on investment, don't get off the drawing board. This is the system in which designers most often work.

In 1970, Milton Friedman, Professor of Economics at the University of Chicago and future Nobel Laurette, wrote an op ed piece for the *New York Times* that was titled "The Social Responsibility of Business is to Increase Its Profits."[98] It was subtitled "A Friedman Doctrine." His argument is that in a free-enterprise, private-property system, a corporate executive is an employee of the owners of the business, typically the stockholders, and the executive's sole responsibility is "to make as much money as possible while conforming to the basic rules of the society." This rejection of any other corporate social responsibilities has had a profound effect in the United States on the business culture and government policies ever since, as we will see in Chapter 16.

The result of these systemic priorities is that while the bottom 50% of the country has lost ground since 1980, well-paying manufacturing jobs have disappeared, drug addiction and poverty have increased in the face of a global pandemic, racism is systemic, and our democracy is under threat, companies worth trillions of dollars are spending hundreds of millions to design a virtual world, driverless cars, and a space tourist industry. Designers are not creating products, services, and government programs that make life better for the majority but for the top 10% or even the top 1%, not because that's where the need is greatest, but because that's where the money is.

In short, I claim, design has lost its moral compass.

The premise that society will benefit by people maximizing their self-interest has made the world worse off, not better. In such a system, people with little or no money don't have much power; they don't own a business and they don't make good customers. If their needs cannot be monetized or generate a profit, they go unmet. And sadly, the worst conditions and the biggest problems in the world happen to those with the least money and political power. Billions are spent to send billionaires into space, but there isn't enough money to build affordable housing for the poor.

In our current system, even well-intentioned designers must both create the solution to urgent, complex problems *and* find the money to fund it. In the face of everything, they not only have to create a design that is great, but also one that has a high return on investment. In such a system, the threshold for this is often too high, and great designs remain only good ideas.

Moral Decisions and Their Consequences

For the most part, we go through our daily lives not having to confront moral issues. We can go days doing our jobs, interacting with colleagues, reading the news, watching TV, playing with our kids, kissing our spouses, all without feeling a need to make a moral decision. When moral issues come up, it is most often with our kids, those in our moral care. When we advise our children, morality seems to be so cut and dry—do this, don't do that; do good; avoid bad.

But morality in the real world is often not so clear; it is situated and often problematic. On occasion, we encounter situations where the moral considerations are more complex or vague, or we are faced with conflicting moral principles. When this occurs, it is often as part of our job and this is particularly so when we are engaged in design. Even when our design purpose is good, trade-off decisions must often be made, decisions that may have both practical and moral consequences.

Often these dilemmas sneak up on us. Our intentions are good; our actions are professional, and yet, here we are in a situation we didn't expect. Or we've made a decision with moral consequences and didn't even realize it at the time. When personally confronted by a moral dilemma, it may be uncomfortable, even risky, to step up and say something, to point out a moral flaw or an inconvenient truth, especially if it means stopping production, going back to the drawing board or contradicting a superior. It's much easier to sidestep the problem. But such dilemmas cannot be morally resolved simply by ignoring them or by saying, "that's not my responsibility," "that's not my job."

The moral implications of our decisions and actions, at work and elsewhere, are entailed whether we acknowledge them or not. That is, ignoring a moral dilemma, side-stepping a moral decision, or tossing it to someone else is itself a moral decision.

Case Study: Boeing 737 MAX 8

Let's look at how everyday moral decisions were played out in the real world in the case of the Boeing 737 MAX 8.

Case Study: Boeing 737 MAX 8

Boeing is one of the largest global aerospace manufacturers in the world and is the largest exporter in the United States by dollar value. Boeing's purpose, as stated on its corporate website is: "Connect, protect, explore and inspire the world through aerospace innovation."[99] And among its enduring values, Boeing once stated: "We value human life and well-being above all else and take action accordingly. We are personally responsible and collectively accountable for safety at all levels: for our teammates, our passengers and those who service our products."[100] (The company has since modified this to say, "We are personally accountable for our own safety and collectively responsible for each other's safety."[101])

In 2011, Boeing's board of directors faced a major challenge. Boeing's competitor, Airbus, launched a brand-new plane, the A320neo, the previous year, and at the 2011 Paris Air Show, and it broke records for the number of planes ordered. To meet the challenge, Boeing's board decided that it would again re-engineer the company's best-selling 737, rather than build an all-new plane, at a cost savings of nearly $10 billion.[102] Named the 737 MAX 8 (see Figure 1.2), the plane was expected to exceed the A320neo in range and fuel efficiency. The plane gained regulatory certification to fly from the Federal Aviation Agency (FAA) in March 2017.

Among the first customers to receive delivery of the new plane was Lion Air. On October 29, 2018, Lion Air Flight 610 took off from Jakarta's international airport in clear weather.[103] Shortly after, the plane plunged into the Java Sea, killing all 189 people onboard. Another early customer was Ethiopian Airlines. On March 10, 2019, Ethiopian Airlines Flight 302 took off from Addis Ababa's international airport, heading for Nairobi, Kenya. Six minutes after take-off, the plane crashed into the Ethiopian highlands, killing all 157 passengers and crew.[104]

A detailed investigation of the crashes identified the Maneuvering Characteristics Augmentation System, or MCAS, as the source of the crash. MCAS is a software program initially designed to kick in and override the pilot's manual control only in extreme circumstances, such as the imminent danger of an aerodynamic stall, thus potentially avoiding a crash and saving lives. However, 2 minutes and 34 seconds into the Lion Air flight, MCAS kicked in and took the plane into a nose dive of 700 feet. Unaware that this component existed, the pilots struggled to bring the plane back up to 5,440 feet until the computer system again took the plane into a dive. This tug of war took the plane down and up more than 20 times before the plane plunged 5,000 feet into the Java Sea at 450 miles an hour. With the Ethiopian flight, the captain reported a flight control problem almost immediately after take-off. Controllers on the ground noticed that the airliner had accelerated to a high rate of speed and was oscillating erratically up and down before the MCAS-controlled plane crashed into the ground going nearly 600 miles an hour.

Figure 1.2 Boeing 737 MAX 8 (Photo by Andreas Zeitler, Shutterstock).

What transformed a component initially designed to avoid crashes and save lives into one that caused crashes that took 346 lives?

During the early development of the 737 MAX 8, before it was certified, MCAS evolved from a relatively minor software and control system into a significant component of the plane's flight operation. Initially, the system was designed to work in the background, and because it was meant to activate only in rare cases, the pilots wouldn't know it was there. However, during early testing of the MAX, a Boeing test pilot was trying out high-speed situations on a flight simulator and the plane wasn't flying smoothly. To fix the issue, Boeing engineers decided to give further responsibilities to MCAS.

MCAS came to compensate for other changes in the plane so as to make the MAX 8 feel the same in the air as the previous 737 models for pilots who were used to flying them. Consequently, MCAS engaged at lower speeds and exercised more control over the flight. Pilots did not receive training about MCAS and weren't even aware of its existence until after the Lion Air accident. Boeing marketed the fact that the plane did not need pilot training as "the 737 MAX 8 advantage."

But people within Boeing knew about MCAS and they knew about problems with it early on, based on corporate emails and text messages that Boeing released as part of the crash investigation. In November 2016, prior to the FAA certification of the 737 MAX 8, the project's Chief Technical Pilot and a Technical Pilot exchanged emails acknowledging they had experienced problems with MCAS in the simulator. The Chief Technical Pilot, the person at Boeing responsible for communicating with the FAA about pilot training, told his colleague that the MCAS was "running rampant in the sim [simulator] on me" and it was "trimming itself like craxy" [sic].[105] The Technical Pilot responded, "that's what I saw on sim one." The Chief Technical Pilot replies that the situation was "egregious."

Despite warning signs, Boeing engineers, in a review of MCAS, decided that the MCAS system was not a safety risk so they didn't bother telling the FAA about the changes.[106] In 2018, after industry lobbying, the congressional act reauthorizing the FAA gave power to the industry for certifying almost every aspect of new planes,[107] authorizing as much as 96% of its own work. Given Boeing's statement that the MCAS was relatively benign and rarely evoked, the FAA approved Boeing's request that the system would not be mentioned in the pilot's manual.

In September 2020, the Congressional Committee on Transportation and Infrastructure released a 238-page report on their investigation of the Boeing 737 MAX 8 debacle.[108] After reviewing the findings, the report castigated both Boeing and the FAA, saying both had failed to do things right and failed to do the right thing. The report cited Boeing for its "culture of concealment" in withholding crucial information from the FAA, its customers, and 737 MAX 8 pilots. The report specifically pointed to a period in time, following Boeing's merger with McDonnell Douglas, when the culture shifted from an emphasis on solving difficult engineering problems to one dedicated to enhancing and expanding the company's financial profits.

In December 2020, the Senate Committee on Commerce, Science and Transportation issued a report on their investigation of the Boeing 737 MAX 8 and the FAA.[109] In it, they concluded that the FAA had a failed culture of safety management, that it was overly cozy with the airline industry, and that it punished people within the FAA who raised issues about airline safety.

How is it that a company with an enduring value of "human life and well-being above all else" and a software program that was designed to prevent stalls and save lives resulted in 346 deaths? What happened along the way that turned an intended good into a harrowing tragedy?

In January 2021, Boeing, charged with fraud and conspiracy, agreed to a $2.5 billion deferred prosecution agreement with the Justice Department over the MAX crashes, which cost Boeing more than $20 billion.[110] In March 2022, the Chief Technical Pilot was tried on charges of misleading U.S. regulators about a MCAS and defrauding Boeing's U.S.-based airline customers of tens of millions of dollars by withholding information when they made their purchase decisions. A Texas jury found him not guilty. In September 2022, Boeing agreed to pay $200 million to settle civil charges by the U.S. Securities and Exchange Commission that it misled investors about its 737 MAX.[111]

But I'm less concerned here with legal responsibility and more concerned with moral responsibility, raising questions about the moral behavior and responsibility of Boeing design engineers, the Chief Technical Pilot and the Technical Pilot, Boeing executives, and about the corporate culture at Boeing and the FAA. What if any of them had asked the uncomfortable questions? What if they had changed the conversation? What if they had stopped and redesigned MCAS or designed pilot training materials to include MCAS? What if all of them, or even one of them, had acted with passion, purpose, and values?

What if each of us act to design a better world?

Your Designs Might Save Us

What makes a design—of a plane or company—good or bad? What are the "oughts"? Are we in safe hands when only "corporate masters," regulators, and politicians are in charge of moral design decisions, to address Parsons's point? What is it about a system or a culture—corporate or societal—that shapes our decisions and our designs? As designers or employees participating in a design, don't we each need to consider the moral implications of our own decisions, actions, and trade-offs? And given all the problems in the world, do we need to think deeply about what we choose to design?

Would you be satisfied with designing the latest version of a first-person shooter video game, creating a virtual shopping mall of nonfungible tokens, or setting up speculative virtual "land" sales in the metaverse?

Or do you go against the grain? Do you think outside the box? Do you design where the need is greatest? Do you make the world a better place?

These are the questions we will explore in this book.

My purpose for this book is to provoke you, to inspire you, and to challenge you to make the world better. Ultimately, we are all confronted by our purpose in life, what the Japanese call *ikigai*: the convergence of one's personal passions, beliefs, values, and vocation.[112] We must all decide on that which influences our career plans and our everyday actions, that which gives us satisfaction and a sense of accomplishment and meaning to our lives. In that personal quest, I hope you will find this book useful, and perhaps, apply what you learn, along with your own passion, purpose, and values, to design a better world.

References

1 Sanger D, Perlroth N. More hacking attacks found as officials warn of 'grave risk' to U.S. government. New York Times. 2021 Jul 19.

2 When seeing is no longer believing [Internet]. CNN [cited 2022, Aug 23]. Available from: https://www.cnn.com/interactive/2019/01/business/pentagons-race-against-deepfakes/.

3 D' Souza S. Bots, trolls and fake news [Internet]. CBC News, 2018, Oct 21 [cited 2022, Aug 23]. Available from: https://www.cbc.ca/news/world/national-us-midterm-elections-bots-trolls-fake-news-1.4863258.

4 Holmes A. Roughly half the Twitter accounts pushing to reopen America' are bots, researchers found. Insider [Internet]. 2020, May 22 [cited 2022, Aug 23]. Available from: https://www.businessinsider.com/nearly-half-of-reopen-america-twitter-accounts-are-bots-report-2020-5?fbclid=IwAR01Wvg5Fj23vS8xYrU4kMMr3D_judavELu04R8OKkZEBBolKX5FSRwwJOk.

5 Palmer D. What is malware? Everything you need to know about viruses, trojans, and malicious software. ZDET [Internet]. 2018, May 30 [cited 2022, Aug 23]. Available from: https://www.zdnet.com/article/what-is-malware-everything-you-need-to-know-about-viruses-trojans-and-malicious-software/.

6 Satter R. Up to 1,500 businesses affected by ransomware attack, U.S. firm's CED says. Reuters [Internet] 2021, Jul 6 [cited 2022, Aug 23]. Available from: https://www.reuters.com/technology/hackers-demand-70-million-liberate-data-held-by-companies-hit-mass-cyberattack-2021-07-05/.

7 Brody B, McLaughlin D. Google, Facebook had illegal deal to rig ad market, Texas says. Bloomberg [Internet]. 2020, Dec 16 [cited 2022, Aug 23]. Available from: https://www.bloomberg.com/news/articles/2020-12-16/google-sued-by-texas-over-abuse-of-dominance-in-antitrust-case.

8 McGrath M. US top of the garbage pile in global waste crisis. BBC [Internet] 2019, Jul 3 [cited 2022, Aug 23]. Available from: https://www.bbc.com/news/science-environment-48838699.

9 Municipal solid waste [Internet]. Environmental Protection Agency [cited 2022, Aug 23]. Available from: https://archive.epa.gov/epawaste/nonhaz/municipal/web/html/.

10 Lebreton L, Slat B, Ferrari F, et al. Evidence that the Great Pacific Garbage Patch is rapidly accumulating plastic. Science Reports [Internet] 8, 2018, Mar 22 [cited 2022, Aug 23]. Available from: https://www.nature.com/articles/s41598-018-22939-w.

11 Hampton O. The hidden faces of hunger in America. NPR [Internet]. 2022, Oct 22 [cited 2023 Jan 7]. Available from: https://www.npr.org/2022/10/02/1125571699/hunger-poverty-us-dc-food-pantry.

12 Benson C. Poverty rate of children higher than national rate: lower for older populations. United States Census Bureau [internet]. 2022, Oct 4 [cited 2023, Jan 70. Available from: https://www.census.gov/library/stories/2022/10/poverty-rate-varies-by-age-groups.html.

13 Food Security Information Network [Internet]. 2020 global report on food crisis [cited 2021, Feb 21]. Available from: https://docs.wfp.org/api/documents/WFP-0000114546/download/?_ga=2.226855131.798553120.1614016647-1131619061.1614016647.

14 Reversal of fortune: Poverty and shared prosperity 2020. World Bank [Internet]. 2022 [cited 2022, Aug 24]. Available from: https://www.worldbank.org/en/publication/poverty-and-shared-prosperity.

15 Sachs J. End of poverty: Economic possibilities for our time. New York: Penguin Books; 2006.

16 Johns Hopkins University. Center for Systems Science and Engineering. COVID-19 Dashboard [Internet] [cited 2022, Aug 24] https://coronavirus.jhu.edu/map.html/.

17 Hess S. The U.S. still has 10 million fewer jobs now than before the pandemic. CNBC [Internet] 2020, Dec 8 [cited 2022, Aug 24]. Available from: https://www.cnbc.com/2020/12/08/the-us-has-10-million-fewer-jobs-now-than-before-the-pandemic.html.

18 Puckett J, Bawab N. Verify: Are 800 small businesses closing each day in the US? K5 [Internet] 2020, Dec 1 [cited 2022, Aug 24]. Available from: https://www.king5.com/article/news/verify/verify-800-small-businesses-closing-a-day/507-1d1f6f90-c558-4307-b5eb-c02b420505f2.

19 Internation Labor Organization. ILO monitor: COVID-19 and the world of work [Internet] 2021, Jan 25 [cited 2022, Aug 24]. Available from: https://www.ilo.org/wcmsp5/groups/public/@dgreports/@dcomm/documents/briefingnote/wcms:767028.pdf.

20 Bernstein, L. Pandemic cut U.S. life expectancy by a year during the first half of 2020. Washington Post 2021, Feb 17.

21 Centers for Disease Control and Prevention. Life expectancy in the U.S. dropped for the second year in a row in 2021. Centers for Disease Control and Prevention [Internet] 2022, Aug 31 [cited 2023, Jan 7]. Available from: https://www.cdc.gov/nchs/pressroom/nchs_press_releases/2022/20220831.htm.

22 Saiidi U. US life expectancy has been declining. Here's why. CNBC [Internet]. 2019, Jul 9 [cited 2022, Aug 24]. Available from: https://www.cnbc.com/2019/07/09/us-life-expectancy-has-been-declining-heres-why.html.

23 Goodnough A, Katz J, Sanger-Katz M. Drug overdose deaths drop in U.S. for first time since 1990. New York Times 2019, Jul 17.

24 Howard J. The US suicide rate is up 33% since 1999, research says. CNN [Internet]. 2019, Jun 21 [cited 2022, Aug 24]. Available from: https://www.cnn.com/2019/06/20/health/suicide-rates-nchs-study/index.html.

25 Ballard J. Many Americans know someone who has died by suicide. Today YouGov [Internet]. 2018, Sep 13 [cited 2022, Aug 24]. Available from: https://today.yougov.com/topics/lifestyle/articles-reports/2018/09/13/americans-depression-suicide-mental-health.

26 Editorial staff. Degrees of separation. American Addiction Centers [Internet]. 2022, Aug 22 [cited 2022, Aug 24]. Available from: https://americanaddictioncenters.org/learn/degrees-of-separation/.

27 Gebeloff R, Ivory D, Marsh B., et al. Childhood's greatest danger: The data on kids and gun violence. New York Times [Internet]. 2022, Dec 14 [cited 2023, Jan 7] Available from: https://www.nytimes.com/interactive/2022/12/14/magazine/gun-violence-children-data-statistics.html.

28 Rosenfeld, R., Abt, T. & Lopez, E. (2020). *Pandemic, unrest, crime and violence in U.S. cities: 2020 year-end update*. Retrieved on February 22, 2021 at: https://context-cdn.washingtonpost.com/notes/prod/default/documents/57ee2ac5-10d1-4854-aa65-e6e768bdbede/note/f79e08b0-2d2a-48b9-bf8e-9672dde2169a.#page=1.

29 In 2021, 3,597 children in the U.S. died by gunfire and guns are now the leading cause of deaths for children ages 1–18 and more die from gunfire than from auto accidents, cancer, or drug overdoses.

30 WMO statement on the status of global climate change in 2019. World Meteorological Organization [Internet]. 2020 [cited 2022, Aug 24]. Available from: https://library.wmo.int/doc_num.php?explnum_id=10211.

31 Dale B, Stylianou N. Climate change: World now sees twice as many days over 50C. BBC [Internet]. 2021, Sep 13 [cited 2022, Aug 24]. Available from: https://www.bbc.com/news/science-environment-58494641.

32 Booth W, Pager T. As climate pledges fall short, U.N. predicts globe could warm. By catastrophic 2.7 degrees Celsius. Washington Post, 2021, Sep 17.

33 https://sf.curbed.com/2019/7/12/20692079/town-destroyed-by-pg-e-fire-loses-92-percent-of-its-population.

34 Wildfire statistics. Congressional Research Service [Internet]. 2022, Aug 1 [cited 2022, Aug 24]. Available from: https://fas.org/sgp/crs/misc/IF10244.pdf.

35 Bogel-Burroughs N, del Rio GMN, Paybarah, A. Texas winter storm: What to know. New York Times 2021, Feb 20.

36 Olmos S, Hubler S. Heat-related deaths increase as temperatures rise in the west. New York Times 2021, Jul 9.

37 Livingston, I. What made Hurricane Ian so intense: By the numbers. Washington Post 2022, Oct 4.

38 Fawcett E, Smith M, Sasani A, et al. Vulnerable and trapped: A look at those lost in Hurricane Ian. New York Times 2022, Oct 21.

39 Intergovernmental Panel on Climate Change. Climate change 2022: Impacts, adaptation and vulnerability [Internet]. 2022 [cited 2022, Aug 24]. Available from: https://report.ipcc.ch/ar6wg2/pdf/IPCC_AR6_WGII_SummaryForPolicymakers.pdf.

40 Mandela, N. Speech delivered by Mr N R Mandela for the "Make Poverty History" campaign. Nelson Mandela Foundation [Internet]. 2005, Feb 3 [cited 2022, Aug 24]. Available from https://db.nelsonmandela.org/speeches/pub_view.asp?pg=item&ItemID=NMS760&txtstr=SLAVERY.

41 King ML. Time to break silence. American Rhetoric [Internet]. 1967, Apr 4 [cited 2022, Aug 24]. Available from: https//www.americanrhetoric.com/speeches/mlkatimetobreaksilence.htm.

42 Parsons G. The philosophy of design. (Kindle edition) (location 903). Cambridge: Polity Press; 2016.

43 Verbeek P-P. What things do. University Park, PA: Pennsylvania State University Press, 2005.

44 Verbeek P-P. Materializing morality: Design ethics and technological mediation. Science, Technology, & Human Values, 2006; 31(3), 361–380.

45 Schwab K. Shaping the future of the fourth industrial revolution. New York: Currency; 2018.

46 Morse code & the telegraph. History [Internet]. 2022, Aug 12 [cited 2022, Aug 24]. Available from: https://www.history.com/topics/inventions/telegraph.

47 Thomas Edison. Wikipedia [Internet]. [cited 2022, Aug 24]. Available from: https://en.wikipedia.org/wiki/Thomas_Edison.

48 ENIAC. Wikipedia [Internet]. [cited 2022, Aug 24]. Available from: https://en.wikipedia.org/wiki/ENIAC.

49 Thomas J. Watson. Wikipedia [Internet]. [cited 2022, Aug 24]. Available from: https://en.wikipedia.org/wiki/Thomas_J._Watson.

50 Schwab K. The fourth industrial revolution. New York: Crown Publishing Group; [2016].

51 Wang A, Ma B, Reith, R, et al. Growth streak for traditional PCs continues during holiday quarter 2021 according to IDC. IDC [Internet]. 2022, Jan 12 [cited 2022, Aug 24]. Available from: https://www.idc.com/getdoc.jsp?containerId=prUS48770422.

52 Forecast number of mobile devices worldwide from 2020 to 2025. Statista [Internet]. 2022, Aug 11 [cited 2022, Aug 24]. Available from: https://www.statista.com/statistics/245501/multiple-mobile-device-ownership-worldwide/.

53 Global digital population as of April 2022. Statista [Internet]. 2022, Jul 26 [cited 2022, Aug 24] Available from: https://www.statista.com/statistics/617136/digital-population-worldwide/.

54 Google search statistics. Internet Live Stats [Internet]. 2020, Aug 24 [cited 2020, Aug 24]. Available from: rhttps://www.internetlivestats.com/google-search-statistics/.

55 Number of monthly active Facebook users worldwide as of 2nd quarter 2022. Statista [Internet]. 2022, Aug 22 [cited 2022, Aug 24]. Available from: https://www.statista.com/statistics/264810/number-of-monthly-active-facebook-users-worldwide/.

56 Global e-commerce forecast 2021. Insider Intelligence [Internet]. 2022 [cited 2022, July 16]. Available from: https://www.insiderintelligence.com/content/global-ecommerce-forecast-2021.

57 Number of sent and received e-mails per day worldwide for 2017-2025. Statista [Internet]. 2022, Jul 26 [cited 2022, Aug 24]. Available from: https://www.statista.com/statistics/456500/daily-number-of-e-mails-worldwide/.

58 Land use, land value & tenure. USDA Economic Research Service [Internet]. [cited 2022, Aug 24]. Available from: https://www.ers.usda.gov/topics/farm-economy/land-use-land-value-tenure/major-land-uses/.

59 Jarus O. 21 of the worst epidemics and pandemics in history. Live Science [Internet]. 2022, Aug 18 [cited 2022, Aug 24]. Available from: https://www.livescience.com/worst-epidemics-and-pandemics-in-history.html.

60 Achievements in public health, 1900-1999: Control of infectious diseases. CEC MMWR Weekly [Internet]. [Cited 2022, Aug 24]. Available at: https://www.cdc.gov/mmwr/preview/mmwrhtml/mm4829a1.htm.

61 Craven J. COVID-19 vaccine tracker. Regulatory Focus [Internet]. 2022, Jun 24 [cited 2022, Aug 24]. Available from: https://www.raps.org/news-and-articles/news-articles/2020/3/COVID-19-vaccine-tracker.

62 Pinker S. Enlightenment now: The case for reason, science, humanism and progress. New York: Penguin; 2020.

63 Roser M, Ritchie, H. Hunger and undernourishment. Our World Data [Internet]. 2019 [cited 2022, Aug 24]. Available from: https://ourworldindata.org/hunger-and-undernourishment.

64 Roser M, Ortiz-Opsina, E. Global extreme poverty. Our World Data [Internet]. 2019 [cited 2022, Aug 24]. Available from: https://ourworldindata.org/extreme-poverty.

65 Ortiz-Ospina E. Global health: Maternal mortality. Our World Data [Internet]. 2020 [cited 2022, Aug 24]. Available from: https://ourworldindata.org/health-meta#maternal-mortality.

66 Roser M, Ortiz-Ospina E. Literacy. Our World Data [Internet]. 2018, Sep 20 [cited 2022, Aug 24]. Available from: https://ourworldindata.org/literacy.

67 Roser M, Ortiz-Ospina E. Primary and secondary education. Our World Data [Internet]. 2013 [cited 2022, Aug 24]. Available from: https://ourworldindata.org/primary-and-secondary-education.

68 Roser M. Economic growth. Our World Data [Internet]. 2013 [cited 2022, Aug 24]. Available from: https://ourworldindata.org/economic-growth.

69 Roser M, Ritchie H, Dadonaite B. Child and infant mortality. Our World Data [Internet]. 2019, Nov [Cited 2022, Aug 24]. Available from: https://ourworldindata.org/child-mortality.

70 Lower secondary completion rate, total. World Bank [Internet]. 2022, Jun [cited 2022, Aug 24]. Available from: https://data.worldbank.org/indicator/SE.SEC.CMPT.LO.ZS.

71 Lower secondary completion rate, female. World Bank [Internet]. 2022, Jun [cited 2022, Aug 24]. Available from: https://data.worldbank.org/indicator/SE.SEC.CMPT.LO.FE.ZS

72 Shares of wealth by wealth percentile groups. Federal Reserve Economic Data [Internet]. [cited 2022, Aug 24]. Available from: https://fred.stlouisfed.org/release/tables?rid=453&eid=813804#snid=813806.

73 Day J. Among the educated, women earn 74 cents for every dollar men make. United States Census Bureau [Internet]. 2019, May 29 [cited 2022, Aug 24]. Available from: https://www.census.gov/library/stories/2019/05/college-degree-widens-gender-earnings-gap.html.

74 https://www.statista.com/statistics/639650/median-household-wealth/.

75 Wilson V, Rodgers W. Black-white wage gaps expand with rising wage inequality. Economic Policy Institute [Internet]. 2016, Sep 20 [cited 2022, Aug 24]. Available from: https://www.epi.org/publication/black-white-wage-gaps-expand-with-rising-wage-inequality/.

76 Semega J, Kollar M. Srider E, et al. Income and poverty in the United States: 2019. 2020, Sep 15 [cited 2022, Aug 24]. Available from: https://www.census.gov/library/publications/2020/demo/p60-270.html.

77 On views of race and inequality, Blacks and Whites are worlds apart. Pew Research Center [Internet]. 2016, Jun 27 [cited 2022, Aug 24]. Available from: https://www.pewsocialtrends.org/2016/06/27/on-views-of-race-and-inequality-blacks-and-whites-are-worlds-apart/.

78 de Brey C, Musu L, McFarland J, et al. Status and trends in the Education of racial and ethnic groups 2018. 2019, Feb [cited 2022, Aug 24]. Available from: https://nces.ed.gov/pubs2019/2019038.pdf.

79 McCarthy N. The American cities with the highest homeless populations in 2019. Forbes [Internet]. 2020, Jan 14 [cited 2022, Aug 24]. Available from: https://www.forbes.com/sites/niallmccarthy/2020/01/14/the-american-cities-with-the-highest-homeless-populations-in-2019-infographic/?sh=5c0e9514a9.

80 Racial inequalities in homelessness, by the numbers. National Alliance to End Homelessness [Internet]. 2020, Jun 1 [cited 2022, Aug 24]. Available from: https://endhomelessness.org/resource/racial-inequalities-homelessness-numbers/.

81 Demographic trends and economic well-being. Pew Research Center [Internet]. 2016, Jun 27 [cited 2022, Aug 24]. Available from: https://www.pewsocialtrends.org/2016/06/27/1-demographic-trends-and-economic-well-being/.

82 Gromis A. Eviction: Intersection of poverty, inequality, and housing. United Nations [Internet]. 2019 [cited 2022, Aug 24]. Available from: https://www.un.org/development/desa/dspd/wp-content/uploads/sites/22/2019/05/GROMIS_Ashley_Paper.pdf.

83 Hillier A. Redlining and the Homeowners' Loan Corporation. Journal of Urban History, 2003, 29(4); 394–420.

84 Sherman E. If you're a minority and poor, you're likely to live near a toxic waste site. Fortune [Internet]. 2016, Feb 4 [cited 2022, Aug 29]. Available at: https://fortune.com/2016/02/04/environmental-race-poverty-flint/

85 Tolbert J, Oregera K, Damico A. Key facts about the uninsured population. Kaiser Family Foundation [Internet]. 2020, Nov 6 [cited 2022, Aug 24]. Available from: https://www.kff.org/uninsured/issue-brief/key-facts-about-the-uninsured-population/.

86 McDermott D, Cox C, Rudowitz R, et al., How has the pandemic affected health coverage in the U.S.? Kaiser Family Foundation [Internet]. 2020, Dec 9 [cited 2022, Aug 24]. Available from: https://www.kff.org/policy-watch/how-has-the-pandemic-affected-health-coverage-in-the-u-s/.

87 Tolbert J, Oregera K, Damico A. Key facts about the uninsured population. Kaiser Family Foundation [Internet]. 2020, Nov 6 [cited 2022, Aug 24]. Available from: https://www.kff.org/uninsured/issue-brief/key-facts-about-the-uninsured-population/.

88 Imhoff J. Health inequality actually is a “Black and White issue”, research says. Michigan Health [Internet]. 2020, Jun 3 [cited 2022, Aug 24]. Available from: https://healthblog.uofmhealth.org/lifestyle/health-inequality-actually-a-black-and-white-issue-research-says.

89 Johnson L. Where the kids across town grow up with very different schools. NPR [Internet]. 2019, Jul 25 [cited 2022, Aug 24]. Available from: https://www.npr.org/2019/07/25/739494351/separate-and-unequal-schools.

90 Report card for America’s infrastructure: Bridges. American Society of Civil Engineers [Internet]. 2021 [cited 2022, Aug 24]. Available from: https://infrastructurereportcard.org/cat-item/bridges/.

91 Backgrounder on the Three Mile Island Accident. United State Nuclear Regulatory Commission [Internet]. 2018, Jun 21 [cited 2022, Aug 24]. Available from: https://www.nrc.gov/reading-rm/doc-collections/fact-sheets/3mile-isle.html#impact.

92 Assessments of the radiation effects from the Chernobyl nuclear reactor accident. United Nations Scientific Committee on the Effects of Atomic Radiation [Internet]. [cited 2022, Aug 24]. Available from: https://www.unscear.org/unscear/en/chernobyl.html.

93 Petroski H. To engineer is human: The role of failure in successful design. New York: St. Martin’s Press; 2982.

94 DuPont lawsuits. Business & Human Rights Resource Centre [Internet]. 2001, Jan 1 [cited 2022, Aug 24]. Available from: https://www.business-humanrights.org/en/dupont-lawsuits-re-pfoa-pollution-in-usa.

95 Eaton J. How a drugmaker bribed doctors and helped fuel the opioid epidemic. AARP [Internet]. 2020, Jan 24 [cited 2022, Aug 24]. Available from: https://www.aarp.org/health/drugs-supplements/info-2019/insys-opioid-bribery-case.html.

96 Garrison J. Insys Therapeutics CED John Kapoor, 4 other excs found guilty in fentanyl bribery case. USA Today. 2019, May 2.

97 Founder and former Chairman of the Board of Insys Therapeutics sentenced to 66 months in prison. U.S. Attorney’s Office, District of Massachusetts [Internet]. 2020, Jan 23 [cited 2022, Aug 24]. Available at: https://www.justice.gov/usao-ma/pr/founder-and-former-chairman-board-insys-therapeutics-sentenced-66-months-prison.

98 Chen J. Veblen good. Investopedia [Internet]. 2020, Nov 30 [cited 2022, Aug 24]. Available from: https://www.investopedia.com/terms/v/veblen-good.asp.

99 Friedman M. A Friedman doctrine—The social responsibility of business is to increase its profits. New York Times, 1970, Sept 13.

100 Our values. Boeing [Internet]. [cited 2022, Aug 24]. Available from: https://www.boeing.com/principles/vision.page.

101 Our principles. Boeing [Internet]. [cited 2022, Aug 24]. Available from: https://www.bia-boeing.com/our-principles.

102 Our principles. Boeing [Internet]. [cited 2022, Oct 22]. Available from: https://www.bia-boeing.com/our-principles. Available from: https://www.bia-boeing.com/our-principles.

103 Boeing 737 MAX. Wikipedia [Internet]. [cited 2022, Aug 24]. Available from: https://en.wikipedia.org/wiki/Boeing_737_MAX.

104 Glanz J, Creswell J, Kaplan, T, et al. After Lion Air crash in October, questions about the plane arose. New York Times; 2019, Feb 3.

105 Glanz J, Kaplan T, Nicas J. In Egyptian Air crash, faulty sensor on Boeing 737 Max is suspected. New York Times; 2019, Mar 29.

106 Read the Boeing pilot messages from 2016: ‘The plane is trimming itself like craxy.’ New York Time; 2019, Oct 18.

107 Nicas J, Gelles D, Glanz J. Changes to flight software on 737 Max escaped F.A.A. scrutiny. New York Times; 2019, Apr 11.

108 Before deadly crashes Boeing pushed for a law that undercut oversight. New York Times; 2019, Jul 29.

109 Majority Staff of the Committee on Transportation and Infrastructure (2020). *The design, development and certification of the Boeing 737 Max.* Washington, DC: House Committee on Transportation and Infrastructure.

110 Aviation safety oversight: Committee investigation report. Washington, D.C.: Senate Committee on Commerce, Science and Transportation; 2020.

111 Boeing charged with 737 MAX fraud conspiracy and agrees to pay over $2.5 billion. United States Department of Justice [Internet]. 2021, Jan 7 [cited 2022, Aug 24]. Available from: https://www.justice.gov/opa/pr/boeing-charged-737-max-fraud-conspiracy-and-agrees-pay-over-25-billion.

112 Shepardson D. Boeing to pay $200 million to settle U.S. charges it misled investors about 737 MAX. Reuters [Internet]. 2022, Sep 22 [cited 2022, Oct 22]. Available from: https://www.reuters.com/business/aerospace-defense/boeing-pay-200-million-settle-civil-charges-it-misled-investors-about-737-max-2022-09-22/

113 Ikigai. Dictionary.com [Internet]. [cited 2022, Aug 24]. Available from: https://www.dictionary.com/browse/ikigai.

2

What Is Design?

All that we do, almost all of the time, is design, for design is basic to all human activity.

Victor Papanek
Designer and
Professor of Design

Everyday Design

When you think of the word *design*, it most often brings to mind some "thing," typically a new artifact of some sort, such as a powerful mechanical device, an exciting computer game, a clever app, a sleek sports car, a trendy dress, an efficient appliance, or a dramatic office building on an urban skyline. It can also be an assemblage of things, such as a modern home interior, a vivid garden arrangement, a waterfront development. Indeed, designer and theorist Christopher Jones defines *design* as, "change in man-made things."[1]

However, in his seminal work *The Sciences of the Artificial*,[2] Nobel Laureate Herbert Simon, takes a more wide-ranging view of design than does Jones, one that goes beyond the designed "thing." Simon (see Figure 2.1) was a polymath: his academic degree was in political science and he made major contributions to the fields of cognitive psychology, computer science, artificial intelligence, and administrative behavior and he received his Nobel Prize in economics.

Simon has had a significant impact on my thinking and career. While an undergraduate political science major at the University of Michigan, I wrote a senior term paper applying Simon's and Allen Newell's General Problem Solver model[3] to the congressional legislative process. Later, as a professor at the University of Michigan, I studied with Simon for a year when I was on sabbatical at Carnegie Mellon University, and I used his work in graduate design courses that I taught and for software that I designed.

For Simon, design is not merely the creation of things, it is the fundamental way that we humans accomplish our goals and respond to our environment, " . . . the designer is concerned with how things ought to be—how they ought to be in order to attain goals, and to function" (p. 4). With our designs, we adapt to our situations and adapt our situations to our needs. Design is a fundamentally human activity. And the condition of our world—indeed its fate—hinges on our ability to do it well.

Designer and design theorist Victor Papanek agrees with this more inclusive conception of design, as reflected in the opening quote of this chapter.[4] So does design historian Victor Margolin.

Make the World a Better Place: Design with Passion, Purpose, and Values, First Edition. Robert B. Kozma.

Figure 2.1 Carnegie Mellon University Prof. Herbert Simon (Public domain, Rochester Institute of Technology, Wikimedia Commons).

In his article "Social Design: From Utopia to the Good Society," he uses the term *design* "in its widest possible sense . . . to recognize the wide range of designed products—whether material or nonmaterial—among which we live: objects, graphics, systems, and even political and legal structures."[5]

So, if we think of designs as material and nonmaterial ways, we accomplish our goals, meet our needs, and change our world; then designed artifacts are not only airplanes, buildings, guns, vaccines, video games, and eye-catching advertisements, but also flight plans, zoning ordinances, business plans, public policies, gun laws, healthcare programs, scientific research projects, and social movements.

Everyday Designers

This inclusive conception of design has important implications for all of us, for it includes all of us as designers. In Simon's view of design, designers are not only the people who have *design* appended to their title: product designer, software designer, game designer, user experience designer, graphic designer, fashion designer. Nor are they only others typically associated with design, such as architects, engineers, and urban planners. For Simon, "Everyone designs who changes existing situations into preferred ones" (p. 129).

So then, designers are also teachers, doctors, lawyers, chemists, song writers, film producers, legislators, managers, consultants, social workers, college students, product managers, social influencers, makers, and hobbyists. A designer is anyone who systematically solves problems and creates, not just buildings, automobiles, wonder drugs, kitchen appliances, handbags, or jewelry, but lesson plans, medical treatments, college term papers, legal briefs, laws, policies, social environments, mass movements, and institutions.

From this perspective, all of us are designers and we design every day. Certainly, as humans, we are all capable of design; it is in our nature. And we all participate in this grand endeavor to adapt our environment to our purposes; we all participate in designs in some way. If we don't directly create artifacts, we invest in their invention, we support their development, we participate in their manufacture and implementation, and we market them, sell them, buy them, use them, and dispose them.

While a single person or small team are often credited with a design, and their contribution justifiably lauded, design is more often than not a collective activity. For example, the iPhone was not only Steve Jobs's idea; its creation involved a team of engineers, software designers, and product designers headed up by Jony Ive, who fleshed out the concept; it was a business team headed up by Tim Cook, who created the supply chain; it was the managers and assemblers at Foxconn, who manufactured it; it was the advertisers and graphic artists at TBWA Media Arts Lab and the "Shot on iPhone" ad campaign; it was Apple's distributors at Apple Stores around the world, who sold them; it was the software designers, who developed the apps for the iPhone; it was the technical support people, who taught customers how to use the them, addressed their problems, and made repairs; and it was the accountants, sales people, secretaries, clerks, and janitors at Apple and other companies, who kept all these companies running. All of these people were needed to bring the iPhone to fruition. But, ultimately, it was the 728 million consumers around the world that made this design—the iPhone—a success.[6]

The importance of this common, human endeavor in the grand scheme of things leads Simon to conclude that "in large part, the proper study of mankind is the science of design, not only as the professional component of a technical education but as a core discipline for every liberally educated person" (p. 138).

We are all designers. We all participate in design in some way. It's what makes us human.

The question is not whether we are all designers; it is whether or not we will do it well.

Design as a Process

Product designers, architects, engineers, doctors, teachers, and other professionals study their craft for years and have degrees and certificates that allow them to claim their titles. They have specialized skills that they practice for decades to excel at their profession. What they do and the artifacts they create are very different from each other; the designs of architects look nothing like those of product designers or of teachers. However, in his effort to create a science of design, Simon characterizes design in a general way that captures all of these specializations.

For Simon, design is purposeful " . . . courses of action aimed at changing existing situations into preferred ones" (p. 111). With this characterization, Simon acknowledges that the word can be used as a verb—a course of action or a process—or as a noun—the outcome of the process, which could be a "thing" or some other human-created, nonmaterial change. Also included in Simon's description is an intended impact or consequence of the design—the *preferred* situation. Given this characterization, design looks something like in Figure 2.2:

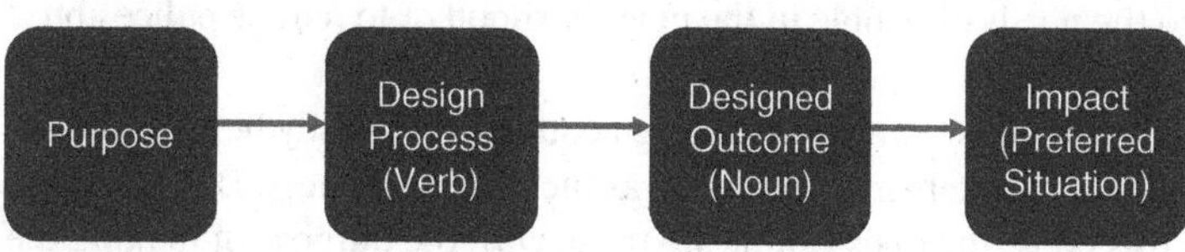

Figure 2.2 Design.

In this book, I will consider all of these aspects of design: the purposes, the design process, the designed outcomes, and their impacts, including those that contribute to a better world and those that don't, with a preference for the former.

Purpose

As a concept, *purpose* goes back to ancient times. For Aristotle, purpose was inherent in the thing, inherent in its nature. The purpose of the lungs is to bring air into the body, and the purpose of the tongue is to taste and to talk.

But the purpose of a design is not inherent in the thing, it is human-made. Purpose is the reason for the design and represents that which is valued in the outcome that is to be created and the impact it has. Purpose is our intention to get us from where we are to where we want to be. It's part of the design process. For Simon, the design is shaped by its purpose and the environment for which it is designed (p. 5).

The purpose of a new product could be to increase convenience, save time, or project a certain social status. The purpose of a service could be to eliminate drudgery, pamper customers, give them an enjoyable experience, or make them look great. The purpose of a social movement could be to change society.

Purpose also directs more immediate, proximal goals. While purposes are over-arching, a goal is a more specific, intermediate state, subordinate to a longer-term purpose. There may be a whole network of hierarchical goals and sub-goals. A purpose may be to have more money; a goal would be to design a profit-making product; a sub-goal may be to specify a design brief for its creation. A purpose may be to be happy; a goal may be to create a comfortable, safe personal environment; a sub-goal may be to read a great book in a cozy chair, listen to enchanting music, or form a close, supportive relationship.

In 2011, Dutch teenager Boyan Slat encountered more plastic in the sea than fish during a diving trip in Greece. This motivated him to begin a design project for his high school science class with the ambitious purpose of cleaning the ocean. Slat's goal was to create a mechanism to do that. His design idea was that rather than expend the energy and money to go around catching the debris, it would be much more efficient to let the plastic come to him by using natural currents to divert it into the waiting arms of platforms anchored in one of several enormous plastic garbage patches. In 2014, he formed a nonprofit organization, The Ocean Cleanup,[7] and was able to obtain funding that allowed him to begin testing his ideas—his sub-goal.[8]

If your purpose is to make the world a better place, your goal may be to create designs that reduce hunger, decrease food waste, enable a paraplegic to walk, or create a service that bridges differences between people and brings them closer together. The goal of a social program may be to provide the homeless with shelter and transition them into employment and long-term housing. The goal of a museum exhibition may be to inform the public about the works of a particular artist and create an appreciation for the beauty of her work. The goal of a new product might be to provide families with inexpensive, nutritious meals. The goal of a social movement might be to make government more responsive to the needs of people in the neighborhood or to reduce police abuse in the Black community.

But if a designer's purpose is only to make money, the design could just as easily be an addictive drug as a playful toy, and it could just as likely increase harm as increase happiness. Design covers a full range of purposes, but in this book, the ones I value are those with the purpose of making the world a better place.

Process

The design process is the course of actions, guided by purpose, that take us from the current state to a preferred one. In his book, Simon refers to design as the "science of the artificial," and as a science, he conceives it to be a rational, analytic process.

One formalism that Simon proposes for the design process is an optimization method. With this method, the desired goal is specified and a list of possible means for achieving it are generated, along with a set of contextual demands that constrain the design. The list of possible means is systematically, perhaps statistically, analyzed to determine the best solution that also meets the constraints. For instance, there are a number of different ways to design a website and a good web designer knows how to optimize it for higher rankings with search engines.

In many situations, optimal solutions are not always possible, given other constraints, in which case, *satisficing* may be the best design approach; that is, a design that meets the minimum requirements but is not necessarily the best design. For example, in 1970, when an oxygen tank in Apollo XIII exploded half way on its trip to the moon, the astronauts onboard had to figure out a way to survive long enough to get them back home. The NASA engineers in Houston threw on a table all the stuff the astronauts had available to them in the space craft. By systematically going through the combinations of things that could be used to give the astronauts enough oxygen, they designed a jerry-rigged solution, just in the nick of time. The solution may not have been the optimal one. Had the engineers had more time, they might have come up with an even better solution. But the one they devised met the crucial time constraint and brought the astronauts back alive. It is considered NASA's finest hour.

However, some situations are so complex they do not lend themselves to this technical, analytic approach. These complex situations are sometimes called ill-defined or "wicked" problems.[9] They are situations where the set of possible solutions is unknown, the desired product is unclear, and its impact is difficult to measure, or perhaps, even to envision. And the purpose that launched the project may be a vague dissatisfaction with the current situation and a general feeling that things must change. The design challenge, in these complex situations, is to convert the aspirational to the actual. The process may be messier, much less rational and more intuitive. The process evolves as the designer works in fits and starts, trials and failures, partial successes or starting over from scratch.

While I will include rational, analytic approaches to the design process in this book, in Chapters 6–10, I will also include processes that are more social and aesthetic in nature, approaches that are, perhaps, more suited to ill-defined, wicked problems.

Outcomes

The creations that come out of the design process are the "things" that we normally associate with design—products, buildings, appliances, clothing, and so on. But with the approach to design taken by Simon, Papanek, and Margolin, design outcomes include a wide range of designed material and nonmaterial products, services, experiences, systems, and structures. So, included in this book are outcomes such as scientific discoveries, social programs, works of art, procedures, policies, organizations, institutions, and mass movements. From this broad perspective, books, musical scores, paintings, legal briefs, surgical procedures, social programs, educational curricula, business plans, term papers, charitable organizations, and labor movements are all design outcomes, anything created to achieve a desired impact.

Often, outcomes of the design process are incremental refinements of a previous design intended to improve the impact or address errors or unanticipated side effects of previous designs. For example, orthopedic casts have been around since ancient times. Hippocrates wrote about them in some detail in the 4th century BC.[10] But in 2016, Alex Wulff, a senior at Skaneateles High School in upstate New York, came up with a new twist on their design.[11] Wulff was concerned with the harmful complications of casts, such as compartment syndrome, skin infection, delayed union, and pain. His response was to develop a system that monitors conditions inside casts and splints while promoting patient healing and comfort. Called "CastMinder," his system consists of a series of embedded sensors that can track conditions such as pressure, moisture, and temperature. The sensors detect potentially harmful changes in the status of the treatment, and communicate this information wirelessly to both the patient and medical professionals, thus avoiding complications before they arise and considerably improving the previous design of orthopedic casts. Wulff went on to attend Harvard University.

On the other hand, some designs are altogether new and transformational. This type of design is the most challenging, and perhaps, the most impactful, for it starts by envisioning something that doesn't yet exist, that hasn't yet been tried, and takes us beyond our current habits, experiences, and assumptions. This was certainly the situation for the 55 delegates from the newly formed American states at the 1787 convention in Philadelphia. Though the process was complex and contentious, the documents and institutions they ultimately designed were more revolutionary than the so-named war that preceded it 11 years earlier. The purpose was to "to form a more perfect Union, establish Justice, insure domestic Tranquility, provide for the common defense, promote the general Welfare, and secure the Blessings of Liberty to ourselves and our Posterity."[12] And the resulting design, although flawed in some ways, was a set of documents and institutions that created a unique form of federal government with three branches, a set of checks and balances intended to assure that none of these branches would prevail over the others, as well as a dynamic process for change. At the same time, a set of amendments laid out the rights of states and individual citizens.

Impact

Impact is what happens after the design is released. It is the consequences of its implementation or use. It implies the criterion for its success: Does the design meet its goal or purpose?

This also implies some assessment or measure. Often, this is specified in the design brief. The goal of a new product might be measured by the number of products sold or the profit made. But it could also be measured by the enjoyment in its use or the learning that results. The impact of a homeless program might be measured by the number of homeless who sleep off the street, and perhaps, transition to more permanent housing. The impact of a museum exhibition may be the number of visitors or the extent to which visitors understand the artist's approach or the emotional response they have to the exhibition. The impact of a social movement may be to create a more just society.

But too often, impacts are measured *only* in the number of sales or the amount of profit a design produces, those things that are easiest to measure. Often things of real value get lost in the numbers. Take, for example, Gross Domestic Product (GDP). GDP is a monetary measure of the market value of all the final goods and services produced by a country in a specific time period. It's easy to count so it is often used to measure the success of our economy. But it lumps together the production of vaccines, educational services, cars, cigarettes, nuclear warheads, semi-automatic rifles, TV programs, video games, and jails. What it doesn't measure is happiness, understanding, equality, justice, relationships, and community, the things that we really value most in our lives.

Only measuring data that is easy to calculate often limits the kinds of designs that might make the world better. Clearly, measuring some impacts is more difficult than measuring other impacts. How do we measure "more equal" or "less unjust"? Using nontraditional or proxy measures can stretch our design goals and broaden the purposes we consider.

For example, the purpose of Big Brothers Big Sisters of America is to help children realize their potential and build their futures.[13] That impact is tough to measure for a number of reasons: the subjectivity of words like "realize their potential" and the fact that, if realized, it wouldn't be until sometime in the future, many years off. It was easy to document that volunteer Big Brothers and Big Sisters served 135,786 children in 2019.[14] But the organization went on to show that children in the program, compared to other children, were less likely to skip school or begin using illegal drugs or alcohol, behaviors that would impair their future. These proxy measures gave them a good sense that the program was meeting its goal and the children they served were indeed going to "build their futures."

Of course, it is essential to measure the intended impacts most directly related to a design's purpose. But we must not neglect the examination of unintended or secondary impacts. Indeed, these impacts may actually be greater than the narrow impact initially intended by the designer. Take the case of Dichlorodiphenyltrichloroethane, commonly known as DDT. This colorless, tasteless, and almost odorless chemical compound was first synthesized in 1874.[15] But its insecticidal action was only discovered in 1939 by the Swiss chemist Paul Hermann Müller. DDT was subsequently used in the second half of World War II to control malaria and typhus among civilians and troops, and it earned Müller a Nobel Prize in Chemistry in 1948. After the war, it was promoted by government and industry for use as an agricultural and household pesticide. However, in 1962, Rachel Carson wrote a book—itself a design—entitled *Silent Spring* claiming that DDT and other pesticides had been shown to cause cancer and that their agricultural use was a threat to people and wildlife, particularly birds.[16] Measuring the unintended impact of this product prior to its introduction would have avoided these problems. As a design, the impact of Carson's book was a large public outcry that led to a ban on DDT's agricultural use in the United States in 1972—one way to measure success.

Good Designs versus Good Impacts

There is a traditional way of thinking about "good designs." When we think of what makes a design good, we often think of characteristics of the "thing": it functions well, doesn't break, it's innovative or enjoyable; or satisfying to hold, wear, or look at. We think of the Mac or iPhone, a Ferrari or Lamborghini sports car, a Frank Gehry building, a Chanel purse, a Dior dress, or a Bvlgari bracelet.

Renowned European designer, Dieter Rams laid out an extensive set of characteristics of good designs.[17] For Rams, good designs are:

1) Innovative—Technological development is always offering new opportunities for original designs, but can never be an end in itself.
2) Useful—It has to satisfy not only functional, but also psychological and aesthetic criteria.
3) Aesthetic—The aesthetic quality is integral because products are used every day and have an effect on people and their well-being.
4) Understandable—The product clearly expresses its function by engaging the user's intuition.
5) Unobtrusive—Their design should be both neutral and restrained, to leave room for the user's self-expression.
6) Honest—It does not make a product appear more innovative, powerful or valuable than it really is.
7) Long-lasting—Unlike fashionable designs, it lasts many years—even in today's throwaway society.

8) Thorough down to the last detail—Care and accuracy in the design process show respect toward the consumer.
9) Environmentally friendly—It makes an important contribution to the preservation of the environment.
10) As little design as possible—Less, but better. Back to purity, back to simplicity.

While these criteria emphasize qualities of the "thing," Simon's characterization of design shifts the emphasis from the thing to its impact. He states that during the design process, the designer " . . . is concerned with how things *ought* to be . . . " [emphasis in the original] (p. 137). In talking about "ought" and "preferred situations," Simon clearly positions design in a normative, ethical, moral space.

From this perspective, all designs have moral implications. The designer's task is to take a situation from where it *is* to where it *should* to be. Creating good designs is not just making beautiful things, but creating designs that result in good impacts, impacts that we ought to aim for.

Beauty in design is important; don't get me wrong. It is part of what we enjoy about its use. But with Simon's characterization, a good design must be judged not only by the characteristics of the outcome of the design process—characteristics of the "thing"—but by the normative value of its impact as well—its "ought."

As important as "oughts" are for Simon, he does not specify them in his book. In developing the science of design, he intentionally avoids normative specifics. The process, he contends, is meant to meet the desired design criteria, whatever those might be (pp. 114–115). But he challenges us to thoughtfully consider the preferred situations—the impacts—that we are trying to achieve with our designs and to think through the purposeful course of actions that lead to an outcome with the preferred impact. Without this consideration, the preferred situation can just as easily be making money from an internet scam as saving a life with an innovative app, just as easily be a police state as a democracy.

I argue that our preferred situation is, to use my dad's words, "a world better than we found it." That is the purpose that drives this book. In the next chapter, I propose that the impact of our designs, those with the purpose of making the world a better place, should be to reduce harm; increase happiness and well-being; advance knowledge, reasoning, and agency; promote equality; address injustice; or build compassionate, supportive relationships, and communities. We will explore the rationale behind these principles, and in Chapters 11–15, we will look at their implications for designs that make the world better.

Everyday Designs and Making the World Better

As described so far, the design process may be so abstract, so general as to lose much meaning. Throughout the book, we will examine a wide range of design examples and case studies to flesh out the concept. We will look at them all through the lens of purpose, process, outcomes, and impacts that allow us to consider them all as designs, even though, on the surface, they all look very different.

Let's look at one of them now.

We can't think of many things that are more every day than food and water. Every day, in rich countries, we eat three meals, sometimes more, sometimes less if we're trying to lose weight. It's something most of us take for granted. Yet, there are many situations around the world where it can't be taken for granted. Even in rich countries, when disaster strikes, food and water are among the first things we need and the first that are lost. It can happen to any of us. And in this world of changing climate, it will happen more and more.

Case Study: Chef Andrés and the World Central Kitchen

It is also hard to think of a more everyday activity than cooking. If you don't do it yourself, your partner does, or the cook at the restaurant around the corner.

José Andrés (see Figure 1) is hardly an everyday cook. He is an award-winning, celebrity chef and restaurateur with establishments all over the United States. He is often credited with bringing small-plate menus to the United States from his home country of Spain.

Figure 2.3 Chef José Andrés (Photo by Lev Radin, Shutterstock)

He's not an everyday cook, but he and his collaborators are everyday designers.

Case Study: Chef Andrés and the World Central Kitchen

A Washington D.C. restaurant listing on *Tock* reads, "Minibar by José Andrés, a two Michelin-starred restaurant, is a study in avant-garde cooking where each bite is designed to thrill the senses by pushing the limits of what we have come to expect—and what is possible—from food."[18] Minibar is one of six restaurants José Andrés has in D.C. and among 18 he has around the United States and abroad. On a typical night, Minibar's kitchen serves 30 lucky people who each pay $295 (before wine) to be served one of Chef Andrés' exciting meals.

On the other hand, on a busy day in March of 2022, in the Polish border town of Przemsyl, Chef Andrés' kitchen distributed around 10,000 simple, nutritious meals for free.[19] As of June 20, 2022, the organization has served over 44 million meals across 8 countries affected by the war in Ukraine (see Figure 2.4).[20]

(Continued)

Case Study: Chef Andrés and the World Central Kitchen (Continued)

Figure 2.4 World Central Kitchen with Ukrainian refugees (Photo by Sodel Vladyslav, Shutterstock).

Chef Andrés' nonprofit organization is World Central Kitchen. It is a very different kind of design than Minibar, and he describes it in his book *We Fed an Island: The True Story of Rebuilding Puerto Rico, One Meal at a Time.*[21]

Chef Andrés launched World Central Kitchen (WCK) in 2010 in response to the disastrous earthquake in Haiti. Since then, WCK has organized meals in the Dominican Republic, Nicaragua, Zambia, Peru, Cuba, Uganda, The Bahamas, Cambodia, Ukraine, and the United States, including Puerto Rico. It has responded to natural and human-made disasters that include hurricanes, tornados, floods, wildfires, pandemics, and mass migration, and has served more than 70 million fresh meals to people in need.[22] In 2020 alone, WCK spent more than $250 million providing meals for communities in the United States and around the world.

The chef elaborates:

> We fed an island after Hurricane Maria destroyed Puerto Rico. We fed tens of millions struggling with the Covid-19 pandemic. We put boots on the ground when a blast devastated Beirut, bushfires ripped through Australia, and a volcano transformed a Spanish island. We were under a bridge with thousands of asylum seekers in Texas, in a demolished Kentucky town after brutal tornadoes, on the Louisiana coast when yet another enormous hurricane made landfall.[23]

Chef Andrés was one of the first people to arrive in Puerto Rico for humanitarian purposes after Hurricane Maria hit. He overcame many obstacles, natural and bureaucratic, to set up the biggest kitchen on the island. On the first day of its operation, the chef and others from a cadre of volunteers known as Chefs for Puerto Rico, prepared 1,000 meals. By the second day, they doubled that and over the following three months they prepared and served 3 million meals throughout the island (pp. ix–x).

The chef was inspired by the organized, volunteer relief efforts of the Southern Baptist Convention, which he first saw in 2012 in response to Hurricane Sandy and has witnessed many times since. He decided to combine its organizational techniques with the food intelligence of local chefs to design a system to respond to disasters.

While inspired by the Southern Baptist Convention, the WCK approach is unique. It is a rapid-response organization. When disaster strikes, its Chef Relief Team mobilizes to the frontlines immediately to start cooking and providing meals. The group is able to act quickly because it leverages local resources and adapts to the local situation in real time. WCK was set up in Puerto Rico within days of Hurricane Maria. While fires were still burning in northern California in 2020, WCK began cooking meals for both first responders and people who had been evacuated.[24] In 2022, it distributed 43,000 meals to families displaced by Hurricane Julia in Venezuela and Guatemala[25] and distributed 825,000 meals to people displaced by Hurricane Ian in Florida.[26] And within a week of the Russian invasion of Ukraine, WCK was set up and distributing meals to refugees, subsequently serving over 170 million meals across eight countries.[27]

The group ensures the food they serve is nutritious. It's not pre-packaged food; WCK sources and hires locally, to jump-start economic recovery through food. The nonprofit does this by partnering with organizations on the ground and activating a network of food trucks or emergency kitchens, to provide freshly made, nutritious meals. The first meal out the door during the California fires was a nourishing beef teriyaki stir fry over cilantro rice served with salad.

In the course of providing food, WCK builds resilient food systems and locally led solutions. Their immediate goal is to revitalize local operations and begin to regrow their capacity for food production, distribution, and sales. WCK's Food Producer Network partners with and supports smallholder farmers, fishers, and small food-related businesses with climate change mitigation and adaptation programs.

But in the long term, the organization aims to contribute to system-wide improvements in food and nutrition security and sustainability by building the capacity of local communities to produce their own food and increase their resilience against future disasters. WCK trains chefs and school cooks, and advances clean cooking practices. And it awards grants to farms, fisheries, and small food businesses while also providing educational and networking opportunities.

In 2021, WCK launched their Climate Disaster Fund: a $1 billion commitment to support communities impacted by the climate crisis over the next decade.[28]

World Central Kitchen is nothing like an iPhone, or a Frank Gehry building, or the latest version of *Grand Theft Auto*. But it is a design, nonetheless. It has purpose, a process, outcomes, and impacts.

There was a basic yet profoundly deep purpose that drove Chef Andrés's work. In reflecting on the project in Puerto Rico, he said, "It was hot, sweaty, exhausting work. But it was also life-changing and inspiring, channeling our love to do something as simple as this: to feed the people" (p. 4).

The simplicity of the goal belied the complexity of the process and it was ingenious. He brought his considerable experience, expertise, and resources to empower local people to address a local disaster. Conditions are different in every situation; there are different problems, different constraints, and different local resources. Responding to a hurricane is very different than responding to a flood or wildfire. Yet, when it comes down to it, everyone needs food and water. The genius of Chef Andrés design is to analyze the local situation and enable, develop, and harness the available resources to respond to the community's own specific needs, to change the situation from what it is to what it ought to be.

There is an outcome. The kitchens he and his collaborators set up and the local process are themselves a very important outcome, as are, of course, the millions of meals they produce.

The impact can be counted in terms of the number of meals prepared and the number of people fed, and that is impressive. But there is, perhaps, an even greater, longer-term impact. As the chef puts it, "After a disaster, food is the fastest way to rebuild our sense of community. We can put people back to work preparing it, and we can put lives back together by fighting hunger."[29]

By working with the local community, by drawing on its resources and empowering people to respond effectively to the tragedy that hit them, the impact of Chef Andrés' design is not only to feed them, but it also rebuilds lives and communities.

Designs Big, Small, and Not at All

In 1968, Garrett Hardin, a biology professor at the University of California, wrote an article in the magazine *Science* entitled "The Tragedy of the Commons."[30] In the article, Hardin described a hypothetical situation in which farmers shared a common meadow for grazing. With each farmer operating out of their own self-interest, it profits each to add cows to their own herd, increasing their income and doing so without incurring additional feeding costs, since the meadow is held in common. But the net result of each farmer following their own self-interest is that the continuous addition of cows results in overgrazing and the meadow collapses. Everyone loses—hence the tragedy.

Hardin contended that there is no way to both keep the meadow in common and to maintain it sustainably. The collapse could only be avoided by either having a central authority design a top-down scheme that determines how many cows from each herd could use it for how long. Or it could be avoided by privatizing the meadow, in which case, the owner would increase the herd only to the extent that the field could be maintained.

This metaphor came to stand for two economic approaches, which we will examine in more detail in Chapter 16. On the one hand, you have "big design"—grand schemes, comprehensively thought through, to create a better world. In economics, big design would be government interventions and regulations that manage the extremes and failures of the free market, of the sort practiced in the United States in the mid-20th century and in many European social-democratic states today, particularly in the Nordic countries. In its extreme form, there is a centrally planned economy and society, such as in the former Soviet Union, in which a committee allocates resources, and sets prices and wages.

From this perspective, the government could save the meadow by statistically analyzing the grass production of the meadow and the number of cows of a certain weight that it can support, and then designing a scheme that allocates a certain number of cows, of a certain weight, that each farmer can have and assigns them certain time slots for use.

On the other hand, you have "no design." This is the laissez-faire, free market approach to the economy advanced by Nobel economists Friedrich Hayek[31] and Milton Friedman, and others. Hayek argued that the price mechanism in the market allows economic actors to achieve ends that serve their own purposes through a principle of spontaneous self-organization, allowing rapid adaptation to the changes in particular circumstances of time and place. From this perspective, no design is needed. In the case of the meadow, the farmer who ended up owning it would figure out the number of cows it can support, based on the market, without government intervention.

For a long time, economists thought these were the only alternatives to save the meadow. However, Elinor Ostrom (see Figure 2.5), a professor at Indiana University and the first woman to

Figure 2.5 Indiana University Prof. Elinor Ostrom (© Prolineserver 2010, Wikimedia Commons).

receive the Nobel Prize in Economics, found another way. Her research around the world identified numerous cases where small, local groups and communities that had access to common pool resources, such as meadows, forests, fisheries, and waterways, could act collectively as a community to design ways of managing the commons' sustainably without resorting to either privatization or central dictates.[32]

In his article on the "Good Society,"[33] Victor Margolin acknowledges the importance of designers who think big and envision the future. He cites Walter Gropius and his manifesto for his Bauhaus design school, which influenced designs around the world for over a century.[34] And he includes the brilliant inventor and engineer R. Buckminster Fuller, his "Operating Manual for Spaceship Earth,"[35] and his World Design Science Decade.

However, while Margolin contends that the visions of these big designers give us a space for aspirations and a beacon toward which we can strive, he argues for a different kind of design, one closer to that found in Ostrom's communities and Chef Andrés's World Central Kitchen. Rather than one big design devised by a team of experts, Margolin envisions thousands of people engaged in designs addressing real-world problems, in real-world situations energized and animated by inspiring ideals (p. 41).

Like Margolin, Chef Andrés is moved by inspiring ideals and bold visions and, like Ostrom, his approach is to draw on the resources of local communities—thousands of chefs, cooks, and volunteers—to design kitchens, meals, and distribution systems that contribute to the common good. All of them confirm the importance of individual ingenuity and creativity in solving the problems we face. All of them attest, as well, to the power of the group in helping us do so. All of them are everyday designers engaged in everyday design. All of them make the world a better place.

References

1 Jones JC. Design methods: Seeds of human futures (p. 6). New York: Wiley, 1970.
2 Simon H. The sciences of the artificial (3rd ed.). Cambridge: MIT Press, 1996.
3 Newell A, Simon H. Human problem solving. Englewood Cliffs, NJ: Prentice-Hall, 1972.
4 Papanek V. Design for the real world (3rd ed.). London: Thames Hudson, 2019.
5 Margolin V. Social design: From utopia to the good society. In Margolin V, Billembourg A, Fuad-Luke A, et al., editors. Design for the good society. Netherlands: naio10, 2015, pp. 27–42.
6 O'Dea, S. Number of Apple iPhone devices in use in the U.S., China and the rest of the world in 2017. Statista [Internet]. 2022, Jul 27 [cited 2022, Aug 24]. Available from: https://www.statista.com/statistics/755625/iphones-in-use-in-us-china-and-rest-of-the-world/.
7 The largest cleanup in history. Ocean Cleanup [Internet]. [cited 2022, Aug 24]. Available from: https://theoceancleanup.com.
8 Slat, B. How we showed the oceans could clean themselves. YouTube [web streaming video]. 2014, Jun 3 [cited 2022, Aug 24]. Available from: https://www.youtube.com/watch?v=QpDxE8BhPSM.
9 Rittel HW, Webber MM. Dilemmas in a general theory of planning. Policy Sciences, 1973. 4(2), 155–169.
10 History of casts. Exosseus [Internet]. [cited 2022, Aug 24] Available from: http://exosseus.com/2018/04/16/history-of-casts/.
11 CastMinder by Intellicast [Internet]. [cited 2022, Aug 24]. Available from: https://www.alexwulff.com/CastMinder/.
12 We the people. National Constitution Center [Internet]. [cited 2022, Aug 24]. Available from: https://constitutioncenter.org/interactive-constitution/preamble.
13 About us. Big Brothers Big Sisters [Internet]. [cited 2022, Aug 24]. Available from: https://www.bbbs.org/about-us/.
14 Mitchell J. 2019 Big Brothers Big Sisters of America annual impact report. Big Brothers Big Sisters [Internet]. 2020, May [cited 2022, Aug 24]. Available from: https://www.bbbs.org/wp-content/uploads/2019-BBBSA-Annual-Impact-Report-FINAL.pdf.
15 DDT. Wikipedia [Internet]. [cited 2022, Aug 24]. Available from: https://en.wikipedia.org/wiki/DDT.
16 Carson R. Silent spring. New York: Houghton Mifflin, 1962.
17 Rams D. (2014). *Less but better*. New York: Publisher: Gestalten, 2014.
18 Minibar by José Andrés. Tock [Internet]. [cited 2022, Aug 24]. Available from: https://www.exploretock.com/minibar.
19 Tillman R. In address to Congress, Chef José Andrés stresses need for humanitarian presence in Ukraine. Spectrum News [Internet]. 2022, Jun 10 [cited 2022, Jun 20]. Available from: https://www.ny1.com/nyc/all-boroughs/news/2022/06/07/chef-jos--andr-s-testify-house-subcommittee-congress-ukraine-humanitarian-crisis.
20 https://wck.org/relief/activation-chefs-for-ukraine.
21 Andrés J. We fed an island: The true story of rebuilding Puerto Rico, one meal at a time. New York: Anthony Bourdain/Ecco Press, 2018.
22 World Central Kitchen [Internet]. [cited 2022, Jun 20]. Available from: https://wck.org.
23 Our story. World Central Kitchen [Internet]. [cited 2022, Jun 20]. Available from: https://wck.org/story.
24 Historic wildfires: WCK cooking across Northern California. World Central Kitchen [Internet]. 2020, Aug 21 [cited 2022, Jun 20]. Available from: https://wck.org/news/california-complex-fires.

25 43,000 meals served in Venezuela and Guatemala after Julia. [Internet]. 2022, Oct 19 [cited 2022, Oct 22]. Available from: https://www.worldcentralkitchen.org/news/julia-update.

26 #ChefsForFlorida: Visual stories. World Central Kitchen [Internet]. 2022, Oct 18 [cited 2022, Oct 22]. Available from: https://www.worldcentralkitchen.org/news/chefs-for-florida-ian.

27 Over 1700 million meals across eight countries. World Central Kitchen [Internet]. 2022, July 16 [cited 2022, Oct 22]. Available from: https://www.worldcentralkitchen.org/relief/activation-chefs-for-ukraine.

28 WCK commits $1 billion to families impacted by the climate crisis. World Central Kitchen [Internet]. 2021, Nov 4 [cited 2022, Jun 20]. Available from: https://wck.org/news/climate-disaster-fund.

29 Our story. World Central Kitchen [Internet]. [cited 2022, Jun 20]. Available from: https://wck.org/story.

30 Hardin G. The tragedy of the commons. Science, 1968,162 (3859), 1243–1248.

31 Hayek F. The use of knowledge in society. The American Economic Review, 1945, 35(4), 519–530.

32 Ostrom E. Governing the commons: The evolution of institutions for collective action. Cambridge: Cambridge University Press, 1990.

33 Margolin V. Social design: From utopia to the good society. In Margolin V, Billembourg A, Fuad-Luke A, et al., editors. Design for the good society. Netherlands: naio10, 2015, pp. 27–42.

34 Gropius W. Program of the Staatliche Bauhaus in Weimar. 1919 [cited 2022, Jun 20]. Available from: https://bauhausmanifesto.com.

35 Fuller RB. Operating manual for spaceship earth. Carbondale: Southern Illinois University Press, 1969.

3

Moral Foundations for Designing a Better World

Every man must decide whether he will walk in the light of creative altruism or in the darkness of destructive selfishness.[1]

Dr. Martin Luther King Jr.
Civil Rights Leader

As we consider what makes good designs and how we can make the world a better place, design philosophy professor Glenn Parsons would object: "… *who* are Designers to be making these ethical decisions?"[2] [emphasis in the original]. He contends that moral judgment is not the designer's responsibility, and since the designer has no particular ethical expertise, his or her ethical decisions are likely to be regarded as arbitrary.

But, frankly, to turn around Parsons's logic, how is anyone else involved in the process more or less ethically expert than the designer? Are "corporate masters" philosophers? Are regulators ethicists or clergy? The net effect of Parsons's position is that, short of including credentialed philosophers, ethicists, or clergy in every design decision, the moral basis for a design is undeterminable and there are no legitimate moral foundations for designs.

If Parsons is correct, in effect, *no one* in the design process is qualified to make a moral decision. Therefore, no one takes on the moral responsibility for a design. Perhaps Parsons's position is precisely how the Boeing 737 MAX 8 catastrophe happened and yet another way we find ourselves with so many terrible designs, with such disastrous impacts on society. Why did 346 people die as a result of the Boeing 737 Max MCAS design? Because, as near as we can tell from the public record, *no one* considered the moral implications of their design decisions—not the design engineers, not the technical pilots, not the Boeing executives, not the FAA. Only one time, in all the reporting prior to Boeing CEO Muilenburg's congressional testimony, were values mentioned and it was in an email from him to corporate employees in which he said that Boeing's safety standards can never be too high.[3] But it was in this same email that he denied any responsibility for the disasters or that Boeing withheld information from pilots about the functionality of the 737 MAX 8.

I contend that *everyone* participating in designs is morally responsible. We are all moral agents. We are morally responsible, individually and collectively, for our decisions, our actions, and their consequences. If the world is to be a better place, we *all* have to participate in the morality of investing in, planning, creating, supporting, buying, or using designs that make the world a better place.

All of us … but *particularly* the professional designers who created them.

In making these decisions, you don't need to be a philosopher, ethicist, or member of the clergy. I contend that, contrary to Parsons's claims, there *are* universal moral principles that designers can draw on to make decisions, principles that are based on our common humanity and that are far from arbitrary.

Make the World a Better Place: Design with Passion, Purpose, and Values, First Edition. Robert B. Kozma.

So, what are the principles we can use to address the moral decisions we encounter as designers? And how do we use these principles to make the world a better place?

The Philosophers and "The Good"

In considering the morality of decisions and behavior, many people draw on their religious faith, their upbringing, and their experience. In this chapter, I will draw on the writings of philosophers, especially those of the English-Scottish Enlightenment and Utilitarianism, philosophers who wrote between the mid-17th century to the mid-19th century. Specifically, I draw on the writings of John Locke, David Hume, Adam Smith, and the Utilitarians Benjamin Bentham and John Stuart Mill.

Even though these philosophers wrote centuries ago and were limited in their thinking by their social privilege, their thinking was profound as it continues to influence our thinking and practices today in ways we often don't acknowledge or even realize. The Enlightenment was a turning point in Western history and it had a tremendous impact on our world. These philosophers helped give birth to the modern age. They replaced superstition with reason. And they are why we teach science in school rather than dogma, why we teach chemistry rather than alchemy, why we teach astronomy rather than astrology. They were the interface between the *Ancien Régime* and now. They inspired the American and French revolutions. They are the reason we have a democratic republic in the United States; the reason we have a president and not a king; the reason there are no dukes, duchesses, lords and ladies; the reason we are citizens and not serfs. Their words appear in the U.S. *Declaration of Independence*, the French *Declaration of the Rights of Man and the Citizen*, and the United Nations's *Universal Declaration of Human Rights*. Their ideas inspired the formation of the *U.S. Constitution*, the League of Nations, the United Nations, and the International Court of Justice. And while they lived 300-plus years ago, their words and ideas surround us today.

Unfortunately, we often do not listen to them. But I recommend their words and ideas to you now, as we consider how to make the world a better place and what that might look like.

I draw primarily on these philosophers for six reasons: 1) Their philosophies build on each other and represent a more-or-less coherent body of thinking. 2) Their philosophies draw on both emotion and reason, and both, I believe, are important considerations in design. 3) They include both moral and scientific principles in their writings, and both are essential for our modern life and our designs. 4) Although their philosophies are abstract and academic, they have real-world applications, including the practice of design. 5) Their philosophies have moral implications for both individuals and society and both are significant when considering how to make the world a better place. 6) Above all, the Enlightenment gave humankind a different way of thinking about the world and about ourselves. It is the notion that with the application of reason, people can understand the world and improve their own condition, and that this ability is available to all people.

The Good

But let's start with the basics. If we want good designs, we must ask: What is "good"? This is a question that humans have been pondering for millennia. In his work *The Republic*,[4] Plato, through the character of Socrates, argues that "The Good" is an abstract idea, or "Form," that exists outside the world, although the quality may be reflected in a person or object (pp. 508–509). Aristotle, in his *Nicomachean Ethics*,[5] disagrees with his teacher and contends that "The Good" exists in the material world, as a quality of some person or thing. The philosophers of the Enlightenment—often called the "Philosophes"—viewed "The Good" as not just a quality of objects or people, but a quality in its enactment, as we shall see. So, "good" is not just a matter of being but doing: not just being good but doing good.

To the Philosophes, goodness is a relationship among intent, action, and its material consequences, toward some earthly end or purpose. More specifically, morality for these philosophers, as for Aristotle, is concerned with making life on Earth good. This was a radical departure, at the time, from the scholastic philosophy of the Middle Ages that focused on good in relation to the hereafter.

In the following sections, I present seven interconnected principles that you can use to guide your designs that make the world a better place. As we will see in Chapters 12–15, they all connect to happiness, the highest good. To draw on Tolkien's image, you can think of happiness as the one ring that rules them all.

Moral Foundations for Good Design

Happiness not harm

Aristotle argues that for all things there is a purpose, or a "final cause," that is an end for its own sake and the reason it exists. For Aristotle, the purpose for humanity is to attain "Good," and the "Chief Good" is that purpose for which all human action is performed (*Nicomachean Ethics*, 1097b). Aristotle believed that the Chief Good for humans is *eudaimonia*, often translated as "happiness," "flourishing," or "well-being." This is not the fleeting feeling or experience most modern people associate with the word *happiness*. It is not pleasure in the physical sense, nor is it fame or wealth because the purpose, the "final cause," of each of these is happiness. For Aristotle, happiness is the end in itself. Whether rich or poor, young or old, happiness is "living well"; it is a way of life.

The Philosophes of the Enlightenment believed that happiness, or well-being, is an emotional primitive. While the Enlightenment is best known for its emphasis on reason, it is emotion—or *sentiment* to use their word—that grounded the philosophers' thinking, particularly their moral thinking. Happiness, or pleasure, is the most valued emotion to these philosophers, and misery, or pain, is the least valued. As John Locke (see Figure 3.1) put it, we have "an unalterable pursuit of happiness in general, which is our greatest good."[6] For the Philosophes, "The Good" is the emotion that makes life worth living, much like Aristotle's concept of *eudaimonia*.

The Philosophes believed that happiness is a universal emotion shared by all people, and it is part of what defined us all as human. As Scottish philosopher David Hume (see Figure 3.2) put it, "All men it is allowed, are equally desirous of happiness."[7] Utilitarianism was an extension of the Enlightenment, and Utilitarian philosopher Jeremy Bentham claimed, "Nature has placed mankind under the governance of two sovereign masters, pain and pleasure. It is for them alone to point out what we ought to do, as well as to determine what we shall do."[8]

Goodness pertains not just to a condition—that of living a good life—but to the actions by which the condition is obtained. As Hume wrote of men and their actions, "that what promotes their happiness is good, what tends to their misery is evil" (p. 756). Similarly, for Locke, the morality of actions is based on their relationship to pleasure and pain: "What has an aptness to produce pleasure in us is that we call good, and what is apt to produce pain in us we call evil" (location 4587). That is, actions—or designs, in our thinking—that bring happiness or pleasure are good, and those that result in pain or misery are bad.

Figure 3.1 John Locke (Line engraving by J. June after Sir G. Kneller, 1697).

Figure 3.2 David Hume (Illustration by Istock World).

Bentham and his Utilitarian colleague John Stuart Mill (see Figure 3.3) argued that the morality of an action is understood in terms of the consequences that result, and a moral action is the one that results in the most good and the least harm.[9] The implication of this principle is that an act is not good in itself but is conditional; it depends on its consequences or impact. The same action may be good at some times but not others, depending on the impact. And, depending on its impact, it may be good for some people but not others.

Figure 3.3 John Stuart Mill (Photo from Everett Collection).

So, what are the moral implications of this philosophy for design and designers? The universal nature of this desire for happiness and the avoidance of misery is the foundation of our shared feelings that there was something profoundly wrong with the Boeing 737 MAX 8 situation, and our shared anger at John Kapoor's decision to bribe doctors to fill off-label prescriptions for his opiate that created drug addicts, our shared sympathy for the misery of the families and friends of those suffering from opiate addiction, for those dying in the cities of Ukraine, or for those suffering a lonely death due to COVID.

These shared feelings are the basis for our first two moral principles that designers should follow in order to make the world a better place:

> *Principle 1. First, do no harm.*

> *Principle 2. Actively reduce harm.*

As with healthcare professionals, the charge not to do harm is the most important moral principle in this book. And its corollary is to actively reduce harm.

You might think these principles go without saying, that they are obvious. But there is a lot of misery in the world—sickness, hunger, poverty, violence, civil strife, as documented in Chapter 2. In one way or another, much of this misery is due to human action and the impact of our designs, whether malicious, thoughtless, or miscalculated.

Designs need not be malicious in intent to be immoral; they can be immoral by their consequences. They can start off good but become corrupted along the way. The intent in the design of MCAS for the 737 MAX 8 was to save lives, but as things developed, Boeing employees neglected this purpose and there was massive loss of life due to the design of MCAS that denied pilots the affordance of controlling the plane.

You may not know all the impacts of a design up front, but this doesn't get you off the moral hook. In what philosophers and jurists call "culpable ignorance,"[10] you cannot take refuge in not knowing the impact when you have a moral responsibility to find out. You are responsible for the harm if you *could* have known. Boeing technical pilots may not have known the ultimate harmful impact of sending out MCAS with the MAX 8, but given the "egregious" problems that the Chief Technical Pilot experienced in the simulator, he could have raised the issue with Boeing engineers, executives, and FAA regulators, despite the implications for the production schedule. That did not happen.

If you find yourself in a situation in which you are working in some capacity and you come to understand or have reason to believe that the purpose or impact of the design results in harm, the application of Principle 1 would say that you must consider the extent of the harm—the number of people harmed, the nature and duration of harm, and so on—against any good that might come from the design. If in balance the design is harmful, you have a moral obligation to bring this up with your employer or client, take it up the chain of command, and push for change or maybe even resign from the project, depending on the client's or employer's response and the nature and extent of the harm.

This was the situation for Tyler Shultz.[11] Tyler was a research engineer at Theranos, a start-up company founded by Elizabeth Holmes to make blood testing equipment. On April 11, 2014, he emailed Holmes saying that failed quality-control checks were being ignored by the company. Holmes responded by forwarding his email to Theranos President Ramesh Balwani, who berated Shultz and said the only reason he bothered replying was because he was the grandson of George Shultz, the former Secretary of State and a Theranos Director. Tyler quit that day. He was harassed by company officers, corporate attorneys, even his grandfather. His response: "I refuse to allow bullying, intimidation, and threat of legal action to take away my First Amendment right to speak out against wrongdoing." He went on to tell his story to the *Wall Street Journal*, which ultimately led to the downfall of the company. Subsequently, Holmes and Balwani were charged with wire fraud and conspiracy to commit wire fraud, alleging they engaged in a multimillion-dollar scheme to defraud investors, doctors, and patients. On January 4, 2022, Holmes was found guilty of one count of conspiracy and three counts of wire fraud.[12] On July 7, 2022, Balwani was found guilty of one count of conspiracy and 12 counts of wire fraud.[13]

Beyond not doing harm, designs are good, according to Principle 2, if they reduce harm. In applying the principle, you might proactively design your products to eliminate any harm they could cause; you might address the harm caused by the designs of others; or you might ameliorate harm due to natural causes. Designs of this sort would be aimed at, for example, curing disease, responding to disasters, or reducing homelessness, poverty, gun violence, plastic in the oceans, or toxic pollution in our drinking water.

For instance, Ivan Owen designs prosthetics to address the harm of lost fingers or limbs and produces them on a 3-D printer.[14] Another example is the company HomeBoy, which was founded to integrate ex-gang members into the workplace and society, and it has become an international network of like-minded organizations committed to turning around lives in their communities.[15]

While reducing harm is important, the Philosophes believed greatest good is creating happiness. Locke claimed, "the highest perfection of intellectual nature lies in a careful and constant pursuit of true and solid happiness" (location 6712). And his words on the pursuit of happiness are woven into our Declaration of Independence. For Utilitarians, the greatest good is creating the most happiness for the most people. Happiness is not only a personal good, according to these philosophers, but a shared good and the foundation of interpersonal relationships and society, more generally. It is not only that *we* want to be happy; we want others to be as well. Hume believed, " . . . everything which contributes to the happiness of society recommends itself directly to our approbation and good will" (p. 748). Social sentiments, such as sympathy and compassion, were acknowledged by

Hume and Adam Smith as those emotions that allowed people to feel the pain and share the joy of others. Smith contended that we not only care about our own happiness but we become happier when others are happy.[16] Which leads to our next principle:

Principle 3. Increase happiness and well-being.

Happiness and well-being are at the center of a network of positive emotions that make life worth living. They are the highest good for the Philosophes. In applying Principle 3, you can make a huge contribution to a better world. Creating the most happiness, the greatest well-being, for the most people with the least harm was the ideal for the Utilitarians. And that should be our charge in designing a better world.

A group of farmers and fellow parishioners in rural Indiana came up with an idea that led to the formation of Heifer International.[17] Its purpose is to improve lives and "end poverty from the ground up." But it also increases well-being. Through this program, people have donated money that provides livestock, training, and capacity building to support the local economy for more than 100 million people in more than 125 countries.[18] Their support begins with an investment of seed, livestock, or agriculture, followed by mentorship to help recipients build a business and gain access to markets. As a result, families are able to earn a living and they, in turn, train the next generation of leaders and help lift up their communities.

The State of North Carolina instituted a program called Smart Start a comprehensive, community-based initiative with the goal of improving the well-being of the state's young children and their families.[19] The program is a network of community-based efforts to improve the health, nutrition, and pre-school literacy skills of children through partnerships with healthcare providers, pre-K teacher training, quality childcare and literacy programs, and improved parental support through parenting education programs and home visits. The results have been improved positive parental support practices and improved health practices and cognitive, social emotional, and language and literacy skills that prepare young children for school success and long-term well-being.

Knowledge, reasoning, and agency

The Enlightenment is perhaps known best for its emphasis on reason. In addition to emotions, the Philosophes believed that rational thought is an essential part of being human and a foundation of our common humanity.

Particularly important in Enlightenment Philosophy is the distinct roles that emotion and reason play together in determining moral actions. The Philosophes believed that while moral sentiments, or emotions, *motivate* action and are the basis on which the rightness or wrongness of actions is judged, reason is used to *determine* those actions that are likely to achieve moral ends. As Hume put it: "Reason . . . directs only the impulse . . . by showing us the means of attaining happiness or avoiding misery" (p. 808). That is, emotion (i.e., "impulse") provides the motivation toward happiness, but reason enables us to figure out how to achieve it for ourselves and others.

Drawing on the empirical principles of the earlier Scientific Revolution, philosopher John Locke believed that experience and reason went hand in hand. The process of empirically deriving ideas through perceptions and then reasoning with them is what Locke called the "fountain of knowledge" (location 2178). Locke contended that experimentation and reason are used to prove the causal relationships between ideas and to remove doubt about these relationships.

These ideas about emotion, reason, and causation have implications both for the design process and for our designs. Passion to do good is an important motivation for your designs. And reason can move you from passion and moral purpose to design and impact that makes the world a better place. The goodness of a design is not just based on its functionality or its aesthetics, but its impact. Your knowledge, experimentation, and reasoning can guide you toward a positive impact. The outcome of the design process—your creative product—is an initial hypothesis about the impact that the affordances of the design will have on its users. Empirically confirming that impact on happiness and well-being validates the design or, if not, can suggest changes that need to be made. Also, experimentation and reasoning about cause and effect can let you know which of several design possibilities results in the best desired impact. And finally, when the design is implemented down the road, empiricism and reasoning can determine whether or not a design worked without unintended, harmful secondary impacts.

Knowledge and reasoning are also important goals for your designs, the user impact you intend. The Philosophes believed that reasoning and the capability of obtaining knowledge are distinctive human qualities and the means by which humans achieve happiness. Providing the users of your designs with knowledge and reasoning skills that they can use to learn on their own and to increase their own happiness, gives them *agency* over their own actions and their consequences. For this purpose, advancing knowledge and supporting reasoning and agency are among the impacts that we should aim to achieve with our designs and the basis for Principle 4:

Principle 4. Advance people's knowledge, reasoning, and agency.

In advancing knowledge and reasoning with your designs, you empower those who acquire these capabilities to take actions and make decisions that increase their own happiness and well-being and that of others. Therefore, increasing users' knowledge and reasoning capability has a multiplier effect and can go a long way to maximizing happiness and making the world a better place.

This principle elevates the importance of education and educators and the special moral opportunities and obligations educators have as designers. Formal educational products, such as curricula, textbooks, instructional software, and assessments, if designed well, can have a significant impact on students' knowledge, and in turn, their success in school and life. So can the everyday designs of classroom teachers, as they implement their well-thought-out lesson plans or they improvise on-the-fly designs to support students who encounter difficulties.

The advancement of knowledge and reasoning can also be included in designs outside formal education, such as the design of commercial products and services. Tutorials imbedded in software products, for example, can be designed not only to help users operate the software, but also understand how it can be used to solve practical problems that improve their lives. A micro-loan program for small businesses that my wife and I encountered in our volunteer work in rural Africa was coupled with training that helps villagers improve their accounting practices and gives them the knowledge needed to use loaned money to contribute to the success of their business. Similarly, Heifer International not only provides animal stock to farmers in need, but also provides training that will allow them to improve their business skills, increase their yields, and reduce poverty.

This principle can even be applied in entertainment. The award-winning, 2015 movie *The Big Short* was an entertaining film that also used unique techniques to inform viewers about difficult financial concepts, such as "collateralized debt obligations" and "sub-prime mortgages." This approach helped viewers understand the moral issues embedded in the housing collapse, a topic we will return to in Chapter 16.

These applications of Principle 4 can be contrasted with the Boeing case, where knowledge was intentionally excluded as a component of the Boeing 737 MAX 8 design in order to save money. Boeing felt that pilots didn't need to know that MCAS existed, and training on it was excluded from the marketing and distribution of the MAX 8. This decision made the plane more competitive in the market, but sadly, it deprived pilots of knowledge and agency and it cost people their lives.

Equality and Justice

Through experimentation and reasoning, the philosophers of the Scientific Revolution were determined to find the universal mechanical and biological principles by which all of nature operated. Building on this quest, the Philosophes wanted to articulate universal principles, especially moral principles as they applied to human nature. Indeed, of justice Hume states it "is so universal, and everywhere points so much to the same rules, that the habit takes place in all societies" (p. 736).

The Philosophes believed that it is in the universal nature of all humans to feel, to reason, and to participate in society. They believed that it is this universality that defines us as humans. For these philosophers, emotion, reason, and social connection were not only a matter of our shared humanity, but also the foundation for Locke's claim that "all men by nature are equal" (p. 667).

This notion of our shared humanity and that all of us are equal was a profound break with thinking up to the Enlightenment. Throughout human history and even as late as the 18th century, it was a common belief that humans were fundamentally unequal. Across Europe at the time, there were kings or queens who ruled by divine right and nobles who by birth had special privileges and wealth, believed to be sanctioned by God. There was another, much-larger class of people, commoners or surfs, who had little wealth, but whose allegiance and labor were owed to the king and noble land owners. Among all classes, women had assigned roles and fewer rights as a matter of their gender. And then there were slaves who were considered property and were owned by others. All of this was taken for granted as the given order. In this context, the Enlightenment notion that all people were equal by birth, by their common humanity, was revolutionary, and in several cases, required a revolution to establish the concept and its attendant rights. The Enlightenment notion of equality, that "all men are created equal" and were due equal rights, was the stated motivation for the American colonies to establish their independence from the British monarchy and aristocracy.

Inequalities do exist, the Philosophes were not naïve about this, but they believed all lives are of equal value and people are to be treated equally as a matter of being human. Inequalities, they argued, were due to differences in circumstances. The Utilitarians, especially Mill, were social reformers and used this principle to argue against social inequalities, especially slavery and the subservient role of women in society. They believed these inequalities could be addressed by improving conditions, such as providing access to quality education, a further argument for Principle 4.

The fundamental equality of all people is directly connected to notions of justice and injustice. Hume contends that "no virtue is more natural than justice" (p. 421) and "justice . . . is absolutely requisite to the wellbeing of mankind and existence of society" (p. 732). And for Mill, "Justice implies something which it is not only right to do, and wrong not to do, but which some individual person can claim from us as his moral right."[20]

The concept of justice is fundamental, but also complex and problematic. Mill examines the concept extensively to untangle its complexity. First of all, he claims that justice or injustice are based on sentiment or emotion, as are other moral principles. He states that justice is a " . . . powerful sentiment . . . resembling an instinct . . . to point to an inherent quality in things; to show that the just must have an existence in nature as something absolute . . . " (p. 42). For example, the desire to punish an injustice comes from the feeling of retaliation or vengeance, in the case of a wrong *done by* someone, and the feeling of sympathy, in the case of a wrong *being done to* someone. These might be the powerful feelings evoked, for example, when you watched the video of George Floyd's senseless murder by Minneapolis police officer Derek Chauvin.

However, justice can be problematic in that injustice can arouse very strong feelings, but the action implied is not clear. This is when emotion must defer to moral reasoning. Mill claims that emotions, in themselves, are not moral; what makes them moral are their implications for society. Our natural feelings become moral by these social implications: the extent to which feelings and actions are associated with the general good. A just person is angered by a hurt to someone else or to society, even though it may not be a hurt to oneself. Likewise, a person feels that a hurt to themselves is unjust only if it is of the sort that would also be unjust if it happened to others. That is, morality is involved when a hurt to oneself is seen as wrong if it were done to anyone.

Mill goes on to contend that justice means that one person's happiness is counted for exactly as much as another's. Mill states, "Equality, which often enters as a component part both into the conception of justice and into the practice of it, . . . constitutes its essence" (p. 46). The converse, of course, is injustice of which Mill states, "all social inequalities . . . assume the character, not of simple inexpediency, but of injustice" (p. 63).

This brings us to our fifth and sixth design principles:

Principle 5. Promote equality.

And its corollary:

Principle 6. Address injustice.

Poverty, of course, is a major source of misery in the world and a major indicator of inequality. Poverty, in turn, breeds poverty, in what economists call a "poverty trap" or a "cycle of poverty" or even "poverty that kills." This is when families have limited or no resources, which makes it virtually impossible for people to do the things that are needed to move out of poverty. Without outside help, poverty becomes self-perpetuating. Once it exists, it can persist across generations.

In 1991, the U.S. Department of Housing and Urban Development (HUD) tested a theory: Could they address long-term poverty and inequality by moving a poor family to a better neighborhood? It was a big social experiment, and they called it Moving to Opportunity.[21] HUD chose thousands of families that lived in public housing in five major cities, and for experimental purposes, split them into three groups by lottery. One of these groups was required to move out of public housing into a low-poverty neighborhood and the government helped them cover rent for their new home. Researchers found that the longer a child spent in a low-poverty neighborhood, the better their outcomes were in adulthood. Kids who moved before they turned 13 were 4 percentage points more likely to go to college and had about 30% higher earnings. As a result of this success, Congress, during the 2019–2020 session, passed bipartisan legislation to run more programs like this.

Let your feelings, your passion, particularly your sense of injustice, motivate your designs. If sentiments are evoked by seeing people who are poor, hungry, homeless, sick, displaced, or imprisoned, it is your calling to do something, to design a world that would be better for them. Representative John Lewis prods us with the quote that leads of Chapter 1: "If you see something that is not right, not fair, not just, you have a moral obligation to do something about it."

However, you don't need to be a U.S. Representative or Federal bureaucrat to promote equality or address injustice. Take the example of Rob Bilott.[22] Bilott is an attorney at a prestigious law firm in Cincinnati, Ohio. In 1998, as a favor to his grandmother, he met with a farmer who was a friend of hers in the rural West Virginia area where he grew up and whose cows were dying of unexplained causes. With his investigations, Bilott found out that a nearby company, Dupont, was using a highly-toxic chemical, PFOA, in their manufacturing process and were pumping hundreds of thousands of pounds of it into the Ohio River and into unlined pits from which the chemical seeped into the ground water which supplied drinking water to more than 100,000 people. He also found out that DuPont knew PFOA is highly-toxic. Due to his dogged investigations over seven years, it was ultimately determined that there was a probable cause between PFOA in the drinking water and a variety of cancers. Through arduous work and a thoroughly documented case, Bilott designed a legal strategy that, in 2017, after an almost 20-year long battle, ultimately resulted in DuPont settling more than 3,500 personal injury lawsuits for roughly $670 million. Bilott's work was lauded in the 2019 movie *Dark Waters*. He did it because "it was the right thing to do."[23]

The social nature of humans

While the pursuit of happiness is often one of self-interest, according to the Enlightenment Philosophers, they viewed humans as fundamentally social. As Hume writes, "Human nature cannot, by any means, subsist, without the association of individuals; and that association never could have place, were no regard paid to the laws of equity and justice" (p. 387). Justice and equality are based on a natural impulse of sympathy, in seeing something happen to others that one would or would not want to happen to oneself, as well as on a desire for their happiness. These sentiments are not only the foundations of morality, they provide a common bond among humans. As put by Smith (see Figure 3.4), sentiment is "the source of our fellow-feeling for the misery of others, that

Figure 3.4 Adam Smith (Getty Images).

it is by changing places in fancy with the sufferer, that we come either to conceive or to be affected by what he feels . . . " (p. 16). And according to Hume, these feelings are the basis for our shared community and society. As he states, "affection of humanity . . . being common to all men, it can alone be the foundation of morals . . . the humanity of one man is the humanity of every one; and the same object touches this passion in all human creatures" (p. 790).

Social relations, in turn, influence and support an individual's moral reasoning and behavior. As Mill notes about social influence, " . . . education and opinion, which have so vast a power over human character, should so use that power as to establish in the mind of every individual an indissoluble association between his own happiness and the good of the whole, . . . so that not only he may be unable to conceive the possibility of happiness to himself . . . but also that a direct impulse to promote the general good . . . " (p. 17). Such social influence develops a community of people who care about each other and this care is returned.

The moral connection between the individual and the group is the foundation of our last principle:

Principle 7. Build compassionate, supportive relationships and community.

Building relationships and community not only fills an important human need, it can have a compounding moral impact. A better world builds on not only individual actions but actions and values of the group—collective actions of a community that draw on its shared principles. Moral feelings begin with our everyday, more personal relationships, according to Hume (pp. 502–503). Family, friends, and work groups have the biggest impact on moral emotions and behavior. These moral feelings then become internalized and extended to other relationships.

For example, in their study of parental discipline techniques, researchers Julia Krevans and John Gibbs[24] found that when the parents of 11- and 12-year-old children disciplined antisocial behavior by expressing disappointment and emphasizing the impact it had on others, their children were more likely to display empathic feelings and prosocial behavior than the children of parents who punished with power-assertive discipline. The children who were punished with power-assertive means were also more likely to display concerns about external consequences of their behavior on themselves rather than a concern of the impact on the welfare of others.

Designs that build relationships and community can take advantage of this compounding effect. Turning Point Scotland is a nongovernmental social service organization with a highly successful approach to homelessness.[25] The organization has stated values of respect, compassion, inclusion, and integrity, and their vision is "of a Scotland where everyone has a safe place to call home, a support network of positive relationships and the chance to fill their time with meaningful and enjoyable activity." Their Glasgow Housing First program provides stable social housing and 24-hour support to individuals who are homeless, aged 18 or over, and are involved in drug misuse. The program first provides stable housing to the homeless, without requiring drug abstinence, and subsequently addresses other issues, once housing is obtained. Turing Point couples this approach with a "harm reduction" program that lessens the negative social and physical consequences of drug addiction. The program provides support, such as access to welfare services and motivational encouragement, and develops positive, supportive relationships with their clients. The program is highly-successful in large part because many of its staff are peer support workers who themselves have histories of homelessness and substance misuse.[26] What they've done is to build a community of compassionate, supportive relationships that not only provides housing but creates the conditions in which addiction can be overcome.

Relationships matter. They matter to you. They matter to me. But most of all, they matter to those most at risk of failure in life. Author Josh Shipp captured this truth in his book *The Grownup's Guide to Teenage Human's* about his foster care upbringing, when he said, "Every kid is one caring adult away from being a success story."[27]

Self and Others

But while it's clear that relationships are important, do we really have obligations to the group? Doesn't a better world come about when each of us take care of our own needs? Can't a design philosophy be built on making the world better merely by supporting each individual's goal of maximizing their own personal happiness?

Self-interest

Indeed, the Philosophes believed that actions are motivated by self-interest, with individuals acting to advance their own happiness or avoid misery. For Locke, this is " . . . the state all men are naturally in, and that is, a state of perfect freedom to order their actions, and dispose of their possessions and persons, as they think fit . . . " (location 213). For Hume, " . . . self-interest is the motive for the establishment of justice . . . " (p. 434). And, most famously, Adam Smith said in his book *Wealth of Nations*, "It is not from the benevolence of the butcher, the brewer, or the baker that we expect our dinner, but from their regard to their own interest."[28]

Some contemporary philosophers, specifically Libertarians, give a moral primacy to self-interest. Harvard professor Robert Nozick was the philosophical standard-bearer for this position, using personal liberty as the organizing moral theme of his book *Anarchy, State, and Utopia.*[29] In his book, Nozick starts with Locke's natural state of perfect freedom and goes on to claim freedom as a right above all other moral considerations. That is, "each person may exercise his rights as he chooses" (p. 166). And, most importantly, no others, individually or collectively, can intervene on anyone's right to do as he or she pleases, as long as that act does not violate someone else's right to do so.

According to Nozick, this restriction applies however much an intervention against an individual's rights might contribute to the common good. Arguing explicitly against any Utilitarian notion of the greatest good for the greatest number, he states, " . . . there is no moral outweighing of one of our lives by others so as to lead to a greater overall social good" (p. 33). Indeed, harm, within this system, is when anyone is restricted from doing what they want, as long as it doesn't interfere with the rights of others to do what they want.

Nozick does not provide any moral principles or responsibilities that might guide what a person does do within this frame of rights, leaving that decision entirely to the individual. Nor does he provide any moral guidance for collective action, other than it not interfere with individual rights. Indeed, Nozick denies that there are any independent moral principles that apply to collective action or political institutions that cannot be derived from the natural rights of their individual members (p. 28).

The philosophy is, Nozick admits, a political one, rather than an overtly moral one (p. 8). As such, its greatest prescriptions are for the actions, or rather limitations, of the group or state, with consequent implications for economic activity. Drawing on the ideas of economists Friedrich Hayek, who we met in Chapter 2, and Milton Friedman, who we met in Chapter 1, Nozick argues that the only legitimate state is a minimal state limited to that of assuring individual rights the provision of security, the protection of property, and the enforcement of contracts (p. 26).

The benefit of such a state to its citizens comes about as if guided by an invisible hand (p. 18). In stating this, Nozick draws on an analogy from Philosophe Adam Smith when Smith says, in talking about "the rich":

> They are led by an invisible hand to make nearly the same distribution of the necessaries of life, which would have been made, had the earth been divided into equal portions among all its inhabitants, and thus without intending it, without knowing it, advance the interest of the society. (*Moral Sentiments*, p. 321)

However, while Nozick uses Smith's invisible hand analogy, he would argue against any notion of such a goal as advancing the interest of society or that society, as such, is even capable of having interests beyond those of the individual (pp. 28–29).

Rational egoism

This Libertarian notion of morality first gained popularity with the writings of Ayn Rand in the 1960s, under the name Objectivism or Rational Egoism. And her philosophy is currently espoused in the United States by a self-select group of influential business titans, celebrities, and politicians.[30] While her philosophy espouses many of the principles stated by Novzick, Rand's position goes beyond that of Nozick in that she viewed actions based on self-interest to be not only a moral right, but also a moral obligation to maximize one's own happiness.

Rand was a novelist, born Alisa Zinovyevna Rosenbaum in 1905, and grew up in late-Czarist Russia and the early Soviet Union. She emigrated to the United States in 1926 where she wrote her best-known novels, *Fountainhead* and *Atlas Shrugged*, in which the main characters—rugged individualists and self-made industrialists—suffer from irrational public opinion and burdensome laws and regulations.

In 1961, she also published a collection of essays on her thoughts entitled, *The Virtue of Selfishness: The New Concept of Egoism*.[31] In one of the essays entitled, "The Objectivist Ethics," Rand asserts, as did the Philosophes, that the highest moral purpose in someone's life is to achieve happiness. However, for Rand, only one's own happiness is life's highest purpose (location 450). The fundamental principle of the Objectivist ethics is that life is an end in itself:

> . . . so every living human being is an end in himself, not the means to the ends or the welfare of others—and, therefore, that man must live for his own sake . . . . (location 448)

As did the Philosophes, Rand also believed in human rationality. She asserts that people have a choice as to exercise their rational capacity (location 316). She claims that happiness is possible only for those that do, those who choose nothing but rational goals and who find joy through rational actions (location 485). For those who don't, Rand contends happiness is a fraud, a whim, a delusion, and a mindless escape from reality (location 475). She refers to such people as irrational brutes, who have never outgrown the primordial practice of human sacrifices.

However, Rand differs from the Philosophes in several ways. Rand never mentions the word *compassion* in her essays. And she uses *equality* only once in her essays and does so in a pejorative way (location 2406). She defines the virtue of "justice" as the taking responsibility for one's own life and never sacrificing one's convictions or desires to the opinions or wishes of another and never seeking or granting that which is unearned and undeserved (location 427). As she puts it, "a man must produce the physical values he needs to sustain his life and must acquire the values of character that make his life worth sustaining—that as man is a being of self-made wealth, so he is a being of self-made soul" (location 441).

For Rand, the foundation for human relationships is not a shared human nature. Nor are the emotions of sympathy and compassion, as they are for the Philosophes. Nor is there a common need for participation in society. Rand believes, as does Nozick, that there is no such entity as society (location 198); society is nothing more than a collection of individuals where, more often than not, they by their numbers or force can impose their whims on others (location 1703).

For Rand, all human relationships are based not on shared emotions but on the rational, ethical principle of "trade": " . . . a free, voluntary, unforced, uncoerced exchange—an exchange which benefits both parties by their own independent judgment" (location 553). For Rand:

> The principle of trade is the only rational ethical principle for all human relationships, personal and social, private and public, spiritual and material. It is the principle of justice. (location 530)

These transactions may be the exchange of object for object, object for money, labor for money, love for love. For Rand, love and friendship are selfish values: love is an expression and assertion of one's own self-esteem, a reflection of one's own values in the person of another, values that earn love (location 787).

Rand does not acknowledge inequalities in these transactions, differences in power or wealth that may give one party a distinct advantage over another, an advantage that is compounded over many transactions, and one that makes the transactions far less free and uncoerced than she speculates. Everything that a person does, according to Rand, is the product of one's own self-interested efforts and justifies whatever it is he possesses (location 342). Any benefit another derives from these efforts is incidental to oneself and due only to the self-interested actions of the other. That some have less is due to their lack of virtue and for them she reserves the terms *parasite, moocher* and *looter* (location 479).

Alan Greenspan, Federal Reserve Chair for Presidents Ronald Reagan, George H. W. Bush, and Bill Clinton and a Rand acolyte, wrote a chapter of another of Rand's books, *Capitalism: The Unknown Ideal,* which he titled "The Assault on Integrity." In it, he claims, " . . . it is precisely the 'greed' of the businessman or, more appropriately, his profit-seeking, which is the unexcelled protector of the consumer."[32] It is unlikely that the families we met in Chapter 1, those of the passengers on Lion Air Flight 610 and Ethiopian Airlines Flight 302, would take solace from Greenspan's moral assurance.

The Philosophes and concern for others

While Nozick draws on the Philosophes' notion of self-interest, he ignores or rejects their position that humans are inherently social, that being in relationships is an important part of our nature and has significant moral implications, implications that we must attend to in our designs. Missing in the philosophy of Nozick and Rand is a concern for others. While such a concern is permissible within the range of individual actions, it does not play a moral role in their philosophy.

For the Philosophes, however, a concern for others was the foundation of morality. For them, acting in one's self interest was not a moral dictum. The tendency to do so, to pursue one's own happiness, is balanced by a concern for others. When talking about justice, for example, Hume goes on to say, " . . . but a sympathy with public interest is the source of the moral approbation, which attends that virtue" (p. 434). And more generally, Hume states:

> . . . the useful tendency of the social virtues moves us not by any regards to self-interest, but has an influence much more universal and extensive. It appears that a tendency to public good, and to the promoting of peace, harmony, and order in society, does always, by affecting the benevolent principles of our frame, engage us on the side of the social virtues. (p. 758)

And in a much less quoted statement than his invisible hand one, Smith claims of humans: "there are evidently some principles in his nature, which interest him in the fortune of others, and render their happiness necessary to him, though he derives nothing from it except the pleasure of seeing it" (*Moral Sentiments*, p. 15).

Moral feelings for others, especially a sense of justice, was for Mill the basis for altruism: "Though it is only in a very imperfect state of the world's arrangements that anyone can best serve the happiness of others by the absolute sacrifice of his own, yet, so long as the world is in that imperfect state, I fully acknowledge that the readiness to make such a sacrifice is the highest virtue which can be found in man" (p. 16).

For Mill, altruistic actions are those that benefit others even if they don't benefit oneself, or even, on occasion, at the cost of harm to oneself. For example, Dr. Joseph Varon is the Chief of Staff at United Memorial Medical Center in Houston. As of December 12, 2020, Dr. Varon had been working 268 straight days without a vacation or as much as a weekend off to treat COVID-19 patients who had been flooding his hospital. "I was meant to do this," he told the *Washington Post*.[33]

On occasion, we call altruistic actions "heroic." In 2012 in Afghanistan, Chief Petty Officer Edward Byers led a team of hostage rescuers into a building under heavy fire, covering the hostages' bodies with his own as he fought off the kidnappers and won freedom for the hostages. For his actions at the risk of his life above and beyond the call of duty, Chief Byers was awarded the Congressional Medal of Honor, the country's highest military honor.[34] On September 11, 2001, hundreds of firefighters charged up the stairs of two burning towers in New York City to save lives; 343 did not return. These heroes did not do this out of self-interest; they did it out of an abiding commitment to others.

But for Rand, altruism is a vile concept. For her, "the appalling immorality, the chronic injustice, the grotesque double standards, the insoluble conflicts and contradictions that have characterized human relationships and human societies throughout history" are all due to misplaced altruistic ethics (location 92). However, Rand defines the term very differently than does Mill, characterizing it pejoratively as "any action taken for the benefit of others is good, and any action taken for one's own benefit is evil" (location 88). She would consider Dr. Varon, Chief Byers, and the September 11 firefighters all to be fools or losers.

For Rand and Nozick, society is a nonentity, unworthy of moral consideration. If designers were to apply Rand's philosophy, in contrast to that of the Enlightenment and Utilitarian philosophers, it would mean they would act only to benefit themselves and the only reason they would help others is if it advanced the designer's own life and their own interests. This describes the actions of John Kapoor not Dr. Varon, of Elizabeth Holmes not Chief Byers or Chef Andrés.

Applied to designs, one would only design products, services, or experiences if it benefitted oneself to do so; any consequent benefit to others would be transactional and incidental, as they pursue their own self-interest. A designer would not be concerned about making the world a better place unless, first and foremost, it benefitted him or her to do so. A warming planet is for later generations to deal with; hungry immigrants fleeing war is not his or her problem.

However, for the readers of this book—those for whom making the world a better place is a moral imperative—society and the well-being of others are of central moral concern. Self-interest is important. But we are unconvinced by Rand that acts that maximize self-interest are moral imperatives. We believe that purposeful courses of action that address both self-interest and a concern for others will take us from where we are to where we ought to be. And we believe, as does Dr. King, in the power of creative altruism.

References

1. King CS. The words of Martin Luther King, Jr. (2nd ed.) (p. 3). New York: William Morrow, 2001.
2. Parsons, G. (2016). *The Philosophy of Design*. New York: Wiley. Kindle Edition, location 3641.
3. Gates, D. Boeing to hold regional meetings with airlines on 737 Max, while execs try to reassure employees. The Seattle Times, 2018, Nov 20.
4. Plato. The republic (D. Lee, ed., trans.) (3rd ed.). New York: Penguin, 2007, originally written around 375 BC.
5. Aristotle. The basic works of Aristotle (D. McKeon, Ed.). New York: Random House, 1941.
6. Locke J. The collected works of John Locke (location 6714). Amsterdam: Pergamon, Kindle edition, 2015.
7. Hume, D. (2011). David Hume: The essential philosophical works. London: Wordsworth, 2011.
8. Bentham J. *Jeremy Bentham Collected Works* (Kindle location 3476). Minerva Classics. Kindle Edition, 2013.
9. Troyer J. (editor). The Classic Utilitarians: Bentham and Mill. Indianapolis: Hackett, 2003.
10. Smith H. Culpable ignorance. The Philosophical Review, 1983, 92(4), 543–571.
11. Carreyrou J. Theranos whistleblower shook the company—and his family. Wall Street Journal, 2016, Nov 18.
12. Theranos founder Elizabeth Holmes found guilty of investor fraud. United States Attorney's Office, Northern District of California [Internet]. 2022, Jan 4 [cited 2022, Aug 25]. Available from: https://www.justice.gov/usao-ndca/pr/theranos-founder-elizabeth-holmes-found-guilty-investor-fraud.
13. Logan, B, Wile R. Former Theranos executive Sunny Balwani is convicted of fraud. NBC News [Internet]. 2022, Jul 7 [cited 2022, Aug 25]. Available from: https://www.nbcnews.com/business/business-news/theranos-trial-verdict-sunny-balwani-elizabeth-holmes-rcna33701.
14. About us. Enabling the Future [Internet]. [cited 2022, Aug 25]. Available from: http://enablingthefuture.org/about/.
15. Homeboy Industries [Internet]. [cited 2022, Aug 25]. Available from: https://homeboyindustries.org.
16. Smith A. The theory of moral sentiments. Excercere Cerebrum Publisher, 2014, originally published 1759.
17. Heifer International [Internet]. [cited 2022, Aug 25]. Available from: https://www.heifer.org.
18. About us. Heifer International [Internet]. [cited 2022, Aug 25]. Available from: https://www.heifer.org/about-us/index.html.
19. Smart Start [Internet]. [Cited 2022, Aug 25]. Available from: https://www.smartstart.org.
20. Mill JS. Utilitarianism (p. 50). Hackett Publishing Company, Inc.. Kindle Edition, 2001, originally published in 1861.

21 Housing Matters [Internet]. [cited 2022, Aug 25]. Available from: https://housingmatters.urban.org/articles/hud-prepares-new-demonstration-what-do-we-know-about-housing-mobility-and-kids-outcomes.

22 Wood M, McHenry, S. The two-decade legal battle with DuPont over a toxic chemical. Marketplace [Internet]. 2019, Oct 15 [cited 2022, Aug 25]. Available from: https://www.marketplace.org/2019/10/15/the-two-decade-legal-battle-with-dupont-over-a-toxic-chemical/.

23 Rich N. The lawyer who became DuPont's worst nightmare. New York Times. 2016, Jan 6.

24 Krevans J, Gibbs J. Parents' Use of Inductive Discipline: Relations to Children's Empathy and Prosocial Behavior. Child Development, 1996, 67, 3263–3277.

25 Turning Point Scotland [Internet]. [cited 2022, Aug 25]. Available from: https://www.turningpointscotland.com.

26 Johnsen, S. Trning Point Schotlan's Housing First project evaluation: Final report. Heriot Watt University [Internet]. 2013, Dec [cited 2022, Aug 25]. Available from: http://www.turningpointscotland.com/wp-content/uploads/2014/02/TPS-Housing-First-Final-Report.pdf.

27 Shipp J. The Grown-Up's Guide to Teenage Humans (location 429). Harper Wave. Kindle Edition, 2017.

28 Smith A. *An Inquiry into the Nature and Causes of the Wealth of Nations* (location 272). Classic Books by KTHTK (Kindle edition), 2022, originally published in 1776.

29 Nozick R. Anarchy, state, and utopia. New York: Basic Books, 1974.

30 https://www.metroactive.com/features/Ayn-Rand-Silicon-Valley-Local-Modern-Business-Icons-Queen-of-Mean.html.

31 Rand A. The virtue of selfishness: A new concept of egoism. New York: Penguin. Kindle Edition, 1961.

32 Greenspan A. Assault on integrity. In Rand, A. (editor) Capitalism: The unknown ideal (p. 126). New York: New American Library, 1946.

33 Villegas P. This doctor has fought COVID-19 in his patients for 268 days straight. "I was meant to do this." Washington Post, 2020, Dec 12.

34 Edward C Byers, Jr. Congressional Medal of Honor Society [Internet]. [cited 2022, Aug 25]. Available from: https://www.cmohs.org/recipients/edward-c-byers-jr.

4

Design within a System

Out of complexity, find simplicity!

Albert Einstein
Nobel Physicist

How do we use the design process and our moral principles to create outcomes that have a positive impact on the world? That's the focus of the rest of this book. But to start, if we want to change the world, we must first understand it.

Design starts with the world as it is, and in some way, big or small, step by step, takes it from there to where we think it should be. To do that we need to understand the complexities of how the world works and how it changes. And then we need to reason about these relationships and processes to create outcomes and beneficial impacts with our designs.

For the most part, the world works in local ways. Short of the universal laws of physics, what happens in one situation is likely to be different than another. While the Earth, moon, and sun uniformly follow the laws of nature, the world of people is more complex and more particular. And while the Philosophes believed human nature was universal, people are also individuals. As much as engineers like to harness the laws of nature to create designs that work reliably and efficiently in all situations, in the world of people, what works here, may not work there. What one person likes, another detests. And in complicated situations, when the unexpected, the unplanned happens, something can always go wrong. If we pretend otherwise, for cost or efficiency's sake, the assumption can have disastrous consequences. Just remember Chernobyl, the Tacoma Narrows Bridge, and the Boeing 737 MAX 8.

For Herbert Simon, a design is at the interface between one system and another.[1] A design creates a fit between a building and its location, between people and their immediate context. So, to design, we must start by looking at the immediate situation, the particular problem—what the world looks like *here*—and design for that. What is the location? Who are the people? What is the immediate context? And how do we create a fit between them?

We must look at how a building can fit the shape of a hillside; how the structure of a bridge might react in the wind turbulence of a particular narrows, how people use your product in an emergency, how an audience responds to your play in this community or this culture. By understanding these two systems and how they relate, we will be able to draw on our accumulated, general knowledge and apply it to the particular situation to create designs that work *here*. This understanding of the design and its local context will also help us understand how the design might work—or not—in other contexts or how it might need to be modified to do so.

Make the World a Better Place: Design with Passion, Purpose, and Values, First Edition. Robert B. Kozma.

Let's illustrate this relationship with an example of a simple situation. Clothing is designed to mediate between two systems: the need of a person to maintain their body temperature and the cold weather of the outer system. We begin to understand the system requirements of the design when we start at that interface and work both inward and outward. To create successful designs, you need to understand the requirements of the users of your designs, the characteristics of their environment, and how they interact. If there is a match between the two systems, no design is needed—clothes aren't necessary, customs aside, if requirements to maintain body temperature and the outside temperature match. If a company's production schedule is meeting the demands of the market, there is no problem and your operations consulting services aren't needed. If people are happy with the trash pickup services as they are, why mess with a good thing?

However, if there is a mismatch, if things aren't working, if something goes wrong, your design can make the difference between someone who is happily warm or miserably cold. You can improve the efficiency of the production line or trash pickup. You can help someone with a disability navigate through a city. You can design a program to find shelter for the homeless.

But if you fail to understand the complexities within and between the two environments, between these two systems, your designs will fail. This chapter gives you concepts and a language that you can use to understand the structure and behavior of systems and help you create designs that work.

Systems: Simple, Complex, and Complex Adaptive

Simple and complex systems

Some systems are quite simple. Your thermostat is a system of electronic sensors and switches with the purpose of keeping the room at about the same temperature. Let's say it's set at 70°F. The room is a system in which the temperature has dropped to 68°F. The thermostat senses this and signals the furnace to kick in and warm the room until it's 70°F, at which point, the furnace turns off. Simple.

As we begin to think of systems and systems within systems, things can get much more complex. Complex systems have multiple components, each with a certain function, each function is connected to other functions, and they work together.

Let's look at another example: a complex mechanical system—the Boeing 737 MAX 8—its inner system, with people on the go, and the outer system, the atmosphere through which it flies. The plane is a design at the interface between the two. The requirements of the inner system—the passengers—demand a pressurized environment with at least the minimum comforts to sustain passengers on a long flight. The outer system consists of air at various densities, temperatures, humidity, wind speed, and turbulence. These all interact to give you flying conditions.

The airplane—the interface between the two—consists of a fuselage, engines, wings, control surfaces, and a control system. Each of these has a specialized function: the fuselage is a pressurized compartment to contain passengers and cargo, the engines move the plane forward, the wings keep the plane aloft, the control surfaces on the wings alter the plane's course, and the control system (including, in this case, the MCAS) is used to navigate the plane. These components must each do their job and work together seamlessly to achieve the purpose or function of the system: to transport people and cargo from one place to another through the air. If the engines are moving the plane fast enough and the control surfaces direct the plane at the proper angle to the airflow, the wings are shaped to give the plane lift, and the control system can be used to get you where you want to go.

An airplane is a complex system, and designing it is a complex task. But aeronautical engineers know the complexities of both planes and their environments and are able to pull off designs that work.

However, if the control surfaces shift the angle of the wings too far up, relative to the airflow, the wings lose lift and the plane stalls and loses altitude. This is what happened when MCAS erroneously kicked in during the flights of Lion Air 610 and Ethiopian Airlines 302. As a result, 346 people died. Apparently, the engineers didn't take *all* of the system's complexities into account, especially when people were involved. When MCAS kicked in, the pilots didn't know how to react or even know that it existed.

Complex adaptive systems

Complex adaptive systems are a whole other level of complexity that applies to a wide range of biological and social systems. Like the 737 MAX 8 and other complex systems, complex adaptive systems are networks of interdependent, interacting parts. But unlike the 737 MAX 8, components in these systems transact, self-organize, and adapt as things change. A change in one part or in the environment can result in changes in other parts elsewhere in the system that interact with and change yet other parts. As the original change ripples through the system and components adjust, these adjustments can, in turn, affect the original change. Designers dealing with complex adaptive systems require an even deeper understanding of the extended network of interdependencies and how one change will affect and be affected by others.

Take, for example, the Amazon rainforest, which is a complex collection of some 40,000 plant, 16,000 tree, 3,000 fish, 1,000 amphibian, 430 mammal, and 400 reptile species.[2] Individual members of these species interact with each other and their environment, each with their own capabilities, variations, and specializations, each with their own needs and drives. They compete or cooperate to obtain the resources they need in order to survive and procreate. There are individual winners and losers, but often agents adapt their subsequent interactions based on feedback from previous interactions to improve their chances of winning next time. From these interactions, self-organizing patterns emerge that create certain structures with physical or functional boundaries, such that a group of monkeys, for example, forage for food, groom each other, share food, and so on, in ways that create a system—a community. Other patterns emerge as these groups interact with yet others. For example, monkeys in the community act to protect each other, maintaining or increasing their numbers, and an increase in the number of monkeys can reduce their food source through overgrazing. But the larger number of monkeys can influence the number of leopards in the jungle that feed off of the monkeys. An increased leopard population, in turn, reduces the number of monkeys but increases the monkey's food source because there is less overgrazing. Through this complex web of emerging patterns, the leopards have an impact on the food source of the monkeys even though they don't directly interact with it.

So, these various relationships and structures are not only self-organizing; they take on their own adaptive and self-maintaining patterns that are more than the sum of their parts. Through their interactions, plants, monkeys, and leopards all adapt to each other, as do other species in the rainforest, and in doing so, the Amazon rainforest becomes a system that maintains itself. No design is needed.

However, occasionally, environmental changes or events go beyond the normal range, such as extreme weather events or fires, or intrusions from outside the environment, such as invasive species or human intervention. These extreme changes can disrupt the regular interaction patterns. Sometimes these disruptions can be so severe that the system is not able to respond adequately or in time and it collapses.

Jerrod Diamond, in his book *Collapse: How Societies Choose to Fail or Succeed*, gives a number of examples throughout history where human systems have collapsed because people didn't understand the complex dynamics of the systems they lived in and both their outer system and the human system failed.[3] Sadly, human disruptions, such as clearcutting and mining, are threatening the survival of the Amazon rainforest system and it may be next, with catastrophic implications for the region and our climate.[4]

Understanding the Amazon rainforest as a complex adaptive system can inform the design of policies that enable us to use resources in the system in ways that don't disrupt or destroy it, that allow us to use them sustainably. To be an effective designer of rainforest policies or anything else that involves people, you need to be a complex adaptive systems thinker.

The Dynamics of Complex Adaptive Human Systems

Complex adaptive systems can help us think about the self-organizing, transactional, emergent patterns of activity in human systems and how designs might mediate between components of the system or if designs are needed at all. As complex adaptive systems, biological systems such as the Amazon rainforest and human social systems have many similarities. Both are composed of agents that interact with each other in patterned ways, changing and being changed by others, cooperating or competing to promote their own interests. And emergence, self-organization, and adaptation occur in both biological and human social systems.

However, there are some significant differences between the two types of systems that make human systems particularly complex.[5] One important difference is the ability of humans to design their environments. Indeed, design is our principle way of adapting. While animals and plants adapt to changes in their environment by changing their behavior, or over time, evolving their species, we are able to redesign our environment for our purposes.

For example, Hardin's farmer, whom we encountered in Chapter 1, can adapt the size of his herd to the amount of grazing land that is available and market demand in order to maximize his profit. That's a design.

Another difference is intentionality. While biological systems have a function, social systems have a purpose. The Amazon rainforest functions to maintain a balance of the species within it. There is no intent. It doesn't serve the purpose of the monkey or the leopard; it just functions. A human system—like the economy—serves certain human intentions or purposes, for example, to facilitate trade, provide needed services, afford employment, generate wealth.

Yet another difference between biological and human social systems is our ability to use language. Language is used by people to internally represent their purposes, values, priorities, intentions, and plans, and to reason about these in their actions. Language is also used to express a person's purposes and intentions in their interactions with other people and through these interactions, shared intentions, purposes, goals, knowledge, practices, beliefs, and values emerge.

The farmers in Hardin's example can use language to express their intentions and mutually negotiate an arrangement where they all make a profit without overgrazing the land, even if none of them is maximizing their individual profit. This is the kind of arrangement Elinor Ostrom found over and over again in her research.[6]

Self-interest, reciprocity, and trust

If human systems were occupied exclusively by purely rational humans driven only by self-interest, the system would be quite simple. This is illustrated by a logic game called Prisoner's Dilemma, invented by Merrill Flood and Melvin Dersher at the RAND Corporation in 1950.[7]

In this game, two criminals (A and B) are caught and charged with stealing. However, the prosecutor has a weak case and admits that if both prisoners refuse to testify she can prosecute them only on a lesser charge. But they will be convicted and each will get 1 year of prison. Since the prosecutor is clever, she says to Prisoner A that if he stays silent but his partner betrays him, he will get 3 years and his partner will go free. If both testify, they will each get 2 years. The same offer is made to Prisoner B. And each must decide separately without knowing what the other will do.

The prosecutor is clever because, in this hypothetical situation, a prisoner motivated by rational self-interest will always betray the other, when he calculates the best payoff, whatever it is the other prisoner does. That is, if A confesses and B also confesses, A gets 2 years, instead of the 3 years if B confessed and A remained silent. And if B remains silent, A goes free, instead of getting 1 year had A also remained silent. So, A confesses. And since the same offer is made to B, it's in B's best interest and he confess, too. Thus, the prosecutor gets two convictions with 4 years of prison combined, where at best she would have gotten otherwise is only 3 years.

However, the best individual solution isn't the best collective solution. That is, if both had remained silent, they would have each gotten 1 year, instead of the 2 years with the "best" individual solution.

If you give this logic game to two very rational computers and they play it over and over, they will always come up with the same answer; they will always betray each other—a very simple system.

But Flood and Dersher found out that humans are much more complex, especially when they interact with same people over and over as they would in everyday situations. What they found is that when real people play Prisoner's Dilemma in an experimental situation and they play the game over and over with the same people, they actually come to cooperate. That is, each player made the decision that is collectively best, even though it is not the best decision in each player's personal self-interest. It seems that humans are "super cooperators," to use Harvard professor Martin Nowak's term.[8] People are motivated both by self-interest *and* trust or concern for others.

The real-world results from this simple game can be used to help us understand very large, extremely complex, human systems such as the economy. Let's see how.

Let's start by considering the economic system at the smallest level of interaction: I am a butcher and you tell me you want to prepare a nice prime rib roast of beef for a large dinner party. It would benefit me most to sell you a poor-quality roast at premium price. It would benefit you most to write me a bad check and leave with the roast.

But we don't. I offer you my best prime rib roast and you pay me a price that I ask. Even though we don't each maximize our individual self-interest, we both win. Your goal is served better than if you kept your money because you can now prepare for your dinner party. And I'm better off because I'm selling my beef to make a profit, which is my goal.

Language is important here. Unlike the Prisoner's Dilemma situation, you and I can talk to each other. You tell me what you need; I tell you what I have and the price. If you feel the roast is worth the price, we have a transaction.

Trust is important, too. You pay the price I'm asking because you trust me when I say the roast is of the high quality you want. And I trust that your check will not bounce when I send it to the bank.

Trust is not taken for granted; it develops. One way that trust develops is through recurring transactions over time. When you have purchased meat from me before, you have always been satisfied with the quality. However, if I tell you I have a top-grade roast and it is actually a poor grade, you may purchase it this time but end up displeased when you serve it to your guests. I may make a bigger profit this once but you would adapt and not do business with me in the future, so I would lose in the long run. But because I haven't cheated you, and you and I have done these mutually self-rewarding transactions over and over, you have come to trust me to do the same in the future and these interactions go on indefinitely. This pattern is what Nowak calls *direct reciprocity*. Direct reciprocity makes the system work.

Trust can be there, even if someone hasn't purchased my meat before, as long as I have a reputation for being trustworthy. Again, language is important. Let's say your dinner party was a smashing success. All 10 people at your party loved the prime rib and asked where you got it. You tell them that you got it at my butcher shop and you do business with me all the time because you know I will give you high-quality meat at a fair price. The next week, all your friends come to my shop because they now believe I am trustworthy. This is *indirect reciprocity*. Indirect reciprocity also makes the system work.

Let's increase the complexity of this hypothetical one-on-one transaction in a way that might begin to explain an entire economic system.

Given your recommendation, I'm now so popular, I've run out of prime rib. I adapt by ordering another side of beef from the distributor with whom I do business. I also realize that my prime rib has become so popular, I adapt by raising its price and increasing my profit. On the other hand, I notice my hamburger hasn't been selling well, so I cut my prices to clear it and I grind less the next time. With these savvy moves, I'm now doing so well, I need to hire another butcher, yet another adaptation. As a result of a series of transactions and my adaptive behavior, I'm better able to serve the needs of my customers and I'm making an even bigger profit.

However, the other butcher in town sees that he has lost customers to me, so he adapts by cutting his prices to gain them back. I may then need to cut my prices in response, reducing my profits. Or I might be able to cut prices but keep my profits by lowering the wages of my employees. But then the other butcher could hire them away from me. This dynamic, adaptive pattern tends to keep prices, wages, and profits in check, and the customers win. Adaptation makes the system work.

According to many economists (and some philosophers such as Nozick) it is this self-organizing, emergent quality of individual transactions that make a free-market, capitalist economy unique.[9] Individual, self-serving transactions, these economists claim, create optimal demand, supply, and prices without the need for any central planning, and these self-organizing dynamics end up serving the common good. This is the invisible hand of Adam Smith and Robert Nozick. With this hand, no design of the economy is needed.

These patterns of rewarding and punishing behaviors have even been noted within groups of apes and higher monkeys. Some anthropologists,[10] primatologists,[11] and evolutionary biologists,[12] including Martin Nowak and Charles Darwin,[13] claim that these reciprocal patterns, which mutually benefit cooperators and punish noncooperators, repeated many many times across a range of transactions over the millennia, account for the emergence of our strong moral norms. And these moral norms move people from maximizing their own gain at the expense of others to cooperating for the survival of the group and to the benefit of all. It even accounts for altruism, where one might engage in a transaction with an individual loss this time, knowing that it maintains a moral system that benefits all, including oneself.

This claim is illustrated by yet another pattern of self-motivated cooperation called *strong reciprocity*.[14] With strong reciprocity, not only I, but the baker, the brewer—all the merchants—provide you and everyone else with their best products at their best prices, and we pay our employees fair wages, even though we could make more money if we acted only to maximize our self-interest. In this group, individuals are not just business owners, customers, and employees; they are also neighbors and friends; they are a community.

This pattern of strong reciprocity is a very different characterization of relationships than that painted by Ayn Rand in the last chapter, in which relationships are merely a collection of one-off self-interested, direct exchanges between parties. In our community, individuals have organized themselves into a network of people who conduct reciprocal, trustworthy interactions. With strong reciprocity, trust and trustworthiness are not just qualities of individuals, they have become a quality of the group, the community.

Social system as a normative culture of trust and caring

For Nowak, this network of people who conduct reciprocal, trustworthy transactions evolves into a culture (p. 275). Culture is the shared traditions, ideas, beliefs, purposes, and values of a group. While the concept of *social system* captures the composition, structure, and patterns of interactions of a group, *culture* refers to the system's shared purpose and values. Culture is the rules of the game—the shoulds and shouldn'ts and priorities of the system. Culture makes a community out of a group of individuals and, contrary to the belief of Rand and Nozick, it is what makes the system more than the sum of its parts.

For the most part, behaviors are shaped by social institutions—the family, church, school, corporations, government. Harvard sociologist Talcott Parsons was an early contributor to systems theory and claimed that individual actions are influenced by macro-level social structures, or institutions.[15] These institutions are not just formal organizations with physical locations, but according to Parsons, they consist of complex patterns of roles and expected behavior that build trust within the community. In these roles, people are not just individuals but dutiful children, nurturing parents, faithful parishioners, studious pupils, productive employees, patriotic citizens. These social structures facilitate the integration of individuals' activities into the cultural purposes and goals of the system.

This culture is constantly renewed, and to some degree, revised in a dynamic, reciprocal process of co-influence: norms shape members' behavior. These behaviors are not only expressions of self-interest but they more or less also conform to and express the community's purposes and values. Others, in turn, respond to these behaviors by expressing or acting out their favor or reproach, based on the community's purposes and values as well as their self-interest. Conversely, individuals' membership in the community is confirmed by their trustworthiness—the extent to which their behavior and interactions conform to the community's values and purposes. In this way, the system—and the culture—work and are maintained.

Culture explains, in large part, the differences in behavior and impact between Boeing and World Central Kitchen. In the Boeing case, the cultural shift to maximizing profits contorted its value of passenger safety, influenced the behavior of the technical pilots, and resulted the deaths of passengers and crew. At World Central Kitchen, the cultural value of addressing harm due to natural disaster and war, and the purpose of feeding people in need, aligned the behavior of thousands of chefs, cooks, and volunteers to prepare and distribute millions of meals to feed hundreds of thousands of people.

So, it seems Smith's and Nozick's invisible hand of self-interest is insufficient, by itself, to explain a moral society let alone a sustainable economy. In a complex adaptive human system, there must be two invisible hands working together to guide transactions toward the common good, one economic and one moral, one of self-interest and the other of caring. It is when everyone is acting *both* out of self-interest *and* concern for others that the pattern of individual interactions work.

Without moral norms, the self-interested hand doesn't work to benefit all, trust erodes and the system fails as we will see in Chapter 16. Indeed, Adam Smith, who was first and foremost a moral philosopher, admits as much when he talks about our natural love for society and its preservation for its own sake.[16]

Ayn Rand would cringe at this thought.

Design to Make the System Work

The cultural purposes and values of a system are of particular importance to designers because they influence the specific purposes and the "oughts" of their designs. There are three interacting levels at which such adaptive changes can be made: the local, micro-level, where individuals act and interact with each other; the macro level of institutions; and the meso or middle level of groups, neighbors, or community.

Courses of action are important to all of them, but they take on a different character in each case. There are multiple systems at each level and these interact and influence each other within and across levels to create a great deal of complexity that makes causality difficult to determine and creates "wicked problems." Because wicked problems have no obvious solution and are difficult to understand, they make designing within complex adaptive human systems very challenging.

Designs at the micro level

At this first level, designs are courses of actions we take individually as we interact with things and people in our immediate environment to achieve the impacts we desire. In the preceding simple economic example, as a butcher, I might make adaptive changes such as: I design my shop to be an attractive place to shop and to be an enjoyable work environment; I hire a graphic designer or a web designer to attract more customers; I organize products and practices in my shop to give you the quality of meat you want at a price you will pay; I take out newspaper or web ads to show how competitive my prices are, and issue discount coupons to make them even more competitive. As for Hardin's farmer who owns the pasture, he would add cows to his herd to the extent I needed more meat from him.

As for you, you take actions to design your perfect dinner: determine a menu, send out invitations, purchase nice wine, and buy a top-quality roast. In doing so, you create a budget for the meal, search the web for a good butcher, read posted reviews. You cook the roast to perfection and set a beautiful table, so as to please yourself and your friends.

At this micro level, people buy products, pay for services or experiences, and interact with others so as to achieve their goals. And others design products, manage their resources, provide services and experiences that meet those demands, and they are rewarded for their efforts.

These are all designs. So, where Nozick sees no designs in a free market, they are happening all the time at the micro level. Designs are built into the system. Each of us is our own everyday designer.

The question is, do we design only for our own self-interests or do we also consider the interests of others? The pattern of behaviors that we see in trust games suggest that we, more often than not, design for both. In designing for both, no one's interests are maximized, but relationships are maintained and deepened and culture is affirmed.

On the other hand, there are transactions, within this micro level system of person-to-person interactions that fail, that result in harm or unhappiness that break trust between parties. These are opportunities for external designers, for outside parties whose focus is on making such transactions work. That is, the task for the designer in this situation or similar ones is to take a situation from where it is to a preferable one. In effect, the designer helps make the system work by supporting the product or service provider, creating a product or service that better satisfies the interests of the consumer. Or the designer helps the consumer create a spectacular party plan that works within her budget. Or the designer becomes a third party in interaction by supporting the relationship and facilitating the transaction.

Related to our moral framework in the last chapter, a designer who is interested in making the world a better place would create a product or service, or plan a party that reduces harm, increases happiness, advances knowledge, promotes equality, and so on. Or the designer could build a supportive, trusting relationship between the two parties that also facilitates the transaction.

Designs at the macro level

While micro level analyses focus on one-on-one interactions, macro systems are much larger, and of course, much more complex. Take, for example, a city or urban region. At the macro level not only are there more people with a greater number interactions, but there is a greater diversity in the kinds of system components and the variety of interconnections among them.

The design profession that is concerned with this complexity are city or urban planners. Cities can emerge on their own as people congregate to live, work, and trade, and they have done so for millennia. But the patterns of living, working, and interacting that emerge can create significant collective problems as cities grow, including traffic congestion, pollution, and homelessness. The job of urban planners is to address these problems and avoid them in the future.

Cities, as complex systems, consist of components such as people, houses, factories, shops, and public buildings and spaces, each serving different purposes and interacting and interconnecting via an infrastructure: roadways, public transportation, utilities, and communication.[17] Looked at in this way: urban planners design public service policies and land use related to housing, transportation, industrial, and commercial purposes so as to serve economic and social purposes.

Planning for systems of such complexity is difficult enough, but the difficulty increases significantly when a city is viewed as a complex *adaptive* system where components not only interact but adapt to changes, such as policies and plans, as they ripple through the system. Viewed from that perspective, planners must acknowledge that changes in the system, such as a factory closing, or the immigration of a new ethic group, have unplanned impacts on the city, despite their best efforts. Policies designed for one purpose may have unanticipated or unwanted effects, such that, for example, single family homes are purchased as part-time rentals, reducing the housing stock, or businesses leave town altogether for friendlier cities or the suburbs.

The good intentions of urban plans are to affect patterns of behavior at the local, micro level such that they contribute to the overall public good, not just to increase economic wealth, but to improve human well-being, improve health, and strengthen bonds among family members, friends, and neighbors.[18] A common error among planners is to underestimate the complexity of the system and create designs based on simplistic assumptions, often leading to disastrous consequences. A particularly disastrous error is to approach the planning process as a technical one and neglect the diverse social, cultural, and political context that surrounds it. And, of course, the consequences of this type of design error are even greater at a national level with its greater level of diversity and complexity.

For designers, the practical challenge in a large system is to follow Einstein's dictum, to find simplicity in complexity. But the means of simplifying the system is crucial. Purpose is an important concept to use in simplifying the complexity of a system. A major difference between natural systems, such as the Amazon rain forest, and human systems is that human systems are filled with intentionality, or purpose. Often there are multiple purposes and these purposes are distributed across the system, such as the different purposes of merchants and customers. Sometimes these purposes conflict but in well-functioning systems the purposes align. So, alignment is another concept that can be used to simplify the complexity of a system. Finally, there is impact, that is the extent to which these purposes are fulfilled.

In his book, *Systems Thinking for Social Change*, organizational consultant David Peter Stroh describes a project of his in which he applied these concepts to address homelessness in Calhoun County, Michigan.[19] Calhoun County has a population of 134,000 people, in rural areas, small towns, and medium sized cities, with 53,000 living in the county's largest city, Battle Creek. Stroh worked with federal, state, and local government officials, along with business leaders, service providers, and homeless people themselves to design a ten-year plan to address homelessness in the county. An initial systems analysis found a complex, interconnected set of factors that contributed to homelessness that included unemployment, drug addiction, mental health issues, and crime. They also found that agencies often addressed one piece of this but worked at cross purposes and competed for funding. Through a series of collaborative sessions, Stroh helped the group create a shared purpose of placing clients in permanent housing with coordinated services. This effort moved some of the agencies from a purpose of helping the homeless cope with their situation through temporary housing, a purpose that actually ended up putting people back on the street, to a coordinated effort across agencies that move temporarily housed people into permanent supportive housing as quickly as possible, where they would also have services that address their needs and help them maintain their housed status.

Purpose by itself, is not sufficient as a simplifying mechanism. But it can be used to identify the most crucial contributing factors, or levers for change, to align agencies and their efforts, and to confirm their effects by assessing impact with measures aligned to purpose. Six years into the Calhoun County ten-year plan, homelessness decreased by 14 percent (from 1,658 to 1,419) despite a 34 percent increase in unemployment and a 7 percent increase in evictions.

Designs at the community level

As mentioned in Chapter 2, Elinore Ostrom found a third way to approach design, a middle way between private planning and grand designs. Her research around the world identified numerous cases where local groups that had access to common pool resources, such as fields, forests, fisheries, and waterways, could act collectively as a community to design ways of managing the commons sustainably without resorting to privatization or central dictates.[20]

Ostrom's work gives us another way to simplify complex systems effectively and create on designs that make the system work—by reducing the scope of the system to the community level and talking collective action. Ostrom and others found that in a wide variety of situations around the world, local groups of users worked together to design schemes that were customized to the particularities of their community. Responding to local opportunities, constraints, and resources, these communities set their own rules, monitored use, shared information, managed conflicts, evaluated impacts, and met the demands and constraints of the larger system, such that the common resource was maintained and it contributed to the common good. In these situations, everyone benefitted, although no one maximized their self-interests.

She also found out why these worked, empirically identifying eight principles of design that communities used to increase the likelihood of success:

1) Set boundaries by identifying those who are in the system.
2) Identify those who have access to resources.
3) Identify those who are responsible for its maintenance and success.
4) Those affected by the rules participate in setting them, and the rules fit to the local situation.
5) Local community members actively monitor the design's implementation and share information so that everyone knows that others are following the rules.
6) Rule-breakers are punished with graduated sanctions.
7) Conflicts are managed by the group before they got out of hand.
8) The rules fit the requirements of the larger system the community lives in.

The net result of applying these design principles is that trust is built and the design is maintained without either privatizing the resource or resorting to formal government intervention.

These design strategies are particularly important in adaptive community responses to limited or diminishing resources, such as dwindling water supplies due to ever-more-recurring drought, reduced forests due to ever-more-recurring wild fires, increased air and water pollution due to human activity, limited street parking in major city centers, and other situations of diminishing common resources. But they are also relevant to the community that uses their collective action to create new common resources, such as coops, credit unions, seed banks, resource sharing, open-source knowledge, and micro-lending schemes that benefit everyone.

Elinor Ostrom and Design for the Common Good

While Ostrom's research focused on small communities and what are called "common pool resources," other researchers and social designers have begun to apply Ostrom's principles more broadly to larger groups, such as cities, and to a larger range of natural resources, such as air, water, and public land use, as well as cultural resources, such as infrastructure, knowledge, and cultural artifacts. They have also gone beyond existing resources to include the creation of new resources, such as those just listed, in what is sometimes called "commoning."

One such group of researchers and social designers is LabGov.[21] And our case study of collective efforts in the city of Baton Rouge illustrates how adjustments in Ostrom's principles can even be used for larger systems.

Case Study: Baton Rouge and "Imagine Plank Road"

Located at LUISS Guido Carli University in Rome and Georgetown University in Washington DC, LabGov expands on and extends Ostrom's insights and design principles, and applies them to the urban context. LabGov conceives of cities as complex systems where multiple actors have opportunities to work collaboratively in order to generate (or regenerate) and enjoy their shared urban spaces and resources. These actors include city residents, civil society organizations, local governments, and the private sector.

LabGov treats the city as a "commons."[22] Not in the sense that all property is commonly owned—they view it as a mixture of privately owned, publicly owned, and open spaces and resources. "Commons" in the sense that the confluence of these private, public, and open spaces and resources in a city creates a set of issues and opportunities that relate to all of its residents who are all entitled to participate in the creation of designs that result in mutual advantage and common benefit. Inspired by Ostrom, their research aims to identify the patterns, themes, and design principles that make certain initiatives successful, sustainable, and accessible to all members of the community and advance distributive justice.

The facilitation function of the lab is run through its various Co-City projects that are being implemented in New York City; Rome; Bologna; San José, Costa Rica; and Baton Rouge, Louisiana, among other cities. Our case study focuses on Baton Rouge.

Case Study: Baton Rouge and "Imagine Plank Road"

Baton Rouge is the capital of Louisiana and the state's second largest city with a population in 2020 of 227,470 and 870,569 in the Greater Baton Rouge area.[23] The city population is 54% African American, 34% White, and 6% Hispanic.

Situated on the bank of the Mississippi River, Baton Rouge is a major industrial, petrochemical, medical, research, and growing technology center of the American South. The city was rated 9th by CNN, among mid-size cities, as a place to start a new business.[24] ExxonMobil and

(Continued)

Case Study: Baton Rouge and "Imagine Plank Road" (Continued)

Figure 4.1 Imagine Plank St. Community Planning Meeting (Photo by Leslie Rose).

Dow Chemical make significant economic contributions. And it is the location of Louisiana State University and Southern University, a historically black university.

In the city, the median household income was $44,470, according to 2019 census estimates, with 24.8% living at or below the poverty line. South Baton Rouge is relatively affluent; poverty is concentrated in north Baton Rouge,[25] remnants of its segregated past.

Plank Road is a main corridor that divides the city east-west, and connects it north-south. Historically, it was the means by which enslaved people and goods were transported between the plantations north of the city and the city's port on the Mississippi River. The system has changed in recent decades. With White flight due to school desegregation and freeway construction that cut through neighborhoods, the area around the road has become blighted, populated with abandon buildings and vacant lots.

In 2009, the East Baton Rouge Redevelopment Authority, later named Build Baton Rouge (BBR), was created by Louisiana legislature to encourage needed rehabilitation, and to provide for the redevelopment of slum or blighted areas.[26] Among its stated values are accountability, equity, community collaboration, innovation, and service.

Imagine Plank Road. After a two-year process, with extensive community input, BBR issued a plan, in late 2019, to revitalize the Plank Road corridor.[27] Community input activities included an envisioning survey, a trolley tour of the area, a food truck event highlighting local food vendors, a street fair and music festival, and a community roundtable. During these events, community members contributed to discussions on perceived problems, priorities, and solutions to the condition of the areas surrounding Plank Road (see Figure 4.1).

The Plan starts with a vision statement that served as a purpose for their design and aligned their efforts: "The Plank Road Corridor is a thriving, socially diverse and walkable network of

Figure 4.2 Plan for Plank St. Civic Center (Illustration by WHLC Architecture).

neighborhoods anchored by good transit, strong local businesses, quality housing, and resilient infrastructure" (p. iv). Specific impact benchmarks and associated metrics were developed to measure the achievement of this vision. The benchmarks included: strengthening Plank Road's role as a place for cultural expression for Black communities in East Baton Rouge; improving the ability of North Baton Rouge residents to participate in commerce and the job market; protecting and growing community wealth; and connecting more people to opportunities through enhanced transportation options.

The activities designed to achieve this vision include: a rapid bus transit and pedestrian-oriented corridor that connect north Baton Rouge with the city center and into the southern part of the city. Development projects along the corridor include a civic center (see Figure 4.2), food hub, housing, essential human services, and a park. The plan also includes a small loan program and technical assistance to support the development of small, locally owned businesses.

A key partner in the Plan and the process that led up to it was the Co-City Project at LabGov. The Co-City/BBR partnership involved the creation, modeling, and testing of novel neighborhood governance, financing, and participatory institutions that provide residents with long-term stakes in economic revitalization.

One of the more innovative projects that came out of the process was the combination of a land bank (LB) and a community land trust (CLT) to form a cooperative LB/CLT structure. LBs are legal structures that can easily acquire vacant, abandon, or tax-delinquent land. But they often lack an efficient way of using that land productively, particularly the case in economically distressed areas, resulting in large overhead costs associated with holding the land. CLTs are structured to use land productively, but have limited capacity to acquire property given high land costs and/or the lack of clear titles to vacant land and parcels.

With a traditional CLT land is treated as a common heritage, not as an individual possession, and is held by a single nonprofit owner that manages these lands on behalf of the community. Land is removed permanently from the market. However, it is put to use by leasing it out for the

(Continued)

Case Study: Baton Rouge and "Imagine Plank Road" (Continued)

construction of housing, the production of food, the development of commercial enterprises, or the promotion of other activities that support the community. All structural improvements are owned separately from the land, with title to these buildings held by individual owners or housing cooperatives. A ground lease lasting many years gives the owners of these structural improvements the exclusive use of the land, while protecting the interests of the larger community.

The cooperative, hybrid LB/CLT structure developed by the Plank Road Plan allows the CLT and LB to work together to address these traditional challenges of either. With the Plan, BBR functions as both the land trust and the land bank. It has the legal authority to create a land bank and acquire abandoned and vacant land, and it can transfer or sell land to the trust for commercial or residential redevelopment. The CLT would maintain ownership of the land, but enter into leases with interested buyers for the use of residential or commercial structures.

The owner would have a 99-year ground lease for a modest monthly fee or no fee at all. The ground lease contains restrictions on the use and resale of all buildings, granting the CLT the right to determine how these buildings or other land uses are operated, owned, improved, and conveyed. When the owner decides to sell the property, the increased equity, if any, is shared between the current owner and the CLT, keeping the property affordable for future low- to moderate-income buyers.

As of this writing, BBR has attracted funding from private, foundation, city, state, and federal funds for the Plan. However, with the COVID pandemic, implementation of the plan was delayed until 2022.[28] Even with that, as of December 9, 2021, it has repaired over 200 homes along the corridor to make them ready for occupancy.[29] Currently, the city is working with the Environmental Protection Agency to address lingering land contamination concerns that would clear property along the Plan Road corridor for development that advances the Plan.[30]

This case study illustrates one way a community can create common resources that benefit the entire community. And it illustrates several of Ostrom's design principles as modified by the LabGov model.

The City of Baton Rouge is a complex adaptive system. It is composed of many components—companies, private associations, public agencies, neighborhoods, families, private individuals—each acting, interacting, and adapting for their own purposes, and on occasion, a concern for others. For the most part, the city has worked, adjusting to changes as needed. But on Plank Road, it did not work and that part of the system collapsed: businesses closed, homes were abandoned, the area was blighted.

Individual self-interests within the market were insufficient to turn the area around. Given the current situation, there were no individuals or corporations that stepped up to purchase abandoned land and invest in this low-income, blighted area.

BBR looked at this situation as a design opportunity, an opportunity to take a situation from where it is to where it ought to be. The agency approached this design space as a commons where all of the components of the system could come together because they all had a stake in turning things around. BBR's process of community input made it clear that turning a blighted area of the city into an economically and socially thriving area was in the entire community's interest.

BBR worked with diverse interests in the community to identify needs and was able to create a plan, much as did Stroh in Calhoun County, to focus on purpose and use that to align key components of the system, and leverage those for larger gains. The purpose was to turn around a crucial but blighted strip of the city, developing residential and commercial properties and a transportation corridor to link them. The design takes abandoned property and makes it productive again, something that needed to happen but the market was not doing on its own.

These actions are facilitated by affordances of the Plan, which uses BBR's legal authority to acquire abandoned and tax-delinquent properties and create a land bank with these properties to make them available to individuals and businesses in ways that benefitted both the recipients and the needs of the community. In parallel, BBR is building a transportation infrastructure to connect different elements of the system—houses, businesses, shops, and public services—to increase the likelihood that those properties will be used productively and contribute to an equitable, sustainable economy for the area. By including those people who would be affected most by the plan in its formulation, as Ostrom would recommend, BBR has increased the likelihood that their individual and collective actions will help the Plan succeed.

Imagine Plank Road is not a master plan for the state, or the country, or even the entire City of Baton Rouge. It does not take on that level of complexity. Rather, it carves out a crucial portion of the city that constitutes a community, yet represents one of the major challenges to the entire urban area. By narrowing the system that it is working on, not just by reducing the size, but by creating a community boundary for the design, BBR makes the problem more manageable and the prospect of collective action more likely.

The Plan neither privatizes resources nor provides central command for how they would be used, as Hardin would contend. Rather, it used a mixed approach, sometimes allocating resources to public services, such as public transportation, and sometimes private enterprises, such as businesses or private homes, all the while maintaining community ownership. At the same time, it engaged all elements in the community to create a shared vision, a vision of what ought to be.

The Appropriate Level of Complexity

You will always be designing within a system. Understanding of the complex, adaptive set of relationships in a particular situation gives you a picture of the situation as it is now, the ways it is and is not working, and what needs to be changed. The challenge, of course, is moving the situation from where it is to where it should be. And if you're trying to make the world a better place that will be some version of reducing harm, increasing happiness, advancing knowledge, promoting equality, addressing injustice, or building relationships.

Even the simplest one-on-one situation of a shop owner offering a product that makes a customer happy or a tutor helping a student learn is complicated by the surrounding context in which it is embedded. And even the most complex situation, such as planning a city or passing a piece of legislation in Congress, is composed of subsystems, districts and neighborhoods or parties and their factions.

At the simplest level, successful designs can come from understanding both the dynamics of the local interactions and the surrounding context. Understanding the context can help you incorporate these dynamics into your local designs and can contribute to success: a shop owner can enlist his customers to attest to his trustworthiness and the quality of his meat to their guests; a tutor can recruit parents to quiz their child on homework. At the macro-level, success comes from finding the right subsystem that can make the solution more manageable, as BBR did with the Plank Road neighborhood, as well as contribute to a larger plan. At both levels, collective action can be the key to success, including others at the micro level, and finding the proper level of sub-system engagement at the macro level.

Reciprocation is essential at all levels of a purposeful, complex, adaptive human system, and it depends on trust and trustworthiness. Reciprocation is when self-interest is matched by concern for others. Direct reciprocation emerges at the micro level through extended interactions that build trust and relationships. Designs that engage and structure face-to-face interaction among small numbers of people can support this emergence.

The size, complexity, and diversity of macro systems make them particularly problematic design contexts. These characteristics increase the likelihood that system problems will arise and that these problems will be more impactful, as their effects ripple through the system, creating wicked design challenges.

Ostrom's design principles for the meso, or middle, level structure interpersonal interactions to play out in positive ways in which groups, neighborhoods, and communities collectively create and use common resources that benefit everyone. The strong reciprocity fostered by this structure creates a culture of trust that builds and sustains the community. Designs that build strong reciprocity at this local, meso level also create opportunities in which more complex, macro level problems can be addressed, as we'll see in Chapter 15.

References

1 Simon H. The sciences of the artificial (3rd ed.), p. 5. Cambridge, MA: MIT Press, 1996.
2 Butler R. The Amazon rainforest: The world's largest rainforest. Mongabay [Internet]. 2020, Jun 4 [cited 2022, Aug 25]. Available from: https://rainforests.mongabay.com/amazon/.
3 Diamond J. *Collapse: How societies choose to fail or succeed*. New York: Penguin, 2005.
4 Nunez C. Deforestation explained. National Geographic [Internet]. [cited 2022, Aug 25]. Available from: https://www.nationalgeographic.com/environment/article/deforestation.
5 Sawyer K. Social emergence: Societies as complex systems. Cambridge, UK: Cambridge University Press, 2005.
6 Ostrom E. Governing the commons: The evolution of institutions for collective action. Cambridge: Cambridge University Press, 1990.
7 Flood M. Some experimental games (RM 789-1). Santa Monica, CA: RAND Corporation, 1952.
8 Nowak M. Super cooperators: Beyond the survival of the fittest. Edinburgh: Canongate, 2011.
9 Hayek F. The fatal conceit: The errors of socialism. University of Chicago Press, Kindle edition, 2011.
10 Klenk, M. (2019). Moral philosophy and the 'ethical turn' in anthropology. Springer Open Access [Internet]. 2019, Aug. [cited 2021, Sep 16]. Available from: https://link.springer.com/article/10.1007/s42048-019-00040-9.
11 De Waal F. Primates and philosophers: How morality evolved. Princeton: Princeton University Press, 2006.
12 Wilson EO. The biological basis of morality. The Atlantic, 1998, Apr, 53–70
13 Darwin C. The decent of man. Amazon Services (Kindle edition, 2014, originally published in 1871.
14 Gintis H, Henrich J, Bowles S, et al. Strong reciprocity and the roots of human morality. Social Justice Research, 2008, 21, 241–253.
15 Parsons T. The social system. New Orleans: Quid Pro Book, 2012, originally published in 1951.
16 Smith A. The Theory of Moral Sentiments (p. 151). Excercere Cerebrum Publications, Kindle Edition, 2014, originally published in 1759.
17 Batty, M. Cities as complex systems. In Myers, R. (editor), Encyclopedia of Complexity and System Science (pp. 1041–1071). Berlin: Springer, 2009.
18 Montgomery C. Happy cities: Transforming our lives through urban design. New York: Farrar, Straus, and Grioux, 2013.

19 Stroh, DP. Systems thinking for social change.

20 Ostrom E. Governing the commons: The evolution of institutions for collective action. Cambridge: Cambridge University Press, 1990.

21 About LabGov Georgetown. LabGov Georgetown [Internet]. [cited 2022, Aug 25]. Available from: https://labgov.georgetown.edu/about_labgov/.

22 Foster S, Iaione C. Ostrom in the city: Design principles and practices for the urban commons. In D. Cole, B. Hudson, & J. Rosenbloom (editors), Routledge handbook of the study of the commons (pp. 235–255). London: Routledge, 2019.

23 Baton Rouge, Louisiana. Wikipedia [Internet]. [cited 2022, Aug 25]. Available from: https://en.wikipedia.org/wiki/Baton_Rouge,_Louisiana.

24 Best places to launch: Baton Rouge, LA. CNN Money [Internet]. 2009 [cited 2022, Aug 25]. Available from: https://money.cnn.com/smallbusiness/best_places_launch/2009/snapshot/28.html.

25 http://www.city-data.com/poverty/poverty-Baton-Rouge-Louisiana.html.

26 Build Baton Rouge [Internet]. [cited 2022, Aug 25]. Available from: https://buildbatonrouge.org.

27 Build Baton Rouge. Imagine Plank Road: A plan for equitable development. Baton Rouge: Build Baton Rouge, 2019.

28 Heckt S. Build Baton Rouge expects Plank Rd improvements to begin in the new year. BRPround [Internet]. 2021, Nov 1 [cited 2022, Aug 25]. Available from: https://www.brproud.com/news/local-news/build-baton-rouge-expects-plank-rd-improvements-to-begin-in-new-year/.

29 Riley R. Build Baton Rouge to move forward as CEO departs. BRPround [Internet]. 2021, Dec 9 [cited 2022, Aug 25]. Available from: https://www.brproud.com/news/local-news/build-baton-rouge-plans-to-move-forward-as-ceo-departs/.

30 EPA selects LDEQ for $2 million brownsfield assessment grant. Louisiana Department of Environmental Quality [Internet]. 2022, May 13 [cited 2022, Oct 23]. Available from: https://deq.louisiana.gov/assets/docs/Brownfields/EPA_Brownfieldsgrants2022_PR.pdf

5

Technology, Activity, and Culture

Technology is nothing. What's important is that you have a faith in people, that they're basically good and smart, and if you give them tools, they'll do wonderful things with them.

Steve Jobs
Co-Founder
Apple Computer

How do technologies fit into design? How can they be used to change our current situation into a preferred one? Are they currently making the world a better place or a worse one?

The contemporary attitude toward technology can be summed up with the headline of a *New York Times* article: "The Tech That Will Invade Our Lives in 2023."[1] Another headline is: "The Long-Term Jobs Killer Is Not China. It's Automation."[2] Another is: "How Technology Wrecks the Middle Class."[3] Yet others are: "How TikTok is Rewriting the World and "The Metaverse is Coming, and the World Is Not Ready for It".[4,5]

To read these articles, you would think that, contrary to Steve Jobs' preceding assessment, technology is far from nothing; it is an all-pervasive, sometimes sinister force that is controlling our lives, economy, and society.

But to hear others, technology is an inevitable force for good. Bill Gates claimed that, "Technology is unlocking the innate compassion we have for our fellow human beings."[6] Sheryl Sandberg, former COO of Meta, stated, "Social media has created a historical shift from the historically powerful to the historically powerless."[7] And Carly Fiorina, former CEO of Hewlett Packard, believes "that technology is the great leveler."[8]

I started my academic career in technology because I was excited by its promise. I believed that it could be used to improve people's lives, particularly in education. During my career, I've seen some amazing developments in technology, as it became an economic juggernaut, moving from room-sized mainframes to personal computers, to smart phones, watches, and apps that were only science fiction when I was a kid. But while the technology sector generated things and a lot of wealth over the past thirty years, I've been disappointed in the extent that these powerful resources were used to make people's lives and the world better.

Then there was 2022. Theranos executives were convicted of fraud, FTX collapsed for the same reason, Twitter became a circus side show, Epic Games agreed to pay $520 million over children's privacy and trickery charges,[9] Meta agreed to pay $725 million in a privacy law suit,[10] and the industry lost $7.4 trillion in value.[11]

Technology has not only lost its mojo; it has lost its moral compass. And just maybe the two are related.

Make the World a Better Place: Design with Passion, Purpose, and Values, First Edition. Robert B. Kozma.

We are surrounded by technology and use it every day in our work and play. But if you are going to use it in your designs—which is inevitable—think of it neither as an alien power to be feared or the savior of the planet to be hailed, but as Jobs would have it, a tool and a resource to be used to do wonderful things. And if technology is to be used to unlock the innate compassion we have for others, if it is to create a historical shift from the powerful to the powerless, if it is to do wonderful things that make the world a better place, it will not do it on its own. It will depend on how you use it to advance moral purposes.

How to Think about Technology

Often, we think of technology as specific devices: computers and mobile phones, audiovisual systems and wireless ear buds, microwaves and smart refrigerators. When taking a techno-centric perspective like this, technology is something that is separate from us, an object that has an effect of its own; something that shapes us; something that acts *on* us rather than something we act *with*. From that perspective, technology does seem like a powerful force that impacts society and changes our lives, for good or bad.

However, in this chapter, rather than focus on the devices, we are going to look at technology as part of the system and how we use it to make situations better. And to make situations better, you have to understand how we interact with technology in ways that enable and constrain what we do, how we think, and how we interact. We will look at this mediational role at three levels: the micro level of person-technology (or resource) use that influences patterns of activity (doing, thinking, and interacting); the middle level, community of relationships and trust; and the macro level where patterns of individual- and community-technology uses shape and are shaped by the cultural context.

It is only by considering this complex set of interactions between and among people and technology to accomplish goals and purposes within a culture that you can advance the moral impacts of your designs.

And consider them we must. Because without considering this complex network of relationships and their impacts, technology and your designs are just as likely to wreck the middle class as create an historical shift toward the powerless; just as likely to invade our lives as unlock our innate compassion for our fellow human beings; just as likely to degrade our society and our planet as to make the world a better place.

Technology at the Micro Level: Affordances and Activity

In considering technology and design, think not only about devices, but also about people *plus* device in an environment: what people do with the device to act, think, and interact and how we can use it to change our environment. In this chapter, I build on systems concepts from Chapter 4 and give you ways to think about technology at the interface between one system—the person—and another—their environment. In doing this, I will draw on Activity Theory, a set of ideas developed by psychologists and anthropologists to describe how people act in their environment, particularly as it applies to their use of technologies as tools.[12,13] With this theory, you can see how people use technology to change the current situation to a preferred one and how you can design the use of technology to help them do that.

According to the theory, technologies are the physical and symbolic resources available to people that *mediate* activity at the inner-outer environmental interface. Technologies include both

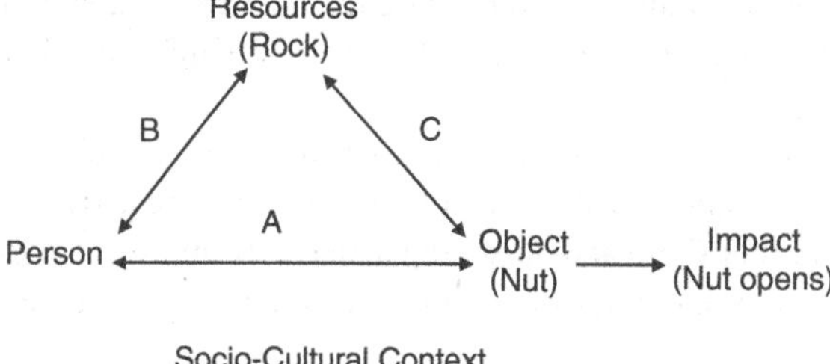

Figure 5.1 Person-resource-activity model.

physical devices, like kitchen microwaves, computers, and smart phones, as well as symbolic resources, such as text, images, numbers, and other symbol systems. And in mediating activity, technologies change the relationship between the internal and external systems. This is the conception of technology I will use in this book.

Person-resource-activity model

Let's start at the micro level by thinking of a simple, everyday activity: a person, an object, and an action on the object with a particular goal in mind. And let's illustrate this with a simple situation: a caveman has a nut and wants to open it for its meat. The outer environment, in this simple case, is the nut, the inner environment is a sense of hunger and the goal to open the nut to change the current situation to a preferred one.

The action on the nut with the person's bare hands is depicted in Figure 5.1 as action "A," an action that is often ineffective in accomplishing the goal. As a caveman, you analyze the situation as it is and consider it as it ought to be and come up with a design to change the current situation—you grab a rock!

In this example, the rock is the tool or a simple technology. But it plays a fundamental role in mediating the relationship between the inner and outer environment by changing the action. Instead of twisting the nut, the person with the rock (action "B") pounds on the nut (action "C") with a very different outcome: opening the nut to get the meat. In effect, the rock changes the action from "A" to "B–C", with the rock participating in that action.

Now, let's build on this simple case to develop a deeper understanding of activity and the role that technological resources can play in it. In this simple example, the immediate goal of getting at the nut meat is subordinate to a longer-term purpose of satisfying hunger, in which the action of opening the nut is just a part of a more complex pattern of actions for hunger-satisfying purposes, such as gathering berries, hunting squirrels, and so on. The technology—the rock—works because it changes behavior to successfully obtain food in this particular situation. A variety of technologies could conceivably be used in the food-getting activity, including spears, traps, and bows and arrows, but they would not work in this situation. And while the rock can be successfully used in this situation to crack open the nut, it would not help in gathering berries.

What is it about these technologies, and designs using them, that makes one more effective in achieving the goal in one situation than another?

Affordances and activity in the outer environment

Picking or creating the right technology for a design is an important task and how the technology is used is an important part of the design. In this regard, it is useful to think not just about the technology, but also about the activities enabled by it and how those align with the situation and the purpose of the design. In considering these activities and technologies, it is helpful to think about a technology's affordances.

Affordance is a specialized term that incorporates the more common notion of a technology's "capabilities" or "features." But included in affordances is also the notion that there are activities that these capabilities and features enable and that these activities are particularly appropriate to the specific situation. That is, affordance captures the relationship among person, resource, action, and object, within a context.

Features are not affordances by themselves, but only in relationship to what can be done with them by a user. The features of a tool, or technology, are affordances only if they enable actions that a person is capable of performing, and these actions move toward goals, which are, in turn, shaped by available objects in the immediate environment and by a social, cultural context. Affordances make acting, thinking, or interacting, in preferred ways, easier or even possible when they would not be so otherwise. And these actions can turn the current situation into a preferred one.

Returning to our person with the nut, the rock *affords* the action of pounding that is not available to the person without it. What the rock affords is because of *both* the features of the rock—its size and weight—*and* the capabilities of a person—among them, being able to grasp the rock, lift it, and pound with it. But pounding is not an affordance of the rock alone; this action cannot be done without a person; the rock would otherwise just sit there. And a boulder does not afford this behavior because a person is not able to grasp and lift it.

Applying the concept to a bow and arrow, the affordance of this technology enables the person with the necessary capability, or skill, to shoot a projectile—the arrow—for many dozens of feet, making it good for obtaining rabbits for food. Its affordances would not make it good for opening nuts any more than a rock would be good for collecting berries. And it doesn't have affordances for someone who doesn't have string-pulling or arrow-aiming capabilities. Consequently, technology must be thought of not just as a physical or symbolic resource, but also as a person-resource-activity unit that changes the interaction pattern, and consequently, the relationship between the inner and outer environment.

Technologies, and the designs we embed in them, are our adaptive response to our environment. The rock is a successful design because it aligns the affordances of the technology with the requirements of the environment, relative to the goal—cracking open the nut. As such, we use technology and designs to change our environment.

But they, in turn, also change us.

How does that work?

Using the rock also requires us to acquire a different set of rudimentary skills: grasping, aiming, and striking hard enough to open the nut but no so hard as to pulverize the meat. As a result, twisting skills give way to striking skills, when it comes to the goal of obtaining food. Add to these food-getting skills the development of string-pulling and arrow-aiming skills, among others, shaped by yet other technologies that come along. Of course, these skills are completely different than yet others required when future, transformational technologies emerge that require the person to go to the supermarket to obtain food.

Now, let's apply the basic model to a more complex, real-world example in a pharmaceutical laboratory where the purpose is to create new drugs. The chemist has a current situation—a set of chemicals on her lab bench—and she has a preferred situation in mind—a new drug. Her design is to engage in a set of activities that synthesize the new chemical compound from the chemicals on her bench. These activities are enabled by certain devices used in different parts of the process to achieve certain goals and sub-goals. One of the activities is to confirm that the resulting compound is the one she had in mind, that she has indeed changed the current situation into the preferred one. Among the technologies that can help with this activity is a nuclear magnetic resonance (NMR) spectrometer.

My colleagues and I at the University of Michigan and at SRI International conducted research by observing a chemist in a pharmaceutical laboratory, whom we called "Susan" in our reporting, as she used an NMR spectrum—the symbolic peaks on a graph generated by an NMR spectrometer in which a compound is placed—to confirm that the substance she had synthesized was a compound with a specific chemical composition and structure that she intended to create.[14] In our observations, we saw Susan methodically map patterns of peaks on the NMR graph onto structural components of the compound that she had in mind, confirming that she did, indeed, synthesize the compound that was her goal. This mapping activity was afforded by the specific symbolic features of the NMR spectrum—its patterns of peaks and dips along the graph—that stood for the composition and structure of the compound. The affordances of the NMR spectrum align Susan's activities to her goals. The beaker and clear solution sitting on her lab bench did not have affordances that could be used to confirm its composition and structure. Thus, the affordances of the NMR technology enabled a set of activities and outcomes that weren't possible without it, and Susan was able to use these affordances in her activities to change the outer environment by synthesizing a new drug.

Affordances and changing the inner environment

As a designer, sometimes your designs are intended to change the outer environment to shape a user's actions to achieve a desired result. For example, you could design a new, more accurate NMR spectrometer to help chemists in their drug synthesize activities.

At other times your designs are intended to change the inner environment, how the user thinks. This is the primary goal of teachers, instructional designers, and curriculum developers, and it corresponds to Principle 4 in Chapter 3.

Let's play out this difference by looking at another chemistry example, this time a situation where high school students who are engaging in instructional activities for the purpose of understanding the invisible, molecular-level processes that are happening on their lab benches. As you can imagine, the inner environments of chemistry students—that is, their current understandings of chemical processes—are very different than those of professional chemists. Susan had a mental image of the composition and structure of the compound she intended to synthesize and the dynamic process of how reagents combine, restructure, and rearrange during her experiments. When chemists consider reactions, they think of them as a dynamic process where reagents continue to collide, forming products and reactants, even as the reaction reaches equilibrium. Students, on the other hand, have a much simpler and often inaccurate or erroneous understanding that includes, for example, the notion that when reagents reach equilibrium and the solution on their lab bench stops changing color, the reaction stops.[15] This is not surprising given that the visual affordances of the lab bench reaction stop changing color at equilibrium.

Changing high school students' inner environment to have them think more like chemists was the goal of a software environment, called *ChemSense*, that my team and I designed.[16] This understanding is a valued goal in the chemistry curriculum. To make this change in the inner environment, we designed a set of laboratory activities and technological resources that included sensors, which students inserted into their experiments, and associated computer software that displayed a dynamic graph of the reagents' concentrations during their experiments. These symbolic resources provided students affordances parallel to those that Susan used in the external environment during her experiments to confirm her products.

We also wanted to give students ways to begin to think about the reaction-in-progress as Susan and other chemists think about it internally, as a dynamic process of compounds colliding and exchanging elements. So, we also gave students a chemical animation tool kit with which they could depict what they thought was happening at a molecular level during the reaction. Students could then post their animations and explanations as a lab report on a classroom-networked environment where the teacher and other students could observe and comment on their inner understanding as they externalized it with their animations. In using these symbolic resources with their dynamic affordances to explain their experiments, we found that the students began to think of reactions as dynamic systems, much like chemists.

Embedded technology

Changing the inner environment involves the temporary use of technology. The intent is to support the development of capabilities that come to be internalized so that, in the case of our chemistry students, they begin to think like chemists, without the animations. But other uses of technology, such as a word processor or a spreadsheet, are designed to be used as a regular part of the task. That is, technology is designed to become embedded in the activity.

The use of embedded technology aids practice by offering affordances, aligned with the purposes of these tools, that perform some part of the task or/and provide the users with support for certain physical or cognitive actions that would have been more difficult or even impossible to perform without it. A simple illustration is our previous example of rock use. The intent of using the rock is not to help a person become better at opening nuts by hand. The purpose of the rock is to make it possible at all. Of course, other means of opening nuts could be designed with affordances better aligned with the goal and situation, given the person's capabilities and the task, such as a nut cracker that uses leverage rather than weight to open the nut, requiring less work and offering more control over the action, and the nut meat is not pulverized along with the shell. In that case, we abandon the rock for a better tool. And coming up with better and better tools and technologies is an important design task.

For a real-world example, we can return to Susan, our pharmaceutical chemist. Her use of NMR spectra is not intended to ultimately enable her to confirm the chemical structures without the aid of NMR spectra. The affordances of the technology are designed to become an integral part of the activity. You can also think of the affordances of tools that enable your designs—computer-aided design/computer-aided manufacturing (CAD/CAM) software, graphics packages, or programming tools.

Technology at the Macro Level: Culture and Impact

Moving from the micro to the macro level allows us to look at another key element of Activity Theory: the sociocultural context in which activity takes place.[17] As we saw in the last chapter, culture is an important part of a person's external environment. Culture is where the patterns of individual actions and interactions over time come to create purposes, values, and social resources that go beyond the sum of individual actions. And cultural purposes, values, and social resources of the group, in turn, influence activity and interactions.

The direction of causal influence is predominantly one-way: Our culture influences our activity. How we were raised, our valued purposes, and our shared worldview shape our life paths. Our culture presents us with options—what and where we study, where we live, what we do for a living. What we choose to do within those options has an impact, most immediately, on us, our family, and our close associates. Culture also influences how we act, think, and interact at work, as it did at Boeing and the FAA.

However, there is a way that we, in turn, shape the culture. For the most part, we shape it by our confirmation. That is, what we do, how we think, how we interact confirms that the system is the way it ought to be. But there are also choices we can make that, perhaps in some small way, go against the current system: enact different values, express different beliefs, form different relationships. Done individually, these changes may have little overall impact on the culture. Done collectively, it creates a different pattern of acting, thinking, and relating that constitutes cultural change.

What role does technology play in culture and cultural change?

There are two ways that technology influences and is influenced by culture. The most common influence is that technology enables and constrains the set of actions, beliefs, and relationships that constitute our current culture. If things change, they do so in what economist Brian Arthur calls "incremental change."[18] These are the changes that make what we do and how think and interact easier, better, faster, or less expensive.

Returning to our pharmaceutical lab, we can see how technology fits into the culture and activity within it. Susan was not conducting her activities in a vacuum. From a sociocultural perspective, the compound Susan synthesized was culturally valued by both her and her company, whose purpose is to develop, test, and sell pharmaceutical products. Her activity with the technology served that cultural purpose: She used the features of the spectrum to confirm to herself she had synthesized the compound she intended. But the technology also served a cultural purpose that confirmed the community and its values. She used the spectra to assert to colleagues that she had created the kind of compound that they all work toward and value. The products she synthesized are passed on to other parts of the company for testing, to federal regulators for approval, to pharmacies for selling, and so on *because* they were confirmed by NMR analysis. Her technology-supported activities were conducted in a corporate culture that values the production of drugs and a larger culture that values the use of drugs to cure diseases. New technologies that make this process easier, less expensive, even more reliable, and so on would also be valued.

The second way technology influences culture is by fundamentally changing what we do, how we think, and how we interact. This is what Arthur calls "transformational change." This is illustrated by another example from chemistry.

Prior to the 18th century, what could be called chemistry was a practical body of knowledge about substances that were used by metal smiths, dyers, distillers, and so on. Substances were named based on their surface features, such a smell, color, taste, and consistency that served these practical purposes.[19] In the late 18th century, French chemist Antoine Lavoisier, had a different purpose in mind for the use of substances, influenced by cultural developments of the time, specifically the developing Scientific Revolution. The purpose of chemistry for Lavoisier was "subjecting different bodies in nature to experiment . . . [so as to] decompose them and . . . examine separately the different substances that enter into combination."[20]

However, affordances of the chemical language at the time did not lend themselves to thinking about their composition. Consequently, Lavoisier set about to invent a new chemical language—a new symbolic technology—that would support that purpose. And it changed what chemists did, how they thought, and how they interacted. A contemporary of Lavoisier, French Enlightenment Philosopher Étienne Bonnot de Condillac wrote at the time, "We only reason well or reason badly in so far as our language is well or badly constructed" (p. 171). With this in mind, Lavoisier developed a new language that enabled chemists to decompose substances in their laboratory, to think about compounds in terms of their composition, and to express their thoughts to other chemists as they coordinated their activities and interactions around these new, shared purposes. These were structured so that elements of the symbol system stood for chemical elements and a combination of the elements stood for compound substances: "water" became "H_2O." The equations had affordances such that by manipulating (combining, decomposing) the symbolic elements in an equation it implied corresponding procedures that chemists would use with reagents on the lab bench: $H_2O \rightarrow 2H + O$. The affordances of these symbols gave material reality to otherwise invisible elements and the affordances of the equations gave chemists ways of thinking about their experiments that changed chemical practice. These are the very things that we saw occurring in our observations in modern chemistry labs.

In designing at the macro level, it is useful to think about the process by which transformational change happens. As Arthur documents, transformational changes didn't come out of nowhere. They were not discovered in the wilds of a jungle or conceived, whole-cloth, in the mind of a genius. Rather, they were built by making novel combinations and connections among parts of technologies, designs, and ideas that already existed, often in other domains, what Arthur also calls "combinatorial evolution."

For example, the first internal combustion engine was invented in 1804 by Isaac de Rivaz, a Franco-Swiss artillery officer and engineer.[21] De Rivaz had previously designed several steam powered carriages. He also had experience with canons. These experiences gave him the idea of designing an engine that combined these two technologies. That is, a cannonball being pushed out of a barrel by igniting a charge, gave him the idea of introducing oxygen and hydrogen into a cylinder and igniting it with a spark to create hot gas that would move a piston, much like heated water moves the piston of a steam engine.

Arthur contends that as more and more technologies are invented, the number and variety of potential combinations increases dramatically and this accounts for the exponential growth in technological innovation that we've witnessed in recent decades. As a designer, you have these possibilities before you: you can create designs that incrementally improve how we act, think, and interact. Or you can think of novel combinations of technologies and ideas to create designs that transform how we act, think, and interact.

But in either case, we must consider this: What are the moral implications of our designs? Does change always mean better? How do we use these tools to, in Steve Jobs's words, do wonderful things?

Moral Impacts of Technology and Our Designs

We are now at a point where we can return to the issue that opened this chapter: Is technology a force for good or ill? We now know that it depends on how it is used. And, using the person-resource-activity model, we know that how it is used depends on the affordances designed into it, relative to the user's goal and the environment. Its use is also shaped by the culture and this behavior, in turn, confirms and occasionally changes the purposes and values of a culture.

With these concepts, we can turn to the consideration of our design task. As we try to make the world a better place, the task becomes: How do we build affordances into our designs that change acting, thinking, or interacting such that they are likely to reduce harm, increase happiness and well-being, advance knowledge and agency, promote equality and address injustice, and build positive, supportive relationships and communities?

There are two approaches to answering this question. One is *prospective*, using what philosopher Peter-Paul Verbeek calls "moral imagination."[22] That is, as you ponder the range of situations in which your design could be used and apply the person-resource-activity model and consider the affordances you might offer by your design, think about how they are likely to shape behavior and the morality of the likely impact of these actions.

The other approach is *retrospective*. That is, once the design goes out the door, you collect data on the ways in which your design is use in various situations and the impact it has, including unintended uses and consequences. Based on the moral desirability of the consequences, you adjust the affordances in the next release. With either approach, you need to understand how the affordances of the design are shaping behaviors, relative to user capabilities, goals, and situations.

Let's see how these moral considerations may get played out in various design situations.

Artificial intelligence and human well-being

One of the most powerful technologies available to designers is artificial intelligence (AI), particularly as it is combined with machine learning and robotics. The array of affordances that can support doing, thinking, and interacting are unparalleled. In 2017, a transformational change in thinking capabilities of the technology occurred as AI architectures moved from expert systems to neural networks. Alphabet's neural network AI system, AlphaZero, taught itself to play three extremely complex games—chess, shogi, and go—at a world champion-level within 24 hours through millions of self-play experiences, given no domain knowledge of the games other than the rules.[23] With this development, AI now has the capacity to go beyond the initial abilities provided by its designers to create its own abilities. This computational affordance allows AI users to analyze very large data sets to augment human thinking, problem-solving, and decision-making.

This capability has been combined with the increasingly powerful capabilities of robots to provide a vast array of "doing" affordances.[24] Robots have become increasingly capable and much nimbler as various forms of locomotion have been added along with visual and tactile sensors, such that robots are able to move around, climb over obstacles; to see and recognize visual patterns; and to pick up objects of various shapes with the appropriate amount of pressure.

"Interactional affordances" include speech recognition and natural language process, to understand what is being said to it, and speech production, such that the interaction affordances of an AI system can resemble those of human-to-human interactions. Chat bots and personal assistants can respond to natural language queries with realistic, natural language responses. For example, ChatGPT, developed by Open AI, is a commonly available system that uses human language input to generate produce sophisticated paragraphs of solidly written English (or French, or Mandarin, or whatever language you choose) texts.[25] It can also create blocks of computer code. These advances are so human-like in their interactions that an engineer at Google claimed that their AI chatbot, LaMDA, was sentient,[26] although the claim was widely disputed.[27]

Sentient or not, the powerful capabilities of AI can be employed in designs to provide person-resource-action affordances that can, indeed, make the world a better place. For example, BioNTech recently partnered with AI start-up InstaDeep to advance its vaccines by using InstaDeep's protein design platform to engineer new mRNA sequences for a range of cancers and infectious diseases.[28] Other biotech companies are using the data analysis affordances of AI to predict virus variants prior to outbreaks.[29]

However, these capabilities could just as easily be used in ways to make some people, such as investors, happy while doing great harm to many others. For example, the automation of assembly tasks has increased corporate profits but has had a major negative impact on U.S. manufacturing and high-paying manufacturing jobs over the past decades.[30] This trend will continue as emerging affordances will eliminate more low skill jobs.[31] And even more powerful AI affordances will have implications for higher-skilled occupations that typically require more education. The net effect of these trends will be a truncation of wages, as wage reductions for high-education, high-wage jobs "catch up" with the earlier reductions in lower-education, lower-wage jobs that have been impacted for some time. At the same time, this level of automation will create a much larger wealth gap between the top 1%, who are likely to gain increased profits that benefit from technological designs, and everyone else.

For example, consider the impact that the AI system DALL-E might have on the graphic arts, photography, and other visual professions. DALL-E is a text-to-image generation software program that uses natural language commands, such as "A woman in a red coat looking up at the sky in the middle of Times Square," to create an image that is indistinguishable from a photograph.[32] Or "A hobbit house designed by architect Zaha Hadid" that depicts a novel structure representing her style. What impact will this have on graphic design and other design professions and how might the negative impact be mitigated? And how might ChatGPT disrupt education, for example, when students can turn in computer generated essays without understanding the subject matter? Could this exacerbate educational inequality and resulting harm?[33]

The moral implications are profound as AI systems advance, become autonomous, and perhaps sentient. While the reasoning capacity of AI systems is far superior to that of humans, their rational decisions are based only on the algorithms and data that they are fed. Studies have already demonstrated racial and gender bias in AI systems when data underrepresent certain groups.[34] For example, Lensa, an AI avatar generating app, produced over-sexualized images when used by an Asian woman, most likely because of the preponderance of such images in anime and pornography.[35] And in recent National Institute for Standards and Technology (NIST) analysis concluded that bias manifests itself not only in AI algorithms and the data used to train them, but also in the societal context in which AI systems are used.[36] Significant harm, inequalities, and injustices can be created by such bias when such AI systems are applied to bank loans, school admissions, healthcare, and criminal justice.[37]

Applications of AI are more likely to improve human well-being (and less likely to destroy the middle class) if their affordances are used to augment human behavior, thinking, and interacting, rather than reduce agency or replace it.[38] With the Boeing case study, we saw what can happen in a plane when a relatively simple software program makes an erroneous decision and preempts a human response. If AI replacement becomes pervasive, such systemic errors could be catastrophic as they ripple through the system. It leaves one's "moral imagination" spinning.

Social media, harm, and community

In February 2017, Meta (Facebook at the time) CEO Mark Zuckerberg posted a letter to the Facebook community saying, "For the past decade, Facebook has focused on connecting friends and families. With that foundation, our next focus will be developing the social infrastructure for community—for supporting us, for keeping us safe, for informing us, for civic engagement, and for inclusion of all."[39]

With 2.9 billion active Facebook users worldwide,[40] at this writing, the potential for building compassionate relationships and communities is tremendous. Facebook is a complex platform with many features. The affordances most relevant to relationships include: the ability to be "friends," to share "content" (text, links, photos, and videos) on your "timeline" that others (all users, friends, or some subset at the user's choice) can see on their "news feed"; the ability to receive posts from others as an updated stream on your news feed; and the ability to react to those posts with preset emojis (like "love," "haha," "wow," "sad," "hate") and to comment on them. All of these affordances can conceivably contribute to building positive relationships.

Other popular social media platforms include Instagram (owned by Meta), Snapchat, and TikTok. Instagram has 1.2 billion active users: TikTok has 1 billion; and Snapchat has 347 million. The features of these sites allow users to upload photos and short videos; tag them by theme,

Figure 5.2 Teenage girls using social media (Photo by SpeedKingz).

person, and place; modify them with filters and other tools; and view and comment on the postings of people they follow as well as see relevant public postings. They also enable chatting, or direct messaging, between users. TikTok is the favorite social media platform among U.S. teens, with 33% of survey respondents indicating their use of it, compared to 31% using Snapchat and 22% using Instagram.[41]

A 2018 Pew study of the social media use of teens, ages 13–17, found that nearly 90% of U.S. teens use social media multiple times a day; 45% said they use the internet "almost constantly."[42] Teens said they post about a wide range of topics, with 49% posting about their accomplishments and 44% posting about their family. More than a third (34%) posted about their emotions; 22%, about their dating life; and 13%, about their personal problems. Many teens belonged to online groups about hobbies or gaming (41%), humor (40%), pop culture (28%), sports (28%), or fashion (26%).

All of this could contribute to relationship building. And for many, it does. The Pew study found that 81% of the teen respondents said social media helps them feel more connected to their friends; 69% said they are more in touch with their friends' feelings; and 68% felt they have people who can support them through tough times. A majority of respondents said that social media helps them interact with people from different backgrounds (69%), find different points of view (67%), and show their support for different causes and issues (66%).

However, 13% of the teens reported that they are overwhelmed by all of the drama in social media (see Figure 5.2). Of the 44% who said they at least sometimes unfriend or unfollow people on social media, too much drama is the reason most often given (78% of the time). In another Pew report, the majority of teens (59%) said that they were subjected to some type of cyberbullying and 42% said they experienced offensive name-calling.[43]

Other studies raised more concerns. For example, one study found that adolescents who used social media more and those who were more emotionally invested in social media experienced poorer sleep quality, lower self-esteem, and higher levels of anxiety and depression than did less frequent users.[44] Another study found more social media use was associated risky behaviors among adolescents, such as substance use or risky sexual behavior.[45] Another meta-analysis found relationships between teen use of social media and depression, anxiety, and psychological distress.[46]

Some of the harm generated within social media is the responsibility of teens who bully and taunt others and some harm comes from the risky behavior of users themselves. But some of it may be due to the attractive social affordances that keep teens engaged in online interactions even if it means sacrificing the quality of face-to-face relationships or their physical or mental health, or due to the opportunity given to those who intend harm.

As we saw in the last chapter, the lack of harm is important to building community. But it takes more than that. Building community is more than attracting a lot of people who post things online and respond to each other with brief texts and emojis. It requires a history of interactions that contribute to trust and ongoing relationships.

How can designers use social media to create supportive communities? And if there is harm, what should be done to reduce it? What role can technology play in that? Are there other affordances that can be designed into social media platforms that reduce harm and build positive relationships?

Artificial intelligence is at the core of social media. But, as it is being used in these platforms, AI is not social in its conception. Whether it is monitoring postings, prioritizing content to be delivered, or delivering consumers to advertisers, the focus is on individual users. There is no community. Groups are treated merely as collections of individuals, nodes in a network. If community emerges, it is through the interaction of individuals not, at present, through the interactional, social affordances of AI.

If social networks are to build supportive, compassionate relationships and communities, social media designers need to think of groups as communities and design the affordances of their technology for them. Communities are not just a collection of individuals to be monetized. They are not just a bunch of users that occupy the same platform, follow the same brand, or play the same games. As we saw in the last chapter and will explore more in Chapter 15, communities are people who have a history of reciprocal, caring, trusting interactions that are shaped by, and over time,

Case Study: AI and Social Media

The business model for social media platforms is to create features that attract users and keep them engaged on the platform so they can to deliver these users to advertisers. AI is an essential part of that business model. The use of AI is the only way that social media platforms can process the billions of postings made on their website each day. AI algorithms can monitor the postings and engagement of users and analyze them for preferences, delivering to advertisers a customized subset of users who are most likely to be interested in their product.[47] AI algorithms have also been used to deliver more customized experiences to the users' feeds, prioritizing postings from the people they interact with most and the content that captivates their interest.

In response to public concern, some platforms have begun to use AI for another purpose, to reduce harm and make their platforms friendlier and safer, particularly for teenagers. Trust is an important part of that, trusting that people online are who they say they are. One way to protect teens is to make sure that users are the age they say they are. Instagram, for example, requires users to be at least 13. And those between 13 and 18 are treated differently on the platform than are adults, such that the default settings for this group reduce their exposure to older people they do not know and age-inappropriate content and advertising.[48] This policy is meant to provide teens with a safe environment in which people and content are less likely to be harmful.

To assure users are the age they say they are, Instagram has partnered with the U.K. company Yoti (Your Own Trusted Identity) to use AI to check age.[49] Yoti technology uses facial analysis to verify age by asking the user to take a video selfie.[50] It then uses algorithms to verify that it is a photo of a real person and estimates their age. The algorithms read the pixels of the image for age identifiers (such as wrinkles, gray hair), but does not "recognize" the image as a face, nor does it store the image, thus protecting privacy. The facial recognition algorithm was tested on diverse group of individuals of different ages, genders, and skin tones.

Instagram is also using AI to monitor content, especially for teens. Beyond their general policy to prohibit nudity and illegal activity on the site, those under 18, do not have access to content that is sexually suggestive, violent, or includes regulated products, such as cigarettes or drugs.[51] Nor are ads permitted that target minors, promoting products, services, or content that are inappropriate, illegal, or unsafe, or exert undue pressure on the age groups targeted.

To enforce this policy, the platform uses an AI tool that can proactively detect and flag images and videos that go against community guidelines and either block it or limit its availability to those under 18.[52] Instagram is also using Meta's DeepText AI to review text comments and automatically remove offensive posts without relying on users to first report them before they are removed.[53]

In addition to these automated services, Instagram provides offline materials for teens and their parents that describe the features of the platform and how they can be used to insure a safe environment. Instagram recommends that parents go over these materials together with their children, discussing the social and emotional issues embedded in social media use, the strategies to use social media wisely, and what to do if things go wrong.

Beyond safety for teens and others, AI is being used in a range of other ways in social media, from facilitating user searches to providing chatbots that engage users in human-like dialog in addressing inquiries. Facebook uses AI to translate foreign languages so posts can be read in other countries and cultures.[54] They also use it to automatically classify images to better deliver customized content. YouTube uses AI to fight misinformation by identifying and flagging videos that are spreading conspiracy theories and fake news. TikTok AI analyzes uploaded videos to serve up content customized to user interests that it learns from analyzing previous use patterns. Social media advertisers can use AI tools that analyze consumer trends and recommend ad strategies and even write ads based on them.

shape a culture—shared traditions, ideas, beliefs, purposes, and values. If they are to build communities, technology affordances need to support these processes.

Supporting the engagement of people outside the platform, much as Instagram structures discussions between parents and their children over platform use, is a good strategy since most communities exist in the physical world. Affordances that designers include within the platform could support platform interactions and AI could be part of that. For example, AI has been trained to detect various emotional states based on tone of voice or facial expressions.[55] This capability can be joined with the facial expression capabilities of virtual reality headsets, such as the Meta Quest Pro, if the user was interacting with others in the metaverse.[56] These affordances could be running in the background, perhaps also coordinated with biometric data from other smart devices, to warn parents of the potential for an emotional event, or to suggest to a teen user in the form of a "personal advisor" that he or she should to talk to a parent or professional about their emotional state.

AI algorithms could also be designed to support community formation and interaction within the platform. For example, they could be trained to analyze patterns and substance of interactions and functionally define a group as a community, as it appears to be forming, prioritizing postings and content to individual or group members that facilitate their community formation.

At the same time, designers can treat the platform as a community of communities. AI can analyze similarities and differences among groups, identify opportunities for different groups to connect around specific issues or actions, and facilitate cross-group interactions that foster innovative thinking. Or it mediates differences or could scaffold moral discussions—all of which can benefit individuals, groups, and society, more generally, contributing to social cohesion and a more just society.

Designing such AI enabled systems requires building in these social affordances. But it also requires a design culture in which building supportive relationships and communities is valued. It also requires that companies value the safety of their customers over making money and assessing the impact of their designs accordingly.

Web 3.0 and the future of community

Web 1.0 is the earliest version of the World Wide Web, generally characterized as the posting of primarily text-based, non-interactive content by a few providers that could be accessed by others.[57] An example would be Encyclopedia Britannica Online. Web 2.0 is the web as we know it now, a system that actively engages users: they can buy things, post content, interact with others. This is the online world of Amazon, PayPal, Facebook, and Instagram.

But there is a group of technologists who are promoting the evolution of Web 3.0 as our online world of the future.[58] Web 3.0 is blockchains, crypto currency, nonfungible tokens (NFTs), decentralized autonomous organizations (DAOs), and the metaverse. Advocates of Web 3.0 see Web 2.0 as the centralized control of the web in a handful of companies that own your data, your profile, your postings, and your interactions. They contrast this with Web 3.0, which is decentralized; a "trustless" online place where everyone owns their own digital content; where that content is monetized and profits the content creators; and where voluntary communities are governed by their members. These advocates see this decentralized world as a preferable situation. If they were presented with Hardin's tragedy of the commons, they would choose to have the meadow privatized.

The preference is based on these technological affordances and assumptions. Blockchains have the affordance of creating a distributed, immutable, public record of transactions and the ability to create "smart contracts" that are self-executable. A typical example of this would be the purchase of a digital artifact using cryptocurrency that is automatically transferred from one account to another upon the verified transfer of the digital artifact. The ownership of the artifact, and its transfer, would be authenticated by an NFT. This transfer would be "trustless," which in the Web 3.0 world means that you don't need to trust the party you are dealing with, or an intermediate facilitator because trades are automatically handled and authenticated by the technology.

The potential uses of Web 3.0 technologies are most vividly illustrated by the metaverse. The metaverse is a virtual or virtually-augmented world of digital artifacts and personas that populate, move, and interact within 3-D spaces, requiring a headset or specialized eyeglasses to visualize. As described and illustrated by Mark Zuckerberg, these affordances can create social spaces in which people physically located anywhere in the world can come together to play virtual games, co-create digital artifacts, work, provide or take advantage of digital services, or just hang out.[59]

Some of the technologies, such as blockchains and NFTs, already exist and are widely used. Many of the technologies needed to fully realize the metaverse are still being developed and built out.

The moral implications of some of these technologies become apparent when you look at the impact of their use. Other implications are apparent only when you dig into the underlying assumptions, purposes, and values and how they are implemented in the technology's affordances and the impact they have.

For crypto, the stated purpose is "electronic payment system based on cryptographic proof instead of trust."[60] While addressing the harm done by. Untrustworthy institutions is important, one must consider the impact this design has on trust. The value of various crypto currencies is determined primarily as it is set by daily conversion rates as they are traded for fiat currencies, such as U.S. dollars, British pounds, or Euros. This fact has dramatically contorted the use of the currency for the purchase of goods and services, virtual or actual, to a speculative asset whose value fluctuates dramatically. For example, between January 1, 2020, and this writing (October 23, 2022), the U.S. dollar value of a bitcoin has fluctuated from a low of $4,861 (March 12, 2020) to a high of $67,554 (November 8, 2021), back down to $16,946 (January 8, 2023).[61] Of course, there are individual losers and winners in these trades, but the trades are voluntary and based on the personal value that each trader assesses at the time. With these massive fluctuations, everyone must question the impact crypto has on harm and trust in both other people and crypto itself. At best, blockchain and crypto technologies morally mute on this question. At worst, there is money laundering, in which crypto gained from ransomware attacks and other illegal activities is converted by anonymous criminals into dollars.[62] Or there are "rug pulls" in which the market is manipulated to the advantage of unscrupulous traders, or paid celebrities, and the harm of "trustless" speculators.[63] And then there is the fraud related to the collapse of crypto exchange FTX, which wiped out billions of dollars in wealth, harming millions.[64] Perhaps it is unsurprising that currently only 8% of Americans have a positive view of cryptocurrencies and 43% have a negative view, according to a CNBC survey.[65]

Also troubling are the assumptions that seem to underlie the economic model within the metaverse, at least as envisioned by Mark Zuckerberg.[66] In his vision, the purpose of the metaverse community seems to be to come together to do, think, and interact within a transactional environment in which creations, relationships, and experiences are tokenized, monetized, bought, and sold in what he refers to as a "massively large creative economy" supported by crypto and NFTs. In this environment, Zuckerberg envisions individuals and teams coming together to co-create digital artifacts and services, such as digital clothes for their avatars or virtual tours of ancient cities, which they own, not the metaverse platform. Users can jointly enjoy these virtual objects and experiences, whether they are games or virtual concerts, but these creations only exist and can only be used in the metaverse. The business model seems to assume that the value of any good, service, or experience is determined only by what it brings in their proprietary marketplace, not by the value it has to the community, and only if it exists in the virtual platform, which Meta owns and profits from, rather than in the real world.

However, an alternative exists to the Web 3.0, market-based approach to the tragedy of the commons. And Elinor Ostrom foresaw it. The alternative is called "Commons-Based Peer Production" communities, or CBPPs. These communities are characterized by peer-to-peer collaboration for the creation or maintenance of shared resources, which are freely accessible and reusable by anyone.[67] Common examples of these efforts include Open Source Software[68] and Wikipedia,[69] as well as resource sharing, such as FreeCycle,[70] and manufacturing, such as FabLabs.[71]

With the collaborative creation of common resources, CBPP communities are fundamentally different than corporately owned or trade-based decentralized communities. And, following Ostrom's design principles, can create different technological resources and affordances with their designs. In such an environment, tools would exist for collaborative creation and experiences, but groups would be treated as communities by providing them with affordances that can be used to determine community membership, formulate group norms and rules, and manage conflicts. From this perspective, designers can craft AI affordances that give communities agency; that engage them in jointly determining their own standards, rules, conventions, and expectations; and help them monitor and enforce them for the benefit of everyone in the group. Affordances such as these help groups become communities that benefit all.[72] Perhaps Web 3.0 and the metaverse can contribute to that, but it will depend on what designers do in these environments. Imagine, for example, if rather than designs that reduce the need for trust, designers build affordances that build trust and trustworthiness among individuals, groups, and institutions. How might this not only build supportive relationships and communities but increase the happiness and well-being of all?

CRISPR and the future of humanity

Perhaps the technology that has the greatest potential for well-being—or harm—for the future of humankind is CRISPR/Cas9. CRISPR/Cas9 (or CRISPR) is a genetic engineering tool and research and development on it won Professors Jennifer Doudna and Emmanuelle Charpentier the 2020 Nobel Prize in Chemistry.[73] CRISPR/Cas9 is a genome cut-and-paste tool that acts on DNA.[74] The affordances of this tool allow the genetic engineer to delete or block unwanted genetic sequences or it can be used to insert desirable sequences. The genetic makeup used can come from anywhere: the desired sequence from the same species, one of another species, or even synthetic material. Because the tool changes DNA, it has a direct effect on the traits of a virus, bacterium, plant, animal, or person that it is used on.

Genome-engineering research on plants and animals are happening right now to, for example, increase plant yield or nutritional value, absorb more carbon, and control the mosquito population responsible for malaria.[75] And CRISPR therapies are currently being used in clinical trials with adults to treat genetic diseases, infectious diseases, and cancer.[76] But, the full potential of this application will be realized as we come to know more about the relationship between specific genes and human genetic characteristics, such that we could eliminate entire classes of genetic disorders.

The moral implications of this technology are most profound when CRISPR is used to conduct what's called "germline editing." This involves DNA edits in an embryo that not only affect an individual as he or she develops, but also his or her progeny, and subsequently, theirs, propagating changes through the population. Theoretically, germline editing could be used not only to correct a mutation in a baby before birth but to redesign the genome of the human species. Scientists are approaching this prospect with both excitement and dread and Professor Doudna has called for a pause in the application of germline editing with humans until the scientific community can discuss all of the ethical implications. There have now been two international summits on the topic, with a third scheduled in London in 2023.[77]

Nonetheless, this technology has already been applied to humans, to the shock of the scientific community. In 2018, Chinese scientist He Jiankui announced the birth of twins whose germline DNA had been altered with CRISPR to disable the genetic pathway HIV uses to infect cells.[78] His work was roundly condemned for using the technology despite the unresolved ethical implications of editing that affects future generations. And in 2019, He was tried and found guilty of illegal medical practices.

The moral challenge of technology

The moral implications of these design decisions are immense as they affect not just individuals but future generations, people who were not able to participate in the decisions made. Most likely everyone would consider the world better off if we totally eliminated the harmful effects of genetic diseases from the human race, such as muscular dystrophy, Huntington's disease, cystic fibrosis, and sickle cell anemia. But what might be the harmful effects if we were to develop a class of "super humans," the select few whose ancestors could afford such treatments, people who are genetically distinct from the rest of us? What might be the social implications of such a development? And what implications would it have for equality, justice, and other fundamental moral values that are based on a humanity that we no longer have in common? The answers to these questions must be widely discussed.

It's hard to think of anything we have more in common—and more important to our future—than our shared humanity. Perhaps AI and Web 3.0 can be used to expand the discussion of these issues to a wider audience that might be able to attend the summit in London on the ethics of CRISPR and to include a wider range of participants from all over the world, not only geneticists, but philosophers, ethicists, medical practitioners, and members of communities suffering from genetic conditions. And perhaps that discussion would benefit from the application of Ostrom's principles within such a technology platform to facilitate rule formation, enforcement, and conflict mediation.

When talking about the perils and promise of AI, Erik Brynjolfsson, Director of Sanford University's Digital Economy Lab, presents the grand challenge of our era.[79] The challenge is to reap the unprecedented benefits of AI, and by extension, other advanced technologies, by understanding how the capabilities of these technologies effect both productivity and inequality such that our technological designs contribute to and augment human capabilities and agency and ways that the wealth and value so created can benefit all of us.

The benefits of technology don't come to us automatically. Designers have a choice. Designers can create Bored Ape NFTs and build virtual real estate for sale in the metaverse. Or we can use technology to reduce harm and increase well-being in the real world. We can create communities of trade or we can build communities of caring. Without moral considerations of the ways we use of technology's powerful affordances, technology will not unlock the innate compassion we have for our fellow human beings or create a historical shift from the powerful to the powerless. It can just as easily bring harm to teenage girls, wreck the middle class, destroy trust, and create an unequal, unjust world. It all depends on how you align the purpose, affordances, and impacts of your designs and technology use to support acts, thoughts, and interactions that make the world a better place.

References

1 Chen B. The tech that will invade our lives in 2023. New York Times [Internet]. 2022, Dec 29 [cited 2023, Jan 7]. Available from: https://www.nytimes.com/2022/12/29/technology/personaltech/new-tech-2023-ai-chat-vr.html

2 Miller CC. The long-term job killer is not China. It's automation. New York Times. 2016, Dec 21.

3 Autor D, Dorn D. How technology wrecks the middle class. New York Times. 2013, Aug 24.

4 Herrman J. How TikTok is rewriting the world. New York Times. 2019, Mar 10.

5 Weinberg, Z. The metaverse is coming and the world is not ready for it. New York Times [Internet]. 2021, Dec 2 [cited 2023, Jan 7]. Available from: https://www.nytimes.com/2021/12/02/opinion/metaverse-politics-disinformation-society.html

6 Gates B. Bill Gates: Here's my plan to improve our world—And how you can help. Wired. 2013, Nov 12.

7 Singer G, Franco J. In hindsight . . . Tech predictions and quotes. TechSpot [Internet]. 2021, Nov 4 [cited 2022, Aug 25]. Available from: https://www.techspot.com/article/754-tech-predictions-and-quotes/.

8 Muro M, Perry A. What tech companies can do to become a force for inclusion. Harvard Business Review. 2018, Aug 24.

9 Singer, N. Epic Games to pay $520 million over children's privacy and trickery charges. New York Times [Internet]. 2022, Dec 19 [cited 2023, Jan 7]. Available from: https://www.nytimes.com/2022/12/19/business/ftc-epic-games-settlement.html

10 Ahn, A. Facebook parent Meta will pay $725M to settle a privacy suit over Cambridge Analytica. NPR [Internet]. 2022, Dec 23 [cited 2023, Jan 7]. Available from: https://www.npr.org/2022/12/23/1145303268/facebook-meta-cambridge-analytica-privacy-settlement

11 Goswami, R. Tech's reality check: How the industry lost $7.4 trillion in one year. CNBC [Internet]. 2022, Nov 25 [cited 2023, Jan 7]. Available from: https://www.cnbc.com/2022/11/25/techs-reality-check-how-the-industry-lost-7point4-trillion-in-one-year.html

12 Vygotsky L. Mind in society: The development of higher psychological processes. Cambridge, MA: Harvard University Press, 1978.

13 Leon'tev A. The problem of activity in psychology. In Wertsch J, editor. The concept of activity in Soviet psychology (pp. 37–71). New York: Routledge, 2019.

14 Kozma R, Chin E, Russell J, Marx, N. The roles of representations and tools in the chemistry laboratory and their implications for chemistry learning. Journal of the Learning Sciences, 2000, 9(2), 105–143.

15 Kozma R, Russell J. Multimedia and understanding: Expert and novice understanding of different representations of chemical phenomena. Journal of Research in Science Teaching, 1997, 34(9), 949–968.

16 Schank P, Kozma R. Learning chemistry through the use of a representation-based knowledge building environment. Journal of Computers in Mathematics and Science Teaching, 2001, 21(3), 253–279.

17 Cole M. The zone of proximal development: Where culture and cognition create each other. In Wertsch J, editor. Culture, communication and cognition: Vygotskian perspectives (pp. 146–161). New York: Cambridge University Press, 1985.

18 Arthur WB. The nature of technology: What it is and how it evolves. New York: Free Press, 2009.

19 Crosland M. Historical studies in the language of chemistry. Cambridge, MA: Harvard University Press, 1962.

20 Anderson W. Between the library and the laboratory: The language of chemistry in eighteenth-century France (p. 136). Baltimore, MD: Johns Hopkins University Press, 1984.

21 De Rivaz engine. Wikipedia [Internet]. [cited 2022, Aug 25]. Available from: https://en.wikipedia.org/wiki/De_Rivaz_engine.

22 Verbeek P-P. Morality in design: Design ethics and the morality of technological artifacts (pp 91-104). In Vermaas P, Kroes P, Light A, et al., editors. Philosophy and design: From engineering to architecture. New York: Springer, 2008.

23 Silver D, Hubert T, Schrittwieser J, et al. A general reinforcement learning algorithm that masters chess, shogi, and go through self-play. Science, 2018, 362(6419), 1140–1144.

24 Boston Dynamics [Internet]. [cited 2022, Aug 25]. Available from: https://www.bostondynamics.com.

25 Mollik, E. ChatGPT is a tipping point for AI. Harvard Business Review [Internet]. 2022, Dec 14 [cited 2023, Jan 7]. Available from: https://hbr.org/2022/12/chatgpt-is-a-tipping-point-for-ai

26 De Cosmo L. Google engineer claims AI chatbot is sentient: Why that matters. Scientific American [Internet]. 2022, Jul 12 [cited 2022, Aug 25]. Available from: https://www.scientificamerican.com/article/google-engineer-claims-ai-chatbot-is-sentient-why-that-matters/.

27 Metz R. No, Google'ss AI is not sentient. CNN [Internet]. 2022, Jun 14 [cites 2022, Aug 25]. Available from: https://www.cnn.com/2022/06/13/tech/google-ai-not-sentient/index.html.

28 BioNTechand InstaDeep announce strategic collaboration and form AI innovation labo to develop novel immunotherapies. BioNTech [Internet]. [cited 2022, Aug 25]. Available from: https://investors.biontech.de/news-releases/news-release-details/biontech-and-instadeep-announce-strategic-collaboration-and-form.

29 Wu LL. Flagship unwraps new AI biotech that looks to predict variants before they're here. EndPoints News [Internet]. 2022, Jul 12 [cited 2022, Aug 26]. Available from: https://endpts.com/flagship-unwraps-new-ai-biotech-that-looks-to-predict-variants-before-theyre-here/.

30 Charles K, Hurst E, Schwartz, M. The transformation of manufacturing and the decline in U.S. employment. National Bureau of Economic Research, Working Paper 24468. Cambridge, MA: 2018, Mar.

31 Webb, M. (January 2020). *The impact of artificial intelligence on the labor market.* Retrieved on September 17, 2021 at https://papers.ssrn.com/sol3/papers.cfm?abstract_id=3482150.

32 Tiku N. AI can now create any image in seconds, bringing wonder and danger. Washington Post [internet]. 2022, Sep 28 [cited 2022, Oct 31]. Available from: https://www.washingtonpost.com/technology/interactive/2022/artificial-intelligence-images-dall-e/.

33 Tufekci, Z. What would Plato say about ChatGPT? New York Times [Internet]. 2022, Dec 15 [cited 2023, Jan 7]. Available from: https://www.nytimes.com/2022/12/15/opinion/chatgpt-education-ai-technology.html

34 Webb M. The impact of artificial intelligence on the labor market. SSRN [Internet]. 2019, Nov 6 [cited 2022, Aug 25]. Available from: https://sitn.hms.harvard.edu/flash/2020/racial-discrimination-in-face-recognition-technology/.

35 Heikkilä M, The viral avitar app Lensa undressed me—without my consent. MIT Technology Review [Internet]. 2022, Dec 12 [cited 2023, Jan 7]. Available from: https://www.technologyreview.com/2022/12/12/1064751/the-viral-ai-avatar-app-lensa-undressed-me-without-my-consent/

36 There's more to AI bias than biased data, NIST report highlights. NIST [Internet]. 2022, Mar 16 [cited 2022, Aug 25]. Available from: https://www.nist.gov/news-events/news/2022/03/theres-more-ai-bias-biased-data-nist-report-highlights.

37 Dyndal GL, Berntsen A, Redse-Johansen S. Autonomous military drones: no longer science fiction. Nato Revi [Internet]. 2017, Jul 28 [cited 2022, Aug 25]. Available from: https://www.nato.int/docu/review/articles/2017/07/28/autonomous-military-drones-no-longer-science-fiction/index.html.

38 De Cremer D, Kasparov G. AI should augment human intelligence, not replace it. Harvard Business Review [Internet]. [cited 2022, Aug 25]. Available from: https://hbr.org/2021/03/ai-should-augment-human-intelligence-not-replace-it.

39 Zuckerberg, M. (February, 2017). *Building global Community.* Facebook [Internet]. 2017, Feb [cited 2022, Aug 25]. Available from: https://m.facebook.com/nt/screen/?params=%7B%22note_id%22%3A3707971095882612%7D&path=%2Fnotes%2Fnote%2F&_rdr.

40 Dixon S. Number of monthly active Facebook users worldwide as of 2nd quarter 2022. Statista [Internet]. 2022, Aug 22 [cited 2022, Aug 25]. Available from: https://www.statista.com/statistics/264810/number-of-monthly-active-facebook-users-worldwide/.

41 Taking stock with teens. Piper Sandler [Internet]. 2022, spring [cited 2022, Aug 25]. Available from: https://www.pipersandler.com/1col.aspx?id=6216.

42 Anderson M, Jiang J. Teens' social media habits and experiences. Pew Research Center [Internet]. 2018, Nov 28 [cited 2022, Aug 25]. Available from: https://www.pewresearch.org/internet/2018/11/28/teens-social-media-habits-and-experiences/.

43 Anderson, M. A majority of teens have experienced some form of cyber-bulling. Pew Research Center [Internet]. 2021, Aug 6, 2021 [cited 2022, Aug 25]. Available from: https://www.pewresearch.org/internet/2018/09/27/a-majority-of-teens-have-experienced-some-form-of-cyberbullying/.

44 Woods H, Scott H. #Sleepyteens: Social media use in adolescence is associated with poor sleep quality, anxiety, depression and low self-esteem. Journal of Adolescence, 2016, 51, 41–49.

45 Vannucci A, Simpson E, Gagnon, S, et al. Social media use and risky behaviors in adolescents: A meta-analysis. Journal of Adolescence, 2020, 79, 258–274.

46 Keles B, McCrea N, Grealish A. A systematic review: The influence of social media on depression, anxiety and psychological distress in adolescents. International Journal of Adolescence and Youth, 2020, 25(1), 79–93.

47 Kaput M. What is artificial intelligence for social media? Marketing Artificial Intelligence Institute [Internet]. 2022, Apr 18 [cited 2022, Aug 25]. Available from: https://www.marketingaiinstitute.com/blog/what-is-artificial-intelligence-for-social-media.

48 How does Instagram decide which ads to show young people? Facebook [Internet]. [cited 2022, Aug 25]. Available from: https://www.facebook.com/help/instagram/1079023176238541.

49 Introducing new ways to verify age on Instagram. Instagram [Internet]. 202, Jun 23 [cited 2022, Aug 25]. Available from: https://about.instagram.com/blog/announcements/new-ways-to-verify-age-on-instagram.

50 Yoti age estimation. Yoti [Internet]. 2022, May [cited 2022, Aug 25]. Available from: https://www.yoti.com/wp-content/uploads/Yoti-Age-Estimation-White-Paper-Executive-Summary-May-2022.pdf.

51 Updates to the sensitivity content control. Instagram [Internet]. 2022, Jun 6 [cited 2022, Aug 25]. Available from: https://about.instagram.com/blog/announcements/updates-to-the-sensitive-content-control.

52 How does Instagram use artificial intelligence to moderate content? Instagram [Internet]. [cited 2022, Aug 25]. Available from: https://help.instagram.com/423837189385631.

53 Elanotta M. How does Instagram make use of AI. Net2 [Internet]. 2021, Aug 7 [cited 2022, Aug 25]. Available from: https://net2.com/how-does-instagram-make-use-of-ai/.

54 Kaput M. AI for social media : Everything you need to know. Marketing Artificial Intelligence Institute [Internet]. 2021, Apr 22 [cited 2022, Aug 25]. Available from: https://www.marketingaiinstitute.com/blog/ai-for-social-media.

55 Somers M. Emotional AI, explained. MIT Management, Sloan School [Internet]. 2019, Mar 8 [cited 2022, Aug 25]. Available from: https://mitsloan.mit.edu/ideas-made-to-matter/emotion-ai-explained.

56 Chen BX. I tried the $1,500 Quest Pro and saw the best of the Metaverse: It's not what Mark Zuckerberg promiseNew York Times [Internet]. 2022, Oct 19 [cited 2022, Oct 31]. Available from: https://www.nytimes.com/2022/10/19/technology/personaltech/quest-pro-review-metaverse.html.

57 Schmitt K. Web 2.0. Investopedia [Internet]. 2022, Feb 3 [cited 2022, Aug 25]. Available from: https://www.investopedia.com/terms/w/web-20.asp

58 Centieiro H. In insane future of Web 3.0 and the Metaverse. Medium [Internet]. 2022, Jan 23 [cited 2022, Aug 25]. Available from: https://medium.datadriveninvestor.com/the-insane-future-of-web-3-0-and-the-metaverse-4cec3f13895a.

59 Meta. The Metaverse and how we'll build it together. YouTube [web streaming video]. 2021, Oct 28 [cited 2022, Aug 25]. Available from: https://www.youtube.com/watch?v=Uvufun6xer8.

60 Nakamoto, S. Bitcoin: A peer-to-peer electronic cash system. [cited 2023, Jan 7] Available from: https://www.ussc.gov/sites/default/files/pdf/training/annual-national-training-seminar/2018/Emerging_Tech_Bitcoin_Crypto.pdf

61 Bitcoin. CoinDesk [Internet]. [cited 2023, Jan 8]. Available from: https://www.coindesk.com/price/bitcoin/.

62 Crypto money laundering rises 30%, report finds. BBC [Internet]. 2022, Jan 26 [cited 2022, Aug 25]. Available from: https://www.bbc.com/news/technology-60072195.

63 SEC charges Kim Kardashian for unlawfully touting crypto security. U.S. Securities and Exchange Commission [Internet]. 2022, Oct 3 [cited 2022, Oct 23]. Available from: https://www.sec.gov/news/press-release/2022-183.

64 Yaffe-Bellany, D, Goldstein, M, & Weiser, B. Two executives in Sam Bankman-Fried's crypto empire plead guilty to fraud. New York Times [Internet]. 2022, Dec 21 [cited 2023, Jan 8]. Available from: https://www.nytimes.com/2022/12/21/technology/ftx-fraud-guilty-pleas.html

65 Liesman, S. Just 8% of Americans have a positive view of cryptocurrencies now, CNBC survey finds. CNBC [Internet]. 2022, Dec 7 [cited 2023, Jan 8]. Available from: https://www.cnbc.com/2022/12/07/just-8percent-of-americans-have-a-positive-view-of-cryptocurrencies-now-cnbc-survey-finds.html

66 Zuckerberg, M. Founder's letter, 2021. Facebook [Internet]. 2021, Oct 28 [cited 2023, Jan 8]. Available from: https://about.fb.com/news/2021/10/founders-letter/

67 Commons-based peer production. RRC Harvard University [Internet]. [cited 2022, Aug 25]. Available from: https://rcc.harvard.edu/commons-based-peer-production.

68 Gavras K. Open source beyond software: Re-invent open design on the common's ground. Journal of Peer Production [Internet]. 2019 [cited 2022, Aug 25]. Available from: https://www.academia.edu/39007673/OPEN_SOURCE_BEYOND_SOFTWARE_RE_INVENT_OPEN_DESIGN_ON_THE_COMMONS_GROUND?email_work_card=view-paper.

69 Wikipedia [Internet]. [cited 2022, Aug 25]. Available from: https://www.wikipedia.org.

70 FreeCycle [Internet]. [cited 2022, Aug 25]. Available from: https://freecycle.org.

71 FabLabs [Internet]. [cited 2022, Aug 25]. Available from: https://www.fablabs.io.

72 Roza D, Tenorio-Fornés A, Díaz-Molina, et al. When Osstrom meets Blockchain: Exploring the potentials of Blockchain for commons governance. SAGE Open [Internet]. 2021, Jan-Mar [cited 2022, Aug 25]. Available from: https://journals.sagepub.com/doi/pdf/10.1177/21582440211002526.

73 Ledford H, Callaway E. Pioneers of revolutionary CRISPR gene editing win chemisty Nobel. Nature [Internet]. 2020, Oct 7 Roza D, Tenorio-Fornés A, Díaz-Molina, et al. When Osstrom meets Blockchain: Exploring the potentials of Blockchain for commons governance. SAGE Open [Internet]. 2021, Jan-Mar [cited 2022, Aug 25]. Available from: https://www.nature.com/articles/d41586-020-02765-9.

74 What is CRISPR? Innovative Genomics Institute [Internet]. [cited 2022, Aug 25]. Available from: https://innovativegenomics.org/education/digital-resources/what-is-crispr/.

75 Climate and sustainable agriculture. Innovative Genomics Institute [Internet]. [cited 2022, Aug 25]. Available from: https://innovativegenomics.org/programs/sustainable-agriculture/.

76 Human health. Innovative Genomics Institute [Internet]. [cited 2022, Aug 25]. Available from: https://innovativegenomics.org/programs/human-health/.

77 Doudna J. The science and ethics of rewriting our DNA. TED [web streaming video]. [cited 2022, Aug 25]. Available from: https://www.ted.com/talks/the_ted_interview_the_science_and_ethics_of_rewriting_our_dna_jennifer_doudna/transcript.

78 Cyranoski D, Ledford H. Genome-edited baby claim provokes international outcry. Nature [Internet]. 2018, Nov 26 Innovative Genomics Institute [Internet]. [cited 2022, Aug 25]. Available from: https://www.nature.com/articles/d41586-018-07545-0.

79 Brynjolfsson E. The Turing Trap: The promise and peril of human-like artificial intelligence. Digital Economy Lab [Internet]. 2022, Jan 12 [cited 2022 Oct 31]. Available from: https://digitaleconomy.stanford.edu/news/the-turing-trap-the-promise-peril-of-human-like-artificial-intelligence/.

Part II

Our Design Traditions

6

The Scientific Tradition

An experiment is a question which science poses to Nature, and a measurement is the recording of Nature's answer.

Max Planck
Nobel Physicist

Design Traditions

The definition of design that I use in this book covers a wide range of creations from bicycles and airplanes to heart-bypass procedures, high-rise buildings, sonatas, and social welfare programs. While these creations are very different from each other in appearance and function, there are cross-cutting themes that make them all designs. They all have a purpose: to change an existing situation to preferred one. Yet they differ significantly in the kinds of purposes they have and how they go about achieving them. They all are creations of some sort. But the characteristics of these creations vary significantly. They all have criteria for successful impact, but the criteria and how they are used to judge success are significantly different. And they were all created within a context and culture that shaped them.

What accounts for the differences? What makes the design of a scientific experiment, for example, similar to other designs, yet different from the design of an automobile or the design of a piece of legislation?

That is what we will explore in the next five chapters. In large part, the differences are due to the fact that they come out of different design traditions, traditions that address different needs and conditions, require different skills, offer us different perspectives, produce different creations, and have different implications for the way we live. As such, each tradition is a sociocultural system that has emerged and evolved, over time, within the larger society to take on its own characteristic purposes, processes, products, and preferred impacts.

However, core to our considerations here are these questions: How have each of these traditions made the world a better place? Have they harmed us? Can they be improved?

For the purpose of our analysis, I will offer five coherent, somewhat overlapping, design traditions: The Scientific Tradition, the Technical-Analytic Tradition, the Human-Centered Tradition, the Aesthetic Tradition, and the Community Organization and Social Movement Tradition. Each, over time, developed its own structures and interaction patterns, and its own purposes and values.

In each of the following chapters of Part II, I will present the historic context out of which each tradition emerged. I will examine their unique purposes, processes, outcomes, and impacts. I will

Make the World a Better Place: Design with Passion, Purpose, and Values, First Edition. Robert B. Kozma.

address the sociocultural, systemic role that each play in our world. And I will consider the moral implications of each tradition.

What we have achieved with our design traditions has been impressive, if not always adding to the happiness of humankind. None of the traditions is inherently moral in character. Each can be used to create a better world if we can shape its purpose to reduce harm, and build happiness, knowledge, equality, justice, and compassionate, supportive relationships. Any of them can, and too often have, created great harm.

In this chapter, I will examine one of the most powerful design traditions: the creation of new knowledge, what has come to be the Scientific Tradition.

Roots of the Scientific Revolution

Prior to the 16th century, humankind had accumulated a huge amount of practical, everyday knowledge that helped it get by in the world. Passed down from generation to generation and modified slowly, and often painfully, over hundreds of years, through a process of trial and error, humans improved their lives by applying this accumulated practical knowledge—knowledge about how to grow crops and manage herds, how to weave and dye cloth, how to cast metal, how to lift and move heavy loads and transport them to other places. They rarely knew, or they misunderstood, *why* things worked the way they did—the conceptual knowledge and principles that accounted for the success or failure of the things they tried. They only needed to know that they *did* work. The caveman with the rock in the Chapter 5 comes to mind. He didn't need to know the physics of rock against the nut, only that it worked better than his bare hands.

This practical knowledge was disseminated from one person to another—parent to child, master to apprentice. With the invention of writing, the human race began to store and disseminate this practical information in ways that went beyond face-to-face communication and the limits of time and human memory. As the infrastructure of this technology deepened, knowledge began to accrue and was disseminated more widely, but limited still by the skills and knowledge needed to understand these special texts, the reading-writing skills that were in the hands of a small number of people.

But beginning in the 16th century, the accrual of those skills and knowledge, and the people who could use them reached a critical mass in Europe, resulting in what came to be called the Scientific Revolution. It changed the way we think about the world and gave us a new mechanism, a new process for generating and sharing knowledge.

Because the purpose of scientific research is to move from current knowledge to a preferred knowledge state—that is, more or better knowledge—and because it is an organized course of action toward that end, it qualifies as a design approach under the definition I use in this book. Scientific research has come to be the primary way, in our culture, by which new conceptual knowledge is created, initially knowledge that explains the workings of the natural world and subsequently knowledge of the complex, dynamic world of people. How the Scientific Revolution started and how it progressed tells the story of how it came to be a design tradition and how that tradition changed our world.

Early Western science

The Scientific Revolution, which started in the 16th century, was built on the thinking of Renaissance intellectuals, such as Da Vinci and lesser known scholars. Eighteen hundred years before that were the Ancient philosophers, and subsequently the Hellenic and Islamic scholars who maintained their work. Aristotle (384–322 B.C.) is generally considered the first scientist in Western history. Although others wrote on astronomy, mathematics, physics, and biology, Aristotle was the first to engage in extended empirical observations of natural phenomena for the purpose of describing the natural world and ascribing causality, the conceptual knowledge that explained how the natural world worked. He got many things wrong, as it turned out, but the process that he used began to shape the way new conceptual knowledge was created.

Aristotle did not conduct experiments in the modern sense. However, he systematically gathered data, observed patterns common across phenomena, and deduced causal explanations based on his observations and the conceptual knowledge that existed at the time. For example, he believed, as was common then, that the world is made up of four elements—earth, air, fire, and water with a combination of properties, hot or cold, and wet or dry.[1] And he believed that there are four types of causes: a material cause—what an object is made of; a formal cause—its form or shape; an efficient cause—how it was made or changed; and a final cause, or a thing's purpose. He believed that all of these causes are involved in explaining natural phenomena. He then drew on these fundamental beliefs to deduce causal explanations of phenomena he observed.

For example, from his observations of objects in motion he deduced a causal principle that an object moves only if acted upon by an efficient cause and it moves only as long as it is acted upon by this cause.[2] Astronomical movements, based on Aristotle's observations, were explained as a series of concentric, transparent spheres rotating on different axes. The model was earth-centric—unsurprising since that's where he was making his observations—with objects positioned in concentric rings moving around a stationary Earth and with the stars located in the outermost sphere.[3] These spheres, Aristotle deduced, were moved by an unmoved mover.

For two years, Aristotle applied his empirical-deductive method to study animals and sea life on the Greek isle of Lesbos. He named and classified about 500 species of birds, mammals, fish, insects, and other invertebrates, describing the internal anatomy of over a hundred animals, having dissected some 35 of them. Aristotle's biological research was substantial. Nearly 25% of his existent work is dedicated to the study of animals. No similarly comprehensive analysis of zoology was subsequently attempted until the 16th century, 1,800 years later.

But he did more than just describe and classify; he explained. For example, he developed an inheritance model to explain how parents' characteristics are transmitted to their offspring.[4] He concluded that the male's semen and the female's menses encode their characteristics of each parent, and in this way, they are passed down to their progeny. According to Aristotle, information in the male's sperm determines the "form" or species of the offspring. The female provides the matter or the "material cause." And if the "heat of the male's sperm" overpowers the "female's cool menses," it determines gender—the offspring will be a male. But the offspring's gender can be influenced by other factors, including temperature, weather, wind direction, diet, and the father's age. Information from both the male and the female define the offspring's traits, such as eye color or nose shape.

The Romans acquired this scientific knowledge when they conquered the Greeks but did not add much to it. When the Rome fell in 476 A.D., much of this work was lost in the West. But it was maintained by the Eastern Roman Empire in Constantinople. The Greeks, especially Aristotle, had considerable influence in the Arab world, which had been part of the Greek empire established by Alexander the Great. During the Islamic Golden Age from the 8th to the 14th century, Islamic scholars added to both the accrued scientific knowledge and scientific methodology. For example, the Islamic physician Rhazes was an early proponent of experimental medicine and clinical research, saying, "If you want to study the effect of bloodletting on a condition, divide the patients into two groups, perform bloodletting only on one group, watch both, and compare the results."[5]

The work of Islamic scholars was introduced to the West with the reconquest of Spain and the fall of the Eastern Empire, which drove many Greek scholars to the West. Also, with these developments, the writings of Aristotle, Plato, and other ancient Greeks were rediscovered. Their works were translated into Latin, and Aristotle's writings, reinterpreted to conform with prevailing Christian theology, became the authoritative conceptual understanding in the Western world as it was incorporated into the medieval university curriculum.

The Scientific Revolution

In the 16th century, the prevailing science began to unravel as the Aristotelian notion of an earth-centered universe, a model that had reached theological status in the Church, was challenged by a heliocentric model. This model was advocated by Nikolai Copernicus, and subsequently, by Galileo Galilei, who based their explanations on calculations and observations aided by the newly invented technology of the telescope, in the case of Galileo.[6]

This breakthrough was cemented when Isaac Newton resolved several unanswered questions about the heliocentric model, such as, if the Earth is spinning, why don't people fly off of it? Newton's law of universal gravitation explained that every mass attracts every other mass in the universe, and the gravitational force between two bodies is proportional to the product of their masses and inversely proportional to the square of the distance between them.[7] Therefore, it is gravity that keeps us bound to the earth's surface, thus resolving a main problem with the Copernican explanation.

Newton's laws of motion were revolutionary; they totally upended Aristotelian science. Newton demonstrated, among other things, that a body at rest stays at rest unless acted upon, but once acted upon, continues to move in a straight line unless it is again acted upon.

During that same period, new methods ultimately replaced Aristotle's empirical-deductive approach. In 1620, in his book *Novum Organum* (translated as *New Tool* or *New Method*), Englishman Sir Francis Bacon developed an investigative method that rejected medieval Aristotelianism and influenced the process by which new scientific knowledge was created.[8] Bacon specified the requirements for making the careful, systematic observations necessary to produce quality facts. He then proceeded to use an iterative process of induction, the ability to generalize from a set of facts to one or more conclusions, followed by gathering additional data to draw additional conclusions. The process is repeated in a stepwise fashion to build an increasingly complex knowledge base from the ground up, one which is supported by the accumulation of observed facts rather than deduction from prior conceptions.

The cumulative findings of these 16th- and 17th-century scholars represented a reset of humankind's conceptual understanding of the natural world, in what philosopher Thomas Kuhn calls a "paradigm shift."[9] This new knowledge and these new methods inspired philosophers of the Enlightenment to think differently about human nature as well. And it was upon their new conception of human nature that they built their philosophy of the good.

Characteristics of the Scientific Tradition

As with the other design traditions, the Scientific Tradition can be characterized by a particular pattern of purposes, processes, outcomes, and desired impacts.

Purpose

The tradition draws on the empiricism of Aristotle and has the same purpose as his: that of producing new knowledge, specifically knowledge that explains natural phenomena. In his 2020 book, philosopher Michael Strevens calls science the "knowledge machine."[10] Indeed, the Latin word for *knowledge* is *scientia*.

The purpose of science was framed as the objective search for universal truths about nature.[11] That is, the goal was to go beyond speculation about the world that is based on opinion, religious faith, or even current understanding to sort true facts and principles from falsehoods. Initially, this purpose was just another way of revealing the truth of the Bible, God's truth as it is written in laws of nature. However, over the centuries, the purpose shifted to become an independent, secular way of finding truth.

Through the centuries, new knowledge has compounded and it coalesced into separate academic disciplines, including astronomy, physics, chemistry, and biology that have become institutionalized as university departments. These disciplines have further specialized with subfields such as organic chemistry, biochemistry, and neurochemistry, each generating a narrower, deeper band of new knowledge.

In the 19th century, the purpose of science has expanded to include the production of knowledge of social phenomena. Disciplines have since emerged that apply the scientific method or variations of it to research on and the study of individuals (i.e., psychology), groups (i.e. sociology), and cultures (i.e., anthropology).

The development of disciplines gave scientists, individually and collectively, a way to understand and manage the exponentially growing body of knowledge by focusing on a particular aspect of that body. These different disciplines came to ask their own unique set of questions and develop specialized skills, tools, and methods for answering them. The term *discipline* was used to reflect the rigorous use of these skills, tools, and methods in the search for truth. This created distinct groups of people (physicists, chemists, psychologists, sociologists, etc.) that had their own academic journals, associations, and cultures but who are all united by the common narrative of the search for truth, which is why even today their common title is the mediaeval *philosophiae doctor*, or Ph.D.

However, while the disciplines enabled scientists to build a deeper, richer understanding of their own particular questions, the process often formed silos of knowledge and people, disconnected from other knowledge and other scholars who could, potentially, address the same question from a different perspective. These disciplinary silos of people and knowledge also became more esoteric and disconnected from practical applications, as the purpose came to be the generation of knowledge for the sake of knowledge.

However, it became clear, more than ever during World War II, that scientific knowledge could be used for practical purposes. Even the most esoteric scientific theories, such as Einstein's theory of special relativity, could be applied to get practical results, most dramatically and tragically demonstrated with the detonation of two atomic bombs over Japan at the end of the war. The practical implications of scientifically derived knowledge moved scientific research beyond the university and into industry. After the war, conceptual knowledge generated by scientific research was increasingly applied in a range of areas, from agriculture and pharmaceuticals to the design of commercial products, such as microwave ovens and computers. Consequently, scientific research came to have a huge impact on society and the economy.

In turn, the purpose of the Scientific Tradition has been broadened to include not just the generation of new knowledge, but also for that knowledge to have an economic and social impact.

The social impact purpose has now become such an important feature that it is included among the criteria for judging the merits of research proposals submitted for funding to the U.S. National Science Foundation even in the "hard science" fields of astronomy, physics, and chemistry.[12]

Process

The Scientific Tradition is known for the unique process it employs for generating new knowledge and this is its primary distinguishing characteristic. As physicist Max Planck's quote at the beginning of this chapter points out, this design tradition is a discourse between the scientist and nature. However, it is a particularly unique kind of discourse, which involves posing the question and then designing experimental conditions in a certain way that allows nature, as observed, to answer the question. However, "nature" is not the way things are in their natural state, but, increasingly, natural phenomena are altered and experiments designed by scientists to answer a specific question. And the design of such experiments to answer such questions is an essential part of the scientific process.

Since the time of Francis Bacon, scientists have used designed experiments and observations to make objective inferences about the truthes of nature. More recently, this truth-discovering narrative was challenged by two philosophers of science, not so much in challenging the purpose of science but in its process. One philosopher, Karl Popper, contended that the limitations of the inferential, experimental method, which characterized science since Bacon, could not establish the truth of a proposition; it could only eliminate the alternative explanations that were tested.[13] Thus, "truth" was tentative, waiting to be modified or even upended by the next set of experiments. The other, Thomas Kuhn, contended that, in fact, scientists were not objective seekers of truth, but rather, engaged in confirming the current "truth," what Kuhn called the prevailing "paradigm" in the discipline. In the practice of what Kuhn called "normal science," scientists were merely elaborating on this paradigm or using it to explain away any anomalies in their findings. It was only when anomalies accumulate to the point of crisis, when the current paradigm can no longer hold up, that the science opens to new, revolutionary ways of thinking that replace the old.

In the practice of normal science, experiments systematically control conditions to prove a theory, or since the writings of Popper, to disprove its competing versions of the truth. The scientific process starts by building on current scientific knowledge and evidence from previous experiments. Additional experiments are designed to verify and extend this knowledge. In these every-day activities and interactions of scientists and technicians, questions are posed, instruments used, measurements taken, and results are analyzed to come to some common understanding of their meaning.[14]

The practice of normal science, within the current paradigm, can be extremely productive, even if it is not revolutionary. For example, in the development of a vaccine, the current knowledge—knowledge gained from basic research and previous epidemics—includes an understanding of the immune mechanisms in the body and how they can be manipulated as well as how molecules can be constructed in ways to affect this process. This knowledge is used to design a possible treatment. The treatment is considered a hypothesis—a best guess that must be validated by research. The validation of a hypothesis depends on how it compares to alternative hypothesis, or competing possible truths.

In the development of a vaccine, such as the BNT162b2 COVID-19 vaccine developed by Pfizer and BioNTech,[15] experiments are designed to answer several questions: Is it effective in preventing infection in a range of people? What dosage is the most effective? Does it have any or an acceptable set of side effects? To answer these questions, experiments are designed to allow for logical conclusions based on a comparison of the effects, or impacts, of each treatment, including a placebo, or null treatment. Initially, the effectiveness and toxicity of treatments are tested on animals, followed by a series of clinical trials with humans. The new knowledge generated by this research serves as of the current knowledge in the next study, thus compounding the generation of knowledge over time.

As a result of animal tests, Pfizer and BioNTech found a candidate, BNT162b2, for human testing. In the ultimate Phase III clinical trial, prior to Federal Drug Administration (FDA) review and approval for widespread use, Pfizer hypothesized that this vaccine would be safe and effective. The company enrolled more than 43,000 people in a randomized, placebo-controlled, double-blind study.[16]

This kind of experimental design is considered to be the scientific gold standard because it eliminates a number of likely alternative causal explanations for the findings.[17] The randomized assignment of people to one treatment or another eliminates any possibility that systematic results between groups would be due to characteristics of the people who participated, rather than the treatment. The use of a non-active placebo, such as a saline solution, in comparison to the active treatment, eliminates results that might otherwise be due to the participants' perception of having received *some* treatment, rather the particular treatment of concern. And in a double-blind design, neither the participant nor the administrator knows which treatment was administered to a particular participant. This eliminates any result that might otherwise be explained by the participants' or administrator's expectation or bias about which treatment is more effective. The elimination of these alternative explanations increases the researchers' confidence that any findings are caused by the treatments being tested. So, when Pfizer researchers found 170 confirmed cases of COVID-19 28 days after the first doses were administered and 162 of these were in the placebo group while only 8 were in the vaccine group, they concluded that these differences were, indeed, due to the effectiveness of the vaccine.

The explanatory power of experiments is significantly enhanced by the use of statistical analyses. Statistical analyses can determine whether the difference between the groups is significant. In the case of the Pfizer COVID vaccine, statistical analysis indicated that the vaccine was 95% effective, and there was less than a 1 in 10,000 odds that this finding was due to chance.

Outcomes

Sometimes the result of the scientific process is a physical entity, something made or discovered. In the case of COVID, billions of dollars were spent by companies and governments to fast-track research that developed a vaccine.

But more generally, and relevant to its purpose, the scientific method, applied in various forms appropriate to the scientific question at hand, has produced a significant amount of new knowledge over the past few centuries. This has included empirical confirmation and refinement of discoveries by Copernicus and Newton; the existence of gases and their properties; the existence of molecules, atoms, subatomic particles and their structure and behavior; electrical charges and the behavior of electricity; the existence of biological cells and cellular mechanisms; the evolution of species and natural selection; the discovery of bacteria, antibiotics, and vaccines; and the molecular structure of DNA and genetic editing. The scientific method has also come to be applied to social phenomenon, augmenting knowledge in fields such as psychology, sociology, political science, and economics.

Indeed, one of the wonders of the Scientific Tradition is that the new knowledge it creates builds on itself to create more knowledge. It is estimated that between the 17th and 21st centuries, new knowledge grew at a rate of 8–9% each year.[18] That equates to a doubling of global scientific output roughly every nine years.

Impact

As mentioned, this conceptual knowledge, generated through the Scientific Tradition, has come to be used in the creation of designs in practical fields, such as mechanical engineering, chemical engineering, agriculture, pharmaceuticals, medicine, clinical psychology, social work, and education. It is easiest to measure the impact of scientific research on the economy. A study looked at the impact of research on economic growth in 65 countries over the period 1980–2016.[19] They found that the amount of research output in a country increased economic growth, primarily through structural changes favoring the industrial sector. They found that academic knowledge was applied in a broad set of industries and that social and physical sciences impact economic growth the most. The impact of the research output of clinical and health sciences, and arts and humanities was characterized by low levels of applications, although they also led to positive economic growth.

Case Study: Mendelian Genetics

In the chapters of Part II, I will use case studies as a mechanism to both give a concrete example of the purpose, process, outcomes, and impact of the design traditions and to illustrate the similarities and differences between them.

One of the most important practical applications of scientific knowledge has been in the area of plant breeding. From early civilization, practical knowledge about selective breeding led, at first, to the domestication of certain grain species, and then to a level of productivity that was able to support larger populations, enabling the growth of villages and then entire cities. Over the centuries, farmers acquired and then passed down practical knowledge about breeding, which allowed them to selectively breed for characteristics they desired, such as more productive grains or hardier stock. But this was a hit-or-miss process; they had no conception of the mechanisms by which specific characteristics were passed on. It wasn't until this process was understood that crossbreeding was systematically applied to increase crop yields, which ultimately resulted in the Green Revolution that fed billions of people around the world. This case study illustrates the process by which a scientist designed a series of studies that launched the entire field of genetics.

Case Study: Mendelian Genetics
Between 1856 and 1863, a humble Augustinian monk conducted a series of experiments that established the rules of heredity that are the foundation for genetics.[20] Gregor Mendel (see Figure 6.1) was born in the small village of Heinzendorf in a part of the Austrian Empire that is now the Czech Republic. As a boy, he worked on the farm and kept bees. He studied at the University of Olomouc, where the Department of Natural History and Agriculture was headed by Johann Karl Nestler, who conducted extensive research on hereditary traits of plants and animals. Part way through, Mendel discontinued his studies because of health and financial difficulties. He became a monk so that he could get an education he could not otherwise afford, joining the community of Saint Thomas's Abbey in Brno. He was then able to attend the University of Vienna, where he studied physics. Upon returning to the abbey, Mendel taught high school science.

Figure 6.1 Gregor Mendel
(*Source:* Wikimedia Commons).

Mendel was very interested in what accounted for the variations within plant and animal species. For example, why are some flowers of pea plants white and others purple? Why aren't they all one color or the other, or mixtures of colors? The general scientific knowledge at the time was that characteristics of a plant where a blend of the characteristics of both its male and female parents. However, in his initial studies, Mendel found that pea plants (*Pisum sativum*) had only white flowers or purple flowers; there were no plants that mixed the two colors to form pink flowers, as the prevailing theory of the time would predict, if these plants crossbred.[21]

So, Mendel conducted a whole series of experiments with pea plants, nearly 30,000 over the years, to see if he could better understand the mechanisms by which traits were passed from one generation to another. Pea plants are a particularly good species to study because they grow and reproduce quickly. Peas also have a simple set of traits that can be visually observed and studied, such as flower color, size, and pea pod shape.

The purpose of Mendel's research was to understand the mechanisms of inheritance, how characteristics were passed on that would explain physical traits of pea plants. He designed experiments to do just that. He identified seven characteristics of pea plants, each with two traits, that he could experimentally manipulate: flower color (white or purple), flower position (in the middle of the plant or at the end of the stem), plant size (long or short), seed shape (smooth or wrinkled), inner-seed color (green or yellow), pea pod color (green or yellow), and pea pod shape (smooth or lumpy). He started with plants that were bred to consistently display only one or the other of the traits, let's say flower color, so that he could start his experiments with a pure inheritance line of white-flowered plants and another line of purple-flowered plants. He then crossbred plants, by careful, artificial pollination to examine the results on the next generation as well as on subsequent generations. What he found were consistent patterns of traits across each of these characteristics that became the basis of a whole new scientific field of genetics.

(Continued)

Case Study: Mendelian Genetics (Continued)

Female / Male	P	W
P	PP	PW
W	WP	WW

Figure 6.2 Punnett Square.

These offspring plants that he started with had inherited genes from each of its parents, one from the prior male side and one from the female side. The plants with white flowers received white-flowered genes from each parent and the purple-flowered plants received purple-flowered genes from each parent, both of whom had purple flowers. Mendel wanted to know what would happen if white-flowered plants were crossed with purple-flowered plants. You might expect that some would have purple flowers and some would have white.

But no; even though all the plants had inherited genetic material, called alleles, from both purple-flowered and white-flowered parents (let's call them PW plants), all those offspring had purple flowers. None of them had white flowers!

Mendel wondered why that was so. He found out why when he bred these crossbred plants again. When he did, he found that now only 75% of the plants in this third generation had purple flours and 25% had white flowers. Why was that so? Why weren't they all purple again or why weren't half of them purple and half white? Or some other combination?

This 75–25 distribution only made sense if you look at the pattern as displayed in what's called a Punnett Square, shown in Figure 6.2. The female parents are on the top row; and the males, on the side. Even though all the second-generation plants in all four squares ended up with purple flowers, each has both purple- (P) and white-flowered (W) genetic material that they inherited from the crossing of their purple-flowered and white-flowered parents. Each of these plants were, in turn, parents for the third generation and would contribute genetic material to those offspring, either P or W. So, the four possible combinations of P and W in the offspring would be PP, PW, WP, and WW. It became clear to Mendel that the 75% is composed of all those plants that had inherited at least one purple-flowered allele (P) and that the 25% of white flowered plants are those with no inherited purple allele, those in the WW square.

Mendel concluded that the purple allele, P, is a dominate gene that expressed its color in any plant that had inherited a P allele. That is, whenever there was a P allele (PP, PW, or WP), the plant would have purple flowers. The white allele, on the other hand, is recessive and the color would be expressed only if both parents had the recessive gene (WW), even if they don't display that trait.

The patterns that Mendel found are the basis of the four Mendelian Principles of Inheritance. The Principle of Paired Factors states a character is represented by at least two factors, or alleles. The Principle of Dominance and Uniformity states that some alleles are dominant while others are recessive, and an organism with at least one dominant allele will display that trait. The Principle of Segregation states that a single allele of two from each parent is passed on for each trait. And the Principle of Independent Assortment states that alleles for different traits are passed on independent from each other.

Mendelian principles came to generate a huge amount of knowledge that has included the discovery of DNA, the mapping of the human genome, and genetic engineering that, most recently, resulted in the design of the mRNA-based BioNTech/Pfizer and Moderna COVID vaccines.

Along the way, technological advances such as X-ray crystallography, allowed scientists to actually observe the underlying molecular structures and genetic processes that Mendel could only infer from his experiments. But it was the process he used to design the experiments and analyze the results that allowed him to make that inference.

Mendel's ability to describe underlying processes, which were not available for direct observation relied on three important factors that illustrate the power of the scientific method. First, he made detailed observations and measurements before, during, and after each set of experiments. Second, his experimental designs controlled variables such that he could make inferences based on the observable results. Specifically, he systematically controlled for the traits of the parents and observed the effect these had on the traits of the offspring. Third, he analyzed patterns to make connections between the variables he controlled and the outcomes of the experiments. These patterns lead to the conclusions that underpin the Mendelian principles.

However, it is important to note several things. First, while Mendel worked on his own in his modest monastery garden, modern scientific research most often requires teams of scientists and significant resources. Over the past half-century, there has been a dramatic increase in the scale and complexity of scientific research that has been accompanied by a shift toward collaborative research, located in research centers at universities, research institutions, and private companies.[22]

Second, the scientific process is not a straightforward, linear accumulation of knowledge that builds on and extends earlier knowledge. Nor is the process as logical and objective as some purport it to be. As Kuhn points out, science is also a subjective, social process by which the validity of conclusions is discussed and debated by other researchers but is subject to biases of the day.[23] The discourse is not just between a scientist and nature, as Plank describes, but also a discourse among scientists about what nature says. That is, it is not the data per se that determines the validity of scientific research but the consensus of scientists about the research, a consensus that is also influenced by the current paradigm.

This was certainly the case with Mendel's work. Mendel presented his paper at two meetings of the Natural History Society in 1865. But other scientists failed to understand his work and it was generally ignored by the scientific community.[24] When Mendel's paper was published in 1866, it was seen as essentially about hybridization rather than inheritance; it had little impact, and was only cited three times over the next 35 years. Mendel's results did not conform to the prevailing belief that inherited traits were a blend of those from the parents, and consequently, the work was ignored. Even Mendel himself thought his findings applied only to certain categories of species or traits. It wasn't until 30 years later that other researchers found the same results and Mendel's work was established as a significant contribution to the understanding of inheritance, which subsequently served as the foundation of the Green Revolution.

The Green Revolution started in Mexico in the 1940s and much of its success depended on development of new strains of seeds, which in turn, depended on Mendelian genetics. The project was headed by Norman Borlaug, a plant pathologist from the University of Minnesota who applied these principles to design strains of sturdy, pest-resistant, high-yielding wheat. In 1944, Mexico was importing half its wheat, but by the time the new strains were widely used in 1956, Mexico was self-sufficient in wheat production. And in 1964, Mexico exported half a million tons of wheat. Borlaug's strain of wheat was also successful when grown in some areas of Asia and Africa.

With its application in India, wheat production increased four times in 20 years, from 12 million tons in 1966 to 47 million tons in 1986. From 1961 to 2018, world cereal production increased by 238%.[25] In 1970, Borlaug won the Nobel Peace Prize for his work, recognized for saving millions of lives from starvation.

Systemic Implications of the Scientific Tradition

The Scientific Tradition is an excellent example of how macro systems influence what people do, how they think, and how they interact. It also demonstrates how micro interaction patterns, purposes, and values can come to influence the larger sociocultural system. But it wasn't this way from the start.

Initially, there was little exchange between the scientific community and the larger system in which it was embedded. The scientific culture valued knowledge for its own sake—what is sometimes called basic research or pure science—with relatively little concern for its practical applications. In turn, science was by and large ignored by the rest of society. For example, there is little evidence that knowledge generated during the Scientific Revolution had much of a direct impact on the Industrial Revolution that followed closely on its heels, although the Industrial Revolution did benefit from the empirical mindset and economic progressivism of the Enlightenment.[26]

However, the 20th century saw significant change in the connections between scientific knowledge and practical applications. The connections increased dramatically during World War II and the Cold War when there was a significant increase in government funding of scientific research in the United States, initially in support of the war effort, and subsequently, for economic and commercial purposes.[27] Corporate funding of basic research increased as well. The increased support for research has corresponded to an exponential growth of new patents over the last 75 years. In 1945, there were less than 20,000 patents granted in the United States, but by 2017, there were 160,000 granted.[28] Nearly a third of these patents relied directly on federal funding of research. The new knowledge generated by the Scientific Tradition has resulted in the design of new materials, technologies, products, and processes with significant commercial implications.

This increase in new knowledge ultimately came to have a huge impact on the United States and world economies, moving them away from manufacturing economies to what has come to be called the "knowledge economy."[29] This term captures a shift in the market value of "things" to that of "knowledge" and "information." This corresponded to a shift in the labor market from factory workers to professional categories as well as to the monetization of knowledge and its impact on economic output. As such, the Scientific Tradition has come to be integrated into the larger socioeconomic culture, emerging as a prime contributor to the economy.

Moral Implications of the Scientific Tradition

Over the centuries, the Scientific Tradition has contributed to the world in many beneficial ways. The results of scientific studies have reduced harm, saved lives, and contributed to happiness. For example, the practical application of genetic research has resulted in the creation of designer grain seeds resulting in plants that are resistant to drought and pests, thus significantly increasing the productivity of food crops that have fed billions of people around the world. And discoveries of vaccines for tuberculosis, polio, and measles, among other diseases, have reduced misery in the world and saved the lives of millions. In 2020, after significant scientific effort worldwide, several vaccines were developed that prevented infection by COVID-19, the virus that has killed over 4.6 million people to date.

But it is important to note that there is nothing inherently moral about the scientific endeavor. Without applying moral principles, research studies and the application of their findings can just as easily be used to create harm as happiness, injustice as equality. This is a particularly important concern when one considers the potentially devastating impact, for example, of applying CRISPR technology to create pathogens that could be used in a war or terrorist extortion.

Beyond harm, the moral implications of the tradition are most relevant to our principle related to the advancement of knowledge. As previously documented, the tradition has served that purpose well. However, there are profound moral issues related to other moral principles, such as the access of that knowledge and how it is used. Is scientific knowledge available to all or is it structured to privilege a very few?

The access issue relates to our equality principle. The typical mechanism by which that knowledge is accessed is through education, particularly higher education where much of the nation's research capacity is located. However, in the United States, the quality of K–12 education that enables people to access higher education is uneven, with the poorest quality schools concentrated in the poorest neighborhoods and people of color disproportionately living in those neighborhoods.[30] Black and Hispanic students and those from high-poverty school districts score consistently lower on national assessments than White students and those from low-poverty districts.[31] Consequently, Black and Hispanic students are less likely to be prepared for higher education and qualify for admission. This achievement-based access problem is compounded for poor students by the significant expense of higher education. The inflation-adjusted annual cost of tuition, fees, and room and board in public 4-year institutions has jumped from $8,981 in 1985 to $20,589 in 2018, in current dollars.[32]

Beyond a concern about equal access to scientific knowledge via education, there is a moral issue of knowledge ownership and the extent to which knowledge is a private good or a public good. The mechanism for assigning private ownership to inventions goes back to England in 1624, when patent laws protected owners of new physical inventions by granting them monopolies for 14 years. This system protected many of the inventions that came out of the Industrial Revolution. But in 1796, the patent system was expanded to include not just inventions but ideas and principles, what are called intellectual property. Currently, intellectual property in the United States is protected for 20 years, in the case of patents, and for the life of an author plus 70 years, in the case of a copyright. This device does not assign ownership to the knowledge per se, only to its expression in a document or instantiation in an object.

But there is a trend toward the use of intellectual property law to restrict not just the expression of knowledge but its use as well. And this raises a question about the extent to which new knowledge, especially that funded by taxpayers, is a private good that benefits a few or a public good that could benefit all.

In 1980, the federal Bayh-Dole Act was passed by Congress to incentivize the commercial application of new knowledge by allowing a university or a researcher to secure the intellectual property rights for an invention whose discovery was funded by public money. The rationale was knowledge that might otherwise only appear in esoteric journals would additionally be applied to benefit the public. But in actuality, the public who paid for the development of much of this knowledge would pay again for its use. Universities and professors, some of them paid by the public, would pocket the profits.

Lawrence Lessig, in his book *America, Compromised*, points out that this confounding of knowledge and profit has a corrupting influence on science.[33] It brings into question the overall purpose of those working in the Scientific Tradition: Is it to create new knowledge or does making money drive the scientific endeavor? Does corporate support for scientific research shape what is or is not studied or bias the findings? How can people maintain their trust in science when science is used to claim, for example, that cigarettes have no negative health effects, prescriptive opioids are not addictive, or the burning of fossil fuels has no impact on our environment?

Other moral issues are perhaps more profound, ones related to the process of producing scientific knowledge and the use of the resulting discoveries. In a study conducted from 1932 to 1972, scientists with the U.S. Health Service researched the disease syphilis. They did this by studying Black males in Tuskegee, Alabama, both those who had the disease and those who did not. Those who had the disease were not offered treatment that scientists knew at the time would have cured the disease, so that they could examine the natural course of the disease.[34] The purpose of advancing knowledge is commendable, according to Principle 4. But it can't be at someone's harm. And to do so without their knowledge is reprehensible.

Perhaps the most atrocious application of the Scientific Tradition is the creation of new knowledge for immoral purposes. The chemical compound Zyklon B was developed in Germany as a pesticide. But after they experimentally determined its lethal effects on Russian prisoners, the Nazis used it to murder over 6,000 Jews a day between 1943 and 1944 in Auschwitz.[35]

To make the world better, we need more scientific research and its applications to reduce harm and increase happiness; we need more research on building trust and cooperation and no more Tuskegee experiments, more modified seed grains that feed millions and no research on genocidal weapons. The potential for Scientific Tradition to reduce harm and improve the world is tremendous, but very much depends on the integration of moral principles into its purposes, processes, outcomes, and impacts.

References

1 Aristotle. Organon. In The Basic Works of Aristotle. New York: Random House, 1941.
2 Aristotle. Physica. In The Basic Works of Aristotle. New York: Random House, 1941.
3 Aristotle. De caelo. In The Basic Works of Aristotle. New York: Random House, 1941.
4 Aristotle. De generatione animalium. In The Basic Works of Aristotle. New York: Random House, 1941.
5 Hajar R. The air of history (Part IV): The great Muslim physician Al Rhazes. Heart Views [Internet]. 2013, Apri-Jun [cited 2022, Aug 25]. Available from: https://www.ncbi.nlm.nih.gov/pmc/articles/PMC3752886/.
6 Wootton D. The invention of science. New York: Harper, 2015.
7 Shapin S. The Scientific Revolution (2nd Ed.). Chicago: University of Chicago Press, 2018.
8 Bacon F. The new organon. In Francis Bacon: The complete works. London: Centaur Classics, 2015.
9 Kuhn T. The structure of scientific revolutions (4th ed.). Chicago: University of Chicago press, 2012.
10 Strevens M. The knowledge machine: How irrationality created modern science. New York: Liveright, 2020.
11 Bacon F. The new organon. In Francis Bacon: The complete works. London: Centaur Classics, 2015.
12 MacFadden B. Broader impacts of science on society. Cambridge: Cambridge University Press, 2019.
13 Popper K. The logic of scientific discovery. New York: Routledge, 2002.

14 Latour B, Woolgar S. Laboratory life: The construction of scientific facts (2nd ed.). Princeton, NJ: Princeton University Press, 1986.

15 Polack F, Thomas S, Kitchin N, et al. Safety and efficacy of the BNT162b2 nRNA Covid-19 Vaccine. New England Journal of Medicine, 2020, 383, 2603–2615.

16 Pfizer and BioNTech conclude Phae 3 study of COVID-19 vaccine candidate, metting all primary efficacy endpoints. Pfizer [Internet]. 2020, Nov 18 [cited 2022, Aug 25]. Available from: https://www.pfizer.com/news/press-release/press-release-detail/pfizer-and-biontech-conclude-phase-3-study-COVID-19-vaccine.

17 Misra S. Randomized double blind placebo control studies, the "gold standard" intervention based studies. Indian Journal of Sexually Transmitted Diseases and AIDS, 2021, 33(2), 131–134.

18 Van Noorden R. Global scientific output doubles every nine years. Nature.Com [Internet]. 2014, May 7 [cited 2022, Oct 24]. Available from: https://www.as.utexas.edu/astronomy/education/spring13/wheeler/secure/scientific_output_9.pdf.

19 Pinto T, Teixeira A. The impact of research output on economic growth by fields of science: A dynamic panel data analysis, 1980-2016. Scientometrics, 2020, 123, 945–978.

20 Gregor Mendel. Biography [Internet]. 2017, Apr 27 [cited 2022, Aug 25]. Available from: https://www.biography.com/scientist/gregor-mendel.

21 Mendel G. Experiments in plant hybridization. Scotts Valley, CA: CreateSpace, 2017.

22 Cooke N, Hilton M. Enhancing the effectiveness of team science. Washington, D.C.: National Academies Press, 2015.

23 Kuhn T. The structure of scientific revolutions (4th ed.). Chicago: University of Chicago press, 2012.

24 Gregor Mendel. Wikipedia [Internet]. [cited 2022, Aug 25]. Available from: https://en.wikipedia.org/wiki/Gregor_Mendel.

25 Ritchie H, Roser M. Crop yields. Our World Data [Internet]. 2021, Jun [cited 2022, Aug 25]. Available from: https://ourworldindata.org/crop-yields.

26 Science and the industrial Revolution. Britannica [Internet]. Science and the industrial Revolution. Available from: https://www.britannica.com/science/history-of-science/Science-and-the-Industrial-Revolution.

27 Evolution of the U.S. research enterprise. National Library of Medicine [Internet]. [cited 2022, Aug 25]. Available from: https://www.ncbi.nlm.nih.gov/books/NBK253892/.

28 Fleming l, Greene H, Li G, et al. Government-funded research increasingly fuels innovation. Science, 2019, 365(6446), 1139–1141.

29 Unger R. The knowledge economy. London: Verso, 2019.

30 Johnson L. Where the kids across town grow up with very different schools. NPR [Internet]. 2019, Jul 25 [cited 2022, Aug 25]. Available from: https://www.npr.org/2019/07/25/739494351/separate-and-unequal-schools.

31 Hussar B. The condition of education 2020. Washington, D.C.: National Center for Education Statistics, 2020.

32 Tuition costs of colleges and universities. National Center for Educational Statistics [Internet]. 2022, Jull 20 [cited 2022, Aug 25]. Available from: https://nces.ed.gov/fastfacts/display.asp?id=76.

33 Lessig L. America, Compromised. Chicago: University of Chicago Press, 2018.

34 The U.S. Public Health Service syphilis study at Tuskegee. CDC [Internet] [cited 2022, Aug 25]. Available from: https://www.cdc.gov/tuskegee/timeline.htm.

35 Gassing operations. United States Holocaust Museum [Internet]. [cited 2022, Aug 25]. Available from: https://encyclopedia.ushmm.org/content/en/article/gassing-operations.

7

The Technical-Analytic Tradition

There's a way to do it better. Find it.

Thomas Edison
American Inventor

What I'm calling the Technical-Analytic Tradition is the one we most often think of when we talk about design. It is the tradition that has given us steam engines, automobiles, airplanes, TVs, and the panoply of consumer products that fill our store-selves and our lives. Given how ubiquitous these designs are, it's hard think what life must have been like without them. But prior to the 19th century, everyday items that we take for granted now were far fewer and made by hand in cottages or small shops. Or, more likely, they didn't exist at all.

The Industrial Revolution changed everything.

Roots in the Industrial Revolution

The Industrial Revolution began with the development of machines that, in the 18th and into the 19th century, dramatically increased the productivity of industrial processes. In the case of textiles, the industry first impacted by the revolution, it was the invention of machines such as the spinning mule, the power loom, and the cotton gin. In the early 19th century the cotton gin increased the output of cotton by each operator by 40%, and made Britain the dominant producer of cotton linen in the world.[1]

This efficiency was again increased mid-19th century in Britain and the United States, with refinements in steam engines that culminated with the Corliss engine, introduced in 1849. These engines ended up powering ships, which had previously been powered only by wind, and initiated the invention of a whole new form of transportation, rail locomotives. They also came to power factory machines that were previously powered by waterwheels. In the last half of the 19th century, steam engines overtook waterwheels as the principle source of industrial power in the United States, increasing from 40,000 engines in 1870 to 56,000 in 1880, compared to 55,000 waterwheels that year.[2] More importantly, the slightly higher number of steam engines generated almost twice as much power, 2.1 million horsepower compared to 1.2 million for waterwheels.

As steam was overtaking water power, a new source of power emerged in the United States. Nikola Tesla invented the electric motor in 1886 and electric power transmission companies were formed, with Westinghouse Electric and Edison General Electric competing for dominance. It was calculated that these new sources cut the cost of power by between 70% and 83%.[3] This efficiency-gain powered U.S. economic growth in the 20th century.

Make the World a Better Place: Design with Passion, Purpose, and Values, First Edition. Robert B. Kozma.

Emergence of the Technical-Analytic Tradition

The continuous striving to design machines and procedures that increased efficiencies refined the development of the factory system, which had come to be characterized by mass production, the division of labor, and product assembly from interchangeable parts, requiring a high level of standardization. Early development of the factory system realized its full potential with Ford Motor Company's production of the Model T.[4]

In the first 1908 Ford plant, teams of workers moved down the line of parts and sub-assemblies with each worker performing a specific task, producing 14,000 automobiles that year. However, in 1913, Ford switched to a system where the cars moved, instead of the teams. Using a conveyer to move the autos standardized the process, and production skyrocketed. That year, a finished Model T rolled off the assembly line every 40 seconds, and production increased to 189,000. In a pattern familiar in our modern economy, this efficiency resulted in the price dropping from $950 to $550. The line reduced chassis assembly time from 12 hours to 1.5 hours, and by 1916, Ford produced over a half-million Model Ts, allowing for a reduction in price to $440 while still generating a profit of $60 million.[5] Ford also reduced the work day from 9 hours to 8 hours, allowing for three shifts a day, instead of two, and giving workers more leisure time. And the company doubled worker's pay to $5 a day, enabling many employees to purchase the automobiles they worked on.[6]

Maximizing efficiency

As Henry Ford was developing his approach to manufacturing, industrial engineers Fredrick Taylor and Frank and Lillian Gilbreth were implementing a new analytic methodology to improve the production process. The approach involved the observation of workers engaged in a task. An analysis of their performance broke the task into component parts and timed each component to identify the most efficient way to perform the task. Based on the physical requirements of tasks, recommendations would be made to managers on the best ways for them to be performed so as to improve productivity. The increased productivity drove dramatic economic growth and prosperity.

In the summers of 1965 and 1966, I was able to benefit from this process first hand. As a young college student, I worked on the assembly line at the Ford truck plant in Wayne, Michigan, to pay my University of Michigan tuition. Every 1 minute and 20 seconds, I installed a steering column and firewall insulation in the cab of a Ford F100 pickup truck as it moved by my work station. I worked the evening shift from 4 p.m. to midnight, six days a week, and my short-term employment allowed full-time workers to take a summer vacation. While I was not eligible to be a union member because my employment was temporary, I made the union wage of $3.50 an hour, plus time-and-a-half for overtime. The work was repetitious and tedious, but the pay from my three months of summer employment was more than enough to cover my tuition, and room and board the next school year.

The Technical-Analytic Approach used at Ford has come to be applied to a wide variety of other industries and work situations. For example, what Henry Ford did for cars, the McDonald brothers subsequently did for hamburgers and French fries: they broke down processes into simple, repetitive tasks.[7] And as a result, they churned out food quickly, cheaply, and consistently to become one of the world's largest retail food chains.[8]

However, despite the increased production resulting from the Technical Approach, autos and other U.S. products were often plagued by quality issues. For example, in 1950 Ford was manufacturing a new car model with transmissions that were being made in both Japan, by Mazda, and the United States, in their Ford factories. Soon after, the car model was introduced, Ford customers were specifically requesting the model with Japanese transmissions rather than the U.S.-made transmissions. Because both transmissions were made to the same specifications, Ford engineers could not understand the customer preference for the model with Japanese transmissions. They decided to take apart the two different transmissions. The American-made car parts were all within specified tolerance levels. But the Japanese car parts were even more exact. If a part was supposed to be one foot long, plus or minus 1/8 of an inch, the Japanese parts were all within 1/16 of an inch. This made the Japanese cars run more smoothly, and customers experienced fewer problems.[9]

Much of what happened with Japan's industrial economy after World War II was due to W. Edwards Deming, an American engineer and statistician who was working with the Allied Command occupying Japan. Deming worked with Japanese leaders to redesign their manufacturing capacity advocating a method of statistical process control that focused on improving quality but also resulted in productivity increases.[10] Deming proposed a continual improvement approach to management whereby organizations could optimize their operations to increase quality and reduce costs. The key to this practice is to treat manufacturing not as bits and pieces, but as a system in which all the components must work together to achieve its purpose. Application of these processes in Japan resulted in what was called the "post-war economic miracle," which brought the country out of the ashes of war and on the road to becoming the second-largest economy in the world. Ultimately, this approach was widely-adopted in the United States as well.

The consumer economy

By mid-20th century, efficient mass production processes became the standard way of manufacturing the wide range of products desired by a prospering middle class that emerged out of the postwar U.S. economy. The postwar industry in North America, and eventually Europe and Japan, produced automobiles, TVs, ranges, refrigerators, dishwashers, vacuum cleaners, and other appliances, making companies that produced these products, like General Motors, Ford, General Electric, and AT&T, among the largest revenue-producing companies in the world.[11]

Production of these goods, coupled with mass advertising—initially through print media, then radio and TV—created the mass-consumption economy and culture that we have today. To sustain its growth, the economy had to be continuously fed with new products that were distinct from those of competitors and from earlier versions of the same products. This need led to product designs that were incremental improvements or stylistic changes to previous products. Sometimes products were intentionally designed so that it was more expensive to repair them when something went wrong than to replace them with a new product.[12] And sometimes the new versions would intentionally invalidate the utility of earlier versions, in what's called "planned obsolescence."[13] A recent example of this is Apple's design practice of slowing down the performance of older iPhones to encourage the purchase of new ones, a practice that cost the company $113 million to settle consumer fraud lawsuits.[14]

Scientific research and transformative innovations

In the mid-20th century, modest improvements and stylistic changes were common; innovative designs were rare and required significant technological breakthroughs. These breakthroughs came as World War II and Cold War military needs harnessed science, an emerging engineering capability, and technological infrastructure to create transformative technologies. It was during this time that the Scientific Tradition came to support the purposes and goals of the Technical-Analytic Tradition.

At universities, government funding pushed academic fields, such as physics, chemistry, biology, and mathematics, to move from pure research to research with military or economic applications. Meeting military needs resulted in a range of technological breakthroughs in materials, computing, networking, and sensors. The subsequent fall of the Soviet Union allowed for civilian applications of these breakthroughs.[15] The U.S. federal agency that funded most of the developments, DARPA (Defense Applied Research Projects Agency), became ARPA and technological know-how was transferred to the private sector to foster a vast array of new designs for consumer use and to fuel economic growth. The fall of the Soviet Union also opened up opportunities in the world economy for globalization and free trade that supported the continuation of economic growth.

Corporations also invested in applied research. Corporate research that supported the creation of new products started in the late 19th century with what came to be called AT&T Bell Laboratories and is now Nokia Bell Labs. Over the years, Bell Labs researchers developed radio astronomy, the transistor, the laser, the photovoltaic cell, the Unix operating system, and the programming languages C and C++. Nine Nobel Prizes have been awarded for work completed at Bell Laboratories.[16] After World War II, other research and development (R&D) labs and institutions emerged out of industry or academia, such as Xerox PARC and SRI International, where I worked for eight years leading teams that designed and evaluated advanced technologies for education. These R&D institutions developed the laser printer, the graphical user interface, the computer mouse, the internet, ethernet, bit-mapped displays, collaborative software, speech recognition, AI, and robotics. This tradition of innovative breakthroughs has continued with Google X, Amazon's Lab126, Apple's Design Lab, Boeing's Phantom Works, and Nike's Innovation Kitchen.[17]

The combining and recombining of the exponentially growing number of innovations, the processes described in Chapter 5, have transformed our economy and society. Innovation in mechanics, computing technology, medicine, and business practices has driven economic growth, raised wages, and helped Americans lead longer and healthier lives.[18]

Characteristics of the Technical-Analytic Tradition

The purpose, process, outcomes, and impact of the Technical-Analytic Tradition are very different from those in the Scientific Tradition. Each tradition requires different training and skills. However, over time, there has grown to be significant overlap that has primarily benefitted the Technical-Analytic Tradition.

Purpose

The purpose in the Technical-Analytic Tradition is to create and manufacture a product that meets some need or takes advantage of or creates a market opportunity. But an essential feature of the tradition has come to be manufacturing the product efficiently and optimizing the production process and this is its distinguishing characteristic. Many technologies and processes have been designed for that purpose.

The purpose or reason for a design in this tradition is typically articulated in a *design brief*. The design brief is a stated plan developed by a designer or by a client who is commissioning the design.[19] In the brief, the stated purpose could be to fill a need, sell a specified amount, capture a particular share of the market, or produce a certain profit. The brief may specify a particular problem to be solved, such as the design of a runway that can handle a certain traffic flow of planes of a certain size and weight, or it may specify a certain advance in efficiency, such as an ebike that minimizes weight and maximizes battery power and longevity. Or the brief may call for certain efficiencies on the production line or production process. The brief may also specify performance standards, constraints and a timeline, and budget for the design project.

Process

Over the centuries, the process by which products were designed and produced has moved from an intuitive craft to a profession, characterized by a self-conscious, logical process of synthesizing forms that best fit contexts.[20] For example, before architecture was a profession it was an informal process carried out by artisans, such as stone masons and carpenters, who rose to the role of master builder. Other products, from woven goods to pots and pans, were created by individual craftspeople, such as weavers and tinkers, in small shops. Over time, the knowledge used to create these products accumulated and became more specialized, requiring extensive training, and architecture and engineering became professions, followed by even more specialized professions, such as mechanical engineering, civil engineering, and electrical engineering.

Along with this professionalization, the process became paramount and the specific product secondary. That is, the knowledge that was acquired was not how to make a specific thing but how things are made. As the Industrial Revolution picked up steam, the engineer became a key figure: the engineer was the person who designed the machines that made things.

Early in the 20th century, Taylor and the Gilbreths brought the production process under quantitative analysis and control. The field of operations research was developed during World War II to coordinate the movement and positioning of massive numbers of troops, weapons, and supplies.

Operations research relies on techniques such as mathematical modeling, statistical analysis, computer simulation, and mathematical optimization, to achieve efficiencies and arrive at optimal or near-optimal solutions to complex coordination problems. After the war, operations research was applied to manufacturing process to, again, increase efficiency. The technique is often linked with technical approaches to decision-making, referred to as management science, characterized as rational, systematic, science-based techniques to inform the design of organizational structures and processes and control operations, so as to maximize productivity. This was the process advocated by Deming.

These organizational and production design processes rely on an in-depth understanding of the current manufacturing situation and the desired situation, as quantitatively expressed. Since the goals, contexts, and success criteria come to be well understood, the prospect is that all possible solutions can be identified and systematically analyzed and can result in an optimal solution. In this regard, the Technical-Analytic Tradition most closely aligns with the design process described by Simon in his book *The Sciences of the Artificial*, referenced in Chapter 2.[21] Complex problems are treated as a system of interconnected subcomponents. Problems are broken down into subproblems that are more susceptible to analyses and the solutions to these problems can be combined for a complete solution. Competing solutions are often implemented as prototypes that can be tested and revised based on performance against alternative designs and against success criteria, and the best one can be selected.

The Technical-Analytic Tradition has benefitted greatly from development of the computer and specialized software. Computer-aided design (CAD) software aids in the creation and modification of product design ideas by making it easy to render them as 3D images that can be rotated for visual inspection. And the software allows for mathematical analysis, testing, and optimization. Computer-aided manufacturing (CAM) software takes CAD output files as input and makes it easy to control machine tools and the design of the manufacturing process. CAM can assist in designing the operations of a manufacturing plant, including planning, management, transportation, and storage, thus optimizing the manufacturing process.

In the mid-1960s, design itself became a profession. A movement was formed among engineers, industrial designers, and architects to apply this Technical-Analytic Approach to the design process so as to systematize it and make it more efficient. This came to be called the "Design Methods Movement" and its principles were most famously articulated by designers J. Christopher Jones,[22] Christopher Alexander, [23] Horst Rittel,[24] and L. Bruce Archer.[25] While these designers varied in the details of their design approaches, they all emphasized design as a logical, step-by-step, analytical process. For example, Jones, in his textbook on design, listed the steps as: issuing the brief, exploring the design situation, transforming the problem structure, describing subsolutions, combining subsolutions into alternative designs, evaluating alternatives, and finalizing the design decision.[26] Archer, a mechanical engineer and professor of design, described an elaborate 229-step process that was divided into phases: data is collected and analyzed, design ideas are synthesized, developed, and communicated. Within these phases, the design subproblems are identified, solutions developed, the proposed design is defined, then tested and validated.[27]

Outcomes

The result of this formal design process is typically some physical outcome, such as a product, device, or tool that fills a need or takes advantage of or creates a market opportunity. The product often must meet measurable criteria specified in the design brief—size, weight, speed, endurance, improved quality, and so on—as well as meet production costs.

The Technical-Analytic Tradition has resulted in the cornucopia of products that fill our showrooms, shelves, and online catalogs, from automobiles and bicycles to kitchen appliances and digital watches. Often these outcomes are incremental changes that make them more competitive with similar products. Occasionally, innovative designs and products are enabled by breakthroughs and recombinations of technologies or materials.

Another outcome of the technical design process could be a new way to increase production efficiencies, such as the design of advanced manufacturing technologies that reduce labor costs and wasted materials, and thus, increase productivity and profits.

Impact

The design impact of the Technical-Analytic Tradition is always objectively measurable, typically in terms of a product's characteristics or performance, the efficiency of the production process, or in the company's or client's bottom line. Adjustments are made to the design until the intended measures are achieved. In effect, the design discussion is between the designer and the impact data. Often, these are things relatively easy to measure: Does the product meet the quantitative specifications? Is it fast enough? Is it error-free? Did it sell enough? Did it make enough profit? If these figures aren't satisfying, the designer tweaks the design or may even go back to the drawing board. Often left unconsidered are things less easy to measure or those the designer would rather not: Is the product harmful? Does it improve people's happiness? Does it create or reduce equality? Does it improve human relationships or create harm?

The long-term impacts of designs in the Technical-Analytic Tradition are often not known or even examined by designers or their clients. For example, the proliferation of the automobile has had a profound impact on U.S. society that was never anticipated or considered by car manufacturers. The loss of population of U.S. inner cities during the last half of the 20th century is often attributed to, among other things, a dramatic increase in the number of automobiles that allowed for the development of a suburban lifestyle. To illustrate, the population of Detroit in 1950 was

1.8 million and it was the 5th largest city in the United States. Today, the population is around 670,000. Meanwhile, the Detroit metro area, which includes the City of Detroit and its surrounding suburbs, grew from 2.7 million in 1950 to 3.5 million today.

The auto industry and its products have also contributed significantly to air pollution and global warming.[28] Collectively, cars and trucks account for nearly one-fifth of all U.S. emissions, amounting to around 24 pounds of heat-trapping emissions for every gallon of gas produced and used. Approximately 5 pounds of this number comes from the production of the gasoline. But the great bulk of the global-warming gases—more than 19 pounds per gallon—is created as the carbon atoms emitted by combustion of the gasoline combines with two heavier oxygen atoms to form carbon dioxide that traps heat in the atmosphere.

Case Study: Ford versus Ferrari

The quest to fine-tune the process and to optimize impact that characterizes the Technical-Analytic Approach is illustrated by our case study for this chapter, Ford versus Ferrari.

Case Study: Ford versus Ferrari

From the beginning, the Ford success story was associated with speed. On October 10, 1901, Henry Ford stepped into his hand-built machine at a racetrack in Grosse Pointe, Michigan, and in front of a crowd of 6,000, beat Alexander Winton, holder of the world track speed record and the most famous name in speed of his day.[29] Ford's top speed was 72 miles an hour on the half-mile straightaway. The victory put him and his car on the automotive map.

When Ford's grandson, Henry Ford II, became President of the company in 1945, it had hit hard times and was losing $9 million a month. Henry II turned around the company by using modern management practices and by introducing a series of new models, including the Thunderbird in 1955, and in 1964, the Mustang took the market by storm.

In 1963, Ford Vice President Lee Iacocca, who was instrumental in developing the Mustang, proposed to Henry II that the company purchase the cash-strapped Ferrari Company as a means of boosting car sales even more.[30] Baby boomers were taking to the road and looking for speed and style, and Iacocca felt Ford could benefit from this trend with the purchase of the iconic Italian carmaker known for these qualities.

Ford approached Ferrari but the company's head, Enzo Ferrari, turned around and used Ford's offer to secure a more lucrative deal with Fiat that allowed him to retain complete ownership of the company. In response, Ford and Iacocca decided to design and build the fastest, most reliable, and technologically advanced racing car in history. To do it, they hired retired race car driver turned designer Carroll Shelby. His charge: to help with the development of a car that could beat Ferrari at its own game, at the most prestigious and brutal race in the world, the 24 Hours of Le Mans race in France. This story was portrayed in the 2019 film *Ford v Ferrari*, staring Matt Damon as Carrol Shelby and Christian Bale as his British driver Ken Miles.

As a driver, Shelby won the 24 Hours of Le Mans in 1959 in an Aston Martin. He had since retired from racing due to a heart condition. Shelby had already proven himself with Iacocca, who invested Ford money with him to put a Ford V8 engine in a lightweight European body to create the Shelby Cobra that trounced the competition on U.S. race tracks, including the Corvette Stingray, the undisputed U.S. sports car leader at the time.[31]

(Continued)

Case Study: Ford versus Ferrari (Continued)

But the challenge Henry II put to Shelby in 1963 was to develop a car that could win at the 24 Hours of Le Mans, a much more demanding race than the short ones in the United States that emphasize only speed. Le Mans has been called the Grand Prix of Endurance and Efficiency, and unlike fixed-distance races whose winner is determined by minimum time, the Le Mans winner is the car that can complete the most laps in a 24-hour period. Teams must balance the demands of speed with the cars' ability to run for that long without mechanical failure. Many cars fail the endurance test for one reason or another. For example, in 2019, only 47 of the 61 qualifying cars ran the full duration.

All of the famous European car manufactures have made their name on the Le Mans track at one time or another: Ferrari, Alfa Romeo, Bugatti, Bentley, Mercedes-Benz, Jaguar, Porsche, Audi, Aston Martin.[32] But, as of 1966, an American-built car had never won the event.

By 1963, Ferrari had become the dominant manufacturer in the race. The company had won 5 of the last 6 races and in that year; it took places 1 through 6.[33] The winning model was the Ferrari 250, powered by a 3.3 liter, 201 cubic inch (cu in) V12 engine producing 320 horsepower. The car won with an average speed of 118.10 miles an hour and completed 339 laps in the 24-hour period.

In 1964, Shelby took design control of the GT40 (see Figure 7.1), the car that Ford was developing for Le Mans at its engineering shop in England. The car was built on the Lola Mk6 chassis, a body that had performed well in the 1963 Le Mans but did not finish. In the Lola, they put a Ford 427, 289 cu in, V8 engine that generated an amazing 450 horsepower. By comparison, the engine that comes standard in a Toyota RAV4, 2020's largest selling automobile, is 2.5 liters or 153 cu in.[34] As one Ford executive put it, the much larger Ford 427 engine was the "way to solve the [Ferrari] problem with a sledge hammer."[35]

However, winning an auto race, especially an endurance race like the 24 Hours of Le Mans, is not just having the biggest engine. It is a combination of many factors, including engine power, low weight, reliable components, and a great race team. And the whole system—the engine, the gear box, the tires, the brakes, the steering, the pit crew, and the driver— must work together at peak performance. If any of these go wrong, it could mean the loss of the race, the car, even the driver.

That year, Ferrari cars again dominated Le Mans, taking first, second, third, fourth, fifth, and sixth places in the race. Shelby spent the rest of 1964 and early 1965 preparing the car for races later that year. Shelby's first victory with the GT40 came with Ken Miles taking the car to victory in the Daytona 2000 in February 1965.[36] One month later, Ken Miles came in second overall and first in prototype class at the 12 Hours of Sebring race.

Figure 7.1 Ford GT40 (Photo by EA Photography, Shutterstock).

Between Shelby's team and other entrants, there were six Ford GT40s entered in the 1965 Le Mans, two of them by Shelby. In the practice runs, one of Shelby's drivers, Phil Hill, shattered the record for the 8-mile track, completing it in 3 minutes 33 seconds at an average speed of 141.362 mph, and he took the pole position for the race.[37] This is when Ford knew they could beat the Ferraris. But the rest of the race was disappointing.

On race day, Shelby's two cars took an early lead over the Ferraris and the rest of the field, running at a mind-bending 195 mph on the straight away. But by the time the checkered flag came down to end the race the next day, both of Shelby's cars and the rest of the GT40s had fallen out of the race, one with clutch problems the other lost the gearbox. The Ferraris finished first, second, and third with the winner finishing 348 laps at an average speed of 121.09 mph.

With next year's race in mind, much more work needed to be done. Back in Ford's laboratories, engineers studied the air intake to the 427 and made alterations to the combustion chambers, achieving an additional 35 horsepower.[38] Electrical engineers designed the wiring system without moving parts that could be damaged by extreme vibrations. They chose windshield wipers that were those used on the Boeing 707 aircraft. Transmission engineers refined the gearbox with a team of two drivers who spent a total of 3.6 hours in the act of changing gears. And experts were assigned to solve the problem of brakes that spiked to more than 1,500°F in mere seconds when the driver hit the brakes at 210 mph.

In Test Room 17D of Ford's Engineering and Research complex, an electronic testbed was made by General Electric at the cost of millions. It was rigged with a sophisticated computer, something that had never been done before in the development of an automobile. Using measurements from an oscillograph that had been mounted in Ken Miles's car at the Le Mans trials, the team programmed the engine speeds and gearshift patterns into the computer, running through a near-exact simulation to improve gear shifting.

When Le Mans race day came on June 18, 1966, Ford entered eight GT40s, all with their 427-cubic-inch engines; three of them from Shelby's team. Ferrari had prepared seven new race cars; three 330 P3s and four 365 P2s. The 330 had 4-liter (244.1 cu in) V12 engine, rated at 390 hp.[39] The 365 (see Figure 7.2) was powered by a 4.4 L (267.9 cu in) V12 engine.

Figure 7.2 Ferrari 365 (Photo by Dan74, Shutterstock).

(Continued)

Case Study: Ford versus Ferrari (Continued)

Henry II was the honorary starter that year and he dropped the flag at 4 p.m.[40] Ferrari's plan was to charge out front at the start and try to bait the Ford drivers into moving too fast too early, breaking their cars. By 8 p.m., two of Shelby's Fords and a Ferrari were on the lead lap. At 10 p.m., it started to rain. But this didn't slow down Shelby's driver Ken Miles. While others slowed their pace, Miles overtook other cars, going faster than them by 50, 60, sometimes 70 mph. Despite being told by the pit crew to slow down, Miles broke the lap speed record that day and then broke his own record two more times. At 3 a.m., Shelby's team was running first, second, and third with Miles in the lead and the nearest Ferrari was in fifth place. At 11 a.m., with five hours to go in the race, four Fords were in the lead, with Miles in first, followed by Shelby teammate Bruce McLaren.

As the race was coming to its conclusion and it was clear that Ford would dominate, Leo Beebe, the Ford executive in charge of their race program, decided it would make a great press splash if the race ended with the GT40 in a 1-2-3 tie. At the time, Miles was ahead by four laps but was ordered to slow down to achieve the photo finish. Miles was furious but cooperated. Trying to engineer a photo finish is difficult to do, particularly at speed. Consequently, even though he led for the last half of the race, Miles came in second to Shelby teammates Chris Amon and Bruce McLaren, who finished the race inches ahead of Miles with 360 laps and a record average speed of 130.98 mph.

In 1967, Dan Gurney and A. J. Foyt teamed up in a GT40 Mk II to win again at Le Mans, with a record average speed of 135.48 mph. Ford GT40s also took first place in 1968 and 1969 before retiring from the Le Mans race the next year.

The purpose of the design of the Ford GT40 was clear and laser-focused: to optimize speed and endurance. The battle between Ford and Ferrari capped an incredible 43-year quest of auto manufacturers for this ideal at Le Mans. From the inception of the race until Ford's win that year, winners completed more and more laps during the 24-hour race each year, jumping from 1,372.94 miles in 1923 to 3,009.36 miles in 1966, with speeds that skyrocketed from the average of 57.2 mph in that first race, to an astounding 125.3 mph in the Ford GT40. Along the way; engines got bigger; the weight ratio was reduced; and parts, crew, and drivers were all fine-tuned.

The challenge was to design a car and assemble a team and then treat it as an integrated system; to squeeze everything possible out of each component yet have them all work seamlessly together. This process became increasingly technical, measured by stop watches, scales, and calipers; measured in cubic inches, horsepower, pounds, drag coefficients, fractions of a mile, and fractions of a second. None of it was good enough unless it lasted 24 hours. And it was not the best unless it came in first. It was a process that took calculations: calculations that were increasingly complex; calculations that ultimately required the use of computers, which themselves became increasingly fast. It took teams of experts—designers, engineers, drivers, pit crew. But the measurements and the competition ruled the process. Stop watches don't lie, and someone was always there to beat you.

The outcome of this process—the legendary GT40 and all the Les Mans race cars up to that point—looked much like street cars, especially street cars made to look fast. But, increasingly, race cars designed since, optimized for speed, have come to be nothing like street cars. Yes, they all had a gas-powered engine, four wheels, a transmission, brakes, and tires. But all of these parts, even the gasoline that was used, were far superior to what you drive on the road. And ultimately, with their aerodynamic profiles, they look nothing like you would have in your driveway.

In this case study, the immediate impact of the design was measured by success: record lap speeds, fastest overall speed, and of course, coming in first. But the ultimate impact of this effort was shaped by the context and it was measured in profit and dollars. Ford was interested in increasing sales of its cars, and race wins were a huge advertising boon that could do that. As the summer of 1963 ended and "Powered-by-Ford" was written on the side of race-winning Shelby Cobras, the *New York Times* made the connection between race car wins and Ford's soaring sales official with a September 7 article on the front page of the Business Section that began "Does winning automobile races sell cars? You bet it does."[41] The piece called the success of racing as a marketing tool "immediate and remarkable." This connection is what drove Ford to succeed on the track at Le Mans.

But Le Mans victories had a price. Not just the increasingly high price of building and racing a car, but also a price in human lives. In the history of Le Mans, 27 drivers have died on the track, including one of Shelby's GT40 drivers in the 1966 race.[42] There have been 159 more drivers die at the four other top race tracks. Additional injuries or deaths include marshals, crew, or spectators, such as the 1955 disaster in which 80 attendees were killed when an on-track crash launched a car going 125 mph into the stands. Nor does the figure include the many deaths at other race tracks. Two months after the Le Mans race, Ken Miles was killed while testing Ford's latest experimental race car. In 1970, Bruce McLaren, Miles's old teammate, died in a crash on a British race track.

Systemic Implications of the Technical-Analytic Tradition

The Technical-Analytic design tradition emerged from the application of steam engines to mass produced woven woolens that were previously produced by hand in cottages or small shops. This dramatically changed the interactions in the micro system from ones that occurred between artisan and materials to meet the needs of a specific client to ones that occurred between engineer and machine that optimized the mass production of products. This also created new structures, such as factories, that supported mass production and that came to be the foundation of modern capitalism. A successful design in this system depends on creating efficiencies and optimizations in speed, production, productivity, and profits which came to be the primary value in the institutional culture.

The value of optimization, typical of the Technical Approach, is dramatically illustrated by our case study. All of the components of the Ford GT40 were treated as integral parts of a system with engine, gearbox, clutch, brakes, tires, and body all tuned to maximize speed and endurance. Humans—the pit crew and drivers—were also considered part of this system. The GT40 was part of a larger system: the Le Mans 24-hour race that set the rules of the game and was composed of Ferraris, Porches, Aston Martins, Audis, Jaguars, and so on, that also maximized speed and endurance. The competition among these companies and their cars keeps moving the bar and pushing the entire system. The ability to measure speed, in terms of a thousandth of a kilometer per hour, and endurance, in terms of the total distance to the thousandth of a kilometer completed in 24 hours, is what allows for optimization and makes the system work. This feeds into yet a larger system in which success is measured in sales and profits. These profits are, in turn, fed back into corporate product development.

The optimization of production and profits was also evident in our case study of Boeing in Chapter 1. In that case, the value of optimizing production and profit prevailed, influencing the interaction patterns within Boeing during the development of the 737 Max 8, and between Boeing and the FAA that ultimately resulted in crashes that took the lives of 346 people.

In many ways, the mutually reinforcing, amplifying feedback loop within the Technical-Analytic Tradition and between it and the larger economic system has come to mutually define each other. These two systems have meshed together to make our world what it is, with all its benefits and problems as documented in Chapter 1. And it has made the Technical-Analytic Tradition the dominant design approach in our society. The design of a vast array of new products and the development and application of efficient production and management processes have resulted in an amazing amount of economic growth the last 150 years. This growth has created a remarkable amount of wealth, which has improved lives around the world.[43] A significant part of this wealth has been reinvested in the same process that produced it and this continues to feed economic growth. But this wealth has been unevenly distributed and the system has benefited a few much more than the many.

The optimization of the Technical-Analytic Tradition can have a negative impact on society as a whole. When operating in a competitive market, there is a strong incentive to take actions that serve the interests of the company at the expense of others, for example by externalizing environmental or climate impacts or reducing labor costs by eliminating jobs.

Moral Implications of the Technological-Analytic Tradition

While the Technical-Analytic Tradition and the economy it has produced have benefitted humankind in many ways, there is nothing inherently good about the approach. Growth and efficiency can just as easily be harmful as helpful; just as easily lead to inequality and injustice. For instance, it hasn't only been race car drivers who have died at the wheel. As the number of cars increased on the road, so did the number of deaths due to auto accidents. In 1966, the year Ford beat Ferrari, over 50,000 people died in auto accidents in the United States, as part of an upward trend at the time since the car's invention.[44]

Seeing this trend develop, American lawyer and activist Ralph Nader published a book the previous year titled, *Unsafe at Any Speed: The Designed-in Dangers of the American Automobile.*[45] The book was a scathing attack on the auto industry and its design practices that ignored their impact on the lives of drivers and pedestrians. He documented the crash effects of steering wheels, steering columns, dashboards, windshields, bumpers, grills, and passenger compartments that on impact produced severe injuries or death for drivers, passengers, or pedestrians. He also documented the contribution that automobiles made to air pollution.

The book became a bestseller, and Nader's testimony in front of Congress in 1966 led to the creation of the U.S. Department of Transportation and the predecessor agencies of the National Highway Traffic Safety Administration. Seat belt laws were passed in 49 states. Initially, the auto industry responded with a campaign of spying, harassment, and smear tactics for which Nader brought a civil suit. and with the winnings, established the independent, no-profit advocacy group the Center for Auto Safety. Since then, the number of automobile-related deaths has come down, despite the increase in the number of cars on U.S. roads. Nader's advocacy also contributed to the creation of the U.S. Environmental Protection Agency and the passage of the Clean Air Act.

When only one number is optimized at the expense of other values—speed on the race track or profit on the ledger—the Technical-Analytic Approach creates moral problems. If only profit is maximized to benefit executives and shareholders, the impact on others—consumers, workers, the general public—is just as likely to be harmful as beneficial. Without a consideration of impact on people, the Technical-Analytic Tradition, with its optimization of speed, efficiency, productivity, and profit can become a tyranny of numbers.

If a culture values only one number—productivity, profit, return on investment, GDP growth—you get more than a market economy. You get what philosopher Michael Sandel calls a *market society*.[46] You get a society where the value of everything is determined by the market and it is denominated in dollars. Where you go to school, what you study, who you marry, where you live, who you befriend, where you work, what you design are all influenced by dollars: dollars you make, dollars you save, dollars you invest, dollars you spend. And, without moral principles, you get the Boeing 737 Max 8 and airplane crashes, Dupont Teflon and PFOA-related cancer deaths, Subsys and opioid addiction, and you get 50,000 auto deaths.

As a result of the efforts of Ralph Nader and others, the auto industry turned a corner and began to design safety features into cars. With these improvements, auto deaths have gone down since the 1960s, despite the population and the number of drivers continuing to go up.[47] It remains to be seen if the improvements in the Boeing 737 MAX 8 will be safe.

To contribute to happiness, knowledge, equality, justice, and supportive relationships, technical designs need to be based on moral principles. Human needs must be design considerations if you want to make the world a better place. And it is this consideration that we turn to next in examining the Human-Centered Design Tradition.

References

1 Ayers R. Technological transformations and long waves. Luxemburg: International institute for Applied Systems Analysis, 1989.

2 Trowbridge W. Statistics of power and machinery. Employed in manufactures. Washington, D.C.: Department of the Interior, Census Office, 1885.

3 Du Boff R. The introduction of electric power in American manufacturing. The Economic History Review, 1967, 20, 3, 509–518.

4 Mass production begins at Ford. Science Encyclopedia [Internet]. [cited 2022, Aug 25]. Available from: https://science.jrank.org/pages/4160/Mass-Production-Mass-production-begins-at-Ford.html.

5 Hubbard G. Essentials of economics (2nd edition) (p. 272). French's Forest, AU: Pearson Australia, 2013.

6 Company timeline 1896. Ford Motor Company [Internet]. [cited 2022, Aug 25]. Available from: https://corporate.ford.com/about/history/company-timeline.html.

7 Harford T. How McDonalds revolutionised business. BBC [Internet]. 2020, Feb 5 [cited 2022, Aug 25]. Available from: https://www.bbc.com/news/business-51208592.

8 The world's biggest restaurants in 2017. Forbes [Internet]. 2017, May 17 [cited 2022, Aug 25]. Available from: https://www.forbes.com/pictures/591c79084bbe6f1b730a5811/2017-global-2000-restaura/#79b2114d6d2a.

9 Ford transmission quality study. YouTube [web streaming video]. 2010, Nov 12 [cited 2022, Aug 25]. Available from: https://www.youtube.com/watch?v=uAfUOfSY-S0.

10 The Deming philosophy looks through a lens that is different from all others. The Deming Institute [Internet]. [cited 2022, Aug 25]. Available from: https://deming.org/the-deming-philosophy/.

11 Fortune 500 1960 Full list. CNN [Internet]. [cited 2022, Aug 25]. Available from: https://money.cnn.com/magazines/fortune/fortune500_archive/full/1960/.

12 Thompson A. The fix is out: Product repairs get tougher in a new age of obsolescence. NBC News [Internet]. 2016, Jul 31 [cited 2022, Aug 25]. Available from: https://www.nbcnews.com/news/us-news/fix-out-product-repairs-get-tougher-new-age-obsolescence-n614916.

13 Gershon L. The birth of planned obsolescence. JSTOR Daily [Internet[. 2017, Apr 10 [cited 2022, Aug 25]. Available from: https://daily.jstor.org/the-birth-of-planned-obsolescence/.

14 Allyn B. Apple agrees to pay $113 million to settle 'Batterygate' case over iPhone slowdowns. NPR [Internet]. 2020, Nov 18 [cited 2022, Aug 25]. Available from: https://www.npr.org/2020/11/18/936268845/apple-agrees-to-pay-113-million-to-settle-batterygate-case-over-iphone-slowdowns.

15 Schafer T, Hyland P. Technology policy in the Post-Cold War world. Journal of Economic Issues, 1994, 28(2), 597–608.

16 Bell Labs. Nokia [Internet]. [cited 2022, Aug 25]. Available from: http://www.bell-labs.com.

17 Nike's Innovation Kitchen and Sports Research Lab. Business Insider [Internet]. [cited 2022, Aug 25]. Available from: https://www.businessinsider.com/coolest-skunk-works-2013-2#nikes-innovation-kitchen-and-sports-research-lab-9.

18 Greenstone M, Looney A. A dozen economic facts about innovation. Brookings Policy Memo [Internet]. [cited 2022, Aug 25]. Available from: https://www.brookings.edu/wp-content/uploads/2016/06/08_innovation_greenstone_looney.pdf.

19 Jones JC. Design methods: Seeds of human futures. New York: Wiley, 1970.

20 Alexander, C. Notes on the synthesis of form. Cambridge, MA: Harvard University Press, 1964.

21 Simon H. *The sciences of the artificial* (3rd ed.). Cambridge, MA: MIT Press, 1996.

22 Jones, JC. (1970). *Design methods: Seeds of human futures*. New York: Wiley.

23 Alexander, C. (1964). *Notes on the synthesis of form* (p. 15). Cambridge, MA: Harvard University Press.

24 Protzen, J-P. & Harris, D. (2010). *The Universe of Design: Horst Rittel's Theories of Design and Planning*. New York: Taylor and Francis.

25 Archer, LB. (1965). *Systematic method for designers*. London: Council of Industrial Design.

26 Jones, JC. (1970). *Design methods: Seeds of human futures*. New York: Wiley.

27 Archer LB. (1965). *Systematic method for designers*. London: Council of Industrial Design.

28 Car emissions and global warming. Union of Concerned Scientist [Internet]. 2014, Jul 18 [cited 2022, Aug 25]. Available from: https://www.ucsusa.org/resources/car-emissions-global-warming.

29 1901 Ford "Sweepstakes" Race Car. The Henry Ford [Internet]. [cited 2022, Aug 25]. Available from: https://www.thehenryford.org/artifact/199258/.

30 Baime AJ. (2010). *Go like hell: Ford, Ferrari, and their battle for speed and glory at Le Mans*. HMH Books. Kindle Edition.

31 Branch J. A quick history of the Shelby Cobra. Silodrome Gasoline Culture [Internet]. [cited 2022, Aug 25]. Available from: https://silodrome.com/history-shelby-cobra/.

32 24 Hours of Le Mans Winners. Ultimate Car Page [Internet]. [cited 2022, Aug 25]. Available from: https://www.ultimatecarpage.com/winners/&race=le_mans.

33 24 Hours of Le Mans. Wikipedia [Internet]. [cited 2022, Aug 25]. Available from: https://en.wikipedia.org/wiki/1963_24_Hours_of_Le_Mans.

34 Capparella J. 25 Bestselling cars, trucks, and SUVs of 2020. 2021, Jan 6 [cited 2022, Aug 25]. Available from: https://www.caranddriver.com/news/g32006077/best-selling-cars-2020/?slide=22.

35 Baime AJ. Go like hell: Ford, Ferrari, and their battle for speed and glory at Le Mans (p. 123). HMH Books. Kindle Edition, 2010.

36 For GT40 Mk II. Wikipedia [Internet]. [cited 2022, Aug 25]. Available from: https://en.wikipedia.org/wiki/Ford_GT40#Mk_II.

37 Baime AJ. (2010). *Go like hell: Ford, Ferrari, and their battle for speed and glory at Le Mans.* HMH Books. Kindle Edition.

38 Baime AJ. (2010). *Go like hell: Ford, Ferrari, and their battle for speed and glory at Le Mans.* HMH Books. Kindle Edition.

39 Ferrari 330. Wikipedia [Internet]. [cited 2022, Aug 25]. Available from: https://en.wikipedia.org/wiki/Ferrari_330#330_GTC/GTS.

40 Baime AJ. (2010). *Go like hell: Ford, Ferrari, and their battle for speed and glory at Le Mans.* HMH Books. Kindle Edition.

41 Ingraham J. Racing victories spur Ford sales. New York Times Archives [Internet]. 1963, Sep 7 [cited 2022, Aug 25]. Available from: https://timesmachine.nytimes.com/timesmachine/1963/09/07/82147907.html?pageNumber=23.

42 List of driver deaths in motorsport. Wikipedia [Internet]. [cited 2022, Aug 25]. Available from: https://en.wikipedia.org/wiki/List_of_driver_deaths_in_motorsport.

43 Pinker S. Enlightenment now: The case for reason, science, humanism and progress. New York: Penguin, 2020.

44 Motor vehicle fatality rate in U.S. by year. Wikipedia [cited 2022, Aug 25]. Available from: https://en.wikipedia.org/wiki/Motor_vehicle_fatality_rate_in_U.S._by_year#cite_note-5.

45 Nader R. Unsafe at any speed: The designed-in dangers of the American automobile. New York: Grossman Publishers, 1965.

46 Sandel M. What money can't buy: The moral limits of markets. New York: Farrar, Straus & Giroux, 2012.

47 US motor vehicle deaths per VMT, deaths per capita, total deaths, VMT, and population. Wikipedia [Internet]. [cited 2022, Aug 25]. Available from: https://en.wikipedia.org/wiki/Motor_vehicle_fatality_rate_in_U.S._by_year#/media/File:US_traffic_deaths_per_VMT,_VMT,_per_capita,_and_total_annual_deaths.png.

8

The Human-Centered Tradition

I do not ask the wounded person how he feels, I myself become the wounded person.

Walt Whitman
American Poet

Roots in the Technical-Analytic Tradition

The more social, Human-Centered Design Tradition had its early roots in the Technical-Analytic Tradition. Within that tradition, the work of Taylor and the Gilbreths emphasized the analysis of the physical requirements of tasks on the assembly line. The emphasis was on the task and how it could be structured and organized to maximize the efficiency and productivity of a typical worker. The military applied these techniques to examine the cognitive as well as physical demands on expert pilots and how these demands affected the pilot's performance, particularly in emergency situations. As such, the focus of the analysis shifted to include not just the structure and demands of the task but the person's capabilities and limitations in response to them. This led to cockpit redesign to accommodate the pilot's abilities. The field of human factors, or ergonomics, was born out of this research, and application of these techniques were expanded into the civilian domain. In keeping with the purpose in the Technical-Analytic Tradition, these applications included the design of equipment, work stations, and work environments that increased productivity and allowed the worker to work longer and safer. In effect, the person was part of the machine system whose operation was to be optimized.

As the computer revolution unfolded and novel software applications were designed to support complex, open-ended tasks, such as writing reports and calculating a profit-loss statement, the field of human factors grew to include the study of "human-computer interaction" (HCI), which extended the analysis to people's work-related purposes, goals, and the contexts of computer use. Based on these analyses, designers would then specify software functions and interface conventions that might meet those requirements in what is called "user-centered design." Still, these techniques were narrowly focused on solo users and the way software functionality could be designed to shape tasks to improve worker performance and productivity. When networked computing became a part of the workplace, HCI was again extended to include "computer-supported collaborative work" (CSCW), which focused on the design of software tools and capabilities that enabled distributed teams to work together efficiently on the same project to accomplish a shared goal. Consequently, more complex social, cultural, and even emotional factors were injected into a design approach that was not otherwise structured to accommodate them.

Make the World a Better Place: Design with Passion, Purpose, and Values, First Edition. Robert B. Kozma.

Human-centered design and design thinking

As the limitations in the Technical-Analytic Tradition became apparent, the design approach was stood on its head. That is, the more user-centered design approaches of HCI and CSCW spawned a more human-focused approach called "Human-Centered Design" or sometimes "Design Thinking." The movement corresponded to a fundamental shift, occurring at the time, from an economy based primarily on products to one based on services, particularly knowledge services.[1] The movement was also a reaction to the overly rational character of the Design Methods movement, acknowledged as so even by some of the initial conceptualizers of Design Methods, such as Chris Alexander, Chris Jones, and Horst Rittel.[2] This new approach was institutionalized at Stanford University's Hasso Plattner Institute of Design and its design school, or "d.school," and at the design agency IDEO. The description of this approach to the design process is articulated by designers Tim Brown,[3] Don Schön,[4] and Horst Rittel.[5]

Characteristics of the Human-Centered Approach

Purpose

Coming out of the Technical-Analytic Tradition, user-centered design focuses on people, but it does so from the starting point of a task or product in which they are engaged, as the term *user* implies. The purpose of the design was to create a product, such as a software package, or to structure a task in a way that optimized efficiency. The human-centered design approach, on the other hand, begins with people, individually or together in social situations. And its purpose is to identify and address their needs, concerns, relationships, and problems.

Starting with people, rather than products, software, tasks, or work, opens up the design contexts to a broader range of considerations that include personal, emotional, social, organizational, and cultural issues. So, the purposes of specific human-centered designs can start off as quite open and rather vague, compared to the highly specified design brief in the Technical-Analytic Tradition. In these complex social situations, the purpose or desired goal, if articulated by the target group at all, may initially be something as vague as the need for a more inspirational work environment, more harmonious interactions with colleagues, or ways of connecting across organizational or neighborhood boundaries to form new relationships or generate ideas. It could be to facilitate work team dynamics so as to restructure team collaboration and increase innovativeness. Or it could be to support small businesses in a rural community by designing a micro-lending service or to help city neighborhoods prepare for disaster.

These design situations are often complex in large part because they frequently involve emotions—frustration, fear, anxiety, the desire for happiness, acceptance, excitement. Thus, designers need to understand not only the physical and cognitive limits of the people they work with, but also the emotions they struggle with or strive for. Empathy is an important component of the analysis, both on the part of the designer and the target group. Role reversals or "walk in my shoes" exercises have been a useful technique to help a designer reveal the purpose of a project.

Process

In the Human-Centered Tradition, the interaction patterns and local structures of the targeted micro-environment are inherently social and another reason why the design situation is complex. The target is people and groups, not primarily the objects to be made or industrial processes that can be optimized; people who are living their daily lives, interacting, working, facing problems, encountering impasses, feeling stress, needing help. These situations are sometimes called "ill-defined problems" or more challenging "wicked problems," ones so complex that they are difficult to define and have no obvious solution, let alone an optimal one. This calls for a very different design process.

The process does not proceed in a logical, stepwise way from purpose to finished product, as is characteristic of the Technical-Analytic Tradition. The process emerges as the designer engages with the target individual or group. Rather than a logical progression, the process can be thought of as a set of overlapping exploration spaces of inspiration, ideation, and implementation, and the designer may go back and forth among these.[6]

With this process, an understanding of the nature of the problem emerges through the interaction between the designers and the target group, and discovering or refining the purpose of the design is part of the process. In coming up with a design to meet this purpose, the challenge for the designer is to impose order and pull a design idea out the sometimes messy, observed, target social situation. This may be a rather arbitrary scheme, based on the designers' experience with similar situations. Or it could be a formal framework or design technique used with the target group to generate ideas.

This generative process might involve role plays or simulations where members are given typical or problematic situations and designers observe their reactions and interactions. To understand people, their purposes, frustrations, and needs, designers watch their clients as they interact with objects and with each other in their work or social situations. These interactions are often coded or video recorded and analyzed for patterns, problems, and impasses that people encounter and the insights they make. Designers also interview people about their needs and everyday activities and analyze what they say.

For example, a design team from human-centered agency ?What If! immersed itself into the lives of persons dealing with Type 2 Diabetes.[7] Its client, AstraZeneca, needed to understand the complex issue of weight control among diabetics before embarking on a 10-year-long drug development program. ?What If! did research with diabetics to reveal the a tension they feel between the need to use insulin that reduces blood sugar and the increase it causes in unwanted weight, a tension that undermined the relationship between physician and patient. These findings confirmed for AstraZeneca the real need for its new drug Byetta that both lowers blood sugar levels and helps reduce weight.

The process of coming up with a measurable impact is another challenge for designers using the human-centered approach, especially since the purpose often addresses deeply held emotions. In response, designers can develop questionnaires that get at emotions through self-report and they can observe corresponding behavior patterns. In the case of AstraZeneca's Byetta, measuring impact of the design went beyond measures of the drug's effectiveness to observing patient drug-use patterns, measuring attitudes—not only about the drug but about their weight—and looking at the impact of this use on the relationship between patients and their physicians.

Outcomes

In the Human-Centered Tradition, the nature of the desired outcome may be unclear at the start as well. With the Technical-Analytic Tradition, the outcome (e.g., a product or process) is usually very clear and the design challenge is to figure out the best or most efficient way to accomplish it. But with the human-centered approach, the designed outcome often emerges through the designer's interaction with the group. Whereas innovations in the Technical-Analytic Tradition usually require a technological breakthrough, innovations in the Human-Centered Tradition usually involve a conceptual breakthrough. The role of the group can be central to this breakthrough.

A variety of techniques can be used to help group members think outside the box, to get them out of the "business as usual" mode and begin to look at things differently. These include brainstorming, role playing, sharing inspirational or nightmare stories, and exercises that generate, mix, and match ideas.[8]

Because the process so often involves the group in formulating the problem, generating solutions, and conceptualizing their impacts, the resulting design becomes a co-creation of the designer and the group. When identified, the outcome could be a product but more often is a service, a new set of interaction patterns, a new set of relationships or the redesign of the group's environment, its organizational structures, or a set of available enabling resources.

For instance, the human-centered design firm IDEO worked with the San Francisco Department of Emergency Management to help people prepare for the 72 hours after a major emergency, such as a significant earthquake, but before official help can be organized. In crafting a response, IDEO interviewed people who'd been through disasters before, from previous earthquakes in San Francisco to the East Coast's Hurricane Sandy.[9] They found that effective response involves connections with other people and with resources. The resulting design was a website, *SF72*.[10] The website helps people prepare for disaster by planning things to cope with the crucial 72 hours that follow. It helps with five important tasks: get connected, gather supplies, watch survival stories, make a personal emergency response plan, and have access to an updated Google map that supplies them with the latest official and crowd-sourced information on conditions and responses. The tool has since been made available to other cities as *City72*.

Impact

It is likely there will be many possible candidate solutions generated for the design. It is also likely there will be no single correct solution. But there could be ones that don't work. And because the outcomes are so underspecified, early testing of ideas to get feedback is essential. "Fail early to succeed sooner" is a slogan often used.[11] The involvement of the target group is essential at this point as well, so that the tryout can be tested against some concrete, local impact. If the design idea includes a physical artifact, a mockup or prototype is useful in collecting feedback. If the design is not a physical artifact but a procedure, service, or organizational restructuring, or if a prototype is not easy to make, role plays or storyboards may be a useful tool to get early feedback from the group.

Determining success in this social domain can be complex and difficult. Many of the goals that emerge during human-centered design sessions can be difficult to measure with any precision, especially emotional goals such as increasing happiness and deepening relationships. Promoting equality and addressing injustice are also difficult to measure. Yet they are all important human needs nonetheless. So, designers may have to rely on patterns of use, changes in behavior, or expressions of satisfaction as proxy measures for hard-to-measure impacts. Acceptable levels of subjective satisfaction or changes in behavior could be specified and used to estimate success.

Case Study: Alight, Kuja Kuja, and IDEO.Org

A particular challenge to a human-centered designer is establishing and defining the nature of the relationship between the designer and the people who are at the center of their designs. A resolution of this challenge is illustrated in the case study of Kuja Kuja, a project of Alight and IDEO.org, the nonprofit arm of the commercial design firm IDEO.

Case Study: Alight, Kuja Kuja, and IDEO.org

Gaetan is an enterprising young man who has been a resident of the Nyabiheke Refugee Camp in Rwanda, for the past 15 years. Gaetan is one of over 14,500 people who occupy Nyabiheke, where most of the people, like Gaetan, are from the war-torn Democratic Republic of the Congo next door. According to ReliefWeb, there are 70.8 million people worldwide who have been forcibly displaced from their homes.[12] Every day, approximately 37,000 people flee their homes due to persecution or conflict. They often live in deplorable conditions.

Nyabiheke Refugee Camp is home to over 163,000 refugees and asylum-seekers from neighboring countries.[13] These refugees are settled in camps across the country. Daniel Wordsworth has visited many of them and observed, "When you visit camps and you see people at the extremity, what you see are really determined, amazing people who are trying to look after their families."[14]

Until recently, Wordsworth was the CEO of Alight, the nonprofit formerly known as the American Refugee Committee (ARC). It is a 40-year-old, Minneapolis-based refugee assistance and development agency. Originally founded to assist those fleeing war-torn Southeast Asia, it now provides healthcare, clean water, shelter, protection, and economic opportunity to more than 3.5 million people in 17 countries each year.[15] Named to *Fast Company's* annual list of the World's Most Innovative Companies for 2019, Alight strives to continually reinvent itself. Alight's website claims, "We're working on how best to help the people we serve find connection, purpose and joy in the challenging situations they find themselves in today."

Wordsworth explains, "As an organization, what we do is we focus on people in those countries that experience the front line of suffering. We are focusing on countries that are experiencing conflict or emerged out of conflict or experienced floods or large-scale disasters."[16] He goes on to say, "There is an army of people who want to do good and the army of people who want to do good is far larger than the small bands of people who want to do bad." With a staff of more than 2,500 paid professionals and volunteers, Alight's mission is to re-imagine humanitarian aid for the 21st century. Wordsworth says, "We provide a platform or pathway for everyday people, whether they live in Minnesota or Washington or anywhere in the world. We allow those people to connect to refugees and make a difference. So, we actually see [Alight] a bit like a servant to the idealism of everyday people." As to its approach: "Human-centered design and co-creation with passionate companies and individuals have been central as we've created new services that respond to what really matters to people we serve."[17]

Gaetan is one of the people Alight serves. He's one of the amazing people whom Wordsworth talks about and he had an idea. Over the past 20 years, Rwanda has become an African tech hub, investing in technology infrastructure with the cooperation of companies likes of Google, Facebook, and Amazon setting up shop. Gaetan saw this as an opportunity. With the nearest internet café 15 kilometers away, he wanted to get a computer lab for Nyabiheke that would also offer IT training, preparing him and his friends for jobs.[18]

Wordsworth said, ". . .we began letting refugees in to create and design with us, one of the first things we thought was that everyone should be able to let us know if we're doing a good job or a bad job."[19] As a result, an app called Kuja Kuja was designed. "It means 'come come' in Swahili. Every day we ask refugees 'Were you happy with us?' They can give us a smiley face if they were satisfied or a frowny face if they weren't. And then we ask them if they have an idea for how we could improve our services. We publish the data in the community and put it all up on the www.kujakuja.com website for the whole world to see." (See Figures 8.1 and 8.2.)

(Continued)

Case Study: Alight, Kuja Kuja, and IDEO.org (Continued)

Figure 8.1 Kuja Kuja workers off to work with clients (*Source:* Alight).

In response to Gaetan's idea, "A group of Minnesotans helped...they funded the construction of a lab and all of the equipment to fill it. And then we found a technology partner in Kigali-based kLab who could pilot a coding school at the computer lab. The Minnesotans [funded] scholarships for 32 refugee youth to become A+ coders and develop skills that can change their futures."

On Alight's webpage for Kuja Kuja, the organization explains, "Understanding our customer more deeply will allow [Alight] to increase the value and impact that its services currently deliver and to make better decisions about new services to design. We're starting by testing Kuja Kuja on our own organization. We believe that Kuja Kuja will revolutionize service design and implementation for nonprofit and for-profit organizations around the world."[20]

"It's shifting from the idea of a refugee as a beneficiary of services to really a customer, and someone that you're providing the best services that you can for," says Adam Reineck, global design director at IDEO.org.[21] IDEO.org is the nonprofit arm of IDEO committed to creating positive impact.[22] IDEO established IDEO.org in 2011 to design products, services, and experiences that improve the lives and livelihoods of people in poor and vulnerable communities around the world. Like its sister organization, it also takes a human-centered design approach to its work. It focuses on four programs: Health XO, sexual health and contraceptive services for teens; Financial Health, financial products and services for low-income communities; Amplify, a series of innovation challenges to invest in early-stage solutions to tough problems; and Launchpad, to understand how business and technology can meet the demands of poverty.

Figure 8.2 A Kuja Kuja worker with a client (*Source:* Alight).

IDEO.org collaborated with Alight on the design of Kuja Kuja. Jennifer Rose, who was the global design director of Kuja Kuja at IDEO.org, described the collaboration process: "The idea for Kuja Kuja came from the American Refugee Committee in Minneapolis. They hired our design team at IDEO to build the first working prototype and brand for this idea that they had. Soon after the project, I transferred from IDEO over to the American Refugee Committee to work on Kuja Kuja full time and to get this venture up and running."[23] She goes on to describe the human-centered design approach of basing design decisions on information from prospective customers: "The research part comes down to making genuine connections and having a genuine curiosity while being in interviews or immersed in the moment. Incorporating the design is happening simultaneously with the research. Those two parts of the process blended together much more while designing Kuja Kuja." Based on interactions with users, the app was designed it "to be a sunny, warm, welcoming brand because we wanted customers to feel like it was a safe trusted space to share their thoughts, dreams, and ideas. Human emotion can become complex, but through our design approach, we can find something that resonates with everyone."

As of September 2021, Kuja Kuja recorded over 2 million conversations with refugees, with over 1,000 actions taken.[24] Since its launch, Alight has seen customer satisfaction rise by 20% in Uganda's Nakivale Settlement, where the nonprofit provides clean water for 85,000 people, and 18% in Rwanda's Mahama Camp, where it manages a health facility for treating 40,000 patients per quarter.[25] In 2018, Kuja Kuja received the Best Service Design Award[26] from Core 77, a publisher and online resource site for designers.[27]

In the face of the complex, desperate plight of refugees, Alight created its organizational purpose: to help its clients find connection, agency, joy, and their own purpose. Alight's purpose is very different than the sort common in the Technical-Analytic Tradition, where problems are typically well-understood, have identifiable solutions, and are amenable to quantification and statistical analyses.

Alight draws on this purpose to understand the problems of the people that are at the center of its designs. They see the refugees in its camps not as victims, but as clients and collaborators who have skills and ideas as well as needs.

In response to these problems, Alight uses a human-centered, design approach, as does IDEO.org, its design partner, to provide healthcare, water, shelter, and economic opportunity services. With the Kuja Kuja platform, Alight continuously collects information and ideas from the community on its needs and preferences. The nonprofit uses this information to come up with new services and improve current ones. And it uses the platform to, in turn, assess the impact of these changes on the community. As a result, there is a high degree of ownership of the designs within the community.

Systemic Implications of the Human-Centered Approach

The design approach taken in the Technical-Analytic Tradition is limited in the way it treats people as part of the system. If their individual needs or concerns are considered at all, it is typically as part of the physical/mechanical system—the driver of a race car, the manager of a production line, or the pilot of a plane. The Human-Centered Tradition evolved specifically to address that limitation to look at the uniquely human aspects of the system. The design question turns from how people can work in the system to how the system can better work for the people in it.

The methods used in the Human-Centered Tradition are very good at looking at human needs and problems, and analyzing the system's micro-interaction patterns and structures to pull out the informal, unarticulated rules that often govern interactions in specific situations. The methods are particularly good for analyzing the dysfunctions in these rules and relationships and coming up with novel repairs.

The methods are also good for identifying and mobilizing networks of groups and organizations in the surrounding system that can be enlisted to support the design. Often the effectiveness of a design involves weaving connections between these supportive groups.

For example, the human-centered design firm Frog Design partnered with two community coalitions, South Bronx Rising Together and Brownsville United, on a project for the charitable organization Robin Hood Foundation.[28] To inform Robin Hood's program for early learning of low-income young children, the Fund for Early Learning (F.U.E.L.), Frog collected community perspectives around parenting goals, strengths, and needs. Frog worked with partners to connect with over 50 parents via contextual interviews and group interviews. The firm presented its community research assessment to Robin Hood, to F.U.E.L.'s Executive Board, and to NYC Children's Cabinet that featured contextual analysis, parents' perspectives and opportunities to support early childhood development at institutional and community levels. The insights and recommendations informed the program on how it could better serve early childhood development needs in the communities of the South Bronx and Brownsville.

However, even though this design approach is human-centered, it very much lives in a larger socioeconomic macrosystem dominated by the Technical-Analytic Tradition that values optimization, efficiency, productivity, and return on investment. Indeed, in many ways, the Human-Centered Tradition has come to be re-absorbed into the Technical-Analytical Tradition from which it emerged. This value-alignment with the Technical-Analytic Tradition and its systemic context moderates the overall social impact of the human-centered approach in four interrelated ways: it limits its client base, it constrains the projects that are selected, it shapes the design process, and it undermines the human-centered design culture, itself.

First, a look at the websites of design agencies that use the human-centered approach—agencies like IDEO, ?What If!, Lunar Design, and Frog Design—shows that their clients are overwhelmingly profit-making companies rather than community groups and social organizations that are most likely to have human-centered purposes and needs. The operating assumption of the Tradition has, in effect, come to be that the way to address the needs of people and groups is by working for or in organizations whose primary purpose is to make a profit. Human-centered design agencies explicitly appeal to this motivation in their advertising. For example, ?What If! states, "We start with a human problem and then use experimentation to de-risk bold solutions, accelerate them to market, and empower a cultural movement to create growth today and tomorrow."[29] This focus on profit, shaped by the socioeconomic context, means that the social groups that may need human-centered design services the most, particularly poor or disadvantaged groups, are not their clients at all.

The alignment of the Human-Centered Tradition with the Technical-Analytic Tradition and its underlying systemic assumptions also shape the projects that are most often taken up by agencies using the human-centered approach. This alignment favors large, profit-generating projects at the expense of other projects that may be worthwhile but generate less profit. For instance, Tim Brown begins his book on human-centered design thinking with an example of a project that IDEO did for Shimano.[30] It resulted not only in a new design for an automatic bicycle transmission that shifts the gears as the bike gains speed or slows down, but they also created a whole new category of bicycling—coasting—designed to reconnect consumers to their experiences as children, and the project tapped into a whole new market for Shimano. In the grand scheme of human problems, needs, and concerns, designing a coasting bicycle may not have been the best choice to lead a book on human-centered design. But the preponderance of examples throughout the book are innovative designs for new products and services that created new markets and generated increased profits rather than ones specifically targeted at human problems to be solved. An online review of the project portfolio of other human-centered design agencies finds a similar pattern.[31]

The dominant technical-analytic paradigm also contorts the human-centered design process. Inherent in the process is the designer's need to impose constraints, so as to make a complex, open-ended situation more manageable. But these constrains are not arbitrary, and the cultural press favors a design process that aligns with the values of optimization, effectiveness, efficiency, and profit. In IDEO's case, the constraints imposed on projects are desirability, feasibility, and viability. Not only must a project design meet the needs of the target group (i.e., be desirable) and be functionally possible within the near future (i.e., be feasible) in must be part of a sustainable business model (i.e., be viable); it must generate income for the client, and presumably, IDEO.

Finally, the alignment with values of the prevailing system also distorts the human-centered design culture. This contortion is subtle, but it invades the thinking of designers in ways that are, at times, contrary to the primary purpose in the Human-Centered Tradition, which is to improve the human condition. While Brown extolls the human-centered design approach as a culture change in which designers apply their skills to problems "that matter," such as improving the lives of people in extreme need; this attitude is moderated by business concerns as reflected in Brown's statement on working with disadvantaged target groups: "The objective is not so much to design for these marginal, outlying populations as to gain inspiration from their passion, their knowledge, or simply the extremity of their circumstances" (p. 216). And designers are "not motivated by an altruistic desire to 'give something back' for a few months after graduation or upon retirement but by the fact that the greatest challenges are always the source of the greatest opportunities."

My analysis in this section is not meant to deprecate the importance of the Human-Centered Tradition, only to point out its limitations within the prevailing socioeconomic context. Human-centered design firms are working within the reality of an economy dominated by the Technical-Analytic Tradition. But it is an ongoing moral challenge for these design firms to push against the constraints of the system if it is indeed going to address human problems and needs that really matter. It is this challenge that we turn to next.

Moral Implications of the Human-Centered Approach

Compared to the Technical-Analytic Design Tradition, the Human-Centered Design Tradition is structured to be much more responsive to social needs or dissatisfaction with the current situation as expressed by some group. While the approach does not specifically cite moral principles, the process used is structured in a way that issues related to happiness, harm, knowledge, and so on could emerge on their own and become the purpose for the resulting design. Consequently, the Human-Centered Design Tradition is much more attuned to the moral principles presented in Chapter 3 than is the Technical-Analytic Tradition. And products, programs, services, or other outcomes designed with the human-centered approach are more likely to address these moral considerations and values are more likely to be embedded in them. As Tim Brown states, and as illustrated by our Kuja Kuja case study, human-centered design thinking can, indeed, be applied to society's most challenging problems, whether on the outskirts of Kampala, in the offices of a social venture fund in New York, or in the classrooms of an elementary school in California.

However, within our economic system, this often requires a special source of funding. If projects are funded by government agencies, nonprofit organizations, or foundations, human-centered design agencies are able to take on projects of limited profitability even within the prevailing socioeconomic context, such as what happened with Frog Design and Robin Hood's F.U.E.L. Or profit-making human-centered design agencies can set up nonprofit sister organizations that are able to take on these projects, as the for-profit design agency IDEO did with its nonprofit sister organization, IDEO.org, that worked with the nonprofit organization Alight in our Kuja Kuja case study.

Within these contexts, application of the human-centered approach can create happiness, reduce harm, advance knowledge and agency, promote equality, address injustice. It can be used to promote supportive relationships and build communities. And these results, without a doubt, make the world a better place. If funding can be found, the approach can be applied within the dominant systemic paradigm, where current services don't include certain groups of people or where current products don't address their needs. The approach can address these errors in the system, and in turn, improve the world for these groups. But these moral outcomes and impacts depend not only on the methodology and the funding, but on building these values into the process. This is a concern we will return to in Chapter 11.

However, even at its best, the human-centered approach likely reaches its limits if the problems are due to fundamental systemic problems, which is often so with the most egregious cases of harm, ignorance, inequality, injustice, and social isolation. As Tim Brown points out, if it comes to something major, like the UN Millennium Development Goals, human-centered design can be applied to enable poor farmers to increase the productivity of their land or to help adolescent girls become empowered and productive members of their community through better education. But, he notes, eradicating extreme poverty or creating gender equality are beyond the scope of the approach. When problems are due to systemic failure and human needs are balanced against profit and efficiency, they are not likely to be addressed and systemic change won't happen. As Brown puts it, "To borrow the language of the computer industry, this approach should be seen not as a system reset but as a meaningful upgrade" (p. 22).

To make the world a better place, to really focus on human needs that matter, we need ways to look at the world differently. And we need design approaches aimed at eradicating extreme poverty, promoting equality, and addressing other systemic problems that are screaming to be solved. Sometimes designers need to look beyond the current system and with passion, purpose, and values, think about fundamental structural and cultural changes, to not only think outside the box but outside the system. And what could be a greater challenge for designers than that, Tim Brown?

References

1. Bell D. The coming post-industrial society. New York: Basic Books, 1976.
2. Cross N. A history of design methodology. In de Vries MJ, Cross N, Grant DP (editors) Design Methodology and Relationships with Science. NATO ASI Series (Series D: Behavioural and Social Sciences), 1993, vol 71. Springer, Dordrecht.
3. Brown T. Change by design: How design thinking transforms organizations and inspires innovation. Harper Collins, 2019.
4. Schön D. The reflective practitioner: How professionals think in action. New York: Basic Books, 1983.
5. Protzen J-P, Harris D. The Universe of Design: Horst Rittel's Theories of Design and Planning. New York: Taylor and Francis, 2010.
6. Brown T. Change by design: How design thinking transforms organizations and inspires innovation. Harper Collins, 2019.
7. Creating impact in the lives of Type 2 Diabetes patients. ?What If! [Internet]. [cited 2022, Aug 26]. Available from: https://whatifinnovation.com/case_studies/astrazeneca/.
8. IDEO.org. The field guide to human-centered design. San Francisco: IDEO.org, 2015.
9. Wilson M. Ideo rebrands disaster preparedness. Fast Company [Internet]. 2014, Jul 29 [cited 2022, Aug 26]. Available from: https://www.fastcompany.com/3031874/ideo-rebrands-disaster-preparedness.
10. Designing a city emergency plan. IDEO [Internet]. [cited 2022, Aug 26]. Available from: https://www.ideo.com/case-study/designing-a-city-emergency-plan.
11. Brown T. (2019). *Change by design: How design thinking transforms organizations and inspires innovation*. Harper Collins.
12. World Refugee Day 2019. Relief Web [Internet]. 2019, Jun 20 [cited 2022, Aug 26]. Available from: https://reliefweb.int/report/world/world-refugee-day-2019.
13. UNHCR Rwanda. UNHCR participatory assessment September and October 2017. UNHCR [Internet]. 2017, Dec [cited 2022, Aug 26]. Available from: https://www.unhcr.org/rw/wp-content/uploads/sites/4/2018/01/PA-2017-REPORT.pdf.
14. Manson M. Daniel Wordsworth on Leadership. The Mary Hanson Show [web streaming video]. 2015, Oct 2 [cited 2022, Aug 26]. Available from: https://www.youtube.com/watch?v=PlUbLqPNV2Q.
15. Alight [Internet]. [cited 2022, Aug 26]. Available from: https://wearealight.org.

16 Manson M. Daniel Wordsworth on Leadership. The Mary Hanson Show [web streaming video]. 2015, Oct 2 [cited 2022, Aug 26]. Available from: https://www.youtube.com/watch?v=PlUbLqPNV2Q.

17 Fast Company 2019 Honoree. Alight [Internet]. 2019 [cited 2022, Aug 26]. Available from: https://wearealight.org/named-most-innovative-2019/.

18 A lab for Nyabiheke. Alight [Internet]. [cited 2022, Aug 26]. Available from: https://wearealight.org/a-lab-for-nyabiheke/.

19 St. Anthony N. Minneapolis-based American Refugee Committee, now Alight, spent a decade changing its approach. Star Tribune. 2019, Jul 12.

20 Kuja Kuja is more than a moral obligation—it's also good business. Alight [Internet]. [cited 2022, Aug 26]. Available from: https://wearealight.org/kuja-kuja/.

21 IDEO.org [Internet]. [cited 2022, Aug 26]. Available from: https://www.ideo.org.

22 About IDEO. IDEO.org [Internet]. [cited 2022, Aug 26]. Available from: https://www.ideo.com/about.

23 Lorenzo D. How and Ideo.org designer created a Yelp for refugees. Fast Company [Internet]. 2019, Jun 19 [cited 2022, Aug 26]. Available from: https://www.fastcompany.com/90365726/how-an-ideo-org-designer-created-a-yelp-for-refugees.

24 About Kuja Kuja. Kuja Kuja [Internet]. [cited 2022, Aug 26]. Available from: https://www.kujakuja.com/en/about.

25 American Refugee Committee is becoming Alight: 2018 annual report. Alight [Internet]. 2018 [cited 2022, Aug 26]. Available from: https://wearealight.org/annual_reports/Annual_Report_2018.pdf.

26 Winner Service Design Award Kuja Kuja. Core77 [Internet]. 2018 [cited 2022, Aug 26]. Available from: https://designawards.core77.com/Service-Design/74284/Kuja-Kuja.

27 About Core77. Core77 [Internet]. [cited 2022, Aug 26]. Available from: https://www.core77.com/about?utm_source=navigation.

28 Robin Hood Foundation F.U.E.L. Frog [Internet]. [cited 2022, Aug 26]. Available from: https://www.frogdesign.com/work/community-empowerment-with-robin-hood-foundation.

29 Our Approach. ?What If! [Internet]. [cited 2022, Aug 26]. Available from: https://whatifinnovation.com/approach/, retrieved 12/15/2020.

30 Brown T. Change by design: How design thinking transforms organizations and inspires innovation. Harper Collins, 2019.

31 See for example [cited 2022, Aug 26]: ?What If! https://whatifinnovation.com/work/; Frog Design https://www.frogdesign.com/work; https://www.lunar.com/work.shtml.

9

The Aesthetic Tradition

A simple line painted with a brush can lead to freedom and happiness.

Joan Miró
Catalan Expressionist Painter

In this chapter and the next one, we're going to look for ways to think outside the system. We will do so by looking at two very different traditions. The first one, at least on occasion, looks beyond the system by disconnecting from it. The other stands up to its faults. One looks at our noblest ideals and deepest emotions, notions of beauty or purpose that transcend the world as it currently is. he other rolls up its sleeves and confronts the grittiest parts of our reality.

Roots in Ancient Human Expression

Artistic creations are among the oldest expressions of the human experience. The earliest preserved human art is Paleolithic paintings on cave walls. The Chauvet Cave, in southern France, dates back 30,000 years and contains hundreds of animal paintings, including horses, aurochs, mammoths, cave lions, leopards, bears, and cave hyenas. There are even paintings of rhinoceroses. Neolithic art, appearing some 20,000 years later, included pottery, statues, and architectural structures formed out of the materials of the time: clay, stone, ivory, and bone as well as, most likely, wood, which did not survive. Some of these artifacts were functional, but all included artistic elements and patterns.

The development of civilizations has been marked by its art. The rise of the Sumerian culture in the 30th century BCE is documented and characterized by its pottery, gold and silver jewelry, finely executed carvings, and base reliefs of deities, kings, priests, soldiers, and people engaged in everyday activities. Sometimes these reliefs marked key events; sometimes they would tell stories. In Sumer, and a bit later in Egypt, elemental pictograms were used initially for accounting, and subsequently stringed together to convey a message or story.

The emergence and ascendance of Assyrian, Babylonian, Egyptian, Greek, Mayan, Nubian, Olmec, Roman, and Shang civilizations were each marked by their distinctive art, which became increasingly sophisticated and came to be expressed in new materials and technologies as they were developed. Sometimes artistic artifacts did not seem to have a practical use, but even practical items, like pottery, armor, and tiled floors, were also adorned with artistic details. Even after the fall of the Roman Empire in 476, when cultural expressions went into decline in the West, monks used artistic flourishes to illuminate bibles and other manuscripts that they copied from earlier times. During the

Make the World a Better Place: Design with Passion, Purpose, and Values, First Edition. Robert B. Kozma.

decline of art in the West, it burgeoned in the Islamic world and the Far East. The religious prohibition of representing animate beings channeled Islamic art into calligraphy and intricate geometric patterns expressed in carpets, pottery, and architecture. The Tang Dynasty (618–907) in China saw a flourishing of fine art in painting, pottery, sculpture, and architecture. In the 15th and 16th centuries, the Renaissance was a rebirth of art in the West, borrowed from ancient empires and expressed in sculptures, paintings, and literature.

Art, design, and industry

Prior to the Industrial Revolution, aesthetic features were often an essential part of the craftsmanship in the West that went into fine, handmade objects, such as furniture, decorative arts, jewelry, and clothes. The aesthetic approach to design continued even as factories were filling the skylines with smoke stacks and churning out pallets of identical products in response to mass consumption.

In the late 19th and early 20th centuries, aesthetic design was most notably expressed in two stylistically different ways in Europe through the Arts and Crafts, and the Aesthetic design movements. Both emphasized the quality, workmanship, and beauty of handmade items using traditional methods and materials, such as wood, glass, fabrics, and metals. The Aesthetic Movement, most often expressed in the decorative arts, celebrated "art for art's sake" and de-emphasized or even denounced any "meaning" or utilitarian value in art. With the new millennium, Art Nouveau designers moved away from traditional motifs and created highly sculptured pieces with curved, sinuous lines often inspired by nature, as displayed by the work of artist Alphonse Mucha and architect Antoni Gaudi. Post-World War I, Art Deco designers left behind the sinuous curves of Art Nouveau and created objects with clean, geometric lines, as typified by the Chrysler Building in New York City or Christ the Redeemer that overlooks Rio de Janeiro.

During these inter-war years, the philosophy of the Bauhaus school of design in Germany aimed to explicitly reconcile aesthetic considerations with modern manufacturing processes. The school emphasized aesthetics but subordinated it to mass production. The school's aesthetic philosophy emphasized clean lines, plane surfaces, and simple forms that dispensed with ornamentation. Designers used new materials, such as plywood, tubular steel, and the pre-plastic material Bakelite to create objects that were easy to manufacture and lent themselves to mass production. Their subordination of form to function launched the Modernist Movement. After World War II, this movement continued in a softer version. In Germany, the Ulm School of Design built on the philosophy of the Bauhaus, particularly through its collaboration with Dieter Rams, the design director for the German manufacturer Braun. Rams, along with designers Jones, Alexander, and Rittel, was one of the originators of "Design Methods." Rams used this logical approach and his criteria for good designs, listed in Chapter 3, to create hundreds of products for Braun—from stereo systems to pocket calculators to clocks—that emphasized both form and function. The designs were sleek and uncluttered, and the functions were simple, clearly labeled, and easy to use. His design principles have had a strong influence on contemporary designers, such as Jony Ive, who designed the look for many of Apple's products.

Characteristics of the Aesthetic Approach

The Aesthetic Tradition not only differs in its historical roots from the other design traditions, it also has a unique set of purposes, processes, outcomes, and impacts.

Purpose

Throughout the ages, artistic artifacts have served a wide variety of social and cultural purposes. Prehistoric instruments made of wood and bone were used to create music that, most likely, accompanied cultural rituals and religious ceremonies that reinforced a common, communal bond. Monumental statues of a winged bull with a man's head guarded the gates of Assyrian citadels with the purpose of creating awe among their citizens and fear among attackers. Greek epic poems filled theaters with as many as 20,000 seats in Megalopolis, which served as the people's collective memory and were sung to share cultural knowledge and create a collective Greek identity. Arches and statues commemorated successful Roman military campaigns. Pictorial decorations adorned the pages of medieval bibles to convey the sacredness of the text. The mid-14th century marked the emergence of recognizable clothing fashion in Europe that amplified class distinctions.

Prior to World War I, European painters, such as Joan Miró, Wassily Kandinsky, and Marc Chagall, began to focus on expressing their personal emotions, rather than depicting reality. Graphic art in post-revolution Russia was used to elevate the status of workers. And in Germany, the films of Leni Riefenstahl lauded the Nazi Party and the "Aryan race." Novels, such as *Grapes of Wrath* and *Catcher in the Rye*, and films, such as *The Graduate* and *Apocalypse Now*, held up a mirror to society, sometimes in unflattering ways. Or fictional works offered a vision of a future, idyllic or dark.

These purposes were very different. But the commonality among the purposes of these works of art was to evoke emotions, sometimes awe or happiness, sometimes fear or dread, a purpose that goes back through time. And sometimes the emotion was sublime, as with Michelangelo's *Ceiling of the Sistine Chapter*, or disconsolate, with Picasso's *Guernica*, so as to direct human aspiration to a higher, more noble purpose.

Process

While the outcomes of the artistic process are readily perceived, the process, itself, is far-less transparent. One can observe the work of a sculpture or a painter, but how the artist is thinking about the work is internal and not available for analysis, with the exception, perhaps, of collaborative projects such as film and theater, where artists are expressing their thoughts to each other as they work. While art critics and art historians describe "schools" or "movements" in the arts, such as Realism, Romanticism, Impressionism, and so on, this often refers to the style of the artwork rather than the process by which it is achieved. There is little that would inform us of how artists engage in the creative process.

However, considerable research has been conducted by psychologists who have studied one particular creative act: the writing process. This research describes a pattern of purpose, process, outcomes, and criteria for success that qualifies the creative arts as a design process, yet one that is distinctive from other design traditions.

Psychologists have formulated a theoretical model for writing in which writers consider two sets of issues while writing: what they want to achieve with their writing and what they have written, so far. [1,2] Of course, there are different kinds of writing and these differences influence the writing process. For instance, we are more likely to associate an informational purpose with journalism, technical writing, or the design of curriculum materials. On the other hand, we associate a more emotional purpose with the writing of literature, where the author may aim to evoke sympathy, fear, wonder, and so on. In either case, part of a writer's goal may also include an idea of a target audience for whom she is writing, an audience with a particular background, set of desires and interests, cultural knowledge, and so on, and this understanding influences the writer's initial conception of what the final product should be like. However, the writer's conception of the product and audience may be more or less vague to start and may become refined as the writing progresses.

These two sets of considerations—her vision of what the piece *ought* to be and what it currently *is*—brings writing into the design domain. But the criteria a writer uses for judging progress from "is" to "ought" is an internal design dialog in which she shifts back and forth between the two, as the writer rereads the piece, measuring it against internal criteria, and refining the text when it doesn't match her vision. Alternatively, the writer may refine or change the goals or clarify an understanding of the audience as a result of this dialog.

The process occurs within a sociocultural context of values that may be explicitly or implicitly incorporated into her criteria . . . or rebelled against. There are a set of conventions and tools for creating the written work, which are related to sentence structure, composition, rhetorical strategies, story structure, and so on, that are modified by such factors as genre and audience. The writer draws on them, as well as a personal style of writing she may have, to create the text. These conventions and considerations are used by the author to judge her work as it progresses. The written work is completed when the writer feels that all the criteria have been sufficiently met. Short of more research on the creative process in other art forms, we may want to hold this process in mind, acknowledging that music, painting, and other nonlinguistic art forms may not have the same cognitive and emotional qualities of the writing process, and may be more intuitive and less planful.

For the visual arts, the artist's perception of the world plays a key role. But what distinguishes visual artists from others is their ability to see the world differently, to go beyond what is normally taken for granted. Indeed, this is borne out by research. Two Norwegian researchers, Stine Vogt and Svein Magnussen, found that when presented with a range of pictures, artists tended to scan the whole picture, including apparently empty expanses of ocean or sky, while the non-artists focused on objects, especially people, suggesting that while non-artists were busy turning images into concepts, artists were taking note of colors and contours.[3]

Perception plays an important role in the dialog between visual artists and their emerging work. For instance, the painter Paul Klee refers to the act of painting in this way: "A certain fire, an impulse to create, is kindled, is transmitted through the hand, leaps to the canvas, and in the form of a spark leaps back to its starting place, completing the circle—back to the eye and further (back to the source of the movement, the will, the idea)" [parentheses in the original].[4] What Klee describes is an emotional, physical interaction between the artist and the work, a discourse between the artist's idea and the emerging work that returns to its origin, the evolving idea, image or "fire." The artist's internal dialog between what is desired and what is currently achieved in the work of art parallels but differs from the external dialog between designer and participants in the Human-Centered Tradition, and between the designer and data in the Scientific and Technical-Analytic Traditions.

One way to look at the Aesthetic Tradition is as a pattern where an emotion, the desire to create something—a story, a painting, a musical composition—and the purpose of that creation is very personal: to express a certain feeling, such as beauty or awe. As dancer Isadora Duncan put it, "My art is an effort to express the truth of my Being in gesture and movement."[5] This purpose is expressed with the affordances and constraints of the artist's selected medium. As conveyed by the person-resource-activity model presented in Chapter 5, the affordances of the technology, or medium, shape what it is the artist can do.

Whether it is one's body and the space of a dance floor, the blank screen and features of a word processor, a white canvas and a palette of colors, or the keyboard of a piano, the artist has at his disposal both an infinite number of possibilities and the reassuring limits of the medium, limits that at times beg to be stretched. As the innovative Russian composer Igor Stravinsky claimed, "I experience a sort of terror when, at the moment of sitting to work, I find myself before the infinitude of possibilities that present themselves . . . I shall overcome my terror and shall be reassured by the thought that I have seven notes of the scale and its chromatic intervals at my disposal. . . . "[6] As Stravinsky points out, a specific medium is characterized by certain elements that constrain and shape the production: note and scale in music; line, shape, form, texture, color, and pattern in clothing fashion; sentence and story structure in literature; rhyme and meter in poetry. This range is further circumscribed by the conventions of the art or genre as well as the culture in which the artist works.

Outcomes

In accomplishing their purposes, artists materialize their vision with the unique affordances and within the constraints of their selected medium, while often pushing its boundaries. The creative outcome is often some artistic work or production. A painting, novel, poem, play, film, dance, or musical score or lyrics come to mind as typical artistic works: da Vinci's *Mona Lisa*, Harper Lee's *To Kill a Mockingbird*, Maya Angelou's *Still I Rise*, Henrik Ibsen's *A Doll's House*, Michael Curtiz's *Casa Blanca*, Alvin Ailey's *Revelations*, Andrew Lloyd Webber's and Charles Hart's *Music of the Night*. But it could be a poster or advertisement. It could even be the aesthetic features or an emotional experience designed into a product or service.

Impact

The intended impact that an artistic work has on an observer or listener is often emotional. Perceivers may experience a sense of joy, calm, or awe from a film, play, novel, or work of art. Or, sometimes, the artist may want to provoke and generate negative emotions of fear, anger, or disgust in front of visually challenging stimuli.

In the research laboratory, these emotions are measured by galvanic skin response, pupil dilation, facial expressions, increased heart rate, or other physiological measures. Neurological studies have shown that the viewing of art or listening to artistic performances activated pleasure generating parts of the brain that are the same as those activated by viewing a love partner.[7]

Outside of the lab, measuring the impact of an aesthetic design is more difficult. More subjective reactions are observed by others as a facial expression or bodily stance. These emotions are sometimes accompanied by cognitions, such as evaluating or analyzing the work. And these emotions may be accompanied by actions. Applause or cheers are often a spontaneous reaction to an in-person performance that is well done and actors and musicians feed off of audience responses to add to their effort. Another action is a purchase, and artists (literally) feed off of these as well. However, the criteria for success are often highly personal, individualistic, and very difficult to measure.

Unfortunately, with the exception of the performing arts, artists most often do not have access to the impacts of their work. They don't have a sense of the emotional effect of their work on a viewer and must rely on their own emotions to guide their work.

Case Study: *Starry Night*

Vincent van Gogh was one of the few artists that commented extensively on his works. The van Gogh Museum in Amsterdam has a collection of more than 800 letters that he wrote to his brother Theo, who was an art dealer in Paris; to his sister Willemien; and to friends and colleagues. These give us an insight into his art and his personality. The case study of van Gogh's *Starry Night* can also give us insights into the passions, purposes, processes, outcomes, and impacts of the Aesthetic Tradition.

Case Study: *Starry Night*

Hanging on a wall on the fifth floor of the Museum of Modern Art in New York City is one of the most famous paintings in the world—Vincent van Gogh's *Starry Night*. Ironically, the painting, estimated to be worth more than a $100 million, was considered by van Gogh to be a failure.

Starry Night is known for its bold brush work and intense color, particularly the various shades of blue that are used to paint the night sky and the shades of yellow to paint the moon and stars. A significant influence on his color and brush work was a two-year stay in Paris, between 1886 and 1888. Prior to this period, van Gogh's style was very dark, as epitomized by his painting *Potato Eaters*. But Paris exposed him to a contemporary community of artists and their use of color, especially the use of contrasting colors, and the brushwork of the Impressionists, Neo-Impressionists, and Pointillists. He was also influenced by colorful Japanese woodcut prints that were fashionable in Paris at the time and he had a large collection of them. This exposure had a profound impact on his subsequent work.

Early in 1888, van Gogh (see Figure 9.1) moved to Arles in the south of France for health reasons and with the hope of forming an artist colony to create the art of the future. The colors of Provence had an immediate effect on him. Shortly after arriving, he wrote to Emile Bernard (letter #587[8]), a fellow artist, and although van Gogh had never been to Japan, he said: "I want to begin by telling you that this part of the world seems to me as beautiful as Japan for the clearness of the atmosphere and the gay color effects. The stretches of water make patches of a beautiful emerald and a rich blue in the landscapes, as we see it in the Japanese prints. Pale orange sunsets making the fields look blue—glorious yellow suns." And to Theo, he wrote in June (#620): "About staying in the south, even if it's more expensive—Look, we love Japanese

Figure 9.1 Vincent van Gogh self-portrait (Illustration from Everett Collection).

painting, we've experienced its influence—all the Impressionists have that in common—and we wouldn't go to Japan, in other words, to what is the equivalent of Japan, the south? So, I believe that the future of the new art still lies in the south after all."

In October of that year, the painter Paul Gauguin moved in with van Gogh as the prospective first member of his artist community. They painted together for several months but had a falling out on their opinions of art. In a fit of depression over what seemed to be the disintegration of his nascent artist colony, van Gogh cut off his own ear, and Gauguin returned to Paris. Shortly after recovering from his wound, he checked himself into an asylum in nearby Saint-Remy, where he remained from May 1889 to May 1890. He had two rooms at the asylum, one of which he used as a studio, and the hospital staff would allow him to paint outdoors. It was a period of struggle for him with his personal demons, but it was also a period in which he painted some of his most famous works. During his stay, he created 142 paintings, including *Starry Night*.

He rarely mentioned the painting in his letters, but there were some letters that give us insight into his thinking in general and his approach to the elements in *Starry Night*. Although many of his paintings in the south were of the sun-drenched fields, van Gogh had for some time wanted to paint at night, going back to his time in Arles. In September 1888, he wrote his sister (#678), "I definitely want to paint a starry sky now. It often seems to me that the night is even more richly colored than the day, colored in the most intense violets, blues and greens. If you look carefully you'll see that some stars are lemony, others have a pink, green, forget-me-not blue glow. And without laboring the point, it's clear that to paint a starry sky it's not nearly enough to put white spots on blue-black." The immediate result of this expressed need were two paintings he did in Arles, *Café Terrace at Night* (see Figure 9.2) and *Starry Night Over the Rhone*.

Figure 9.2 *Café Terrace at Night* (Illustration from Vovalis).

(Continued)

Case Study: *Starry Night* (Continued)

In these two paintings, he began to develop themes he would use in *Starry Night*. In the first of them, *Café Terrace*, painted in September 1888, the night sky is a mere backdrop for the glowing interior of the terrace, lit by a gas lamp, played out in brilliant yellows and greens with bold brush strokes as the lamp illuminates the café walls. Across the street is a row of houses, receding into the distance. The moonless night sky is blue, done in subtler brush strokes than the terrace, and the sky is filled with small stars painted in yellow, contrasting with their white haloes and with the blue night sky. Of this painting, he writes to his sister (#678), "The gables of the houses on a street that leads away under the blue sky studded with stars are dark blue or violet, with a green tree. Now there's a painting of night without black. With nothing but beautiful blue, violet and green, and in these surroundings the lighted square is colored pale sulphur, lemon green."

Starry Night Over the Rhone, painted a bit later that month, is a more fulsome development of the night sky. The sky, again moonless, is painted in various shades of blue with stars in white with yellow haloes. On the horizon are the lights of the town, painted in yellow, that spill in ripples across the dark blue waters of the Rhone. Of this painting, he writes to Theo (#691): "The sky is green-blue, the water is royal blue, the areas of land are mauve. The town is blue and violet."

Painted in June 1889, *Starry Night* (see Figure 9.3) was the view out his window at the asylum, altered to make the composition more interesting. For example, the village cannot actually be seen from his window. The canvas is divided on the diagonal by the skyline of the Alpilles Mountains and it is divided on the left by a tall cypress tree. The canvas is dominated by a swirl of colors: brilliant shades of blue for the night sky, punctuated by an intense, lemon-yellow moon and many yellow stars with white and yellow haloes.

Figure 9.3 *Starry Night* (Photo by Bumble Dee).

> Clearly, based on his comments in prior letters, color played an important role in this creation. But, unfortunately, in his 820 surviving letters, there are very few that mention *Starry Night* that would let us understand what his goal or purpose was for this specific painting, perhaps because he considered it a failure. This was expressed in one of his letters to fellow-artist Emile Bernard (#822) in November 1889, in which he refers to the painting and comments, "However, once again I'm allowing myself to do stars too big, etc., new set back. Enough of that."

Van Gogh does not mention a purpose for *Starry Night*, so how can we even consider the painting a design, given the important role that purpose plays in the definition of *design* I use in this book? I will leave it to art critics to elaborate on some intent that van Gogh himself does not ascribe; I would rather rely on his letters to understand his work. In doing so, we find that, perhaps, we are looking too narrowly at purpose when considering the arts.

In 1880, nine years prior to painting *Starry Night*, when Vincent was in his mid-20s and deciding to become an artist, he wrote to Theo (#151) about his thoughts on the emerging role that art would have in his life, "But what's your ultimate goal, you'll say. That goal will become clearer, will take shape slowly and surely, as the croquis[i] becomes a sketch and the sketch a painting, as one works more seriously, as one digs deeper into the originally vague idea, the first fugitive, passing thought, unless it becomes firm." By the time he was 29, in 1882, he wrote (#261): "I feel the power to produce so strongly within myself, I'm aware that there will come a time when I'll finish something good, so to speak, *daily*, and do so regularly. . . . I'm doing my very best to put all my energy into it, for I long so much to make beautiful things. But beautiful things require effort—and disappointment and perseverance."

Failure was part of this process; van Gogh wrote (#270), "Success is sometimes the outcome of a whole string of failures." But this success was based on an inner criterion (#252): "The duty of the painter is to study nature in depth and to use all his intelligence, to put his feelings into his work so that it becomes comprehensible to others. But working with an eye to saleability isn't exactly the right way in my view, but rather is cheating art lovers. The true artists didn't do that; the sympathy they received sooner or later came because of their sincerity."

This perspective provides a contrasting way to study nature, different from the scientific approach, one based on feelings. He used an inner criterion, that of "sincerity," to determine his success. Yet his intent, like that of scientists, was to make this understanding of nature comprehensible to others, a comprehension based on emotions rather than reason.

Meeting this inner criterion was his reward (#327): "In my view I'm often *very rich*, not in money, but rich (although not every day exactly) because I've found my work—have something which I live for heart and soul and which gives inspiration and meaning to life." From Arles in 1888, Vincent told Theo (#673), "Ah, my dear brother, sometimes I know so clearly what I want. In life and in painting too, I can easily do without the dear Lord, but I can't, suffering as I do, do without something greater than myself, which is my life, the power to create."

These letters tell us a lot about van Gogh and his work, and they help us understand characteristics of the Aesthetic Tradition. While he doesn't express a specific purpose for the work, *Starry Night* is nested in a larger purpose of van Gogh's life: to express his feelings in a way that is comprehensible to others by making beautiful things. He values sincerity and integrity, and believes

---

i A croquis is a rough drawing often used as a foundation for another work of art, such as a painting.

this will be recognized by others as the basis for the value of his work. The purpose of *Starry Night* and all his other works was his passion to create. And his ability to create gave meaning and purpose to this life.

Several letters allude to the process he was going through to create *Starry Night*. Clearly, he desired to paint a night sky. And his use of color to express his feelings was his motif in doing so. He saw the night sky not as black but richly colored with blue, violet, and green. And the stars were not white but "lemony, pink, green, and forget-me-not blue." This ability to see the world in a different way, expressed so passionately, is what makes *Starry Night* jump off the wall at the Museum of Modern Art and have such an emotional impact.

While van Gogh was interested in the acceptance of his work, achieving fame was not his purpose and saleability was not his criterion for success. He was his own source of purpose and success, or lack thereof, and both successes and failures drove him. He only sold one painting in his life, but to him, this was not a failure. He was doing something that was greater than himself; he was looking beyond the world as it is and creating something that would change the way people saw the world.

And perhaps for us as designers *that* is the moral imagination we need to make the world a better place.

Systemic Implications of the Aesthetic Tradition

As a tradition, the arts take a more detached stance to the larger system than do most of the other traditions. While the Scientific, Technical-Analytic, and Human-Centered Traditions work within the larger economic system, in the idealized, classic version Aesthetic Tradition the artist works outside of and is intentionally isolated from the larger system—the image of the "starving artist" comes to mind. As such, it is a relatively closed, self-referential system. Similar to science-for-science's-sake in the Scientific Tradition, the Aesthetic Tradition has often promoted art for art's sake. Creating such a self-reinforcing system was the motivation of van Gogh when he tried to launch his artists' community in the south of France.

In this context, the purpose of the artistic act is often highly personal and the interaction pattern is between the artist and her medium, often influenced by the community of other artists. Artists often look at the world in a different, more emotional way, sometimes idealized, sometimes critical. In doing so, artists serve an important role of helping us, as well, to think outside the system, to think differently about the world. This was certainly characteristic of van Gogh and his work.

But as much as the Aesthetic Tradition aspires to a different world, it lives in and has been shaped by our current world, the world of the dominant Technical-Analytic Tradition and the consumer culture it has spawned. Even with the classic view of the Aesthetic Tradition in mind, the artist's work was often enabled by a rich patron. Van Gogh was dependent on his brother for financial support.

This financial dependence on the larger system has had an inevitable effect on the tradition. In numerous ways, aesthetic considerations have come to be incorporated into the Technical-Analytic Design Tradition and the cultural milieu of optimization, efficiency, and profit that it has helped to create.

In the contemporary world, design agencies draw heavily on artists and include aesthetic elements in the look and feel of products they design. And the expressive arts are essential to the business of advertising. Modern advertising originated with techniques introduced with tobacco ads in the 1920s and agencies used illustrators and photographers to create emotional associations between their products and desirable lifestyles. For example, cigarette companies created magazine and ads intended to have an emotional appeal to women by associating their products with fashion, romance, and a slender figure attributed to smoking's suppression of appetite.[9] In the post-war 1940s and 1950s these advertising techniques were used to sell everything from automobiles to household products and fast food. Later, as this new medium emerged, graphic and photographic artists were joined by video producers and actors in ad productions to sell desirable lifestyles that were associated with products.

The net effect has been that creative arts are used not only to sell specific products but sell, or at least confirm, the dominant culture created by the Technical Tradition described in Chapter 7, with all its benefits and inequalities. And, rather than holding up a critical mirror, art has too often become so enmeshed in the cultural system that it projects the dominant values of the culture as taken for granted or unquestioned, even if it isn't overtly selling it. Take, for example, the 2011 American movie *Limitless*, in which the main character, played by Bradley Cooper, is a down-and-out writer suffering from writer's block. He runs into an old friend who introduces him to a revolutionary new drug that will give him access to "100% of his brain." Upon taking the pill, he finishes his novel over a weekend and decides to go on to bigger and better things. Does he write more novels? Does he cure cancer or solve homelessness? No, he uses this brain power to parley a small amount of money into a huge fortune on Wall Street, buys designer clothes and flashy cars, and gets laid by beautiful women. At the end of the movie, he is running for the U.S. Senate with his eye on the presidency.

Within this commercial environment, art itself has become monetized, not necessarily to the benefit of the artist. Fine art always was, of course, available for purchase only by the very rich. Van Gogh lived in near poverty and sold only one painting during his lifetime. But van Gogh's *The Portrait of Doctor Gachet* sold for $82.5 million in 1990, then an auction record, equivalent to almost $150 million now.[10] *The Card Players* is widely considered the best Cézanne in private hands and was reportedly purchased for $250 million in 2011. In November 2017, *Salvator Mundi*, attributed by some to Leonardo da Vinci, sold for $450 million at Christie's in New York City, becoming the most expensive painting ever sold at auction.

Beyond fine art, aesthetic productions from novels and films to streaming music and video games have become mass market items and have come to define popular culture. The creative arts contributed $763.6 billion to the U.S. economy in 2015.[11] This accounted for 4.2% of U.S. gross domestic product (GDP) and employment for 4.9 million workers, who earned $372 billion in total income. The arts, including museums, performing arts, movie and video productions, photography, publishing and printed goods, art education, architecture and interior design, and advertising, added four times more to the U.S. economy than the agricultural sector and $200 billion more than transportation or warehousing. The creative arts have made America a world leader in the mass production of cultural goods, and the arts produced a $20 billion trade surplus in 2015, leading with movies and TV programs.

Moral Implications of the Aesthetic Tradition

Despite these compromises with the systemic context, the Aesthetic Tradition holds promise for creating designs that contribute to a better world. This role is magnified by the ability of aesthetic products and productions to tap into basic human emotions and the role, in turn, that emotions play as the foundation for morality, as asserted by the Enlightenment philosophers.

Novels, films, songs, and plays can document harm that evoke feelings of sympathy or injustice that can, in turn, motivate change. For instance, the documentary movie *13th* vividly establishes the history of unjust incarceration and forced labor of Black males in the South after Reconstruction—resulting, in effect, in their re-enslavement. That film and the documentary *Central Park Five* shows the structural racism that is rampant in the current U.S. judicial and corrections system. Arthur Miller's play *Death of a Salesman* and David Mamet's play and film *Glengarry Glenn Ross* bring home, in gut wrenching fashion, the personal tragedy of being an average male in a culture that only values success. Billie Holliday's song *Strange Fruit*, about the lynching of Blacks in the South, and August Wilson's Cycle Plays, including *Fences* and *Ma Rainey's Black Bottom*, dramatize the harm and tragedy caused by racism and the limitations race imposes in accessing the American dream. (These themes were combined in a recent Broadway revival of *Death of a Salesman*, starring Black actor Wendell Pierce as the salesman Willy Lowman.) Margaret Attwood's novel and TV series *The Handmaid's Tale* depicts a dystopian world in which women are subservient in an oppressive, male-dominated religious society. And George Orwell's *1984* vividly describes a world in which a person's every action, including the vocabulary that they speak, is monitored and shaped by the state for its own benefit and continued existence.

Voices of those harmed convey their frustration, anxiety, anger, or even rage based on their experiences, which can serve as the basis of sympathy and compassion, and motivate the actions of others to address injustice. Their emotions have been expressed in films, such as *I'm not Your Negro*, based on James Baldwin's experiences with racism; or essay, such Ta-Nehisi Coates's *Letter to My Son*, about being Black in America; or the book *Heart Berries: A Memoir* by Terese Marie Mailhot about her trials, family trauma, and a distinct type of oppression of Native American women that was a *New York Times* Best Seller and named one of the best nonfiction books of 2018 by *Time* magazine.

Conversely, aesthetic productions can inspire us with examples of harm reduced, justice restored, or meaningful happiness. Take, for example, Cynthia E. Smith's 2022 curated exhibit *Designing Peace* at New York City's Cooper Hewitt, Smithsonian Design Museum, a collection of 40 designs from 25 countries that include objects, models, installations, maps, images, textiles, video games, and films that promote peace. "As America's design museum, Cooper Hewitt can advance public understanding that design can be a force for good," Smith says of the exhibit's purpose.[12]

Or take the movie *Happy*, by Roko Belic, which explores profound questions such as: What makes you happy? Does money make you happy? Kids and family? Your work? Do you live in a world that values and promotes happiness and well-being? Are we in the midst of a happiness revolution? The film *Finding Hygge* provides the Danish answer to these questions by illustrating the art of creating joy and coziness in life's everyday moments, that are so important in that culture.

Speculative works, going back to Plato's *Republic*, have provided us with aspirational visions, stories, or narratives of alternative futures and systems built on moral principles that help us think about how the world might be a better place. Sir Francis Bacon's *New Atlantis*, published in 1627, outlines his vision of a perfect society founded on peace, enlightenment, and public spirit.

Science fiction has made its contribution. Ursula Le Guin's book *The Dispossessed*, published in 1974, is a novel about two worlds: one is essentially a 1970s United States replete with capitalism and greed. The other is an "ambiguous utopia" inspired by a female revolutionary whose philosophy was that men and women were equals and who advocated solidarity, the decentralization of power, and a society without laws. This society was based on mutual respect and guided by simple principles, such as help those in need, never intentionally harm or take advantage of others, and contribute to society by doing what you can do best. Le Guin portrays both worlds in good light and bad, thus the ambiguity. The main character moves between the two worlds in his adventures to judge which is better and in what ways.

The *Star Trek* TV and movie series, which ran from 1965 to 2010, depicted a multigender, multiracial, multispecies crew, each with their own unique role and function in the social system and each with special knowledge, expertise, and powers, who worked together as a team to explore the universe and deal with a range of moral issues that included war and peace, authoritarianism, imperialism, class warfare, economics, racism, religion, human rights, sexism, feminism, the value of personal loyalty, and the role of technology in society. In his purpose for the series, creator Gene Rodenberry stated, "[By creating] a new world with new rules, I could make statements about sex, religion, Vietnam, politics, and intercontinental missiles. Indeed, we did make them on Star Trek: we were sending messages and fortunately they all got by the network."[13]

Literary works have even generated social movements. Edward Bellamy's novel *Looking Backward, 2000–1887* was published in 1888 when the United States was witnessing the full impact of the Industrial Revolution. Working days were as long as 12 hours, 6 days a week, and working conditions were dirty, noisy, and dangerous.[14] There were no health or retirement benefits, factories were employing large numbers of children, and labor unions were on the rise.[15,16,17] Inequality was on the rise. Bellamy's novel is a story of a young American, who falls into a deep, hypnosis-induced sleep toward the end of the 19th century and wakes up 113 years later to find himself in utopian America where working hours were reduced drastically, everyone retires with full benefits at age 45, and the benefits of society are equally distributed to all its citizens. The novel was very popular in North America and Britain, and it hit an emotional cord. Hundreds of "Bellamy Clubs" and societies sprang up to discuss and propagate the book's ideas and it inspired a generation of urban planners and designers.[18] *Looking Backward* even spawned several utopian communities as did other novels.[19]

However, the Aesthetic Tradition is no more inherently moral than the other traditions. There are numerous examples of movies, books, music, and video games that condone or even glorify racism, misogyny, and violence. Books, such as *Mein Kampf*, *The Turner Diaries*, and *The Protocols of the Elders of Zion* have spread hate rather than happiness. The films *Birth of a Nation* (1915), *Mandingo* (1975), *Se7en* (1995), *Sicario* (2015), and *The Joker* (2019), and video games such as *Carmageddon*, *Custer's Revenge*, and a long list of first-person shooter games and misogynistic porn films are artistic productions that made money but degrade people and values of our culture.

However, with their passion, purpose, and values, artists can make a unique contribution to making the world a better place, one that goes beyond the boundaries of the current system to offer us moral imagination, different visions of the world, better ones. They can tap into our emotions and inspire us toward new worlds to achieve or deter us from those to avoid, in ways that the Technical-Analytic or even the Human-Centered Traditions cannot.

References

1 Flower L, Hayes R. (1981). A cognitive theory of the writing process. *College Composition and Communication*, 32:4, 365–387.

2 Berieter C, Scardamalia M. The psychology of written composition. Mahwah, NJ: Lawrence Erlbaum Associates, 1987.

3 Vogt S, Magnussen S. Expertise in pictorial perception: Eye-movement patterns and visual memory in artists and laymen, Perception, 2007, 36(1), 91–100.

4 Klee P. Art History [Internet]. [cited 2022, Aug 26]. Available from: https://www.arthistory-famousartists-paintings.com/PaulKlee.html.

5 Duncan I. My life (p. 7). New York: Norton, 1927.

6 Stravinsky I, Petrushka LA Phil [Internet]. [cited 2022, Aug 26]. Available from: https://www.laphil.com/musicdb/pieces/2700/petrushka-rev-1947.

7 Ishizu T, Zeki S. Toward a brain-based theory of beauty. Plos One [Internet]. 2011, Jul6 [cited 2022, Aug 26]. Available from: https://journals.plos.org/plosone/article?id=10.1371/journal.pone.0021852.

8 Numbers refer to letters in the online collection of van Gogh's letters. Vincent van Gogh: The Letters. Van Gogh Museum [Internet]. [cited 2022, Aug 26]. Available from: http://www.vangoghletters.org/vg/letters.html.

9 Sivulka J. Soap, sex, and cigarettes: A cultural history of American advertising. Boston: Wadsworth, 2012.

10 Fernández G. The 200 most valuable paintings in private hands. Art Wolf [Internet]. 2022, May [cited 2022, Aug 26]. Available from: http://www.theartwolf.com/articles/most-valuable-private-art.htm#over-200-million.

11 The arts contributed more than $750 billion to the U.S. economy. National Endowment for the Arts [Internet]. 2018, Mar 6 [cited 2022, Aug 26]. Available from: https://www.arts.gov/news/press-releases/2018/arts-contribute-more-760-billion-us-economy.

12 Moonan W. Designers build a provocative road map for world peace. Smithsonian Magazine [Internet]. 2022, Aug 3 [cited 2022, Aug 26]. Available from: https://www.smithsonianmag.com/smithsonian-institution/designers-and-creators-build-a-provocative-road-map-for-world-peace-180980514/?utm_source=smithsoniandaily&utm_medium=email&utm_campaign=20220803-daily-responsive&spMailingID=47191575&spUserID=MTE1NDM2MjA3MDY5NQS2&spJobID=2300313079&spReportId=MjMwMDMxMzA3OQS2.

13 Johnson-Smith J. American science fiction TV: Star Trek, Stargate, and beyond (p. 59). Middletown, CT.: Wesleyan University Press, 2005.

14 The Struggles of Labor [Internet]. [cited 2022, Aug 26]. Available from: http://countrystudies.us/united-states/history-82.htm.

15 History of child labor in the United States. Monthly Labor Review [Internet]. 2017, Jan [cited 2022, Aug 26]. Available from: https://www.bls.gov/opub/mlr/2017/article/history-of-child-labor-in-the-united-states-part-1.htm.

16 Tenement sweatshops. National Museum of American History [Internet]. [cited 2022, Aug 26]. Available from: https://americanhistory.si.edu/sweatshops/history-1880-1940.

17 Labor movement. History [Internet]. 2021, Mar 31 [cited 2022, Aug 26]. Available from: https://www.history.com/topics/19th-century/labor.

18 Nelson, GD. The splendor of our public and common life. Places [Internet]. 2019, Dec [cited 2022, Aug 26]. Available from: https://placesjournal.org/article/edward-bellamy-urban-planning/?cn-reloaded=1.

19 Utopian communities inspired by novels. Teaching with Themes [Internet]. 2020, Jan 6 [cited 2022, Aug 26]. Available from: https://teachingwiththemes.com/index.php/2020/01/06/utopian-communities-inspired-by-novels/.

10

The Community Organization and Social Movement Tradition

The greatness of a community is most accurately measured by the compassionate actions of its members.

Coretta Scott King
Civil Rights Activist

Roots in Systemic Harm

While the Aesthetic Tradition looks at the world as it could be, or shouldn't be, the Community Organization and Social Movement Tradition very much looks at the world as it is. Community organizing and social movements are not typically thought of as designs, let alone a design tradition. But I include them here, as a single entity, because they meet the definition of design as I lay it out it in Chapter 2: a purposeful course of action aimed at changing existing situations into preferred ones. It is a particularly important and powerful design tradition because it targets systemic problems and aims to advance goals by changing the structure of the system and its cultural values. One-off designs, whether scientific, technical, human-centered, or aesthetic, will have a minimum impact on ignorance, inequality, and injustice if the systemic structure and values that created the situation in the first place do not change. And it may only be by making transformational changes in the system and culture that we solve the biggest problems that we face.

Not only are community organizing and social movements a design approach, there is a distinct history to them that constitutes a tradition. Actually, there are several distinct but inter-connected historical strains in the United States that include the Labor Movement, Civil Rights Movement, Women's Movement, Environmental Movement, and Gay Rights Movement. While each of these movements has a unique but overlapping origin, focus, and history, there are themes that cut across them related to purpose, process, outcomes, and impact. Each movement has created a community where often one did not exist and each mobilized the community to take collective action that addressed harm. Each has taken courses of action to move society from where it is to where they believe it should be.

The Labor Movement

The Labor Movement in the United States emerged early in the Industrial Revolution and started with the 1827 formation of the Mechanics' Union of Trade Associations in Philadelphia.[1] Initially the movement focused on skilled trades. But the rise of the factory system in the late 1800s and

Make the World a Better Place: Design with Passion, Purpose, and Values, First Edition. Robert B. Kozma.

early 1900s, with its use of unskilled labor, resulted in oppressive working conditions, especially for women and children that included 10- to 12-hour work days, hazardous working conditions, low pay, and no benefits. These conditions made labor unions attractive and they came to represent about 10% of the U.S. labor force prior to World War I, growing afterward in response to the Great Depression. The influence of labor unions resulted in the passage of New Deal legislation during the Great Depression, such as the 1933 National Industrial Recovery Act and the 1935 National Labor Relations Act that protected unions and allowed workers to collectively bargain for wages and working conditions.

In post-war 1946, labor exerted its power when 400,000 steel workers walked off the job and more than 5 million American workers were involved in strikes. Union power was increased when two large labor federations—the American Federation of Labor, founded by Samuel Gompers, and the Committee for Industrial Organization, led by John L. Lewis—joined forces in 1955 to represent workers in the automobile industry, steel, food, construction, public employees, and many other industries. At its peak, the AFL–CIO included nearly 20 million members. From 1955 until 2005, the AFL–CIO's member unions represented nearly all unionized workers in the United States.

With the combined organizations and increased membership, collective bargaining, backed by strikes, was an effective tool to improve the lives of workers. These techniques performed impressively after World War II, more than tripling weekly earnings in manufacturing between 1945 and 1970, gaining for union workers security against old age, illness, and unemployment, and strengthening their right to fair treatment at the workplace.

The Civil Rights Movement

In 1876, with the end of the post-Civil War Reconstruction effort in the South that attempted to assure equality to the formerly enslaved people, legislative control was returned to the former Confederate States. This resulted in a series of state constitutional amendments that disenfranchised African Americans, and the passage of Jim Crow laws that institutionalized economic, educational, and social inequality for Blacks living in the South.[2]

The Civil Rights Movement started in 1955 with Rosa Park's refusal to give up her seat to a White person and the Montgomery bus boycott. It continued into the 1960s with sit-ins, freedom rides, voter registration drives, and protest marches. A highlight in the movement was Martin Luther King Jr.'s 1963 March on Washington that drew over 250,000 people. The goal of the movement was to change public opinion and pressure national legislators to pass legislation that would address discriminatory laws at the state and local level that were among the reasons for the abominable condition of Blacks in the United States. These efforts resulted in the passage of major laws, such as the 1964 Civil Rights Act and the 1965 Voting Rights Act, which addressed the legal status and rights of Blacks in the South and across the country.

Of particular significance in changing public opinion was the depiction of brutal violence against Blacks in the South, such as church bombings, lynchings, police dog attacks, and police beatings. The 1965 violent police response to a peaceful march from Selma to Montgomery was graphically shown on the increasingly influential medium of TV. All of this had a dramatic impact on national public opinion. Whereas nearly 65% of the American public in the mid-1950s felt Blacks should have equal access to jobs, 50% supported integrated schools, and less than 5% approved of interracial marriage; by the mid-1970s, nearly 100% believed in job equality, 90% approved of integrated schools, and 30% approved of interracial marriage, although White support for affirmative action was only 20%.[3]

The Women's Movement

Dissatisfaction with women's lack of voting rights in the United States grew with the movement to abolish slavery in the mid-1800s. After the Civil War, in the late-1800s, this dissatisfaction became organized as the women's suffrage movement.[4] While women's rights to own property and control their own income after marriage were addressed through legislation in many states in the 1800s, women's right to vote remained elusive.

Two organizations, the National American Woman Suffrage Association (NAWSA), headed by Susan B. Anthony, and the Women's Christian Temperance Union led the fight and won limited voting rights in some states. Alice Paul, Chair of NAWAS's Congressional Committee, advocated militant, nonviolent action, and in 1913, she organized a Washington, D.C., demonstration in which 5,000 women marched and 300,000 people reportedly watched. In 1916, Paul formed the National Woman's Party, a militant group of women who picketed the White House in support of a national amendment to assure women the right to vote. Over 200 women were arrested; some went on hunger strike and endured forced feeding after being sent to prison. The efforts of these groups culminated with the passage of the 19th Amendment in 1920 conferring women's right to vote, although the amendment left out Black women, who still faced discrimination.

Betty Friedan's 1963 book *The Feminine Mystique* rekindled the Women's Movement in the mid-1960s. Lead by the newly formed National Organization for Women (NOW), the goal became to seek liberation from a domestic role imposed on women by the culture and to bring women into full, equal participation in the mainstream of American society, with all its privileges and responsibilities. Rallies, pickets, strikes, protests, lobbying, and runs for elected office ultimately resulted in Congress passing the Equal Rights Amendment in 1972. It did not however, garner approval from 38 states, which was required for its ultimate confirmation. By the mid-2010s, U.S. attitudes about egalitarian roles for women holding political office, shared family roles, and working mothers all reached nearly 80%.[5]

The Environmental Movement

The early roots of the Environmental Movement in the United States came from 19th-century conservationists such as John Muir and Henry David Thoreau, who wrote about the importance of living in nature and the need to preserve nature for its own sake.[6] Environmental organizations established from the late 19th to the mid-20th century were primarily middle- and upper-class lobbying groups concerned with nature conservation, wildlife protection, and the pollution that arose from industrial development and urbanization. Some scientific organizations were also concerned with natural history and with biological aspects of conservation.

In 1962, Rachel Carson's book *Silent Spring* was published. It raised public consciousness about the impact that human activity, particularly the use of pesticides, was having on the natural environment, including air and water pollution. The book became an immediate bestseller and has never been out of print. The concerns raised by the book, and the popular response to it, culminated in 1970 with the first Earth Day, in which 20 million people in the United States joined rallies and teach-ins in support of the environment. That year also saw passage of the Clean Air Act and establishment of the Environmental Protection Agency (EPA). A year after that, Congress passed the Endangered Species Act, and soon after, the Federal Insecticide, Fungicide, and Rodenticide Act.

A growing alarm since the 1970s, increasing in the last decade, has been focused on the extent of human impact on the global climate, extensively documented by scientists around the world.

Because of the global nature of climate change, several environmental organizations, such a Green Peace, Friends of the Earth, and the World Wildlife Fund, established offices and chapters across the globe, and their central offices coordinated local and international lobbying and direct-action efforts. This resulted in a series of international conferences, agreements, and treaties, culminating with the Paris Agreement, adopted in 2015, in which 196 countries committed themselves to mitigate greenhouse gas emissions.

In recent years, the movement has become more grassroots, especially among young people who have the most to lose with the long-term impact of an increasingly degraded environment. In 2018, a 15-year-old Swedish girl, Greta Thunberg, launched a school strike for climate change outside the Swedish Parliament. In 2019, she was invited to speak at the United Nations General Assembly, where she told world leaders, “You have stolen my childhood and my dreams with your empty words.” During that week, 300,000 people turned out to hear her launch Global Climate Strike in New York City,[7] and over 6 million people took to the streets around the world.[8] By 2020, two-thirds of Americans felt the government should be doing more about climate change.[9]

The Gay Rights Movement

One of the earliest organized efforts to protect and improve the rights of gay men in the United States was the Mattachine Society, established in 1950 by Harry Hay in Los Angeles.[10] But it wasn't until the 1970s that a vigorous Gay Rights Movement emerged in the United States. While police raids of gay establishments were a common way to suppress gays, the movement was galvanized in 1969 by riots in New York City in response to a raid of the Stonewall Inn, a gay bar in New York City's Greenwich Village. A commemorative march one year later drew 5,000 marchers on the city's Sixth Avenue that foreshadowed the modern-day pride marches.

This emergent social movement was fostered and their tactics were inspired by other social movements of the time, such as the Anti-War Movement, the Civil Rights Movement, and the Women's Movement. However, large-scale involvement in the movement was impeded, in large part, because homosexuality was still illegal and attached to a huge social stigma. Early organizational efforts were focused primarily on enlisting people in the movement through self-identification (i.e., “coming out”) and gay pride. Initially male-oriented, the movement grew to include lesbians, and ultimately, the full range of sexual orientations, and an estimated 75,000 people participated in the 1979 National March on Washington for Lesbian and Gay Rights.

In the 1980s, the momentum of the movement was disrupted by the devastating impact that HIV-AIDS had on the community, which carried into the 1990s. In 1996, the U.S. Supreme Court ruled that the Second Amendment of Colorado's State Constitution, denying rights to gays and lesbians, was unconstitutional. However, that was also the year Congress passed the Defense of Marriage Act, which limited marriage to a man and a woman.

States had begun decriminalizing sodomy in 1961, and in 2003, the U.S. Supreme Court ruled as unconstitutional laws in the few remaining states that criminalized it. In the 21st century, the movement adopted a strategic, customized, federal-and-national effort to establish same-sex marriage through the courts, legislatures, and ballot boxes. In states that were so inclined, the movement pushed to establish the foundations for marriage equality. In other states, it was more feasible to push for approval of domestic partnerships. And generally, the movement engaged in a variety of efforts to create cultural change to incorporate gays into society and to accept the idea of gay marriage, more specifically. More gay characters appeared in TV, movies, and plays. And at the same time, more people who were coming out meant more straights had family, friends, or neighbors who were gay. By the time the U.S. Supreme Court had confirmed marriage equality in 2015, American approval of same sex marriages had switched to 55% from 31% in 2004.[11] In 2022, support stands at 71%.[12]

Characteristics of the Social Movement Tradition

While these social movements varied in their histories, organizational structures, and tactics, there are commonalities that make them worth considering together as a design tradition having similar purposes or goals, processes or methods, outcomes, and impacts.

Purpose

These movements were in response to harm done within a context of systemic inequality. Often the responses started out as spontaneous protests or riots, before they were formally articulated as a movement. However, the articulation of purpose was often one of the early stages in the development and this expression is often what made it into a movement. The purpose that runs across these movements, as articulated by organizers, such as labor organizer Saul Alinsky, Dr. Martin Luther King Jr., Susan B. Anthony, and Harry Hay, is to empower a community to take control over its own condition and to change the structure of the immediate system so as to address some harm or accomplish some goal that is not met within the larger prevailing socioeconomic system.

However, the ultimate purpose of a social movement is often to change the values of the socioeconomic system, so as to advance equality, address injustice, and increase overall happiness and well-being. For the Civil Rights Movement, the immediate purpose was to strike down Jim Crow laws, but ultimately, it was to create a culture where "little black boys and black girls will be able to join hands with little white boys and white girls as sisters and brothers."[13] For the Gay Movement, the immediate purpose was to protect gays and establish their rights. Ultimately, gays wanted a cultural change that would value them as people and allow them to integrate into the community as full members.

There is some tension within the tradition around the purpose of gaining power: Was it a means to an end or an end in itself? This tension is best contrasted by quotes from Dr. King and Saul Alinsky. For King, "power properly understood is nothing but the ability to achieve purpose. It is the strength required to bring about social, political and economic change."[14] For Alinsky, "Power is the reason for being of organizations."[15] The difference can be viewed as a matter of emphasis since both believe that power provides the agency for collective action and for change to happen. But the emphasis can be important in terms of the movement's moral stance. Alinsky, for example, claims in relation to power that "the end justifies almost any means."[16] But King states, "power without love is reckless and abusive."[17] The purpose of achieving power, if not balanced by values, can work against the purpose of changing the larger culture.

Process

One reason that social movements are not thought of as a design tradition is the ambiguity that exists about who the "designers" are and what the "design process" is. The title "designer" isn't used in the social movement literature but there are leaders or organizers of the movement who are trying to change the existing situations into preferred ones. The tactics for doing this constitute the design process as I define it. Sometimes designers/organizers are trained professionals who come into the community from the outside, such as labor organizers or social workers. And sometimes they are local leaders in the community who respond to events or are turned into leaders by these events.

The design process for social movements happens at the interface between a community, and the larger network of systems surrounding it. And the process often involves changing both the inner environment—the community—and the outer environment—the surrounding network of systems that is causing it harm. In response, one or the other or both need to change to reduce systemic harm.

The process of changing the inner environment is called "community organizing," or sometimes, "community development." The word *community*, in this context, needs some clarification. Community organizer Saul Alinsky wrote: "'community' means community of interests, not physical community."[18] From this perspective, a community can be all gay men or all the workers in a factory or it may be a neighborhood made into a community by its concern over a chemical spill. Or it could be a more dispersed, national, or international group of people generally concerned about water or air pollution or climate change.

However, a community, as such, may not yet exist. That is, there may be a group of under-paid workers, passed-over women, or abused youth who don't yet identify with each other or believe they have a shared problem or common cause. They may feel that the harm they are experiencing is happening only to them or even that it was their own fault. In that case, the first step in organizing a community is to create positive, supportive relationships where they don't yet exist.[19] It is bringing people together who may believe they have nothing in common, demonstrate their commonality, and create a common identity, so as to achieve a shared goal. The first step creates relationships based on compassion and shared purpose, relationships that go beyond a single event to them agency, to empower them to do together what cannot be accomplished individually.

Whether a sense of community already exists or shared identity had to be formed, the process then involves organizing the community into something more than a mere response to a specific incidence of harm. Labor organizer Jane McAlevey starts her organizing with an analysis of the inner system: understanding the current structures and sources of power within the community.[20] This involves identifying the community's indigenous leaders, social influencers, active participators, and those with special skills as well as describing the knowledge, skills, connections, and values that people have. The analysis involves identifying the institutions and organizations people belong to and act through: churches, social groups, unions, clubs, teams. It involves describing the purposes and programs of these organizations and their impacts on the community. And the analysis of this system identifies the ways it is and isn't working to accomplish its goals and purposes.

With this understanding, community organizer Lee Staples describes the process of internal development of the community and its resources so as to empower them and make them more effective.[21] Community development draws on community members' own knowledge, skills, and resources, and engages them in constructive activities that create improvements, common resources, opportunities, structures, and goods and services. This builds the community's capacity, creates agency that empowers the community, and increases well-being. Examples of these internally focused activities include creating a community garden in a neighborhood that has access only to fast food restaurants; forming groups around healthy living and building their knowledge about helpful and harmful health practices; and forming self-help groups among gays and lesbians to provide personal support.

But the process also includes a focus on the external environment that is both the source of potential allies and the source of systemic harm. The systems analysis continues, McAlevey contends, with an examination of the larger system that surrounds and influences the community. The analysis involves identifying sources of power and influence among corporate executives, directors, political leaders, and so on, and the companies, government agencies, universities, and so on to which they belong. It involves an analysis of the flow of information and money among them that is the source of their power and influence. This analysis allows for the effective targeting of collective action.

The analysis of the external system also involves identifying other groups that may be natural allies and crossing group boundaries to build positive, supportive relationships with them. These relationships may be based on common sources of harm, such as connections between gays and lesbians; or on common benefits from collective action, such as connections between unions working with different corporations; or on common moral principles, such as a commitment to equality and justice. Creating these relationships enlists others in collective action that can dramatically increase the power of the community.

Collective action against the larger systems involves bringing the community members together to convince, pressure, or coerce external decision-makers to advance the goals of the community. These externally focused actions are strategies and tactics designed to alter the actions, behaviors, and attitudes of outside groups and institutions that are the source of harm. Gene Sharp, Senior Scholar at the Albert Einstein Institution in Boston, has written a comprehensive book on social action strategies.[22] He describes and gives examples of nearly 200 methods of collective action that escalate from persuasive methods, such as public speeches and letters of opposition; to noncooperation, such as consumer boycotts and withholding rent; to disruptive methods, such as strikes and civil disobedience; to more unorthodox interventions, such as guerilla theater and creating alternative markets.

Disruptive actions are powerful because consumers, workers, and citizens refuse to fulfill their roles, as defined by the system, and make it difficult for the system to operate, thus reducing harm to the community caused by the system, and perhaps, ultimately reorganizing the system to be less harmful and more helpful. Disruptive actions need to be selected carefully, based on an understanding of the structure and interactions of the system, so that the strategic application of effort is most effective. Disruptions may also bring the group's situation to the attention of a larger audience who are potential allies. Because allies are so important to making a movement succeed, the action must be executed with discipline. If a strike or peaceful march turns into a riot, especially with burning and looting or hurting innocent people, it will very likely work against the purposes of changing the larger culture.

All of the collective action methods that Sharp promotes are nonviolent, as are the methods advocated by Mahatma Gandhi, Dr. Martin Luther King Jr., and most social movement organizers. Nonviolence has both practical and moral advantages over violent methods, such as destruction of property, beatings, and killings.[23] First, nonviolence can be more effective than violent methods, in part, because, when it comes down to it, the opposition is more heavily armed and much more skilled in the use of violence than is the protesting community. Second, nonviolence confirms the purpose of the action as fundamentally moral—to reduce harm, increase well-being, promote equality, or address injustice—while violence undermines the morality of the community's position. This moral foundation opens the community to alliances with other groups that don't have a direct stake in the outcome. Finally, nonviolence also confirms the shared humanity of the opposition, which is the foundation for moral principles.

That is not to say that nonviolence will always be met with nonviolence in return. There are many instances where nonviolent marches have been met with police tear gas, beatings, rubber bullets, and even live ammunition. But the asymmetry of the system's response both validates the morality of the community's actions and reveals the lack of moral standing of the system. And it is likely to evoke support for the movement among people not otherwise affected by the system's harm. This lack of the system's moral standing was powerfully demonstrated for the world to see when police violently charged the nonviolent march for voting rights by Black Americans and their allies at the Edmund Pettus Bridge in Selma, Alabama, in 1965. This resulted in massive support of people not directly affected by Jim Crow laws and it led to the 1965 Voting Rights Act. The morality of the group's actions also contributed to a cultural change about race in the United States that is still felt—and still incomplete—to this day.

Outcomes

The most immediate product or outcome of a social movement is the residual organization it creates, the sense of community it develops, along with the capabilities and resources it develops. This may be a formal organizational structure, such as a union or an association, with a professional staff that coordinates activities. Or it may be a less formal, decentralized network of people, such as a neighborhood watch group or a national network of grassroots chapters that coordinate local actions.

Establishing a formal organization was a key goal of the Labor Movement: to certify a local union chapter at a specific factory. This approach not only organizes the community, but it also changes the system by adding a new component and that alters the system's dynamics—a company must deal with the union around certain issues rather than act on its own. And having a formal organization in place with a professional staff can carry the movement beyond a specific incident to maintain the movement's momentum and monitor the implementation of agreed-upon changes.

But there are certain downside risks to formal organizations. As they become a part of the formal system, the organization may end up merely reinforcing the underlying cultural assumptions of the system in its somewhat reconstituted form. The organization has a seat at the table, but the net effect may be that the purpose of the larger system stays the same—systemic values are maintained that are contrary to the interests of community. Another potential problem of formal structure is that its purpose may become corrupted, shifting from advancing the needs of the community it represents to advancing the needs of the professional staff and perpetuating itself as an organization. This has been an unfortunate part of the history of the Labor Movement.

On the other hand, if the outcome of organizing efforts is a decentralized network, there are many advantages. Decentralized networks bring more people into the movement and distributes power across the group, giving agency to more people.[24] More people, particularly those who are otherwise marginalized, participate in determining the goals and the direction of the group. Decentralization also creates opportunities for the emergence of more leaders. Decentralization is based on the belief that many activists and many leaders are needed to create transformative change and that these leaders should come from the communities themselves.

The development of these local leaders can itself be an important outcome of the process.[25] Local leaders may already exist or they may emerge in response to a particular incident of harm. But in some cases, an outside organizer can facilitate the development of an indigenous organizational structure by working with local leaders to improve their organizational skills, introduce them to outside knowledge and practices that may be helpful, and broker organizational connections that can extend the reach and impact of the group. However, when an outside organizer becomes the leader or creates an organizational structure detached from community members, it works against local empowerment and agency. It is important that outside organizers be clear about the difference between themselves and people in the community, and they understand the unique contribution they might make in creating local, sustainable organizations.

Impact

The impact of inward-oriented community development is the increased agency within the community; people have more power and more involvement in local decision-making that can directly benefit community members. These benefits might be improved health as a result of a community garden that provides fresh, healthy produce, improving the diet and health of the community. Or it may be a sense of well-being that results from the capacity of a group of gays or lesbians to help their members make it through personal crises.

The outward-oriented impact of collective action taken by a movement may be to stop the system from working and reducing its harmful effects on the community, at least, in the short term. The target may be a company, a developer, or a city and its police department. And the action may reduce harmful working conditions, clean up a toxic dump, or get an abusive policeman fired.

But the long-term impact of a successful social movement is to change the structure and dynamics of the system and values of the culture. The intended impact is to redistribute power so that community members have more control over their own situation, resulting in higher pay and better working conditions, the hiring of police officers who are more considerate of the concerns of community members, or the hiring of teachers who better reflect the composition of the community. The community might share in government decisions about building in its neighborhood, resulting in a much needed community center or neighborhood school. The successful long-term impact of a social movement might change the culture to make it more just, a culture where all community members are treated equally and with respect.

Case Study: Black Lives Matter (BLM)

The Civil Rights Movement of the 1960s was able to accomplish many things, primarily through legislative action, which we will examine in more detail in Chapter 16. But issues of racial inequality and injustice have continued to plague the United States, most recently demonstrated with a series of shootings of unarmed Blacks by police officers and the social unrest associated with it. Black Lives Matter (BLM) is the latest effort to address this lingering problem and it illustrates in more detail the purpose, process, outcomes, and impact of the Community Organization and Social Movement Tradition.

Case Study: Black Lives Matter (BLM)

On the evening of July 13 2013, a young Black woman, Patrisse Cullors (see Figure 10.1), sat on a bed in a motel room in Susanville, California.[26] She had come to Susanville to support a Black male friend who was imprisoned there. As she sat on the bed, she saw breaking news flash across her computer screen: The man who shot Trayvon Martin, an unarmed Black boy, was just acquitted. Martin's killer would walk free while the young man she was visiting was sentenced to 10 years in prison for a robbery in which no one was physically harmed. So many feelings flooded into her: shock, disbelief, confusion, shame. She cried. She shouldn't be crying; she was supposed to be strong. But how could this happen? How was this fair?

She reflected on the details of Martin's murder. On the night of February 26, 2012, 17-year old Martin was walking to the home of his relatives in a gated community in Sanford, Florida. He was talking to a friend on the phone. He had a box of candy and an iced tea in his pocket. Martin was followed by a man who was the neighborhood watch coordinator and was armed. The man called the police to report a suspicious person in the neighborhood. He was told not

(Continued)

Case Study: Black Lives Matter (BLM) (Continued)

Figure 10.1 Patrisse Cullors, one of the Black Lives Matters Founnders (Photo by Ashley Graham, Wikimedia Commons).

to follow Martin; he did anyway. An altercation took place; Martin was shot and killed. There was no question about who killed Martin or that he was unarmed. But the man claimed self-defense. Standing your ground to the point of killing someone is legal in Florida, so he was released. It was only after 6 weeks of protests and the occupation of the governor's office for the killer to finally be arrested.

Cullors was confronted that night by the killer's acquittal that came 17 months later. She transformed her disbelief, confusion, and shame to righteous anger and determination.

Then Alicia Garza, a friend of hers, wrote on Facebook in response to the verdict: "I continue to be surprised at how little Black lives matter. And I will continue that. stop giving up on black life. black people, I will NEVER give up on us. NEVER."

To that, Cullors responded: "#BlackLivesMatter."

Cullors met Garza at a political gathering several years before. Both women had a history of community organizing since high school, Cullors in LA, Garza in Oakland. Over the next few days, they brainstormed what they could do. They knew they wanted to develop something with a global reach. Garza reached out to her friend Opal Tometi, an organizer in New York. They decided together that they wanted to build power; they wanted to build a movement. Tometi created a website and accounts on Twitter, Facebook, and Tumblr.

And BLM was born.

Cullors wrote on Facebook: "I hope it impacts more than we can ever imagine."

Subsequently, each woman organized protest marches: in LA, Oakland, and New York City. In LA, their initial demands were narrow: bring federal charges against Martin's killer, no more new jail or prison construction in LA, community control over all law enforcement. But their aim is systemic cultural change; a system in which Black lives will be long, vibrant, and healthy; a system without prisons and punishment; a shared culture of mutual respect and dignity.

In August 2013, BLM took on a more substantive form in response to yet another travesty: On August 9, an unarmed Black man, Michael Brown, was shot and killed by a Ferguson,

Missouri, policeman. The Black community in Ferguson organized a series of protests that began peacefully but were met with police in riot gear.

Cullors and Darnell Moore, an early BLM organizer, decided to organize a national ride during the following Labor Day weekend, called the Black Life Matters Ride. Over 600 people showed up: organizers, lawyers, policy experts, journalists, artists, and healers. Cullors and Moore made two commitments: to support the team on the ground in St. Louis and to go back home and do the work there. They worked with local organizers and religious leaders to provide a space for organizing, talking, painting banners, speaking out. It is here that BLM first gets positive news coverage.

When they left Ferguson, organizers from 18 different cities went back home and developed BLM chapters in their communities. An organization was being built. Cullors, Garza, and Tometi did not want to control it. They wanted it to spread like wildfire. Their goal is to support the development of new Black leaders as well as create a network where Black people feel empowered to determine their destinies in their own communities. Consequently, other groups, organizations, and individuals used BLM to amplify their own message across the country.

Subsequently, they created the BLM Global Network infrastructure.[27] It is an adaptive, decentralized network with a set of guiding principles and 40 member-led chapters in the United States, Canada, and England. Professor Melina Abullah, an early BLM organizer, says "It was students, artists, organizers and mommas. We knew it was our sacred duty to step up."[28] An emphasis from the beginning was on "group-centered" leadership, according to Abullah, and leadership was not just about oratory, "it's also about facilitation, planning, bringing arts into the movement, things that don't get much recognition." Women are often chapter leaders, and the movement is inclusive of people regardless of economic status, ability, disability, sexual identity, gender identity, religious beliefs or disbeliefs, immigration status, or location.

The group's stated mission is to eradicate White supremacy and build local power to intervene in violence inflicted on Black communities, to create space for Black imagination and innovation, and to center Black joy.[29]

In May 2020, BLM became a full-fledged social movement. On May 25, George Floyd was arrested in Minneapolis for allegedly passing a fake $20 bill.[30] He was handcuffed and thrown on the ground, face-down. A police officer, put his knee on George Floyd's neck and held it there for 9 minutes and 29 seconds, even for a full minute and 20 seconds after paramedics arrived; despite Floyd's pleas that he couldn't breathe, despite pleas from bystanders. The policeman lifted his knee only after paramedics told him to. By then, George Floyd had died.[31]

Spontaneous protests took place in Minneapolis–St. Paul metropolitan area beginning May 26. That day, graphic video taken by witnesses and security cameras were released. Protests continued in Minneapolis–St. Paul and began to spread to other cities, some of them turning violent. By June 2, activists used social media to take protests beyond Floyd's death to include a more general expression of anger over police brutality to Blacks and in support of BLM.[32]

On June 6, half a million protestors turned out in nearly 550 places across the United States.[33] From late May to late June, there were more than 4,700 demonstrations in all 50 states in large cities and small towns, an average of 140 protests per day (see Figure 10.2). There were demonstrations in at least 1,360 counties, more than 40% of counties in the United States. Nearly 95% of counties are majority White and nearly three-quarters are more than 75% White. While BLM did not direct each protest, it provided materials, guidance, and a framework for activists. It is estimated that somewhere between 15 million and 26 million people

(Continued)

Case Study: Black Lives Matter (BLM) (Continued)

Figure 10.2 BLM protest (Photo by Aspects and Angels, Shutterstock).

participated in demonstrations, making it one of the largest collective actions in American history. About half of the protestors surveyed said it was their first time getting involved in any kind of protest.

While it is still too early to tell what the long-term impact of the BLM movement will be, there are some indications that the actions of BLM have had an impact on our culture.[34] Some local governments have been more responsive to police incidents against Blacks, producing video and identifying and disciplining officers more quickly. Some have launched efforts to re-imagine their police departments. In Minneapolis, the City Council pledged to dismantle its police department; although it has since modified its stand.[35] In New York, lawmakers repealed a law that kept police disciplinary records secret.[36] Mississippi lawmakers voted to retire their state flag, which prominently includes a Confederate battle emblem, and statues of Confederate soldiers have been removed.[37] Cities and states across the country passed laws banning choke-holds and enacting other police reforms.[38] Sports teams have taken a knee in support of the movement and their owners have approved; a significant change from years ago when such a protest by San Francisco 49er quarterback Colin Kaepernick left him without a team to play for.[39] Companies such as CitiGroup, Netflix, Microsoft, IBM, and Salesforce are also supporting the movement.[40]

But perhaps the most important impact is cultural, as borne out by polls that were taken shortly after the mass demonstrations.[41] In 2014, only 43% of Americans felt that Michael Brown's death was part of broader problem of treatment of African Americans by police; after George Floyd's death and the protests that followed, 74% of Americans felt so. In another poll, 84% of Americans felt that peaceful protests against police mistreatment of Blacks was justified. As for attitudes about BLM, more specifically, a national survey of Americans, released by the Pew Research Center in 2016, found that only 43% of Americans were strongly or somewhat supportive of BLM, 40% of White respondents and 65% of Black respondents felt that way.[42] In a survey released by Pew in June 2020, it was found that a majority of Americans, 67%, were strongly or somewhat supportive of BLM: 60% of White, 86% of Black, 77% of Hispanic, and 75% of Asian respondents.[43]

However, a March 2022 Pew Research Center poll found that overall support for the BLM movement had dropped to 57% among U.S. adults, although it was still high at 70% among U.S. teens.[44] This shift emphasizes the moderating effects of increased crime rates, the passage of time, and the immediate and perhaps long-term adverse effect of riots on the intended impact of the movement.

The success of BLM, to date, illustrates several components of the Community Organization and Social Movement Tradition that make it such a powerful design approach. First, the purpose of BLM, and social movements more generally, is to change the system: the structures, interconnections, and the cultural values of the system that are harmful to a group, and in the case of BLM, oppress Black lives. While BLM focuses on specific incidents of racism and police brutality, it continues to connect these incidents to other inter-related, systemic issues that include the criminal justice system, economic conditions, voter suppression, healthcare, and gun laws.

Second, acquiring and using power is the means by which the BLM intends to change the system. With BLM, power was acquired by using critical incidents, such as the acquittal of Trayvon Martin's killer, and Michael Brown's and George Floyd's deaths, to leverage a small number of people to mobilize a large number of people. Emotion plays a big part in this process. The video of George Floyd's killing was particularly compelling, and BLM used social media and the creative arts to amplify this emotional impact. It was particularly effective in taking moral outrage and using it to engage people in collective moral action.

Third, the organization that Cullors, Garza, and Tometi created is a coordinated, distributed network of grassroots groups. Not all mass movements are organized in this way. But in her book *How Change Happens*,[45] Leslie Crutchfield describes the characteristics of successful mass movements, and in her recent article in *The Chronicle of Philanthropy*,[46] she applies these criteria to BLM. Crutchfield notes that a principle feature of BLM that contributes to its success is its approach to leadership. Rather than a few, high-profile leaders who consistently represent the movement, BLM's emphasis is on developing and deferring to local leaders. They rely on grassroots efforts and allow victims, survivors, and people with personal experience to stand in front of protest marches. This "leaderful" approach expands the power base of the movement and minimizes the risk of the movement being compromised by the death, controversy, or fatigue of a single, high-profile leader.

Crutchfield also notes that BLM's decentralized but highly coordinated approach tailors its strategies to local political systems and cultural milieus, much as did the Gay Rights Movement in its efforts to support various forms of gay relationships, depending on the local situation. BLM local chapters, which are aware of local laws, power structures, political dynamics, and attitudes, have significant control over BLM activities in their area. And she points out that BLM is not just committed to changing government policy, but also impacting cultural norms and attitudes. Finally, Crutchfield attributes BLM's success to recruiting companies, including sports franchises, that have not only donated funding to the BLM network but have included BLM messages in their advertising, thus amplifying BLM's efforts to impact public opinion.

Systemic Implications of the Community Organization and Social Movement Tradition

The systemic implications of the Community Organization and Social Movement Tradition are profound because it is the one tradition that has as its purpose making fundamental changes in the system. If the structure and dynamics of the socioeconomic system and its underlying cultural purposes, values, and beliefs are at the root of profound harm and inequality, then the other design traditions are not structured to address these conditions. This is why the Community Organization and Social Movement Tradition can make such an important and unique contribution to a better world.

Both the local and the larger, harm-causing systems must be addressed. Locally, this involves organizing a harmed group into an effective alternative system, often creating a community where none existed previously. This process includes creating a sense of group identity out of the common harm of its members. But it also includes identifying the knowledge, skills, resources, supportive relationships, and interaction patterns that already exist among individuals within the group and can serve as the basis for collective action. An important part of this skill-building is the nurturing and development of local leaders.

The focus of the community's collective action is the larger system that is the source of harm. Essential to an effective response is a power-structure analysis of the system. This involves describing the structures and interaction patterns of the larger system and identifying the influential people, and the roles and dynamics among them that are the source of the power that works against the community. Important to this systemic analysis is the identification of allies so as to leverage the power the community has and increase its impact. Understanding the structure, power-roles, and interaction patterns of the system enables the movement to interdict or otherwise influence the system to reduce harm and to gain power over its own situation.

The ultimate goal of a movement is not just to interdict the structure and function of the social system, but to also change the cultural purpose, values, and beliefs that underpin the larger system to make it more just and equitable. This may involve going beyond the local system to impact the systems at a state or national level, coordinating the community's actions with a network of other groups to create a mass movement.

Moral Implications of the Community Organization and Social Movement Tradition

Despite the moral themes of harm reduction, well-being, knowledge, equality, justice, and supportive relationships that underpin the social movements previously described, there is nothing inherently moral about social movements. The approach can be used to address the harm, actual or perceived, of one group to harm others.

Since the 2010 global financial crisis, several contemporary populist movements have emerged in the United States. Movements such as the Tea Party, militia, and sovereign citizens movements were energized by Donald Trump's presidential campaign, who drew on the anger of harmed groups to create nationalist, anti-globalist, us-versus-them narratives that railed against immigrants, racial minorities, and political and intellectual elites.[47] These movements have used many of the same organizational and tactical methods used in earlier community organization movements.[48] But rather than draw on moral principles based on our common humanity, these groups have used the techniques to pit group against group, intimidate minority groups, and suppress voting for their own self-interests. This rise of populism has corresponded to an increase in hate crimes from 2014–2020, primarily against ethnic (Black, Hispanic, and Asian) and religious (Jewish and Muslim) minorities.[49] On January 6, 2021, thousands of people mobilized by these sentiments attacked and ransacked the U.S. Capital Building, resulting in 9 deaths and 150 police officers injured.[50]

In the 1990s, the National Rifle Association (NRA) fanned and capitalized on the fear and insecurity of some in the United States to create a movement that promotes the purchase and use of guns not just for self-defense but to fight a perceived tyrannical government.[51] The NRA and its allies used many of the techniques employed by other social movements, including rallies, marches, and local and national advocacy and lobbying efforts. Among the outcomes of their efforts are laws and court decisions that have deregulated ownership and use of guns and passed Stand Your Ground laws in 35 states that allow people to shoot others if they feel threatened. The impact of this movement has been an increase, rather than a decrease, in firearm homicides.[52] We have seen vigilantly street shootings, tragic school shootings, and mass casualties from gun violence in theaters, shopping centers, bars, and music concerts. We've also seen protesters armed with semi-automatic weapons occupy state capitals. Violent White supremacist, anti-government acts have come to be the primary domestic terrorist threats in the country.[53]

Creating designs that address the systemic harm to those with the least money, that are the least well-educated, the hungriest, the sickest, the most likely to be imprisoned, the most likely to live next to a toxic site, and the most likely to be homeless is the greatest moral challenge we face as designers and as people. This challenge must address any harm to all groups, Black or White, male or female, whatever their religious or sexual orientation. We are all humans and we all deserve to be treated fairly and with respect.

If we are to design a better world, we must start, not just by discovering new knowledge, not just by designing better products and services, not just by creating inspiring art, but by designing a better system, one that addresses injustice, promotes equality, builds supportive relationships, and advances knowledge for the purpose of increasing happiness especially to those most harmed by the system as it currently is. Without drawing on these fundamental moral principles in our designs, the world will continue to produce scientific knowledge that harms, products that kill, services that work at the margins, and art that entertains, while also generating populist social movements that prey on the harm these designs create.

Summary of Design Traditions

Each design tradition has developed and refined a unique set of processes or methods for a unique set of purposes, outcomes, and impacts. They all operate within a system, focusing on different aspects of the cultural environment; influencing and being influenced by it in different ways.

Each requires a different set of skills and knowledge. And each offers us a different lens, a different way of looking at design. Yet each is a course of actions aimed at changing existing situations into preferred ones that constitute it as a design tradition.

Over the decades, the traditions have intertwined and overlapped as they have influenced each other, coalescing around the Technical-Analytic Tradition, which has come to dominate. Yet each has retained its distinctiveness.

Each, in its own way, has made the world a better place. The Scientific Tradition has given us an amazing amount of knowledge about the natural and social world. The Technical-Analytic Tradition has given us a bounty of products and processes for producing them efficiently.

The Human-Centered Tradition has addressed some of our needs, problems, and concerns. The Aesthetic Tradition has given us beauty and splendor that pulls at our emotions. And the Community Organization and Social Movement Tradition has aimed at remediating the worst tendencies in our society.

Yet, each tradition has done us harm; each has degraded our world in some way. None has a special moral advantage. The only way for us to design our way out of our current plight is to use what we have learned about design and our design traditions to design with passion, purpose, and values. Together, these traditions provide us with multiple perspectives and alternative tool sets that we can use to customize our designs to specific purposes and goals for particular situations. And along with our passion, purposes, and values, they can be used to reduce harm; increase happiness and well-being; advance knowledge, reason, and agency; promote equality; address injustice; build compassionate, supportive relationships and communities; and make the world a better place.

References

1 Dray P. There is power in a union: The epic story of labor in America. New York: Doubleday, 2010.

2 Bullard S. Free at last: History of the civil rights movement and those who died in the struggle. New York: Oxford University Press, 1993.

3 Krysan, M. Racial attitudes. University of Illinois, Institute of Government and Public Affairs [Internet]. [cited 2022, Aug 26]. Available from: https://igpa.uillinois.edu/programs/racial-attitudes.

4 Dicker, R. (2016). A history of U.S. feminism. Berkeley, CA: Seal Press.

5 Meagher K, Shu, X. Trends in U.S. gender attitudes, 1977–2018: Gender and educational disparities. SOCIUS, 2019, 5(1–3). [cited 2022, Aug 26]. Available from: https://journals.sagepub.com/doi/pdf/10.1177/2378023119851692.

6 Spears EG. Rethinking the American environmental movement post-1945. New York: Routledge, 2020.

7 Gieger O. Global climate strike: Greta Thunberg and huge crowds protest. Forbes [Internet]. 2019, Sept 20. [cited 2022, Aug 26]. Available from: https://www.forbes.com/sites/oliviagieger/2019/09/20/global-climate-strike-greta-thunberg-and-huge-crowds-protest/#2a9f631c36fb.

8 Taylor M, Watts J, Barlett, J. Climate crisis: 6 million people join latest wave of global protests. The Guardia [Internet]. 2019, Sep 27 [cited 2022, Aug 26]. Available from: https://www.theguardian.com/environment/2019/sep/27/climate-crisis-6-million-people-join-latest-wave-of-worldwide-protests.

9 Tyson A, Kennedy B. Two-thirds of Americans think government should do more about climate change. Pew Research Center [Internet]. 2020, Jun 23 [2022, Aug 27]. Available from: https://www.pewresearch.org/science/2020/06/23/two-thirds-of-americans-think-government-should-do-more-on-climate/.

10 Downs J. Stand by me: The forgotten history of gay liberation. New York: Basic Books, 2016.

11 Attitudes on same-sex marriage. Pew Resear Center [Internet]. 2019, May 14 2020, Jun 23 [2022, Aug 27]. Available from: https://www.pewforum.org/fact-sheet/changing-attitudes-on-gay-marriage/.

12 McCarthy J. Same-sex marriage support inches up to new high of 71%. Gallup [Internet]. 2022, Jun 1 [cited 2022, Oct 1. Available from: https://news.gallup.com/poll/393197/same-sex-marriage-support-inches-new-high.aspx.

13 The voice of Martin Luther King. New York Times [Internet]. 1968, Apr 7 [cited 2022, Aug 27]. Available from: https://archive.nytimes.com/www.nytimes.com/books/98/01/18/home/king-quotes.html?scp=7&sq=I%2520Want%2520You%2520%255B1966%255D&st=cse.

14 King Jr ML. The Essential Martin Luther King, Jr. (Location 2451). Beacon Press. Kindle Edition, 2013.

15 Alinsky S. Rules for Radicals (p. 113). Knopf Doubleday Publishing Group. Kindle Edition, 2010.

16 Alinsky S. Rules for Radicals (p. 29). Knopf Doubleday Publishing Group. Kindle Edition, 2010.

17 King Jr ML. The Essential Martin Luther King, Jr. (Location 2460). Beacon Press. Kindle Edition, 2013.

18 Alinsky S. Rules for Radicals (p. 120). Knopf Doubleday Publishing Group. Kindle Edition, 2010.

19 Garza A. The purpose of power: How we come together when we fall apart. New York: One World, 2020.

20 McAlevey J. No shortcuts: Organizing for power in the new gilded age. New York: Oxford University Press, 2016.

21 Staples L. Roots to power: A manual for grassroots organizing (3rd ed.). Santa Barbara: Praeger, 2016.

22 Sharp G. The politics of nonviolent action. Boston: Albert Einstein Institution, 2020.

23 Fischer L (ed.). The essential Gandhi: An anthology of his writings on his life, work, and ideas. New York: Vintage Books, 1962.

24 Garza A. The purpose of power: How we come together when we fall apart. New York: One World, 2020.

25 McAlevey J. No shortcuts: Organizing for power in the new gilded age. New York: Oxford University Press, 2016.

26 Khan-Cullors P, Bandele A. When they call you a terrorist: A Black Lives Matter memoir. New York: St. Martin's Griffin, 2018.

27 Herstory. Black Lives Matter [Internet]. [cited 2022, Aug 27]. Available from: https://blacklivesmatter.com/herstory/.

28 Maqbool A. Black Live Matter: From social media post to global movement. BBC [Internet]. 2020, Jul 10 [cited 2022, Aug 27]. Available from: https://www.bbc.com/news/world-us-canada-53273381.

29 About. Black Lives Matter [Internet]. (cited 2022, Aug 27]. Available from: https://blacklivesmatter.com/about/.

30 Hill E, Tiefenthäler A, Triebert, C, et at. How George Floyd was killed in police custody. New York Times [Internet]. 2020, May 31 [cited 2022, Aug 27]. Available from: https://www.nytimes.com/2020/05/31/us/george-floyd-investigation.html.

31 Levenson E. Former officer knelt on George Floyd 9 minutes and 29 seconds—not the infamous 8:46. CNN [internet]. 2021, Mar 30 [cited 2022, Aug 27]. Available from: https://www.cnn.com/2021/03/29/us/george-floyd-timing-929-846/index.html.

32 Blankenship M, Reeves R. From the George Floyd moment to Black Lives Matter movement, in tweets. Brookings [Internet]. 2020, Jul 10 [cited 2022, Aug 27]. Available from: https://www.brookings.edu/blog/up-front/2020/07/10/from-the-george-floyd-moment-to-a-black-lives-matter-movement-in-tweets/.

33 Buchanan L, Bui Q, Patel J. Black Lives Matter may be the largest movement in U.S. history. New York Times [Internet]. 2020, Jul 3 [cited 2022, Aug 27]. Available from: https://www.nytimes.com/interactive/2020/07/03/us/george-floyd-protests-crowd-size.html.

34 Ankel S. Minneapolis lawmakers vowed to disband the city police department less than two weeks after Floyd death. Business Insider [Internet]. 2020, Jun 24 [cited 2022, Aug 27]. Available from: https://www.businessinsider.com/13-concrete-changes-sparked-by-george-floyd-protests-so-far-2020-6#minneapolis-lawmakers-vowed-to-disband-the-citys-police-department-less-than-two-weeks-after-floyds-death-4.

35 Herndon A. How a pledge to dismantle the Minneapolis police collapsed. New York Times [Internet]. 2020, Sep 26 [cited 2022, Aug 27]. Available from: https://www.nytimes.com/2020/09/26/us/politics/minneapolis-defund-police.html.

36 Beer T. New York Senate votes to repeal law that kept police records secret. 2020, Jun 9 [cited 2022, Aug 27]. Available from: https://www.forbes.com/sites/tommybeer/2020/06/09/new-york-senate-votes-to-repeal-law-that-kept-police-records-secret/?sh=56282ffc.

37 Mizelle S. Mississippi lawmakers pushing to remove Confederate emblem from state flag. CNN [Internet]. [cited 2022, Aug 27]. Available from: https://www.cnn.com/2020/06/11/politics/mississippi-lawmakers-push-to-change-the-state-flag/index.html.

38 Changes to policing policy in the states and 100 largest cities, 2020. BallotPedia [Internet]. [cited 2022, Aug 27]. Available from: https://ballotpedia.org/Changes_to_policing_policy_in_the_states_and_100_largest_cities,_2020.

39 Haislop T. Colin Kaepernick kneeling timeline: How protests during the national anthem started a movement in the NFL. Sporting News [Internet]. 2020, Sep 12 [cited 2022, Aug 27]. Available from: https://www.sportingnews.com/us/nfl/news/colin-kaepernick-kneeling-protest-timeline/xktu6ka4diva1s5jxaylrcsse.

40 McGirt E. Cititgroup, Netflix and Microsoft among companies making statements in support of Black lives and justice. Fortune [Internet]. 2020, Jun 1 [cited 2022, Aug 27]. Available from: https://fortune.com/2020/06/01/citigroup-netflix-microsoft-racism-george-floyd-police-brutality-statements-business/.

41 Cheung H. George Floyd death: Why US protests are so powerful this time. BBC [Internet]. 2020, Jun 8 [cited 2022, Aug 27]. Available from: https://www.bbc.com/news/world-us-canada-52969905.

42 Horowitz JM, Livingston G. How Americans view the Black Lives Matter movement. Pew Research Center [Internet]. 2016, Jul 8 [cited 2022, Aug 27]. Available from: https://www.pewresearch.org/fact-tank/2016/07/08/how-americans-view-the-black-lives-matter-movement./

43 Parker K, Horowitz JM, Anderson M. Amid protests, majorities across racial and etnic groups express support for the Black Lives Mater movement. Pew Research Center [Internet]. 2020, Jun 12 [cited 2022, Aug 27]. Available from: https://www.pewsocialtrends.org/2020/06/12/amid-protests-majorities-across-racial-and-ethnic-groups-express-support-for-the-black-lives-matter-movement/.

Part III

Design with Passion, Purpose, and Values

11

Design with Passion and Purpose

Always remember, you have within you the strength, the patience, and the passion to reach for the stars to change the world.

Harriet Tubman
American Abolitionist

In many ways, our design traditions have served us well. Science has given us a deep understanding of the natural, biological, and social worlds—the mechanics of how they work, the foundations of life, the dynamics of social systems. We have used this knowledge and the technical tradition to invent medicines that cure our diseases and improve our health; we've developed products and the means to produce them that make life easier and our work more productive. We've designed services that meet our human needs. We've created art that makes the world more beautiful and life more enjoyable. We've organized our communities to reduce harm and to address injustice to benefit all.

Yet, designs and designers have also failed us in many ways. There is still much harm, unhappiness, ignorance, inequality, injustice, isolation, and loneliness in the world. Some of this is due to our designs, whether unintended, inconsiderate, or malicious. And much is due to the fact that we have failed to create designs to explicitly address these problems. While tech companies are busy creating first-person shooter games, self-driving cars, non-fungible tokens, a space tourist industry, and the metaverse, many people are crying—and in some cases dying—for improvements in the real world.

There is something deep in us that resonates with this cry, that calls us to do something about the suffering we see, that inspires us to envision something better.

In this book, I contend that if we are to make the world a better place, if we are to take it from where it is to a preferred state, it will be because of the passion, purpose, and values of everyday designers—you, me, all of us. You can draw on your passion and the power of our various design traditions to improve the world, but only if you harness your passion to the purpose of crafting designs that reduce harm, increase happiness, advance knowledge and agency, promote equality, address injustice, and build compassionate, supportive relationships and communities.

Passion

What is the role of passion in design? Can't we just reason our way to a better world?

Emotions are an essential part of who we are. They played an important role in the evolution of our species and they do so in our everyday lives. The biggest role they play is to drive actions. They motivate

Make the World a Better Place: Design with Passion, Purpose, and Values, First Edition. Robert B. Kozma.

us to get what we need to prosper and to avoid threats to our survival. They motivate us to connect with other people. They also motivate us to design; to adapt our environment to our purposes and needs.

And passion is one of our most intense emotions. It motivates us to actions that we might not otherwise do; the ones that take significant effort, the ones that might even be at our short-term cost. Passion motivated Civil Rights nonviolent protestors to face nightsticks, tear gas, and mounted police at the Edmund Pettus Bridge on Bloody Sunday in 1965.

Happiness

The Philosophes were sentimentalists. That word has a different connotation today than it did in the 18th century. Today, we associate it with a tender birthday card, a touching note, or a tearful eulogy. But for the Enlightenment philosophers, sentiments are the deeply held feelings that give our life meaning. Happiness, ours and that of others, is the greatest good and the source of great meaning.

Sentiment is the joy Ivan Owen must have felt in making an artificial hand for a child who lost one in an accident, and happiness is what the child must have felt in being able to pick something up with it.[1] Sentiment was the intense passion that Carroll Shelby drew on to succeed at Les Mans and the thrill he must have felt to see his cars cross the finish line. And sentiment was the joy and sense of beauty that Van Gogh expressed in his art.

For the Philosophes, sentiments are not just emotions; they are foundations of morality; they are shared social feelings that bind us together; and they are the profound sense we have of right and wrong. These philosophers believed that moral behavior is motivated by passion: a sentiment for the happiness of humankind and a resentment of its misery, as Hume put it.

Empathy and compassion

For Adam Smith, compassion is the emotion that we feel for the misery of others, when we either see it or think of it in a vivid way. And empathy (or *sympathy*, to use their term) is the emotional source of that sentiment. Smith believed that sympathy is the means by which we feel how others feel, even though we are not directly experiencing their condition. We do so by conceiving of how we ourselves would feel in that situation. But these "conceptions" are not rational inferences, they are sympathetic feelings directly evoked in us by the condition of a fellow human being, feelings evoked when we see a last-second, game-winning, end-zone pass; when we hear the cry of a child in pain; when we see a son holding the hand of his dying father; when we see the devastation in Ukraine.

The beliefs of these 18th-century philosophers are shared by contemporary psychologists, such as New York University's Jonathan Haidt[2] and Harvard's Joshua Greene.[3] These scientists and others cite empirical evidence that suggests we are evolutionarily pre-programmed to treat others with affection and to respond to suffering with compassion. These feelings promote cooperation, group cohesion, and collective action, behaviors that increase the survival prospects of the group.

These sentiments are automatic, not rational. Greene agrees with Hume; emotions come first; cognitive functions follow as we figure out what we must do in response to these feelings. In Haidt's terms, moral emotions are the tail that wags the rational dog.

Anger and moral outrage

While we all agree that positive feelings are good, we often think of fear and anger as undesirable emotions. But they, too, have served us well. It is fear that may get you out of a life-threatening situation. And it may be anger that pushes you past the most difficult barriers.

Of course, social norms and rational thoughts keep those feelings from being expressed in violent, antisocial ways that would harm others and destroy the group. They keep you from throwing things when you don't get what you want, from punching out your boss when he doesn't like your report, or from trashing your office when your computer doesn't work.

But negative feelings have also served an evolutionary function when they are beneficial to the group.[4] The response of our ancestors to cheating with feelings of anger and to betrayal with punishment had its own way of promoting cooperation and group survival.

Moral outrage is the more focused, justifiable anger we feel when we perceive that a moral norm has been violated.[5] It is an emotional response to the immoral behavior of others, the flip side of guilt that we feel in response to our own immoral behavior. This outrage is expressed when people believe that it will prevent future violations or promote social justice.[6]

Moral outrage is particularly powerful when it promotes collective action, which happens most often when anger is accompanied by a sense of group identity, social support, and a shared belief that the group has been disadvantaged and has the agency to do something about it.[7] We saw this over and over in the last chapter, as social movements catalyzed group anger in response to disadvantaged conditions of labor, race, gender, environment, and sexual orientation.

Moral outrage can extend beyond the group one identifies with, as when one is angered by harm done to disadvantaged others, especially when those who are suffering are seen as innocent and not the cause of their own harm. Moral outrage can be an important source of action in response to injustice.

But outrage is a two-edged sword. It was the feeling whipped up in the crowd that gathered in Washington, D.C., on January 6, 2021. And it was the feeling that many of us had as we saw people sack the Capitol Building. It's what you do with the outrage that makes it moral.

From moral motivations to moral plans

You have a lot of mental resources that can be activated by your moral outrage. Modern brain research using 21st-century neuro-imaging technology supports 18th-century notions of morality showing that moral feelings also activate deep cognitive structures and can be used to devise an effective response when we encounter a moral wrong.[8] Multiple studies looked at the brain activity of people while they interact with a variety of morally loaded tasks, such as a making a choice in a moral dilemma, and found that moral judgments regularly engage brain structures that are associated with both emotion and reasoning.

For example, in his brain research, Professor Greene found that the initial response in moral situations draws on people's emotion-based brain structures that are intuitive and reflexive. But they also stimulate people's logical brain structures that are goal-oriented and planful. While the emotion-based structures direct autonomic responses, the moral-reasoning structures allow us to formulate actions based on detailed and explicit knowledge of the situations we face, along with general knowledge about the world and how it works.

The emotional responses can serve as powerful motivators for significant accomplishments, according to University of Pennsylvania psychologist Angela Duckworth.[9] In her research, Duckworth found strong associations between what she calls "grit" and success in the military, workplace sales, high school, and marriage. Duckworth defines *grit* as passion and perseverance for long-term goals. Certain personal traits, such as intelligence quotient (IQ) or physical ability, are well-established correlates with success. But we all know people who are more successful than others with greater intelligence or physical talent. Duckworth contends that this difference is due to grit. Beyond raw ability, it is passion and perseverance that enabled soldiers in her study to complete a Special Forces selection course, sales employees to succeed at their jobs, students to graduate from high school, and people to stay married.

Quite likely, it was passion and perseverance that motivated Gregor Mendel through those 30,000 experiments with pea plants. Surely, it was grit that drove Carroll Shelby past failures to develop the fastest car at Le Mans. Grit and moral outrage took Patrisse Cullors, Alicia Garza, and Opal Tometi to the streets to advance the quality of Black lives. Perhaps van Gogh was the grittiest and most passionate of them all, generating over 2,100 works of art, despite constant doubt about his ability and the fact that he sold only one piece during his lifetime.

Your emotional response to the condition of the world, your feelings in response to how it is now and how it should be, can serve as an essential motivator for your efforts to design a better world. Your feelings of empathy, compassion, or sadness in response to those suffering from homelessness, poverty, hunger; or your moral outrage at our poisoned rivers and trashed oceans; or your anger at the ignorance, inequality, injustice, and division in our country; or your hopefulness about the future, those feelings can serve as the moral foundation for your work. And it will be those sentiments, that passion, along with your perseverance, that help you prevail and make a difference in the world with your efforts.

Take as a model Ms. L. and Lee Gelernt.

Ms. L. (referred as such to protect her anonymity) is a Catholic woman from the Democratic Republic of the Congo, where Catholic churches have been regularly attacked and parishioners killed.[10] In 2017, fearing for her life and that of her 6-year old daughter, S., Ms. L. fled the Congo, traveling 4 months across 10 countries and 3 continents, often walking barefoot, begging for food, all so she could find safety for her and her daughter in the United States. On November 1, 2017, she and her daughter lawfully presented themselves at the San Ysidro Port of Entry between Mexico and the United States, seeking asylum based on religious persecution, one of five classes protected by the U.S. Immigration and Nationality Act. Immigration and Customs Enforcement (ICE) agents separated them, handcuffed Ms. L., and took her daughter to another room screaming, "Mommy, don't let them take me away!"

Lee Gelernt is a father of two sons and a lawyer at the American Civil Liberties Union. In February 2018, Lee met Ms. L., wearing an orange jumpsuit, in the San Diego detention center, and Ms. L. told him her story. Her story had a profound emotional impact on him. "The trauma inflicted on the children and the parents is just unthinkable," he said in an interview.[11] The U.S. Circuit Court suit that Lee subsequently devised claimed that Ms. L. had entered the country legally, that there was no evidence that Ms. L. was an unfit mother, and that there is overwhelming medical evidence that the separation of a young child from her parent has a devastating negative impact on the child's well-being and that the damage can be permanent.[12] The suit asked that Ms. L. and her daughter be released or at least detained together. The court ruled in his favor and on March 16, 2018, after four and a half months of separation, Ms. L. and her daughter were reunited. Reflecting on his efforts and that reunion, Gelernt said, "There are times when this work is so tiring but something like this, if people could only see this, I think it could change the way some of them think about these issues. This isn't abstract policy, this is a mother and a daughter who have been through more than we can imagine. It was the rawest possible emotion."[13]

But you don't need to be a lawyer to bring emotion into your designs.

On August 3, 2019, Ruben Martinez was 11 years old, living in El Paso, Texas. While riding with his mother, they drove by their Walmart and saw a large number of emergency vehicles there. They learned that 46 people were shot there that day; 22 died. His mother told BBC News, "Ruben was anxious after seeing that and hearing about what happened. He then asked me if there was a delivery service that could bring us groceries so we wouldn't have to go to the mall again. I told him you cannot live in fear and asked him if there was something he wanted to do to help. That's when he came to me with the note about the challenge."[14] Ruben came up with the idea of posting a social media challenge on Facebook and Twitter that he called #elpasoCHALLENGE. To honor each person who died, he asked readers to do 22 acts of kindness, such as mowing someone's lawn, visiting a nursing home, or comforting someone when they are sad or distressed. "This will show the world that people from El Paso, Texas, are kind and care for each other," Ruben exclaimed. Ruben probably doesn't think of himself as a designer, but his purposeful actions had an impact. By August 7, 7,000 people from across the country had shared the post, many of them saying what they were going to do.

Purpose

While our emotional responses are primal and sometimes raw, it is our ability to reason that allows us to go beyond our autonomic responses to create plans and to change our world. Purpose is the bridge between emotions and reason. In a larger sense, purpose gives our lives meaning and it also coordinates our actions.

Purpose has been getting a lot of press lately.[15] For the past several decades, there has been a movement among businesses to be purpose-driven organizations. The movement pushes executives to go beyond organizational structure and business strategy to articulate a purpose—the reason the organization exists.[16] The assumption, backed by data, is that purpose motivates employees[17] and creates loyal customers,[18] which in turn, contributes to the bottom line.[19]

In a 2020 survey of 1,000 employees of U.S. companies, McKinsey & Company found that 82% felt it was important for a company to have a purpose, 72% felt that purpose should be more important than profit, and 62% said their company had a stated purpose.[20] But only 42% said that the purpose drove the organization's impact.

While corporate purpose of your employer could be helpful to you in your desire to improve the world, it is your own purpose that is more likely to build on your passion and motivate your actions and designs. In this context, you might think about your own life purpose. What is it that you want your career and your life to count for?

Psychologist Michael Steger reviews the extensive body of research on life meaning, which he equates with having a purpose, mission, or overarching aim in life.[21] He notes that hundreds of studies have linked meaning in life to less suffering and greater well-being, both psychologically and physically. People who have meaning and purpose in their lives take better care of themselves and are psychologically and physically healthier. They have closer relationships; family connections and marital satisfaction are particularly associated with meaning and purpose. Purposeful people give back to their relationships and communities, through volunteering, providing donations, and relationship-improving activities. People who have meaning or purpose in their life are happier and more satisfied with their lives, express more positive feelings and opinions about themselves, and score higher on measures of self-esteem, self-acceptance, and positive self-image. Purpose is linked to a positive perception of the world as well as an optimistic orientation toward the future and striving to make it better.

Some motivational speakers and career consultants say that you find life's purpose at the intersection of what you love, what you're good at, what the world needs, and what you get paid for.[22] This may be the ideal balance of factors that influence one's life. The what-you-get-paid-for part is more important at some points in your life than others. Of course, money is a major concern for many people who are in early or mid-career and need to support a family and pay for college tuition. Getting paid is probably less important for those who find their life's purpose—or discover a new one—when they retire. My wife's definition of *retirement* is "being able to do what you love, whether it makes money or costs money."[23] For a lot of people, doing what they love is far more important than making a big salary. And doing what you love and what you're good at can make the world a better place, whether it makes money or costs money.

Take the example of Walter Meyer, an author and speaker living in southern California.[24] When he spoke on his purpose in life, he said, "For a class in high school we had to write a mission statement for our lives. Mine was simple: to use my writing to better the world. And I have tried to live up to that. I have written about the environment, diversity and bullying as well as a host of other topics. But I was happiest when I wrote something that addressed a problem and even happier when I would get feedback saying that my writing touched someone."[25]

The life purpose I offer you in this book is one that my father conferred on me, one that motivated Walter Meyer's writing, and one that inspired Amanda Gorman's elegant inaugural poem: it is to leave the world a better place than you found it. For Professor Duckworth, purpose is the top-level goal that organizes all our day-to-day goals in the service of passion and perseverance. The articulation of purpose is the first step in the long process of design that takes our world from where it is to where we want it to be.

What is your passion? What is your purpose?

Perhaps you have the passion for justice that motivated Patrisse Cullors, Alicia Garza, and Opal Tometi to launch Black Lives Matter. Perhaps your purpose is like that of van Gogh, who was compelled to make beautiful things, resulting in *Starry Night*, among other stunning paintings. But making the world better can be the overarching purpose that organizes everything else that you do. It can be the top-level goal that fosters and supports other goals related to your social life and your work. And it can motivate and organize powerful, impactful designs.

Purpose and design

Purpose is built into the design process. It is the starting point for your designs. It is the goal you are striving toward, the change you want to see, the "ought" that guides the rest of the process. The question is: What do you want that purpose to be?

At the micro level, purpose is used to align the affordances of the design with the specific situation and intended impacts. Purpose is well-articulated in the Technical-Analytic Tradition and articulating a purpose is often the first challenge in the Human-Centered Tradition. But once stated, purpose serves to focus subsequent design efforts, outcomes, and impacts.

The problem is more complex for designs impacting larger systems, such as companies or communities, and more complex yet for even larger systems, such as economies or societies. While purposefulness is a distinguishing feature of human systems, compared to physical or natural systems, such as the Amazon rain forest, there are multiple, often competing purposes at work in large human systems that make it the design process more complicated. For example, is the purpose of our economy to generated wealth, facilitate trade, create jobs, meet human needs, or all of these? In a decentralized economy, no one is in a position to say. Yet, each has different implications for designs within the economy and economic policy.

In such cases, one must infer an effective purpose by examining the impact of its activity. *This effective purpose* of a large human system is its impact—the current state of the system. One can design in a way that aligns with and confirms this purpose, as is done within the Technical-Analytic Tradition, or design to alter that purpose, as in the Community Organization and Social Movement Tradition.

Designer Victor Margolin, in his writings on designing for the good society, sees the purpose of design is to create "a new world based on fairness, justice, and equality."[26] The New Economy

Coalition, a network of nonprofits that work with communities most harmed by the current economic system, has the purpose of building a just and sustainable economy that prioritizes people and the planet over profit and growth.[27] The Creative Reaction Lab sees itself as "redesigners for justice" and with this purpose it trains and challenges Black and Latinx youth to become leaders who design healthy and racially equitable communities.[28]

But, as we saw above, purpose also has a personal dimension for designers. The year 2021 witnessed an unprecedented number of people quitting their respective job, in what has come to be called "the great resignation." A record 4.43 million quit in September of that year, alone.[29] Of course, there are many reasons for such a trend. One major driver appears to be that many workers were no longer willing to put up with the pay or working conditions they may have accepted prior to the pandemic. "I certainly think that the pandemic has led many people to reevaluate their work and their priorities and what they want to do," Elise Gould, senior economist at the Economic Policy Institute said in a statement to Business Insider.[30]

Perhaps you find yourself unsatisfied with tinkering at the margins, with making one more refinement to a product that provides convenience but not substance, with creating ads that promise happiness for products but don't deliver it, with polishing the look and feel without delivering impact, with making movies or video games that give thrills but not insight. If so, then a new purpose can build on your passion and turn it into products, places, services, experiences, art, relationships, organizations, and policies that improve the world and make it a better place.

Moral Reasoning and Moral Dialog

Getting from passion and purpose to real products, services, experiences, works of art, policies, and other designs, requires reasoning—figuring out how you can accomplish your purpose and goals; how you can build on resources, ideas, and experiences; and perhaps, how you can recombine them to create new ones that transform the world. Designs that improve the world will involve moral reasoning not just design thinking. Moral problems stimulate brain structures that are involved in emotion as well as those that are involved in cognition as we saw with Professor Greene's research. But while there are only a few emotional brain structures activated by moral situations, there are many cognitive structures that are activated, indicating complex processes are involved, such as abstract reasoning and problem-solving, and these can guide moral behavior. While the emotional tail wags the rational dog, in Jonathan Haidt's words, the dog is still important for moral behavior and its consequences.

In Chapter 2, I described the basic structure of the design process, a process that varies with the different traditions, as we saw in Chapters 6–10. In Chapter 3, I laid out seven moral principles and advocated that designers use them to reason about moral situations that guide designs to make the world better. In that chapter, I claimed, as did the Enlightenment philosophers, that these principles are universal; they are part of how we became human, and they apply to all of humankind. But as you apply these principles to your designs, they get particular. General principles look different in different situations, and these situations imply different responses.

So, how do you use these general principles to create specific designs for particular situations?

In this section and the next several chapters, I will explore the moral implications for design in more detail and look at how these principles are applied in different situations.

Design is the means of getting from "is" to "ought." Hume stated that you can't get from "is" to "ought" by reasoning alone. (Hume p. 409) While "is" is a descriptive statement, "ought" is a normative one that must rely on a sense of morality. From this perspective, every design is a moral statement—explicit or implied, intended or otherwise—about a preferred state, a more desirable condition for ourselves or the users of our designs, perhaps a better world for all. To get from our current state to a morally preferred one, and to get from our passion and purpose to designs with moral impact, it takes reasoning about the connections between moral principles and design purposes, processes, outcomes, and impacts.

Moral reasoning

For the Philosophes, it is morally-reasoned action that turns moral sentiments into moral consequences, action that gets to "ought." But reasoning about complex, adaptive, social systems is, well . . . complex. The causal chains are many and compounded, and the impacts are difficult to predict with a high degree of certainty. A change here may bring on unexpected consequence there, as the system adapts. Defunding police may reduce police abuse but increase the crime rate. Building shelters for the homeless may take people off the street but bring more homeless to your city. Applying universal moral principles is difficult.

Harvard Professor Michael Sandel (see Figure 11.1) describes moral reasoning as a process of creating a fit, or alignment, between concrete situations and universal moral principles with implications for action.[31] The process involves moving back and forth between the specifics of situations and the generalities of moral principles. This back-and-forth reasoning between the situation and the principle results in a better understanding of both the situation and the principle.

Moral reasoning is about determining the appropriateness of the principle to the situation: Is this instance of harm due to ignorance, inequality, or injustice? In this particular situation, can I increase happiness by advancing knowledge or building compassionate, supportive relationships? Can I reduce harm by promoting equality or addressing injustice? If more than one principle applies, is one better than the other? Must I choose between them? Do the implications derived from one principle conflict with the other? If so, how are those conflicts resolved?

In answering these questions, in resolving these issues, particularly within a design context, it is important to remember that the morality of an action is based more than on the goodness of what you do; it is also based on the goodness of the consequences, or the impacts, of your design. Drawing on the Utilitarian philosophers, a course of action—a design—is good if it produces more happiness for all affected by it and it produces no harm or less harm than any alternative action or

Figure 11.1 Michael Sandel (*Source:* Wikimedia Commons).

design. But in many situations, moral reasoning involves making inferences about a complex network of cause-and-effect relationships between alternative designs and desired impacts when the level of confidence about consequences may be low. It therefore requires hypothetical reasoning, or what Peter-Paul Verbeek calls "moral imagination," [32] about various possible impacts and the relative impact on some people compared to others.

How might this process of moral reasoning and moral imagination play out in a particular situation? Let's return to the case of the Boeing 737 MAX 8. Could moral reasoning have saved lives when the aircraft and its software were designed?

Moral reasoning depends on emotion and this is, perhaps, why the decisions of Boeing test pilots went off the rails. If not confronted by immediate emotions, Boeing's stated value of "human life and well-being above all else" is necessary but not sufficient to motivate moral reasoning. Without the immediate feelings of sadness, shame, or anger evoked by the actual crash, the emotional distress at the loss of life needs to be foreshadowed. In this situation, designers need to continually ask: What would it be like if our decision resulted in injuries or death? How would our passengers, their families, our investors feel? How would *we* feel if we were on that plane? If our families were? How would we feel about the work we had done, about our responsibilities?

It is when these feelings are evoked that the value of life becomes as urgent or as important in the design of the MCAS software program as the feelings evoked by the pressures of getting the airliner out on time.

Without this emotional moral foundation to start, there was a major disconnection in moral reasoning between the goal of saving lives and the company's actions. There was a failure to actively consider the alignment between the way MCAS affordances, the way they were being implemented, the way it was behaving in the simulator, and the purpose of saving human lives, even though there was someone whose responsibility it was to address safety issues. Had moral reasoning been evoked, the technical pilots may have responded differently to data from the flight simulator. Had their explicit task been to assess this data from the perspective of its moral impact, rather than merely its financial implications, they might have informed Boeing engineers of the danger of MCAS and may not have gamed the FAA agents. Engineers could have made modifications in the design of MCAS or/and produced technical training for pilots to address its inappropriate onset. They could have then retested MCAS in the simulator to see if the problems were addressed. Confirmation of its appropriate behavior would have given Boeing executives and FAA officials assurance of the plane's safety. Even with this assurance, the early results might prompt Boeing's test pilots to monitor impact through pilot reports from the field, once the MAX 8 was released, to assure the soundness of their redesign.

Unfortunately, it seems that this moral reasoning did not take place, perhaps because there was a greater concern among Boeing executives for a production schedule that would contribute more quickly to the bottom line than there was a concern for assuring safety. As a consequence, the ultimate impact was significant harm done to passengers, crew, clients, investors, and to Boeing's bottom line and its reputation for caring about human life and well-being above all else.

The social nature of morality

This reconsideration of the Boeing case highlights the sociocultural nature of moral reasoning. The back-and-forth interaction between principle and situation, according to Sandel, can be an internal dialog, as when we argue through a moral problem with ourselves. Or moral reasoning can be a public endeavor that involves an interlocutor—a friend, a neighbor, a co-worker, a rabbi, fellow citizens.

Extending the sociocultural discussion of Chapter 4, the development of morality evolves from the network of dialogs within and across families, groups, congregations, and communities as they discuss, debate, resolve, and enact moral values in a range of situations. This process is internalized in ways that can be used by individuals and groups to address subsequent moral situations.[33] As such, even individual moral reasoning is fundamentally social in character as it recapitulates the external discussions that preceded it.

Indeed, George Washington University Professor Amitai Etzioni contends that public moral dialog is the basis for shared values and the foundation of community in a democratic society.[34] In important ways, it is through moral dialog, or what Etzioni calls "values-talk," that a community identifies and draws on shared values to resolve moral issues in specific situations and come to better understand the values they share. It is by discussing values in the context of their practical implications that communities come to have a common understanding of happiness, equality, justice, and relationships, and become a moral culture.

Had "values talk" been a feature of the corporate culture at Boeing, perhaps 346 people would still be alive today.

From moral dialog to collective action

For Sandel, moral discussions are not merely philosophical exercises; they are not mere intellectual jousts between sharp-witted academics at the university club over port. They are everyday conversations over things that matter in everyday communities. They are more than discussions of values; they have implications for actions. And for Elinor Ostrom such dialogs have implications for collective action.

Moral actions, much like moral reasoning, are social even if they are individual acts that entail individual moral responsibility. These individual acts are framed by prior discussions with parents, friends, teachers, and priests, and they have impacts on others, sometimes joyous impacts, sometimes devastating ones.

But by *collective action*, Ostrom means more than this. She means a group of people acting together for mutual benefit. These are actions that we observe in everyday life: Teams work together to make a product. Families plan a vacation together. Farmers act to preserve a meadow. And citizens of Baton Rouge create a vibrant social and commercial strip when previously is was populated by abandon buildings.

Of course, not everyone chooses to participate in collective action or does so all of the time. There is an individual, free-rider advantage to those who can benefit when others do the work. However, in her research, Ostrom empirically derived design principles that create conditions under which collective action is more likely to happen.

As discussed in Chapter 4, Ostrom found that common goods from collective action can be maintained when it is clear who is in the group, that is, who can benefit and who must contribute; when the group's rules fit the local situation; when the group has the authority to make the rules; when those affected by the rules participate in making them; when following the rules is monitored; when not following them incurs graduated sanctions; when there are mechanisms to resolve conflicts easily; and when the group's actions fit with the larger system.

Communities that followed these design principles were able to design or maintain common resources that benefitted everyone. While it can be assumed the net impact was to increase happiness and well-being in the community, the community norms that Ostrom focused on were trust, trustworthiness, and reciprocation, norms that are essential to maintain collective action.

But what would it look like if the moral dialog of Sandel and Etzioni was combined with the collective action principles of Ostrom?

Design as a Moral Dialog among Co-Creators

Private moral reasoning and the creations of individual designers or small design teams can play a significant role in improving the world. But the notions of Sandel, Etzioni, and Ostrom suggest a more impactful, transformational approach to design. They suggest that the group can be brought into the design process to create a moral dialog between designers and those affected most by the moral consequences of their designs. In doing so, you—as an everyday designer and group member—not only create designs that improve the situation, but also restructure roles and interaction patterns of the group in a positive way, one that empowers the group and confirms the importance of morality in the design process.

This collaborative approach is particularly important when a group has an ongoing relationship, such as work groups, church congregants, club members, companies, neighbors, or family. And it is also relevant to those who share the same culture, such as the residents of the Nyabiheke Refugee Camp in the Chapter 8 case study, or who share a moral investment in the outcome of the design, such as those involved Black Lives Matter, the case study in Chapter 10.

To engage the group in a moral design dialog, I have three recommendations:

Be grounded in your own moral foundation

First, start with *your* interpretation of moral principles, what they mean to you. Be firmly grounded in them. Be committed to these values in your personal and professional life and purpose. Draw on feelings related to these values to pick the company you work for, to select your design projects, to determine which ones are most important to you and which ones you would turn down. Build these values into the purposes for your design work and draw on your passion to fuel your projects and your perseverance in your work. Use them to reason about the outcomes and impacts of your designs.

If you are a professional, there are ethical standards in your field and these will frame the morals of your professional practice. They are the starting place for your consideration but they typically don't cover all the bases. For instance, there are standards related to the use of ""human subjects" in the Science Tradition and standards regarding product safety in the Technical-Analytic Tradition. These ethical standards set the outside boundaries for the work of professionals; they say what *shouldn't* be done or the minimum that *must* be done. But such standards often don't guide designers in what they should aspire to do or what needs to be done. They don't say what scientific questions you *should* pursue; they don't say what products you *should* create, what buildings *should* be built, and so on. The Chapter 3 moral principles provide a foundation for the shoulds. And moral reasoning supplies the how.

These principles need to be considered deeply from your perspective and from that of others. What, in your mind, is happiness and well-being? How would you feel in someone else's shoes? What harms and injustices do you see in the world? Which disturb you most? What is equality? Where do you see injustice? Who suffers from it most? What knowledge do you have that you can use and share? What kinds of relationships do you feel most strongly about? You will bring these principles to specific situations and your understanding of the principles will guide your designs. At the same time, applying these principles to the specifics of the situation will deepen and refine your understanding of the principles.

The moral grounding of these considerations is important whether you are a professional designer developing a product for a company, a doctor deciding on a treatment for a patient, a lawyer crafting a defense for a client, a teacher designing a lesson plan for students, a parent guiding your children, or a leader or member of a community designing an activity to improve the neighborhood. Deeply understanding your own moral foundation and priorities will guide and energize your work.

Scaffold moral discussions

Second, introduce moral principles into your design discussions. Moral principles that might guide designs are rarely explicitly discussed during the design process, which is probably the very reason why there are so many poor and harmful designs. I argue that they should be discussed.

By beginning your client discussions with moral considerations, you are weaving values into the design process from the very start, increasing the likelihood these values will come to be embedded in the design outcomes and their impacts. Support these discussions by asking questions and engage those affected most by your designs in answering them: What does happiness and well-being mean to them? What harms are they suffering? What inequalities or injustices do they feel? By introducing questions related to happiness, harm, knowledge, agency, equality, justice, and supportive relationships, you are legitimizing moral concerns as an overt part of the design process. You are going beyond surface issues to show your concern for the community at the deepest level. You are supporting the discussion of issues that are important to them but which they may not otherwise think are appropriate for a design discussion, issues they may be reluctant to bring up on their own, and consequently, that may go unexplored. You are treating community as more than just an opportunity to make money. And you are confirming that the ultimate purpose of the design will be to advance moral outcomes and impacts and improve people's lives.

This emphasis on values is clear in the work of Professor Batya Friedman and her colleagues at the University of Washington who have developed a methodology they call Value Sensitive Design.[35] With their approach to designing technological systems, moral values such as human welfare, ownership, privacy, trust, informed consent, calmness, and environmental sustainability are explicitly embedded in the design of the software they use to structure their interaction with clients. Consequently, moral issues are addressed throughout the design process. They have applied their approach to a variety of design projects that range from informed consent mechanisms for the use of cookies in a browser to the development of an urban planning simulation that facilitates decisions of integrated land use, transportation, and environmental impact.

Use these discussions to co-create designs

My third recommendation is that you build on the Human-Centered and Social Movement design traditions and make your design process collaborative. As Ostrom recommends enlist the group in co-creating designs. This is an approach in which designs are collaboratively produced, culturally relevant, socially applicable, and empowering, contrasted with design processes that are imposed on users and products that are owned by outside designers.[36]

This values-centered, collaborative methodology is characteristic of the Scandinavian Participatory Design approach, as described by Judith Gregory, a Professor of Informatics at the University of Oslo.[37] There are three principles to its design practice: a striving for democratization of the design process, explicit inclusion of values in design discussions and imagined futures, and the regarding of conflicts and contradictions as resources in the design process.

The approach democratizes the process by drawing on people's expertise of their day-to-day activities with other people and technologies relevant to the design situation. Relevant stakeholders and communities are given a central position in the process and an authoritative voice in the dialog, much as with the Kuja Kuja project and people of the Nyabiheke Refugee Camp in the Chapter 8 case study. The designer defers to the lived experiences of the community, understanding that solutions cultivated from afar must be subordinate to the beliefs, knowledge, experiences, and perspectives of the people affected most by the issues and problems that emerge from the discussion.

With the explicit inclusion of values in discussions, the moral purposes of the design are embedded in strategies and decisions. This increases the likelihood that the outcome of the process and its impact will address the moral concerns of the group.

The approach uses conflict to acknowledge differences in interests and perspectives of diverse stakeholders as well as contradictions among values to forge a more robust design response to the situation. Morality in its application is typically contested. Even though the principles in Chapter 3 are universal, as the Philosophes claim, it doesn't mean that everyone would agree on their meaning in a specific situation. What happiness is to one person may not be to another or even to the same person in a different situation. Or what happiness is for one may be harm for another. Conflict is an opportunity to gain a deeper understanding of the underlying multiple, complex sources of harm and how it affects people differently, as we will see in the Chapter 14 case study of the City of Austin and reimagining public safety. This deeper understanding of conflicting perspectives can even be the source of radical breakthroughs and design innovation that can be transformative. The Scandinavian approach has been applied to architecture, urban planning, and health information services, among other design situations.

While there are aspects of this the co-design approach that are similar to the Human-Centered Tradition, it differs in important ways. First, while expressions of values may emerge in human-centered design discussions, they are not an explicit focus of the design process and the resulting products, services, or experiences are less likely to embody the values of the group. Second, while group or community participation is important in human-centered design, the designer has a privileged role in the design process; the designer's purpose is at the center of the discussion, not the purpose of the community. Third, in the Human-Centered Tradition, the designer owns the output of the process. The designer's role is typically to harvest information and ideas from the group that can be taken back to the studio or to the client and developed into a product or service that profits designers and their clients. The group may be asked to participate in testing out versions of the design, but in the end, the design firm or its client owns the design. With collaborative co-creation, the community owns the design, shares ownership, or the ownership is negotiated as part of the process. Consequently, this approach changes the interaction patterns within the microsystem, empowers community members to become designers themselves, and creates a macro-culture in which morally grounded design processes are perpetuated and morally center designs are valued.

Case Study: Burning Man and Radical Inclusion

How does such a community of co-creators look in the real world? What does the design process look like?

Burning Man started very modestly in 1986 with two men, Larry Harvey and Jerry James, collecting a group of people on a beach in San Francisco with no particular purpose other than to party among friends. But it has since become an annual convocation of over 70,000 people who come together in the Black Rock Desert of northern Nevada to share art, music, and experience, organized around a set of guiding principles.

Burning Man is now also a formal organization. Its mission is to produce the Burning Man event each year and to "nurture and protect the more permanent community created by its culture."[38] And they believe that "the experience of Burning Man can produce positive spiritual change in the world."

The transition from a modest beginning to an international social event and cultural movement is a compelling story of how community, art, technology, and values can combine to foster change. As such, there are many lenses through which to look at Burning Man—experiential, organizational, technological, cultural—and many elements—the Burn, the art, its international network, Fly Ranch, Burners Without Borders. For the purpose of this chapter, I will look at one particular lens—moral—and one particular element—collaborative design.

Case Study: Burning Man and Radical Inclusion

My playa name is "Wisdom Seeker." I attended "the Burn" in 2012. It was a life-changing experience.

It's hard to describe a Burning Man experience (see Figures 11.2, 11.3, and 11.4) to someone who hasn't been there. But it is even more difficult to describe the Burning Man culture. The one-week Burning Man experience in the Nevada desert is so overwhelming that it is difficult to see the rest of the story, the depth of the culture, the year-round passion and commitment of the people who are at the core of that culture; the paid staff—yes—but more importantly, the thousands of volunteers that add their talent, insight, creativity, and effort to the community.

The culture of Burning Man unfolds like the layers of an onion if you let it. On the sand, or playa, you experience the beautiful art, much of it monumental and interactive; the playful costumes; the crazy mutant vehicles; the pounding music and dancing; the skillful performances; the flashing lights and flames.[39] It all pulls you in, the raw experience. You can luxuriate in it, let it surround you and embrace you.

But you can also reflect: There is a fully planned infrastructure, nearly 2 miles in diameter, spread out in front of you that grew up out of the barren desert over the previous weeks and in another two weeks it will return to the desert without a trace. Its existence is puzzling. No public taxes went toward building the temporary infrastructure. Was this centrally planned or a set of independent actors that showed up in the desert on a particular date?

Figure 11.2 The Man and the crew that built the base (Photo by Vanessa Franking).

Figure 11.3 Burners on the playa at dusk (Photo by Vanessa Franking).

Figure 11.4 Burners and art on the playa at (Photo by Vanessa Franking, sculture by Michael Benisty).

(Continued)

Case Study: Burning Man and Radical Inclusion (Continued)

This is not a commercial event. There are no wages for artists and musicians. The nurses and doctors in the medical tent are volunteers. There are no clothing vendors, no food booths. There is no merchandise, no swag. No one makes a profit.

How does this happen, year after year?

The culture

As I dug deeper into the Burning Man community, went to meetings, met organizers and volunteers, volunteered myself, I began to understand. Burning Man is not just—or even primarily—an event; it is a culture and a social movement. As Burning Man CEO Marian Goodell described it at a TEDx session, "Burning Man is more than an event. It actually is a way of life. And it is a way of looking at yourself in the world. Burning Man changes people. It causes a cultural shift in the way we communicate and the way we relate to each other."[40]

At the center of this culture are the Burning Man Principles. Burning Man didn't start with principles; they evolved organically, captured by co-founder Larry Harvey in 2004.[41] Among the principles are radical self-reliance. You bring your own RV or tent, all your food and water, everything you're going to wear. Another principle is radical self-expression. People dress in costume, adopt a playa name, decorate their living space and bicycle, all to express who they really are and to delight others. Gifting is a major principle. People bring food to share, set up a bar for free drinks, offer performances. Groups of people organize theme camps to provide services, entertainment, art, and other creative interactive experiences for everyone at Burning Man. These could be yoga workshops, dance lessons, or free food or drinks. Some individuals and camps have spent months creating spectacular art that they display on the playa. But no one charges for these delights; no one makes any money; de-commodification is another principle. All of this is a gift to the Burning Man community.

These principles are articulated and practiced during the event. The Burning Man organization does not specify who should bring what or who will do what. They do not book bands or DJs. What happens is created by the people who attend and shaped by the principles of the community. And these principles serve as a way to engage the community in an ongoing, reflective discussion about what Burning Man is and what it means to be a Burner.[42]

Radical inclusion

Radical inclusion is yet another principle. Among the many things I was impressed with when I attended the event was the wide range of people who were there. There were young people and old; males, females, and nonbinary; skilled crafts people, artists, and technicians; New Age hippies and Tech Bros; people from all walks of life.

But in 2020, the racial protests that followed George Floyd's death changed the discourse within the Burning Man community, as it did for many others, and the "radical inclusion" principle came to take on a new, deeper meaning.

This was first expressed as a statement of support for Black Lives Matter and solidarity with the Black community.[43] But in the subsequent months, the response became a reflective, moral dialog on the extent to which the community was an open, welcoming place for People of Color and what could be done to make it more so. While the community and the event were inclusive in many ways, racial inclusion had not explicitly been one of them. For example, in 2020, only 6%

of the 140-person staff was Hispanic; 4%, Asian; and 2%, Black. At the 2019 Burn, only 5% of the attendees were Hispanic; 5%, Asian; 1%, Black; and less than 1%, Native American.[44]

In response to this realization, the organization set up a multiracial Radical Inclusion, Diversity, and Equity (R.I.D.E.) Stewardship.[45] However, R.I.D.E. was created not just as an organizational structure; it is an ongoing community discussion and set of activities to deepen the community's understanding of the racial inclusiveness principle and increase the range of participation of various racial groups in the community.

In October 2020, the organization held a virtual town hall to discuss the value of racial inclusion and actions the community might take to implement this value.[46] Over 500 people joined the call. And 33 Burners shared their experiences and anxieties as Black, Indigenous, or a Person of Color at the Burning Man event.

Take, for example, Ed Fletcher. Fletcher is a filmmaker, journalist, and president of a nonprofit community organization. He is also a Black man. He recalls his anxiety about attending his first Burn in 2008, thinking he wouldn't fit in and would end up going back home in the middle of the week. He ended up staying and has gone regularly ever since and is committed to diversity. As he says, "If we think Burning Man is good medicine for society, then should we want all people to have access to it?"[47]

What came out of the meeting was an increased awareness of the ways that decisions and actions of community members can be unintentionally racist and exclusory; the special vulnerability that People of Color experience during the event, given the armor they create in response to societal racism, that Whites are shielded from; and the need for community action to address the problems.

A wide variety of actions have followed, so far, spearheaded by the R.I.D.E. group.[48] These include: An Anti-Racism Pledge[49]; a training curriculum on inclusiveness for staff and the larger community; a statement of support of Asian Americans and Pacific Islanders[50]; changes made to increase the attendance of People of Color at the event; and outreach to the Native American community, on whose ancestral land the event is held. For example, the organization gives out several hundred free passes to the Paiute tribe adjacent to the Black Rock desert. R.I.D.E. also facilitates regularly scheduled community-wide conversations about racial justice, identity, systemic racism, and restorative justice.

Due to COVID, the Burning Man event was not held in 2020 or 2021. And as of this writing, the 2022 census of attendees has not been completed. So, it is not clear yet what impact these efforts will have on attendance. But the voices of People of Color have already been included in the community discourse.

The distinctiveness of Burning Man as a moral, co-created community experience is best understood when compared to another internationally known festival in the desert, Coachella, which is held annually in Indio, California.[51] Coachella is primarily a music festival, for which bands and DJs are booked by the festival's producers for the event's five stages. Big-name music groups are headliners, and A-list celebrities attend to see and be seen. Costumes are worn but as much to impress as express. It is a huge moneymaker for the producers and local businesses.[52] It is an event, not a community. There are no principles that organize the event. Attendees don't participate in creating the festival; they come to be entertained. At the end of the Coachella event, attendees go home, having had a good time. At the end of Burning Man, many Burners go home changed and live the principles of this community.

There are many aspects of this case that are illustrative and compelling. It illustrates the process of co-creative design through moral dialog. Aside from the city infrastructure provided by the Burning Man organization, nothing would be there—no music, no art—nothing would happen that isn't created by the community, unlike Coachella. And what happens is guided by Burning Man's 10 principles.

Radical inclusion has been a stated value of the community since 2004 and has been actively practiced in their events. However, it took another event, the racial demonstrations of 2020, to push the community to reconsider what this principle *really* means. It was the back-and-forth moral dialog among community members, and with people most impacted by this principle—People of Color—as they applied this principle, leading to a deeper understanding of both the principle and the situation to which it applied. And it led to collective action to address a moral harm.

The case also illustrates some important aspects of Ostrom's design principles, as they apply to collective action problems. Her first principle is defining group boundaries—who will contribute to the group, who will benefit, who belongs. This was the central question at issue in this case and it is a moral issue. It is often easier to solve a collective action problem by limiting the community to a handful of like-minded people. It is much more challenging to solve it in a large, diverse group. But if your mission is to change the world for the better, you will ultimately be faced with the dialog and collective effort that confronted Burning Man: to include people different from you.

As with another of Ostrom's design principle, the Burning Man community included those who would be affected most in their decisions and their planning of collective action. And the community is committed to monitoring the impact and making necessary adjustments.

But most of all, this case study illustrates the purpose and passion a community has to a set of fundamental values. This, among other things, distinguishes Burning Man from other cultural festivals, such as Coachella or Lollapalooza. Their principles and the Burning Man event reflect a joyous commitment to human happiness and well-being. The case study vividly demonstrates the community's commitment to equality and justice. And perhaps most of all, the case study shows Burning Man's value of relationships and community, and the effort needed to build and maintain them. As co-founder Larry Harvey said, "Communities are not produced by sentiment or mere goodwill. They grow out of a shared struggle. Our situation in the desert is an incubator for community."[53] It is moral struggle through dialog and collective action that has made Burning Man what it is and what it will become.

CEO Marian Goodell may not think of herself as a designer. But what she and all the other Burning Man organization everyday designers, past and present, have designed is a community of co-creators that use values and their own passion to make the world a better place.

New Roles for Designers

Creator, maker, and innovator are roles often associated with designers. But if you are going to engage people in the collaborative co-creation of moral designs, there are new roles that are needed, ones that even go beyond those of the human-centered design approach. And these roles require the acquisition of different skills and engagement in different interaction patterns.

Facilitator

As a *facilitator*, the designer works with the group to convene meetings, set agendas, and guide the design process. But it is important that these functions serve the goals of the group, rather than, or at least in addition to, the personal or corporate goals of the designer, and that the designer structures and scaffolds discussions around the group's well-being, knowledge, equality, justice, and relationships.

However, as a facilitator, the designer also collaborates. The designer defers to the values and lived experiences of the group, but at the same time, as a collaborator, the designer draws on their own passion, purpose, values, and adds them to the discussion. While honoring the group's situated expertise, the designer adds her or his own outside knowledge, resources, and expertise, in service to the group or community.

Mentor

In the related role of teacher or mentor, the designer scaffolds the knowledge and skill development of individual group members and the group as a whole. By allowing others to take on and try out some of the designer's roles and by providing encouragement and supportive feedback, the designer scaffolds interactions in a way that members become more able to manage their own design processes. With this leaderful approach, the designer contributes to the group's knowledge and agency, increasing their ability to address problems and design solutions on their own, thus embedding the moral principle of advancing knowledge and agency into the design process.

Mediator

As a mediator, the designer can manage the tensions that are likely to arise during the design process and use them in productive ways, as implemented in the Scandinavian design approach. One type of tension may be between different values or desired end states within the group, which emerge in the discussion as values are applied to the particular situation. Discussing, honoring, and elaborating on differences can deepen people's understanding of each other's goals, purposes, and values. If common understanding can be found, it can sharpen the group's purpose and strengthen the group's bonds. But even if it cannot, the discussion can identify multiple value positions that must be addressed and impact criteria that must be met if the design is to be successful.

Another type of tension may be differences within the group on the design, itself. Within a diverse group, there are likely to be different visions of where the design should go and what it might be like. Conflicts in design solutions can be used as the source of new design ideas, if managed properly. Otherwise, it can spiral into discord and destructive personal attacks. The designer can help the group reason through the logic of aligning design affordances with the specifics of the situation and expected impact to the advantage of one design option or another. Or the designer can propose that early prototypes of multiple designs be tried out with the group to see if advantages can be confirmed or consensus achieved. Or the designer can help to group playoff competing ideas against each other to come up with novel recombinations that lead to innovative, even transformative, breakthroughs.

Broker

While shared moral values are essential social elements of a group or community, they can also create a silo in which the group sees the world in its own narrow way. This supports group cohesion but it can also result in designs that work only in certain situations or only to the benefit of the group and to the determent of others.

The designer can serve an important role by brokering relationships between the group and others who are impacted by the group's actions. Of course, this role needs to be used selectively, where greater moral purposes can be served and more people can benefit from the resulting design. But it will inevitably introduce complexities, and likely, conflict. In which case, skills of the mediator will be needed.

Creating a Collaborative Culture of Moral Design

With new design approaches and new roles, designers can not only create designs that increase happiness, reduce harm, advance knowledge, promote equality, address injustice, and promote relationships, they can also help to create a culture, one which harnesses the passion and purpose of the community and engages them in an ongoing, collective action of design that makes the world better.

We all participate in design in one way or another. It is part of who we are, the way we alter our environment to serve our purposes. If we don't design something ourselves, we participate in its making, we invest in it, we buy it, we use it. Individually and collectively, we create the world we live in. I propose that collectively we can design a better world.

Before concluding this chapter, I want to return to Glenn Parsons's assertion, mentioned in Chapter 1, that designers have no role in dealing with "larger problems."[54] I assert that we, as designers—as people—are always dealing with the larger problems. The question is, do we deal with them in a moral way? Or do we, as Parsons would have it, leave our morals at the door?

I hope I've made the case that in making the larger problems of society the purpose of our designs, we claim our highest moral purpose.

All designs are moral artifacts. And design is not merely a technical process. It is also an emotional, rational, and moral one. It is by harnessing your passion as well as your moral agency as a designer that you will create designs with the purpose of addressing these "larger problems" to make the world a better place. And it is by sharing our purpose, passion, values, and process with others—our design team, our company, our church, our neighborhood, our legislators, our community—that we build a foundation for collective action and create a culture of moral design.

References

1 About us. Enabling the Future [Internet]. [cited 2022, Aug 27]. Available from: http://enablingthefuture.org/about/.
2 Haidt J. The righteous mind. New York: Pantheon Books, 2012.
3 Greene J. Moral tribes: Emotion, reason and the gap between us and them. New York: Penguin Books, 2013.
4 Gintis H, Bowles R, Fehr E. Moral sentiments and material interests: Origins, evidence, and consequences (pp. 3–40). In Gintis, H, Bowles, S, Boyd, R., et al. (editors). Moral sentiments and material interests: The foundation of cooperation in economic life. Cambridge, MA: MIT Press, 2005.
5 Goodenough WH. Moral outrage: Territoriality in human guise. Zygon, 1997, 32(1), 5–27.
6 Salerno J, Peter-Hagene L. The interactive effect of anger and disgust on moral outrage and judgments. Psychological Science, 2013, 10, 2069–2078.

7 van Zomeren M, Spears R, Fischer A, et al. Put your money where you mouth is! Explaining collective action tendencies through group-based anger and group efficacy. Journal of Personality and Social Psychology, 2004, 87(5), 649–664.

8 Prinz J. Sentimentalism and the moral brain (pp. 45–73). In Liao M (editor). Moral brains: The neuroscience of morality. New York: Oxford University Press, 2016.

9 Duckworth A. Grit: The power of passion and perseverance. New York: Scribner, 2016.

10 Rafei L. Family separation, two years after Ms. L. ACLU [Internet]. 2020, Feb 26 [cited 2022, Aug 27]. Available from: https://www.aclu.org/news/immigrants-rights/family-separation-two-years-after-ms-l/.

11 Louis E. Lee Gelernt: Fighting Trump in the courts. Spectrum News NY1 [Internet]. 2019, Feb 6 [cited 2022, Aug 27]. Available from: https://www.ny1.com/nyc/all-boroughs/you-decide-with-errol-louis/2019/02/06/you-decide-with-errol-louis-podcast-lee-gelernt--fighting-trump-in-the-courts-.

12 Ms. L v. ICE—Complaint. ACLU [Internet]. 2018, Feb 26 [cited 2022, Aug 27]. Available from: https://www.aclu.org/legal-document/ms-l-v-ice-complaint.

13 Lovell, J. Can the A.C.L.U. become the N.R.A. for the Left? New York Times [Internet]. 2018, Jull 2 [cited 2022, Aug 27]. Available from: https://www.nytimes.com/2018/07/02/magazine/inside-the-aclus-war-on-trump.html.

14 Sini R. #ElPasochallenge: Boy responds to shooting to help community heal. BBC [Internet]. 2019, Aug 7 [cited 2022, Aug 27]. Available from: https://www.bbc.com/news/world-us-canada-49244249.

15 McLeod L. From bottom lines to higher callings: The new era of purpose-driven boards. Forbes [Internet]. 2020, Aug 20 [cited 2022, Aug 28]. Available from: https://www.forbes.com/sites/lisaearlemcleod/2020/08/20/from-bottom-lines-to-higher-callings-the-new-era-of-purpose-driven-boards/?sh=566dc21b7502.

16 Bartlett C, Ghoshal S. Beyond strategy to purpose. Harvard Business Review [Internet]. 1994, Nov-Dec [cited 2022, Aug 28]. Available from: https://hbr.org/1994/11/beyond-strategy-to-purpose.

17 Quinn R, Thakor A. Creating a purpose-driven organization. Harvard Business Review [Internet]. 2018,Jul-Aug[cited2022,Aug28].Availablefrom:https://hbr.org/2018/07/creating-a-purpose-driven-organization.

18 Americans more loyal and willing to defend purpose-drive brands, according to new research by Cone. Cision PR Newswire [Internet]. [cited 2022, Aug 28]. Available from: https://www.prnewswire.com/news-releases/americans-more-loyal-and-willing-to-defend-purpose-driven-brands-according-to-new-research-by-cone-300656014.html.

19 Why Amazon, Facebook, and AirBnB place purpose first. BBC [Internet]. [cited 2022, Aug 28]. Available from: http://www.bbc.com/storyworks/capital/the-purpose-driven-company/purpose-driven-companies

20 Purpose: Shifting from why to how. MicKinsey [Internet]. 2020, Apr 22 [cited 2022, Aug 28]. Available from: https://www.mckinsey.com/business-functions/organization/our-insights/purpose-shifting-from-why-to-how?cid=other-eml-alt-mcq-mck&hlkid=a42bd855dc6c4257538c464ea86da6&hctky=2772198&hdpid=5229a444-7ece-47a0-98af-49047e307135.

21 Steger M. Meaning in life and wellbeing. In Slade M, Oades L, A. Jarden, A (eds.). Wellbeing, recovery and mental health (pp. 75–86). Cambridge: Cambridge University Press, 2017.

22 Purpose venn diagram. Human Business [Internet]. 2017, Feb 8 [cited 2022, Aug 28]. Available from: http://www.humanbusiness.eu/purpose-venn-diagram/.

23 Personal communication from Sharon Malone.

24 http://www.waltergmeyer.com.

25 Meyer W. [Internet]. [cited 2022, Aug 28]. Available from: https://www.trackinghappiness.com/life-purpose-examples/#8220My_purpose_in_life_is_to_solve_problems_by_changing_the_status_quo822.1
26 Margolin V. Social design: From utopia to the good society (p. 28). In Margolin V, Brillembourg A, Fuad-Luke A, et al. (eds.). Design for the good society. Utrecht: Utrecht Manifesto, 2014.
27 What is the new economy coalition? New Economy [Internet]. [cited 2022, Aug 28]. Available from: https://neweconomy.net/about.
28 A method of co-creating equitable outcomes. Creative Reaction Lab [Internet]. [cited 2022, Aug 28]. Available from: https://www.creativereactionlab.com/our-approach.
29 Richter F. The great resignation. Statista 2022, Jan 11 [cited 2022, Aug 28]. Available from: https://www.statista.com/chart/26186/number-of-people-quitting-their-jobs-in-the-united-states/.
30 Hoff M. Leisure and hospitality workers are quitting their jobs at more than twice the record national average. Business Insider [Internet]. 2021, Nov 13 [cited 2022, Aug 28]. Available from: https://www.businessinsider.in/policy/economy/news/leisure-and-hospitality-workers-are-quitting-their-jobs-at-more-than-twice-the-record-national-average/articleshow/87675555.cms.
31 Sandel M. Justice (p. 21). New York: Farrar, Straus and Giroux, 2009.
32 Verbeek P-P. Morality in design: Design ethics and the morality of technological artifacts (p. 100). In Vermaas P, Kroes p, Light A, et al. (eds.), Philosophy and design: From engineering to architecture. New York: Springer, 2008.
33 Tappan M. Mediated moralities: Sociocultural approaches to moral development. In Killlen M, Smetana J (editors). Handbook of moral development (pp. 351–374). New York: Taylor & Francis, 2005.
34 Etzioni A. (2000). Moral dialogues in public debates. Public Perspective, March/April, 27–30.
35 Friedman B, Hendry D. Value sensitive design: Shaping technology with moral imagination. Cambridge, MA: MIT Press, 2019.
36 Janzer C, Weinstein L. (2014) Social design and neocolonialism, Design and Culture, 6(3), 327–343.
37 Gregory J. Scandinavian approaches to participatory design. International Journal of Engineering Education, 2003, 19(1), 62–74.
38 What is Burning Man? Our Mission. Burning Man [Internet]. [cited 2022, Aug 28]. Available from: https://burningman.org/about/our-mission/.
39 What is Burning Man Like? Burning Man 2019. YouTube [web streaming video]. 2019, Sep 6. [cited 2022, Aug 28]. Available from: https://www.youtube.com/watch?v=C5zKA66H5Rw.
40 Burning Man: Marian Goodell and TEDxTokyo 2014. YouTube [web streaming video]. 2014, May 30 [cited 2022, Aug 28]. Available from: https://youtu.be/OofYn1asJ0Y.
41 What is Burning Man? The 10 Principles. Burning Man [Internet]. [cited 2022, Aug 28]. Available from: https://burningman.org/culture/philosophical-center/10-principles/.
42 Posts about the Ten Principles. Burning Man [Internet]. [cited 2022, Aug 28]. Available from: https://journal.burningman.org/category/philosophical-center/tenprinciples/.
43 Burning Man 2020. Jack Rabbit Speaks [Internet]. 2020, Jun 9 [cited 2022, Aug 28]. Available from: https://jackrabbit.burningman.org/t/ViewEmailArchive/t/6E079E0463679F112540EF23F30FEDED/C67FD2F38AC4859C/.
44 Sociodemographic characteristics. Black Rock City Census [Internet]. [cited 2022, Aug 28]. Available from: http://blackrockcitycensus.org/sociodemo.html#ethnicity.
45 Staff data. Burning Man [Internet]. [cited 2022, Aug 28]. Available from: https://burningman.org/about/about-us/diversity-radical-inclusion/#reference-materials.

46 Tan B. 2020 Diversity + Radical Inclusion Town Hall: What we heard and what we're doing. Burning Man Journal [Internet]. 2021, Feb 26 [cited 2022, Aug 28]. Available from: https://journal.burningman.org/2021/02/philosophical-center/tenprinciples/ride-town-hall/.

47 Debucquoy-Dodley D. Diversity & radical inclusion: Ed Fletcher and the good medicine of Burning Man. Burning Man Journal [Internet]. 2020, Feb 13 [cited 2022, Aug 28]. Available from: https://journal.burningman.org/2020/02/opinion/serious-stuff/diversity-radical-inclusion-ed-fletcher/.

48 What we've done and what we're doing. Burning Man [Internet]. [cited 2022, Aug 28]. Available from: https://burningman.org/about/about-us/diversity-radical-inclusion/.

49 Burning Man Project. Burning Man Project's Radical Inclusion, Diversity, & Equity (R.I.D.E.) anti-racism. Medium [Internet]. 2021, Aug 17 [cited 2022, Aug 28]. Available from: https://medium.com/beyond-burning-man/burning-man-projects-radical-inclusion-diversity-equity-r-i-d-e-anti-racism-pledge-16415254f9fa.

50 Burning Man Project stands in solidarity with Asian, Asian American, and Pacific Islander communities in the fight for racial justice. Instagram [Internet]. [cited 2022, Aug 28]. Available from: https://www.instagram.com/p/CN5hv9arwS2/.

51 Booth J. What is Coachella? We won't tell anyone you asked. Hello Giggles [Internet]. 2019, Apr 15 [cited 2022, Aug 28]. Available from: https://hellogiggles.com/news/what-is-coachella/.

52 Gonzalez C. Coachella 2022: Festival return leaving local businesses dancing. Fox 11 Los Angeles [Internet]. 2022, Apr 15 [cited 2022, Aug 28]. Available from: https://www.foxla.com/news/coachella-2022-festivals-return-leaving-local-businesses-dancing.

53 Tan B. 2020 Diversity + radical inclusion town hall: What we heard and what we're doing. Burning Man Journal [Internet]. 2021, Feb 26 [cited 2022, Aug 28]. Available from: https://journal.burningman.org/2021/02/philosophical-center/tenprinciples/ride-town-hall/.

54 Parsons G. The Philosophy of Design. New York: Wiley, 2016.

12

Reduce Harm and Increase Happiness

Human happiness and moral duty are inseparably connected.

George Washington
Founding Father
First U.S. President

Values

With our passion and purpose to make the world a better place, I offer seven moral principles in Chapter 3 that are the values that can guide our designs in getting us there.

But what do these values really mean? What is happiness? What is knowledge and agency? What is equality and justice? And why are relationships important in design? But perhaps the most important question for designers is the practical one: How do we use these values to guide our designs?

The Enlightenment Philosophers believed these values are universal and based on experiences common to all humans. But they are also situated. The terms are abstract enough that everyone can agree on their value. However, the meaning of these values becomes tangible only when they address the needs and concerns of particular people in a particular situation and at a particular time and place. In this and the following three chapters that make up the remainder of Part III of this book, I want to drill down into these values and give you some things to think about when considering what they mean to you and how they can be applied to your designs.

Cause No Harm

If we're going to make the world a better place, we must first not make it worse, and doing no harm is the first moral principle in Chapter 3. It seems that doing no harm would be a straight-forward proposition. When you think of the most harmful people in the world or the organizations doing the most harmful things, you think of dictators who oppress their people, generals with genocidal tendencies, radical religious leaders and their terrorist followers, mob bosses and their illegal enterprises, or state-sponsored and lone-wolf hackers who destroy network systems or hold them for ransom. The U.S. government, Johnson & Johnson, Facebook, or Boeing probably wouldn't come to mind.

It would be easy to avoid harm if it simply meant not getting involved with dictators, drug cartels, or terrorist organizations. But many people doing great harm are not genocidal generals, mobsters,

Make the World a Better Place: Design with Passion, Purpose, and Values, First Edition. Robert B. Kozma.

or hackers, and their organizations are not illegal. They are companies you could work for or organizations you could join without getting arrested; yet they do great harm to their customers, employees, other businesses, the environment, or society in general.[1,2,3,4] They are companies that make products and sell them in the open market, but in the process, pollute our environment, heat the planet, or create mountains of waste. Or their products are unsafe, addictive, don't work as advertised, or degrade public discourse. Or they are organizations or websites that spew racist tropes or spread malicious conspiracy theories that destroy trust. Or they are companies that sell services or products to dictators, war lords, or drug cartels. Or they buy out and destroy competitors, eliminate jobs, pay their employees as little as possible, run operations in a way that threatens the health and safety of their employees, offshore their work to companies that abuse their workers, or offload corporate expenses and risk to gig workers, all to maximize their profits.

Harm comes when companies and individuals don't think first and foremost about the harm that could come from their decisions. Had Boeing made harm avoidance a priority, the 737 MAX 8 disaster likely wouldn't have happened. Had Insys been more concerned about harmful addictions than profit, more people would be alive and healthy today. Had Immigration and Customs Enforcement agents thought of this principle, Ms. L. wouldn't have been separated from her daughter while her application was being processed.

Athena Herrmann, Head of Design at Toronto-based design house Architech, recommends five ways to ensure you do no harm: 1) Make a conscious choice to do no harm. 2) Understand the motives and goals behind a client's strategy so you can suggest other ways of achieving it if it looks like harm might be done with the strategy they propose. 3) Understand the ultimate users of the design so that you can anticipate how the design might impact them. 4) Remember that you are responsible for the impact of what you create. 5) Test the impact to be sure there is no harm.[5]

Organizations and their leaders who create harm are able to do so because a vast array of people they employ—designers, managers, salespeople, assemblers, secretaries, software developers—and their investors and customers are ignorant of or chose to ignore the harmful impacts of the organization's practices. To avoid doing harm, it is important to not be one of those designers, investors, employees, or customers. Landing a lucrative design contract, getting a great return on your investment, buying products at a lower cost, or getting an impressive salary may increase your own comfort or wealth, but it may harm employees, customers, the environment, or society as a whole. Be aware of the impact of an organization's practices. If you follow our first principle, do not participate in harmful ones.

Take, for example, Jeffrey Wigand. Wigand is a biochemist and former vice president of research and development at Brown & Williamson, a tobacco company. With leading brands like Kool and Viceroy, Brown & Williamson was selling more than 90 billion cigarettes annually in 1994.[6] At that time, over 2 million annual deaths in the United States were attributed to tobacco-related cardiovascular and respiratory disease, according to the Centers for Disease Control.[7] Cigarette smokers are exposed to a toxic mix of over 7,000 chemicals when they inhale cigarette smoke.[8] The harmful chemicals in cigarette smoke can damage nearly every organ in the body. Cigarettes, or more accurately the nicotine in them, are highly addictive. In 1996, Wigand appeared on the CBS news program "60 Minutes" and stated that Brown & Williamson had intentionally manipulated its tobacco blend with chemicals such as ammonia to increase the effect of nicotine in cigarette smoke.[9] Brown & Williamson hired investigators to discredit Wigand, but its efforts backfired when the claims were examined. After leaving Brown & Williamson, Wigand became a high school physics teacher and was named Teacher of the Year for the state of Kentucky. Wigand's story was dramatized in the 1999 movie *Insider*, starring Russel Crowe.

Brown & Williamson was established in 1894. It no longer exists.

Reduce Harm

Beyond doing no harm, there is so much harm that has already been done in the world and there is much you can do as a designer to alleviate it. As documented in Chapter 1, there are people suffering severe harm from poverty; hunger; drug addiction; racism; depression; sickness; mental illness; job loss; and lack of access to clean water, housing, and safe environments, particularly during a pandemic. If you see this harm in the world, do something about it. As John Lewis said in the quote that began Chapter 1, "If you see something that is not right, not fair, not just, you have a moral obligation to do something about it."

Politicians, lawyers, healthcare workers, pharmacologists, engineers, teachers, and community organizers can play a particularly important role in this regard. However, their efforts are often underfunded and they are overwhelmed by forces working in the opposite direction. Many more resources could and must be brought to bear if these harms are to be eliminated. We, as tax payers, could do more. And those of us working in the Scientific, Technical, Human-Centered, Aesthetic, and Community Organization and Social Movement Traditions can do more. We can make harm-reduction the purpose of our efforts.

Take, for example, the Americans with Disability Act (ADA). As of 2019, there were 41 million people in the United States, or 12.7% of the population, who had a disability.[10] These disabilities range broadly from 20.8 million with an ambulatory disability to 15.8 million with a cognitive disability to 11.5 million with a hearing disability, and to 7.4 million with a vision disability. The disabilities of over 15 million people make it difficult or impossible for them to live independently. These disabilities may result from diseases, genetic disorders, or accidents, and accidents may occur at home, in a vehicle, in the workplace, or in combat. The disabilities people bring with them to situations have a profound impact on a person's life, restricting their education, employment, mobility, and general quality of life. Consequently, of people with disabilities between the ages of 18 and 64 in the United States, 26% live in poverty. This compares with 11.4% of people in the same age group without a disability.

Patrisha Wright of the Disability Rights and Education Defense Fund, along with Justin Dart Jr. of the American Association of People with Disabilities and others, grew a grassroots effort during the 1980s, proposing an Americans with Disabilities Act (ADA). The ADA was passed by Congress in 1990, to address some of the harm experienced by those with disabilities. Among the provisions in the act are requirements that all public entities (such as national, state, and local government agencies, public schools, etc.) and public accommodations and commercial facilities provide equal access to their services for people with disabilities.[11] This resulted in the widespread installation of ramps, curb cuts, and elevators for those with mobility disabilities. The ADA also mandated the use of assistive technologies, what in Chapter 5 I called embedded technologies, by public entities, accommodations, and commercial facilities to allow those with disabilities to participate fully in society. In 2010, technical design standards were issued to give detail to these requirements.[12]

This legislation set a framework that shaped the local laws and services that addressed the harm experienced by those with disabilities. Two research and policy institutes were established with funds from ADA to further develop policies and technologies that would advance this cause: The Center for Inclusive Design and Environmental Access at the University at Buffalo's School of Architecture and Planning and The Center for Universal Design at North Carolina State University's College of Design. Many graduate courses and degree programs have since been designed in colleges and universities to teach the ideas and techniques of what came to be called Universal Design[13] or Inclusive Design.[14] Hundreds of state and local government programs and services were established to assist the disabled and those serving them.

The ADA also created a market for products and services used by the disabled and those that serve them. Since the passage of ADA, there have been thousands of products designed for the wide range of disabilities that people suffer.[15] Among these products are computer-enabled, sip-and-puff- or eye-movement-controlled wheel chairs and other adaptive devices that allow a range of functions for those with severe, multiple disabilities. Other products are home and vehicle modifications, communication devices for the blind or deaf, and smart phone apps that help the hearing impaired, sight-impaired, or those with cognitive disabilities. The affordances designed into these technologies allow people with disabilities to participate more fully in the economy and social community.

The social movement and resulting ADA legislation, as well as the funding, programs, services, and technologies it provided, serve as a model for how other harms, such as poverty, hunger, unemployment, and drug addiction might be addressed. But beyond the systemic structures that enable such programs, it is the design efforts of local individuals and groups, such as those of Chef Andrés, Ivan Owen, Patrisha Wright, and Justin Dart that are so important.

Case Study: WestGate Water

It may surprise you to know that 60% of the human body is water.[16] Generally, an adult needs 3 quarts of water each day.

Fortunately, 72% of the surface of the world is water.[17] Unfortunately, 97% of Earth's water is in the oceans and only 3% is drinkable fresh water; however, most of that is locked up in glaciers or polar ice caps. Or it is too polluted to drink. Only .5% of Earth's water is available for drinking. And it is even more unfortunate that even that small percentage of water is not evenly distributed around the world.

In fact, some 1.1 billion of the world's 7.9 billion people do not have access to fresh water and 2.7 billion lack it for at least some months of the year.[18] In fact, according to the World Economic Forum (WEF), water insecurity is one of the world's major problems with potentially the biggest harmful impacts.[19]

But a church in San Jose, California, designed a novel way to reduce that harm.

Case Study: WestGate Water

WestGate Church is a nondenominational Christian church of about 3,500 congregants spread across three campuses in the greater San Jose area (https://www.westgatechurch.org). In describing itself, the website states: "We're trying out hardest to understand what it looks like for us to become fully devoted followers of Jesus Christ. We want to love and live like Jesus. And we want to do this together in community."

Calvin Breed is one of those congregants. For 18 years, Calvin worked at the California Water Service Company, a public utility. His job was to make sure the city's water was clean.

In 2012, Breed was part of a volunteer team working with the organization Living Water International (https://water.cc) that drilled a well in a Guatemalan rural village with no access to fresh water. The mission of Living Water is to mobilize churches and communities to cultivate sustainable water, sanitation, and hygiene programs around the world, as a witness to the gospel of Jesus Christ.

While working in the village, Breed met a young boy named Milton. Milton was about 8 years old and sick due to dehydration. His sister, Breed learned, had died from complications when she drank contaminated water. That's when he realized that not only were they providing clean water to the community but they were saving lives.

This so moved Breed that he asked, what more can I do? What can we do?

His answer was to share his experience and passion with others at WestGate, and in 2013, they started *WestGate Water.*[20]

They started by asking the entire church community to bring in their bottles and cans for recycling. People collected them from their home, their office, and their neighbors. And teams of volunteers trained by Breed collected, sorted, crushed, and redeemed these bottles and cans for money (see Figure 12.1). They used the money to build clean water projects across the globe.

They called people young and old, rich and poor, Christian and non-Christian. They recruited individuals, families, groups, elementary school kids, and high school students (including my grandkids) to serve. In serving, they donated their recyclables, they gave their time, they gave their money, and in serving, they saved lives.

Very often it was Breed himself, wearing his gloves and his ball cap, crushing and sorting.

On occasion, people even volunteered to travel to foreign countries to work on the water projects.

And they did this every week for eight years.

Figure 12.1 WestGate congregants collecting recyclables (*Source:* WestGate Church).

(Continued)

Case Study: WestGate Water (Continued)

Since Calvin's return from Guatemala, thanks to his advocacy and that of other people, WestGate Church has raised more than $2.6 million and built 362 wells that provide clean water to more than 224,000 people (see Figure 12.2).

Figure 12.2 Villagers with a new well (*Source:* WestGate Church).

During the past couple years, COVID made things difficult. The church didn't have its normal in-person weekly services, so it adapted to monthly drop-off times. It couldn't have volunteers gather, so the church staff crushed and sorted. And through all that, they were still able to raise more than $33,000 for wells in 2020. In 2021, the project collected 56 tons of plastic and more than 20 tons of aluminum, raising more than $350,000 for 70 clean water projects in 17 countries.

In addition to their recycling program through WestGate Water, the church also raised money for other water projects through a special offering during Christmas. In 2021, the church raised nearly $700,000 with the offering.

Breed was asked to reflect on his work. He thought of Milton and it reminded him that it isn't just about raising money. Access to clean water is a life-or-death situation. "I think of Milton and the impact it had on his life," he mused, "And we can impact other lives. And that's the reason I do what I do."[21]

This case study illustrates how designs can reduce harm and make the world a better place. In their design, everyday designers Calvin Breed and his WestGate friends combined their passion, purpose, and values: they believe all lives have value and it is important to serve. In serving, they not only dug wells and saved lives, they built relationships and they built community in San Jose. This community strengthened communities around the world.

Increase Happiness

Happiness, or well-being, is the greatest good according to Aristotle and the Philosophes. And the pursuit of it is claimed as an unalienable right in the U.S. Declaration of Independence. Yet many people in the United States are unhappy, even depressed. In 2020, the year of COVID, job loss, stay-at-home isolation, and racial unrest, only 14% of Americans reported they are very happy, the lowest figure in nearly 50 years according to a poll by the University of Chicago.[22] At the same time, 23% reported that they are not happy. You might think that it is only the poor, uneducated, and unemployed that are unhappy. But according to federal health statistics, about 13% of Americans have taken antidepressants in the last 30 days, with the highest rate among women, Whites, and college-educated people.[23] This goes beyond COVID, as it has been an upward trend over the last 18 years.

Much can be done by designers to increase happiness. But before we think about what that might be, we need to think more deeply about what we mean by the term.

What is *happiness* and how it can be influenced? For some, happiness is a promotion or raise. For others, it's a game winning strikeout. Yet others find happiness hanging out with friends, curling up with a page-turner, or cuddling with a loved partner. However, as different as these all are, they all generate feelings that we call happiness.

Philosophers and psychologists have thought about happiness in two different ways. For Utilitarian philosopher Jeremy Bentham, happiness is pleasure, "What happiness consists of, we have already seen: enjoyment of pleasures, security from pains."[24] Sometimes called *hedonic happiness*, it is a sensation, an immediate emotional experience—one is happy right now. On the other hand, Aristotle thought of it as a condition of one's life—one is leading a happy life. While pleasure is an important part of life, Aristotle asserted that it is subordinate to overall happiness or well-being, what he called *eudemonic happiness*.

Psychologists have conducted research on both meanings, as have neuroscientists. It turns out there is a lot of overlap between them, although they operate in different ways, even in our brain. For example, hedonic happiness is associated with a chemical in the brain called dopamine, which is released in the primitive, subcortex and portions of the higher-level, frontal cortex. Dopamine generates feelings of pleasure related to sexual orgasms, drugs, chocolate, and music (and video games).[25] It's quite addictive and it played an important evolutionary role in keeping us alive and procreating. On the other hand, well-being, social bonding, trust, and emotional support are associated with the release of the chemical oxytocin. This chemical supports our social connectedness and also played an important evolutionary survival factor in advancing the group.

Happiness as pleasure

To examine happiness in the moment, there have been many research studies that question participants during their everyday lives at randomly selected moments via a pager questionnaire or an app. They are asked what they are doing and where they are. Then they are asked to make a subjective assessment of their happiness.[26] Across studies, it was found that happiness at the moment was positively associated with being with other people, being in nature, or being engaged in physical activity. Working was negatively associated with happiness, although that relationship was moderated by work environment, including working with others. School activities are rated low, although participants who are involved in social activities at school are happier.[27]

Studies have also looked at the intensity of happy feelings—are they merely pleasant experiences or profound ones, bordering on ecstasy? In his book *Flow*, psychologist Mihaly Csikszentmihalyi talks about the times when, on occasion, we have a focused engagement in what we are doing; we lose a sense of time and place and we feel happy, content, or a sense of exhilaration, a deep sense of enjoyment that becomes a landmark in memory and what we think life should be like.[28] This is what Csikszentmihalyi means by *optimal experience* and what he calls *flow*. His research was initially done with experts—artists, athletes, musicians, chess masters, and surgeons—to understand their peak experiences. But the patterns he found with them were replicated with everyday people in cultures around the world.

What Csikszentmihalyi found was that optimal experience, whether it was while playing the piano or cuddled up reading a book, was composed of two things: challenge and skill. But challenge and skill don't have to be physical. Challenge can be an activity that requires great concentration, such as the attention required to follow a compelling plot twister, and skill can be cognitive, such as those involved in solving complex puzzles. Csikszentmihalyi found that during these moments of flow, participants felt in control of their actions, masters of their own fate; they felt a sense of agency. Csikszentmihalyi claims that, in the long view, many such optimal experiences add up to a sense of a happy life. So, it turns out that even momentary happiness often has a deeper meaning associated with more enduring feelings of happiness and well-being that people strive for.

Perhaps this momentary sensation is what Miró meant when he said, "A simple line painted with a brush can lead to freedom and happiness." And perhaps this was the emerged sense of happiness van Gogh was searching for in his painting when he said, "In my view I'm often very rich, not in money, but rich (although not every day exactly) because I've found my work—have something which I live for heart and soul and which gives inspiration and meaning to life."

Happiness as well-being

Aristotle's term of *eudemonia* can be translated from Greek as "happiness," "flourishing," or "well-being." In his 1998 Presidential Address to the American Psychological Association, University of Pennsylvania Professor Martin Seligman challenged the field of psychology to shift from its traditional, narrow focus on pathology and treating mental illness and social disorders. He advocated for a new emphasis on *positive psychology* that documents actions that lead to well-being and promote positive individuals, flourishing communities, and a just society.[29]

This redirection not only has important implications for the field of psychology, but also for design. While research on pathology and mental illness focused on where we don't want to be, positive psychology focuses on where we want to be and on how to get there. It helps us understand happiness and well-being and the conditions that foster them. This understanding is crucial to design.

In his book *Flourish: A Visionary New Understanding of Happiness and Well-Being*, Seligman takes up his own challenge. He develops a theory of happiness with the acronym PERMA.[30] The theory is comprised of five elements that create the foundation of a flourishing life: Positive emotions, Engagement, Relationships, Meaning, and Accomplishments. Each of these elements has three properties: it contributes to well-being; people pursue it for its own sake, not just to attain the other elements; and each is measured and defined independently from the other elements. The movement of positive psychology inspired a large body of research and clinical practice to promote long-term, eudaimonic happiness. Much of the research I draw on in this book comes from this new tradition.

But what does a happy life look like in the everyday world?

In popular culture, a happy life is often associated with physical attractiveness, having a lot of money, professional success, fame, or social status and its associated symbols, all of which are linked to happiness in advertisements for products and services. But positive psychology research results run contrary to many of these common beliefs.

For example, while physical attractiveness has proven, over numerous studies, to be an important factor in selecting a mate, a series of recent studies by Harvard Professor Christine Ma-Kellams and her colleagues found that a high degree of physical attractiveness did not correspond to long-term marital happiness.[31] In one study, senior high school yearbook photos from the late 1970s were rated for their physical attractiveness and then researchers examined the subsequent life experiences of these students. Those rated higher on physical attractiveness were more likely to have been married for a shorter period of time and more likely to be divorced 35 years later. Another of their studies replicated these findings with high-profile actors and celebrities. Those rated higher on attractiveness (holding age and net worth constant) were more likely to be divorced and more likely to have shorter first marriages.

Similarly, studies of money and happiness show only a limited association between the two. The lack of money—poverty—is clearly a source of unhappiness. Research has shown that less income is associated with more sadness and more income associated with less sadness.[32] However, there is not a direct relationship between having more money and being happier. Studies have found that additional income increases happiness up to a certain amount (about $75,000 in one U.S. study[33]; about €28,000 in a European study[34]). But beyond some middle level of income, having more money has little effect on happiness. Indeed, an examination of 175 studies finds that there is a negative relationship between materialism and personal well-being.[35] Across these studies, people who focus on the importance of acquiring money and possessions are less satisfied with life and less happy.

Being rich also seems to have a negative effect on social behavior. In a series of naturalistic and experimental studies by University of California psychology professor Paul Piff and his colleagues found that wealthier people, relative to lower-income individuals, were more likely to break the law while driving, display unethical decision-making tendencies, take valued goods from others, lie in a negotiation, cheat to increase their chances of winning a prize, endorse unethical behavior at work, and have a more-favorable attitude toward greed.[36] On the other hand, relatively poor individuals proved to be more generous, charitable, trusting, and helpful compared with their upper-income counterparts, perhaps because poorer individuals orient to the welfare of others as a means to adapt to their more hostile environments and this orientation gives rise to greater prosocial behavior.[37]

In fact, giving money away seems to increase happiness. In an experimental study, one group of participants was given money and asked to spend it on themselves; another group was asked to spend it on someone else.[38] The group that spent it on someone else was happier than those who spent it on themselves. Along this line, in a study in Japan, researchers asked one group of participants to record their acts of kindness for a week.[39] The control group did not keep track of their kindness activities. The two groups scored the same on happiness at the beginning of the week. But the happiness score for those that kept track of their acts of kindness was higher at the end of the week than the scores for those that did not keep track.

As mentioned in the last chapter, life meaning or purpose is associated with less suffering and greater well-being, both psychologically and physically.[40] People who have purpose in their lives are psychologically and physically healthier and have closer relationships, family connections, and marital satisfaction. They are happier and more satisfied with their lives.

A long-term study at Harvard University suggests that one of the most important predictors of whether you live a long, happy life is not fame or the amount of money you amass.[41] A much better predictor of long-term health and well-being is the strength of your relationships. The Harvard Study of Adult Development has tracked and examined the lives of more than 700 men in two groups over 75 years. One group was a sample of Harvard students, at the time, and the other was a group of young men from some of Boston's poorest neighborhoods. Over the decades, the Harvard men have gone into all walks of life. Some became lawyers, doctors, and businessmen. Some became alcoholics, had disappointing careers, or descended into mental illness. Looking at factors across the decades, the researchers found that people were protected against chronic disease, mental illness, and memory decline when they were in strong relationships with others, especially spouses—even if those relationships had many ups and downs. The study concluded that close relationships, more than money or fame, kept people happy throughout their lives. Of course, correlation is not necessarily causation. But by following subjects for many decades and comparing the state of their health and their relationships early on, these Harvard researchers are fairly confident that strong social bonds play a causal role in long-term health and well-being.

Designs that connect people to others and to nature are more likely to increase happiness. Ads designed to associate a product with wealth or attractiveness may sell more products, but those products are less likely to result in more happiness.

Happy cultures

In 1998, Bhutan's prime minister introduced the idea of Gross National Happiness to the United Nations as an alternative development measure to GDP, economic Gross Domestic Product.[42] The speech launched conferences and spawned a global industry in happiness. In 2022, the Sustainable Development Solutions Network at Columbia University issued its 10th *World Happiness Report*, which examines well-being around the world and the role that society and culture play in supporting it.[43] The report examines data from more than 146 countries, much of it collected by the *Gallup World Poll*.[44] Interestingly enough, the 2021 report, which focused on the impact of the COVID pandemic, found that there was relatively little change in the overall status of happiness, suggesting that there is a resilient quality about happiness that can carry people through difficult times.[45]

The report ranks countries on a compound measure of happiness that includes two national measures (per capita GDP and national life expectancy at birth) and national averages of individual participants' responses to questions related to support of family or friends, freedom to choose what to do with one's life, personal generosity, perceptions of corruption in government and business, and the experience of positive feelings and negative feelings during the previous day. An interesting finding is that all five of the Nordic countries ranked in the top 10, with Finland and Denmark the top 2. The United States ranked 16th out of the 146 countries.

Beyond the national rankings, the report explored the factors that seem to account for personal and national happiness, and more specifically, the reasons behind the uniformly high happiness ratings among Nordic countries. The researchers found that environment matters. City dwellers in poorer countries are happier, most likely because of increased opportunities. On the other hand, the relationship is opposite in richer countries; city dwellers are less happy, perhaps because of high levels of stress. They found a negative relationship between happiness and air pollution. And, in a special side study of London residents, they found that a respondent's mood at the moment was positively affected by being in parks or near rivers, by being outdoors instead of indoors, and it was negatively affected by being at work, although all of these factors were positively influenced by being with someone else at the time.

But the key finding of the report is that measures of having someone to count on, having a sense of freedom to make key life decisions, generosity, and trust in government and business account for a disproportionate amount of a country's overall happiness ranking. Parallel to the findings in the Harvard study, high scores on these measures moderate inequalities, such as lower income and poorer health. Nordic countries consistently scored high on all these measures. The researchers concluded that if all European countries had the same average levels of social connections, social trust, and trust in institutions as are found in the Nordic countries they would score 8% higher on overall happiness.

The emphasis on social environment in Nordic cultures is illustrated by the concept of *hygge* (pronounced "hoo-ga").[46] It's a Danish word without a precise translation to English and it's an important part of the Danish culture. Hygge is about creating a cozy environment: candles, a blazing fire, warm blankets and fuzzy slippers, comfortable pants (*hyggebukser*), and woolen socks (*hyggesokker*). But hygge is not a solitary experience. Danes plan *hyggelig* evenings of cooking together or playing board games. It's possible to have hygge while curled up on a snowy evening watching TV, but it's so much better if it's part of a casual gathering.

Japan has a similar concept in their culture: *ikigai*. Translated literally, *ikigai* is two kanji characters that stand for "life" and "value," but roughly translated it means "the value of life" or "happiness."[47] However, there is a difference between *shiawase*, the common Japanese word for happiness, and *ikigai* in that *ikigai* carries with it the idea of moving toward the future. *Ikigai* is the process of finding the joy in everyday life that the Japanese believe will result in a fulfilling life as a whole; it's seeing the value in the present moment as a pathway toward that future. *Ikigai* can be as simple as the reason to get up in the morning, accompanied by a ritual tea ceremony. Or it can be a grand purpose, such as aiming to cure cancer, which is the grit, to draw on Professor Duckworth's term, that motivates years of study and research.

In 2017, the First Minister of Scotland Nicola Sturgeon gave a TED talk in which she described the unique policy goals of Scotland, Iceland, and New Zealand, a network of countries called the Well-being Economy Governments, which she referred to in a humorous way as the "SIN countries."[48] The title of her talk was "Why Governments Should Prioritize Well-Being." Motivated by the ideas of the Enlightenment, to which Scottish philosophers made important contributions, she described the efforts of these three countries to create a vision of society that has well-being, not just wealth, at its very heart, and to establish policies and measurements that support this vision.

At the macro level, governments can do things to increase a country's happiness, at a minimum, by keep institutions uncorrupt and trustworthy, but happiness also relates to healthcare and quality education, and aesthetically pleasing public spaces.[49] But it seems interpersonal connections account more for happiness, the sense that I not only care about my happiness but yours as well.

Government policies and programs are often shaped by measures of economic growth. New laws are framed as "job creators" or "inflation busters" when GDP is the primary measure of impact. But if Gross National Happiness was a measure, other government designs would have priority, those that emphasized supportive relationships and communities, quality education, and a healthy, happy life. Maybe if these were the programs governments emphasized, we would not only be happier, we would have more trust in government institutions.

Designing for Happiness

How can we use what we've learned here to create designs that advance happiness?

There are tons of self-help books on how to make yourself happy, such as Paul Dolan's book, *Happiness by Design: Change What You Do, Not How You Think*,[50] or Tal Ben-Shahar's book *Happier: Learn the Secrets to Daily Joy and Lasting Fulfillment*.[51] In our culture, it is often seen that we are responsible for our own happiness or misery.

Of course, taking charge of your own happiness is an important source of agency. However, when it comes to design, we think about how *we* can make *other people* happier. We are concerned with how the products, services, environments, experiences, and social communities we build influence people's happiness. But often this goal gets warped in translation. Sometimes when companies think about how to make their customers happier they are actually thinking about things they should do to avoid making customers unhappy, like listening to customers when they speak, treating customers as individuals, or keeping promises.[52] This is important, of course, but it's not the same thing.

Other companies start with a great idea for a new product or service, and then rely on their advertising agency to convince consumers that it will make them happy.[53] Indeed, this is the principle purpose of marketing. But happiness is more likely to happen if designs start with the purpose of increasing happiness rather than selling products.

For example, engaging people in happy moments is the goal Austrian graphic designer Stefan Sagmeister. He created an installation at the Philadelphia Institute of Contemporary Arts in 2012 entitled *The Happy Show.*[54] With this installation, Sagmeister invited the visitor to vicariously participate in his 10-year exploration of his own happiness with an entire floor of visual and tactile experiences. Through graphic exhibits, multimedia displays, and playful interactive stations, Sagmeister engaged visitors in experiencing happy moments and thinking about what happiness means and about their own happiness. By peddling a stationary bike, visitors would see a series of neon light displays that remind them of the need to engage in purposeful activity to increase their sense of satisfaction. Or visitors were encouraged to take a gum ball from one of a series of vertical glass tubes, labeled 1 to 10, that correspond to how happy they are feeling at the moment, thus participating in a visually dramatic display of the impact of the exhibit on people's happy feelings.

Happy Schools is a project of the Bangkok office of United Nations Education, Scientific and Cultural Organization (UNESCO). Countries participate with the purpose, as the name implies, of promoting the importance of happiness in schools by enhancing holistic development and learner well-being.[55] The program uses Professor Seligman's positive psychology model, PERMA, to develop a framework and set of criteria that education ministries and schools can use to create curricula and activities that engage teachers, students, and parents in supporting students' happiness and well-being. For example, the program encourages the use of teaching and learning methodologies that develop a sense of belonging to a common humanity, a sharing of values and responsibilities, empathy, solidarity, and respect for differences and diversity. The program encourages learner freedom, creativity, and engagement through activities that allow learners to express their opinions and to learn without the fear of making mistakes. It also encourages parents to get involved in classroom activities, and students to get involved in community issues and activities, creating connections beyond the school.

Of course, happiness comes in two flavors as illustrated by the two previous examples. While Sagmeister's show provides momentary experiences of fun, whimsy, and delight, the Happy Schools program provides a framework for extended engagement intended to influence the student for a lifetime. Designs that target hedonic or eudemonic happiness would be quite different from one another.

Toys and games are obviously designed to elicit hedonic happiness. A wide range of products can be designed with the look, feel, and function that generates this momentary experience. In his book *Emotional Design: Why We Love (or Hate) Everyday Things*, psychology professor and design consultant, Donald Norman identifies three factors designers must consider to create products and services that affect emotions.[56] One is to consider the visceral, perceptual impact of the product or experience. What is the user's reaction upon looking at it? Touching it? Smelling it? The second consideration is the behavior aspect: Is it easy to use or frustrating? Does it accomplish what the user wants to do? And the third consideration is what Norman calls "reflective," its cultural meaning. Are you proud to be seen with it? Does it reflect who you are, as a person?

Another source of information for happiness designers is a study out of the Imperial College London, which asked participants to identify products and services that made them happy.[57] Respondents identified 87 products and services that made them happy, which the researchers divided into six categories: digital devices (such as computers, mobile phones, and computer games), food, vehicles, books, clothing and accessories, and sports equipment. The researchers then looked for themes in the experiences that the respondents reported that they associated with these products and services. They found that food was primarily associated with connecting with loved ones but also associated, less so, with being entertained and with a feeling of comfort. Sports equipment was associated with doing things freely but also mastering an activity and connecting with loved ones. Books were associated with learning new knowledge and comfort. Experiences with vehicles were most often connected to doing things freely but sometimes included experiences of mastering the activity of driving, entertainment, and connecting with others. Respondents' stories sometimes included ideas about developing self-image, as did some experiences reported about sports equipment. This was also the primary theme when respondents mentioned their experiences with clothing and accessories. Stories about digital devices included all these themes, perhaps because the category included a broad range of devices and perhaps because these devices can be used in variety of ways.

The user-generated stories in this study give designers insight into what people consider happy experiences and what makes them happy. These are important findings for designers who have the purpose of actually making people happy rather than trying to convince customers they should be happy with their product or service.

Many of the themes in the Imperial College study, such as comfort, entertainment, and doing things freely, refer to feelings of the moment and relate to hedonic happiness. Others, such as mastery and relationships connect more directly with longer-term, eudaimonic happiness. Designing for eudaimonic happiness, or well-being, is more difficult, in part because it is an experience or sense of happiness that is developed over a longer period. Drawing on both philosophy and research, the goal of designing for eudaimonic happiness might involve advancing knowledge and a sense of autonomy or agency, or creating compassionate, supportive relationships.

All designers can think about ways that their products, services, and programs can contribute to hedonic happiness. But the goal of influencing long-term, eudaimonic happiness is particularly important for those designers who create products and experiences that users engage with frequently or for extended periods of time, such as designers of educational curricula, social support services, government programs, regularly used computer programs, work spaces, homes, office buildings, interiors, and urban environments. This brings us to our next case study.

Case Study: Happy Cities

People spend most of their time working, playing, and living in rooms, buildings, and spaces created by architects, interior designers, and urban planners. These designers, perhaps most of all, should be concerned with designs that support eudaimonic happiness. This is the case with Charles Montgomery and Happy Cities.

Case Study: Happy Cities

Charles Montgomery is an urban planner and author of the book, *Happy City: Transforming Our Lives Through Urban Design*.[58] Drawing on the ideas of Aristotle and the Enlightenment philosophers as well as research findings in public health, neuroscience, sociology, behavioral economics, and environmental psychology, Montgomery founded the international urban planning consultancy, Happy Cities, headquartered in Vancouver, British Columbia. The firm has had projects in the United Arab Emirates, Mexico City, Rotterdam, Denver, West Palm Beach, and Vancouver, among other cities.

A foundational assumption of Happy Cities is that there is a direct connection between people's happiness and environmental factors. Chief among those environmental factors is social connections. As Montgomery states, "The happy city is a social city above all."[59] From this perspective, "Our roads, our buildings, our parks, our neighborhoods, our streets are emotional infrastructure."

Happy Cities aims to solve problems at the intersection of urban design, policy, engagement, and human well-being.[60] It takes an evidence-based approach to link design and systems to human emotions, behavior, and health. When designing a project, the firm considers nine factors. The first—core needs—is necessary but not sufficient for well-being: food, water, shelter, sanitation, and safety. After core needs are met, social relations are the most powerful driver of well-being. Health is also essential to well-being. The other factors are equity and social inclusion, ease of coping with everyday challenges, positive memories and a sense of joy, meaning of life, a sense of belonging, and resilience. The agency staff believes that by including these considerations in the design process, buildings, places, spaces, and systems can maximize relationships, health, inclusion, and happiness. And the firm's well-being metrics, guidelines, and tools help its clients become leaders in happy community design.

Figure 12.3 Happy Cities Modular Housing Set Up for Aboriginal Day Ceremony (Photo by Happy Cities).

Among the agency's specialties is the planning of multifamily housing (see Figure 12.3). In 2015, funding from the Housing and the Real Estate Foundation of British Columbia enabled Happy Cities researchers to conduct studies on the relationships among social interaction, well-being, and multifamily housing. They found that thoughtful design can help address social isolation and build community resilience in multifamily settings.[61]

Every night, at least 35,000 Canadians find themselves without a home; some find a spot at an emergency shelter, but the majority are forced to weather the outside elements.[62] This number can be added to nearly 50,000 uncounted Canadians who are part of the hidden homeless population, many of whom are women fleeing violence and abuse. Women, indigenous peoples, and members of the LGBTQ+ community are disproportionately represented in homeless figures. The homeless population in British Columbia is often afflicted by various levels of substance use and addiction that requires specific supportive services. In addition to battling drug addiction, between one third and one half of B.C.'s homeless population is struggling with mental health and physical challenges. All these factors must be considered in developing housing for the homeless and are a challenge for urban planners.

Since 2017, over 1,300 temporary modular housing units have been built across British Columbia. These units provide a safe, clean, new, and dignified space for people to live in. But Happy Cities asked: What role do these buildings actually play in promoting well-being?

The Canadian Mortgage and Housing Corporation (CMHC), the agency of the Canadian government responsible for developing affordable housing, funded Happy Cities for a project entitled "Social Wellbeing in Modular Housing: Co-Creating Designs to Nurture Health and Social Support for Vulnerable People."[63] The project focuses on indigenous people in the Vancouver area who have experienced homelessness. The purpose of the project is to understand how the design of existing temporary modular housing can impact well-being. The goals of the project are to create a user-centered representation of the current state of temporary modular supportive housing and its successes and challenges; to understand the priorities and challenges that indigenous residents experience on their journeys out of homelessness; and to translate well-being learnings from residents, housing operators, housing managers, policy-makers, and design experts into actionable design, programming, and policy recommendations.

Happy Cities is using a five-phase process to develop the recommendations. First, in the Definition Phase, the agency established the scope and issues to develop a focus of the project.

In the second, Discovery Phase, Happy Cities researchers engaged residents, key experts, and other stakeholders in exercises and interviews about their perspective on issues related to temporary modular housing for indigenous people. Among the themes they discovered in their interviews was a need to create shared spaces in temporary housing that invite people to linger and talk, supporting social connections that are vital to well-being. There is a need for social services to be integrated into housing development, to help residents build skills and find jobs. And it is important to include features in the design that reflect indigenous culture.

In Phase 3, the next phase at the time of this writing, researchers will conduct workshops, facilitate discussions among residents and other stakeholders, conduct collaborative activities, and shadow housing staff to get a clearer picture of the current state of temporary modular housing. This will help understand the needs and priorities and get ideas for recommendations.

(Continued)

Case Study: Happy Cities (Continued)

In the Prototyping and Testing Phase, Phase 4, Happy Cities researchers will co-develop ideas that boost well-being, find creative ways to prototype them, and implement promising ones, iterating with residents and stakeholders to identify scalable solutions.

At the end of the project's final phase, Happy Cities staff will deliver a roadmap that cities, designers, and operators can use to design and implement resident-centered, temporary, modular housing that supports well-being. Implementation of these evidence-based recommendations can not only provide the homeless with shelter, but also create an environment of well-being that can be the foundation for a better life.

The interface between inner and outer environment for Happy Cities' design projects is not just between the physical need of the homeless and their immediate physical surroundings, but also includes the social and emotional needs of the homeless and their larger social environment. The firm's goal was not just to get them off the street and out of sight. Happy Cities designers wanted to create happiness and community.

Happy Cities staff understands that to promote eudemonic happiness, designers need to go beyond the immediate microsystem interactions and look at the community as a system. Like LabGov that we encountered in the Chapter 4 case study, Happy Cities views a city as a common social and emotional infrastructure. It does not just look at harm reduction—the physical requirements of a place of shelter—but the social interactions and services that would be needed to support happiness in temporary, modular housing. In doing so, Happy Cities included the cultural aspects that would be needed to build relationships and community, all things that support happiness and well-being.

This is also an example of how a design team can use collaborative design that explicitly includes moral values in the design process, as we discussed in the last chapter. With the discovery phase of the project, the Happy Cities design team conducted research and interviewed stakeholders with the explicit goal of developing a well-being framework for the project. During the development phase, they worked with residents to co-develop prototyping ideas for modular homes.

This case can help you think about how you can create happiness with your designs, and particularly, how you can contribute to long-term, eudemonic happiness. The key point is to make creating happiness the explicit purpose of your products, services, buildings, experiences, and programs. Make it the purpose of your company. Make it the purpose of your life. Once that is established, focus on creating happiness-making designs. Find out what the current situation is; what is making people happy or unhappy. Have them tell you what happiness means to them; co-create happiness designs.

Start with major themes like advancing knowledge and agency, equality, justice, and supportive relationships. Have them tell you stories about their happy experiences. Engage them in the design process, much as does Imagine Plank Road, Kuja Kuja, or Burning Man. Work with them to co-create products, services, and experiences around their happiness. Be evidence-based. Happiness is difficult to measure, like many important things. Scientists use measures of galvanic skin response, heart rate, pupil dilation, and facial expression to get precise data about emotions, but equipment for these measures is intrusive and the data, while accurate, are often only loosely associated with the specific emotion of interest. So, for a designer, self-report is often sufficient for your purposes. Ask them. Watch them as they use your designs. Are your designs making them happy?

For Aristotle and the Philosophes, happiness is the greatest good. It is the good to which all other values, such as knowledge, equality, justice, and relationships contribute and around which they are organized. For designers, contributing to happiness is one of the most important things you can do to make the world a better place.

It just might make you happy too.

References

1 The evil list. Slate [Internet]. 2020, Jan 15 [cited 2022, Aug 29]. Available from: https://slate.com/technology/2020/01/evil-list-tech-companies-dangerous-amazon-facebook-google-palantir.html.

2 Dirty dozen: Special Corona Virus edition. National Council on Occupational Safety [Internet]. 2020 [cited 2022, Aug 29]. Available from: https://nationalcosh.org/sites/default/files/2020%20Dirty%20Dozen%20Report.pdf.

3 Monopoly by the numbers. Open Market Institute [Internet]. [cited 2022, Aug 29]. Available from: https://www.openmarketsinstitute.org/learn/monopoly-by-the-numbers.

4 Riley T. Just 100 companies responsible for 71% of global emissions, study says. Guardian [Internet]. 2017, Jul 10 [cited 2022, Aug 29]. Available from: https://www.theguardian.com/sustainable-business/2017/jul/10/100-fossil-fuel-companies-investors-responsible-71-global-emissions-cdp-study-climate-change.

5 Herrmann A. The ethics of design: 5 ways to ensure you "do no harm." Akēdi [Internet]. 2018, Jun 14 [cited 2022, Aug 29]. Available from: https://www.akendi.com/blog/the-ethics-of-design/.

6 Brown and Williamson Tobacco Corporation. Encyclopedia.Com [Internet]. [cited 2022, Aug 29]. Available from: https://www.encyclopedia.com/books/politics-and-business-magazines/brown-and-williamson-tobacco-corporation.

7 Smoking-attributable mortality and years of potential life lost—United States, 1984. Center for Disease Control [Internet]. 1987, Oct 30 [cited 2022, Aug 29]. Available from: https://www.cdc.gov/mmwr/preview/mmwrhtml/lmrk131.htm.

8 Cigarettes. U.S. Food & Drug Administration [Internet]. [cited 2022, Aug 29]. Available from: https://www.fda.gov/tobacco-products/products-ingredients-components/cigarettes.

9 Wigand J. The big tobacco whistleblower. 60 Minutes [Internet]. 2018, Dec 16 [cited 2022, Aug 29]. Available from: https://www.youtube.com/watch?v=1_-Vu8LrUDk.

10 Annual disability statistics compendium. Rehabilitation Research & Training Center [Internet]. 2020, [cited 2022, Aug 29]. Available from: https://disabilitycompendium.org/sites/default/files/user-uploads/Events/2021_release_year/Final%20Accessibility%20Compendium%202020%20PDF_2.1.2020reduced.pdf.

11 Americans with Disability Act. ADA [Internet]. [cited 2022, Aug 29]. Available from: https://www.ada.gov.

12 2010 ADA standards for accessible design. ADA [Internet]. 2010, Sep 15 [cited 2022, Aug 29]. Available from: https://www.ada.gov/regs2010/2010ADAStandards/2010ADAStandards.pdf.

13 Center for Universal Design. CUD [Internet]. [cited 2022, Aug 29]. Available from: https://projects.ncsu.edu/ncsu/design/cud/about_ud/udprinciples.htm.

14 Inclusive design toolkit. University of Cambridge [Internet]. [cited 2022, Aug 29]. Available from: http://www.inclusivedesigntoolkit.com/whatis/whatis.html.

15 Assistive technology. Massachusetts's Initiative to Maximize Assistive Technology 9AT) in Consumer's Hands [Internet]. [cited 2022, Aug 29]. Available from: https://www.massmatch.org/find_at/at_catalogs.php.

16 Water Science School. The water in you: Water in the human body. US Geological Survey [Internet]. 2019, May 22 [cited 2022, Aug 29]. Available from: https://www.usgs.gov/special-topics/water-science-school/science/water-you-water-and-human-body.

17 Water facts: Worldwide water supply. Bureau of Reclamation [Internet]. [cited 2022, Aug 29]. Available from: https://www.usbr.gov/mp/arwec/water-facts-ww-water-sup.html.

18 Water scarcity: Overview. World Wildlife Federation [Internet]. [cited 2022, Aug 29]. Available from: https://www.worldwildlife.org/threats/water-scarcity.

19 Water crises are a top global risk. World Economic Forum [Internet]. 2015, Jan 16 [cited 2022, Aug 29]. Available from: https://www.weforum.org/agenda/2015/01/why-world-water-crises-are-a-top-global-risk/.

20 WestGate Water. WestGate Church [Internet]. [cited 2022, Aug 29]. Available from: https://www.westgatechurch.org/water.

21 WestGate Water. WestGate Church [web streaming video]. 2016, [cited 2022, Aug 29]. Available from: https://vimeo.com/188729547.

22 Lush T. Poll: Americans are the unhappiest they've been in 50 years. AP [Internet]. 2020, Jun 16 [cited 2022, Aug 29]. Available from: https://apnews.com/article/0f6b9be04fa0d31944018217266550.

23 Brody D. Antidepressant use among adults: United States, 2015-2018. Center for Disease Control. 2020, Sep [cited 2022, Aug 29]. Available from: 2018. https://www.cdc.gov/nchs/products/databriefs/db377.htm.

24 Bentham J. Collected Works of Jeremy Bentham (location 5477). London: Minerva Classics. Kindle Edition, 2013.

25 Compton W, Hoffman E. (2020). Positive psychology: The science of happiness and flourishing (3rd. ed). Los Angeles: Sage.

26 De Vries L, Baselmans B, Bartels M. Smartphone-based ecological momentary assessment of well-being: A systematic review and recommendations for future studies. Journal of Happiness Studies, 2020, [cited 2022, Aug 29]. Available from: https://doi.org/10.1007/s10902-020-00324-7.

27 Csikszentmihalyi M, Hunter J. Happiness in everyday life: The uses of experience sampling. Journal of Happiness Studies, 2003, 4(2), 185–199.

28 Csikszentmihalyi M. Flow: The psychology of optimal experience. New York: Harper Collins, 2008.

29 Seligman M. The President's Address (Annual Report). American Psychologist, 1999, 54, 559–562.

30 Seligman M. Flourish: A visionary new understanding of happiness and well-being. New York: Free Press, 2011.

31 Ma-Kellams C, Wang M, Cardiel H. Attractiveness and relationship longevity: Beauty is not what it is cracked up to be. Personal Relationships, 2017, 24, 146–161.

32 Kushlev K, Dunn E, Lucas R. Higher Income Is associated with less daily sadness but not more daily happiness. Social Psychological and Personality Science, 2015, 6(5), 483–489.

33 Kahnamen D, Deaton A. (2010). High income improves evaluation of life but not emotional well-being. Proceedings of the National Academy of Sciences 107 (38), 16489–16493.

34 Muresan G, Ciumas C, Achim M. (2020). Can money buy happiness? Evidence for European countries. Applied Research in Quality of Life, 15, 953–970.

35 Dittmar H, Bond R, Hurst M, Kasser T. (2014). The Relationship Between Materialism and Personal Well-Being: A Meta-Analysis. Journal of Personality and Social Psychology, 107, 5, 879–924.

36 Piff R, Stancato D, Côté S. Higher social class predicts increased unethical behavior. PNAS, 2012, 109(11), 4086-4091. Available from: https://www.pnas.org/content/109/11/4086.short.

37 Piff P, Kraus M, Côté, et al. Having less, giving more: The influence of social class on prosocial behavior. Journal of Personality and Social Psychology, 2010, 99(5), 771–784. Available from: https://psycnet.apa.org/record/2010-14101-001.

38 Dunn E, Aknin L, Norton M. Spending money on others promotes happiness. Science, 2008, 319, 1687–1688.

39 Otake K, Shimai S. Tanaka-Matsumi J, et al. Happy people become happier through kindness: A counting kindness intervention. Journal of Happiness Studies, 2006, 7(3), 361–375.

40 Steger M. Meaning in life and well-being. In Slade M., Oades L, Jarden A. (eds.), Well-being, recovery and mental health (pp. 75–86). Cambridge: Cambridge University Press, 2017.

41 Mineo L. Good genes are nice, but joy is better. Harvard Gazette [Internet]. 2017, Apr 11 [cited 2022, Aug 29]. Available from: https://news.harvard.edu/gazette/story/2017/04/over-nearly-80-years-harvard-study-has-been-showing-how-to-live-a-healthy-and-happy-life/.

42 McCarthy J. The birthplace of 'Gross National Happiness' is growing a bit cynical. . .NPR [Internet]. 2018, Feb 12 [cited 2022, Aug 29]. Available from: https://www.npr.org/sections/parallels/2018/02/12/584481047/the-birthplace-of-gross-national-happiness-is-growing-a-bit-cynical.

43 Helliwell, J, Layard, R, Sachs, J, et al.World happiness report, 2022. Sustainable Development Solutions Network [Internet]. 2022 [cited 2023, Jan 14]. Available from: https://worldhappiness.report/ed/2022/.

44 How does the Gallup World Poll work? Gallup [Internet]. [cited 2022, Aug 29]. Available from: https://www.gallup.com/178667/gallup-world-poll-work.aspx.

45 World Happiness Report [Internet]. 2021 [cited 2022, Aug 29]. Available from: https://worldhappiness.report/ed/2021/.

46 Tolin L. What is "hygge"? Get to know Denmark's secret to happiness—and how Americans can cultivate it. NBC News [Internet]. 2020, Jun 26 [cited 2022, Aug 29]. Available from: https://www.cnbc.com/2020/06/26/hygge-denmarks-secret-to-happiness-how-americans-can-cultivate-it.html.

47 Mitsuhashi Y. Ikigai: Giving every day meaning and joy. London: Kyle Book, 2018s.

48 https://www.ted.com/talks/nicola_sturgeon_why_governments_should_prioritize_well_being/transcript.

49 Sturgeon N. Why governments should prioritize well-being. TED [web streaming video]. 2019 [cited 2022, Aug 29]. Available from: https://wellbeingindex.sharecare.com/research/identifying-county-characteristics-associated-with-resident-well-being-a-population-based-study/.

50 Dolan P. Happiness by Design: Change What You Do Not How You Think. New York: Avery, 2014.

51 Ben-Shahar T. Happier: Learn the Secrets to Daily Joy and Lasting Fulfillment. New York: McGraw-Hill, 2007.

52 Top 15 ways to keep your customers happy. Measure-X [Internet]. [cited 2022, Aug 29]. Available from: https://measure-x.com/top-15-ways-to-keep-your-customers-happy/.

53 Woodford N. Why do so many brands choose to evoke happiness in ads? Unruly [Internet]. 2019, Jan 29 [cited 2022, Aug 29]. Available from: https://unruly.co/blog/article/2019/01/29/happiness-ads-insights/.

54 Sagmeister S. The happy show. Stefan Sagmeister [Internet]. [cited 2022, Aug 29]. Available from: https://sagmeister.com/work/the-happy-show/.

55 UNESCO. Happy schools! A framework for learner well-being in the Asia-Pacific. Paris: UNESCO, 2016.

56 Norman D. Emotional design: Why we love (or hate) everyday things. New York: Basic Books, 2005.

57 Xi Y, Marco A, Mackrill J, et al. (2017). On products and experiences that make us happy. In Maier A, Škec S, Kim H, et al. (editors, Proceedings of the 21st International Conference on Engineering Design Vol. 8: Human Behaviour in Design [internet]. 2017, Aug 21–25 [cited 2022, Aug 29]. Available from: https://www.designsociety.org/publication/39868/On+the+products+and+experiences+that+make+us+happy.

58 Montgomery C. Happy city: Transforming our lives through urban design. New York: Farrar, Straus and Giroux, 2013.

59 https://thehappycity.com/project/the-happy-city-experiment/.

60 Montgomery C. A recipe for urban happiness. Medium [Internet]. 2019, Apr 9 [cited 2022 Aug29]. Available from: https://medium.com/happy-cities/happiness-framework-ead6430997ca.

61 Hebert M, Elokda H, Rios P, et al. Recommendations and roadmap for social wellbeing in modular housing. National Housing Strategy [Internet]. [cited 2022, Aug 31]. https://admin.happycities.com/wp-content/uploads/2022/01/Happy-City-Solutions-Lab-recommendations-and-roadmap-2021-12-14-1.pdf.

62 Gaetz S, Dej E, Richter T, et al. The state of homelessness in Canada. Homeless Hub [Internet]. 2016 [cited 2022, Aug 31]. Available from: https://www.homelesshub.ca/SOHC2016.

63 Social wellbeing in modular housing solutions Lab: Co-creating designs to nurture health and social support for vulnerable people. Canada Mortgage and Housing Corporation [Internet]. 2021, May 11 [cited 2022, Aug 31]. Available from: https://www.cmhc-schl.gc.ca/en/nhs/nhs-project-profiles/2019-nhs-projects/social-wellbeing-modular-housing-solutions-lab.

13

Advance Knowledge, Reasoning, and Agency

. . .knowledge is power. . .knowledge is safety. . .knowledge is happiness.

Thomas Jefferson
Founding Father
Third U.S. President

How long did you go to school? Sixteen years? Eighteen? Twenty?

Why did you spend all those years in school? For a better job? To make more money? Because you loved learning and you were good at it? Because you thought it would make you a better person, the person you really wanted to be?

Or maybe you dropped out at some point, bored or frustrated that you weren't learning. Or you felt what was being covered wasn't worth the effort.

In this chapter, we will look at knowledge and its purpose. We will look at how we use it and how it helps us to live a better life. And we will look at how you use your own knowledge, reasoning, and agency to create designs and how your designs can advance knowledge, reasoning, and agency in others.

The Enlightenment philosophers had a huge impact on Western knowledge and thought, not in the least because they did a lot of thinking about it. Both John Locke and David Hume wrote treatises on human understanding. And while they disagreed on a few points, together, their work represented a major shift in the thinking about knowledge, reasoning, and agency. Both believed that knowledge was derived from experience, which was then applied through reasoning. And knowledge and reasoning had a purpose: to inform intentional action toward happiness. As philosophy professor William Bristow puts it in his essay on the Enlightenment, "The faith of the Enlightenment—if one may call it that—is that the process of enlightenment, of becoming progressively self-directed in thought and action through the awakening of one's intellectual powers, leads ultimately to a better, more fulfilled human existence."[1]

The Enlightenment was a cultural paradigm shift. It moved from a cultural situation where thought was based on dogma and superstition, where action was directed by tradition and authority, and where interaction was in one-direction—people were told to what to do and to accept their plight in life. And it moved to the beginning of modern age, a situation in which humans came to believe they can increase their happiness through knowledge, reasoning, and actions that give them control over their environment and improve their condition. It is this realization of the Enlightenment that is the underpinning of moral Principle 4 in Chapter 3, the goal of advancing knowledge, reasoning, and agency.

Make the World a Better Place: Design with Passion, Purpose, and Values, First Edition. Robert B. Kozma.

Knowledge at the Micro Level

While the Philosophes had many observations about knowledge, reasoning, and action, we have since learned much more, thanks to the Scientific Tradition. What we have learned takes up many books and volumes of research journals. But in this chapter, I will focus on a few findings that I think are particularly salient to designers interested in advancing knowledge, reasoning, and agency.

Knowledge in the head

Significant gains were made in the last half of the 20th century on knowledge and reasoning when the field of psychology moved from a focus on behavior to a focus on cognition: on how people acquired, structured, and used their knowledge.[2] Much of the early research on cognition looked at how those with a lot of knowledge in a domain (i.e., experts) are different in the way they structure and used their knowledge from those with only a little of it (i.e., novices). We saw some of the differences between experts and novices in our examination of chemists and chemistry students in Chapter 5. Decades of research on the differences between experts and novices in a wide range of fields, from chess and physics to restaurant order-taking and computer programming, tell us lot about knowledge, how people get it, and how they use it.[3]

Among the findings of these studies are that expertise comes from a lot of experience, just as the Philosophes claimed. Typically, experts in a field have spent over 10,000 hours practicing or applying their knowledge, often over a period of 10 years, or more.[4] But it is not just that the more experienced expert has more knowledge than the less experienced novice; the knowledge is organized differently in memory. Expert knowledge is organized into patterned networks of deeply interconnected concepts and principles that are also connected to situations in which the knowledge can be used. The knowledge of novices is incomplete, often inaccurate, and it is disconnected from other knowledge and from situations and action.

These findings are illustrated in a study that examined differences in knowledge structures, related to the pulmonary system, between two kinds of domain experts (respiratory therapists and pulmonary physicians) and two levels of relative novices to the domain (middle school students and their teachers). [5] Unsurprisingly, given significant differences in amount of their training and experience, the knowledge structures for pulmonary physicians and respiratory therapists were much deeper than for teachers and their students. But what was interesting in the findings was the nature of the structures between and among novices and experts. First of all, the differences between the groups in their knowledge of the components of the pulmonary system were less significant than the differences in their knowledge of the function of the system.

But of particular interest were findings related to differences in the knowledge structures between the two kinds of experts. Whereas respiratory therapists organize their knowledge around the actions they must take in addressing respiratory distress, pulmonary physicians organize it more around the interconnected functions that maintain healthy respiratory systems. That is for experts, information is organized in patterns that relate to situations in which they use it.

Knowledge in the environment

Late in the 20th century and early 21st, research on knowledge expanded to recognize that, while knowledge in the head is important, the knowledge that we use to think and solve problems also exists in the world and it has material form.[6] It exists in books, movies, songs, databases, online, and electronic devices. It also exists in the heads of other people and in the culture. From this knowledge-in-the-world perspective, knowledge and reasoning are distributed among people and devices. And this expanded view looks at how people use knowledge in the head with knowledge resources in the world to act, think, and interact with other people and things to create more knowledge, use it, and share it. But as we know from the person-resource-activity model in Chapter 5, changes in resources mean changes in activities.

My research team and I saw this in our research in chemistry labs when we looked at how a chemistry professor, David, interacted with his graduate student, Tom, as they used a nuclear magnetic resonance spectroscope (NMR) in their research, much as Susan did, whom we encountered in Chapter 5. David, the professor, had a deep knowledge about chemicals, the ways they are structured and how they interact.[7] Tom, the graduate student, also had a lot of deeply structured knowledge and was learning more. The NMR has a lot of knowledge embedded in its design and affordances about the behavior of nuclei in a strong magnetic field when excited by radio signals. We observed David and Tom reason with each other and with the NMR to determine if they had the product they were trying to synthesize.

What we saw was an intricate pattern of interactions between the two chemists, and between the chemists and the instrument as they shared knowledge and used them together to understand the information that was generated by the NMR. In the process, new knowledge was co-constructed between knowledge in their heads and knowledge in the world. Tom wasn't just memorizing how the NMR worked. Together with these resources—chemical compounds, the NMR spectra, and David's guidance—he was coming to use the NMR to understand the composition and structure of compounds he synthesizes.

Knowledge and how to acquire it

Learning is a course of actions getting from the current situation to the preferred one. And teaching is a course of actions to help someone do that. The particulars of the current situation are crucial in getting from here to there, for knowledge is built on knowledge. It is an elaboration of what is currently known and a connection with other known things.

For novices, often the things that are known are incomplete, as with the high school chemistry students we encountered in Chapter 5 who didn't understand how chemicals interact and react at a molecular level. And sometimes they are inaccurate, as with chemistry students who believe at equilibrium, a chemical reaction stops. Learning for novices means adding to, correcting, and inter-connecting their knowledge.

Two additional concepts from Activity Theory, which we discussed in Chapter 5, are helpful here: the *zone of proximal development*, or ZPD, and *scaffolding*.

ZPD is the performance zone between what someone can do on their own, unaided, and what he or she cannot do at all.[8] ZPD is the space in between, where a person can do something with support from a more knowledgeable parent, helper, software, peer, or teacher that they can't yet do on their own. As such, it is an important concept for a student or teacher who is trying to get from the current situation to a preferred one. ZPD is where internal change happens, where performance improves and where development and learning take place. Development occurs at the leading edge of the ZPD, over time, as external patterns of activity are internalized.

Within the ZPD, *scaffolding* is the specific set of resources and activities designed to aid performance change with the goal of achieving interaction patterns unaided.[9] Scaffolding could be thought of as procedures, structures, prompts, questions, modeling, templates, reminders, mnemonics, tutoring, or guided apprenticing that people can use to move from being less skilled to becoming more expert. This concept is particularly important for teachers, trainers, instructional designers, managers, and others who are trying to help people improve. It can even be useful for students. Understanding this concept can help you analyze how resources are currently being used in a situation and how your design could be structured such that the resources could be used differently or how different resources could be used in your designs to improve the situation.

To examine these concepts, let's return to the chemistry lab and look at the intricate pattern of interactions between the professor, David, and his graduate student, Tom, as they used the NMR spectrometer to confirm composition and structure of the compound they synthesized. The pair exhibited the same activity pattern as did Susan, solo, except David asked certain questions that supported Tom's reasoning with the spectrum, similar to what Susan was doing on her own. By the end of the session, Tom had picked up this interaction pattern such that he began to take the lead and started using the spectrum's affordances to make unaided statements to David that confirmed the compound's structure elements and confirmed Tom's emerging skill.

David and Tom were working within Tom's ZPD as he was coming to learn how to read an NMR spectrum but couldn't yet do it on his own. With his modeling and questions, David was scaffolding Tom's reasoning using the affordances of the NMR spectrum, as Tom demonstrated that he was successfully acquiring this interaction pattern. Had Tom demonstrated that he was having trouble understanding David's comments, it would have been evidence that David was working beyond Tom's ZPD and he would have adjusted his modeling and questions accordingly.

Reasoning: What We Do with Knowledge

Knowledge is not merely a good in itself; we can reason with it to inform and direct our actions. It enables us to do things that improve our situation and that of others. With knowledge we can explain how the world works. We can make decisions and solve problems. And, with knowledge, we can design, innovate, and create a better world.

Explain

With experience and knowledge, we develop personal theories, or mental models, about the world and how it works. Knowledge is often organized in memory as informal theories, usually expressed mentally as a network of probabilities, causal mechanisms, or stories.[10] Sometimes these theories are acquired in school, as part of our formal education. And sometimes they are acquired informally, as we experience the everyday world around us. We use these theories to explain how our world works, to make predictions, and to act accordingly.

For example, a key purpose of science is not just to describe the world but to use this knowledge to explain how it works. One of Newton's great discoveries is his explanation of motion: In a frictionless environment, a body in motion stays in motion, unless another force acts upon it.

But many young people have a theory, based on their personal experience in a world of frictional forces: that things only move as long as they continue to be acted upon, contrary to the formal, Newtonian explanation.[11] Part of a science teacher's task it to scaffold students' reasoning to take them from their informal, "naïve" explanations to more accurate understandings and explanations.

We not only have theories that explain the world, we have theories that explain each other and ourselves. In her book *Mindsets: The New Psychology of Success*, Stanford University psychology professor Carol Dweck summarizes two kinds of theories people can have about people and themselves and how the way they think influences what they do.[12] In her research, she found that some people have a *fixed mindset*. They think that traits in people are permanent; you're either smart or not and this does not change. People with a fixed mindset who believe they are not smart also feel that it's not worth putting in the effort to learn something new and they will avoid it if they can. Or, if they have to, they will do what they need to look like they're doing a good job, even if it sometimes means they have to cheat. In the event of failure, it affirms that they are deficient and it will reduce their motivation even more. Even people who believe they are smart, but have a fixed mindset, will do less when they encounter failure at some point because they believe they have reached the limits of their ability. In general, people with a fixed mindset feel the world needs to change, not them.

On the other hand, people with what Dweck calls a *growth mindset* believe that success comes from effort. They believe that people differ in intelligence and other traits but that these can be developed. They value self-improvement and mastery. And when they encounter a challenging learning situation, they love it and do more. When they encounter failure, they are not demotivated. Rather, they believe they need to apply more effort or/and they believe that in failure they have learned something new about learning. People with a growth mindset are not only more likely to do well in school, but they also enjoy better emotional and physical health, and have stronger, more positive social relationships with other people.

Make decisions and solve problems

For decades, psychologists were focused on a general process for solving problems.[13] A famous article by mathematician George Pólya laid out a process to be used in solving all kinds of problems, a process that parallels the design model presented in Chapter 2. The process begins with understanding the problem by asking questions, collecting information, analyzing the situation, and so on. Next, one devises a plan by using reasoning, eliminating possibilities, considering special cases, and so on. The third step is implementing the plan, followed by the final step of reviewing it and thinking about other situations in which the solution might be useful.

But recent research has found that, in many situations, a general problem-solving process is not enough; knowledge plays an important role in the process. This is why experts are better than novices at solving problems in their field. Expert knowledge comes into play in specific ways when solving problems. When novices are given a problem, they immediately plunge into an attempted solution, based on superficial understandings of both the problem situation and the domain. Experts begin by using their deep knowledge of situations to analyze the characteristics of the particular problem.[14] They then connect the specifics of the situation to their deep understanding of principles in their domain knowledge structure to quickly come up with the solution.

So, it turns out that rather than expert problem-solvers, there are experts who use their knowledge to solve problems in their domain. But expertise in one area doesn't make you an expert in another. I wouldn't want a chess master to operate on my hernia, however expert he is in his end game. However, experts can improve their ability to solve out-of-domain problems if they are able to extract general principles used within the domain, such as "control the center" in chess, and think of ways the principle might be applied in totally different problem situations, such as how "controlling the center" can be used to convince people of one's position at a town hall meeting, for instance.[15] Nonetheless, "control the center" probably doesn't help with a hernia repair.

Create, innovate, and design

Economist Brian Arthur, who we encountered in Chapter 5 when looking at technological innovation, found that transformational innovations rarely come as a spark of genius out of nowhere, but from the novel combinations of technologies, ideas, and designs that already exist, what he calls combinatorial change.[16] These innovative combinations, in turn, provide the foundation for yet other combinations and innovations.

In his book *Group Genius*, University of North Carolina psychology professor Keith Sawyer reviews a long research tradition to show that when finding the solution of novel problems with no previously known solution, teams are more effective than individuals. [17] Think of the Wright brothers and the first airplane, Watson and Crick and the discovery of DNA, and Doudna and Carpentier and CRISPR Cas9. Or think of the highly innovative teams at companies such as Bell Labs, Xerox PARC, SRI, Google X (now Alphabet X), Amazon's Lab126 and A9, and Jony Ive's Apple design lab.

The success of these innovative groups relies on the deep knowledge of highly qualified experts, with complementary skills, yet different perspectives who work in an environment that supports their collaboration. Groups of experts in the same domain represent silos of deep knowledge, but they all share the same ideas. If groups of experts go across different domain boundaries, they have more ideas from which they can create novel combinations. For example, the novel chemistry animation software that we developed at SRI International came from a team composed of instructional psychologists, a computer scientist, and a chemistry professor, and we worked with high school chemistry teachers and their students.[18]

The process by which innovators come up with ideas is more organic than linear and strictly rational. You may recall from Chapter 7 on the Technical-Analytic Tradition that in the mid-1960s the Design Methods movement proposed a design process that progressed in a formal, rational way, from design brief through to implementation and testing. Chapter 8 on the Human-Centered Tradition described the design process more appropriate to complex, social problem situations, as a set of overlapping exploration spaces of inspiration, ideation, and implementation.

Research on how professional designers, such as architects and product engineers, actually do their work elaborates on this process. It turns out that rather than work in a linear, step-by-step fashion, designers work much as do writers, working back and forth between their goals and the emerging text. Designers work iteratively, moving between their deep knowledge of designs in their field and the requirements of the specific situation, proposing a tentative solution and working it against the situation, which in turn, deepens their understanding of the situation and modifies the design.[19]

So, with deep knowledge in an area, you can explain complicated situations, use it to solve complex problems in your area, and come up with creative, innovative designs. This is particularly so if you combine knowledge from multiple people with complementary expertise who work together on the same problem or project.

The limits of knowledge and reasoning

For the Philosophes, experience generated knowledge, and knowledge informed reason. Emotion motivated actions, and reasoning directed them. But our current scientific knowledge suggests a more complicated relationship than that.

Herbert Simon, who you may remember meeting in Chapter 2, received his Nobel Prize in Economics for his work on decision theory that was a novel combination of economics, psychology, and computer science. The theme of his 1978 Nobel lecture was *bounded rationality* in decision-making.[20]

The classic model of "economic man," or *homo economicus*, assumes that people are purely rational and have knowledge of all the alternative choices, know the consequences that would follow from each of the alternatives, and make the choice that maximizes their self-interest. Simon confronted that model, claiming that, in actuality, people do not know all possible alternatives, do not know or are uncertain about consequences, and are often not capable of determining which option is optimum. Instead, Simon contended that rationality is bounded, or limited, and people make decisions that satisfice rather than optimize outcomes, much as did the Apollo XIII engineers in an emergency situation. Knowledge and reasoning are particularly bounded when trying to solve problems in complex, adaptive human systems where interactions are dynamic and ever-changing.

Not only is rationality bounded, it is influenced by other things. Emotions don't just motivate reasoning, they also play a big role in making decisions less than purely rational.[21] For example, the emotional state that someone happens to be in at the time a decision is made will influence the decision. A person who is happy at the time will make optimistic judgements, while someone who is depressed will make pessimistic decisions, even though the mood has nothing to do with the nature of the decision itself. Someone in a good mood increases the likelihood they decide to buy a Porsche, for example, even though reason would say it is a financial stretch to do so. Someone depressed may decide not to take a trip that is offered for free, even though there is a good reason to believe it would lift their spirits.

But emotions evoked by the decision itself can have a bigger effect on decisions. Financial anxiety induced by the Porsche's price tag will decrease the likelihood of purchasing it. Someone who is afraid of flying may decide to drive, even though flying is safer than driving. Emotions evoked by the anticipated outcome can also affect the decision. Envisioning the thrill of driving the Porsche through the open countryside may overcome the financial anxiety. The prospect of seeing a beloved relative may result in a decision to fly, despite the fear.

Knowledge still comes into play. Expertise allows those that have it to distinguish between decision-relevant emotions and extraneous emotions, and filter out the latter when making decisions, at least in their area of expertise.[22] In regular situations, an experienced pilot may also follow emotions and buy the Porsche when she can't really afford it. But she can factor out extraneous emotions and use situation-relevant emotions to focus concentration and heighten awareness in landing a plane under extreme conditions that make it a white-knuckle flight for passengers.

Agency: How Knowledge Empowers Us

The Philosophes believe that knowledge and reasoning make people's lives better. That is, it empowers them. Personal agency is when people take responsibility for their actions, and ascribe success and failure to the goals they choose, the resources they mobilize, and the effort they expend.[23] It is through personal agency that we take charge of our lives to avoid harm and increase happiness, our own and others'. In the context of knowledge and reasoning, the terms *metacognition* and *self-regulated learning* are used to describe the ability to take charge of one's own thinking and actions.

Metacognition

Metacognition—literally, thinking about thinking—refers to the deliberate conscious control of cognitive activity.[24] As such, metacognition is not different in process than cognition. Rather, one's thinking is what one thinks about. With metacognition, people monitor their cognition to create a mental model of what they are thinking or learning about and use this model to control that process, evoking different strategies to help them reason or learn, as they assess whether they are doing well or poorly in the process.

An example of metacognitive knowledge would be if you know that you are a savvy investor, that you've done a lot of investing and made some good money at it. But you also know that all your investments have been in stocks and you don't know much at all about bonds. A metacognitive experience would be that a friend starts talking about the tax advantages of municipal bonds and you realize you're not really following what she is saying. But since your goal is to retire in the next five years, you decide that investing in bonds may contribute to that goal, so you deliberately pay closer attention to what she is saying and ask questions when you don't understand something. You figure you can follow up by doing some reading and consult with your financial advisor.

There is an important connection between metacognition and knowledge. Experts are not only able to use their vast knowledge to solve problems, but they also reflect on their thought processes and strategies, and this improves their performance.[25] They know what they know and what they don't know as well. Their expertise involves both engaging in the problem to be solved while also consciously reflecting on their problem-solving strategies, modifying and adjusting them and knowing when to back-track or start over if a particular strategy is not fruitful and needs to be modified or abandoned.

You don't have to be an expert in a field in order to engage in metacognitive thinking, but engaging in metacognitive thinking helps in developing expertise. Earlier I mentioned that experts have often practiced for thousands of hours over many years to become an expert. But it turns out that practicing is not sufficient.[26] We are all familiar with attaining a certain level of ability in tennis or chess or in our profession and then leveling off without improvements in performance, no matter how many more years we continue to work at it. It turns out that becoming an expert requires not just practice, but also *deliberate practice*,[27] practice that involves the continual monitoring and control of performance and refinement based on reflection and modification—that is, metacognition. Experts tend to set stretch goals for their practice, put great concentration and effort into each instance of practice, and generate feedback about what they did right or wrong. They are particularly interested in analyzing why they got something wrong and what they can do about it. For example, it has been found that in addition to practice, metacognitive strategies such as self-explanation and reflection have been effective in developing expertise in advanced medical students.[28] Without monitoring and refinement, years of practice is merely doing the same one year of practice over and over.

Self-regulated learning

Self-regulated learning is a related concept that combines metacognition, motivation, knowledge, and agency, and applies them to the learning process. Psychologist Barry Zimmerman defines self-regulation during learning as, ". . .self-generated thoughts, feelings, and actions that are planned and cyclically adapted to the attainment of personal goals."[29] From this perspective, learning is a constructive activity that learners engage in proactively, for themselves, rather than something that happens to them or is directed by a teacher. Learners—whether young or old, whether in school or outside of school—are self-regulated to the degree that they are metacognitively, motivationally, and behaviorally active participants in their own learning process.

The self-regulatory processes can be thought of as a three-phase cyclical model involving forethought, performance, and self-reflection while learning. With forethought processes, the learner may evoke certain theories she has about herself, her learning, and her interest in a topic. The learner may tap into emotions and motivations about the topic to identify her learning goals. This sets the stage for the performance phase, where the learner consciously picks strategies designed to achieve her goals. Self-monitoring assures that these strategies are being implemented, identifies difficulties in doing so, and assesses their effectiveness in different learning situations. Self-monitoring also feeds forward, affecting forethought goals for subsequent learning efforts—completing the self-regulatory cycle. Students with a growth mindset are more likely to engage in these strategies; those with a fixed mindset feel that the effort would not make a difference.

An example of self-regulated learning would be when a college freshman knows that she has done well in her high school math courses but did not take advanced placement calculus, so she questions how well she understands it. She has since decided she wants to be an engineer and she knows that she will need a sound understanding of calculus to do well in her engineering courses. But she is confident if she takes the course in college and puts in the effort and seeks help from the instructor if she encounters a problem, she can ace the course. She uses certain strategies during lecture, such as making connections between what is being said to what she already knows from high school. And if she doesn't understand something she will ask for an explanation that may allow her to make a connection. She also has certain strategies for doing homework, such as drawing diagrams that connect ideas to other ideas and coming up with practice problems of her own. She monitors her progress in a notebook and connects it to the strategies that she's using. And she figures that by the end of the course, she should have a pretty good idea about her prospects for success in subsequent engineering courses.

We now have a picture so far of how people acquire, organize, and use knowledge in their head and in the world. Knowledge comes from experience. Those with more experience and more knowledge structure it in memory as deep interconnected knowledge structures composed of concepts, principles, stories, and theories and these are connected to situations in which they would be used. People also interact with others and with resources to elaborate and extend their knowledge and to scaffold that process in others. The more people engage in deliberate, reflective experiences, the more expert they become. Those who have a growth mindset engage in experiences in this more mindful, self-regulated way, and with passion and persistence, they succeed. People with a fixed mindset and poor self-regulation often lack the motivation and passion to persist. With knowledge and agency, you are able to explain situations, make decisions, solve problems, and create designs that improve our world.

Designing for Knowledge and Agency at the Micro Level

This understanding can help you think about how designs at the micro level can help people learn, whether you are a teacher, trainer, college professor, manager, service provider, or even a product developer or UX designer. Knowing what your student, trainee, or user already knows can help you adjust your design to their ZPD and scaffold their reasoning and learning to advance their knowledge. If they have a high degree of agency and self-regulated learning skills, they can arrange much of the learning experience on their own and your design will be minimal. If they have less knowledge and fewer self-regulated skills, your design will be more important and you will need to scaffold both their learning of new knowledge and their development of self-regulated skills and mindset. The technology you use and the designs you create would not de-skill learners by making all the learning decisions for them, but help them become better self-regulated learners. All of this argues for the need that designs be personalized for the specific learner.

Early in my career I was a public-school elementary math teacher in the inner-city of Detroit. I participated in a federally funded experimental program that allowed me to do just that—experiment. I organized my class as a self-study hall. Even though it was a specific grade, 3rd grade one year, 4th the next, each student was working on a particular math concept, which they chose, at their own level of understanding. For the learning goal they selected, they used self-study materials I designed. When they finished their self-study, each had to demonstrate to me, in a one-on-one session, that they had mastered of the concept before moving on to the next concept. While they were studying, if they had problems understanding, they could ask another student for help or come to me. All my interactions with students were one-on-one or in small groups of students working on the same concept. During these interactions, I probed their understanding, adapting my strategies based on their responses. I demonstrated the concept using a combination of symbols, physical objects, and real-world examples. I asked students questions, and within their zone of proximal development, scaffolded their connection of new concepts with ones I knew they had already mastered. And I guided their performance, as they demonstrated and explained their understanding. It was only after they solved a number of problems, explaining how they did so, that I marked them as having mastered the concept.

These inner-city students were not used to success in learning. Many of them were classified as learning problems. But they succeeded, demonstrating mastery of learning goal after learning goal, at whatever level they were, week after week for the entire year. And they learned how to learn. If I needed to be absent, the lesson plan I left for the substitute teacher was simple. It said, "These students know what to do. Let them do it and answer any questions they may have." Invariably, the teacher would report that they were amazed at what the students could do on their own. My students were excited about their success. And their excitement excited me. The time with these students was among the most rewarding of my professional career.

Knowledge and Institutions at the Macro Level

When we come into the world, we're not blank slates or empty vessels. Nature and evolution have given us a complex and wondrous brain that seems to be particularly well structured to acquire language without much effort. However, beyond this structure and our amazing language acquisition capability, there's no knowledge of the world. We certainly aren't experts at anything at the beginning. From the moment we're born, we must rely on our environment to provide us with the resources and experiences we need to develop into successful adaptors and contributors in the complex, adaptive system that is our society. Eventually, many of us become self-regulated learners and have the capability—the agency—to arrange our own resources and experiences.

In between, we need to rely the social structure designed to get us there: schools. What it is that you learned as a young person and how you learned it was very much affected by this institution.

Sadly, education in the U.S. is facing a crisis. The COVID-19 pandemic caused historic learning setbacks for America's children, erasing decades of academic progress and widening racial disparities, according to results on the "Nation's Report Card".[30] Across the country, math scores saw their largest decreases ever. Reading scores dropped to 1992 levels. Nearly four in 10 eighth graders failed to grasp basic math concepts.

At the same time that qualified, experienced teachers are needed most, they are leaving the profession in droves, stressed and dejected. Caught in the middle of the nation's culture wars and the impact of the COVID pandemic, often requiring them to teach remotely, some 300,000 public-school teachers and other staff left the field between February 2020 and May 2022, a nearly 3% drop in that workforce, according to Bureau of Labor Statistics, leaving schools across the country critically understaffed.[31] Given the importance of education to both students and society, designs that advance knowledge, reasoning, and agency—as well as help teachers—could make a huge impact on improving the world.

Schools and education

The education system is the institution that society has designed to help individuals become members of our society. Formal education has a long history that goes back to the earliest civilizations.[32] But it was very different than schooling as we know it today. Formal education was effectively limited to the aristocracy or the wealthy and to males. For the rest, education was informal. For the most part, boys learned skills such as those needed to raise crops, or a trade through apprenticeship, typically from their fathers. And girls learned household skills from their mothers. Cultural knowledge was propagated through oral stories. Most people were illiterate.

In Western countries throughout the Middle Ages, formal education was the primary responsibility of the church, with its focus on Bible reading, religious teachings, and the training of future clergy and civic leaders. In the late 19th century, most European governments began to provide free elementary education in reading, writing, and arithmetic to the general public, and secondary education was open to those who could afford it.

In the 19th century, the United States followed the example set by European countries. Horace Mann, Secretary of Education for the state of Massachusetts, created a statewide system of professional teachers and public education, based on the Prussian model of "common schools," a movement that spread across the North. By 1930, every state required students to complete elementary school to provide students with a basic education in reading, writing, and arithmetic.

Early in the 20th century, a more-or-less uniform model of schooling developed across the country that came to be referred to as the "factory model" of education (see Figure 13.1). This model was based on "scientific management" and the principles of Fredrick Taylor and the Gilbreths, whom we met in Chapter 6 on the Technical Tradition.[33] The model emphasized efficiency, productivity, and standard measurements of results that prepared students for work in the factory system and assured taxpayers that their money was well spent. But school was also thought of as a factory. The model was characterized in 1916 by Elwood Cubberley, Dean of the School of Education at Stanford University:

Figure 13.1 Factory model of education (Photo contributor LiliGraphie).

> Our schools are, in a sense, factories in which the raw products (children) are to be shaped and fashioned into products to meet the various demands of life. The specifications for manufacturing come from the demands of the twentieth-century civilization, and it is the business of the school to build its pupils to the specifications laid down. This demands good tools, specialized machinery, continuous measurement of production to see if it is according to specifications, the elimination of waste in manufacture, and a large variety in the output.[34]

There was a counter-movement, developed by University of Chicago professor John Dewey and referred to as *Progressive Education*, which built on the purpose that "to prepare (the student) for the future life means to give him command of himself; it means so to train him that he will have the full and ready use of all his capacities."[35] The movement emphasized learning by doing, collaborative learning projects, problem-solving and critical thinking, the development of social skills, lifelong learning, and education for social responsibility and democracy. While the movement generated a lot of discussion in academia, it was applied in a relatively few schools and those were typically associated with university colleges of education.

For the most part, principles of the factory model dominated U.S. education even into the 21st century. With the passage of the "No Child Left Behind Act" of 2002, there was an infusion of new education money to the states, but it required them to measure student progress with standardized state exams in math and language skills, and to punish schools that were not meeting goals.

Throughout the 20th century, this education model worked well for many people, and primarily, for the economy. By 1940, 50% of young adults had earned a high school diploma. The acquisition of knowledge in subject areas prepared students for more challenging jobs in the manufacturing economy and the education system created a workforce that powered the United States to economic preeminence and spawned a vibrant middle class.

However, while the factory model did well in supporting a manufacturing-based economy, it began to show its limitations as the 21st century began and the country moved toward a knowledge economy and information society, enabled by new technological developments. A standardized education seemed to have significant limitations in responding to an ever-increasingly complex society with ever-more complicated problems, problems that didn't need standard solutions but creative, innovative ones. Calls began for systemic education reform, including changes in curriculum, instruction, teacher preparation, assessment, and the integrated use of technology that would prepare students for the new century.[36]

Building on this movement, I worked with the United Nations Education, Scientific and Cultural Organization (UNESCO) to help national education systems think about how to reform their education system using technology as a catalyst. We designed a framework that laid out a systemic scheme to help education systems move from basic education and knowledge acquisition, that characterized the factory model, to a system that would support a deeper understanding of knowledge, much like that of experts, which is needed to solve complex, open-ended problems, and to support the creation of new knowledge, skills needed for an economy based on continuous innovation.[37] In this framework, the curriculum emphasizes deep understanding of subjects needed to solve complex, real-world problems and inquiry, information management, goal setting and self-monitoring, critical thinking, and creativity skills, reminiscent of the Progressive Movement a century earlier. Teacher professional development emphasizes the teacher's own deep knowledge and development of their ability to employ new technology-enhanced teaching methods. Such methods include collaborative projects, scientific investigations, data collection and analysis, and assessment by student reports, multimedia productions, and performances that correspond to the kinds of products valued in a knowledge economy and information society.

Learning in Communities

Within and outside of formal education structures, education environments are being reconceptualized as communities of learners, rather than as physical classrooms. And designers have used both physical resources and social relationships to enrich these environments and support learning.

Knowledge Building Communities (KBCs)

Among the innovative educational approaches that came out of the education reform movement were Knowledge Building Communities (KBCs), an idea developed at the University of Toronto by Professors Marlene Scardamalia and Carl Bereiter. The fact that information products and services now account for a greater proportion of the U.S. economy than manufactured goods has significant implications for the role of knowledge creation in contributing to and benefitting from the knowledge economy and participating in the information society. As Scardamalia and Bereiter put it, "This presents a formidable new challenge: how to develop citizens who not only possess up-to-date knowledge but are able to participate in the creation of new knowledge as a normal part of their lives."[38]

KBCs address this challenge. Rather than thinking of a class as a group of individual learners, this approach considers learners as a community whose practice is creating and sharing knowledge of value to the group. Established knowledge is still important. But rather than a curricular end point, established knowledge, including knowledge previously created by students themselves, is a starting point in the generation of new knowledge. In KBCs, learners collaborate to establish common goals; hold group discussions; use technology-based tools to gather, analyze, and share information; and synthesize ideas to advance their collective knowledge of a valued topic. The product of these efforts is "knowledge artifact"—such as a joint publication, a presentation, a research report, a designed artifact, an illustrated model, or a theory—which other learners can then build on and use to advance their own understanding of that subject.

The concept of knowledge building takes agency up a notch. It goes beyond metacognition and self-regulated learning in at least two ways. One is that people are more in control of the process. While self-regulated learning is typically done within the confines of a curriculum and a school environment structured by someone else, knowledge building is controlled by the people doing it. Second, while metacognition and self-regulation are solo activities to advance personal goals, knowledge building is a joint activity in which members construct and share new knowledge that has value to the community and where the community supports knowledge building work. These are the sorts of activities, skills, and people involved in innovative, highly productive work teams.[39]

An example of knowledge building is illustrated by the chemistry software environment that my team and I designed to help students think more like professional chemists, referenced in Chapter 5.[40] With this networked environment, high school and college chemistry students used a variety of symbolic resources to collectively discuss chemical phenomena they were examining with their laboratory experiments. Students and their instructors were able to pose research questions and hypotheses, post graphs of their experimental findings, create and share animations that represented their thinking about what was happening at a molecular level, and comment on each other's postings. In the process, they developed individual knowledge and skills, and created a mutual understanding of chemical processes that paralleled that of professional chemists.

Communities of practice (CoP)

But this community-based approach to knowledge acquisition, use, and agency goes beyond formal educational institutions. The workplace analog to KBCs are communities of practice (CoP).

The concept of CoP was presented in the book *Situated Learning*[41] by cognitive anthropologist Jean Lave and educational theorist Etienne Wenger, and it is further developed by Wenger in the subsequent books, *Communities of Practice*[42] and *Cultivating Communities of Practice*.[43]

With a CoP, a community of practitioners share experiences and build relationships in order to learn from and with each other. Members of the community are real practitioners from a specific field. Membership is based on personal passion and shared concerns about practice. Members can be employees of the same company with the same or related jobs but membership is voluntary. They can be from different organizations with parallel responsibilities or tasks, or they can be a group with diverse jobs and responsibilities that are all concerned about the same issues, perhaps for different reasons. And members don't have to be co-located; they can be a virtual community that collaborates online in discussion boards or various groups, or chatrooms on social media sites.

A CoP is focused on a particular area of interest or set of problems. However, members are not merely sharing knowledge for knowledge's sake, but for the purpose of informing shared practices, for taking collective action. In pursuing this purpose, the community develops shared resources. The knowledge areas of focus are generated by the group and are related to practice: experiences, stories, tools, guidelines, procedures, model practices. The knowledge is systematically gathered and stored, typically online, and organized around these issues so that it can be easily retrieved as members encounter practical issues and problems.

An example of the usefulness of CoPs is demonstrated by COP-RCORP, Communities of Practice for Rural Communities Opioid Response Program. In response to the opioid crisis, Ohio University, with funding from the Ohio Department of Mental Health and Addiction Services, set up COP-RCORP in 2018 as a CoP dedicated to addressing and preventing opioid use disorder. The CoP was convened by researchers and included leaders from four community-based opiate task forces located in Ohio's rural and Appalachian region.[44] Using videoconferencing technology, CoP met regularly and members identified barriers to healthcare service, shared local solutions, and brainstormed action plans. During the third year of meetings, COVID hit, and it hit their communities particularly hard. However, because the CoP had become a virtual space for sharing innovative local efforts and exchanging resources, it provided a forum for community leaders to discuss the challenges presented by COVID.

What is common about KBCs and CoP is that both focus on advancing knowledge, developing agency, and building community. They engage in many of the design principles found by Ostrom in her research, such as participants setting their own rules and monitor results. The cumulative effect of these collective actions is to build stronger bonds and mutual trust within the community, as well as support learning.

The development of such a community is dramatically illustrated by our next case study, High Tech High.

Case Study: High Tech High

According to the U.S. Department of Labor, only 33% of recent high school graduates are enrolled in college.[45] And this is at a time when 75% of the new jobs that were added to the U.S. economy between 2008 and 2017 required college degrees or higher, and nearly two thirds of the labor force is composed of workers without college degrees.[46]

This has left school districts and communities struggling to find ways of making schools better. San Diego is one of them.

Case Study: High Tech High

The idea for High Tech High started in 1996 when members of San Diego's civic and high-tech industry, convened by the San Diego Economic Development Corporation and Business Roundtable, gathered to discuss the shortage of high school grads prepared in science, technology, engineering, and math (STEM).[47] The members met regularly for the next two years to discuss how to engage and prepare local students for high-tech careers.

Larry Rosenstock was one of the members. Rosenstock was originally a carpenter on the East Coast and, when working on a darkroom for a local organization for immigrant families, he ended up showing the kids how to do carpentry. One thing led to another, and he became a teacher. Before moving to San Diego, Rosenstock directed several schools and he was a lecturer at the Harvard Graduate School of Education. In developing one of his schools, Rosenstock and his team developed three design principles to guide their efforts: personalization, real-world connection, and common intellectual mission.[48]

When Rosenstock moved to San Diego, the group asked him to head up its new school.

The school opened in 2000 with 450 students in grades 9 and 10. It is now a network of 16 schools with 6,300 students in the greater San Diego area: 6 high schools, 5 middle schools, and 5 elementary schools.[49]

High Tech High built off of Rosenstock's experience and ideas, and those of many others to move the school away from the factory model toward the progressive ideas of John Dewey. And the school is built around design as a theme. The three design principles that Rosenstock brought with him have now morphed into four: equity, personalization, authentic work, and collaborative design.

Equity

With this principle, teachers address student inequities and help them develop their full potential. Students are drawn through a lottery, by zip codes in the San Diego area, so the students are very diverse and represent the makeup of the area. Whatever their abilities, all students are challenged to meet high expectations and are provided with the resources to do so. The goal is for all graduates to be prepared for college and the world of work. Achieving equity within this diversity is addressed through advisory groups. All students stay with the same group throughout their high school experience. All the teachers and staff members have a group and they meet weekly with the same group, across the years. Consequently, the teachers and students get to know each other very well and students talk about academic issues, social issues, and preparation for college and life beyond school. These group meetings are supplemented by supportive individual consultations, parent meetings, and home visits.

Personalization

Instruction is learner-centered and project-based. Students, often working in groups, pursue their passion in choosing their own learning projects, within an integrated, challenging academic curriculum. Students maintain a digital portfolio of their work, which follows them through the grades. Each semester, students pick a project and develop it through their work in their various academic and technical classes. At the end of the semester, each student gives a 15- to 20-minute presentation of their learning project to peers, parents, community members, and teachers.[50] For example, one group gave a presentation entitled "A Fight with Gravity,"

(Continued)

Case Study: High Tech High (Continued)

in which they documented their own physics experiments in order to fight gravity using kites, balloons, and other flying objects of their own creation. Another group read plays by three Greek writers before adapting them into an onstage version following themes of genocide, war, refugees, and the treatment of women.

Authentic work

Students' projects are based on real-world situations or/and have real-world consequences. They often consult with outside experts in conducting their projects. And in the 11th grade, students are required to have a semester-long internship at a local business or organization. Assessments are also authentic. That is, rather than being assessed on their learning with standard, multiple-choice tests, student knowledge is applied to solve complex real-world problems and applied in their learning projects. The outcomes of students' projects are also real-world, such as fully illustrated books, devices, working models, performances, and PowerPoint presentations. A student's senior year project is the culmination of her or his personalized academic work at High Tech High. The project spans their entire academic year, and requires her or him to set large goals, demonstrate independent learning, manage complex and challenging tasks, and present substantive work to a panel of experts (see Figure 13.2).

Collaborative design

Design runs throughout the school. Not only do students work collaboratively on design projects, but also teachers are first and foremost designers. New teachers attend Design Camp, at HTH's Graduate School of Education, in which they learn how to work with students to design their projects.[51] In Design Camp, teachers use a common framework for developing their designs that looks an awful lot like human-centered design. It starts with empathizing with students, moves to defining a problem, ideating possible solutions, drafting prototypes, testing them, and giving critiques. Teachers also collaborate to combine math and physics, for example, or English and history, and they engage in peer evaluations and reflective discussions.

Figure 13.2 High Tech High students designing a project (*Source:* High Tech High).

As High Tech High teachers design curriculum for their courses, they consider the California academic content standards, which call for students to: master core academic content, think critically, solve complex problems, work collaboratively, communicate effectively, learn how to learn, and develop academic mindsets. As a result, all HTH academic core courses have been approved by the University of California.[52]

But teacher concerns go beyond academics. HTH schools create safe, inclusive classroom environments where all students feel a sense of belonging, are supported with socioemotional needs, develop strong relationships, and experience joy. Teachers work to develop a culture of belonging by coming to know their students well and addressing their socioemotional needs in nonpunitive, non-adversarial ways. Teachers are able to do this because these are priorities of the school, they are provided with the skills to do this, and their classes are small.

Collaboration with researchers

HTH schools also collaborate with researchers.[53] With a grant from the William and Flora Hewlett Foundation, HTH approached the Carnegie Foundation for the Advancement of Teaching to bring their scientific improvement approach to the school. HTH sent a team to the Foundation's Improvement Summit to learn about improvement science and their version of communities of practice which they call NICs, or Networked Improvement Communities. Through a series of improvement projects, teachers, administrators, and researchers worked together on specific strategies to address data-identified problems. As a result, HTH graduate attendance at a four-year college jumped from a modest 65% to an impressive 73%. This approach has since been applied to other data-identified problems, and NICs have become a standard way for teachers to take collective action for improvement.

High Tech High is an excellent case study in many ways as you consider how design can advance knowledge, reasoning, and agency. At the micro level, teachers work closely and individually with students to personalize instruction, in the way I did with my math students in Detroit. Students not only acquire deep knowledge but work together to apply it to solve specific problems in real-world situations, much as do Scardamalia and Bereiter's Knowledge Building Communities. As a result, they come to develop the agency of motivated, self-regulated learners and designers.

At the institutional level, the school is organized around design principles that guide and support teacher and student work. Teachers are provided with the temporal, physical, and strategic resources they need to design curricula with other teachers and projects with their students.

At the community level, the school has created collaborative design communities among teachers, between teachers and students, and among students, using design principles much like those of Elinor Ostrom. These are communities that value design and organize their practices around it. Even more, the school caries this design theme beyond the school, supporting design collaboration between teachers and researchers, teachers and parents, and teachers and businesses and organizations in the San Diego community.

This collaborative, community-based design is made even more powerful by connecting to knowledge, its application, and student agency with moral values, such as equity and the joy of learning, and by embedding these values in reflective discussions within the community.

It makes you wish you were a teacher or could start high school all over again, doesn't it?

References

1 Bristow W. Enlightenment. Plato [Internet]. 2017, Aug 20 [cited 2022, Aug 30]. Available from: https://plato.stanford.edu/entries/enlightenment/#RatEnl.
2 Bransford J, Brown A, Cocking R. How people learn: Brain, mind, experience and school. Washington, DC: National Academy Press, 2000.
3 Glaser R, Chi M. Overview. In Chi M, Glaser R, Farr M (eds.), The nature of expertise (pp. xv–xxviii). Hillsdale, NJ: Erlbaum, 1988.
4 Chase W, Simon H. The mind's eye in chess. In W. G. Chase (Ed.), Visual information processing (pp. 215–281). New York: Academic Press, 1973.
5 Hmelo-Silver C, Liu L. Fish swim, rocks sit, and lungs breath: Expert-novice understanding of complex systems and designs for learning. Journal of the Learning Sciences, 2007, 16(3), 307–331.
6 Committee on How People Learn II. How people learn: Learners, contexts, and cultures. Washington, DC: National Academy Press, 2018.
7 Kozma R, Chin E, Russell J, et al. The roles of representations and tools in the chemistry laboratory and their implications for chemistry learning. Journal of the Learning Sciences, 2000, 9(2), 105–143.
8 Zinchenko V. Developing activity theory; The zone of proximal development. In Nardi B (editor), Context and consciousness (pp. 283–324). Cambridge, MA: MIT Press, 1996.
9 Wood D, Bruner J, Ross G. The role of tutoring in problem solving. Journal of Child Psychology and Psychiatry, 1972, 17, 89–100.
10 Sloman S, Lagnado D. Causality in thought. Annual Review of Psychology, 2015, 66, 3.1–3.25.
11 diSessa A. Toward an Epistemology of Physics. Cognition and Instruction, 1993, 10 (2–3), 105–225.
12 Dweck C. Mindset: The new psychology of success. New York: Random House, 2006.
13 Pólya G. How to solve it. Princeton, NJ: Princeton University Press, 1945.
14 Glaser R, Chi M. Overview. In Chi M, Glaser R, Farr M (eds.), The nature of expertise (pp. xv–xxviii). Hillsdale, NJ: Erlbaum, 1988.
15 Perkins D, Salomon G. (1989). Are cognitive skills context-bound? Educational Researcher, 1989, 18(1), 16–25.
16 Arthur WB. The nature of technology: What it is and how it evolves. New York: Free Press, 2009.
17 Sawyer K. Group genius: The creative power of collaboration. New York: Basic Books, 2017.
18 Schank P, Kozma R. Learning chemistry through the use of a representation-based knowledge building environment. Journal of Computers in Mathematics and Science Teaching, 2001, 21(3), 253–279.
19 Cross N. Expertise in professional design. In K.A. Ericsson, R. Hoffman, A. Kozbelt & A.M. Williams (eds.), The Cambridge Handbook of Expertise and Expert Performance (pp. 372–388). New York: Cambridge University Press, 2006.
20 Simon H. (1978). Rational decision-making in business organizations. Nobel Memorial Lecture in Economics [Internet]. 1978 [cited 2022, Aug 30]. Available from: https://www.nobelprize.org/uploads/2018/06/simon-lecture.pdf.
21 Lerner J, Li Y, Valdesolo P, Kassam K. Emotion and decision making. Annual Review of. Psychology, 2015, 66, 799–823.
22 Mosier K, Fischer U, Hoffman R, et al. Expert professional judgments and "naturalistic decision making." In Ericsson KA, Hoffman R, Kozbelt A, et al. (eds.), The Cambridge Handbook of Expertise and Expert Performance (pp. 453–475). New York: Cambridge University Press. Kindle Edition, 2006.

23 Paris S, Byrnes J, Paris A. Constructing theories, identities, and actions of self-regulated learners. In Zimmerman B, Schunk D (eds.), Self-regulated learning and academic achievement: Theoretical perspectives (2nd ed.) (pp. 239–271). Hillsdale, NJ: Lawrence Erlbaum Associates, 2001.

24 Winne P. Cognition, metacognition, and self-regulation. Oxford Research Encyclopedia of Education [Internet]. 2021, Aug 31 [cited 2022, Aug 30]. Available from: https://doi.org10.1093/acrefore/9780190264093.013.1528.

25 Glaser R, Chi M. Overview. In Chi M, Glaser R, Farr M (eds.), The nature of expertise (pp. xv–xxviii). Hillsdale, NJ: Erlbaum, 1988.

26 Feltovich P, Prietula M, Ericsson KA. Studies of expertise from psychological perspectives: Historical foundations and recurrent themes. In Ericsson KA, Hoffman R, Kozbelt A (eds.), The Cambridge Handbook of Expertise and Expert Performance (pp. 59–83). New York: Cambridge University Press, 2006.

27 Ericsson KA. The influence of experience and deliberate practice on the development of superior expert performance. In Ericsson, KA, Hoffman, R, Kozbelt A, et al. (eds.), The Cambridge Handbook of Expertise and Expert Performance (pp. 683–703). New York: Cambridge University Press, 2006.

28 Schmidt H, Mamede S. How cognitive psychology changed the face of medical education research. Advance in Health Sciences Education, 2020, 25, 1025–1043.

29 Zimmerman B. Attaining self-regulation: A social cognitive perspective. In Boekarts, M, Pintrich P, Zeidner M (eds.), Self-regulation: Theory, research, and applications (pp. 13–39). Orlando, FL: Academic, 2000.

30 Associated Press. Test scores dropped to lowest levels in decades during pandemic, according to nationwide exam. NBC News [Internet]. 2022, Oct 24 [cited 2023, Jan 14. Available from: https://www.nbcnews.com/news/us-news/test-scores-dropped-lowest-levels-decades-pandemic-according-nationwid-rcna53659.

31 Dill, K. School's out for summer and many teachers are calling it quits. Wall Street Journal [Internet]. 2022, Jun 20 [cited 2023, Jan 14]. Available from: https://www.wsj.com/articles/schools-out-for-summer-and-many-teachers-are-calling-it-quits-11655732689.

32 https://en.wikipedia.org/wiki/History_of_education.

33 Callahan R. Education and the cult of efficiency. Chicago: University of Chicago Press, 1962.

34 Cubberley E. Public school administration. Quoted in Callahan R. Education and the cult of efficiency (p. 151). Chicago: University of Chicago Press, 1962.

35 Dewey J. My pedagogic creed. School Journal, 1897, 54, 77–80.

36 Partnership for the Twenty-First Century. Learning for the 21st century. Washington, DC: Partnership for the 21st Century, 2003.

37 Kozma R. A framework for ICT policies to transform education. In R. Kozma (ed.) Transforming education: The power of ICT policies (pp. 19–36). Paris, UNESCO, 2011.

38 Scardamalia M, Bereiter C. Knowledge Building. In Encyclopedia of Education (2nd ed., pp. 1370–1373). New York: Macmillan, 2003.

39 Sawyer K. Group genius: The creative power of collaboration. New York: Basic Books, 2017.

40 Schank P, Kozma R. Learning chemistry through the use of a representation-based knowledge building environment. Journal of Computers in Mathematics and Science Teaching, 2001, 21(3), 253–279.

41 Lave J, Wenger E. Situated learning: Legitimate peripheral participation. New York: Cambridge University Press, 1991.

42 Wenger E. Communities of practice: Learning, meaning, and identity. New York: Cambridge University Press, 1998.

43 Wenger E, McDermott R, Snyder W. Cultivating communities of practice. Cambridge, MA: Harvard Business School Press, 2002.

44 Burggraf C, Milazo L, Raffle H, et al. Stronger together: The role of a community of practice in implementing a culturally relevant response to the opioid epidemic during the COVID-19 pandemic. Family & Community Health, 2021, 44(3), 113–116.

45 Table 1. Labor force status of 2021 high school graduates and 2020-2021 high school dropouts 16 t0 24 years old. U.S. Bureau of Labor Statistics [Internet]. 2021, Oct [cited 2022, Aug 30]. Available from: https://www.bls.gov/news.release/hsgec.t01.htm.

46 Pandey E. The college degree barrier to work. Axios [Internet]. 2021, Apr 27 [cited 2022, Aug 30]. Available from: https://www.axios.com/college-degree-barrier-work-08048e08-2685-4b25-87f9-89b216a32d06.html.

47 Questions for Larry Rosenstock. Voice of San Diego [Internet]. 2006, Sep 2 [cited 2022, Aug 30]. Available from: https://voiceofsandiego.org/2006/09/02/questions-for-larry-rosenstock/.

48 Larry Rosenstock. Wikipedia [Internet]. [cited 2022, Aug 30]. Available from: https://en.wikipedia.org/wiki/Larry_Rosenstock.

49 Connecting the classroom to the world. High Tech High [Internet]. [cited 2022, Aug 30]. Available from: https://www.hightechhigh.org.

50 Project School Site. High Tech High [Internet]. [cited 2022, Aug 30]. Available from: https://www.hightechhigh.org/project_school_site/high-tech-high/.

51 HTH design process. PBL Design Camp [Internet]. [cited 2022, Aug 30]. Available from: https://pbldesigncamp.org/about/.

52 2019-2020 School profile. High Tech High [Internet]. [cited 2022, Aug 30]. Available from: https://www.hightechhigh.org/hth/wp-content/uploads/sites/22/2021/10/HTH_School_profile-2019-20-1.pdf.

53 Bryk A. Improvement in action: Advancing quality in America's schools. Cambridge, MA; Harvard University Press, 2020.

14

Promote Equality and Address Injustice

If you are neutral in situations of injustice, you have chosen the side of the oppressor.

Archbishop Desmond Tutu
South African Religious Leader

Equality and justice were important concepts in the Enlightenment. More than any others, these two concepts capture our sense of what is right or wrong in the world. And the two concepts are inseparable. As Utilitarian John Stuart Mill put it, "all social inequalities. . .assume the character, not of simple inexpediency, but of injustice."[1]

But what do we mean by *equality*? How is it that we can say all people are created equal when there are obvious differences between us, differences that shape our lives and influence our happiness? And what is a just society?

We will explore these questions in this chapter. However, we won't leave them as abstract ideas only discussed by philosophers. We will look at them as they are played out in our society. And we will ask the questions: How can we address equality in our designs? How can we create a more justice society?

Equality

Equality in the Enlightenment was revolutionary in its conception. To realize how revolutionary the concept was, we need to step back in time to a world in which society was profoundly and systemically unequal. Going back to antiquity, notions of inequality prevailed. Inequality of classes and genders were presumed as natural in the philosophies of Plato and Aristotle, and it was enshrined in Greek, and subsequently, Roman political and cultural institutions. Huge social and economic inequalities continued through the Middle Ages and into the Renaissance, again considered part of the natural order.

The Medieval period in Europe was dominated by a feudal, or in England, manorial economic and social system that was the embodiment of inequality, which pervaded Europe. It was an agricultural system in which a lord held land, and his peasants were bound to the land and required to work on the lord's fields and provide military service. Ownership of the land was linked to aristocratic title, nobility, or royalty, headed by the monarch, who also had special rights and privileges that are passed on by birth. The linkage between land and title locked the system in place.

Make the World a Better Place: Design with Passion, Purpose, and Values, First Edition. Robert B. Kozma.

Equality by design

In England, this system began to unravel with the bloody Civil War of 1642–1651, in which Parliament, especially the House of Commons, wrested power from the King. The bloodless Glorious Revolution of 1688 and the English Bill of Rights in 1689 confirmed the power of Parliament over the diminished power of the King. During the 17th century, there was also a growing class of nontitled land owners, merchants, traders, and professionals who were creating economic wealth outside the feudal system. This lead up to the Industrial Revolution, in the late 18th century, in which wealth was based not so much on ownership of land and agricultural production, but the ownership of capital and industrial production, ownership that was independent of title.

The Enlightenment emerged in the early 18th century during a period in which England and the Continent were experiencing significant and disruptive economic and social change, transitioning from the Medieval to the Modern periods. As such, ideas of the Enlightenment were both an intellectual articulation of the change that was happening and an influence that amplified the change.

Within this historical context, John Locke, who lived between 1632 and 1704, made some startling—indeed revolutionary—statements. Locke claimed that all men were capable of reason and in human's natural state "all the power and jurisdiction is reciprocal, no one having more than another" and "equal one amongst another without subordination or subjection."[2] This was in profound conflict with a worldview that considered inequality as natural and established by divine law.

Within this historical context, the notion of equality that emerged did not pertain to all sorts of equality. Titled nobility still existed, as did a vast population of peasants and even slaves. It was not social or economic equality that Locke claimed but political equality—equal treatment under the law. Even this equality was limited to free adult males. In Locke's words, it was "equality, which all men are in, in respect of jurisdiction or dominion one over another."[3] The American colonists built on this idea of political equality when, in declaring a new nation in 1776, Jefferson penned the words, "All men are created equal and endowed by their Creator with certain unalienable rights, that among these are life, liberty, and the pursuit of happiness."

Inequality by Design

However, even as Jefferson declared the equality of all men, inequality had already been baked into the laws and culture of the new country. The early colonists did not consider others equal to themselves, specifically neither the Native American population that occupied the land for millennia before them nor the enslaved Africans who worked their plantations. Over time, these attitudes were designed into the laws and policies that governed the colonies, and ultimately, the new nation that the Founders designed.

Native Americans

When the English settlers arrived on the North American continent in 1585 and established their first colony at Roanoke, in what is now North Carolina, they were met by natives who were not their technological equal. Ready to battle the competing Spanish conquistadors, if encountered, the colonists were supplied with light armor, steel swords, long bows with steel-tipped arrows, steel tipped pikes, muskets, pistols, and canons on their ship, which they were also prepared to use against the natives.[4] The Native Americans were armed only with clubs and swords of wood, and bows and arrows tipped with stone or shells. However, the indigenous people were not only technologically unequal, they were different: They looked different, had different customs, and different religious beliefs.

The Virginia Company of London was established in 1606 with a charter from King James granting it a large swath of North America for the purpose of settling it and profiting from the trade of natural resources of the land, particularly the mining of gold, silver, and copper and the produce from plantations, with a share of profits going to the king and the rest to the company.[5] It granted self-governance to the company, consistent with the king's approval. Expeditions were funded by the sale of common stock to those expecting a return on their investment.[6]

The first venture of the company arrived in 1607 at Jamestown, in what is now the state of Virginia. The relationship between the Jamestown settlers and local Native Americans was complex. The food settlers needed to survive depended on trade with the locals, whom they referred to in their chronicles as "savages."[7] The natives both feared and distrusted the colonists, wanting friendship but concerned that the colonists would harm them or aid enemy tribes to do so. Mutual distrust erupted into conflict that escalated over time to a point where settlers attacked and burned local villages, and the natives ultimately abandoned the immediate area to the settlers.

To fully understand the relationship between natives and colonists, it helps to know the legal and cultural position regarding indigenous people that was incorporated, implicitly and explicitly, into the charter that governed the colonists' actions in Virginia, and later, other English colonies. The Virginia charter referred to the native inhabitants as people living in darkness and ignorance of God, and it charged colonists with bringing them to the Christian religion.[8] The charter also referred to them as "savages" and "infidels." The legal status of infidels at the time was that of a perpetual enemy against whom war was legally and morally justified. Consequently, not only did the Virginia Company "own" the land, granted to them by the king, the colonists were operating under a moral duty to convert the natives and were legally justified in warring against them if not converted. Furthermore, it was common for the colonists, and in the English culture more generally, to consider the natives not as people but as "wild beasts" in the forest.

The relationship between the natives and colonists was compounded by commercial concerns. Gold, silver, and copper were not found in Virginia, but the colony started to be profitable with the export crop of tobacco, which was introduced earlier to Europe from America by the Spanish and had become popular in England.[9] In response, the land was cleared and used to grow tobacco, which was exported to England at a profit and which made some of the colonists rich. As the number of settlements grew, so did the need for more planation land, increasing the conflict with Native Americans.

By 1776, 13 colonies had been established, and the population of the British colonies had grown from 350 to over 2 million.[10] At the same time, the native population had been reduced from an estimated 100,000 at the time of the first colony to about 30,000 as a result of European diseases to which natives were not immune, wars with the colonists, and relocation west of the Allegany Mountains.[11] Or they were sold off as slaves for use in Caribbean plantations.[12]

The legal status of natives varied from colony to colony, but they were generally not treated as equal to Whites. Nor did the Constitution treat Native Americans as citizens of the new country; rather, it considered native tribes as distinct entities to be dealt with as were other nations. And since Native Americans generally sided with the British against the colonists and the natives were out-numbered and out-armed, they were treated as conquered nations subjected to the terms of the conquerors. Generally, this meant that natives were confined to reservations or forced to move west, arrangements that were confirmed by treaties forced by government troops.

As the nation expanded westward, the political rights and sovereign status of Native American nations were variously respected, ignored, terminated, and unilaterally modified by the federal government, perpetrating great harm on the tribes as thoroughly documented in the book *Uneven Ground: American Indian Sovereignty and Federal Law* by David E. Wilkins and K. Tsianina Lomawaima.[13] The purpose, outcome, and impact of these policies were that land was made available to settlers, who paid the government to own it, and Native Americans were deprived of their traditional hunting grounds and means of living. Suffice it to say that Native Americans have not been among the "all men created equal" referenced by the Declaration of Independence.

Nor were the enslaved people from Africa.

Enslaved Africans

In 1619, shortly after the Virginia colony was established and before the *Mayflower* landed on Plymouth rock in 1620, an English privateer with a cargo of enslaved people stolen from a Portuguese slave ship stopped off the coast of the Virginia colony and traded "20 and odd Negroes" for food. These were the first enslaved Africans in the English colony.[14]

The legal status of Africans was initially that of indentured servants who worked with no wage for a specified period before being freed and children born to Africans at the time were legally free.[15] However, in practice, they were held in servitude for life, and in 1640, a Virginia court ruled that children born to Africans were the property of their owner, which was the first official act of enslavement in the colonies. In 1641, the Massachusetts colony passed a law institutionalizing slavery and later in the 17th century passed a series of laws further defining the institution, including making it legal to sell children of enslaved people and to limit the movements of Black people.[16] In 1662, Virginia passed a law, contrary to all laws at the time, that determined the legal status of a person based on that of their mother rather than their father, enslaving even the children of enslaved women that were fathered by their owners.[17]

By the end of the 17th century, chattel slavery was legally established in all the English colonies in North America. Chattel slavery means that enslaved people were not considered human beings, but merely the property of the owner who were treated however the owner saw fit. They had no rights, could be bought or sold, and their value was determined by the open market.

During the 15th through 19th centuries, the slave trade in the Atlantic had become a big business, engaged in by all the European naval powers, with an estimated 12 million Africans sent to the Americas after killing at least as many in their procurement and their sea passage.[18] The brutal harm and suffering inflicted on enslaved people once they were sold is also documented in the book *Inhuman Bondage: The Rise and Fall of Slavery in the New World* by Yale professor David Davis.[19] And, of course, depriving Africa of a large portion of its productive population had a profound effect on its subsequent development of that continent. Over time, an elaborate body of economic, moral, and racial thought evolved to justify the institution.[20]

By 1790, nearly 3.9 million people were counted as inhabitants of the country, of which approximately 964,000, or 25%, were slaves.[21] The Constitution of 1787 does not refer directly to slaves, but leaves it up to the states to determine who is qualified to vote. Women, minors, Native Americans, and slaves were not included. However, the Constitution indirectly referred to enslaved people. At the insistence of slave-holding states, representation in the House was apportioned based on three-fifths of "all other persons." As a consequence, states with a high proportion of slaves had a higher representation in the House than did nonslave holding states or those with relatively few, even though enslaved people could not vote for the people who nominally represented them.

However, things were changing in some states, changes that would come to divide the nation. By 1790, slavery had been outlawed in Massachusetts and Maine, and enslaved people were freed.

In 1808, Congress passed a ban on the importation of slaves into the country, although the smuggling of slaves was common afterward.

But slavery continued to be an essential part of the plantation economy in the South and it continued to be an important institution in the country, even though a growing number of states outlawed it. In 1850, the Fugitive Slave Act was passed in Congress that compelled nonslave states, of which there were 16 at the time, to return runaway slaves to owners in the 15 states in which slavery was legal. The Kansas-Nebraska Act of 1854, along with the Missouri Compromise of 1820, were successful efforts of southern states to maintain their balance of power in the Senate, to match that in the House, regarding the admission of new slave versus nonslave states.

In 1858, the U.S. Supreme Court decided against a case brought by Dred Scott, an enslaved man who claimed he was free because his owner now lived in a free state. In ruling against Scott, the court ruled generally that African Americans had no claim to freedom or citizenship. In writing for the majority, Chief Justice Roger B. Taney stated:

> [Negroes] had for more than a century before been regarded as beings of an inferior order, and altogether unfit to associate with the white race, either in social or political relations; and so far inferior, that they had no rights which the white man was bound to respect.[22]

As in this judgement, the federal government generally deferred to the states in passing laws that affected the status of enslaved people. To protect their system of slavery, southern states passed slave codes that restricted the gathering and movement of slaves, limited their right to marriage or to learn to read, authorized slave patrols for the purpose of pursuing runaway slaves, and enabled owners to punish slaves in any way they saw fit, the brutality of which is well documented.[23]

In November 1860, Abraham Lincoln, an Illinois Republican running on a platform that would limit the number of slave states admitted into the Union, was elected President. On February 8, 1861, even before Lincoln was sworn into office on March 4, 11 southern slave states formed the Confederate States of America. On April 12, the Confederates declared war on the United States, attacking the Union fort at Charleston, South Carolina, after which four more states joined the Confederacy.

The purpose of the Confederacy was made clear in a speech by Alexander Stephens, its Vice President:

> [The Confederacy's] corner-stone rests upon the great truth that the negro is not equal to the white man; that slavery subordination to the superior race is his natural and normal condition. This, our new government, is the first, in the history of the world, based upon this great physical, philosophical, and moral truth.... With us, all of the white race, however high or low, rich or poor, are equal in the eye of the law. Not so with the negro. Subordination is his place. He, by nature, or by the curse against Canaan, is fitted for that condition which he occupies in our system.[24] (p. 335)

During the conflict, President Lincoln freed slaves in the rebellious states with the hope they would flee to the North and join Union forces, which approximately 180,000 did.[25] The war resulted in an estimated 620,000 military deaths, including more than 30,000 Black troops, and the wounding of 476,000 more.[26]

After losing the war, during a period of Reconstruction, the rebellious states were allowed to rejoin the Union if they ratified the newly passed 13th Amendment to the Constitution, which prohibited slavery, accept a punishment for a crime, and reformulate their state constitutions to conform to it. Federal troops were stationed throughout the South to protect freed slaves and assure that states complied with federal requirements.

Reconstruction ended when federal troops were pulled out of the South as part of a compromise that resolved the disputed presidential election of 1876 between Republican nominee Rutherford Hayes and Democrat Samuel Tilden. This launched a period during which the former Confederate states used legal, and through White citizen groups such as the Ku Klux Klan, extra-legal means to dismantle any gains made by Blacks and to reestablish White supremacy.[27] "Jim Crow" was the name given to the new legal and social order that segregated Blacks from White society, effectively eliminating their political power and rights, and subjugating them to White rule. The exception of criminality, embedded in the 13th Amendment, was used to re-enslave Blacks by arresting them for breaking laws specifically designed for the purpose.[28] Otherwise, terrorism was used to enforce this social order on anyone who resisted.

State constitutions were rewritten, removing reforms imposed by the Reconstruction. For example, in 1890, Mississippi adopted a new state constitution with a poll tax and arbitrary literacy tests for voting, sections designed to disenfranchise newly franchised African Americans. As U.S. Senator and future Governor James Kimble Vardaman put it: "There is no use to equivocate or lie about the matter. Mississippi's constitutional convention was held for no other purpose than to eliminate the nigger from politics; not the ignorant—but the nigger."[29]

This attitude and the corresponding treatment of Black Americans as second-class citizens has, since the Reconstruction, reverberated throughout not only in the Old South, but also the entire United States in legal, political, and cultural practices. In the North, laws, policies, and practices were designed to separate Blacks from the rest of society, such as the practice of redlining, which restricted where Black could own homes, or the post-World War II GI Bill, which denied home loans to Black veterans.[30] The impact of these laws, policies, and cultural practices was not only to segregate Blacks from White society and impose on them a hierarchy of human worth, but also to reduce their access to the primary means of accumulating intergenerational wealth, home ownership.[31] These policies resulted in far fewer Blacks owning homes, and the homes they owned had far less value, significantly contributing to the racial wealth gap. And, of course, lack of wealth reduced access to quality education and the opportunities for improvement that come along with it, compounding the impact.

While court rulings and laws have been passed to address some of these issues, such as the 1954 *Brown v. Board of Educatio*n Supreme Court ruling and the 1964 Civil Rights and 1965 Voting Rights Acts, the United States remains a country in which "equality" and "race"—Black or Native American—remain conflicting concepts. Consequently, the Enlightenment principle of equality upon which the country was founded remains elusive. Sadly, much of that has been by design. And if that elusive concept will be realized for our country, it will also be by design, by taking us from where we are to where we ought to be.

Merit and Its Tyranny

With the founding of our country, a meritocratic social, legal, and to some extent, moral system replaced one that valued humans based on their nobility and birth. In theory, meritocracy says that everyone has an equal chance to pursue happiness and success. The theory goes that in such a system, inequality and wealth exist because of differences in talent and effort, rather than by an accident of birth. In this system, the most talented people will rise to the top, making the system better and benefitting everyone. Those who take advantage of opportunities in this system have a right to whatever rewards they reap. On the flip side is the moral claim that those who are unsuccessful have nothing or no one to blame but themselves for lack of developed talent or effort.

Harvard philosophy professor Michael Sandel, in his book *The Tyranny of Merit*, contends otherwise.[32] In it, Sandel makes the points that the meritocratic system fails on its first principle: we don't all have equal opportunity. The meritocratic system ignores the role of intergenerational wealth in creating unequal opportunity, and that this advantage is compounded across generations.

Merit and morality

But Sandel goes on to make a deeper point. Meritocracy, the way it is practiced in our society, is corrosive to civic well-being. In downplaying the compounding effect of intergenerational wealth and the role of sheer luck, meritocracy creates an attitude that successful people are that way because they are inherently better people. It confounds wealth and social status with human value and morality.

This head start advantage is illustrated by an informally-reported experiment conducted by Professor Paul Piff and his team of psychologists at the University of California, Irvine.[33] In this experiment, researchers invited pairs of strangers to play a rigged Monopoly game where a coin flip designated one player rich and one poor. The rich players received twice as much money as their opponent to begin with; as they played the game, these players got to roll two dice instead of one; and when they passed "Go," they collected $200 to their opponent's $100. As the game progressed, "rich" players began to act—through body language and boasting about their wealth, by smacking their pieces loudly against the playing board and by making light of their opponents' misfortune—as though the poor players deserved their lot and they deserved the good fortune that was largely a result of a lucky flip of the coin. At the end of the game, when researchers asked the rich players why they had won the game, not one person attributed it to luck. "They don't talk about the flip of the coin. They talk about the things that they did. They talk about their acumen, they talk about their competencies, they talk about this decision or that decision," Piff reported.

That the "rich" players were not actually rich, indicates that the relative worth of successful people in a meritocratic society has pervaded the culture. Being successful not only means that you have more resources; it means you are better than others and that you deserve to be so.

These differences also corrode the morals of the meritocratic elites. In a series of other studies, Piff found that people who are better off act differently from their poorer peers.[34] His findings include that, for example, while 90% of California drivers follow a law requiring them to stop for pedestrians at crosswalks, people who drive luxury vehicles are three to four times more likely not to. Or, in an experiment where people were left in a video-monitored room with a bowl of candy they were told was for kids coming by later, wealthy people took twice as much candy as poorer participants. And in a test of honesty in reporting dice rolls where the prize for the best roll was $50, he found that people making $150,000 a year cheated four times as much as someone who made $15,000 a year. The findings apply equally to liberals and conservatives, whether rich or poor. And the results were consistent across 30 studies on thousands of people all over the United States.

Sandel claims that the lack of compassion or empathy among meritocratic elites has diminished the value of all work and workers that aren't of high status. This, in turn, has engendered a populist backlash against elites and experts, such as scientists and other professions; by those who have been disadvantaged by the system against those who have been most advantaged and look down on them.

For our society to be just, Sandel asserts, we need to acknowledge the dignity of all work and all contributions that improve our world. The moral and economic significance of this need was demonstrated during the COVID pandemic when farmers, delivery workers, child care workers, grocery clerks, nurse assistants, maintenance workers, truckers, warehouse workers, and home-care workers put their health at risk to provide everyone with essential services, often in stressful conditions for little pay.

Work is not only about making a living, but also about contributing to the common good and being recognized for it. And we need to make life better for those who lack a college degree but make essential contributions to our society. Sandel closes his case by quoting a speech Dr. Martin Luther King Jr. gave to striking sanitation workers the night before his assassination, "the person who picks up our garbage, in the final analysis, is as significant as the physician, for if he doesn't do his job, diseases are rampant. All labor has dignity."[35]

The compounding effect of inequality

Sandel's book emphasizes the compounding effect of merit: those who have more get more. This is no more apparent than in the current news that during a pandemic, when millions of people lost income or even their jobs, the world's richest people got incredibly richer.[36]

The inverse is also often true. Those at the bottom not only don't get richer, they also often get poorer. There is a compounding effect of inequality. This compounding happens at both micro and macro levels. And inequality is compounded both across factors and over time. Let's look at this with three inter-related indicators of inequality: wealth, education, and home ownership.

Between 1989 and 2016, the gap in wealth between the poorest and richest in the United States more than doubled, growing significantly with the 2008 housing crisis and its aftermath.[37] This relative inequality in wealth persisted and grew more during the pandemic, nearly doubling again.[38] Sadly, after more than a year into the pandemic, while fewer White and Hispanic Americans were reporting lost income, the percentage of Black Americans growing poorer increased.[39]

Wealth is also connected to access to other opportunities, such as education. University of Michigan sociology professor Fabian Pfeffer, did a study that examined differences between wealth groups and college attainment.[40] What he found is that wealth inequality in college graduates rose between those born in the 1970s and those born in the 1980s, with the college graduation rates of children from higher wealth backgrounds surging while children from lower wealth levels are left behind.

This rapid increase in wealth inequality in college degree attainment is especially concerning because the stakes of college completion have also been rising. The difference in median earnings between individuals with a bachelor's degree and those who completed high school was larger in 2019 than 2010.[41] In 2010, the median earnings of those with a bachelor's degree was $17,600 higher than the median earnings of those who completed high school; in 2019, this difference was $20,800 in real dollars. During this period, there was a massive decrease in the number of jobs available to the noncollege educated, particularly right after the 2008 housing crisis.[42] At the same time, there was been a dramatic sevenfold increase in education debt from 1995 to 2017, which makes it more difficult for low-income students to get ahead and adds to inequality rather than reducing it.[43]

Thus, the primary mechanism in our society to create opportunity for upward mobility—college education—is failing in the U.S. College education is not addressing inequality; it is contributing to it. Unsurprising, nearly 40% of Americans say that colleges and universities are having a negative effect on the country.[44]

The third leg of this inequality stool is home ownership, the American dream and the primary vehicle in the United States for accumulating wealth. Home ownership was at a high of 69.1% in 2005 and began dropping dramatically during the housing crisis, hitting a low of 63.5% in 2016.[45]

It recovered a bit subsequently, but dropped again during the pandemic, standing 65.6% at the end of 2021.

The Fair Housing Act of 1968 prohibited discrimination concerning the sale, rental, and financing of housing based on race, religion, national origin, sex, and as amended, handicap and family status. This practically eliminated blatant discrimination, such as redlining. But buying a home and accumulating wealth, as a result, is still a challenge for Black Americans and other minorities.

This is documented in a study that used data from the Department of Housing and Urban Development in neighborhoods of 28 U.S. cities to find strong evidence that discrimination constrains the neighborhood choices of minorities in their housing search, across the country.[46] They found that minorities are significantly more likely to be steered toward neighborhoods with lower quality schools and neighborhood human capital, and higher rates of assault and pollution exposure. And an experimental study using email correspondence with mortgage loan originators, across all 50 states, using racially distinctive names and other qualifications equal, found a net discrimination effect on African Americans equivalent to having a credit score that is 71 points lower.[47] Holding location preferences and income constant, these discriminatory steering practices can alone explain a disproportionate number of minority households found in high poverty neighborhoods that contribute to racial gaps in intergenerational income mobility.

In sum, the mechanism our society offers to improve your lot—meritocracy and hard work—has not worked as claimed. Within the context of societal inequality, merit merely solidifies and perpetuates the inequality. To make the world a better place, we need designs that disrupt these patterns and remediate this harm. To make the world a better place, we not only need to acknowledge the equal value and worth of all human lives and design for more than just the well to do, we need to address injustice.

Justice

What makes a society just? And how can we design a more just world, particularly in light of the inequality that exists?

While notions of political equality were novel in the 18th century, notions of justice and what makes a just world have been around at least since ancient times. But some studies show that a sense of justice may be embedded in our genetic code, going back in our evolutionary history.

What is just?

In a study of capuchin monkeys, primatologists Sarah Brosnan and Frans de Waal found an interesting set of behaviors we can all relate to.[48] Capuchins like both grapes and cucumbers as food but vastly prefer grapes. In an experiment, two monkeys in side-by-side cages in which they could observe each other's behavior were given tokens that they could exchange for food. Initially, each monkey was given a cucumber when they gave the experimenter a token. But after a while, one monkey was given a grape while the other was given a cucumber in exchange for the token. In this situation, 45% of the monkeys subsequently receiving a cucumber refused to complete the exchange, often expressing dissatisfaction with screeches or by throwing the food back at the experimenter.

In another condition, when the companion monkey was given a grape without the requirement to exchange the token, while the experimental monkey was required to give a token in exchange for a cucumber, the refusal rate was even higher—80%. Among these monkeys, there seemed to be a common sense of what's fair, something along the lines of equal effort (i.e., both give a token) must result in equal return (i.e., both given a grape). And according to the capuchin conception of justice, it is extremely unjust when you have to give up something for a cucumber and another monkey gets a grape for doing nothing.

Researchers speculate that such unjust behaviors among monkeys deteriorate group cohesion needed for its survival, and social responses evolved to keep it in check. For example, in a review of research, Brosnan identified studies that documented the behavior of the highest-ranking males in the group to recognize inequalities in group interactions and act to break up fights on behalf of the loser in order to maintain group stability.[49]

In human history, a strong central leader has often played a role in establishing fairness and maintaining stability in societies. Among the earliest recorded human expressions of justice or fairness is Hammurabi's Code, written in ancient Babylon around the 18th century, B.C.[50] It is a set of 282 laws; do's and don'ts intended to maintain social order and settle disputes within the kingdom. Most are very specific, such as:

> If a man has a debt lodged against him, and the storm-god Adad devastates his field or a flood sweeps away the crops, or there is no grain grown in the field due to insufficient water—in that year he will not repay grain to his creditor; he shall suspend performance of his contract and he will not give interest payments for that year.

And:

> If a builder constructs a house for a man but does not make it conform to specifications so that a wall then buckles, that builder shall make that wall sound using his own silver.

Of the 282 laws, many are associated with punishments for their infractions, such as:

> If a man breaks into a house, they shall kill him and hang him in front of that very breach.

And the classic:

> If a man should blind the eye of another, they shall blind his eye.

But justice was in bits and pieces. There are no general principles expressed in the code that underlie these laws, although some implicit principles can be inferred. For example, the latter two laws and many others are retributive in principle. That is, if someone breaks the law they should be punished, and perhaps, the punishment should in some way fit the crime—an eye for an eye.

When Aristotle took up writing about justice in the 4th century B.C., setting out the principles underlying the concept of justice was a major part of his task. Justice, for Aristotle, is not only important for the order of society but important for the common good; it is justice that makes for a good society.[51] Articulating the principles of a just society was very important to Aristotle. And one of the principles he articulated, implicit in Hammurabi's code—and the behavior of capuchin monkeys—is reciprocity. For Aristotle, a society is just when everyone gets what is fair, when the distribution of merit or effort and benefits is just; what he calls "distributive justice." There is also what Aristotle calls "corrective justice," sometimes referred to as "restorative" or "reparative" justice. That is, when a situation is not just, there needs to be a correction that restores justice. This implies a need, for example, to return to someone what was taken unjustly, or in the case of Hammurabi's builder, restore it to its original condition.

But it is important to understand that for Aristotle the equality of this justice was only for those who were "equal" in a world that took the natural condition to be one of inequality, as it was for Hammurabi. That is, the "fairness" of the distribution of effort and benefits was proportional to merit. And, in Athenian society, the merit of women, children, and slaves was inherently unequal to that of men. It was only among free men of equal status that Aristotle believed that the distribution between effort and benefit must be equal. For people of different status or merit, it was just that it be unequal. This notion of proportional justice was carried through the Middle Ages.

It was with the Enlightenment notion of equality that this conception of proportional justice came to be revised. The pre-Enlightenment philosopher, Thomas Hobbes, writing during the bloody English Civil War, believed that justice was an artifact (or a design), constructed by humans to address their natural state that was, in his view, a war of all against all.[52] Equality for Hobbes was the assessment that all men are equal enough, in practical terms, such that even the weakest could kill the strongest, by trickery or by teaming up with others, and that no one man is of such power that he could prevail over all. In Hobbes's war, there is no right or wrong, no law, no property, no justice, only force and fraud. To set aside this all-out war, to get to a better place, according to Hobbes, men enter into a covenant, or social contract, creating, in government, a greater power that enforces security, peace, and justice on everyone, much as did Hammurabi's Code. In such a state, each man follows the covenant, or law, trusting that others will do so as well, knowing that to break the law would be considered unjust and punished, the form of retributive justice that Hammurabi imposed on his people.

It was during the time of the bloodless Glorious Revolution that John Locke wrote of a different, imagined, natural state, one of equality and independence with equal rights to life, liberty, and property.[53] For Locke, the purpose of government was to affirm this natural state. However, Locke believed, as did Aristotle, that women, children, and slaves were inherently unequal to free men. Locke differed from the notions of Aristotle, who believed there were inherent differences among free men, such as that those who ruled were inherently better or meritorious than others (or the converse, those who were inherently better had the right to rule). Thus, the burdens and benefits would be unequally distributed, with those superior men getting more privileges and say than others. Locke rejected this notion of inequality among free men and argued, for example, that all men had a right to their property and that they acquired property through their own labor.

It was up to others, as the Enlightenment progressed, to extend this new conception that "all are created equal" to others and to examine the implications it had for the conception of justice.

Equality and justice for all

With David Hume, the Enlightenment came to differ from Locke in the conceptualization of human nature. For Locke, the common foundation of humanity is the universal capacity to reason and the assumption that we all shared this was the basis for his claim that all men are created equal. Hume, who along with Adam Smith, is considered a Moral Sentimentalist, contended that, beyond reason, it is our shared emotions or sentiments that are the foundation of our common humanity. These sentiments constitute an innate sense that something is right or wrong, much as the capuchin monkeys sensed there was something wrong about one getting a cucumber in trade for a token while another monkey was getting a grape in trade or for doing nothing at all. For Hume, while emotion plays an important role in our sense of fairness,[54] it is up to reason to figure out how to accomplish a good outcome, unlike, perhaps, the behavior of the monkey, which is to screech and throw things.

Justice for Hume, as for Hobbes, is an artifice that people rationally and cooperatively construct. It is the device society uses to guide reasoned behavior. But for Hume and Smith, unlike for Hobbes, the establishment of justice is in response to this common sense of fairness or unfairness, based not just on one's own experience, but through the sentiment of sympathy, the experience and emotions of others. It isn't a social contract that is the foundation of a just society, as it was for Hobbes, but the bonds of emotions and shared experiences that are common to all.

It was up to the Utilitarians Jeremy Bentham and John Stuart Mill to make the connection between equality and our shared emotions explicit, particularly the emotions of happiness and suffering. They did not claim that equality was a natural state, but claimed, as a moral imperative, that the happiness of each person should be considered equally in making laws or public policies. It is on this basis that the Utilitarians consider the best society one that achieves the greatest happiness for the greatest number.

At about the time the U.S. Civil War was brewing, Mill wrote in Scotland that, "[The Greatest Good] principle is a mere form of words without rational signification, unless one person's happiness, supposed equal in degree (with the proper allowance made for kind), is counted for exactly as much as another's."[55] And, as Mill attributed to Bentham, "everybody to count for one, nobody for more than one." Mill concludes:

> The entire history of social improvement has been a series of transitions, by which one custom or institution after another, from being supposed a primary necessity of social existence, has passed into the rank of universally stigmatized injustice and tyranny. So it has been with the distinctions of slaves and freemen, nobles and serfs, patricians and plebeians; and so it will be, and in part already is, with the aristocracies of color, race, and sex. (p. 63)

Mill used this contention to argue for the abolition of slavery and the equal treatment of women. And with the Utilitarians, Locke's notion of political equality was extended to the larger social realm and included all of humankind.

A just society

In 1971, Harvard Philosophy Professor John Rawls (see Figure 14.1) authored a book entitled *A Theory of Justice* that was considered to be one of the most influential books in the 20th century.[56] Rawls begins with the premise, as did Locke, that all people are free and equal, although unlike Locke, he includes everyone. He also assumes, as does Hume and Smith, that we all have common emotions, and in particular, a sense of fairness. And he uses this sentiment as the basis for justice. But the task he takes on is how do we determine what is just based on these assumptions: freedom, equality, and a sense of fairness. That is, like Hume, he wants to use reason to get from emotion—a sense of fairness—to desirable behaviors—a situation of justice.

With these assumptions, Rawls took the rational position, called the "original position," that we can determine what is just by considering it through what he calls "a vail of ignorance" about our own personal condition. That is, we must consider a moral proposition as if it would apply to any of us, without us knowing what our current condition is. We don't know if we are young or old, Black or White, rich or poor, male or female or nonbinary (not his word). If we didn't know our own condition, how would we decide on the design of policies of products that would be just?

In such a situation, Rawls contends, we would all opt for equal treatment. It would be just to treat all people the same. All would benefit equally from society and since we might find ourselves in any situation, we would benefit too. But Rawls goes on with what he calls the *difference principle*. That is, if we treat anyone differently, if someone benefits more than others by their

Figure 14.1 John Rawls (*Source:* Wikimedia Commons).

participation in society, it would be just only if those inequalities result in benefits to all, especially those in society that are worst off. That is, if one person acquires more riches or more power than others, it would only be just if the results, in one way or another, through taxation, for example, benefitted everyone else, as well, especially the least wealthy and powerful. Rawls' philosophy had a significant effect on the design of U.S. social policies and programs for many years.

Robert Nozick is another Harvard philosophy professor who we met in Chapter 3. In his book *Anarchy, State, and Utopia*, he took issue with his colleague and friend Rawls.[57] Nozick starts with the position of Locke's state of nature, a state of perfect freedom in which people have a right to order their actions and dispose of their property as they see fit, bound only by law of nature that requires no one harm another in his life, health, liberty, or possessions. He denies that there are any independent moral principles applying to collective or political institutions that cannot be derived from the natural rights of their individual members.

Nozick argues that the only legitimate state is a minimal state limited to the provision of security, the protection of property, and the enforcement of contracts. He differs the most with Rawls in denying that there is a moral reason to mitigate social and economic inequality, arguing instead that, in the case of taxation, for example, that it is as wrong as theft or forced labor for any reason other than the protection of individual rights. Nozick claims that it is unjust to steal from others, or defraud them, or enslave them, seizing their product or land, and people who do so are subject to the rectification of injustice in holdings. However, he concedes that it is difficult, in practice, to determine the history and extent of such harm and the amount of rectification without violating that person's rights, which are supreme.

Professor Sandel takes on them both.[58] Contrary to Rawls, Sandel believes that we don't determine what is just in any particular situation by starting with a position of ignorance. You don't treat people as equal by ignoring their race, gender, beliefs, values, history, or their current situation. Sandel believes that all of these things are an important part of who we are. And Sandel challenges Nozick's contention that we have no obligation to others nor that the only obligation of the state is to protect individual rights.

For Sandel, justice is not an idealized end-state; it is a process. And it is socially embedded in particular situations. In a particular situation, justice is not determined by conducting thought experiments behind a vail of ignorance, as would Rawls, nor by imagining someone's feelings or how it would be to walk in someone else's shoes, as would Smith. We don't ourselves individually determine what is just, in Sandel's view. We do it in community, but not only in reasoning with others of our kind—those in our field of expertise, our social class, our neighborhood, our religion, our political party. In a pluralistic society, such as ours, Sandel asserts that we determine what is just by actually engaging with people who are different than us—who differ in race, gender, social class, wealth, sets of beliefs, history; people who are unequal in conditions of privilege, suffering, or pain. In any particular situation, we engage everyone who has a stake in the outcome, everyone who will be impacted by the results.

For Sandel, we don't treat people as equal by ignoring their background, their condition, their history. We treat them as equal by interacting with them civilly, by treating everyone with dignity. All are due respect, whether CEOs or grocery clerks, scientists or truck drivers, farmers or software developers. No one in this discussion is a nigger or a kike, a redneck or a snowflake. In a pluralistic society there are differences and there will be disagreements. By respectfully engaging with others to seek justice, we express our position, sometimes passionately. We try to persuade. We also listen and learn. Sometimes we will reach agreement; sometimes, perhaps often, we will not. But in understanding we get closer to a just society.

Designs that Promote Equality and Address Injustice

What have we learned from these philosophers? First, that equality is a natural right. As humans, all of us have the capacity to reason; all of us have emotions. All of us desire happiness and avoid suffering. And, as our Declaration of Independence puts it, "all men are created equal, that they are endowed by their Creator with certain unalienable rights, that among these are life, liberty, and the pursuit of happiness."

All of us should be treated equally; everybody to count as one, nobody for more than one.

And yet, equality is not our current situation. Even as the Declaration was being written, Native Americans were being killed and dispossessed of their land, and Africans were enslaved. And these conditions were codified in our Constitution, laws, and policies. Studies abound that show that our society is, in many ways, unequal and unjust.

How do we get from where we are to where we ought to be?

Hobbes and Hume contend that justice is a human artifice, a human design. If we are to have a just society, we must create it, collectively and individually with our actions and their consequences. Governments, companies, associations, churches, communities, block clubs, and work teams build an equal and just society. Legislators, judges, lawyers, bureaucrats, police, ministers, social workers, teachers create equality and justice with their laws, policies, programs, and practices. Manufacturers, product designers, engineers, computer programmers, experience designers, graphic designers, user experience designers, movie producers, writers, poets, sculptors, and musicians can create equality and justice with their products, services, performances, and works of art. . .or they can create inequality and injustice

So, how do they—how do *we*—create designs to advance equality and address injustice?

We learned from Professor Sandel that justice is a moral dialog within a diverse community. This returns us to the discussion in Chapter 11. Through collaborative design in a community of moral discourse, we not only design a product, formulate a good corporate policy, develop a public project, design a lesson plan, produce a film, or pass a law, we can move toward a just and equitable society. There will not be uniform agreement on its justness. But by engaging those who will be affected by it, it will likely be more just. On the other hand, if we think that our designs are neutral and have no impact on inequality and injustice, we are contributing to them.

However, by focusing moral discussions around our designs, we make moral concepts more concrete, more specific. Justice and injustice, equality and inequality are not just abstract concepts and we can contribute to a more just society. They are lived experiences that are played out in specific situations. And participants affected most by these situations draw on their experiences to propose solutions that will improve their condition. Yet these solutions may harm others. The product of these discussions has a concrete manifestation in a designed object, service, or experience, designs that have consequences that can be measured, although sometimes with difficulty. And it is in this way that we can shape the world and, to use Professor Verbeek's words, we "materialize morality."[59]

Case Study: The City of Austin and Reimagining Public Safety

On May 26, 2020, a video was released of the murder of George Floyd by Minneapolis policeman Derek Chauvin. The video was shocking. Across the country and around the world, massive demonstrations broke out. Rather than protecting and serving them, communities of color felt that police were harassing them and perpetuating a system of racial inequality and economic injustice. Protestors of all races demanded police reform, often under the slogan "defund the police." Major U.S. cities, including Minneapolis, New York, Los Angeles, Chicago, Philadelphia, and Austin responded by reducing police budgets. But with a 2021 spike in violent crime and shifting public attitudes, many of these cities backtracked and increased their budgets for police, even beyond their earlier funding.[60]

It turns out that "defunding the police" was a counterproductive blind alley. Reducing police funding did not address the root causes of inequality and injustice, and, in our complex, adaptive human system, it had many unintended effects that created an intense blowback.

But where does that leave us? How do we address the racism that has racked our country for 400 years? How do we act on our anger at such moral harm?

The case of Austin and the reimagining of its public safety is a good example of what we can do.

Case Study: The City of Austin and Reimagining Public Safety
Austin is a city of 960,000 citizens, the 11th largest city in the country by population.[61] It is a multi-ethnic city; 32% of its citizens are Hispanic; 9%, Asian; and 7%, Black. It is the capital of the state and the seat of the University of Texas. It is a prosperous city. It has a median household income of $75,400, an employment rate of 71.6%, a poverty rate of 12.2%, and 55% of the population has a bachelor's degree or higher. It is a liberal bastion in the heart of a conservative state.

(Continued)

Case Study: The City of Austin and Reimagining Public Safety (Continued)

However, Austin is not without its problems. In January 2020, before George Floyd's killing, the city's Office of Police Oversite issued a study on police racial profiling that found Black people constituted 15% of those pulled over by police and 25% of those arrested, although they constitute only 7% of the population. Hispanics accounted for 33% of vehicle stops and 44% of people arrested. Whites, according to the data, had a negative chance of being pulled over.[62]

There had also been several controversial police killings. In March 2019, Javier Ambler, a Black man, died while being arrested and tased multiple times after he was chased by sheriff's deputies for not reducing his brights to oncoming traffic.[63] In July of that year, Austin police shot and killed an Asian scientist, Dr. Mauris DeSilva, who was having a psychotic break down and threatening his own life with a knife.[64] And in April 2020, police killed Michael Ramos, a Black man, while attempting to apprehend him after they received a report about a drug deal by an armed man. He did not have a gun.[65]

Over a several-day period after George Floyd's murder, as in the rest of the country, there were multiple crowds, building to thousands of people, that demonstrated in front of the state capital, city hall, and the police headquarters against police actions in Minneapolis and Austin (see Figure 14.2).[66] There were peaceful marches through the first two days, with protesters carrying handmade signs saying things like "I can't breathe," "Black Lives Matter," "We will not be silenced," and "No Justice, No Peace." Or they chanted "George Floyd," "don't shoot," "hands up."

The initial demonstrations were organized by the Austin Justice Coalition, but it called off subsequent protests after demonstrations ended violently. As the second day progressed, some shops were vandalized, a car was set on fire, and a large number of nonviolent demonstrators

Figure 14.2 Protests in Austin (*Source:* IMAGN).

occupied an interstate highway adjacent to police headquarters, bringing traffic to a halt. The police responded by firing tear gas canisters, 12-gauge pellet bags, and rubber bullets into the crowd.[67] During the course of the demonstrations, 19 protesters were severely injured by non-lethal police rounds, including a university student who was not the intended target, but was critically injured with head and brain damage.[68]

At an emergency meeting following the demonstrations, the City Council heard emotional testimony from citizens demanding police reform. At its meeting the next week, the City Council passed a resolution committing the city to "reimagine public safety." It directed the city manager to submit a budget to freeze the number of new officers, explore ways of redistributing police resources to other units, increase the staff for mental health responders, and fund revisions of the police training curriculum. In response, City Manager Spencer Crock presented the City Council with a budget that reduced funds for the Police Department by $120 million and recommended the formation of a community task force to consider the task.

In August, the City Council authorized the formation of the Reimagining Public Safety Task Force and passed a city budget that included a $150 million reduction for police and the police academy (see Figure 14.3).[69] The task force membership included representatives of a range of community organizations that had participated in protests, such as the Austin Justice Coalition, Communities of Color United, and Grassroots Leadership as well as the Greater Austin Crime Commission, a group more supportive of police. There were also members of the City Manager's Office, the Office of Police Oversight, and the city's Equity Office.

In December, the task force issued a statement articulating the shared values behind its efforts.[70] These values included equity, the need to include those most harmed, a focus on systems and root causes, and divesting in system components that cause harm. The following April, the task force issued a report with recommendations.[71]

Figure 14.3 Austin City meeting among citizens and police (*Source:* IMAGN).

(Continued)

Case Study: The City of Austin and Reimagining Public Safety (Continued)

The report stated that a significant segment of the Austin community felt harmed by the police system and the broader socioeconomic system. People felt that the socioeconomic harm, which included poverty, homelessness, drug addiction, and the lack of access to mental health services, was at the root of many problems in their community that involved the police and that reimagining a safe community would require changes that must also address these problems. Among recommended police reforms were the elimination of the use of deadly weapons, horses, and police dogs; revision of the police academy curriculum to eliminate paramilitary training and emphasize community service and de-escalation; the decoupling of the city's police force from traffic stop enforcement; and the hiring and training of unarmed civil servants to direct traffic and make stops for moving violations. The more systemic recommendations included a limitation on rent increases, the testing of a guaranteed income program that would distribute $1,000 a month to 200 households, and the creation of neighborhood hubs, managed by local grassroots organizations, for resource distribution.

The city manager took the numerous recommendations and designed a proposal he thought the City Council could pass. The task was confounded by a recently passed Texas state law, specifically aimed at Austin, which dictated that no large city in the state could reduce their budget for police lower than the 2019–2020 budget. This restricted the city's ability to respond to proposals that involved defunding elements of the police budget and allocating them to other areas.

In July, the city manager presented the proposal to the City Council. It took the form of a $4.5 billion budget proposal for 2021–2022 fiscal year programs.[72] The manager was able to get many of the task force proposals adopted and funded, including a new curriculum for the police academy, new ways of responding to mental health emergencies, and investments in a family violence shelter. To this was added other recommendations outside the Police Department with money from the general budget, including that for homeless shelters and childcare. The City Council passed the proposed budget unanimously.[73]

Since then, public safety practices have been restructured to send unarmed civilian police employees to traffic accidents and to take reports on thefts and burglaries. Trained mental health workers are dispatched to 911 calls that require psychological interventions that don't involve violence. The Police Academy curriculum has been rewritten and implemented to include not only physical conditioning, but also to provide officers with skills that will help them handle complex, stressful, and potentially dangerous situations, emphasizing emotion management and de-escalation.[74] The academy restarted in 2021 with its most diverse class of cadets yet, which graduated in February 2022. Austin's reimagining public safety program was featured on "60 Minutes" and touted as a potential model for the rest of the country.[75]

The Reimaging Public Safety case illustrates how abstract moral principles can be applied to promote equality and address injustice. First, in its work before the George Floyd incident, the city identified that minorities were not being treated equally by law enforcement nor treated with respect. Indeed, many people had been harmed by police prior to the George Floyd protests and during them. The situation was aggravated by police actions in response to the George Floyd demonstrations. That was the current situation.

The City Council acknowledged this situation and wanted to make it better. To do so, they set up a diverse task force of multiple voices but disproportionately representative of those most harmed by the current situation. The task force engaged in a moral dialog based on the principles of equality and harm reduction. They also engaged in systemic thinking to recognize that harm was due not just to police actions, but also systemic problems of poverty, homelessness, and mental health services.

The task force came up with design recommendations to improve the situation. These designs included changes in police training and police actions. But they also included a broader range of potential solutions that included rent control, guaranteed income, and community hubs. These designs required the engagement of a broader community in the dialog. The result was less than the task force recommended. Yet the changes were concrete, changes that included police training and public services.

Are citizens in Austin now equal? Is law enforcement there now just? Most likely not. But most certainly it is more equal and more just.

Moral Discourse to Promote Equality and Address Injustice

In reimagining public safety, the Austin task force engaged in what Professor Verbeek calls "moral imagination," thinking about how a more equal, more just city might look. Designs that engage a community in moral imagining and moral discourse can promote equality and address injustice.

These designs can be group exercises that help people think about what equality and justice mean in everyday situations, not only equality and justice for me but that for others, particularly those least advantaged, most harmed. No one–Black or White, Red or Blue–wants to be harmed and shifting the discussion to this basic, shared human desire can bridge differences. Shifting the focus can help groups discuss what a society might be like, imagine what institutions, relationships, and everyday behaviors and experiences would be like that support equality and justice in various situations so that no one is harmed. These discussions can consider not only laws and government policies, but also products, services and experiences that might contribute to injustice and how they could be improved.

But most importantly, these designs need to turn discussions into actions. The discussions need to result in the creation of a more equal, more just society. They need to articulate human-centered, corporate, and government policies and programs that promote equality and address injustice. But these discussions and actions need to go beyond corporate policies and government laws. Just as important are everyday designs that embed the values of equality and justice in video games, social media platforms, consumer products, human services, ad campaigns, and user experiences. And designs need to mobilize communities to take collective actions that address the harm of inequality and injustice. Not to address them with our designs is to confirm a society that is otherwise.

References

1. Mill JS. Utilitarianism (p. 63). Hackett, 2001.
2. Locke J. The Collected Works of John Locke: The Complete Works (Kindle edition) (location 225). Oxford: Pergamon, 2015.
3. Locke J. The Collected Works of John Locke: The Complete Works (Kindle edition) (location 616). Oxford: Pergamon, 2015.
4. Arms and armor of the Roanoke colonists. National Park Service [Internet]. [cited 2022, Sep 1]. Available from: https://www.nps.gov/fora/learn/education/arms-and-armor-of-the-roanoke-colonists.htm.

5 The first charter of Virginia; April 10, 1606. Avalon Project at Yale Law School [Internet]. [cited 2022, Sep 1]. Available from: https://web.archive.org/web/20050301092128/http://www.yale.edu/lawweb/avalon/states/va01.htm.

6 The Virginia Company of London. Jamestown Settlement and American Revolution Museum at Yorktown [Internet]. [cited 2022, Sep 1]. Available from: https://jyfmuseums.org/wp-content/uploads/2014/06/VA_Company.pdf.

7 Timeline of Paspahegh-English interaction. Paspahegh [Internet]. [cited 2022, Sep 1]. Available from: http://www.virtualjamestown.org/paspahegh/timeline.html.

8 Williams R. The American Indian in western legal thought: The discourses of conquest. New York: Oxford University Press, 1990.

9 Mark J. A brief history of tobacco in the Americas. World History Encyclopedia [Internet]. [cited 2022, Sep 1]. Available from: https://www.worldhistory.org/article/1677/a-brief-history-of-tobacco-in-the-americas/.

10 United States population chart. Open Educational Resources [Internet]. [cited 2022, Sep 1]. Available from: https://courses.lumenlearning.com/suny-ushistory2os2xmaster/chapter/united-states-population-chart/.

11 The Native American population of Britisch America. The American Revolution [Internet]. United States population chart. Open Educational Resources [Internet]. [cited 2022, Sep 1]. Available from: http://www.ouramericanrevolution.org/index.cfm/page/view/p0140.

12 Gallay A. The Indian slave trade. New Haven: Yale University Press, 2002.

13 Wilkins D, Lomawaima KT. Uneven ground: American Indian sovereignty and Federal law. Norman, OK: University of Oklahoma Press, 2002.

14 Hannah-Jones N, Roper C, Silverman I, et al. The 1619 Project. New York: New York Times, 2021.

15 First enslaved Africans arrive in Jamestown, setting the stage for slavery in North America. History [Internet]. Mark J. A brief history of tobacco in the Americas. World History Encyclopedia [Internet]. [cited 2022, Sep 1]. Available from: https://www.history.com/this-day-in-history/first-african-slave-ship-arrives-jamestown-colony.

16 First slaves arrive in Massachusetts. Mass Moments [Internet]. [cited 2022, Sep 1]. Available from: https://www.massmoments.org/moment-details/first-slaves-arrive-in-massachusetts.html.

17 Enactment of Hereditary Slavery Law Virginia 1662-Act XII. National Park Service [Internet]. [cited 2022, Sep 1]. Available from: https://www.nps.gov/ethnography/aah/aaheritage/chesapeake_pop2.htm.

18 Segal R. The Black diaspora: Five centuries of the Black experience outside Africa. New York: Farrar, Straus and Grioux, 1996.

19 Davis D. Inhuman bondage: The rise and fall of slavery in the New World. Oxford: Oxford University Press, 2006.

20 Jenkins W. Pro-slavery thought in the old South. Durham, NC: University of North Carolina Press, 1935. Available from: https://babel.hathitrust.org/cgi/pt?id=mdp.39015005309268&view=1up&seq=15.

21 Schedule of the whole number of persons within the several districts of the United States. Census Bureau [Internet]. [cited 2022, Sep 1]. Available from: https://www2.census.gov/library/publications/decennial/1790/number_of_persons/1790a-02.pdf.

22 The Dred Scott decision: opinion of Chief Justice Taney. Library of Congress [Internet]. [cited 2022, Sep 1]. Available from: https://www.loc.gov/item/17001543/.

23 Northup S. 12 years a slave. Vancouver, BC: Engage Books, 1853/2014.

24 Wilkerson I. Caste: The origin of our discontent. New York: Random House, 2020.

25 Black troops in Union blue. Constitutional Rights Foundation [Internet [cited 2022, Sep 1]. Available from: https://www.crf-usa.org/black-history-month/black-troops-in-union-blue.

26 Civil War casualties. American Battlefield Trust [Internet]. [cited 2022, Sep 1]. Available from: https://www.battlefields.org/learn/articles/civil-war-casualties.

27 Gates H. Stoney the road: Reconstruction, white supremacy, and the rise of Jim Crow. New York: Penguin Books, 2019.

28 Gilmore K. Slavery and prison: Understanding the connections. Social Justice, 2000, 27(3), 195–205.

29 Gates H. Stoney the road: Reconstruction, white supremacy, and the rise of Jim Crow (p. 28). New York: Penguin Books, 2019.

30 Blakemore E. How the GI Bill's promise was denied to a million Black WWII veterans. History [Internet]. 2021, Apr 20 [cited 2022, Sep 1]. Available from: https://www.history.com/news/gi-bill-black-wwii-veterans-benefits.

31 Ray R, Perry A, Harshbarger D, et al. Homeownerhip, racial segregation, and policy solutions to racial wealth equity. Brookings [Internet]. 2021, Sep 1 [cited 2022, Sep 1]. Available from: https://www.brookings.edu/essay/homeownership-racial-segregation-and-policies-for-racial-wealth-equity/.

32 Sandel M. The tyranny of merit: What's become of the common good? New York: Farrar, Straus and Grioux, 2020.

33 Brancaccio D, Conlon R. Why rich people tend to think they deserve their money. Marketplace [Internet]. 2021, Jan 19 [cited 2022, Sep 1]. Available from: https://www.marketplace.org/2021/01/19/why-rich-people-tend-think-they-deserve-their-money/.

34 PBS News Hour. Why those who feel they have more give less. YouTube [web streaming video]. 2013, Jun 21 [cited 2022, Sep 1]. Available from: https://www.youtube.com/watch?v=IuqGrz-Y_Lc.

35 King ML. All Labor Has Dignity (p. 172). Boston: Beacon Press, 2010.

36 Wealth of world's 10 richest men doubled in pandemic, Oxfam says. BBC [Internet]. 2022, Jan 17 [cited 2022, Sep 1]. Available from: https://www.bbc.com/news/business-60015294.

37 Schaeffer K. 6 facts about economic inequality in the U.S. Pew Research Center [Internet]. 2020, Feb 7 [cited 2022, Sep 1]. Available from: https://www.pewresearch.org/fact-tank/2020/02/07/6-facts-about-economic-inequality-in-the-u-s/.

38 Weller C. Wealth inequality on the rise during pandemic. Forbes [Internet]. 2021, Dec 22 [cited 2022, Sep 1]. Available from: https://www.forbes.com/sites/christianweller/2021/12/22/wealth-rises-at-all-income-levels-but-faster-at-the-top/?sh=22b2ff0f6524.

39 Donnell M, Bearden M, Guthrie L, et al. The road to recovery. Capital One Insights Center [Internet]. 2021 [cited 2022, Sep 1]. Available from: https://ecm.capitalone.com/WCM/stories/pdfs/capital_one_insights_center_the_road_to_recovery_2021_report.pdf.

40 Pfeffer F. Growing wealth gaps in education. Demography. 2018, 55(3), 1033–1068. Available from: https://read.dukeupress.edu/demography/article/55/3/1033/167883/Growing-Wealth-Gaps-in-Education.

41 Annual earnings by educational attainment. National Center for Educational Statistics [Internet]. 2022, May [cited 2022, Sep 1]. Available from: https://nces.ed.gov/programs/coe/indicator/cba.

42 https://www.bls.gov/opub/mlr/2017/article/employment-trends-by-typical-entry-level-education-requirement.htm.

43 Student debt has increased sevenfold over the last couple decades. Here's why. Peter G. Peterson Foundation [Internet]. 2021, Oct 26 [cited 2022, Sep 1]. Available from: https://www.pgpf.org/blog/2021/10/student-debt-has-increased-sevenfold-over-the-last-couple-decades-heres-why.

44 Parker K. The growing partisan divide in views of higher education. Pew Reseach Center [Internet]. 2019, Aug 19 [cited 2022, Sep 3]. Available from: https://www.pewresearch.org/social-trends/2019/08/19/the-growing-partisan-divide-in-views-of-higher-education-2/.

45 Quarterly residential vacancies and homeownership. Census Bureau [Internet]. 2022, Aug 2 [cited 2022, Sep 1]. Available from: https://www.census.gov/housing/hvs/files/currenthvspress.pdf.

46 Christensen P, Timmins C. Sorting or steering: The effects of housing discrimination on neighborhood choice. National Bureau of Economic Research [Internet]. 2021, Jun [cited 2022, Sep 1]. Available from: https://www.nber.org/papers/w24826.

47 Hanson A, Hawley Z, Martin H, et al. Discrimination in mortgage lending: Evidence from a correspondence experiment. Journal of Urban Economics, 2016, 92, 48-65. Available from: https://epublications.marquette.edu/cgi/viewcontent.cgi?referer=https://scholar.google.com/scholar?as_q=racial+discrimination+application+experiment+&as_epq=&as_oq=sales+loan+ownership&as_eq=&as_occt=any&as_sauthors=&as_publication=&as_ylo=&as_yhi=&hl=en&as_sdt=0%2C5&httpsredir=1&article=1557&context=econ_fac.

48 Brosnan SF, De Waal FB. Monkeys reject unequal pay. Nature, 2003, 425(6955), 297–299.

49 Brosnan SF. Justice and fairness related behaviors in nonhuman primates. Proceedings of the National Academy of Sciences, 2013, 110, 10416–10423.

50 King LW (translator). The Code of Hammurabi. Lillian Goldman Law Library [Internet]. [cited 2022, Sep 1]. Available from: https://avalon.law.yale.edu/ancient/hamframe.asp.

51 Aristotle. Nicomachean ethics. The basic works of Aristotle (D. McKeon, ed.). New York: Random House, 1941.

52 Hobbes T. Leviathan. New York: Cambridge University Press, 1991.

53 Locke J. An essay concerning the true original, extent and end of civil government. The collected works of John Locke (location 6714). Amsterdam: Pergamon, Kindle edition, 2015.

54 Hume D. A treatise of human understanding. David Hume: The essential philosophical works. London: Wordsworth, 2011.

55 Mill JS. Utilitarianism (p. 62). Indianapolis, IN: Hackett Publishing, 1861/2001.

56 Rawls J. A theory of justice. Cambridge, MA: Belknap Press, 1971.

57 Nozick R. Anarchy, state, and utopia. New York: Basic Books, 1974.

58 Sandel M. Justice: What's the right thing to do? New York: Farrar, Straus and Grioux, 2009.

59 Verbeek P-P. What things do. University Park, PA: Pennsylvania State University Press, 2005.

60 Jackson J. America's biggest cities to invest $450M more in police following 2020 defund. Movement. Newsweek [Internet]. 2021, Dec 19 [cited 2022, Sep 1]. Available from: https://www.newsweek.com/americas-biggest-cities-invest-450m-more-police-following-2020-defund-movement-1663599.

61 Austin city, Texas. Census Bureau [Internet]. [cited 2022, Sep 1]. Available from: https://data.census.gov/cedsci/profile?g=1600000US4805000.

62 Cronk S. Analysis of the Austin Police Department's racial profiling report. City of Austin Memorandum [Internet]. 2020, Jan 30 [cited 2022, Sep 1]. Available from: https://www.austintexas.gov/edims/pio/document.cfm?id=334984.

63 Plohetski T. "I can't breathe!" Video released from 2019 death of Austin-area black man in deputies' custody. KVUE ABC [Internet]. 2020, Jun 9 [cited 2022, Sep 1]. Available from: https://www.kvue.com/article/news/investigations/defenders/javier-ambler-death-investigation-williamson-county-sheriffs-live-pd/269-9065fe1e-bb16-439f-a008-fa74f741d5b4.

64 Knight D. Police identify man killed in officer-involved shooting in downtown Austin. KVUE ABC [Internet]. 2019, Aug 2 [cited 2022, Sep 1]. Available from: https://www.kvue.com/article/news/local/police-responding-to-officer-involved-shooting-in-downtown-austin/269-9ae26db2-0796-46ab-8fe3-46e0922a176d.

65 Chute N. What do videos capturing Michael Ramos shooting by Austin police show? Austin American-Statesman [Internet]. 2021, Mar 11 [cited 2022, Sep 1]. Available from: https://www.statesman.com/story/news/2021/03/11/michael-ramos-austin-video-christopher-taylor-austin-police-shooting-bodycam-footage/4645804001/.

66 Flores R. A week's worth of protests against police brutality in downtown Austin. KVUE ABC [Internet]. 2020, Jun 5 [cited 2022, Sep 1]. Available from: https://www.kvue.com/article/news/local/austin-protests-george-floyd-michael-ramos-june-4/269-2d5fb341-db26-47ab-8942-fe8155223858.

67 Swaby A, McCullough J, Pollock C. Texas police using tear gas and rubber bullets on protesters incites more violence, experts say. Texas Tribune [Internet]. 2020, Jun 3 [cited 2022, Sep 1]. Available from: https://www.texastribune.org/2020/06/03/texas-police-force-protests-george-floyd/.

68 Ruiz A. Austin surgeons shocked by injuries protesters sustained by bean bag rounds. Fox 7 [Internet]. 2020, Aug 14 [cited 2022, Sep 1]. Available from: https://www.fox7austin.com/news/austin-surgeons-shocked-by-injuries-protesters-sustained-by-bean-bag-rounds.

69 Spencer B. Austin City Council cuts millions of dollars from APD budget, approves fiscal year budget. Fox 7 [Internet]. 2020, Aug 13 [cited 2022, Sep 1]. Available from: https://www.fox7austin.com/news/austin-city-council-cuts-millions-of-dollars-from-apd-budget-approved-fiscal-year-budget.

70 Reimagining Public Safety Task Force values. [cited 2022, Sep 1]. Available from: https://www.austintexas.gov/sites/default/files/files/RPS%20Task%20Force%20Values%20Document.pdf.

71 Austin City-Community Reimagining Public Safety Task Force. 2021 mid-year Recommendations report. City of Austin [Internet]. [cited 2022, Sep 1]. Available from: https://www.austintexas.gov/sites/default/files/files/Completed%20RPS%20Taskforce%20Mid-Year%20Recommendations%20Report.pdf.

72 Proposed budget snapshot, fiscal year 2021-22. City of Austin [Internet]. [cited 2022, Sep 1]. Available from: https://assets.austintexas.gov/budget/21-22/downloads/Proposed/2022_Proposed_Budget_Snapshot.pdf.

73 Chukwu D. Austin City Council unanimously approves fiscal year 2021-22 budget. KVUE ABC [Internet]. 2021, Aug 13 [cited 2022, Sep 1]. Available from: https://www.kvue.com/article/money/economy/austin-city-council-approves-budget/269-aeef289d-3821-439c-8205-70c686177bf6.

74 Austin Police Department: Review and assessment of training academy. City of Austin [Internet]. 2021, Apr 23 [cited 2022, Sep 1]. Available from: https://www.austintexas.gov/edims/document.cfm?id=359317.

75 Pelley S. How Austin is leading the nation in police reform. 60 Minutes [Internet]. 2021, Nov 21 [cited 2022, Sep 1]. Available from: https://www.paramountplus.com/shows/60_minutes/video/35ln5MBc8c4Li9mYeznfP8aou_rXsBZp/how-austin-is-leading-the-nation-in-police-reform/.

15

Build Supportive Relationships and Communities

No man is an island entire of itself; every man is a piece of the Continent, a part of the main . . . any man's death diminishes me, because I am involved in Mankind; and therefore, never send to know for whom the bell tolls; it tolls for thee.

John Donne
16th-Century English Poet

The seventh principle in our set of moral guidelines for designs that make the world better is "Build compassionate, supportive relationships and communities."

Why are relationships so important? Can't we do just fine, each of us operating out of our own self-interest? Doesn't this invisible hand of self-interest, multiplied across billions of transactions, benefit us all?

In this chapter, we will explore how relationships affect us at the micro, person-to-person level, at the community level, and at the macro, societal, level. We will then consider these implications for designs that make our social world better.

Moral and Survival Foundations of Relationships

"Love thy neighbor as thy self" runs through both the New and the Old Testaments of the Bible and variants of the dictum exist in many other religions. For the Philosophes, being human meant being social, and social emotions were the foundation of both morality and society.

However, for Ayn Rand and Robert Nozick, whom we met in Chapter 3, society is a mere collection of individuals rather than an entity, itself.[1] The actions of each person are motivated only by self-interest, and maintaining one's own life and pleasure is a moral imperative and one's highest purpose, according to Rand's moral philosophy. "Love thy self" would be her one and only commandment.

According to Rand, "The principle of trade is the only rational ethical principle for all human relationships . . . ."[2] Love and friendship are selfish values, an expression of one's own self-esteem in the person of another. One would never help a stranger at one's own expense. And altruism, for Rand, is a betrayal of the value of oneself. It is the renouncing of one's own self-interests for the sake of one's neighbor and it was abhorrent to her.

This position is profoundly different than that of the Enlightenment Philosophers who believed humans, by their nature, are social beings. They believed that people strive for their own happiness, but that this motivation is moderated by a feeling of compassion for others that is an essential

Make the World a Better Place: Design with Passion, Purpose, and Values, First Edition. Robert B. Kozma.

part of being human. For David Hume, human nature cannot subsist without the association of others and "society is absolutely necessary for the well-being of men."[3] And the fact that we are all humans produces in each of us emotions similar to those felt by others—their interests, their passions, their pains and pleasures.

The Utilitarian philosopher Jeremy Bentham stated that "An action then may be said to be conformable to the principle of utility . . . when the tendency it has to augment the happiness of the community is greater than any it has to diminish it."[4] Similarly, for John Stuart Mill, it's not just one's own happiness that is of value but the happiness of all concerned.[5] The most virtuous act a person can perform, according to Mill, is deferring one's own happiness to increase the total amount of happiness in the world.

Even for Adam Smith—the one to whom all this self-interested trading is attributed—striving for the happiness of others is just as much a part of our nature as striving for our own, even though we may derive nothing from their happiness other than the pleasure of seeing it.[6] And seeing others in pain evokes our own pain. These shared "fellow feelings," Smith contends, are the foundation of our desire that the union of humankind be preserved for its own sake.

These fellow feelings have been with us since the beginning. In her book *How Compassion Made Us Human: The Evolutionary Origins of Tenderness, Trust & Morality*, University of York anthropologist Penny Spikins documents prehistoric burial digs, from Vietnam to Europe, that showed our earliest ancestors cared for those afflicted in their midst, from a paraplegic injured in his teens who survived into his thirties to people with various congenital deformities who were buried with the same respect as others and from all evidence treated the same in life.[7]

Spikins starts her book by asking if our capacity to identify with others through powers of empathy and acts of compassion is a relatively recent development in our species or has existed in us all along. She ends the book stating that compassion is what makes us human, "everything seems to argue that basic human kindness, compassion, a spirit of helping others out was not just there, but everywhere, vital to survival . . . " (p. 315).

Caring for an invalid is not a trade; nursing them, feeding them, cleaning them, carrying them from place to place. There is very little that is returned. But that capacity to go beyond our self-interest is, according to anthropologist Margaret Mead, what made us a civilization.[8]

Loving each other is not just a nice sentiment; as in the past, we may again find that it is essential to our survival as a civilization and a species. If we are going to make the world a better place, we need to understand how relationships are built and how our designs can make them better.

Relationships and Well-Being: The Micro Level

Relationships are the most fundamentally expressed at the micro level, between one person and another. Relationships have both inner, emotional components and outer, behavioral, interactional components.

Emotions and relationships

When we say that that being social is in our nature, it's not just a figure of speech. Sociability is hardwired in our brains. Psychological research has clearly established that the need for relationships is a fundamentally human one,[9] as the Philosophes claimed. There is an internal mechanism we each have that drives us to seek relationships. And emotions are the basis for this need.

There are more than seven billion people in the world. You pass by some of them on the street every day; there is no connection, no relationship. But for a small number of people in your life, there is a connection and it is emotional. You see them on the street and you smile. Brain imaging shows that people have a cognitive and emotional response to viewing familiar faces, more so than viewing unfamiliar faces or even faces of famous people.[10]

For a few people, the emotional response is profound. When you experience an emotional connection with another person, a complex set of biochemical reactions occur inside you.[11] Oxytocin, the "feel good" hormone mentioned in Chapter 12, is released into certain parts of your brain. Oxytocin impacts prosocial behaviors and other emotional responses, contributing to relaxation, trust, and a sense of security. It reduces fear, stress, and anxiety. And it triggers the release in the brain of two other neurotransmitters: serotonin and dopamine. Serotonin influences mood and is associated with the emotions of happiness and well-being. Dopamine is associated with feelings of satisfaction and pleasure, but also has a behavioral component, motivating you to come back for more.

These inner responses to other people are the chemical, physiological basis of relationships and they create bonds that we call "family" and "friends." While self-interested trading with the butcher, baker, and co-workers may help us adapt to the world's everyday demands, interactions with family and friends are the source of our happiness. And as we build on these feelings, we come to include the butcher, baker, and co-workers among our friends.

Family

The important role of family in creating well-being begins at the earliest moments of our lives and it becomes the basis for all other relationships. A study of extended parent-infant care during the postpartum period found that skin-to-skin contact releases oxytocin in both babies and mothers and this release changes the interactions between the two.[12] For the mother, higher levels of oxytocin stimulate the milk production and are associated with caring, nurturing behaviors toward the baby. For the infant, the hormone stimulates the left frontal area of the brain, which is implicated in higher-order cognitive and emotional regulatory skills; with skin-to-skin contact, babies cry less. There is a powerful feedback loop, where the presence of oxytocin generates more oxytocin, amplifying its effects. The net effect of this neurochemical-behavioral link is to create a strong bond between mother and child.

The subsequent relationship between parent and child builds on this early bonding. Indeed, it appears that early close relationships have an impact throughout a lifetime. This conclusion is based on research on infants who have been raised with minimal human touch and emotional attention, often housed in orphanages, and have been found to have lower baseline oxytocin levels and their stress hormones are much higher. [13] These children are at higher risk for behavioral, emotional, and social problems as they grow up. Adults who were abused as children have lower oxytocin levels.[14]

Parent-child interactions have important implications throughout childhood. Parent talk with toddlers is an important influence on language development: not just the quantity of parent talk, but its semantic quality and the number of times the parent elicits responses from the child.[15] An influential element of the interaction is the degree to which the parent adjusts their talk to the child's emerging zone of proximal development.[16] An appropriate progression from "baby talk" to adult conversation aids the child's advancing understanding and use of language. Development of the children's reading skills benefits from parents reading aloud to them. Indeed, throughout their young lives, children depend on interactions with adults and others to help them learn how to use their culture's resources, such as numerical and written symbol systems and technical tools, such as computers. And the development of these skills, has a compounding effect on subsequent learning.

These positive, supportive parent-child relationships have a profound impact on well-being throughout life. A longitudinal study conducted in the United Kingdom with 5,362 people over a 65-year period collected data on parenting practices and well-being of offspring in their teens, mid-life, and later life. The study found a consistent positive relationship between parental care, of both mothers and fathers, and offspring behavior control practices and well-being throughout life.[17]

Married couples

Close bonding plays an essential role in that other component of the family—the couple. In Chapter 12, we looked at a study done at Harvard University that tracked the lives of more than 700 men over 75 years.[18] The study found that marriages played a particularly important role in longevity, health, and happiness, even if the marriages had experienced difficult times.

It's obvious to all of us that have been in one that an intimate, coupled relationship is intensely emotional, the emotion we call *love*. In her book *Love 2.0*, University of North Carolina psychologist Barbara Fredrickson characterizes this emotional response as a synchrony between the biochemistry and behaviors of two people, reflected in the "motive to invest in each other's well-being that brings mutual care."[19] Note that this synchrony of biochemical, emotional, and behavioral responses parallels the relationship between mother and baby. Yes, sex is part of this love in a coupled, intimate relationship, but that physical connection draws on and adds to the strong emotional part that is the foundation of the relationship.

Note also that this emotional relationship gets played out at a behavioral level. Many studies have shown that successful marriages are based on interaction, both the amount and the nature of the communication between individuals. Studies have found that compared to dissatisfied couples, couples who are satisfied with their marriage are more mutually supportive, laugh together more, withhold comments that might be received negatively, and agree more about a variety of topics.[20]

In other words, what predicts marital success over the long haul is not how similar partners are or how wealthy or even if they have great sex. It is interactions, not transactions, as Rand would contend, that are the basis of relationships that foster well-being. It's the day-to-day, moment-by-moment positive interactions that maintain their bond and provide an emotional bank account of connection and trust that couples can draw on to get through the tough times.

Friends

Friends are also important to happiness. Among adults, both the closeness of friends and the amount of socializing with friends are highly correlated with well-being.[21] A sense of well-being can be derived from having close friends with whom one can have meaningful conversations or talk to about problems. Or it can come from spending a lot of social time with friends, eating together and attending social events. And, of course, these often go hand in hand.

Friendships and romantic or family relationships serve different purposes; each type makes a unique contribution to well-being, life satisfaction, and happiness.[22] When satisfaction in a romantic relationship is high, the level of friendship satisfaction does not predict life satisfaction. However, if intimate relationship satisfaction is low, people are only happy if they have good quality friends.

For children, the emotional bond between them and parents serves as a base of security from which they can explore relationships with others. But the friendships children make serve a different and important functional role than the friendships do for adults.[23] As children grow to become adolescents, their personal challenges move from basic cognitive and physical development and the acquisition of language skills to more complex psychological and social issues, such as self-concept, identity, self-esteem, and moral development, and this is a particularly vulnerable developmental period.[24] Studies have documented the role of supportive peer relationships in developing a sense of self, social competence, academic performance, and protection against feelings of loneliness.[25] And the lack of supportive peer relationships is linked to negative outcomes, including social withdrawal, risk-taking behavior such as early commencement of smoking, drinking, and sexual relationships, increased risk of juvenile delinquency, and long-term mental health consequences.

Development of relationships over time

Economists—and Ayn Rand—have trouble explaining how relationships and cooperative behavior persist over time, based on the assumption that people act out of pure self-interest in transactions. As we saw in Chapter 4, for the purely self-interested person, the rational choice in a transaction would be noncooperative, and your payoff would be big if the other person cooperates out of their self-interest but you don't. They lose; you win. Yet people cooperate all the time. What does our exploration of relationships tell us about that?

The fascinating thing about the inner, emotional and the outer, behavioral aspects of relationships is how they change over time to support cooperation. Research shows us how external transactions between strangers become interaction patterns that are the basis of relationships and persistent cooperation. And these changes are charted at a neurochemical level.

Multiple brain studies have documented how mental representations of transactions change over time. Findings suggest that the inner mechanics of transactions between two people who do not know each other are different than those who have a close relationship and the mechanics change with repeated, subsequent interactions.[26] Decisions to conduct an initial exchange with strangers engages parts of the brain associated with the calculation of risk. Subsequent interactions with the same person engage those parts associated with anticipation of reward with expected reciprocation. These subsequent interactions also activate the dopamine pathways associated with sociality that are activated when friends or loved ones interact.

That is, evidence suggests that a series of transactions with strangers begins with the calculation of risk, shifts to an anticipation of reward, develops into an assumption of trustworthiness, and ultimately, transitions into the feelings associated with close relationships. Related to our earlier example in Chapter 4, while the initial transaction with a butcher may evoke feelings of potential threat of being cheated and risk calculations, a successful initial transaction and subsequent ones engender trust and evoke expectations of rewards, and as the two become friends over the months and years, the interactions become not just transactions but interactions that are also an expression of their friendship.

Relationships at the Community Level

When we scale up relationships beyond family and friends to consider more complex social arrangements, relationships clearly become . . . well, more complex. We need ways to think about these more complex situations.

Beyond family and friends, the term that first comes to mind is *community*. But because *community* is used by many people in many different ways, we must think of it as a complex, adaptive system. And to think of how we might improve relationships in a community to contribute to well-being, we need to think of community beyond a collection of co-located individuals and begin to understand how larger numbers of people interact and how that network of interactions works and doesn't work. We need to think of community functionally. We need to think in terms of joint activity and collective action, and how our designs might facilitate that.

Our towns, our community

In their book *Our Towns*, journalist James Fallows and his wife Deborah flew their Cirrus 4-seater airplane to dozens of small and medium-sized communities across the United States over a five-year period. [27] They visited towns from Maine to California and in many fly-over states in between. They were interested in places that had faced adversity of some sort, from crop failure to job loss to political crisis, and had collectively looked for ways to respond. They wanted to document the powerful things that communities can do when people work together.

During their travels, the Fallowses saw towns that had grown and prospered and those that had shrunk and suffered. What they found was that successful towns were characterized by patterns of functional relationships, shared resources, and collective actions. They found that successful towns focused on practical local possibilities, rather than allowing disagreements about national politics to keep them apart. Community members, from mayors and business titans to artists and saloon-keepers, stepped forward as leaders who took action. Government and public agencies formed partnerships with local businesses to make a difference. These communities also cared about education. They developed innovative public schools, as we saw in San Diego in the Chapter 13 case study. They supported community colleges, and partnered with research universities. And these institutions, in turn, cared about the community.

The successful towns had big plans, a vision of how to make the town better in the future. With an intensity of local civic life that generally escaped any outside notice, these communities found ways that neighbors could draw on their local relationships and resources to design a better community.

My wife Shari and I saw similar functional pattern relationships, resources, and actions when we worked in a poor rural village in Kenya in 2005, volunteering with the Millennium Villages Program of Columbia University's Earth Institute and the United Nations Development Programme. Bar Sauri is a village of about 5,000 people in Nyanza Provence in western Kenya near the city of Kisumu and Lake Victoria. The population is majority ethnic Luo and their primary economic activity in the village is subsistence farming. Between 60% and 70% of the population lived on less than $1 per day at the time.[28]

Where we thought we might find poverty-induced despair, we found community and action. Among the community actions we encountered were women's groups that self-financed purchases, which for them were relatively large, such as school uniforms or tuition. Normally, such amounts of money would take weeks to save up. But each week, the women pooled small contributions from each woman to allow one of the women to make the purchase. The scheme, which they called a "merry-go-round," allowed all women to make the purchase earlier than they would have had each woman relied on her own accumulated weekly savings, except for the last women, who would make the purchase no later. The arrangement also had the advantage of providing a bit of security, in that increasingly large amounts of money that was otherwise saved weekly was ripe for pilfering.

Looking at Bar Sauri in terms of functional patterns, the community is not just a group of people who happen to live nearby; it is a number of close-knit networks—in this instance, networks of women—who give resources to others—in this case, small amounts of money—trusting that they will ultimately benefit as well. The structure in this case is a small group of 15 or so, each interacting with all others. There was no group leader. They met weekly to pool their latest contribution and to exchange gossip. The function of the group was to allow women to have enough money to buy school uniforms for their children in less time, or at least no more time, than it would take for each of them to save alone. All gave equally and benefitted equally.

The patterns of relationships and interactions, the resources people create and use together is what turns a collection of individuals into a community.

Communities and collective action

These functional patterns of relationships, resources, and actions are reminiscent of the Communities of Practice we examined in Chapter 13 on designing for knowledge, where a group of practitioners builds relationships and shares experiences in order to learn from and with each other, create common resources, and improve their practice. We are also reminded of collective action taken by congregants for WestGate Water and the citizens of Baton Rouge and Austin. And we are reminded by Saul Alinsky, in Chapter 10, that a community doesn't need to be physically co-located. It can be a community of those with shared values, need, or harm that comes together physically or virtually to take collective action for mutual benefit.

Burning Man, our case study in Chapter 11, is an example of that. Burning Man is not just an iconic cultural event in the Nevada high desert. It is also an extensive network structure of bonding and bridging links that supports collective action. A structure in which each member is connected to every other member, what is called a "bonding structure," or "strong ties." This kind of network facilitates the sharing of information and resources and supports individual and collective action. A structure in which some members of the community have links with members of other communities is called a "bridging structure," or "weak ties," and it brings new ideas into the group. Weak, bridging ties are associated with innovation and its spread.[29] These bridging ties can be the source of combinatorial change that Brian Arthur told us about in Chapter 5, changes that can transform systems. Strong ties are associated with getting things done.[30]

The merry-go-round groups in Bar Sauri are characterized by strong ties. Each woman gives their money to every other woman in the group and all women benefit. It worked because each woman trusts that in their group, they can give away their money, week after week, perhaps for months, but at some point they will get enough money back to buy a school uniform for their child.

At the center of Burning Man is the formal organization, Burning Man Project, also a tight-knit group of strong ties, people who have worked on the event for many years, some since its beginning in 1986. Surrounding this organization is a loose network of weak ties, hundreds of volunteer carpenters, artists, musicians, technicians, and workers. These bridging ties are a source of combinatorial, transformational change that characterizes Burning Man.

In 2019, the year of the festival before the pandemic required cancellations, the network came together to build and assemble, in the middle of the desert, a 61-foot wooden "man," a massive temple, over 400 fantastical art installations, dozens of creative musical and dance performances, and the infrastructure for a city of nearly 80,000 people that included a sanitation service, a medical clinic, a café, a radio station, and a temporary airport.[31] Within a week after "the Burn" everything was gone, without a trace, and the land was given back to the desert.

None of that could have happened by a collection of individuals merely engaged in a series of self-benefitting transactions. Burning Man is a community of shared values, and mutual trusters engaged in collective action for the benefit of all.

Relationships at the Macro Level

Corporations, cities, states, nations, even multinational groups can be viewed as systems of functional networks. But unlike Bar Sauri or small towns in the United States, these networks are more often characterized by formal structures, mechanisms and roles, rather than interpersonal relationships. These enable the system to work, even as specific individuals come and go.

Relationships in cities

If you live in a major city, most of the interactions you have with people who are not your relatives or friends are formal relationships, defined not by affiliation and socioemotional bonds but by institutions and functional roles. These are the devices that have evolved in society to handle a vast array of necessary transactions that must occur, even if you don't know the other person. When you go to the supermarket or the post office or take a taxi, it is very likely you are not friends with the butcher, postal clerk, or taxi driver. You may not have even encountered them before, let alone established a trusting relationship. Yet you are still able to trust that your meat will be good, your package will get to the recipient, and you will get to your destination across town. This is because the function is built into the role and the role is supported by the organizational structure of institutions.

These structures also shape the relationship within them. You have interactions with your coworkers not because you are personal friends, but because your interactions are defined by the roles you have within the organization. You report to your boss who gives you a new assignment. You work on this assignment with your team members and you hand it off to others who get the project implemented, distributed, sold, and so on. What you do, how you do it, and with whom is pretty much defined by your role and by the organizational structure. If you become friends with your co-workers, it's a byproduct of the process not the purpose or goal of the organization.

For the most part, these large systems work. But what is often missing is the neurochemical production and bonding that is generated by ongoing relationships. What is missing is emotion.

Charles Montgomery and Happy Cities, our case study in Chapter 12, are trying to change that. Montgomery contends that "the most important psychological effect of the city is the way in which it moderates our relationships with other people."[32] For Montgomery, "the city is ultimately a shared project, like Aristotle's polis, a place where we can fashion a common good that we simply cannot build alone" (p. 41). Montgomery believes cities must be viewed as systems and that they should be shaped to improve human well-being and happiness.

Much of building relationships in cities is creating a shared infrastructure for happiness. Enrique Peñalosa did that when he was the mayor of Bogotá, Columbia. Peñalosa's focus "has always been social—how you can help the most people for the greater public good . . . . Although income equality as a concept does not jive with the market economy, we can seek to achieve quality-of-life equality."[33]

While mayor, Peñalosa's administration built a number of spaces and resources in the city that gave residents more opportunity for recreation, education, transportation, and the chance to take pleasure in their surroundings together. They established or improved 1,200 parks and playgrounds throughout the city, and planted 100,000 trees. They created the longest network of protected bikeways in the developing world and created the world's longest pedestrian street. And they built 52 new schools, refurbished 150 others, and built 3 central and 10 neighborhood libraries. These shared resources are of the sort that people said made them happy, in the research reported in Chapter 12.

Trust and social capital

What makes social networks like Bar Sauri and small U.S. towns work? What makes large structures like corporations, cities, and nations work?

University of Chicago sociologist James Coleman has an explanation. He says that such systems work because of the trustworthiness of the social environment, the networking or information-flow capability of the social structure, and institutions or community norms accompanied by rewards and sanctions, all of which facilitate action.[34] He calls these community resources *social capital*. Social capital is like physical capital, such as machines and technology, and human capital, such as knowledge and skills, in that it allows for the achievement of certain ends that would be difficult or impossible without it. But unlike either physical or human capital, social capital is not a quality of individual things or of individual people; it is a quality of a group, specifically, the level of trustworthiness in a group, its interconnectedness, its resource flow, and its norms.

This trustworthiness is the aggregate history of interactions within a community that establishes cooperation as a common practice. Networking is the degree of interconnectedness among members that allows for easy flow of resources and information within a community. The network plays a key role in the dissemination of information on cooperative behavior of specific members. And community norms, backed by institutions, establishes the value of trust and the expectation of cooperation, along with formal positive and negative incentives in response to specific behaviors.

The trustworthiness, networking, and institutional and social norms that constitute a community's social capital benefit both individual members and the community as a whole. High levels of social capital are associated with both personal and aggregate levels of well-being, health, and economic prosperity.[35] And Harvard political scientist Robert Putnam, author of the book *Bowling Alone*, contends that it is social capital and mutual trust that serve as the foundation of our democratic form of government.[36] Not only are high levels of social capital associated with high levels of civic engagement, they are associated with the voluntary compliance of laws. The operating assumption is that I pay my taxes because I trust everyone else is, and as a result, we all benefit. It depends more on a shared expectation of civic responsibility and less on an Internal Revenue Service (IRS) audit.

While a network of trusting connections serves to bond people within the community, there is another source of social capital in communities and that's a network of bridging connections. A major study reported in *Nature* examined anonymous data from millions of Facebook users across the U.S. to find that locations in which networks of friends crossed socio-economic boundaries, that is, places where low income users had a higher rate of connection with high income users, were characterized by higher rates of upward economic mobility. So, where bonding social capital sustains a community's trustworthiness, bridging social capital supports its dynamism.[37]

However, trust networks and social capital are not always a force for good. The Medellín Cartel was a Colombian drug distribution network and terrorist-type criminal organization led by Pablo Escobar. The cartel operated from 1972 to 1993 in many countries in South and Central America as well as the United States and Canada. The cartel smuggled multiple tons of cocaine each week into countries around the world and brought in up to $60 million daily in drug profits.[38] The cartel depended heavily on trust in the group, on a network of resource flow, and on norms—trust that no one would betray the group, a network that reliably produced and distributed drugs, and a norm of group loyalty.

As Putnam puts it, "it is important to ask how the positive consequences of social capital—mutual support, cooperation, trust, institutional effectiveness—can be maximized and the negative manifestations—sectarianism, ethnocentrism, corruption—minimized."[39] If social capital is to result in good, it will need to be used to build compassionate relationships that advance knowledge, promote equality, and address injustice in support of increased happiness and harm reduction.

The impressive collective efforts of the Burning Man network are distinguished from that of the Medellín Cartel not by the trust among members, which characterizes both these networks, or the existence of culture norms per se. What distinguishes Burning Man are the particular values of the culture. While the cartel was a commercial organization that valued money and profit and punished betrayal with death, Burning Man is based on a very different set of principles that include decommodification, gifting, radical inclusion, radical self-expression, communal effort, and leaving no trace behind.[40] They created a network of social capital for good.

Social capital in nations

The benefits of social capital scale beyond the local level to national groups. Research at a national level—sometimes with the term *social capital*, used by the OECD (Organization of Economic Cooperation and Development) and sometimes the related term *social cohesion* (the European Union)—has documented differences among countries as a whole. An OECD study of 38 of the world's most developed countries found positive correlations between measures of social capital and measures of well-being that included material conditions, individual aspects of life quality, and relational aspects of life quality.[41] In Europe, Denmark, Finland, and Sweden show the highest levels of social cohesion, and Lithuania, Bulgaria, and Romania show the lowest.[42] Social capital is associated with national economic success but these personal benefits go beyond the extent to which well-being is influenced merely by a country's gross income. The EU study found a significant relationship between social cohesion and individual well-being of their citizens, such that higher levels of social cohesion within a country corresponds to better psychological functioning, less negative affect, higher life evaluation, and greater well-being.

Perhaps the biggest benefit of high levels of social capital within a group is the potential for collaboration among members in collective action to benefit all. That is, members can act together to accomplish something that could not be accomplished by individual members each acting alone, as Putnam claims.

Loss of Relationships and Trust

Loss of friends

Despite the established importance of relationships, social capital, and trust, there is a pronounced relationship deficit in the United States. A 2021 U.S. poll by the Survey Center on American Life found that in the past three decades, American friendship groups have become smaller and the number of Americans without any close confidants has risen sharply.[43] While in 1990, 47% of respondents reported having six or more close friends, in 2021, it was only 25%. In 1990, 4% reported they had only one close friend and 3% reported they didn't have any. In 2021, 7% reported they had only one close friend and 12% reported they had none.

Of course, the COVID-19 pandemic was a significant factor in the national friendship decline, according to the Survey Center on American Life study, with nearly half (47%) of respondents reporting having lost touch with at least a few friends during the pandemic and 9% reporting having lost touch with most of their friends.

However, the relationship crisis predated the pandemic, as documented by a 2018 study in which 46% of respondents reported sometimes or always feeling alone.[44] Fifty-four percent of the respondents said they always or sometimes feel that no one knows them well and 43% felt like "they lack companionship," that their "relationships aren't meaningful," and that they "are isolated from others." A surprising 39% said they were not close to anyone.

With all this, it's not surprising that the United States has among the highest depression rates in the world, according to the World Health Organization (WHO).[45] And the COVID pandemic and the need for social distancing has compounded the problem significantly. According to a report for the organization Mental Health America, the number of people looking for help with anxiety and depression has skyrocketed by 93% during the pandemic, with 37% of people who sought help reporting that they regularly had thoughts of suicide.

Loss of interpersonal trust

Along with a decline in relationships and an increase in loneliness has come a lack of trust in each other, according to a 2019 Pew Research Center national poll.[46] When asked to report on their fellow citizens' confidence in each other, almost 80% said people have too little confidence in each other. Nearly half (49%) of respondents said they think citizens' trust in each other has fallen because people are not as reliable as they used to be.

When asked to report on their own trust in others, 47% said that "most people can't be trusted"; 58% responded that "others would try to take advantage of you if they got a chance"; 62% said that people "just look out for themselves"; and 35% gave nontrust answers to all of these questions, with 46% of young adults falling into this group.

There are also significant negative attitudes about those of a different political party. For example, in a 2019 Pew survey, 55% of Republicans responded that Democrats are "more immoral" when compared with other Americans; 47% of Democrats said the same about Republicans.[47] And 63% of Republicans said that Democrats are "more unpatriotic" than others, while 23% of Democrats said the same about Republicans. On the other hand, 75% of Democrats said Republicans are "more closed-minded" than other Americans, while 64% of Republicans say the same about Democrats.

Loss of institutional trust

With a loss of personal trust we must rely more on our institutions. Tragically, there has been a corresponding loss of trust in institutions as well. Perhaps the most disturbing has been the loss of trust in the federal government. A 2022 Pew national study reported that people's trust that the national government would "do what is right" was only 21%.[48]

Similarly, a series of Gallup polls documented a drop of trust in various government institutions.[49] While a high of 72% of the respondents expressed confidence in the U.S. President in 1991, the figure dropped to a low of 23% in the most recent 2022 survey. For Congress, the drop was from a high of 42% in 1973 to a low of 7% in 2022. For the U.S. Supreme Court, the drop was from 56% in 1985 to 25% in 2022.

While the trust ratings in the Pew study dropped significantly for both Republicans and Democrats, the ratings between the partisans differ depending on who is in office. For example, while 36% of Republicans and those who lean Republican reported they trusted the government in Washington during the Trump Presidency, only 12% of Democrats and those leaning Democrat reported they trusted the government. On the other hand, in the early months of the Biden Presidency, 29% of Democrats reported that they trusted Washington to do what is right; only 9% of Republicans said so.

But it is not only the national government among our institutions that scores low in trust. In the 2022 Gallup poll previously cited, while 68% reported confidence in small business; 64%, in the military; and 64%, in science, a much smaller amount of confidence was expressed in the medical system (38%), "the church or organized religion" (31%), public schools (28%), organized labor (28%), banks (27%), large tech companies (26%), newspapers (16%), internet news (16%), big business (14%), and TV news (11%). Significantly, while 45% responded with confidence in the police, only 14% reported confidence in the criminal justice system.

Loss of trust and social media

As mentioned in the case study for Chapter 5, Facebook CEO Mark Zuckerberg claimed that the company's new focus in 2017 would be on developing the social infrastructure for community.

But how has social media affected trust and community?

A study of Facebook use over an extended period by adults found a negative association between amount of use and overall well-being.[50] Both liking others' content and clicking links significantly predicted a subsequent reduction in self-reported physical health, mental health, and life satisfaction. In fact, Facebook's own internal researchers estimated that about 12.5% of users, corresponding to about 360 million people, reported using the platform so much it affected their sleep, work, parenting, or relationships.[51]

But beyond the impact of its use on individual well-being, it appears that social media use has a significant negative social impact, contributing to misinformation, anger, and mistrust. A study by Yale University researchers used content posted to Facebook and Twitter during the 2016 U.S. Presidential election and found that misinformation news evoked more moral outrage than factually accurate news, and the more outrage-evoking the misinformation was the more users were engaged with likes, shares, and replies.[52] This was particularly so on Facebook, where misinformation was associated more strongly with outrage than with any other emotion. The researchers concluded that this cycle of outrage evoked by posts, which are in turn, re-shared amplifying the anger online is a key component of the spread of misinformation online.

It turns out this phenomenon is part of Facebook's business model. Frances Haugen, who before she quit for ethical reasons was a product manager in Facebook's civic integrity department, shared thousands of internal Facebook documents and research that showed, among many other things, that the company's algorithms were designed to optimize content delivery to users that gets the most engagement.[53] Facebook's own research showed that content that is most engaging is hateful, divisive, and polarizing, and is the kind that inspires people to anger more than to other emotions. Haugen claimed that the company recognized that if it changed the algorithm to be safer, people would spend less time on the site, they'll click on less ads, and the company would make less money. In an interview with "60 Minutes," Haugen said, "The thing I saw at Facebook over and over again was there were conflicts of interest between what was good for the public and what was good for Facebook, and Facebook over and over again chose to optimize for its own interests, like making more money."[54]

The net effect of all these findings is alarming.

Research has clearly established that close social relationships are a source of personal well-being, health, and happiness. Trusting relationships are the basis of collective community action as well as the foundation of economic activity, development, and prosperity. Yet social relationships have unraveled and personal and institutional trust has eroded, fanned by social media postings and profit. We have lost trust in each other, in our information sources, in our corporations, in our educational and medical systems, and in our government. And corporations and other actors are profiting by sowing anger and mistrust.

All of this mistrust has grown precisely at a time when our collective action is desperately needed to address crucial, moral problems that face us, such as global warming, poverty, hunger, homelessness, and racial injustice, problems we cannot solve alone. When social capital of a group, community, or country disintegrates, the group is a mere collection of people. And if each person acts only for their own self-benefit, a community, society, or nation no longer exists. This seems to be happening now in the United States.

Case Study: Braver Angels

How do we get from where we are to where we need to be? How do we create designs that repair relationships and build communities? How do we design for trust? Our case study of Braver Angels helps us think about that.

The United States is clearly in the throes of political divisiveness. Democrats and Republicans hold diametrically opposite views on a number of important issues, and their attitudes are pulling further apart. In recent Pew polls, 81% of Democrats or those leaning Democrat felt gun laws should be made stricter, while only 20% of Republicans and Republican leaners felt that way, with 27% feeling they should be less strict.[55] The respondents who favored granting permanent status to immigrants who came into the country illegally as children was 91% among Democrats, but 54% among Republicans.[56] A majority (80%) of Democrats felt abortion should be legal in all or most cases; a minority (38%) of Republicans felt that way.[57] A 2021 George Washington University poll found that 91% of Democrats responded that dealing with global climate change as somewhat or very important; only 28% of Republicans did.[58] A very large majority of Democrats (78%) felt that voting is a right; 67% of Republicans responded that it's a privilege. And in a CBS poll, 69% of Republicans responded that there was widespread voter fraud in the 2020 Presidential election; only 7% of Democrats believed that.[59]

In a 2021 George Washington University poll, over half of Republicans (55%) supported the possible use of force to preserve the "traditional American way of life" compared to 15% of Democrats.[60] And when asked if a time will come when "patriotic Americans have to take the law into their own hands," 47% of Republicans agreed, as opposed to just 9% of Democrats.

The only thing that majorities of the two parties seem to agree on is that political polarization will get worse.[61]

How can our society handle such political disagreement? How can our government function when people cannot trust each other or the government? How can we step back from the brink? Braver Angels is trying to figure that out.

Case Study: Braver Angels
In December 2016, after a bruising, divisive Presidential election, two friends, David Blankenhorn and David Lapp, felt there must be a better way.[62] Along with family therapist Bill Doherty, they came up with an idea for a neighborhood gathering that might heal the divide. They assembled 21 neighbors from South Lebanon, Ohio, 10 Trump supporters and 11 Clinton supporters. Among those gathered were factory workers, a political organizer, a gunsmith, a psychologist, a retired RN, and a retired auto worker. The goal of the meeting was to see if Americans could still disagree respectfully, and just maybe, find common ground. The weekend was the beginning of beautiful friendships between conservatives and liberals in the community, and after the first workshop proved to be a success, another was planned for their friends. This was the beginning of a grassroots organization that came to be known as Braver Angels (www.braverangels.org), taking its inspiration from Abraham Lincoln's inaugural address. After National Public Radio gave them a full hour of exposure, the group started getting calls from people around the country hoping they could help bring their communities together. In response to the demand, the group organized a bus tour the summer of 2017, starting in

(Continued)

Case Study: Braver Angels (Continued)

Waynesville, Ohio, and ending in Philadelphia, PA. Another tour in the fall started in Washington, D.C. and ran through North Carolina and ended in Nashville. The group held workshops as they went, eventually training over 100 workshop moderators (see Figures 15.1 and 15.2).

Braver Angels mission, as stated on its website is challenging: "Our work is about building civic trust in the USA. It is about healing the wounds between left and right .... Our work is about supporting a more perfect union. Our work is about inspiring the beloved community."

Their principal way of doing this is with what they call "Red-Blue Workshops." The workshops are organized with an even number of Democrat and Republican participants, typically 5–8 each. Independents are also welcome to attend, although for the purposes of the workshop, they are asked to identify as leaning either Red or Blue. Additional people can attend as observers.

The goals of the workshop are to help participants better understand the experiences and beliefs of those on the other side of the political divide, to see if there are areas of commonality in addition to differences, and to learn something that might be helpful to others in the community and the nation. Two moderators, trained by Braver Angels, lead the workshop, ensuring that ground rules are followed and that everyone is treated respectfully.

After a round of brief introductions and discussion of ground rules, to start the workshop, moderators engage participates in a series of exercises. These include a Stereotypes Exercise, in which separate red and blue groups generate a list of the most common false stereotypes or misconceptions people have of their side, why these stereotypes are wrong, what is true instead, and whether there is a kernel of truth in the stereotype.

Figure 15.1 Braver Angels Red-Blue Workshop (*Source:* Braver Angels).

Figure 15.2 Braver Angels Red-Blue Workshop (*Source:* Braver Angels).

There is a Fishbowl Exercise, in which one group sits in chairs in the middle and the other group sits around them to listen and learn. Then the two groups switch positions. Afterward, people on both sides are invited to share what they learned about how the other side sees itself and if they see anything in common.

In the Questions Exercise, separate groups of Reds and Blues meet to generate "understanding questions" they then ask the other side in the merged group to gain genuine understanding of the views and experiences of people on the other side.

With the How Can We Contribute Exercise, everyone fills out an action grid handout. The questions are: What can each of us do individually, what can our side do, and what might both sides do together to promote better understanding of differences and search for common ground? Participants then pair up with someone of the other side to share responses and pick one action step with the whole group.

In addition to the Red-Blue Workshops, the organization has since developed two other workshops that include Common Ground workshops that allow participants from Red-Blue workshops to dig deeper into specific issues, and Race Conversations, that enable participants to talk about race in an inquisitive, nonjudgmental way.

They've also developed several other formats, including Corporate Offerings, College Debates, Town Halls, and 1:1 Conversations. They're latest program is Braver Politics, where they are offering cross-party workshops to legislators and their staff.

All of their events are guided by stated principles that allow participants to state their views without fear, engage with those with whom we disagree, treat people with whom disagree with honesty and respect, avoid exaggeration and stereotypes, look for common ground where it exists, and in disagreements, learn from each other.

As of November 2021, Braver Angels has 80 chapters, spanning all 50 states, and over 10,000 members. They've trained over 2,000 volunteer workshop moderators and organized thousands of events.

The goal of Braver Angels is to bridge the division between warring groups, to use empathy and compassion to emphasize our similarities, rather than our differences. It addresses major political, social trends at a local, interpersonal level. Its exercises create "walk in my shoes," "see things from my perspective" experiences that tap into our shared humanity as a way to create trust and community.

Braver Angels is still a relatively young organization and there hasn't been a lot of research on its impact. Most of the studies so far are merely descriptive. But one study holds out promise. A collaborative study by nine researchers at different universities randomly assigned undergraduate students from Republican and Democrat clubs at four college campuses to either participate in a day-long Braver Angels workshop or merely fill out pre-and post-questionnaires.[63] Cognitive, affective and behavioral measures were taken. The focus of the study was on the impact of the workshop on partisan attitudes and feelings, rather than trust per se. But the researchers found that workshops significantly reduced polarization, although the effects dissipated some over time, and they increased participants' willingness to donate to programs aimed at depolarizing political conversations. These effects were found for both Democrat and Republican students.

If we are to build compassionate, supportive relationships, if we are to save our communities and civil society, we must begin by building relationships and re-establishing trust. Trust doesn't happen overnight. It happens over extended one-to-one interactions, initially furtive, becoming more trusting based on success, and then perhaps, turning into friendships. With Braver Angels, these interactions occur around important issues, issues with moral implications, much as do Michael Sandel's moral discussions.

Designing for Relationships and Community

Designs to support relationships

The basis for human relationships is the deep emotion we feel when we're connected. These emotions are expressed as safety, trust, pleasure, happiness. These feelings are natural, but it takes intentional effort to turn feelings into the long-term relationships that lead to happiness and well-being. These long-term connections get created, acted out, and maintained in everyday, micro-level interactions.

Designs that create social environments can help build relationships. These can be physical environments, such as public parks or community buildings, or digital environments, such as social media platforms. These environments create public spaces in which regular encounters can turn into relationships.

However, for relationships to develop into friendships, more intimate interactions need to occur. Intimate relationships of the sort that support well-being over a lifetime result from ongoing communications in which likes and dislikes, hopes and dreams, triumphs and traumas are shared; communications that respond positively to bids for attention and affection and result in mutual change and shared meaning.[64]

The kinds of environments that support emerging intimacy need to be safe and respectful, and require communication skills that allow people to open up and be vulnerable with each other. Investing in designs that support these kinds of interactions can have huge interpersonal payoffs in health, longevity, and well-being. Designs that build compassionate, supportive relationships come most often from parents, loved ones, marriage and family therapists, group counselors, and pastors, those who can assure safety and work with people to scaffold their interactions and skill development to build intimacy.

As we have seen, social media environments, as they are currently designed, do not provide the safety and trust needed for the development of compassionate, supportive relationships, and may, indeed, be hostile environments that threaten such relationships. However, as we discussed in Chapter 5, safe environments could be specially designed, perhaps using AI, that can support relationship development by excluding people with mal-intent, and structuring and supporting compassionate interactions.

Designs to repair relationships

If mistakes are made in a relationship, if trust is betrayed, it can lead to a vicious cycle of recriminations and reciprocal betrayals that destroys the relationship. Withdrawal of trust is an understandable self-defense mechanism. But forgiveness and reconnection create a path for the positive interactions that drive long-term success.[65] Marriage and family therapists, counselors, and pastors can help with these repairs on a one to one, micro level. Braver Angels is addressing these interpersonal disconnections over political issues.

However, many of the everyday relationships are not, at least at the start, close, interpersonal connections, but are based on roles or institutional structures: the relationship between manager and employee, merchant and consumer, producer and supplier, doctor and patient, teacher and student. These relationships are vital to the everyday functioning of society, yet, without the strong interpersonal connections to fall back on, they are most vulnerable to conflict. This conflict most often gets played out in the legal system.

Dispute System Design is a process used by lawyers, mediators, and human resources (HR) personnel to prevent, manage, and resolve conflict with the overarching purpose of promoting justice and fairness.[66] The approach builds on the work of Elinor Ostrom to craft designs through a process, aided by third-party dispute resolvers, in which stakeholders are identified and they express their goals and interests. They are involved in the systemic analysis of sources of disputes, current communication processes, and the surrounding context and culture to identify overlapping interests and values. And they are involved in processes for resolving these disputes. The design of these mechanisms can be customized to the situation, but might involve direct negotiation, mediation, arbitration, or as a last resort, litigation, and criteria are designed for moving from one to the other. Part of the design is also the means for monitoring its implementation and impact that can serve to foster trust and maintain the relationship.

Repairing trust among people who are different and who don't normally have an opportunity to interact face-to-face is the most difficult situation. Too often, we have opinions about "others" that put them in a box and dehumanize them. Organizations like Braver Angels and events like America in One Room[67] design safe environments and experiences that make the impersonal personal by creating understanding that can serve as the beginning of a trusting relationship.

Designs to support collective action and build communities

Collective action creates common resources that could not be created by individual action alone, resources that can benefit everyone. We saw this with the Plank Road project in Baton Rouge. We saw this with WestGate Water, Happy Cities, and Burning Man. Designs can create opportunities and provide tools that enable communities to engage in collective action. These can be digital resources and collaborative tools that support collective action, as we saw with communities of practice. And they can be designs that generate digital or physical resources that the community can share and enjoy together, as we saw with Kuja Kuja and High Tech High. And as we learned from Elinor Ostrom's research, community members can design ways to manage these share resources for their mutual benefit.

The ability of a community to act together will become more and more important in the face of mounting problems, such as challenges to our democracy and threats from climate change, problems that affect us all and that can't be addressed by individual actions or market forces alone. And actions at the community level are especially important when collective action at the national level hits a wall, as we will explore in the next chapter.

Designs can generate the social capital needed to address emerging problems by creating opportunities for local dialogs that focus on problematic situations, vital to the community, and apply moral principles, rather than just technical fixes, as we explored in Chapter 11. But these designs need to provide a safe and respectful environment in which the dialog takes place in order to build on and contribute to the trust within the community.

Design activities of this sort not only involve social workers, community leaders and organizers, pastors, and elected officials, they must involve everyone who is affected by the design. Our differences can erode trust, push us apart, and bring us down. Or they can be the source of new ideas that are our strength. If that is to be so, there must be multivocal dialog, representing, perhaps, deep divisions and passionate emotions. It is only by hearing each other out, while treating all with dignity and respect, that we can address our common problems, and as Michael Sandel points out, move forward, bit by bit, to a more just society.

References

1 Rand A. The virtue of selfishness: A new concept of egoism. New York: Signet, Kindle Edition, 1961.
2 Rand A. The virtue of selfishness: A new concept of egoism (location 530). New York: Signet, Kindle Edition, 1961.
3 Hume D. An enquiry concerning the principles of morals, Section 5. Hume: The essential philosophical works. Herdsfordshire, England: Wordsworth, 2011.
4 Bentham J. Collected Works of Jeremy Bentham (location 3556). Minerva Classics, Kindle Edition, 2013.
5 Mill JS. Utilitarianism. Hackett Publishing Company, Inc.. Kindle Edition, 2001.
6 Smith A. The theory of moral sentiments. Excercere Cerebrum Publisher, 2014.
7 Spikins P. How Compassion Made Us Human: The Evolutionary Origins of Tenderness, Trust & Morality. South Yorkshire: Pen & Sword Books, 2015.
8 Byock I. Quote from his book, The Best Care Possible: A Physician's Quest to Transform Care Through the End of Life. Avery, 2012. Available from: https://i.stack.imgur.com/Tdobe.jpg.
9 Baimeister R, Leary M. The need to belong: Desire for interpersonal attachments as a fundamental human motivation. Psychological Bulletin, 1995, 117(3), 497–529.
10 Gobbini M, Leibenluft E, Santiago N, et al. Social and emotional attachment in the neural representation of faces. Neuroimage, 2004, 22(4), 1628–1635.
11 Breuning L. Habits of a happy brain. New York: Adams Media, 2015.
12 Hardin J, Jones N, Mize K, et al. Parent-training with Kangaroo Care impacts neurophysiological development and mother-infant neuroendocrine activity. Infant Behavior and Development, 2020, 58, 101416.
13 Harmon K. Touch and emotional engagement boost early childhood development, but can children recover from neglectful environments? Scientific American [Internet]. 2010, May 6 [cited 2022, Sep 2]. Available from: https://www.scientificamerican.com/article/infant-touch/.
14 Heim C, Young L, Newport D, et al. Lower CSF oxytocin concentrations in women with a history of childhood abuse. Molecular Psychiatry, 2009, 14910, 954–958.

15 Owens R. Language development: An introduction (10th ed.). Hoboken, NJ: Pearson, 2020.

16 Vygotsky L. Mind in society: The development of higher psychological processes. Cambridge, MA: Harvard University Press, 1978.

17 Stafford M. Kuh D, Gale C, et al. Parent-child relationships and offspring's positive mental wellbeing from adolescence to early older age. Journal of Positive Psychology, 2016, 11(3), 326–337.

18 Mineo L. Good genes are nice, but joy is better. Harvard Gazette [Internet]. 2017, Apr 11 [cited 2022, Sep 2]. Available from: https://news.harvard.edu/gazette/story/2017/04/over-nearly-80-years-harvard-study-has-been-showing-how-to-live-a-healthy-and-happy-life/.

19 Fredrickson B. Love 2.0: Our supreme emotion affects everything we feel, think, do, and become (p. 17). New York: Hudson Street Press, 2013.

20 Gottman J, Silver N. Seven principles for making marriage work. New York: Crown Publishers, 2015.

21 Kaufman, V, Perez, J, Reise S, Bradbury T, Karney B. (2021). Friendship network satisfaction: A multifaceted construct scored as a unidimensional scale. Journal of Social and Personal Relationships [Internet]. 2021, Aug 3 [cited 2022, Sep 2]. Available from: https://journals.sagepub.com/doi/abs/10.1177/02654075211025639.

22 Kaufman V. Social relationships and well-being: Rediscovering the importance of adult friendship. Dissertation, University of California Los Angeles. 2020 [cited 2022, Sep 2]. Available from: https://escholarship.org/content/qt8k5970m1/qt8k5970m1_noSplash_efe6a78e9cf713d2a9017de335903191.pdf.

23 Bretherton I. The origins of attachment theory: John Bowlby and Mary Ainsworth. Developmental Psychology, 1992, 28 (5),759–775.

24 Berk L. (2018). Development through the lifespan (7th ed.). Hoboken, NJ: Pearson.

25 Mitic M, Woodcock K, Amering M, et al. Toward an integrated model of supportive peer relationships in early adolescence: A systematic review and exploratory meta-analysis. Frontiers in Psychology: Developmental Psychology [Internet]. 2020, Feb 25 [cited 2022, Sep 2]. Available from: https://www.frontiersin.org/articles/10.3389/fpsyg.2021.589403/full.

26 Wu Y, Veerareddy A, Lee M, et al. Understanding identification-based trust in the light of affiliative bonding: Meta-analytic neuroimaging evidence. Neuroscience and Biobehavioral Reviews, 2021, 131, 627–641.

27 Fallows J, Fallows D. Our Towns. New York: Pantheon Books, 2018.

28 Sauri, Kenya. Millennium Villages [Internet]. [cited 2022, Sep 2]. Available from: http://www.mv-aid.org/mv/sauri.html.

29 Granovetter M. The strength of weak ties. The American Journal of Sociology, 1973, 78(6), 1360–1380.

30 Rost K. The strength of strong ties. Research Policy, 2011, 40, 588–604.

31 Burning Man [Internet]. 2019, Aug 25-Sep 2 cited 2022, Sep 2]. Available from: https://burningman.org/timeline/2019.

32 Montgomery C. Happy City: Transforming Our Lives Through Urban Design (p. 37). New York: Farrar, Straus and Giroux, 2013.

33 Walljaspers J. How to design our world for happiness. On the Commons [Internet]. [cited 2022, Sep 2]. Available from: http://www.onthecommons.org/sites/default/files/how-to-design-our-world.pdf.

34 Coleman JS. Social capital in the creation of human capital. American Journal of Sociology, 1988, 94, S95–S120.

35 Helliwell JF. Well-being, social capital and public policy: What's new? Economic Journal, 116, C34–C45.

36 Putnam R. Bowing alone. New York: Simon & Schuster, 2001.

37 Chetty R, Jackson M, Kuchler, T, et al. Social capital I: Measurement and associations with economic mobility. Nature, 2022, 608, 108–121.

38 Llana S. Medellín, once epicenter of Colombia's drug war fights to keep the peace. Christian Science Monitor [Internet]. 2010, Oct 25 cited 2022, Sep 2]. Available from: https://www.csmonitor.com/World/Americas/2010/1025/Medellin-once-epicenter-of-Colombia-s-drug-war-fights-to-keep-the-peace.

39 Putnam R. Bowling alone. New York: Simon & Schuster, 2001, p. 22.

40 What's Burning Man? The 10 principles of Burning Man. Burning Man [Internet]. [cited 2022, Sep 2]. Available from: https://burningman.org/culture/philosophical-center/10-principles/.

41 OECD. How's Life? 2020: Measuring Well-being. OECD [Internet]. 2020 [cited 2022, Sep 2]. Available from: https://www.oecd-ilibrary.org/economics/how-s-life/volume-/issue-_9870c393-en.

42 Social cohesion and well-being in the E.U. Bertelsmann-Stiftung [Internet]. [cited 2022, Sep 2]. Available from: https://www.bertelsmann-stiftung.de/en/publications/publication/did/social-cohesion-and-well-being-in-the-eu-en?tx_rsmbstpublications_pi2%5BfilterSprache%5D%5B2%5D=1&tx_rsmbstpublications_pi2%5Bpage%5D=2&cHash=dd3b33f0d50157474b22176af7cb.

43 Cox D. The state of American friendship: Change, challenges, and loss. Survey of American Life [Internet]. 2021, Jun 8 [cited 2022, Sep 2]. Available from: https://www.americansurveycenter.org/research/the-state-of-american-friendship-change-challenges-and-loss/.

44 U.S. loneliness index. Cigna [Internet]. 2018, May [cited 2022, Sep 2]. Available from: https://www.multivu.com/players/English/8294451-cigna-us-loneliness-survey/docs/IndexRepor t_1524069371598-173525450.pdf.

45 Depression and other common mental disorders. World Health Organization [Internet]. 2017, Jan 3 [cited 2022, Sep 2]. Available from: https://www.who.int/publications/i/item/depression-global-health-estimates.

46 The state of personal trust. Pew Research Center [Internet]. 2019, Jul 22 [cited 2022, Sep 2]. Available from: https://www.pewresearch.org/politics/2019/07/22/the-state-of-personal-trust/.

47 Partisan antipathy: More intense, more personal. Pew Research Center 2019, Oct 10 [cited 2022, Sep 2]. Available from: https://www.pewresearch.org/politics/2019/10/10/partisan-antipathy-more-intense-more-personal/.

48 Public trust in government: 1958–2022. Pew Research Center [Internet]. 2022, Jun 6 [cited 2022, Sep 2]. Available from: https://www.pewresearch.org/politics/2021/05/17/public-trust-in-government-1958-2021./

49 Confidence in institutions. Gallup [Internet]. 2022 [cited 2022, Sep 2]. Available from: https://news.gallup.com/poll/1597/confidence-institutions.aspx.

50 Shakya H, Christakis N. Association of Facebook use with compromised well-being: A longitudinal study. American Journal of Epidemiology, 2016, 185(3), 203–211.

51 Wells G, Seetharaman D, Horwitz J. Is Facebook bad for you? It is for about 360 million users company surveys suggest. Wall Street Journal [Internet]. 2021, Nov 5 [cited 2022, Sep 2]. Available from: https://www.wsj.com/articles/facebook-bad-for-you-360-million-users-say-yes-company-documents-facebook-files-11636124681.

52 Brady W, McLoughlin K, Doan T, et al. How social learning amplifies moral outrage expression in online social networks. Science Advances [Internet]. 2021, Aug 13 [cited 2022, Sep 2]. Available from: https://www.science.org/doi/10.1126/sciadv.abe5641.

53 Horwitz J. The Facebook whistleblower, Frances Haugen, says she wants to fix the company, not harm it. Wall Street Journal [Internet]. 2021, Oct 3 [cited 2022, Sep 2]. Available from: https://

www.wsj.com/articles/facebook-whistleblower-frances-haugen-says-she-wants-to-fix-the-company-not-harm-it-11633304122.

54 Pelley S. Wistleblower Facebook is misleading the public on progress against hate speech, violence, misinformation. 60 Minutes [Internet]. 2021, Oct 4 [cited 2022, Sep 2]. Available from: https://www.cbsnews.com/news/facebook-whistleblower-frances-haugen-misinformation-public-60-minutes-2021-10-03/.

55 Schaeffer K. Key facts about Americans and guns. Pew Research Center [Internet]. 2021, Sep 13 [cited 2022, Sep 2]. Available from: https://www.pewresearch.org/fact-tank/2021/09/13/key-facts-about-americans-and-guns/.

56 Krogstad J, Americans broadly support legal status for immigrants brought to the U.S. illegally as children. Pew Research Center [Internet]. 2020, Jun 17 [cited 2022, Sep 2]. Available from: https://www.pewresearch.org/fact-tank/2020/06/17/americans-broadly-support-legal-status-for-immigrants-brought-to-the-u-s-illegally-as-children/.

57 Hartig H. About six-in-ten Americans say abortion should be legal in all or most cases. Pew Research Center [Internet]. 2022, Jun 13 [cited 2022, Sep 2]. Available from: https://www.pewresearch.org/fact-tank/2021/05/06/about-six-in-ten-americans-say-abortion-should-be-legal-in-all-or-most-cases/.

58 GW politics poll shows lack of trust by Republicans by Republicans in Biden won states. George Washington School of Media & Public Affairs [Internet]. 2021, Jul 26 [cited 2022, Sep 2]. Available from: https://smpa.gwu.edu/gw-politics-poll-shows-lack-trust-republicans-biden-won-states.

59 CBS News Poll Adults in the U.S. CBS News [Internet]. 2021, Jul 6–15 [cited 2022, Sep 2]. Available from: https://drive.google.com/file/d/1YPTDHhnieNZ0SCB0eRksWkdyewuvdWL7/view.

60 Parra D. GW politics poll finds varying confidence in state and local elections. GW Media Relations [Internet]. 2021, Jul 26 [cited 2022, Sep 2]. Available from: https://mediarelations.gwu.edu/gw-politics-poll-finds-varying-confidence-state-and-local-elections.

61 Parker K, Morin R, Horowitz J. Looking to the future, public sees an America in decline on many fronts. Pew Research Center [Internet]. 2019, Mar 21 [cited 2022, Sep 2]. Available from: https://www.pewresearch.org/social-trends/2019/03/21/public-sees-an-america-in-decline-on-many-fronts/.

62 Braver Angels [Internet]. [cited 2022, Sep 2]. Available from: https://braverangels.org.

63 Baron H, Blair R, Choi D, et al. Can Americans depolarize? Assessing the effects of reciprocal group reflection on partisan polarization (2021). OSF Preprints [Internet]. 2022, Jan 20 [cited 2022, Sep 2]. Available from: https://osf.io/3x7z8.

64 Gottman J, Silver N. The seven principles for making marriage work. New York: Crown Publishers, 2015.

65 Nowak M. Super cooperators: Beyond survival of the fittest; why cooperation, not competition, is the key to life. Edinburgh: Cannongate, 2011.

66 Amsler L, Martinez J, Smith S. Dispute system design: Preventing, managing, and resolving conflict. Stanford, CA: Stanford University Press, 2020.

67 America in One Room. Deliberative Democracy Lab, Stanford University [Internet]. [cited 2022, Sep 2]. Available from: https://cdd.stanford.edu/2019/america-in-one-room/.

Part IV

Redesigning the System

16

The Economy, Government, and Design

No society can surely be flourishing and happy, of which the far greater part of the members are poor and miserable.

Adam Smith
18th-Century Philosopher and Economist

We can envision many things as designers, but what we actually do is both enabled and constrained by the economic and the governmental systems in which we work. Economic and political structures and processes shape our activities, including our designs. The political economy we live in has spawned an incredible number of innovations, as documented in Chapter 1. And it has enabled and supported the Scientific, Human-Centered, Aesthetic, and Technical-Analytic Design Traditions, with a clear preference for the latter, while the Community Organization and Social Movement Tradition has been relegated to the periphery.

Yet, many of the world's greatest needs are not addressed because the economic or political systems have not been structured to address them. Projects that get funded are the ones that benefit some groups and harm others. Some designs are valued; other ideas that would make the world better are ignored.

In this chapter, we will consider the nature of the relationship among the economy, government, and design. And Garrett Hardin can help us think about it.

Tragedy of the Commons

We encountered Hardin and *The Tragedy of the Commons* in Chapter 2. In his *Science* magazine article by that name, Hardin described a hypothetical situation in which farmers shared a common meadow, with each farmer operating out of his own rational self-interest.[1] It is in the interest of each farmer to add cows to his own herd, doing so without incurring additional cost since the meadow is held in common, thus increasing profits. But the tragic result of each person following his own self-interest and adding additional cows is the destruction of the meadow as it is overgrazed and collapses.

This hypothetical dilemma reflects many of the real-world concerns we have today,as we consider the impacts of our activities including our designs, on our society and planet. We reflect on our designs' impacts on our common resources: How do they affect the quality of our air and water, our limited natural resources, and the sustainability of our species in a changing climate? But there are other things we hold in common: our accumulated knowledge, our social bonds, our

Make the World a Better Place: Design with Passion, Purpose, and Values, First Edition. Robert B. Kozma.

cultural heritage, our mutual trust—our social capital. Our actions and designs benefit from all of these. Our designs can also contribute to them . . . or degrade them.

When thinking about the fate of our commons, Hardin offers some alternatives. He contends that there is no way to both keep the meadow in common and to maintain it sustainably. The collapse could only be avoided by either privatizing the meadow, in which case the owner would increase the herd only to the extent that the field could be maintained. Or, it could be avoided by having a central authority devise a top-down scheme to determine how many cows from each herd could use it for how long, so as to maintain the meadow.

In effect, he supplies us with two approaches to solving world problems that can frame our designs: individual transactions within an open economy or government command. In the first case, our design offerings are among the individual transactions that get negotiated within the economy. In the second case, comprehensive designs direct economic activity. The competition between these alternative approaches influenced much of the global economic activity from the 20th century up to today.

In this chapter, we will examine the implications of these alternatives, as well as a third approach that we examined in Chapter 4, that offered by Elinor Ostrom, the collective action of a community.

The Economy and Self-Interest

Capitalism as a coherent system of economic thought was first articulated in the 18th century as the Industrial Revolution began in England. The multitalented Adam Smith, whom we met in Chapter 3 as a moral philosopher of the Scottish Enlightenment, is also considered the father of modern economics. Smith contends in his book *An Inquiry into the Nature and Causes of the Wealth of Nations* that the economy is driven not by some grand design or by a government master plan, but by the accumulated actions of individuals driven by their own rational self-interest, much like in my butcher shop example in Chapter 4.

Smith conceives of the economy as a self-organizing system of rational individuals—producers and consumers, sellers and buyers—whose reasoned actions optimize their self-interest. This concept is captured in the Latin term, *homo economicus*, or economic man—the idea is that humans are purely rational agents, acting in their own self-interest.

Smith contends that, in the aggregate, the independent activities of self-interested agents have consequences that go beyond their immediate transactions to benefit society as a whole. This is Smith's famous "invisible hand." In Hardin's example of the commons, Smith would advocate for the privatization of the field and let the farmer adjust the number of cows he has, based on their impact on the land and on market demand. It is through his self-interest that he sustainably provides his products to the market and thus benefits society.

However, there is a downside to self-interest in the economy.

The neoliberal turn

The self-interested, rational, *homo economicus* model of human action and the self-organizing conception of the market was most forcefully articulated by the Chicago School of Economics in the mid-20th century and was turned into a moral philosophy by Robert Nozick and Ayn Rand, whom we met in Chapter 3. The "School" was a body of economic thought rather than a formal academic institution, although many of its most ardent adherents were on the faculty of the University of Chicago, including its most prominent advocates, Nobel Laureates Friedrich Hayek and Milton Friedman, whom we met in earlier chapters.

The principal notion of the Chicago School was that market issues such as levels of production, consumption, prices, and wages are all determined by the market through the rational, self-interested actions of individual investors, consumers, employers, and workers—that is, Smith's "invisible hand"—and the government does not need to intervene in this process. Friedman referred to this philosophy of political economics as *neoliberalism*.[2]

During his career, Friedman advocated for deregulation of the market, international free trade, low taxes, and the privatization of public services, such as education, arguing that free market dynamics would improve the quality of these services and reduce costs to the public. In his book, *Free to Choose*, Friedman claimed:

> . . . when workers get higher wages and better working conditions through the free market, when they get raises by firms competing with one another for the best workers, by workers competing with one another for the best jobs, those higher wages are at nobody's expense. They can only come from higher productivity, greater capital investment, more widely diffused skills. The whole pie is bigger—there's more for the worker, but there's also more for the employer, the investor, the consumer, and even the tax collector.[3]

Friedman and the Chicago School version of free market capitalism had a profound impact on government policies in the United States and England, and Friedman was an economic advisor to both the administrations of U.S. President Ronald Reagan and U.K. Prime Minister Margaret Thatcher. His prescriptions influenced economic policies in those countries during the 1980s and dominated political economic policies until 2008. In many ways, they continue to do so today.

Neoliberal policies in the United States actually began under the administration of Democrat President Jimmy Carter. Carter had inherited both a recession and inflation from President Gerald Ford, and in an effort to stimulate the economy, Carter deregulated trucking, airlines, rail freight, and lending institutions. These initial efforts were expanded significantly under President Regan, who had a well-articulated economic program that came to be known as "Reaganomics." According to Friedman, "Reaganomics had four simple principles: lower marginal tax rates, less regulation, restrained government spending, noninflationary monetary policy. Though Reagan did not achieve all of his goals, he made good progress."[4]

Reagan implemented large, across-the-board tax cuts to stimulate economic growth.[5] He also cut regulations in the banking and natural gas industries. Federal price controls were eliminated on airfares, oil and natural gas, long distance telephone services, and cable TV.[6] The Environmental Protection Agency (EPA) relaxed its interpretation of the Clean Air Act, and the Department of the Interior opened up large areas of the federal domain, including offshore oil fields, to private development. And Reagan began deregulating trade by signing the Canada–United States Free Trade Agreement in 1988, which was the impetus for the North American Free Trade Agreement, known as NAFTA.

Reagan cut or reduced the budgets of nonmilitary programs, including Social Security, Medicaid, food stamps, education and job training programs, and the EPA. He slashed federal assistance to local governments by 60%, cutting the budget for public housing and rent subsidies in half, and eliminating the antipoverty Community Development Block Grant program.

George H.W. Bush intended to continue the Reagan policies, but in an effort to reduce a lingering deficit left over from the Reagan period, he signed a compromise bill that cut spending on domestic programs but also raised taxes. The tax increase was considered a betrayal by his supporters and it contributed to Clinton's victory after Bush's first term. Business-friendly, free-market policies continued into the Clinton Administration when he signed NAFTA, deregulated the telecommunications industry, continued the deregulation of the financial sector, and made major cuts in welfare. The administration of George W. Bush accelerated deregulation of the financial sector and reinstituted tax cuts.

Neoliberal policies also launched a decades-long trend that turned over a wide range of enterprises previously associated with government ownership and responsibility to the private sector. In the United States this has come to include education, prisons, water utilities, transportation, even portions of national defense. Internationally, privatization became part of the Washington Consensus package of economic reforms that was required of developing countries by the International Monetary Fund (IMF) in order to obtain loans or receive debt forgiveness.[7]

Neoliberalism gets played out

While neoliberal policies and the free market created innovations, businesses, jobs, and wealth, it also created devastation and harm. During a period between 1986 and 1995, 1,043 savings and loan institutions failed as deregulation allowed them to increase the risk of their investments and these risky loans failed.[8]

Later in the 1990s, low Federal Reserve interest rates[9] and a newly lowered capital gains tax rate[10] contributed to speculative investments in a plethora of new internet-based "dot-com" companies between 1995 and 2000, with the NASDAQ composite index rising from 726 points in January 1995 to 4,590 points in February 2000, only to fall to 1,139 points in October 2002 when many of these companies failed. The economy went into recession in March 2001, and unemployment peaked at 6.3% in 2003.

But the biggest market failure was the 2008 subprime housing crisis, otherwise known as the "Great Recession." The buildup to this crisis, known as the "housing bubble," occurred as the financial industry was increasingly deregulated over a 10-year period beginning in the late 1990s until 2008. Deregulation of the sector launched a variety of creative financial designs. Among them were derivative investments offerings called "collateralized debt obligations," or CDOs. Investment banks created these derivatives by purchasing mortgages from lending institutions and bundling them into packages that they could turn around and sell to investors. These packages were primarily home mortgages, but could include auto loans, student loans, commercial loans, and other kinds of debt. Because these loans were bundled, it was difficult to assess the true risk of the product.

At the same time, three other things were happening that together set the stage for disaster. 1) Lenders were issuing mortgages to higher risk customers, dangling in front of them low initial rates on adjustable loans, or "teaser rates," with the possibility of achieving the American Dream: owning a home. Lenders took on these risks because they made money up front from loan fees and they could then pass off the risk to investment banks that were attracted by the higher interest rates on these subprime loans. They would then bundle them with other, less risky loans. 2) The rating agencies, such as Moody's and Standard and Poor's, which were paid by the investment banks to rate their products, gave these bundled products their highest AAA investment rating, even though it was difficult to assess the true risk. 3) Finally, insurance companies, such as AIG, designed their own derivatives, called "credit default swaps," that they would sell to investment banks as hedges against default. With deregulation, AIG could sell these policies to anyone who wanted to bet against these debt packages, even if they didn't own them. At the same time AIG's risk was multiplied: deregulation meant that it did not need to have capital to cover its policies in case of default.

All of this worked as long as housing prices were increasing, which was the case until the mid-2000s. In the early to mid-2000s, all of these financial institutions were making enormous profits, and their executives and traders were collecting huge bonuses.

But it all unraveled in 2008.

In any complex adaptive system, a relatively small event within a network of interlocking relationships can trigger other events that cascade through the system with potentially catastrophic consequences. This is most likely to happen when people exploit or game the system for their self-interest and at the expense of the system's self-regulating functions. Early in 2007, housing prices peaked and began to drop.[11] As teaser rates on adjustable-rate loans converted to higher rates, low-qualified home owners began to default on their loans. By 2008, investment banks were holding large amounts of debt because they were having trouble selling their bundled packages. At the same time, they increased their bets against the packages they were trying to sell, knowing that they were poor investments.

On September 9, the dominos began to fall. Lehman Brothers announced losses of $3.2 billion. Its stock price collapsed and it declared bankruptcy. As the debt packages failed, AIG, which insured them, was not able to pay. On September 16, the Federal Reserve Bank provided AIG with what ended up being $182 billion to prevent that company's collapse, enabling it to, in turn, pay the investment banks that bet against these risky loan packages that they originated.[12]

Feeling that these institutions were "too big to fail" and fearing a total economic meltdown if they did, Congress passed, and, on October 3, President George W. Bush signed, the Emergency Economic Stabilization Act, which provided $700 billion to purchase toxic bank assets.[13]

The banks turned around and used the federal money to pay bonuses for the previous year's performance. For example, Citigroup gave employees $5.3 billion in bonuses for 2008, with 738 staff getting more than $1 million each.[14] Goldman Sachs paid out $4.8 billion in bonuses to its staff, and Morgan Stanley paid $4.5 billion in bonuses.

At the same time, the stock market continued to drop, losing half of its value between its high in October 2007 and its low in November 2008.[15] Domestic auto production dropped by more than 70%.[16] The national debt increased dramatically.[17] The U.S. economy went into an extended, 18-month recession, taking the rest of the world with it.

The social impact of pure self-interest

While investment banks and their executives were rescued by the federal government, government support for home owners proved to be meager and ineffective,[18] and mortgage foreclosures continued to rise through 2010. As housing prices began to fall in 2007, owners found that their houses were worth less than what they owed and foreclosures began, wiping out homeowner wealth. In 2008, there were over 2.3 million foreclosures.[19] It is estimated that the 2008 housing collapse resulted in a $10.2 trillion loss of wealth in the United States, including $3.3 trillion lost in home equity.[20] Over 30 million people lost their jobs.[21] And U.S. unemployment rose to 10% in 2009.[22] Household net worth dropped by more than $10 trillion during the recession—the largest loss of wealth since the federal government started keeping records of wealth accumulation 50 years ago.[23] In 2010, homelessness in the country peaked at 1.6 million, but persisted at 1.4 million up to the pandemic, which aggravated the situation.[24]

The recession led to an unequal impact across groups on wealth, health, and well-being. With the collapse of 2008, the value of assets of the top 10% of the wealthiest households took a temporary hit, recovering their full value in 2013 and more by 2015.[25] The upper-middle group also took a hit and didn't recover to their 2008 level until 2015. However, the value of the assets for the bottom 50%—their home equity—fell through the floor.

The overall impact of neoliberal policies has been unequal across the population. In 1989, the wealthiest 1% of the population owned 23.6% of the nation's total net worth and the bottom 50% owned only 3.7%.[26] By 2022, the top 1% owned 32% of the wealth and the top 10% owned 69%. The bottom 50% never owned more than 4.3% of the wealth according to modern records. That sank to a mere .3% of total wealth in 2011. As of Q1 2022, the bottom 50% own only 2.8% and the bottom 90% own only 31%.

Studies that examined the impact of the recession on health and well-being documented a decline in fertility and self-rated health, and an increase in morbidity, psychological distress, and suicide on the population as a whole, but particularly among those who personally suffered job, income, or housing loss, and greatest among men and racial and ethnic minorities.[27] In 2010, there were 38,329 reported drug overdose deaths.[28] The number climbed to over 93,300 in 2020.[29]

Business and the loss of trust

Soon after the housing disaster and the bailout of investment banks and their insurers, the public was both angry and fearful. In a 2009 international survey in six major economies, only 38% of the U.S respondents indicated trust in corporations, 20% lower than the previous year and the lowest level of trust among all countries.[30]

In 2011, a group called Occupy Wall Street started as a march of some 2,000 people in the Wall Street area of lower Manhattan that mushroomed to approximately 1,000 similar demonstrations across the country against corporate greed and undue influence in government.[31]

Even as recently as 2021, a Pew survey showed 60% of the respondents expressed little or no confidence that business leaders would act in the best interests of the public.[32]

Individual ingenuity and creativity have resulted in many innovative designs, from the World Kitchen and mRNA vaccines to collateralized debt obligations and credit default swaps. However, if a design is only based on self-interest—the principle on which neoliberal philosophy is based—it is likely to benefit only some at the expense of others, sometimes catastrophically so. Given neoliberal policy's enrichment of a few at the expense of many, the private, self-interest option of Hardin's two possibilities cannot be counted on to reliably resolve the tragedy of the commons.

The Economy and Government Control

The alternative Hardin offers to private self-interest is government control. Historically, the economic philosophy of the Chicago School was developed at a time that the economic philosophy of British economist John Maynard Keynes was ascendant, and the philosophy was offered as an alternative to Keynes. The Keynesian school, which was most influential in the United States during the Great Depression, advocated strong government intervention in the market, if needed to stimulate demand that promoted economic growth.

Keynesian economics and government policy

Classical economic theory, of which the Chicago School is part, claims that in an economic downturn, investors would take advantage of the low cost of labor and material to increase supply and correct the decline. In contrast, Keynes claimed that, in a depression, unemployment and low wages inhibit demand, which reduces incentive to invest in production, perpetuating the recession. He advocated government intervention to correct the situation by stimulating demand. Interventions might include increasing the money supply by reducing central bank interest rates, reducing taxes, or increasing government spending which would, in turn, support hiring and increase purchasing power that would lead to a demand for goods.

Keynes illustrates how his theory works to counteract unemployment during a depression with a government hydroelectric project, which employs people to build it:

> The government pays out money, which it borrows, to the men employed on the scheme. But the benefit does not stop there. These men . . . spend these wages in providing themselves with the necessaries and comforts of existence—shirts, boots and the like. The makers of these shirts and boots, who were hitherto unemployed, spend their wages in their turn, and so set up a fresh wave of additional employment, of additional production, of additional wages, and of additional purchasing power. And so it goes on, until we find that for each man actually employed on the government scheme, three, or perhaps four, additional men are employed in providing for his needs and for the needs of one another. [33]

Thus, Keynes contends, a relatively small government intervention has a major effect that not only jumpstarts a stalled economy by its compounding employment effect, but in this case, provides the common good of an electric power plant.

Keynes' ideas influenced the Roosevelt Administration New Deal policies that brought the United States out of the depression.[34] Based on Keynesian ideas, the Roosevelt Administration created three agencies designed to stimulate job growth early in his administration: The Work Progress Administration (WPA) provided jobs to unemployed Americans, eventually employing more than 8.5 million Americans. The Civilian Conservation Corps (CCC) employed more than 3 million workers who helped create National Parks, worked in flood management, protected historic sites, and more. And the National Recovery Administration (NRA), which wrote codes and issued mandates related to wages, collective bargaining, monopolies, and price-cutting.

The impact of these programs was significant. While the United States had an unemployment rate 24.75% in 1933, when Roosevelt was in office, it had dropped to 9.9% by 1941, and 1.9%, by the time he died in 1945, although this last figure was influenced by the war effort.

However, there is a downside to government intervention in the economy.

Government control gets played out

The Keynesian economic policy of the time was not the only context in which the neoliberal philosophy was developed. In the background was the Soviet Union, which was becoming a major economy in the 1930s and which presented the world with an alternative economic approach to capitalism. While Keynes advocated relatively small interventions to address the failings of capitalism, the Soviet Union proposed a comprehensive design: the centrally planned economy that is Hardin's second alternative.

Beginning shortly after the Bolshevik Revolution of 1917 in Russia, the Communist Party and the newly established Soviet government designed a series of plans to make fundamental changes in the economy with the purpose of turning it from a feudal agrarian system to an industrialized system, applying Marxist principles in which "scientific procedures will be put into practice, with a resulting leap forward which will assure to society all the products it needs."[35] The Communists were looking at the entire society as a grand system and their scheme was to coordinate among all of its components. During the revolution, the state confiscated all the land and minerals and almost all of the capital along with it; the state controlled virtually all activity in industry, mining, construction, transportation, wholesale trade, communications, health, research and development, and education.[36]

The Communists played out their scheme in a sequence of "five-year plans." The goals of each plan were set by the Central Committee of the Communist Party, which was headed by Joseph Stalin after Lenin's death. The implementation of each plan was conducted by various bureaucracies coordinated by the State Planning Committee (GOSPLAN), aided by scientific statistical analysis and prediction.[37]

The first five-year plan that started in 1929 focused on agriculture, turning large feudal estates into factory-farms that hired farm laborers, and leaving small-holder farmers to sell their excess products at state-determined prices. It was a disaster in the early 1930s, with nation-wide famine killing millions, resulting from crop failures and from small-holder farmers who held back their grain to feed animals, which brought higher state prices, rather than sell the grain at discounted, state prices. Ultimately, individual farming gave way to a more efficient system of collective farming, which was more amenable to mechanization. The plan was particularly successful in building a mass production industrial base, which was used to develop a railway system that stitched the huge network of republics together and to develop the country's military capability, rather than to produce consumer goods. But the plan's implementation was backed by brutal force and dissent was met with violent repression.

The second five-year plan continued to develop the country's heavy industrial capability, such that it came to be not far behind that of Germany. GOSPLAN continued to assert its control over all aspects of the economy, setting production goals and price controls under the authority of the Central Committee and supported by a systemic statistical, analytic capacity. The massive economic growth of the second and third five-year plans were impressive, especially compared to the West, which was still suffering from the Great Depression. The continued focus on development of military capacity proved invaluable when the country was attacked by Germany in 1941 and contributed to the Soviet Union's ultimate victory over the Nazis.

After World War II, the Soviet Union had control over the Eastern European countries that it liberated from the Nazis, and it imposed its form of state-controlled, centralized economies on these countries as well, integrating them into its own economy. During the 1950s, the Soviets invested heavily in education and technological development and its economic growth rate exceeded those in the United States and United Kingdom.

This set the stage for the Cold War with the West, which dominated world politics from the 1960s through the 1980s. Ultimately, the Soviet Union not only lost the Cold War, but on December 26, 1991, it collapsed.

The social impact of a government-controlled economy

There are many reasons for the collapse of the Soviet Union. Large among them is the ultimate failure of its centralized economic system. But the reasons also include: economic plans were responsive to the needs and expectations of central leaders, rather than to the general public that had to implement them. Price controls and an emphasis on the production of military capacity meant chronic shortages of consumer goods and a standard of living that significantly lagged behind the West. Bureaucrats and managers gamed the system for personal and political gain, and they reported exaggerated numbers upon which the scientific statistical analysis for planning was based. Ultimately, economic events evolved in complex ways, unanticipated by the plans, resulting in a great gulf between plans and outcomes such that the very term *planned economy* was illusory. Toward the end, the situation was so unrealistic and unworkable that the whole planning process was abandoned.

Not only did government plans and actions result in deaths from famine, the forced collectivization, and the violent repression of dissent, state planning did not deliver the shared prosperity that it promised would come from centrally controlled, industrial-based economic growth.[38] The elite few had access to the best housing, healthcare, and education, while each was substandard for the large majority of people. An estimated 40% of the entire population could be classified as poor, with poverty disproportionately high among rural groups that constituted the majority of the country's population. Alcoholism was rampant and accounted for reduced economic productivity and large numbers of deaths due to alcohol poisoning.

While both a free-market economy and government economic intervention offer some advantages, it appears that neither a government-controlled economy nor an unregulated free-market economy can reliably solve the tragedy of the commons as Hardin predicts. But there is view of government's role that is alternative to one of economic control.

Government and Collective Action

Whereas a case can be argued that the U.S. economy is self-organizing, unaided by design, the U.S. government was most definitely designed. As with all designs, it is worth beginning its consideration by examining its purpose.

Public good as the purpose of government

The purpose of government was clearly stated in the founding documents. Early in the Declaration of Independence, it states:

> . . . to secure these [unalienable rights of life, liberty and the pursuit of happiness], Governments are instituted among Men, deriving their just powers from the consent of the governed.

The Constitution starts with:

> We the People of the United States, in Order to form a more perfect Union, establish Justice, insure domestic Tranquility, provide for the common defence [sic], promote the general Welfare, and secure the Blessings of Liberty to ourselves and our Posterity, do ordain and establish this Constitution for the United States of America.

These stated purposes are elaborated through published statements of participants in the design process. For example, Thomas Jefferson, the author of the Declaration of Independence and the nation's third President wrote:

> The care of human life and happiness, and not their destruction, is the first and only object of good government.[39]

John Adams, co-author of the Declaration of Independence, the nation's first Vice President, second President, and author of the Massachusetts' Constitution wrote:

> Government is instituted for the common good; for the protection, safety, prosperity and happiness of the people; and not for the profit, honor, or private interest of any one man, family, or class of men.[40]

And James Madison, a principle author of the Constitution and the fourth President, states:

> the public good, the real welfare of the great body of the people, is the supreme object to be pursued.[41]

With these statements, it is clear that the Founders established the federal government as an institution for collective action: the ability of states and people to act together through their government to do what solo individuals cannot achieve on their own: secure rights and promote the public good.

Government as an institution for collective action

The notion of government as an institution of collative action is confirmed in the Declaration of Independence, where independence was claimed by "one people" who are dissolving the political bonds that were connecting them to another. And the U.S. Constitution starts by declaring that "we the people" are forming a more perfect union.

The process by which the government was designed was itself a collective action. It was not the work of one person or even a small group but of 55 representatives of 12 of the 13 states that met in Philadelphia, Pennsylvania, between May 25 and September 17, 1787. The Constitution, which was the outcome of that process, set up a new Congress as two chambers where the House could take collective action by the representatives of the people and where representatives of the states could act collectively in the Senate. The Constitution had to be approved through collective action by the existing Congress, and subsequently, by the people of each state, acting collectively through their state conventions.

The outcome of these actions were our founding documents and the institutions and processes they established: The Presidency, Congress, the Judiciary, and the deliberative processes that they engage in to achieve the public good. The government was designed as a republic, which Madison defines as "Government which derives all its powers directly or indirectly from the great body of the People."[42]

At the same time, some of the Founders, specifically James Madison and John Adams, were concerned that the collective action of some might work against the rights of others. In *Federalist 10*, Madison wrote that "measures are too often decided, not according to the rules of justice, and the rights of the minor party, but by the superior force of an interested and overbearing majority."[43] For this reason, a number of limits were built into the structures and mechanisms of the new government, and it required a higher level of consensus for collective action to be taken.

Structural limits of collective action through government

For this very reason, the Constitution structured government with two legislative bodies, the Senate and the House of Representatives, and a majority within each of these two bodies had to agree on legislation and then that legislation had to be agreed to by the President. And the legislation was further subject to review by the courts.

The first three sections of the Constitution define and limit the powers of each of these branches. In effect, the Founders designed each branch such that it had a check on the actions of the others. And given that all three branches had to, in effect, cooperate in order for collective action to be taken, it makes collective action that much more difficult to occur. In addition, the first 10 amendments to the Constitution—the Bill of Rights—limits the types of actions the government can take, relative to the rights of individuals and states.

The difficulty is compounded by another structural feature of the federal government, the Senate filibuster. While not a design element specified in the Constitution, the document does allow the Senate to decide on its own rules and the filibuster has been a rule of procedure in the Senate for over 200 years. The rule allows any senator or group of senators an unlimited amount of time to speak on any topic and it takes a vote of 60 senators for "cloture," to close the discussion. In effect, this means to pass any bill about which one or more senators object, it takes a super majority to pass it, even if 51 senators are in its favor.

Originally, the rule required the senator to actually speak during the entire time, but a rule change in 1975 that evoked the 60-senator cloture rule merely by giving a notice there would be a filibuster, making defection easier and the passage of a bill, and therefore, collective action, that much more difficult to achieve. Over the last couple decades, there has been an exponential growth by both parties in the use of the once rarely used rule.[44]

Political parties and collective action

Another feature of the U.S. government—one not mentioned in the Constitution—is the two-party system. While both Hamilton and Madison expressed their concern in *The Federalist Papers* about the destructive influence of what they called "factions," political parties have been a feature from the start. Indeed, Hamilton and Madison were involved in the formation of the first two parties, ironically on opposite sides.

Parties have been an important mechanism for collective action. According to Indiana University political scientist Marjorie Hershey, it is the major parties that have the incentive to create majorities out of disparate interests in order to win a wide range of elections over a long period, increasing the prospects for collective action.[45] Also, party leaders can use the carrots and sticks to induce their colleagues to make truly national policy, rather than just "Christmas tree" legislation that consists of government-spending ornaments for particular interests.

In the absence of strong parties, government could be gridlocked by competing special interests that could not muster a majority for their cause or could be dominated by a few powerful, well-funded, single-issue factions that do not represent a majority of the people. That is, between the two major parties, they aggregate the wide range of issues and special interest groups to present voters with two rather coherent, compelling choices that represent alternative, overarching visions with specific implications for legislative action that has a chance of being passed by a majority of representatives. It is the two-party system that has a reasonable chance of crossing the formidable structural requirements and take collective action across the finish line.

America compromised: Corruption of the design

However, in his book *America, Compromised*, Harvard law professor, Lawrence Lessig contends that the U.S. government, and particularly, the House of Representatives has become corrupted.[46] He's not claiming that representatives, as a group, are corrupt, in the sense that they take bribes. He is using the word in the sense that a computer program has become corrupted—it no longer does what it was designed to do. It does not provide the public a means for taking collective action for the common good.

Lessig points to a study out of Princeton University to back his claim. In this study, Martin Gilens and Ben Page looked at 1,779 policy issues between 1981 and 2002 in which a U.S. survey of the general public asked a favor/oppose question about a proposed policy change.[47] They also looked at respondents' income level, comparing those at the top 10% to the median income of 50%. And they looked at the positions on these issues of special interest groups, both business-oriented groups (such as the Chamber of Commerce and the Health Insurance Association) and mass-based groups (such as the American Association of Retired Persons [AARP] and the Christian Coalition). They then analyzed any congressional action that may have been taken on each of the policy issues.

What they found was that while the actual decisions of our government correlated well with attitudes of the economic elite and with the policies of organized interest groups, they had no correlation with the views of the average voter. As the researchers describe it, "When the preferences of economic elites and the stands of organized interest groups are controlled for, the preferences of the average American appear to have only a minuscule, near zero, statistically nonsignificant impact upon public policy."

No impact on public policy by the people in whose name the representatives were designed to govern. Why is this?

One of the reasons that Lessig points to is campaign financing and money in politics. For example, Open Secrets, an independent, nonpartisan, nonprofit, research group, documented a total federal candidate fundraising amount for the 2020 election to be a record $6.8 billion, more than twice as much as the 2016 cycle.[48]

There is nothing inherently wrong about money in politics unless contributions influence policy in ways that favor those with more of it. A more accurate measure of this corrupting influence is not small donations by millions of people, but unlimited contributions, particularly by anonymous donors. Direct campaign contributions have a limit of $5,000 per candidate per election cycle, and they often benefit from many much smaller donations. On the other hand, donations to nonprofit fundraisers called Super-PACs, which can advocate against one candidate or for another candidate, but are nominally uncoordinated with the candidate's campaign, are uncapped and can be anonymous. By design, these sources benefit most from wealthy donors. For example, in the 2020 federal election, these Super-PACs raised $5.6 billion from individuals and organizations (such as corporations and labor unions) in support of their favored candidates.[49] The top 1% of the donors contributed 97% of that total.[50] And in the 2022 mid-term elections, the 50 biggest donors collectively pumped $1.1 billion into political committees and other groups advancing their positions.[51] Again, this is not money that goes into the pockets of candidates, but it can influence the political process in corrupting ways.

Self-interest and identity politics

Beginning in the late 1960s, there was a dramatic shift in U.S. politics. Whereas, previously, the two parties often created majorities by aggregating a range of issues and special interest groups to present voters with two rather coherent policy choices, as Professor Hershey describes, in that decade, the two parties began to shift away from a policy orientation to what American historian Arthur Schlesinger calls "identity politics."[52] This is the segmentation of society around specific characteristics, such as religion, occupation, race, or ethnicity.

These characteristics exist, of course, and people do identify with them. And they have real-world implications, such as the economic hardship experienced by farmers in a drought or the injustices imposed on Blacks and Native Americans. But identity politics is the notion that it is these characteristics that have moral weight, that you have a right to something not because of our shared humanity but because you are entitled to it as a member of a particular identity group, a farmer, a Black, a Christian, a gay.

The shift toward identity politics was accompanied by political campaigns based on "wedge issues." This is an effort by a political party to take a position on a particular issue or set of issues with a two-fold objective: to divide the opposition, depress voter turnout, and realign their voters, on the one hand and on the other to unify their own party around a specific identity and its associated privileges, grievances, and resentments.

For example, in the 1960s, Richard Nixon took advantage of Johnson's alienation of southern Democrats with his civil rights and voting rights legislation, to craft the "Southern Strategy" by which the position of the GOP, which supported Black Americans since Lincoln, came to appeal to White segregationists in the south. The strategy got him elected and turned the South into a Republican bastion.

Government and the loss of trust

Even though the U.S. government was designed to derive all its powers directly or indirectly from the people, the people are not happy with it. According to Gallup polls, only 20% of those surveyed approve of the way Congress is handling its job and 75% disapprove as of February 2022.[53] It has been over 18 years since the approval ratings were higher than the disapproval ratings: 48% approval, 45% disapproval in January 2004. You have to go all the way back to June 2003 to find that more than 50% of the people approved of Congress's job handling.

There has also been the loss of trust in the federal government, as mentioned in the last chapter. In the 63 years that Pew has conducted its National Election Study, it has seen a drop in people's trust that the national government would "do what is right," from a high of 77% in 1964 to 17% in 2019, standing at 21%, as of April 2021.[54]

Why have people lost confidence in the government that is designed to represent them and advance their happiness? When asked by a 2019 NBC News/Wall Street Journal poll, 70% of U.S. respondents said that they were angry because the political system seems to only be working for the insiders with money and power.[55]

In a 2022 New York Times/Siena College poll, 58% of American voters, across nearly all demographics and ideologies, believe our system of government is not working.[56] Both Republicans and Democrats said the country needs major reforms or a complete overhaul, although they didn't agree on the reasons. For Republicans, it is their widespread, unfounded doubts about the legitimacy of the nation's elections. For Democrats, it is the realization that even though they control the White House and Congress, it is the belief that Republicans who are the ones achieving their political goals.

Each year, the Economist Intelligence Unit, a sister organization to the *Economist* magazine, issues a Democracy Index Report, analyzing and rating each of the world's countries on a number of democratic qualities. Over the years the report has documented a gradual decline in democracy in the United States, such that the 2021 report labels the U.S. a "flawed democracy."[57] Where we fall short is on the EIU's measures of political culture and government functioning. The biggest threats to democracy in the United States, it notes, are not only the institutional gridlock and lack of action on many important issue,s but the collapse in social cohesion and consensus over fundamental beliefs, such as those related to election outcomes and public health practices.

Designs to Resolve the Tragedy

Neither business nor government are inherently moral or immoral. Both can serve the common good as well as self-interest. Both can and have been used to solve the tragedy of the commons. And both have implications for designs that do so.

Business and the common good

For Milton Friedman, the sole responsibility of a corporation and its executives was to "make as much money for its stockholders as possible."[58] However, over the past several decades, an alternative vision of business has emerged, referred to as *stakeholder capitalism*, that goes beyond the limits of self-interest in the private sector.

World Economic Forum founder Klaus Schwab describes stakeholder capitalism as a system in which the interests of all stakeholders in the economy and society are considered and companies optimize for more than just short-term profits.[59] Salesforce CEO Marc Benioff states this new vision of the firm "requires that they focus not only on their shareholders, but also on all of their stakeholders—their employees, customers, communities and the planet."[60]

The Business Roundtable, an association of chief executive officers of America's leading companies, calls on its members to ascribe to a new corporate purpose that commits the company to delivering value to customers, investing in employees, dealing fairly and ethically with suppliers, supporting the communities in which they work, protecting the environment by embracing sustainable practices, and generating long-term value for shareholders.[61] The document was signed by 181 CEOs from major corporations. If these CEOs and their companies follow through on these commitments, they will make a significant contribution to a better world.

Government and the common good

Governmental collective action can work. It has never been pretty. There have always been disagreements, sometimes passionately expressed. There have always been compromises, which means no one gets everything they want.

Our national government has, on occasion, found ways to take action that addressed the significant problems facing the people of our country, in the face of the significant barriers built into our system. One way is raw power, a party that occupies the White House and has a majority in the House and enough votes in the Senate to overcome the filibuster. Even with this, factions and regional differences within the party may mean compromise is necessary.

Another way to get things done takes moral imagination, a vision of what could be better with collective action, an appeal to our shared humanity to create the popular support and bipartisanship needed to pass significant legislation. This can be illustrated by the Civil Rights Act of 1964 and the Voting Rights Act of 1965, which delivered on the promise of the 15th Amendment of 1870 to ensure the vote for Black Americans.

This moral approach takes converging and sometimes coordinated efforts between civic groups and politicians. In this case, the Reverend Martin Luther King Jr. (see Figure 16.1) and his allies in the Southern Christian Leadership Conference (SCLC) and the Student Nonviolent Coordinating Committee (SNCC) brought the plight of Black Americans to the nation's attention through a series of peaceful demonstrations that lead up to one in the city of Selma, Alabama, where they were met by violent police resistance that was televised to the nation, resulting in general outrage.[62]

Dr. King framed the lack of voting rights as a moral issue, particularly in the face of police brutality and KKK beatings, in response to nonviolent action. On March 25, 1965, after the Selma to Montgomery march for voting rights, Dr. King said:

> But if we will go on with the faith that nonviolence and its power can transform dark yesterdays into bright tomorrows . . . . We must come to see that the end we seek is a society at peace with itself, a society that can live with its conscience. And that will be a day not of the white man, not of the black man. That will be the day of man as man . . . . How long? Not long, because the arc of the moral universe is long, but it bends toward justice.[63]

Figure 16.1 Dr. Martin Luther King Jr. addressing a rally (Photo by Yoichi Yakamoto. *Source:* Wikimedia Commons).

An important factor in the bills' success was the role President Johnson played as moral leader, who on March 15, 1965, addressed a joint session of Congress in support of the Voting Rights Act. With the Selma beatings as a background, he spoke:

> . . . the cries of pain and the hymns and protests of oppressed people have summoned into convocation all the majesty of this great Government—the Government of the greatest Nation on earth. Our mission is at once the oldest and the most basic of this country: to right wrong, to do justice, to serve man."[64]

He continued:

> Their cause must be our cause too. Because it is not just Negroes, but really it is all of us, who must overcome the crippling legacy of bigotry and injustice. And we shall overcome.

However, while the Democrats controlled both the House and the Senate, representatives and senators from southern states, who were uniformly Democrats at the time, were against both acts, and in the Senate, mounted filibusters. This required Johnson to rely on sympathetic Republicans and he approached an old Senate colleague and Minority Leader, Everette Dirksen of Illinois. Dirksen also used a moral theme to rally his Republican colleagues.

On June 10, 1964, Senator Dirksen rose to give what is regarded as his most important speech of his career, an argument to end the filibuster of the Civil Rights Act, what he called a "moral issue whose time had come."[65] In the speech, he evoked a fellow Illinoisan and Republican Abraham Lincoln in his Gettysburg Address when he spoke of "a new nation, conceived in liberty and dedicated to the proposition that all men are created equal." And Dirksen went on to say, "We have a duty to get that job done."

It was the morality of Dr. King's cause that provided a common purpose that united enough Republicans and Democrats to pass both the Civil Rights Act and the Voting Rights Act. It was King's appeal to our common humanity; it was Johnson's appeal justice and righting wrongs; and it was Dirksen's appeal the equality of every person that proved sufficient to overcome political divides and provide a governmental basis for nation's collective action.

Community and the common good

However, when the market fails and the federal government is gridlocked, it falls to the community and everyday designers to take the situation from where it is to where it ought to be. Even national and world problems get played out at the local level. A factory of a national company closes in this community putting many people out of work and stressing small businesses. A big box store opens in that community, threatening the downtown that has been the town's social gathering place. A police officer stops a Black man with a broken tail light in another and ends up with a death. Climate change results in droughts and crop failure in this community, floods in that one, wild fires in yet another. These situations reflect national or even global problems but it is local, everyday designers must come together and figure out solutions, much as they did in the towns visited by James and Deborah Fallows, discussed in the last chapter.

And they often are played out in different ways in different places. A school shooting in one community may have racial overtones; in another, it may due to school bullying or mental illness. Although harmful in all cases, poverty and homelessness are very different from one community to the next and need local solutions.

Racial mistreatment by police and urban decline are national problems that can benefit from national economic and governmental action. But the cities of Austin and Baton Rouge showed us how to design local solutions to these problems. Everyone needs food and water. But different communities lack them for different reasons—because of war, natural disaster, or undeveloped infrastructure. Disconnection and depression are national problems. But everyday designers like Chef Andrés, the folks at WestGate Church, and those at Burning Man take on problems that governments and private enterprise have often not addressed. They base their designs on values. They use their moral discourse and moral imagination to take collective action that makes their community and the rest of the world better. And they materialize morality with their designs.

Through our everyday discussions and collective actions, through our everyday designs, we design not only products and services, we co-create our neighborhoods, our communities, our economy, and our society. We can take them from where they are to where they ought to be, from situations that only benefit ourselves to those that also benefit many.

Everyday designs and the invisible hands of a moral society

This narrow focus on maximizing self-interest and economic, profit or the exclusive political or even moral, right of a person or company to do whatever they want, regardless of their social impact, is a profound misinterpretation of Adam Smith's meaning of "self-interest" and the "invisible hand" of the free market and a free society.

There was an implicitly moral aspect to Smith's "invisible hand." Smith was first and foremost a moral philosopher, and his economic observations and assumptions are embedded in a view of humans as fundamentally social and compassionate. In his 1759 book *The Theory of Moral Sentiments*, he states:

> How selfish soever man may be supposed, there are evidently some principles in his nature, which interest him in the fortune of others, and render their happiness necessary to him,

> though he derives nothing from it except the pleasure of seeing it. Of this kind is pity or compassion, the emotion which we feel for the misery of others, when we either see it, or are made to conceive it in a very lively manner. (p. 15)

It is clear from this quote, we are not just *homo economicus*, we are also *homo socialis*, *homo moralis*; we are social, moral humans. We are guided not just by rational self-interest, but by the social emotions we feel for the misery and well-being of others.

Smith uses the "invisible hand" analogy for the first time in *Moral Sentiment* in describing the rich landlord:

> They consume little more than the poor, and in spite of their natural selfishness and rapacity, though they mean only their own conveniency, though the sole end which they propose from the labours of all the thousands whom they employ, be the gratification of their own vain and insatiable desires, they divide with the poor the produce of all their improvements. They are led by an invisible hand to make nearly the same distribution of the necessaries of life, which would have been made, had the earth been divided into equal portions among all its inhabitants, and thus without intending it, without knowing it, advance the interest of the society, and afford means to the multiplication of the species. (pp. 319–320)

While the last several decades in the U.S. economy have proven both Smith's assumption of the frugality of the rich and his conclusions about the impact of greed to be faulty, his intent is clear. For Smith, the invisible hand was the presumed mechanism by which the self-organized economy did good. And the good, for Smith, was also clear: The moral purpose of the invisible hand is to advance the interests of society and all its inhabitants. This value is reiterated by Harvard philosopher John Rawls when he says that if someone benefits more than others by their participation in society, it would be just only if those inequalities result in benefits to all, especially those in society that are worst off.[65] It is reiterated by professor Michael Sandel when he says that it is by coming together to discuss how general moral principles fit particular situations that we become a more just society. And it is reiterated by professor Elinor Ostrom when she gives us design principles by which we can take collective actions for the common good.

Economy can't only be about generating wealth. And the effective purpose of an economy in a moral society can't be to redistribute that wealth to the top. Government can't only be about promoting economic growth. Self-interest and "my right" can't be our only value. Our civil discourse can't be limited to the words competitive advantage, "return on investment," "market share," "consumer spending," or even "job creation." Nor can our collective success be measured only by GDP. "Happiness," "knowledge", "equality," "justice," "relationships," and "community" must fill our discussions as much as products fill our selves. And it is our differences in these discussions, sometimes passionately held but respectfully stated, that can provide the unique and innovative combinations of ideas that can be transformational.

Making the world a better place is not just an economic or political task, but a moral one. Our economy, our political system, our technologies, our everyday designs are shaped not only by business titans and political leaders, but also by our everyday actions and decisions. They can be jointly generated resources that make the world better. But only if we apply moral principles in their design.

So, there must be two invisible hands that guide the economy, the government, and our community in a just and moral society. One is the self-organizing economic hand of self-interest, which benefits us and incidentally, but not always, benefits others. The other hand is our cultural norms, our trust and trustworthiness, and our concern for others that guides our individual and collective actions, our economic and political activities toward our collective happiness and well-being, as we produce and consume, buy and sell, employ and work, socialize and play with our family and friends, and as we govern ourselves.

If that second hand is missing, more harm than good is likely to result from our self-interested actions. It is this second hand that must also guide our designs.

References

1 Hardin G. The tragedy of the commons. Science, 1968, 162(3859), 1243–1248.
2 Friedman M. Neoliberalism and its prospects. Collected works of Milton Friedman, Hoover Institution [Internet]. 1951 [cited 2021, June 1]. Available from: https://miltonfriedman.hoover.org/objects/57816/neoliberalism-and-its-prospects.
3 Friedman M, Friedman A. Free to choose: A personal statement (pp. 246–247). New York: Harcourt, 1980.
4 Friedman M. The real free lunch: Markets and private property (p. 7). Cato Policy Report, 1993, 14(4), 1, 12, 14–15.
5 Barlett B. Reagan's tax increases. Stan Collender's Capital Gains and Games [Internet]. 2010, Apr 6 [cited 2021, June 1]. Available from: https://web.archive.org/web/20120625075018/http://capitalgainsandgames.com/blog/bruce-bartlett/1632/reagans-tax-increases.
6 Kenton W. Reaganomics. Investopedia [Internet]. 2021, May 25 [cited 2022, Sep 4]. Available from: https://www.investopedia.com/terms/r/reaganomics.asp.
7 Washington Consensus. Global Trade Negotiations [Internet]. 2003, April [cited 2022, Sep 4]. Available from: https://web.archive.org/web/20170715151421/http://www.cid.harvard.edu/cidtrade/issues/washington.html.
8 Savings and loan crisis. Corporate Finance Institute [Internet]. 2021, May 17 [cited 2022, Sep 4]. Available from: https://corporatefinanceinstitute.com/resources/knowledge/credit/savings-and-loan-crisis/.
9 Mills D. Who's to blame for the bubble? Harvard Business Review [Internet]. 2001, May [cited 2021, Jun 5]. Available from: https://hbr.org/2001/05/whos-to-blame-for-the-bubble.
10 Here's why the Dot Com Bubble began and why it popped. Business Insider [Internet]. 2010, Dec 15 [cited 2021, Jun 5]. Available from: https://www.businessinsider.com/heres-why-the-dot-com-bubble-began-and-why-it-popped-2010-12.
11 Median sales price of houses sold for the United States. Federal Reserve Economic Data [Internet]. 2022, Sept 4 [cited 2022, Sep 4]. Available from: https://fred.stlouisfed.org/series/MSPUS.
12 Greider W. The AIG bailout scandal. Nation [Internet]. 2010, Aug 6 [cited 2022, Sep 4]. Available from: https://www.thenation.com/article/archive/aig-bailout-scandal/.
13 Amadeo K. TRP bailout program. The Balance [Internet]. 2021, May 9 [cited 2022, Sep 4]. Available from: https://www.thebalance.com/tarp-bailout-program-3305895.
14 Inman P. Wall Street bonuses under fire. The Guardian [Internet]. 2009, Jul 30 [cited 2022, Sep 4]. Available from: https://www.theguardian.com/business/2009/jul/31/wall-street-bonuses-bailout.
15 NASDAQ Composite Index. Federal Reserve Economic Data [Internet]. 2022, Sept 4 [cited 2022, Sep 4]. Available from: https://fred.stlouisfed.org/series/NASDAQCOM.
16 Domestic auto production. Federal Reserve Economic Data [Internet]. 2022, Sept 4 [cited 2022, Sep 4]. Available from: https://fred.stlouisfed.org/series/DAUPSA.

17 Federal debt: Total public debt. Federal Reserve Economic Data [Internet]. 2022, Sept 4 [cited 2022, Sep 4]. Available from: https://fred.stlouisfed.org/series/GFDEBTN.

18 Naylor, B. Homeowners rescue program shows slim benefits. NPR [Internet]. 2009, Feb 3 [cited 2023, Jan 7]. Available from: https://www.npr.org/2009/02/03/100163398/homeowners-rescue-program-shows-slim-benefits.

19 Foreclosures in the U.S. in 2008. Pew Research Center [Internet]. 2009, May 12 [cited 2022, Sep 4]. Available from: https://www.pewresearch.org/hispanic/2009/05/12/v-foreclosures-in-the-u-s-in-2008/.

20 Carney J. America lost $10.2 trillion in 2008. Business Insider [Internet]. 2009, Feb 3 [cited 2022, Sep 4]. Available from: https://www.businessinsider.com/2009/2/america-lost-102-trillion-of-wealth-in-2008.

21 Song J, von Wachter T. Long-term unemployment and job displacement. Kansas City Federal Reserve Bank [Internet]. 2014 [cited 2022, Sep 4]. Available from: https://www.kansascityfed.org/documents/4547/2014vonWachter.pdf.

22 https://fred.stlouisfed.org/series/UNRATE.

23 Jacobsen L, Mather M. U.S. Economic and social trends since 2000 (2010). Population Bulletin, 65(1), 1–16. Retrieved on July 12, 2021. https://www.prb.org/resources/u-s-economic-and-social-trends-since-2000.

24 https://www.huduser.gov/portal/sites/default/files/pdf/2018-AHAR-Part-2.pdf.

25 Kuhn M, Scularick M, Steins U. Asset prices and wealth inequality. VOX-EU CEPR Research-Based Policy Analysis and Commentary from Learning Economists (August 9, 2018). Accessed on June 6, 2021. https://voxeu.org/article/asset-prices-and-wealth-inequality.

26 Unemployment rate. Federal Reserve Economic Data [Internet]. 2022, Sept 4 [cited 2022, Sep 4]. Available from: https://fred.stlouisfed.org/release/tables?rid=453&eid=813804#snid=813806.

27 Margerison-Zilko C, Golldman-Mellor S, Falconi, A, et al. Health impacts of the Great Recession: A critical review. Current Epidemiological Report, 2016, 3(1), 81–91.

28 Overdose death rates. National Institute on Drug Abuse [Internet]. [cited 2022, Sep 4]. Available from: https://www.drugabuse.gov/drug-topics/trends-statistics/overdose-death-rates.

29 Drug overdose deaths in the U.S. up 30% in 2020. Center for Disease Control [Internet]. 2021, Jul 14 [cited 2022, Sep 4]. Available from: https://www.cdc.gov/nchs/pressroom/nchs_press_releases/2021/20210714.htm.

30 Trust. Edelman Trust Barometer [Internet]. 2009 [cited 2022, Sep 4]. Available from: https://www.edelman.com/sites/g/files/aatuss191/files/2018-10/2009-Trust-Barometer-Executive-Summary.pdf.

31 Anderson J. Some say Occupy Wall Street did nothing. It changed us more than we think. Time [Internet]. 2021, Nov 15 [cited 2022, Sep 4]. Available from: https://time.com/6117696/occupy-wall-street-10-years-later/.

32 Kennedy B, Tyson A, Funk C. Americans' trust in scientist, other groups declines. Pew Research Center [Internet]. 2022, Feb 15 [cited 2022, Sep 4]. Available from: https://www.pewresearch.org/science/wp-content/uploads/sites/16/2022/02/PS_2022.02.15_trust-declines_REPORT.pdf.

33 Keynes JM. The Essential Keynes (p. 433). Penguin Publishing Group, 2015.

34 Sayen B. How Keynes influenced FDR's New Deal. Future Hindsight [Internet]. 2020, Nov 13 [cited 2022, Sep 4]. Available from: https://www.futurehindsight.com/how-keynes-influenced-fdrs-new-deal/.

35 Marx K, Engels F. Manifesto of the Communist Party. Marxists [Internet]. 1848 Feb [cited 2022, Sep 4]. Available from: https://www.marxists.org/archive/marx/works/download/pdf/Manifesto.pdf.

36 Ericson R. The classical Soviet-type economy: Nature of the system and implications for reform. Journal of Economic Perspectives, 1991, 5(4), 11–27.

37 Ellman M. Socialist planning (3rd ed.). Cambridge: Cambridge University Press, 2014.

38 Johnson B, Raynes, E. Quality of life in the Soviet Union: A conference report. University Center for International Studies, University of Pittsburgh [Internet]. 1984 [cited 2022, Sep 4]. Available from: https://www.ucis.pitt.edu/nceeer/1984-629-2-Johnson.pdf.

39 Jefferson T. To the republicans of Washington County, Maryland. Founders Online [Internet]. 1809, Mar 31 [cited 2022, Sep 4]. Available from: https://founders.archives.gov/documents/Jefferson/03-01-02-0088.

40 Lessons on the rights and responsibilities of. Massachusetts citizens. Massachusetts History [Internet]. [cited 2022, Sep 4]. Available from: https://www.masshist.org/2012/juniper/assets/ed-curricula/wallingford_unit_3_.pdf.

41 Madison J. Federalist No. 45. Hamilton A, Madison J, Jay J, et al. The Federalist & The Anti-Federalist Papers: Complete Collection. Chicago: e-artnow, 2018.

42 Hamilton A, Madison J, Jay J, et al. The Federalist & The Anti-Federalist Papers: Complete Collection (p. 113). Chicago: e-artnow, 2018.

43 Hamilton A, Madison J, Jay, J, et al. The Federalist and The Anti-Federalist Papers: Complete Collection (p. 79). e-artnow, 2018.

44 Modelling COVID-19's death too: There have been 7m-13m excess deaths worldwide during the pandemic. Economist [Internet]. 2021, May 15 [cited 2022, Sep 4]. Available from: https://www.economist.com/taxonomy/term/42/0?page=22.

45 Hershey M. Party politics in America (18th ed.). New York: Routledge, 2021.

46 Lessig L. America, compromised. Chicago: University of Chicago Press, 2018.

47 Gilens M, Page B. Testing theories of American politics: Elites, interest groups, and average citizens. Perspectives on Politics, 2014, 12(3), 564–581.

48 Unprecedented donations poured into 2020 state and federal races. Open Secrets [Internet]. 2020, Nov 19 [cited 2022, Sep 4]. Available from: https://www.opensecrets.org/news/2020/11/2020-state-and-federal-races-nimp.

49 2020 outside spending, by Super PAC. Open Secrets [Internet]. [cited 2022, Sep 4]. Available from: https://www.opensecrets.org/outsidespending/summ.php?cycle=2020&chrt=V&disp=O&type=S.

50 Super PACs: How many donors give. Open Secrets [Internet]. [cited 2022, Sep 4]. Available from: https://www.opensecrets.org/outside-spending/donor-stats.

51 Melgar L., Alcantara C., Stanley-Becker I., et al. Meet the mega-donors pumping millions into the 3033 midterms. Washington Post [Internet]. 2022, Oct 24 [cited 2022, Oct 29]. Available from: https://www.washingtonpost.com/politics/interactive/2022/top-election-donors-2022/.

52 Schlesinger A. The disuniting of America: Reflections on a multicultural society. New York: Norton & Company, 1998.

53 Congress and the public. Gallup [Internet]. 2022, Jul [cited 2022, Sep 4]. Available from: https://news.gallup.com/poll/1600/congress-public.aspx.

54 Public trust in government: 1958–2022. Pew Research Center [Internet]. 2022, Jun 6 [cited 2022, Sep 4]. Available from: https://www.pewresearch.org/politics/2021/05/17/public-trust-in-government-1958-2021/.

55 Dann C. "A deep and boiling anger": NBC/WSJ poll finds a pessimistic America despite current economic satisfaction. NBC News [Internet]. 2017, Mar 4 [cited 2022, Sep 4]. Available from: https://www.nbcnews.com/politics/meet-the-press/deep-boiling-anger-nbc-wsj-poll-finds-pessimistic-america-despite-n1045916.

56 Epstein R. As faith flags in U.S. government, many voters want to upend the system. New York Times [Internet]. 2022, Jul 13 [cited 2022, Sep 4]. Available from: https://www.nytimes.com/2022/07/13/us/politics/government-trust-voting-poll.html.

57 Economist Intelligence Unit. Democracy Index 2021: The China challenge. London: EIU, 2021.
58 Friedman M. A Friedman doctrine—The social responsibility of business is to increase its profits. New York Times [Internet]. 1970, Sep 13 [cited 2022, Sep 4]. Available from: https://www.nytimes.com/1970/09/13/archives/a-friedman-doctrine-the-social-responsibility-of-business-is-to.html.
59 Schwab K. Stakeholder Capitalism. New York: Wiley, 2021.
60 Clifford C. Billionaire Marc Benioff: Capitalism has led to horrifying inequality' and must be fixed. NBC News [Internet]. 2019, Oct 14 [cited 2022, Sep 4]. Available from: https://www.cnbc.com/2019/10/14/marc-benioff-capitalism-led-to-horrifying-inequality-must-be-fixed.html.
61 Our commitment. Business Roundtable [Internet]. [cited 2022, Sep 4]. Available from: https://opportunity.businessroundtable.org/ourcommitment/.
62 Garrow D. Protest at Selma: Martin Luther King, Jr., and the Voting Rights Act of 1965. New York: Open Road, 2015.
63 King ML. How long? Not long. Voices of Democracy [Internet]. 1965, Mar 25 [cited 2022, Sep 4]. Available from: https://voicesofdemocracy.umd.edu/dr-martin-luther-king-jr-long-not-long-speech-text/.
64 Lyndon Johnson on voting rights and the American promise. The American Yawp Reader [Internet]. 1965 [cited 2022, Sep 4]. Available from: https://www.americanyawp.com/reader/27-the-sixties/lyndon-johnson-on-voting-rights-and-the-american-promise-1965/.
65 Dirksen E. The Civil Rights Bill. U.S. Senate [Internet]. 1964, Jun 10 [cited 2022, Sep 4]. Available from: https://www.senate.gov/artandhistory/history/resources/pdf/DirksenCivilRights.pdf.

17

Where Do We Go from Here?

We can change the world and make it a better place. It is in our hands to make a difference.

Nelson Mandela
President, South Africa

Which of Two Roads?

If we are all designers and we take Simon's definition of *design* as purposeful ". . .courses of action aimed at changing existing situations into preferred ones," what is our preferred situation? Where do we go from here? Where do we want to end up? And how do we—individually and collectively—get there? I've tried to address these questions all along, but here is the place to pull all the chapters together in answer to these questions and to review what is at stake. Here, I want you to use your moral imagination.

I see two roads diverge before us. Clearly, there are more. But I would like to juxtapose these two as alternatives both to clarify the issues ahead of us and to examine the consequences of the decisions and actions that face us.

The road less traveled

One is the road less traveled. This, in my mind, is a vision of where we would like to be. This vignette is fictional. It is an idealized vision but I will try not to make it too utopian. I will build it off of the principles expressed in this book, but with footnote references, ground it in hopeful bits of reality that we see today. The road is less traveled but not untraveled, and I will draw on the experiences of those who have already gone down this road.

The second road continues the one we are on. Its familiarity comforts us. It tempts us with beauty and riches for some, perhaps you. If you're young, educated, and White the future promised to you down the road is bright. If you're retired, the road has worked for you. It is the direction that our designs are currently taking us. We know how to get to where we're going because we're already on our way there. But it may not be clear exactly where "there" is, where it is we will end up. Like Scrooge on Christmas Eve, we may need help envisioning the future, based on what we are doing now. In providing this vision, I will not make up some apocalyptic dystopia as some novels and films do. No need for *Mad Max, The Handmaid's Tale, 1984*, or *Brave New World.* I will extrapolate from research and current newspaper articles, with a dash of history, all footnoted, to

Make the World a Better Place: Design with Passion, Purpose, and Values, First Edition. Robert B. Kozma.

give you what I think is a realistic picture of where we might end up. The terminus of the road we are on is not pretty, but the vision is all too realistic. . .and all too likely.

It is likely but not inevitable. If it is to be different, if it is to be better than where we are now, it will be because we design our way there. To get there, we need to "take the road less traveled". . .and it will make "all the difference"[1] in the world.

* * *

One evening, my wife and I invited some of our neighbors over for dinner. We love the community we live in. We've lived here for 10 years and have made many friends. We met them all at the community center during one of the center's social events or activities. The community has many such gatherings: book clubs, theater outings, card clubs, and discussion groups on various topics. These social groups enrich our lives tremendously.[2] One of the couples we invited is Charles and Ruth; he is a high tech executive and she is a multimedia artist. The other couple is Shawn and LaToya. Shawn is a nurse and has been active in advancing community health. LaToya is a teacher and the reason we all know each other so well.

We are all active in our community center's tutoring group and we volunteer at the local elementary school. LaToya organized the group and is giving us tips on how to work with kids and how to make sure that our tutoring supports teachers' goals and fits with the curriculum.[3]

There is a lot of community involvement in schools in our neighborhood.[4] Some volunteers, like Ruth, participate out of their spare time. Ruth works with student teams on their multimedia productions and skills. Some volunteers are college students participating for tuition loan forgiveness and some, like Charles and Shawn, are volunteers through their company's community service program.[5] They tutor in their area of expertise—math, science, accounting, programming, and so on. Charles not only works with the school's teachers to develop their tech skills, he works with the school's technology coordinator and draws on his company's resources to supplement those the school gets from their regular budget. Others, like Shawn, supply teachers with real-life problem situations and case studies from their business or organization that teachers use in their lessons and students can use for their projects.[6] Yet others, like Shari and I, are retired and use their free time tutoring individuals or small groups of students. [7]

I'm a retired professor and scientist; Shari is a retired realtor. I help science students design their science projects; Shari tutors for an applied math class.[8] We've worked with the same kids for the last year. We're excited to see their progress and have gotten to know their parents. There is also a program designed by the teachers that allows student volunteers to tutor other students, either in their own grade or lower grades, and it has benefitted both tutors and tutees.[9] Students at the school give back to the community as well with public music and dance performances, poetry recitals and story readings, project presentations, and public science and art fairs.

Our dinner conversations are lively. That evening, Charles mentioned how gratified he was that the school had so many technological resources and that the students we're using them regularly for their projects. The school district made laptops available to all students, but his company provided each of the students in our school with their own VR personal device and he was working with teachers to incorporate them into their lessons. I congratulated him but cautioned that more technology wasn't always a good thing, reminding him that Facebook had harmed teens by allowing the posting of caustic comments that resulted in student stress and depression. He acknowledged that it was important to keep students safe and informed us that Facebook and several other social media platforms had employed AI to analyze the emotional loading of postings, while maintaining user anonymity, to identify teenagers who may be feeling lonely, isolated, in distress, or be considering suicide. The platform then sends private notes suggesting the teen get help from parents or professionals. It also shapes the contacts and streamed postings of other teens who might end up being friends. He indicated that initial studies showed positive impacts on both teen well-being and relationship development.

LaToya reminded us that the quality of public education has improved significantly over the past decade, in part, because federal officials and national business leaders made it a priority when they realized that future social well-being of the country will increasingly depend on the development of well-educated, highly productive, creative workers and citizens.[10] "This realization is shared by parents and others and has resulted in a higher tax base for schools and more community involvement," she said as she smiled at us. Teachers are highly regarded professionals and well paid and this has, in turn, attracted passionate, committed, highly qualified people into the profession. Teaching methods and the curriculum are focused on the creative application of academic knowledge to solve real-world problems and this has resulted in knowledgeable, growth-minded students,[11] self-regulated learners, and creative problem-solvers.

That night over dinner, our friends also discussed what happened in our lives that week, as we typically do. We discussed what was going on in our community and in the world and what we might do about problems or issues that come up. We help each other out in our individual efforts and often take on a project together. For example, the previous month, Shawn mentioned that one of the girls we tutored was diagnosed with cancer. All her medical expenses were covered by health insurance, but the family was financially impacted because her father took a leave of absence from work to care for her. Our group recruited other neighbors to provide emotional support to the family and launched a crowd funding campaign to help with finances.

In addition to being head nurse at the community health center, Shawn is one of the leaders of an advocacy group called Community Now. That evening, she mentioned that the city planning department received an application for a new office building in a section of the city that is currently stores and apartment buildings occupied by primarily-Hispanic merchants and renters who would be displaced by the new building. We discussed the tension between the need for new jobs that the office building would provide and the displacement of current minority businesses and residents. Shawn made the point that the many new, high-paying jobs would increase the inequality of the city, and she asked us to join her group in demonstrating to block the development. Shari proposed that we support the project if there were shops on the street level and the first several floors of the build there were apartments that would all be offered to current businesses and residents a below-market rates, subsidized by the developer, and that those people be involved in planning the building. We all agreed.

We don't always agree on the changes that have happened. Indeed, dinners with our friends are enlivened by respectful, informed discussions of our differences. We've met several of our friends at the neighborhood Braver Angels events that bring together people with different political and philosophical views to exchange views on current issues.[12] And we bounce off our ideas for change with them. We will with our building proposal as well.

We're optimistic about the reception it will get since there has been a big change among businesses in recent years, as they have come to be full participants in the social and cultural fabric of the city. Early work on stakeholder capitalism by the Business Roundtable[13] changed the culture and values of businesses in the 2020s. And the federal government began to measure Gross National Well-being (GNW)[14] as well as GDP as an assessment of the nation's prosperity. Several leading companies formed the Alliance of Stakeholder Businesses and they co-developed, along with the newly established Association of Stakeholders, a set of social and environmental principles that member companies are committed to. Consequently, many companies have come to value the well-being of employees, customers, suppliers, and communities, along with profits. These commitments have been reflected in employee pay and benefit packages and in their contribution to the welfare of their communities and the environment. Well-being has come to be reflected in the products and services they design as well.

Businesses have made huge research and development investments in cutting-edge solar and wind technology and zero emissions conversion of buildings and homes that reduce climate impact. Other companies have shifted the emphasis of their product development. For example, Electronic Arts has introduced a popular series of collaborative problem-solving games that use augmented reality to connect distributed, problem-solving teams to each other and to real-world problem situations and environments. The series includes problem situations that use math, science, economics, and history to solve challenging yet fun real-world problems. The popularity of the games has resulted in a reality TV series that follows teams through their virtual problem-solving sessions while they compete with other teams to solve the problems and win the weekly prize.

There has been a significant increase in the nation's productivity and GDP, not only because of continued innovation in the technology sector, but because of the creative use of these technologies by highly trained employees who design needed products and services and reduce waste. Collaboration within and across institutions and between the private sector, government, and community interests has been the engine of co-creation and innovation and the generator of new, high-paying jobs. Many of these collaborative efforts have been supported by the National Innovation Agency, a federally funded organization set up to post design challenges that identify urgent, high-priority national and local problems and support precompetition research and innovation to address them.[15]

Design is among the most highly regarded professions for the value it adds to society. The Society of Designers with Purpose was formed a decade ago to incorporate values into designs, whether products, services, experiences, or policies, and to spread value-based design practices that benefit society throughout the public and private sectors.

Despite the success of businesses in creating high-paid jobs, the application of new technologies has created a highly productive economy and economic growth but with a net loss of jobs. In response, the President, her Council of Economic Advisors, the Business Roundtable, advocacy groups, and key legislators designed two complementary programs: The Citizens' Basic Income (CBI)[16] program and the Jobs for the Public Good (JPG) program.[17] CBI funds ensure families and individuals that they will at least have the minimum money needed to stay out of poverty, and the services and training that will integrate them productively into society.

The JPG is an acknowledgement that even as productive as the private sector is, it cannot generate all the jobs needed by society and job creation is a joint private-public responsibility. Among the program's priorities, JPG funds jobs for the development of public art and community spaces. This includes the development of community social and physical activity spaces, such as parks and community centers, and public art, such as public performances and artistic works in government buildings, streets, shorelines, and parks. Our community center was built with this funding.

Many of the economic and social projects of the JPG were selected through design challenges and competitions. These have become the mechanisms of choice by governments, companies, foundations, and community organizations to find focused, effective solutions to complex problems they face. Design challenges have been effective ways of generating innovative ideas, projects, and programs related to zero carbon emissions energy solutions, pop-up homeless and emergency shelters, food insecurity and distribution problems, and severe weather event remediation.

Ruth, our multimedia design dinner partner, was involved in a winning project for a challenge that focused on racial justice. This was jointly funded by a foundation and JPG for a 10-week, multigenerational saga of two Black families that were descendants of enslaved people. The series was designed to help Americans better understand the historic and contemporary factors behind persistent racial tensions. Based on true stories, the series portrays the plight and challenges of African Americans throughout U.S. history. Early episodes show the moral travesty of the slave trade and the living-working conditions of enslaved people. Later episodes follow subsequent generations through the Civil War, the Jim Crow South, migration and segregation in the north, the Black experience during both world wars, and contemporary variations on discrimination. In a final episode, one descendant becomes a beloved university professor who is accidentally killed by police in his own front yard. The series had a huge social impact, in large part, because it was accompanied by background materials and study-group activities that prompted discussions about equality and justice in many communities, including ours. It resulted in the first serious national discussion about the justification of and difficulties in implementing reparations programs for slavery.

Reforms of the public safety and criminal justice systems have improved social trust and well-being in the Black community. Police reforms have included the use of unarmed teams of social and mental health professionals who respond to nonviolent situations,[18] a revision of police practices in the use of deadly force, and more community involvement in police policies. Justice system reform included revised sentencing guidelines, the discontinuation of private prisons, revised probation and parole procedures, and major investments in rehabilitation programs. Rehabilitation programs included jail-to-work, jail-to-college, and other transition programs that developed skills and mindsets and engaged convicts in productive pursuits and guided them in creating positive supportive relationships. These efforts resulted in reduced crime, reduced incarceration, and reduced recidivism.

As part of a settlement of a fraud suit by the New York District Attorney's Office,[19] the National Rifle Association (NRA) fired its current leadership. The subsequent leadership more accurately represented the attitudes of gun owners who supported certain gun violence prevention policies, including background checks and red-flag prohibitions for individuals with domestic violence restraining orders.[20] The NRA has also instituted a suicide prevention program, including a suicide hotline for gun owners, resulting in a decline in suicides. The U.S. Supreme Court found that state stand-your-ground laws are discriminatory and violate victims' right to life and due process.[21]

As political divisiveness took the country to the brink in the 2020's, religious leaders, universities, and civic groups, along with private foundations, launched social connection programs to develop empathy and build personal trust across diverse groups. Leading the efforts were two organizations, Braver Angels[22] and America in One Room that developed training and sensitivity materials used by churches, schools, and community groups, including ours. As I mentioned, we've met several of our closest friends of opposite political persuasions after participating in the sessions.

Rebuilding trust has been a major economic, political, and cultural theme for the last decade. The Association of Stakeholder Companies has done a lot to rebuild trust in the business community, and JPG's cultural programs have done a lot to rebuild trust across racial and ethnic lines. In government, campaign finance laws were passed that met U.S. Supreme Court tests that reduced the influence of special interest groups and the appearance of corruption in the political process. As a result, Congressional legislation is more often seen as addressing society's many problems and reflecting the will of the people, and trust in government has increased dramatically.

Our dinner conversations are intense and exciting but exhausting.

* * *

Is this a future that we want? Maybe something like this. Perhaps your vision is better. Each of us has our own ideas, our own vision, our own moral imagination. But my point here is that we need a collective vision. Something we can all work toward: collective, local visions of a preferred future, one that is happier, fairer, and more caring and more just than the one we have now. This will take moral discussions, discussions we're not yet having. As this vision evolves, each of us, individually needs to determine how what we do with our lives, careers, and actions contributes to that vision and fits into the overall system.

But what if we don't do that? What if we continue down the familiar road, the comfortable one?

The road more likely?

What might the future look like when happiness and well-being are not our collective priorities? When we all look out only for our own well-being? When harm is someone else's problem? When knowledge and reason are not valued or are only private goods? When equality and justice are my right and for my people, but not yours? When people and institutions are untrustworthy, when relationships are tenuous, and when the social fabric is frayed? It might look something like this:

* * *

The constant action of people to promote their own welfare at the expense of others has eroded the trust people have in each other.[23] There is a record-high percentage of people who have not married as well as those who are currently divorced.[24] The lack of personal trust has resulted in increased depression and anger[25] and a dramatic increase in the number of people who have considered suicide.[26] The suicide rate continues to climb,[27] as has the drug overdose death rate.[28] Multiple stressors have resulted in a dramatic increase in cases of domestic violence.[29] At the same time, there was a dramatic increase in the number of people in teaching, healthcare, and other social services leaving out of stress and the lack of value placed on them by the public.[30]

Acts of gun violence portrayed in movies and media have increased dramatically.[31] With incidents of gun violence and crime reported daily in the news media, a general sense of fear has been created.[32] In response, states have passed laws making gun ownership easier.[33] Correspondingly, there has been a significant increase in the availability of guns and an increase in the number gun-related deaths, both homicides and suicides, over the past 10 years.[34] And mass shootings have been on the rise for 20 years.[35] Teachers carry guns;[36] public schools are locked and patrolled by police and have the feel of prisons.

There has been a significant restructuring of the labor market. The loss of high-paying manufacturing jobs, which have given those with less than a college degree access to the American Dream, has continued a four-decade decline,[37] now compounded by the use of self-driving trucks,[38] advanced robotics[39] and other technologies that have eliminated a broader range of well-paying jobs. For many years, farm labor and service jobs supported large numbers of low-wage workers,[40] although many people needed to work multiple jobs to make ends meet.[41] Now robots have been designed to pick fruit[42] and handle food services,[43] eliminating many of those jobs and further depressing wages for those that remain. Efforts were made to train displaced workers for higher-skilled jobs, but these efforts failed as artificial intelligence applications with high-level capabilities, such as reasoning, decision-making, and managing have become widespread, depressing wages or eliminating positions for retail sales, medical technicians, programmers, financial analysis, legal aids, and other professional fields.[44, 45,46] With all these trends, there has been an overall decline in workforce participation.[47]

The quality of the education system continues to be inadequate, with over 60% of students scoring less than proficient on national assessments of reading, math, and science,[48] especially in high-poverty school systems that, for lack of teachers, have had to rely on remote learning.[49] In response to the lack of quality in public education, a few private companies have made huge profits by developing software that "reduces the need for teachers" or by francizing branded schools that produce higher scores on tests—and higher profits—by selecting only the best students. Public schools suffer from a significant lack of qualified teachers as students see education as an underpaid, overly-politicized, disrespected profession.[50] Those teachers who remain, many uncredentialled, are often considered by the public as nothing more than over-paid babysitters. However, a handful of elite private schools have highly qualified, creative teachers that cater to the rich. As a result of these trends, less than 30% of the population has confidence in education leaders.[51] Only 3% believe that colleges are doing a great job at preparing graduates for the current workforce.[52] And a majority of people now believe that a college education actually has a negative effect on society.[53]

Poor education, job loss, and the use of automation and AI have resulted in a decline in wages for middle-income workers, a stagnation of wages for low-wage workers, and a windfall for a very few.[54] The country's middle class has been hollowed out. And for the poor, the number that are homeless has increased, particularly in the nations' large cities.[55] Many of them suffer from addiction, mental illness, and other health-related problems.[56]

With job loss, poverty, and reduced regulation in the healthcare industry, insurance companies have designed their policies to cater to the wealthy and healthy,[57] and there is a record number of people who lack healthcare insurance.[58] Healthcare and insurance stocks have performed well on Wall Street. But with the lack of insurance, the outbreak of a new, virulent strain of COVID[59] had a huge impact on the United States, as many could not afford to seek healthcare. The new strain emerged in Africa, having mutated on that continent in a country that was never adequately immunized during the 2020–2022 pandemic.[60] A group of anti-vaxxers in the United States, initially claimed the new virus was a hoax.[61] When it hit the African American community the hardest, it was relabeled the "Black Plague" and random acts of violence against Blacks increased across the country. Then anti-vaxxers claimed the strain was developed by the large pharma companies to increase their profits, and this increased the percentage of the population refusing to be vaccinated.

Increases in poverty and drug addiction have resulted in increases in crime and incarceration, with one third of all nonworking 30-year-old men either in prison or unemployed former prisoners.[62] Men of color are a majority of this group.[63] With increases in arrests came increased claims of police brutality and the number of deaths during police arrests increased. The United States became the world leader in the percent of the population that is incarcerated.[64]

It has gotten to the point that the number of prisoners has grown beyond the capacity of jails and prisons to handle. Consequently, private companies have been contracted to design internment camps to handle those arrested. To maximize their profits, these camps loan out convicts to private businesses and maintain minimal services, and those are focused on restraint and containment with none focused on rehabilitation.[65]

In the corporate world generally, companies have designed innovative ways to reduce taxes, [66,67] avoid regulations,[68] lower wages,[69] and increase profits. On top of now-traditional ways to reduce costs such as automation and shifting jobs to less expensive labor markets overseas, large multinational companies have developed ways to off-load risks onto suppliers and to quickly and inexpensively move corporate "headquarters," facilities, and jobs to other states and countries that have lower wages, less regulation, and the lowest corporate tax rate.[70,71,72] In an effort to attract these companies, there has been competition among states and countries to lure companies there in a race to the bottom. This has been coupled with a coordinated and aggressive effort on the part of companies to influence state, national, and international policies that would favor their interests.

The resulting corporate-friendly policies have dramatically and negatively impacted small businesses, which are no longer able to compete in the new economic environment.[73] Policies have also enabled companies to externalize their costs in the form of pollution and carbon generation that has added to climate change.[74]

Sophisticated, shadowy criminal enterprises have emerged that have designed schemes to hack and lock up individual, corporate, and governmental systems, holding them ransom for big payouts[75] or just emptying accounts[76] into nontraceable cryptocurrency accounts.[77] The availability of easy-to-use genetic engineering tools has allowed these organizations to design pests, bacteria, and viruses that they threaten to release on entire countries if their demands for huge sums of money are not met.[78]

The income and wealth gaps have continued to increase. The rich have become even richer during the most recent pandemic. And the top 1% of U.S. households now hold 15 times more wealth than the bottom 50% combined.[79] In 2026, the world saw Jeff Bezos become the world's first trillionaire,[80] which is more money than the annual GDP of all but 17 of the world's countries.[81] This was quickly followed by a dozen more trillionaires in the subsequent years. The ultra-rich control, if not own outright, the handful of conglomerates that constitute the global economy.

Many boutique and concierge businesses[82] have designed a vast array of services, hobbies, and amusements for the rich and ultra-rich.[83] And while many of the ultra-rich have enjoyed their wealth in exclusive neighborhoods in the United States, the deterioration of the nation's infrastructure and society has prompted them to look elsewhere for comfortable living. While many of them had purchased their own island,[84] they are now concerned that with increased sea levels they need to look elsewhere. Consequently, a corporate mechanism, owned by the ultra-rich, was designed to purchase a country and set up a government that would cater to their personal interests.[85] The ultra-rich also enjoy having multiple passports that allow them to freely roam the world looking for locations to set up shell companies that advantage them the most.[86]

In the United States, Super PACs have funneled a record amount of corporate and private campaign contributions into elections.[87,88] Between campaign donations and lobbying, the rich and their companies have come to have a tremendous amount of power over government. As a result, Congress has designed legislation that favors the rich and corporate interests,[89] and has become less and less attuned to public sentiment, with large majorities of voters favoring legislation in areas such as gun control,[90] climate change,[91] and minimum wage[92] that occasionally gets proposed but never gets passed. There is a perpetual stalemate in Congress with compromise considered a dirty word. Politicians in opposing parties don't trust or respect—indeed, they vilify—each other. As a result, popular trust in both parties and each of the branches of government are at record lows. For many, the distrust in government has turned to anger and a radicalized or unstable few have drawn on that anger to attack politicians and their families, those expressing support for the other party, and even poll workers in their homes or where they work.[93]

Political parties have used misinformation and lies to gain and maintain power. And once in power, have used it to design district boundaries that benefit their party[94] and to pass legislation that suppresses opposition voters.[95]

Demonstrations against the government and social conditions, more generally, have become common place. The demonstrations have increasingly become violent, with armed confrontations of partisans on both sides.[96] And the government response to demonstrations has become increasingly militarized.[97] The number of private militia groups has grown in support of the current government and politicians have encouraged or tacitly condoned their participation in demonstrations, often leading to violence and even deaths.

The least trusted institution in the country is the news media; less than 20% express confidence in news organizations. However, there are significant differences in *which* news sources are found credible by people of different political affiliations.[98] Fake news has increased dramatically from a variety of domestic and foreign sources amplified by social media.[99] A recent deepfake video, designed to discredit the leader of the opposition party, shows her taking money from a foreign agent and has resulted in violent demonstrations to have her removed from office.[100] Indeed, the ready availability of easy to use AI-generated video tools has resulted in a huge number of fake videos, flooding the internet, depicting politicians, church leaders, corporate executives, even the girl next door in sex acts with children.[101]

On the international front, alliances, institutions, and agencies have been severely weakened.[102] The United States pulled out of the U.N. and several alliances, stating that they did not sufficiently benefit U.S. interests. After the United States withdrew from the Asia-Pacific Economic Cooperation forum, China ramped up its efforts to assert power in the South China Sea[103] and most Asian countries acknowledged China's claims. Australia and New Zealand initially resisted but eventually followed suit after they realized that the United States was not going to check China's power in the region. Without a strong alliance against it, China designed economic policies that put an economic squeeze on Taiwan and it ultimately took over the island without an invasion, executing many local leaders.[104]

Russian intelligence agencies designed an effective covert social media campaign to fan distrust among European nations.[105] This has added to the tensions between the European Union and Eastern European members, with Hungary and Poland claiming that Brussels was asserting too much authority over national policies. The two countries were among the first to recognize the new Russian-backed government in the Ukraine after they completed their invasion.[106] With the European Union neutralized and the United States indifferent to the actions of authoritarian, anti-democratic regimes, Russia subsequently invaded an incorporated Moldovia and Georgia, and threatened Lithuania, Latvia, and Estonia.

Within this global chaos, Iran developed nuclear weapons,[107] and both Iran and North Korea are constantly threatening the international order, such as it is. Saudi Arabia has also acquired nuclear weapons and threatens to use them against Iran.[108]

The United States, again, pulled out of the Paris Agreement, stating that Russia and China were cheating on their commitments and the agreement was hamstringing the U.S. economy.[109] After ignoring their commitments for several years, Russia formally withdrew after its careful analysis of the climate data found that the country would actually benefit significantly from a warmer Siberian climate that would dramatically increase its food production.[110] Having done the same calculations, Canada, Norway, Sweden, and Finland pulled out of the agreement as well. With cheap oil from Russia and with that country's encouragement, Eastern European countries also pulled out and the agreement collapsed.

With these withdrawals and increased corporate pollution and greenhouse gas emission, the world not only failed to meet the 1.5°C goal, but the 2.0°C goal was also missed and mean global temperatures have increased by 2.5°C. This has had a variety of interconnected catastrophic effects resulting in massive wildfires, crop failures due to drought and floods, the die-off of many species, coastal loss due to the rise in sea levels, and increased extreme weather events, such as devastating hurricanes, typhoons, tornadoes.[111] There has also been major secondary social fallout[112] such as massive immigrations due to crop failures or coastal loss. This has increased tension at the southern border of the United States with enormous numbers of immigrants trying to cross illegally[113] and vigilante groups patrolling the border that have killed people caught in the act of crossing.[114]

These stresses were compounded by unrelated events, such as a major earthquake and a volcanic eruption, that went beyond the capability of a nation to respond, especially given the worldwide reduction in the tax base. And the reemergence of the COVID virus resulted in hundreds of millions of people being infected and tens of millions dying, so far, as health systems collapsed.[115] The impact has been the greatest among the poor countries and the poor within rich countries.

Countries varied in their national response to the new pandemic with many initially downplaying it for fear that a lockdown would destroy an already fragile national economy.[116] But all international flights were cancelled, the global trade and supply chain collapsed, and the economic impact has been devastating, despite belated efforts to address the pandemic's impact.

* * *

Is this our future? Does it sound familiar? Perhaps that's because, if you followed the footnotes, much of it is where we already are. If we continue to follow our current design practices, it will only get worse.

We are at a juncture. The situation is dire and it is urgent. Our future is on the line. We—individually and collectively—have decisions to make. . .by commission or by default. If some version of this dark, Hobbesian future is not to be ours, it will be because good designs will come to be based on values, not just function and look-and-feel, not just self-interest. It will be because our designs contribute to happiness, reduce harm, and create a more just, compassionate society. It will be because our government, our economy, our culture, and our communities promote these values and these designs. And it will be because people—people like you—care and do something about it.

Finding a Home. . .or Building One

So, where do you go from here? What do you do next?

If you are to have any chance to change the world, to make it a better place, to make a difference, it will be because you put yourself in a position where making those changes are valued and supported, where you connect with others who have similar values, because you can't do this on your own. Consequently, an essential component to designing with passion, purpose, and values is first finding a home in which you can do that, or it is creating one.

There are four important ways you can put yourself in a position to create designs with values, depending on where you are in your life: by selecting a career in which you can improve the world, by selecting a workplace where you can do good, by volunteering your time for an effective organization, or by creating your own design space.

Design as a career

Let's say you're young and idealistic and want to change the world. You have applied for college admission or want to enter a graduate program that will give you the skills and credentials to enter a profession. Design can be a central part of that choice.

There are many design traditions from which to choose that fit your interests and skills: Scientific, Technical, Human-Centered, Aesthetic, or Community Organization and Social Movement. You may be pulled toward research in the physical, biological, or social sciences. You may be interested in a technical career in engineering, computer science, or medicine. You could be interested in a human-centered design program, such as product design, architecture, interior design, or urban planning. Or it could be a social profession, such as psychology, education, social work, or law. You may have a talent for the arts, such as theater, film, writing, or graphic arts. You may have a passion for social activism and want to develop a career in community development and aspire to launch a mass movement.

What career do you choose? Or how can you capitalize on your interests and career to improve the world?

One way to think about a career is to consider yourself an "effective altruist."[117] As an effective altruist, you would choose a career that turns your passion and values into the biggest impact by working on important problems where one person can make an added difference. Teaching, for example, has a huge potential to advance knowledge, increase happiness and build supportive, positive relationships. There is a wide range of teaching subjects to match your interests, from mathematics, to natural sciences, social sciences, literature, and the arts. Using numbers from the U.S. National Center for Educational Statistics,[118] a typical high school teacher has a class size of 27 students. With 5 periods a day, the teacher would potentially impact 135 students each year. Over a 20-year career, the teacher will influence the lives of 2,700 young people. This is powerfully motivating. Indeed, a national survey of teachers, conducted by Scholastic and the Bill and Melinda Gates Foundation, found that 85% of the respondents said they chose teaching as a career to make a difference in the lives of children. And 98% agreed that teaching is more than a profession; it is how they make a difference in the world.

Take, for example, Chris Dier, Louisiana's 2020 State Teacher of the Year and a finalist of the National Teacher of the Year.[119] Dier teaches World History and Advanced Placement Human Geography at Chalmette High School. He is a proud product of the St. Bernard Parish public school system. He has two Master's degrees from the University of New Orleans, one in education administration and one in teaching. In 2016, Dier was selected as a Hollyhock Fellow at Stanford University, a program that brings educators together to work collectively toward creating more inclusive classrooms. He also has participated in a professional development program at Harvard Business School that focuses on case method teaching, in which he works to find solutions to real-world problems and challenges in the classroom. Dier's passion is providing an equitable education to all and he attributes it to his mother, who was also a teacher: ". . .there were so many times that people would stop my mom to thank her and voice their appreciation. Seeing the influence she had on others throughout my life growing up was life-changing," Dier reported.[120] "When I was in college and deciding on a career choice, my mom invited me to observe her at Chalmette High School. I saw in real-time that influence as it manifested itself. I then got into teaching and I never looked back."

Many types of careers can make a difference in the world. There is a service that can help you pick one. 80,000 Hours is a program of the Centre for Effective Altruism at Oxford University's Future for Humanity Institute.[121] Its premise is that each of us has about 80,000 hours in our work career and the way to make the biggest difference with our lives is to choose a career that improves the world every day. The purpose of 80,000 Hours is to solve the most pressing skill bottlenecks in the world's most pressing problems. It does this by providing research and support to help people start or switch into careers that effectively tackle these problems. It is both explicitly moral and practical.

If you want to make the world a better place and are at or nearing the point of picking or changing a career, you will want to consider their advice. 80,000 Hours has extensive practical recommendations on career and job selection for a range of people, from those with expertise, interest, and skill in technical fields, like physics, biology, engineering, and computer programming; to business skills, such as management and marketing; and to the social sciences and humanities professions, such as psychology, philosophy, education, law, public policy as well as those with strong writing and visual skills.[122]

Design where you work

If you already have your degree and have picked a profession, you may be looking for an employer whom you can work with to make a difference in the world. You may not have a lot of control over the work you do or projects you take on, especially in a large company. The corporate culture of the company you work for can greatly affect your ability to do good in the world. Picking the right company will be critical.

There are a number of services that rate or rank companies on their corporate social responsibility, and these ratings can help you decide where you would like to work. Helpful organizations and websites include Just Capital,[123] the Reputation Institute,[124] *Newsweek*,[125] and *Corporate Responsibility Magazine*.[126] Their rating criteria typically include considerations of the company's "'ESGs": their *environmental* or climate impact, their *social* goals or impact on workers or community, and their corporate *governance*. Other services provide companies with certificates, indicating they have passed a review of their policies and practices.

For example, B the Change Media and its B Lab provides certificates to companies that meet rigorous standards of social and environmental performance, accountability, and transparency.[127] And the U.S. Green Building Council has developed the Leadership in Energy and Environmental Design (LEED) Certificate, recognizing best-in-class building strategies and practices for architechs.[128]

Some companies are highly rated because of the nature of the products or services they provide. The happiness resulting from use of the products of companies like Disney, Lego, Ben & Jerry's can't be denied. But the good that is done by these highly rated companies often goes beyond the goods and services they provide or is based on corporate polices or practices that improve the world or the communities in which they are located. For example, the Walt Disney Company announced during the pandemic that it would continue to pay employees during park closures and provide refunds to anyone planning a visit that had to be cancelled.[129] Warby Parker not only reduces harm due to poor eyesight with its high-quality, affordable eyewear, but its good is also compounded by donating glasses to people in developing countries. Google achieved 100% renewable energy use in 2017, reducing harm to our environment. To minimize the harm caused by the COVID pandemic, clothing stores Patagonia, Allbirds, Urban Outfitters, and Nike all give full pay to their workers even as they closed most stores worldwide. And the Microsoft Giving Program has donated over 5 million volunteer hours of its employees' time over the last 13 years and is on track to give away $2 billion to charities.[130]

Perhaps the ideal place for a designer to work is in a design firm. There are several nationally and internationally renowned firms and many local firms that are committed to design thinking or implementing the human-centered design approach, firms such as IDEO, ?What if!, Fjord, Jump Associates, Lunar, Frog, and Claro. These agencies have innovative teams that include product designers, service designers, and business innovation consultants who have play key roles in building innovative startups like AirBnB, Tesla, and Nest.

But you don't need to join a design firm to find a good design job. A recent trend in large companies is to incorporate some of the ideas from design firms, like IDEO, into their everyday operations. This trend has gone beyond companies like Apple and Ikea, companies where design is an organizing theme, to a wide range of companies like Lloyds Banking, 3M, IBM, Pepsico, Kia Motors, Starbucks, Johnson & Johnson, Salesforce, Walt Disney, Pixar, Auberge Resorts, Philips, and Proctor & Gamble. This trend is organizationally expressed in the position of Chief Design Officer or Chief Creative Officer, people who represent the design process on corporate boards. Terms such as *design culture*, *design-led organizations*, or *design-driven organizations* are often used to express an organizational emphasis on and valuing of the design process, across the company.[131]

Values reflected in the designs of these companies are often expressed in their statement of purpose on their websites or in their brochures. For example, Ben & Jerry's website states that its social mission compels it to use the company in innovative ways to make the world a better place.[132] The website for Salesforce states, "We have a broader responsibility to society, and aspire to create technology that not only drives the success of our customers, but also upholds the basic human rights of every individual."[133] The Levi Strauss website states, "We put our profits, people and products to work in more than 100 countries to champion equality, support vulnerable communities and build a more sustainable future for our planet."[134]

However, it's important not to take the company's words for granted. Do your background research to see how the company's culture and values are implemented in their products, services, actions, and impacts. For example, Johnson & Johnson, one of the companies that has adopted a design culture claims on its website that "At Johnson & Johnson, we believe good health is the foundation of vibrant lives, thriving communities and forward progress."[135] But in 2020, the Missouri Court of Appeals upheld a landmark jury verdict that said long-term use of Johnson & Johnson's talc products had caused ovarian cancer in 22 women.[136] The Court of Appeals stated, "A reasonable inference from all this evidence is that, motivated by profits, defendants disregarded the safety of consumers." In June 2021, the U.S. Supreme Court refused to consider the company's appeal, rejecting its argument that a trial with 22 cancer patients from 12 states was unfair because it added undue emotional weight to the proceedings.[137] And in February 2022, Johnson & Johnson and three other companies agreed to pay $26 billion to settle claims that they fueled the opioid crisis.[138]

Volunteer your time

Another way to help make the world a better place is to volunteer your time through an effective nonprofit organization. If you are retired or have spare time after work or on the weekends, if you're a student with time during summer break, or if your employer supports community volunteer work, there are many opportunities to use your spare time to improve the world. Organizations in the United States, such as the Red Cross,[139] Habitat for Humanity,[140] Burners without Borders,[141] or AmeriCorps[142] provide opportunities to rebuild a community after disaster, mentor and tutor kids, help veterans, or work with local communities to alleviate poverty. For example, Shannon Perry is a development and communications manager with Hemisfair Conservancy in San Antonio, Texas. Between 2006 and 2007, she joined AmeriCorps VISTA to serve with Habitat for Humanity. In reflecting on her service, she states, "While in college, I participated in two alternative spring break trips to build with Habitat in Greensboro, North Carolina, and in York, Pennsylvania. Both experiences made me feel like I was making a difference. . .. To know that my hard work to create a house would impact someone's life the way my childhood home impacted mine—to be a place for security, growth and love—made me extremely happy."[143]

Retirement presents many opportunities to contribute. In the United States, in 2018, there were 52 million people age 65 and older as the Baby Boom Generation hit retirement age. While retired people vary significantly in their health and finances, one thing they typically have in common is more flexible time than they did while working. The use of this time by anyone, but particularly by those who were in the professions, can be a valuable contribution to making the world a better place. The American Association of Retired People's Experience Corps[144] and the Senior Corps of the Corporation for National and Community Service[145] are among the resources you can use to find ways of making valuable contributions and feeling fulfilled at the same time. Among the possibilities are mentoring children or young adults; serving as a foster grandparent; volunteering at food banks, schools, libraries, museums, or parks.

For example, Delores Bell committed herself to work between 5 and 15 hours a week at her local Baltimore elementary school through AARP's Experience Corps volunteer program. Students tutored by volunteers made faster-than-expected literacy gains according to a standardized assessment.[146] The experience also benefitted Doris, "During my short time with Experience Corps I've felt like my life has meaning. I have a reason for getting up in the morning, knowing that I am going to help a child. When they say, 'Miss Bell, I need some help,' or 'Miss Bell, will you help me,' it gives me a feeling that I am needed. You cannot imagine the joy that it brings me. I now have a purpose to get up in the morning, knowing that there are children waiting for me."[147]

Doris Bell and Shannon Perry make the point that helping out can reward the helper as well. There is a growing body of evidence that indicates that altruistic acts, such as giving money and time to charitable organizations, not only helps those in need but increases the happiness of those who give, particularly if the giving is voluntary, is connected to evidence of impact and if it creates or strengthens social relationships.[148]

Create your own design space

When it comes down to it, you may find that the best place to make the world a better is the place you design yourself. Over the past 15 years, traditional Do-It-Yourself hobbyists in crafts, woodworking, and metalworking have been joined by those interested in computer programming, electronics, robotics, and 3D printing and have evolved into a community and culture of Makers and Hackers. The community values the creation of new devices and tinkering with existing ones. They share ideas about designs, published on websites and maker-oriented publications, and support the learning of practical skills and their application to designs. During in-person and online group events around the world, such as Maker Faires and Hackatons, participants engage in competitions and share ideas, skills, tools, and techniques. While many of these events celebrate skills and accomplishments for their own sake, they often have a focus on socially relevant issues.

An example of the hacker spirit is Ivan Owen, mentioned in earlier chapters. Ivan is an interdisciplinary artist, designer, and educator who owns MechMaddness Designs, a shop that designs and fabricates armor, mechanical props, and costumes for theatrical productions. In 2011, Ivan received an email from Richard, a carpenter in South Africa who lost his fingers in a woodworking accident.[149] Ivan had created a crazy, manipulatable metal hand to wear to his first Steampunk Convention. Richard found Ivan and his mechanical hand on the internet. Because a prosthetic finger would cost Richard around $10,000, Richard had been trying to design his own. In searching for information, he came upon the video that Ivan had uploaded about his mechanical hand and Richard reached out for help. This email inspired Ivan to do some research, and he not only designed a prosthetic finger for Richard, but along with colleagues, he developed the online global community e-NABLE that provides 3D printed prosthetics for those who have lost fingers or hands in accidents or war.[150] The e-NABLE Community is a diverse group of over 20,000 volunteers in over 100 countries: teachers, students, engineers, scientists, medical professionals, tinkerers, designers, parents, children, scout troops, artists, philanthropists, dreamers, coders, makers, and everyday people who want to make a difference and "Give the World a Helping Hand."

Another example of this innovative spirit is Boyan Slat, mentioned in Chapter 2. When he was 16 years old, Slat was diving in Greece and encountered a depressing sight: there was more plastic in the sea than fish. As a high-school science project, he and a friend looked at research on the topic and he came to realize it was a complex problem that would involve collecting massive amounts of plastic, without collecting sea life, in five enormous ocean areas, with plastic ranging in size from massive fishing nets to molecules, and then getting it back to land and disposing of it. Cleaning the ocean became his life's passion. When he went off to university, he continued to study the problem. While the traditional idea for collecting plastic debris is to send out ships with nets, it would likely take thousands of years to collect the plastic using such methods. Slat's idea was it would be much more efficient to let the plastic come to him by using natural currents to divert it into the waiting arms of platforms anchored in one of these enormous plastic garbage patches. He was able to test out these ideas with some crowd-sourced funding. In 2014, he formed a nonprofit organization, The Ocean Cleanup,[151] and was able to obtain funding that allowed him to begin testing his ideas.[152] He put together a volunteer team and began engaging in an iterative process that included research, testing, failing, revising, and repeating.[153] Since then, the focus of the organization has included the cleanup of rivers, the largest source of plastic pollution. As Slat reflects on his work, he says, "What motivates me to work on this every day is that I believe we have an opportunity here is not just to solve a global problem that affects billions of people and thousands of other species but to inspire the world to act together to do something. Problems are solved. . .by rolling up our sleeves and get working on something."[154]

Creating a Culture of Everyday Design for a Better World

If you've gotten this far in the book, it is because you've made a personal decision. You have decided that a purpose in your life is not only to improve your own condition but that of others. Like van Gogh, you may have said you found "something greater than myself, which is my life, the power to create." You have decided to build on that passion and contribute designs that make the world a better place. This is a huge personal commitment and leaves you with a lot of work ahead.

But let me pick up a proposal I made in Chapter 11. While it takes the passion and ideas of each of us to make change and every positive change is important, the world will not change until a large number of us make this commitment and until the larger system changes to support us. In addition to whatever we do to with our free time, our jobs, our careers, our enterprises, and our personal life, we must learn from the Community Organization and Social Movement Tradition. We must organize our design community and look for kindred spirits, for alliances, for opportunities to create a culture of design with shared values.

There already is an emerging movement in the professional design community among those who think differently, those who see the need for a more comprehensive, aspirational, transformative role for design. This movement goes by many names: Massive Change,[155] Design for the Other 90%,[156] Service Design,[157] Social Design,[158] Design for Social Impact,[159] Design for Social Justice,[160] Design for Wellbeing,[161] Equity-Centered Community Design,[162] Value Sensitive Design,[163] and Design for the Good Society.[164] While these terms imply slightly different meanings with different emphases, they all address the designer's moral responsibility to create a better world; they are all based on the belief that there is a role for design beyond feeding, promoting, and confirming our current consumer culture. Explore these groups and consider joining one.

Another example of this movement is the First Things First Manifesto of graphic designers, art directors, and visual communicators who state, in part, "We propose a reversal of priorities in favor of more useful, lasting and democratic forms of communication—a mind shift away from product marketing and toward the exploration and production of a new kind of meaning."[165] Allied Media Projects, a Detroit-based network of designers and projects believes "Our liberation is an ongoing process of personal, collective, and systemic transformation. . .to create the world we need."[166] The Design Justice Network, an international group of designers, "challenges the ways that design and designers can harm those who are marginalized by systems of power" and they "use design to imagine and build the worlds we need to live in—worlds that are safer, more just, and more sustainable."[167] We must connect with and build on these efforts.

Several efforts are working toward the redesign of design education. University of California, San Diego Design Lab founder Donald Norman and Karel Vredenburg, Director of Global Design Leadership at IBM, put together a group of design faculty members to rethink design education and design, more generally,[168] a topic Norman also discusses in his new book, Design for a Better World: Meaningful, Sustainable, Humanity Centered.[169] The goal of this effort is to go beyond human-centered design to consider the broader consequences of our designs on all of humanity and embed these considerations in the education of professional designers. University of Michigan College of Engineering Dean, Alec Gallimore, is spearheading People First Engineering, a national effort to reformulate engineering education so that engineers have a positive impact on the world and build a future that will elevate all people.[170] And if we agree with Herbert Simon's conclusion that the proper study of mankind is the science of design as a core discipline for every liberally educated person, then design would be incorporated not just into the schools of art, engineering, and business but other professional schools, such as education, social work, law, and medicine. And also into the undergraduate curricula of natural sciences, social sciences, and the humanities.[171] That has yet to happen.

Beyond our individual decisions and efforts, we must move toward design as a mass movement if we are to avoid our second scenario. Revised curricula for the design professions is important. But so are the everyday actions of everyday designers within a community. In addition to finding a design home, joining or creating a local design community can be an important next step for you. The community may not have "design" in its title. It could be a church group, women's or men's group, book club, community center, political club, maker group, or advocacy group—any group that might be interested in changing things as they are to what they should be. But *that* is design.

Of course, deciding how things should be is an important discussion among moral co-creators. And it is by populating our society with diverse groups that are all working toward making the world better that we can transform society. Like-minded groups that hold the same beliefs and values are more likely to get things done, particularly if these bonding, "strong tie" groups have a range of complementary skills. However, it is the "weak tie," bridging of groups with diverse ideas that can fuel unique combinations of ideas and efforts that can lead to the transformations we need to avoid the second scenario.

For design to transform our society, to make it better, the moral principles that we share as humans must be an explicit thread that runs throughout design: its purpose, process, outcomes, and impacts. First and foremost, the purpose must be to increase happiness. This can be done by advancing knowledge, agency, equality, justice, and supportive relationships. These principles must be considered in the local context of harm, ignorance, inequality, injustice, or depression, isolation, and loneliness. These values must be embedded in the research studies, products, services, aesthetic productions, and other mass movements that we create with our designs. These purposes must guide the impacts we strive for and the results that we measure.

If we are to avoid the second scenario, if we are to make the world a better place, these values must become paramount in our culture, ones that are designed into the structures and roles of our local, and ultimately, national social, economic, and political systems. We must each find or create a design home and then continue to build and extend our design community, building it around our shared purpose and values and the harm we see in the world. We must empower ourselves and our colleagues by developing morally based design skills and moral discourse, as described in Chapter 11. And we must act to change our larger culture to be one guided not just by the invisible hand of self-interest, but by the hand of compassion, caring, and trust.

Ultimately, it is in this way that these values will come to be embedded in our individual and collective everyday actions and designs as well as in our economy and government. This is when we will have transformed design and our designs will be transformative. This is when we will be well along the road less traveled toward making the world a better place. It will be because of the creativity and moral imagination of everyday designers. And it will be because, like van Gogh, we find a purpose great than ourselves.

We began this book thinking about design as the fundamental way the humans change their world to make it better, to take it from where it is to where it should be. In conclusion, the question that hangs in the air is: Better for whom? Will our designs continue to serve only our interests and those of people like us? Or will they address the needs of all, based on our common humanity? Will they bring us together? Will they contribute to our common well-being and continued survival?

We are aware of the current situation; we know about the problems, the inequality, the injustice in our world. We've made the commitment to act; we've agreed to the values and goals of our Constitution, the Paris Climate Accords, and the UN Sustainable Development Goals. History will not judge us kindly—assuming that history continues to exist—if we do not act, if we do not use our passion, purpose, and values to co-design a better world.

> Be the change that you wish to see in the world.
> *Mahatma Gandhi*
> *Nonviolent Leader in India's Independence*

> This is my chance in the world. . .I'm right here, right now and I want now to be the Golden Age. . .if only each generation would realize that the time for greatness is right now when they're alive . . .the time to flower is now.
> *Patti Smith*
> *Singer, Song Writer, Punk Poet Laureate*

> If you wanna make the world a better place, take a look at yourself and then make the change.
> *Michael Jackson*
> *Man in the Mirror*

> A journey of a thousand miles begins with a single step.
> *Chinese Proverb*

References

1 Frost R. Road not taken. Poetry Foundation [Internet]. [cited 2022, Sep 4]. Available from: https://www.poetryfoundation.org/poems/44272/the-road-not-taken.

2 Anaby D, Miller W, Eng J, et al. Participation and well-being among older adults living with chronic conditions. Social Indicators Research, 2011, 100, 171–183.

3 Mozolic J, Shuster J. Community engagement in K–12 tutoring programs: A research-based guide for best practices. ERIC [Internet]. 2015 [cited 2022, Sep 2]. Available from: https://files.eric.ed.gov/fulltext/EJ1123811.pdf.

4 California Volunteers [Internet]. [cited 2022, Sep 2]. Available from: https://www.californiavolunteers.ca.gov/education/.

5 Bengtson B. Reimagine your corporate volunteer program. Harvard Business Review [Internet]. 2020, Dec 18 [cited 2022, Sep 2]. Available from: https://hbr.org/2020/12/reimagine-your-corporate-volunteer-program.

6 Curtis D. Project-based learning: Real-world issues motivate students. Edutopia [Internet]. 2001, Nov 1 [cited 2022, Sep 2]. Available from: https://www.edutopia.org/project-based-learning-student-motivation.

7 A triple win for students, volunteers, and communities. AARP Foundation [Internet]/[cited 2022, Sep 2]. Available from: https://www.aarp.org/experience-corps/.

8 One-on-one English language tutoring. Teach [Internet]. [cited 2022, Sep 2]. Available from: https://www.teachempowers.org/programs-and-resources/community-based-tutoring/.

9 Van Keer H, Vanderlinde R. The impact of cross-age peer tutoring on third and sixth graders; reading strategy awareness, reading strategy use, and reading comprehension. Middle Grades Research Journal, 2010, 5(1), 33–45.

10 Kotschy R, Sunde U. Can education compensate the effect of population ageing on macroeconomic performance? Economic Policy 2018, 339960, 587–634. Available from: https://academic.oup.com/economicpolicy/article-abstract/33/96/587/5068947?redirectedFrom=fulltext.

11 Gouëdard P. Can a growth mindset help disadvantaged students close the gap? PISA in Focus [Internet]. 2021 [cited 2022, Sept 2]. Available from: https://www.oecd-ilibrary.org/docserver/20922f0d-en.pdf?expires=1620832652&id=id&accname=guest&checksum=BB2A0B9C0 1F89558465809409D6A1550.

12 Helping loved ones divided by politics. Braver Angels [Internet]/[cited 2022, Sept 2]. Available from: https://braverangels.org/calling-family-members-divided-by-politics/?link_id=1&can_id=ace0714a4e354004e43acd1749622ecb&source=email-helping-loved-ones-divided-by-politics-2&email_referrer=email_1300059&email_subject=helping-loved-ones-divided-by-politics.

13 Business Roundtable redefines the purpose of a corporation to promote 'and economy that serves all Americans.' Business Roundtable [Internet]. 2019, Aug 19 [cited 2022, Sept 2]. Available from: https://www.businessroundtable.org/business-roundtable-redefines-the-purpose-of-a-corporation-to-promote-an-economy-that-serves-all-americans.

14 Gross National Happiness USA [Internet]. [cited 2022, Sept 2]. Available from: https://gnhusa.org/gross-national-happiness/.

15 Advanced Research Projects Agency-Energy [Internet]. [cited 2022, Sept 2]. Available from: https://arpa-e.energy.gov.

16 Holder S, Mock B. What a national guaranteed income could look like. Bloomberg [Internet]. 2021, Jul 8 [cited 2022, Sept 2]. Available from: https://www.bloomberg.com/news/articles/2021-07-08/what-a-national-guaranteed-income-could-look-like.

17 How government jobs programs could boost employment. Urban [Internet]. 2020, May 6 [cited 2022, Sept 2]. Available from: https://www.urban.org/features/how-government-jobs-programs-could-boost-employment.

18 Albuquerque Community Safety. City of Albuquerque [Internet]. [cited 2022, Sept 2]. Available from: https://www.cabq.gov/acs.

19 Mak T. New York Attorney General moves to dissolve the NRA after fraud investigation. NPR [Internet]. 2020, Aug 6 [cited 2022, Sept 2]. Available from: https://www.npr.org/2020/08/06/899712823/new-york-attorney-general-moves-to-dissolve-the-nra-after-fraud-investigation.

20 Most gun owners favor gun violence prevention policies. Boston University School of Public Health [Internet]. 2020, Jul 28 [cited 2022, Sept 2]. Available from: https://www.bu.edu/sph/news/articles/2020/most-gun-owners-favor-gun-violence-prevention-policies/.

21 Murphy L, Bellamy J. Written statement of the American Civil Liberties Union. Submitted to the Senate Subcommittee on the Constitution, Civil Rights and Human Rights, 2013.

22 Braver Angels [Internet]. [cited 2022, Sept 2]. Available from: https://braverangels.org.

23 Rainie L, Keeter S, Perrin A. Trust and distrust in America. Pew Research Center [Internet]. 2019, Jul 22 [cited 2022, Sept 2]. Available from: https://www.pewresearch.org/politics/2019/07/22/trust-and-distrust-in-america/.

24 Horowitz JM, Graf N, Livingston G. The landscape of marriage and cohabitation in the U.S. Pew Research Center [Internet]. 2019, Nov 6 [cited 2022, Sept 2]. Available from: https://www.pewresearch.org/social-trends/2019/11/06/the-landscape-of-marriage-and-cohabitation-in-the-u-s/.

25 Ng T, Sorensen K, Zhang Y, et al. Anger, anxiety, depression and negative affect: Convergent or divergent? Journal of Vocational Behavior, 2019, 110(Part A), 186–202.

26 The state of mental health in America. Mental Health America [Internet]. [cited 2022, Sept 2]. Available from: https://www.mhanational.org/issues/state-mental-health-america.

27 Suicide. National Institute of Mental Health [Internet]. [cited 2022, Sept 2]. Available from: https://www.nimh.nih.gov/health/statistics/suicide.

28 Overdose death rates. National Institute on Drug Abuse [Internet]. [cited 2022, Sept 2]. Available from: https://www.drugabuse.gov/drug-topics/trends-statistics/overdose-death-rates.

29 Boserup B, McKenney M, Elkbuli A. Alarming trends in US domestic violence during the COVID-19 pandemic. American Journal of Emergency Medicine, 2020, 38(12), 2753–2755.

30 Yong E, Why health-care workers are quitting in droves. Atlantic [Internet]. 2021, Nov 16 [cited 2022, Sept 2]. Available from: https://www.theatlantic.com/health/archive/2021/11/the-mass-exodus-of-americas-health-care-workers/620713/.

31 Have movies become more violent over the years? Common Sense Media [Internet]. 2020, Jun 4 [cited 2022, Sept 2]. Available from: https://www.commonsensemedia.org/articles/have-movies-become-more-violent-over-the-years.

32 Callanan V. Media consumption, perceptions of crime risk and fear of crime: Examining race/ethnic difference. Sociological Perspectives [Internet]. 2012, Mar 1 [cited 2022, Sep 2]. Available from: https://journals.sagepub.com/doi/10.1525/sop.2012.55.1.93 .

33 Many states are pushing through more permissive gun laws. Economist [Internet]. 2021, May 6 [cited 2022, Sep 2]. Available from: https://www.economist.com/united-states/2021/05/06/many-states-are-pushing-through-more-permissive-gun-laws?utm_campaign=the-economist-this-week&utm_medium=newsletter&utm_source=salesforce-marketing-cloud&utm_term=2021-05-06&utm_content=ed-picks-article-link-4&etear=nl_weekly_4.

34 A public crisis decades in the making: A review of 2019 CDC gun mortality data. Educational. Fund to Stop Gun Violence [Internet]. 2021, Feb [cited 2022, Sep 2]. Available from: https://efsgv.org/wp-content/uploads/2019CDCdata.pdf.

35 Smart R, Schell, T. Mass shootings in the United States. Rand [Internet]. 2021, Apr 15 [cited 2022, Sep 2]. Available from: https://www.rand.org/research/gun-policy/analysis/essays/mass-shootings.html.

36 As school year starts, Ohio teachers can now carry guns in class with less training. Cincinnati Edition [Internet]. 2022, Aug 16 [cited 2022, Sep 2]. Available from: https://www.wvxu.org/show/cincinnati-edition/2022-08-16/ohio-teachers-carry-guns-class-less-training.

37 Charles KK, Hurst E, Schwartz M. The transformation of manufacturing and the decline in U.S. Employment. National Bureau of Economic Research [Internet]. 2018, Mar [cited 2022, Sep 2]. Available from: https://www.nber.org/papers/w24468.

38 Driving automation systems in long-haul trucking and bus transportation. U.S. Department of Transportation [Internet]. 2021, Jan [cited 2022, Sep 2]. Available from: https://www.transportation.gov/sites/dot.gov/files/2021-01/Driving%20Automation%20Systems%20in%20

Long%20Haul%20Trucking%20and%20Bus%20Transit%20Preliminary%20Analysis%20of%20Potential%20Workforce%20Impacts.pdf.

39 Brown S. A new study measures the actual impact of robots on jobs. It's significant. MIT Management [Internet]. 2020, Jul 29 [cited 2022, Sep 2]. Available from: https://mitsloan.mit.edu/ideas-made-to-matter/a-new-study-measures-actual-impact-robots-jobs-its-significant.

40 Kelly J. The frightening rise in low-quality, low-paying jobs: Is this really a strong job market? Forbes [Internet]. 2019, Nov 25 [cited 2022, Sep 2]. Available from: https://www.forbes.com/sites/jackkelly/2019/11/25/the-frightening-rise-in-low-quality-low-paying-jobs-is-this-really-a-strong-job-market/?sh=1a2effbf4fd1.

41 Bailey K, Spletzer J. Using administrative data, Census Bureau can now track the rise in multiple jobholders. U.S. Census Bureau [Internet]. 2021, Feb 3 [cited 2022, Sep 2]. Available from: https://www.census.gov/library/stories/2021/02/new-way-to-measure-how-many-americans-work-more-than-one-job.html.

42 Gossett S. How Root AI's agricultural robots are powering the farmtech revolution. BuiltIn [Internet]. 2020, May 19 [cited 2022, Sep 2]. Available from: https://builtin.com/robotics/harvesting-robots-agriculture-root-ai.

43 Correa C. The 11 coolest food service robots on the market. Eater [Internet]. 2015, Sep 20 [cited 2022, Sep 2]. Available from: https://www.eater.com/2015/9/20/8791845/cool-food-related-robots-motoman-makr-shakr.

44 The future of jobs report 2020. World Economic Forum [Internet]. 2020, Oct [cited 2022, Sep 2]. Available from: http://www3.weforum.org/docs/WEF_Future_of_Jobs_2020.pdf.

45 Semuels A. Millions of Americans have lost jobs in the pandemic—and robots and AI are replacing them faster than ever. Time [Internet]. 2020, Aug 6 [cited 2022, Sep 2]. Available from: https://time.com/5876604/machines-jobs-coronavirus/.

46 Rainie L, Anderson J. The future of jobs and jobs training. Pew Research Center [Internet]. 2017, May 3 [cited 2022, Sep 2]. Available from: https://www.pewresearch.org/internet/2017/05/03/the-future-of-jobs-and-jobs-training/.

47 Civilian labor force participation rates. U.S. Bureau of Labor Statistics [Internet]. 2022, Aug [cited 2022, Sep 2]. Available from: https://www.bls.gov/charts/employment-situation/civilian-labor-force-participation-rate.htm .

48 Report on the condition of education 2022. Institute of Education Sciences [Internet]. 2022, May [cited 2022, Sep 3]. Available from: https://nces.ed.gov/pubs2022/2022144.pdf.

49 Goldhaber D, Kane T, McEachin A, et al. The consequences of remote and hybrid instruction during the pandemic. Center for Education Policy Research, Harvard [Internet]. 2022, May [cited 2022, Sept 3]. Available from: https://cepr.harvard.edu/files/cepr/files/5-4.pdf?m=1651690491.

50 Natanson H. "Never seen it this bad": America faces catastrophic teacher shortage. Washington Post [Internet]. 2022, Aug 3 [cited 2022, Sep 3]. Available from: https://www.washingtonpost.com/education/2022/08/03/school-teacher-shortage/.

51 Carter J. The American public still trusts scientists, says as new Pew survey. Scientific American [Internet]. 2020, Sep 29 [cited 2022, Sep 3]. Available from: https://www.scientificamerican.com/article/the-american-public-still-trusts-scientists-says-a-new-pew-survey/.

52 Press G. Is AI going to be a jobs killer? New reports about the future of work. Forbes [Internet]. 2019, Jul 15 [cited 2022, Sep 3]. Available from: https://www.forbes.com/sites/gilpress/2019/07/15/is-ai-going-to-be-a-jobs-killer-new-reports-about-the-future-of-work/?sh=e2aab84afb24.

53 Parker K. The growing partisan divide in views of higher education. Pew Reseach Center [Internet]. 2019, Aug 19 [cited 2022, Sep 3]. Available from: https://www.pewresearch.org/social-trends/2019/08/19/the-growing-partisan-divide-in-views-of-higher-education-2/.

54 Horowitz J, Igielnik R, Kochhar R. Trends in income and wealth inequality. Pew Research Center [Internet]. 2020, Jan 9 [cited 2022, Sep 3]. Available from: https://www.pewresearch.org/social-trends/2020/01/09/trends-in-income-and-wealth-inequality/.

55 New NAEH report describes trends in homelessness. National Low Income Housing Coalition [Internet]. 2020, *May 26* [cited 2022, Sep 3]. Available from: https://nlihc.org/resource/new-naeh-report-describes-trends-homelessness.

56 Homelessness and health: What's the connection? National Health Care for the Homeless Council [Internet]. 2019, Feb [cited 2022, Sep 3]. Available from: https://nhchc.org/wp-content/uploads/2019/08/homelessness-and-health.pdf.

57 Archer D, Marmor T. Medicare and commercial health insurance: The fundamental difference. Health Affairs [Internet]. 2012, Feb 15 [cited 2022, Sep 3]. Available from: https://www.healthaffairs.org/do/10.1377/hblog20120215.016980/full/.

58 Abelson R, Goodnough A. If the Supreme Court ends Obamacare, here's what it would mean. New York Times [Internet]. 2021, Jun 17 [cited 2022, Sep 3]. Available from: https://www.nytimes.com/article/supreme-court-obamacare-case.html.

59 Lapid N. Virus variants found to be deadlier, more contagious; some may thwart vaccines. Reuters [Internet]. 2021, Mar 17 [cited 2022, Sep 3]. Available from: https://www.reuters.com/article/us-health-coronavirus-science/virus-variants-found-to-be-deadlier-more-contagious-some-may-thwart-vaccines-idUSKBN2B92U7.

60 Mallapaty S. Where did Omicron come from? Three key theories. Nature [Internet]. 2022, Jan 28 [cited 2022, Sep 3]. Available from: https://www.nature.com/articles/d41586-022-00215-2.

61 Thompson D. Anti-vaxxers wage campaigns against COVID-19 shots. WebMD [Internet]. 2021, Jan 29 [cited 2022, Sep 3]. Available from: https://www.webmd.com/vaccines/covid-19-vaccine/news/20210129/anti-vaxxers-mounting-internet-campaigns-against-covid-19-shots.

62 Looney A, Turner N. Work and opportunity before and after incarceration. Brookings [Internet]. 2018, Mar [cited 2022, Sep 3]. Available from: https://www.brookings.edu/wp-content/uploads/2018/03/es_20180314_looneyincarceration_final.pdf.

63 Kerby S. The top 10 most startling facts about people of color and criminal justice in the United States. American Progress [Internet]. 2012, Mar 13 [cited 2022, Sep 3]. Available from: https://www.americanprogress.org/issues/race/news/2012/03/13/11351/the-top-10-most-startling-facts-about-people-of-color-and-criminal-justice-in-the-united-states/.

64 Criminal justice facts. Sentencing Project [Internet]. [cited 2022, Sep 3]. Available from: https://www.sentencingproject.org/criminal-justice-facts/.

65 Williams T. Inside a private prison: Blood, suicide and poorly paid guards. New York Times [Internet]. 2018, Apr 3 [cited 2022, Sep 3]. Available from: https://www.nytimes.com/2018/04/03/us/mississippi-private-prison-abuse.html.

66 Thornton A. 11 ways the wealthy and corporations will game the new ta law. American Progress [Internet]. 2018, Jull 25 [cited 2022, Sep 3]. Available from: https://www.americanprogress.org/issues/economy/reports/2018/07/25/453981/11-ways-wealthy-corporations-will-game-new-tax-law/.

67 Furhmann R, How large corporations avoid paying taxes. Investopedia [Internet]. 2022, Aug 22 [cited 2022, Sep 3]. Available from: https://www.investopedia.com/financial-edge/0512/how-large-corporations-get-around-paying-less-in-taxes.aspx.

68 Newsham J. Uber, Lyft save big by avoiding regulations. Boston Globe [Internet]. 2014, Dec 25 [cited 2022, Sep 3]. Available from: https://www.bostonglobe.com/business/2014/12/25/uber-lyft-save-big-avoiding-regulations/pQAMk1KMOavlyZhWi4XIaJ/story.html.

69 Foster B. How to reduce labor costs in your business. Money Crashers [Internet]. 2021, Sep 20 [cited 2022, Sep 3]. Available from: https://www.moneycrashers.com/reduce-labor-costs-business/.

70 Kagan J. Corporate inversion definition. Investopedia [Internet]. 2022, Aug 7 [cited 2022, Sep 3]. Available from: https://www.investopedia.com/terms/c/corporateinversion.asp.

71 Stoian CR. Why big businesses move their headquarters around the world—tax, talent and trepidation. Conversation [Internet]. 2019, Feb 22 [cited 2022, Sep 3]. Available from: https://theconversation.com/why-big-businesses-move-their-headquarters-around-the-world-tax-talent-and-trepidation-110913.

72 Bueloow D. Confidential: Should we move headquarters? Chief Executive [Internet]. [cited 2022, Sep 3]. Available from: https://chiefexecutive.net/confidential-should-we-move-headquarters./

73 Ordway D-M, Kille LW. The impact of big-box retails on communities, jobs, crime, wages and more: Research roundup. 2015, Dec 16 [cited 2022, Sep 3]. Available from: https://journalistsresource.org/politics-and-government/impact-big-box-retailers-employment-wages-crime-health/.

74 Popovich N, Albeck-Ripka L, Rierre-Lous K. The Trump administration rolled back more than 100 environmental rules. Here's the full list. New York Times [Internet]. 2021, Jan 20 [cited 2022, Sep 3]. Available from: https://www.nytimes.com/interactive/2020/climate/trump-environment-rollbacks-list.html.

75 Sanger D, Perlroth N. F.B.I. identifies group behind pipeline hack. New York Times [Internet]. 2021, May 10 [cited 2022, Sep 3]. Available from: https://www.nytimes.com/2021/05/10/us/politics/pipeline-hack-darkside.html?campaign_id=2&emc=edit_th_20210511&instance_id=30565&nl=todaysheadlines®i_id=55366183&segment_id=57726&user_id=6cf7991ceef7a9264934e7e295e11519.

76 Layton R. Hackers are targeting U.S. banks, and hardware may give them an open door. Forbes [Internet]. 2021, Mar 17 [cited 2022, Sep 3]. Available from: https://www.forbes.com/sites/roslynlayton/2021/03/17/hackers-are-targeting-us-banks-and-hardware-may-give-them-an-open-door/?sh=6b3d49fd14dc.

77 McWhinney J. Why governments are wary of Bitcoin. Investopedia [Internet]. 2022, Mar 19 [cited 2022, Sep 3]. Available from: https://www.investopedia.com/articles/forex/042015/why-governments-are-afraid-bitcoin.asp.

78 Wadhwa V. The genetic engineering genie is out of the bottle. Foreign Policy [Internet]. 2020, Sep 11 [cited 2022, Sep 3]. Available from: https://foreignpolicy.com/2020/09/11/crispr-pandemic-gene-editing-virus/.

79 Beer T. Top 1% of the U.S. households hold 15 times more wealth than bottom 50% combined. Forbes [Internet]. 2020, Oct 8 [cited 2022, Sep 3]. Available from: https://www.forbes.com/sites/tommybeer/2020/10/08/top-1-of-us-households-hold-15-times-more-wealth-than-bottom-50-combined/?sh=7ec9ba555179.

80 Molina B. Jeff Bezsos could become world's first trillionaire, and many people aren't happy about it. USA Today [Internet]. 2020, May 14 [cited 2022, Sep 3]. Available from: https://www.usatoday.com/story/tech/2020/05/14/jeff-bezos-worlds-first-trillionaire-sparks-heated-debate/5189161002/.

81 GDP. World Bank [Internet], [cited 2022, Sep 3]. Available from: https://data.worldbank.org/indicator/NY.GDP.MKTP.KD?most_recent_value_desc=false&view=chart.

82 Parker J. The 11 best luxury concierge services in the world. Luxe Digital [Internet]. 2022, Mar 3 [cited 2022, Sep 3]. Available from: https://luxe.digital/lifestyle/scene/best-luxury-concierge/.

83 Living the good life: 10 hobbies of ultra-wealthy people. In Flight [Internet]. 2020, Feb 19 [cited 2022, Sep 3]. Available from: https://inflightpilottraining.com/2020/02/19/living-the-good-life-10-hobbies-of-ultra-wealthy-people/.

84 11 celebrities who own private islands. Style [Internet]. 2021, Apr 21 [cited 2022, Sep 3]. Available from: https://www.scmp.com/magazines/style/celebrity/article/3130299/11-celebrities-who-own-private-islands-beyonce-and-jay-zs.

85 Blankfeld K. Countries billionaires could buy. Forbes [Internet]. 2009, Sep 30 [cited 2022, Sep 3]. Available from: https://www.forbes.com/2009/09/29/forbes-400-gates-dell-walton-charney-rich-list-09-billionaires-vs-world.html?sh=29772bc41050.

86 Arlidge J. The ultra-rich are now buying 'pandemic passports' so they can move to safer countries. Robb Report [Internet]. 2020, May 4 [cited 2022, Sep 3]. Available from: https://robbreport.com/travel/destinations/super-rich-buying-pandemic-passports-multiple-nationalities-2918500/.

87 Horncastle W. The scale of US election spending explained in five graphs. The Conversation [Internet]. 2020, Oct 15 [cited 2022, Sep 3]. Available from: https://theconversation.com/the-scale-of-us-election-spending-explained-in-five-graphs-130651.

88 2020 election to cost $14 billion, blowing away spending records. Open Secrets [Internet]. 2020, Oct 28 [cited 2022, Sep 3]. Available from: https://www.opensecrets.org/news/2020/10/cost-of-2020-election-14billion-update/.

89 Silva D. Who benefited most from the tax cuts and jobs act? Policy Genius [Internet]. 2021, Dec 28 [cited 2022, Sep 3]. Available from: https://www.policygenius.com/taxes/who-benefited-most-from-the-tax-cuts-and-jobs-act/.

90 Page S. Americans back tougher gun laws but GOP support plummets even after Atlanta, Boulder shootings, exclusive poll finds. USA Today [Internet]. 2021, Mar 24 [cited 2022, Sep 3]. Available from: https://www.usatoday.com/story/news/politics/2021/03/24/poll-views-gun-laws-after-atlanta-boulder-show-even-deeper-divide/6963810002/.

91 Tyson A, Kennedy B. Two-thirds of Americans think government should do more on climate. Pew Research Center [Internet]. 2020, Jun 23 [cited 2022, Sep 3]. Available from: https://www.pewresearch.org/science/2020/06/23/two-thirds-of-americans-think-government-should-do-more-on-climate/.

92 Dunn A. Most Americans support a $15 federal minimum wage. Pew Research Center [Internet]. 2021, Apr 22 [cited 2022, Sep 3]. Available from: https://www.pewresearch.org/fact-tank/2021/04/22/most-americans-support-a-15-federal-minimum-wage./

93 Suliman A. What we know about the Paul Pelosi attack and suspect David DePape. Washington Post [internet]. 2022, Oct 29 [cited 2022, Oct 30]. Available from: https://www.washingtonpost.com/politics/2022/10/29/paul-pelosi-attack-david-depape/.

94 Epstein R, Corasaniti N. The gerrymander battles loom, as G.O.P. looks to press its advantage. New York Times [Internet]. 2021, Nov 17 [cited 2022, Sep 3]. Available from: https://www.nytimes.com/2021/01/31/us/politics/gerrymander-census-democrats-republicans.html.

95 Perry A, Barr A. Georgia's voter suppression bill is an assault on our democracy. Brookings [Internet]. 2021, Apr 19 [cited 2022, Sep 3]. Available from: https://www.brookings.edu/blog/the-avenue/2021/04/19/georgias-voter-suppression-bill-is-an-assault-on-our-democracy/.

96 Ali S. Where protesters go, armed militias, vigilantes likely to follow with little to stop them. NBC News [Internet]. 2020, Sep 1 [cited 2022, Sep 3]. Available from: https://www.nbcnews.com/news/us-news/where-protesters-go-armed-militias-vigilantes-likely-follow-little-stop-n1238769.

97 Gross T. Militrization of police means U.S. protesters face weapons designed for war. NPR [Internet]. 2020, Jul 1 [cited 2022, Sep 3]. Available from: https://www.npr.org/2020/07/01/885942130/militarization-of-police-means-u-s-protesters-face-weapons-designed-for-war.

98 Jurkowitz M, Mitchell A, Shearer E, et al. Ideology reveals largest gaps in trust occur between conservatives and liberals. Pew Research Center [Internet]. 2020, Jan 24 [cited 2022, Sep 3]. Available from: https://www.journalism.org/2020/01/24/ideology-reveals-largest-gaps-in-trust-occur-between-conservatives-and-liberals/.

99 Ordway D-M. Fake news and the spread of misinformation: A research roundup. Journalists Resource [Internet]. 2017, Sep 1 [cited 2022, Sep 3]. Available from: https://journalistsresource.org/politics-and-government/fake-news-conspiracy-theories-journalism-research/.

100 Galston W. Is seeing still believing? The deepfake challenge to truth in politics. Brookings [Internet]. 2020, Jan 8 [cited 2022, Sep 3]. Available from: https://www.brookings.edu/research/is-seeing-still-believing-the-deepfake-challenge-to-truth-in-politics/.

101 Tracy P. AI-generated fake porn is on the rise—and it has huge implications. Daily Dot [Internet]. 2021, May 22 [cited 2022, Oct 30]. Available from: https://www.dailydot.com/debug/deepfake-assisted-fake-porn/ .

102 Kahler M. President Trump and the future of global governance. Council on Foreign Relations [Internet]. 2017, Jan 31 [cited 2022, Sep 3]. Available from: https://www.cfr.org/blog/president-trump-and-future-global-governance.

103 South China Sea: What's China's plan for its "Great Wall of Sand"? BBC [Internet]. 2020, Jul 14 [cited 2022, Sep 3]. Available from: https://www.bbc.com/news/world-asia-53344449.

104 Watt L. Pressure and pineapple wars: Taiwan fears quieter Chinese threat as U.S. warns of invasion. NBC News [Internet]. 2021, May 5 [cited 2022, Sep 3]. Available from: https://www.nbcnews.com/news/world/taiwan-fears-quieter-chinese-threat-u-s-warns-invasion-n1266216.

105 Helmus T, Bodine-Baron E, Radin A, et al. Russian social media influence: Understanding Russian propaganda in Eastern Europe. Rand [Internet]. 2018 [cited 2022, Sep 3]. Available from: https://www.rand.org/content/dam/rand/pubs/research_reports/RR2200/RR2237/RAND_RR2237.pdf.

106 Ash T. For Europe, losing Britain is bad. Keeping Hungary and Poland could be worse. The Guardian [Internet]. 2020, Dec 10 [cited 2022, Sep 3]. Available from: https://www.theguardian.com/commentisfree/2020/dec/10/for-europe-losing-britain-is-bad-keeping-hungary-and-poland-could-be-worse.

107 Norman L, Rasmussen S. What is the Iran nuclear deal? What it means, from nuclear weapons to the price of oil. Wall Street Journal [Internet]. 2022, Mar 16 [cited 2022, Sep 3]. Available from: https://www.wsj.com/articles/iran-nuclear-program-11610564572.

108 Saudi Arabia. Nuclear Threat Initiative [Internet]. [cited 2022, Sep 3]. Available from: https://www.nti.org/learn/countries/saudi-arabia/.

109 McGrath M. Climate change: US formally withdraws from Paris agreement. BBC [Internet]. 2020, Nov 4 [cited 2022, Sep 3]. Available from: https://www.bbc.com/news/science-environment-54797743.

110 Global warming boosts the economies of some. 70 countries. Consultancy [Internet]. 2020, Sep 28 [cited 2022, Sep 3]. Available from: https://www.consultancy.eu/news/4964/global-warming-boosts-the-economies-of-some-70-countries.

111 Global warming of 1.5°C. IPPC [Internet]. 2020, Mar 12 [cited 2022, Sep 3]. Available from: https://www.ipcc.ch/sr15/.

112 Climate impacts on society. EPA [Internet]. [cited 2022, Sep 3]. Available from: https://19january2017snapshot.epa.gov/climate-impacts/climate-impacts-society_.html.

113 Berardelli J, Niemczyk K. "We have to go": Climate change driving increased migration from Central America. CBS New [Internet]. 2021, Feb 17 [cited 2022, Sep 3]. Available from: https://www.cbsnews.com/news/climate-change-migration-central-america./

114 How armed vigilante groups are detaining migrants on US-Mexico border. Independent [Internet]. 2019, Apr 25 [cited 2022, Sep 3]. Available from: https://www.independent.co.uk/news/long_reads/us-mexico-border-militia-vigilante-migrants-united-constitutional-patriots-a8886186.html.

115 Woodruff J. COVID crisis: Why India's health system is on the "brink of collapsing." PBS [Internet]. 2021, Apr 26 [cited 2022, Sep 3]. Available from: https://www.pbs.org/newshour/show/covid-crisis-why-indias-health-system-is-on-the-brink-of-collapsing.

116 Hollingsworth J. Prime Minister Narendra Modi could have prevented India's devastating COVID-19 crisis, critics say. He didn't. CNN [Internet]. 2021, May 1 [cited 2022, Sep 3]. Available from: https://www.cnn.com/2021/04/30/india/covid-second-wave-narendra-modi-intl-hnk-dst/index.html.

117 Singer P. The most good you can do: How effective altruism is changing ideas about living ethically. New Haven, CT: Yale University Press, 2015.

118 Characteristics of public and private secondary schools in the United States. Institute of Education Sciences [Internet]. 2020, Sep [cited 2022, Sep 3]. Available from: https://nces.ed.gov/pubs2020/2020142rev.pdf.

119 Chris Dier. National Network of State Teachers of the Year [Internet]. [cited 2022, Sep 4]. Available from: http://nnstoy.org/chapter/louisiana/recipients/chris-dier/.

120 Equity in Education. Classroom Chronicles [Internet]. [cited 2022, Sep 4]. Available from: https://www.louisianabelieves.com/docs/default-source/newsroom/classroom-chronicles—august-2019-(chris-dier).pdf.

121 80,000 Hours [Internet]. [cited 2022, Sep 4]. Available from: https://80000hours.org.

122 Todd B. Have a particular strength? Already and expert? Here are the socially impactful careers 80,000 Hours suggests you consider. 80,000 Hours [Internet]. 2018, Oct [cited 2022, Sep 4]. Available from: https://80000hours.org/articles/advice-by-expertise/.

123 2022 Overall rankings. Just Capital [Internet]. 2022, Jan 11 [cited 2022, Sep 4]. Available from: https://justcapital.com/rankings/.

124 Valet V. The world's most reputable companies for corporate responsibility 2019. Forbes [Internet]. 2019, Sep 17 [cited 2022, Sep 4]. Available from: https://www.forbes.com/sites/vickyvalet/2019/09/17/the-worlds-most-reputable-companies-for-corporate-responsibility-2019/#4f5325cf679b

125 Cooper N. America's most responsible companies. News Week [Internet]. 2020 [cited 2022, Sep 4]. Available from: https://www.newsweek.com/americas-most-responsible-companies-2020.

126 3BL Media announces 100 Best Corporate Citizens of 2022. SBL CSR Wire [Internet]. 2022, May 18 [cited 2022, Sep 4]. Available from: https://www.csrwire.com/press_releases/744051-3bl-media-announces-100-best-corporate-citizens-2022.

127 Make business a force for good. B Corporation [Internet]. [cited 2022, Sep 4]. Available from: https://bcorporation.net.

128 Guide to LEED certification. USGBC [Internet]. [cited 2022, Sep 4]. Available from: https://www.usgbc.org/cert-guide.

129 Doing and saying the right thing during a crisis: How businesses have responded to COVID-19. RepTrak [Internet]. 2020, Mar 27 [cited 2022, Sep 4]. Available from: https://www.reptrak.com/blog/doing-saying-right-thing-during-crisis-how-businesses-responded-covid19./

130 Singer-Velush N. The great giving machine: driven to make an impact, employees turn giving into a way of life. Microsoft [Internet]. 2018, Apr 18 [cited 2022, Sep 4]. Available from: https://news.microsoft.com/life/employee-giving./

131 Design culture. InVision [Internet]. [cited 2022, Sep 4]. Available from: https://www.invisionapp.com/design-defined/design-culture/.

132 We believe that ice cream can change the world. Ben & Jerry's [Internet]. [cited 2022, Sep 4]. Available from: https://www.benjerry.com/values .

133 Intentional innovation. Salesforce [Internet]. [cited 2022, Sep 4]. Available from: https://www.salesforce.com/company/ethical-and-humane-use./

134 We believe. . .Giving back never goes out of style. Levi Strauss & Co. [Internet]. [cited 2022, Sep 4]. Available from: https://www.levistrauss.com/values-in-action/social-impact/.

135 About Johnson & Johnson. Johnson & Johnson [Internet]. [cited 2022, Sep 4]. Available from: https://www.jnj.com/about-jnj.

136 Rabin R. Women with cancer awarded billions in baby powder suit. New York Times [Internet]. 2020, Jun 23 [cited 2022, Sep 4]. Available from: https://www.nytimes.com/2020/06/23/health/baby-powder-cancer.html.

137 Dunleavy K. Johnson & Johnson's last-ditch appeal of $2 B talc verdict falls short at Supreme Court. Fierce Pharma [Internet]. 2021, Jun 1 [cited 2022, Sep 4]. Available from: https://www.fiercepharma.com/pharma/supreme-court-tells-j-j-to-take-a-powder-over-2-1b-missouri-talc-verdict.

138 Mann B. 4 U.S. companies will pay $26 billion to settle claims they fueled the opioid crisis. NPR [Internet]. 2022, Feb 25 [cited 2022, Sep 4]. Available from: https://www.npr.org/2022/02/25/1082901958/opioid-settlement-johnson-26-billion.

139 You can make a difference. American Red Cross [Internet]. [cited 2022, Sep 4]. Available from: https://www.redcross.org.

140 We build strength, stability and self-reliance through shelter. Habitat for Humanity [Internet]. [cited 2022, Sep 4]. Available from: https://www.habitat.org.

141 International disaster relief and community initiatives. Burners Without Borders [Internet]. [cited 2022, Sep 4]. Available from: https://www.burnerswithoutborders.org.

142 What's at your core? AmeriCorps [Internet]. [cited 2022, Sep 4]. Available from: https://www.nationalservice.gov/programs/americorps.

143 Habitat AmeriCorps alumni share why they served. Habitat for Humanity [Internet]. [cited 2022, Sep 4]. Available from: https://www.habitat.org/stories/habitat-americorps-alumni-share-why-they-served.

144 A triple win for students, volunteers, and communities. AARP [Internet]. [cited 2022, Sep 4]. Available from: https://www.aarp.org/experience-corps/.

145 Make giving back your second act. AmeriCorps [Internet]. [cited 2022, Sep 4]. Available from: https://www.nationalservice.gov/programs/senior-corps.

146 Narratives: Executive summary. AmeriCorps [Internet]. [cited 2022, Sep 4]. Available from: https://americorps.gov/sites/default/files/grants/15SI172320_424_2.pdf.

147 Experience Corps: Our stories. AARP Foundation [Internet]. [cited 2022, Sep 4]. Available from: https://www.aarp.org/experience-corps/our-stories/.

148 Aknin L, Whillans A. Helping and happiness: A review and guide for public policy. Social Issues and Policy Review [Internet]. 2020, Aug 6 [cited 2022, Sep 4]. Available from: https://spssi.onlinelibrary.wiley.com/doi/abs/10.1111/sipr.12069.

149 About us. Enabling the Future [Internet]. [cited 2022, Sep 4]. Available from: http://enablingthefuture.org/about/.

150 Enabling the Future [Internet]. [cited 2022, Sep 4]. Available from: https://enablingthefuture.org.

151 Ocean Cleanup [Internet]. [cited 2022, Sep 4]. Available from: https://theoceancleanup.com.

152 Slat B. How we showed the oceans could clean themselves. YouTube [web streaming video]. 2014, Jun 6. [cited 2022, Sep 4]. Available from: https://www.youtube.com/watch?v=QpDxE8BhPSM.

153 Slat B. How we will rid the oceans of plastic. YouTube [web streaming video]. 2017, May 14 [cited 2022, Sep 4]. Available from: https://www.youtube.com/watch?v=du5d5PUrH0I.

154 Slat B. Boyan shares some perspective on the Ocean Cleanup mission. YouTube [web streaming video]. 2021, Apr 22 [cited 2022, Sep 4]. Available from: https://www.youtube.com/watch?v=Mn8VpSrbfAo.

155 We work with leaders to envision an abundant future and accelerate massive sustainable change and positive impact for their organizations and the planet. Massive Change Network [Internet]. [cited 2022, Sep 4]. Available from: https://www.massivechangenetwork.com.

156 Smith C. Design for the other 90%. New York: Assouline, 2007.

157 Stickdorn M, Lawrence A, Hormess M, et al. This is service design doing. Sebastopol, CA: O'Reilly, 2018.

158 Resnick E. (ed.). The social design reader. London: Bloomsbury Visual Arts, 2019.

159 Sercombe J. The power of designing for social impact. Medium [Internet]. 2019, Sep 1 [cited 2022, Sep 4]. Available from: https://medium.com/this-is-hcd/the-power-of-designing-for-social-impact-4297611079.

160 Design for Social Justice [Internet]. [cited 2022, Sep 4]. Available from: https://www.designforsocialjustice.xyz/home.

161 Petermans A, Cain R (eds.). Design for wellbeing: An applied approach. London: Routledge, 2020.

162 Our approach: A method for co-creating equitable outcomes. Creative Reaction Lab [Internet]. [cited 2022, Sep 4]. Available from: https://www.creativereactionlab.com/our-approach.

163 Friedman B, Hendry D. Value sensitive design: Shaping technology with moral imagination. Cambridge MA: MIT Press, 2019.

164 Margolin V, Brillembourg A, Faud-Luke A, et al. (eds.). Design for the good society. Utrecht: Utrecht Manifesto, 2014.

165 Barnbrook J, Bell N, Blauvelt A, et al. First things first 2000: A design manifesto. Reading Design [Internet]. 2000 [cited 2022, Sep 4]. Available from: https://www.readingdesign.org/first-things-first.

166 About. Allied Media Projects [Internet]. [cited 2022, Sep 4]. Available from: https://alliedmedia.org/about.

167 Design Justice Network [Internet]. [cited 2022, Sep 4]. Available from: https://designjustice.org/about-us.

168 https://www.futureofdesigneducation.org.

169 Norman D. Design for a better world: Meaningful, sustainable, humanity centered. Cambridge: MIT Press, 2023.

170 People-first Engineering. University of Michigan College of Engineering [Internet]. [Cited 2022, Oct 30]. Available from: https://strategicvision.engin.umich.edu/people-first-engineering/.

171 Simon H. The sciences of the artificial (3rd ed.). Cambridge: MIT Press, 1996.

Index

Note: Page numbers in *italics* denote figures.

Make the World a Better Place: Design with Passion, Purpose, and Values, First Edition. Robert B. Kozma.

e

f

g

h

k

l

m

r

s